Stories Heard and Stories Told
A Memoir

by

G. Peter Schieferdecker

Dedication

Storytelling is the oldest form of communication between people. It has over time created a bond between generations as younger people would learn from their elders how they lived and what kind of life their forbears had. This memoir is intended to be such a narrative and was written by me over many years, slowly building the story I wanted to tell my sons and daughter, their spouses and especially my grandchildren. Much of what is related here as family history was gathered from speaking with people who are no longer with us and from letters, journals and other written documents they left behind. While it is now possible to produce documents in electronic form, I have deliberately chosen to use the format of a book in an attempt to create something more tangible and of perhaps more lasting value. The onslaught of modern technology has profoundly impacted the way in which people communicate with each other. It has diminished the art of conversation, of correspondence and above all the link between the generations. It is my hope that this story will in its own small way be a bridge between the generations of our family.

Peter Schieferdecker

Table of Contents

I : A Beginning

Through our entire life we struggle to find the meaning of our existence on earth. It is said that—"to find the meaning of our life is to triumph over death." Sadly we often find there is no meaning-except perhaps for the limited significance our existence may have to those who are close to us. Still, we all want to be remembered. We want to leave a "footprint in the sand". We certainly want to be remembered by our own family, our close friends and our relatives. We want to make our brief stay in this world worthwhile and meaningful to ourselves and to others. So if our existence does have meaning, it is rooted in the family and in the circle of friends one has in life and in the manner in which we influence each other. If we look at history, it is in those relationships with smaller groups of people that the family of man developed to what it is now.

Our roots are important, our family is important, our career and our achievements in life are also important, but in my view much less so. In these smaller groups storytelling has throughout history been an important medium to pass on family lore. Today there is hardly any time to listen to a story and the written word conveyed by letter or in books or essays is also becoming extinct. Photographs are being replaced by digital images and nobody knows how long these will last. I am writing a history of our family mainly to leave those who come after me with some notion of our roots, of the people that preceded us, and how they lived and of the places in which they lived. Of course I also want to be remembered myself. Don't we all? I certainly do not see myself as a "great man," but I did leave some footprints in the sands of time, and I hope those who read this will enjoy retracing these footprints with me. Longworth wrote:

> *Lives of great men do remind us*
> *We can make our lives sublime*
> *And departing leave behind us*
> *Footprints on the sands of time*

I am especially keen on leaving a record of our family because those who come after Netty and me will most likely continue to live in America. They may like to know how we lived and they may want to have a clear sense of the background we came from. I want to tell them about members of our family and about our friends and about others who were significant in the world we lived in. There is no question in my mind that it is of great importance to everyone to know as much as possible of one's own roots and of the many people and events that played a role in molding our lives. I will try to relate what I learned and what I heard from those who went before us, and I will include my own impressions. Unavoidably, this family history will become mostly a personal memoir. It cannot be otherwise. In addition, whether this is grammatically or stylistically correct or not, I will freely mix the first person singular with the first person plural and use "I" when relating personal memories or thoughts and "we" when speaking about the many experiences Netty and I have had together in our wonderful life and when I reflect opinions I think are shared by both of us. I hope I will succeed in creating something of value to my own family and perhaps also to others who read this. And I hope I will have the satisfaction of finishing a task I urged myself long ago to begin and now feel strongly I have to complete.

Our move to America in 1958, when Netty and I came here with our two sons George and Adriaan, was perhaps the most important event in our lives. To go to another country on another continent with two small boys meant a new life for our small family. It placed us at a considerable geographical distance from our parents, grandparents and other relatives who, if we had stayed in Holland, would have contributed more and better to our common memories and would have helped us in passing on a better understanding of our common background to our children. In addition, we created a subtle barrier in culture and language when we began to speak English more and more and adopted another culture–different from our European background but not too alien from it. George and Adriaan were born in The Netherlands and came with us to America at a very young age. Our son Richard and daughter Janet were born in America. They are the two members of our family who never lived in Holland as children. Our family grew. First, George married Maggie Murray, but they found they were not suited for each other so they divorced. Happily, there was no acrimony. Later George married Diane Alexander who quickly became a most welcome member of our clan. They now have a son, George Alexander and a daughter, Eloise Jeannette. More recently Richard married Julie Anathan, adding another female member to our "male dominated" family.

After several years of marriage, Julie unfortunately decided that she had to follow another path through life that did not include marriage. In 2010 Richard found a new love and in 2011 he married Toyoko Kawabata, a Japanese young lady who is a most welcome addition. The birth of our two grandchildren and my eightieth birthday, now well behind me, added further urgency to getting on with the task of writing a record before I get too old and memories begin to fade.

A long time ago I began to collect data, photographs, tape recordings and other family records. Much of this material would now be lost to posterity if I had not made a beginning, but it is now high time to start using it and linking it together by writing about our lives and those of our relatives. I also collected books and articles about the history and the places where we and our ancestors lived. On the Schieferdecker side I was greatly helped in my efforts for historical information by my father who put together a comprehensive file on his own parents and grandparents after I asked him to do so. I am glad I asked because most of what he gave me would now be lost. He wrote me in 1968 that he found it an interesting job that he would not have dared to start had I not insisted. In addition to my father's information, I have tape recordings I made years ago when I interviewed my parents and Netty's mother and her aunt Margaret. Tante Margaret was the widow of Netty's uncle Eelco van Kleffens who served as the Dutch Minister of Foreign Affairs during the war and also was, for one session, chairman of the General Assembly of the United Nations in New York. Our son Adriaan made an interesting videotape of my parents while he lived in Europe. This gives a good impression of my parents in their very old age. Relatives of Netty's father compiled useful information on the van Kleffens family going back many years in a book prepared long ago. The family history of Netty's mother, the van Someren Gréve family, is described in a Dutch publication called *Het Nederlands Patriciaat* where families who are inclined to do so list their ancestry. When visiting Holland I discovered a government-supported institution where one can browse among an immense collection of birth, death and marriage records of Dutch municipalities, stored on micro-fiche. A most interesting and reliable source. I fear I will not find much on people who lived outside the Netherlands, specifically my Grandfather Schieferdecker's ancestors as so much was destroyed in Germany during the last war. I will do my best to describe people I have known, fairly and accurately. Above all I will try to describe their environment in such a way that it will give those who come after us an understanding of the world of their forefathers. It is my fervent hope that our family will grow further as time goes by so that we will see more and more footprints in the sand.

My life and Netty's and that of my family has been strongly influenced and shaped by our parents, our grandparents, and to a lesser extent by our friends, our teachers and others who played a role in our lives. But obviously our lives were also affected by many extraneous events, almost all beyond our control. Our grandparents were born in Europe or in Indonesia, in countries that were mostly peaceful and prosperous. The century of political order and balance of power, which stretched from 1815 when the domination of the continent of Europe by the Empire of Napoleon ended until 1914 when World War I started, was an immensely important period for Europe. It is seen as the era that witnessed the beginning of modern history. In this period Europeans conquered most of the world known to man and made colonies of a good part of it. They created many important new inventions, dominated the art world and set cultural standards. America, while independent from European dominance was not yet a world power and was seen as a cultural backwater. This all changed in 1914 with the beginning of World War I, the most horrible of all wars. America joined this war at its very end, enabling the exhausted Allies to score a victory over the equally exhausted Germans who had almost won. The Versailles peace treaty that concluded this war was such a bad arrangement that it spawned virtually all the wars, revolutions and other upheavals that followed until this day.

For sure, Europe was not entirely peaceful in the nineteenth century. There were wars such as the one between Prussia and France in 1870 – 71 and many problems were swept under the rug, but for most of Western Europe it was a period of political stability and of tremendous industrial and economic expansion. In America there was, of course, the Civil War. This terribly bloody war really only affected America and may have been the origin of many admirable American traditions such as patriotism, respect for laws and a strong military tradition of bravery and willingness to sacrifice for a just cause. The end of World War II signaled the beginning of America's role as a world power and the beginning of the decline of Europe's power. After the disintegration of the Soviet Union and the flattening out of the economic growth of Japan, the U.S. has emerged as the dominant world power, militarily as well as economically. This begs the question of what will happen if and when the U.S. power declines.

Against this background, I think our families managed quite well, for many generations, despite or perhaps because of a large number of historically important events that occurred in the lives of our ancestors and in our own lives. Many of our ancestors, our grandparents, parents and we ourselves lived in many far flung parts of the world. They experienced political and economic upheavals, including several wars, and managed to survive them all. Actually, we did not only survive, we did well and we improved our lot. I am proud to say we and our immediate ancestors almost always reacted intelligently to the challenges our environment presented. We positioned ourselves well in the world in which we lived. We prospered - we educated our children as well as we could and we avoided most personal disasters. We obviously benefited greatly from the coincidence that we were living in the right part of Europe and Netty and I moved to America when that country was economically very strong and offered a good base for success. This family record may to some extent be due to good luck, but I believe firmly that God only helps those who help themselves. I also believe that a proactive attitude towards the environment we live in and a good understanding of the economic and political factors that shape it are essential for successful survival in this world. I believe we as a family have shown a willingness to adapt, to take risks where necessary, and to do well. In fact I believe we did "better than average" and outperformed our environment, which is in my opinion tremendously important. It is all too easy to slide back into lower layers of society. I will try to deal with the historic events our families encountered on their path as well as I can. These events can probably best be summarized as "sociopolitical, economic and technological events" such as:

- Political shocks, revolutions and wars.
- Economic shocks: economic growth and economic failures.
- The end of the colonial empires long controlled by Western European nations.
- Technological and scientific developments, both beneficial and detrimental to mankind.
- Societal changes causing greater freedom, tolerance and enjoyment of life for all of mankind, but also causing an increase in antisocial behavior and excesses.

How did change affect us? In the beginning of the 1980's a book called *Future Shock* written by Alvin Toffler was published in America. This book became a best seller in a very short time because the author hit a sensitive nerve when he developed a theme that revolved around the realization that the evolution of mankind moves faster and faster. Toffler observed that the last two or three generations had seen as many new inventions and as much technological progress as all preceding generations that had existed since the beginning of man's known history on earth. His conclusion was that man must adjust to change at an ever accelerating rate of speed and may have trouble doing so. The book was well timed. It appeared around the time of the so-called Oil Shock, which stunned the western world and confronted it with the realization that it was using up its principal source of energy. The world suddenly understood that growth may have its limits. As I read the book, I could not help but relate its theme to our life and that of our parents, particularly my father's career. I recognized that my father's generation and my own life had been strongly influenced by the tremendous growth of science and technology we witnessed in our lifetime and by the attendant consumption of energy. I think it is fair to state that my father always reacted positively to the changes he saw developing in his world. He saw them as basically good and felt he could cope with them. Others, particularly my mother and Netty's father had a somewhat more negative view of change. They preferred to leave things as they were and tended to speak fondly of the past.

At that time a fearful reaction to change was expressed on a very high level, by the "Club of Rome," a powerful group of mostly European economists, scientists and politicians who almost coincidentally with the Oil Shock published an in-depth study of the world's resources and potential growth titled "The Limits to Growth." Their study found a large audience and many people immediately accepted their thesis which said that the world as we knew it would have to reduce its rate of growth drastically because we were facing a serious deficiency in food and natural resources and equally serious overcrowding. We were told that we were running out of living space and out of food to feed our constantly growing population and we soon would not have the technological resources to support so much life on earth. The conclusions of this interesting study largely reflected European fears of growth and European desires to control economic development through government action, often called "social engineering," and to hang on to what the Europeans regarded as their rightful patrimony, saving and conserving what they had. Americans have always had a more optimistic outlook on life and its prospects and generally resist government regulation. Americans tend to use resources, often voraciously, so life can be lived to its fullest. They do not worry too much about the future. At least they used to. Their behavior is changing now. They still reject social engineering or what they see as the control of human behavior by government action. The Europeans still lean more towards conservation, caution and pessimism and a belief that government regulation is necessary and should serve the interest of the citizenry. As is so often the case, the true course most likely lies somewhere in the middle. The tremendous impact the study by the Club of Rome made was useful and well deserved and its theme was worth remembering, but in the years since its publication most of its predictions have proven to be wrong or seem to have found a different resolution because its basic concepts were too broad. The Club of Rome also forgot that large parts of the world were underdeveloped and that the people living there desired to achieve the same levels of prosperity as the Western world. The West was collectively acting like a person squeezing aboard a very crowded train and turning around to say to the person directly behind, "you can't get on, this car is full." Now, many years later, we are still confronted with these problems but do not seem to care too much about them. There is plenty of fuel, prices of crude oil have gone down and stabilized and then risen again to unknown heights and the world continues to grow, albeit in fits and starts. What is more, projections of a gradual decline in the world population are now generally believed to be accurate. Nevertheless, the controversy surrounding the "Limits to Growth" represents a theme that played a major role in the differences between the European world of our ancestors in which Netty and I grew up and America, the country we chose to live in and in which our children were raised.

America has been good to us and we are strong supporters of our new country. We recognize its many faults and shortcomings, but we will always be grateful for the opportunity it offered us and for allowing us to become American citizens and to become part of the very diverse American population. We consider ourselves fortunate to have been able to raise our children in America and to prosper in it. Today America continues to offer the same opportunities to countless other newcomers, and its vigor and growth are clear examples of the positive result of its open-door policy. Despite the occasional bouts of xenophobia, and the racial problems and religious bigotry one may find in America's history and in its society of today, American legal traditions and societal attitudes welcome anybody who wants to live here. I can think of many other countries, particularly in Europe and Asia, where a family of newcomers like us would not have been received with open arms. Just try to become a Swiss citizen or settle in Japan, for example. Here in America we found many close friends and achieved success without ever hearing anybody say a negative word or showing any hint of jealousy, hate or opposition to our presence here.

There are, in our minds, no grounds for the misplaced feelings of superiority many Europeans display when they are visiting America or engage in discussions about it. The perceived superiority of European culture, education and "style," is a trait we have noticed among many newcomers or casual visitors from Europe, but we have also been pleased to note that in most cases these feelings disappeared and were replaced by a more objective and balanced opinion after some time had elapsed and there had been more exposure to America as a country and to those who live there.

It is in our view best to look at each country and its people as separate places with separate individuals who are different, sometimes to one's liking and sometimes not, but who are nevertheless all human beings who share the foibles of all of mankind. Once again, there is much in American society that is wrong or even disastrous, but over time I have come to the conclusion that the American system of government of laws and of politics somehow manages to create a society that after much unavoidable turmoil and suffering finds workable solutions that allow a reasonable amount of freedom and economic growth. The "American experiment" is a truly phenomenal success story. It created a successfully working democracy in an enormously big country, welcoming people of vastly different racial, ethnic and cultural backgrounds. In this family history I will try to remain objective and give the best possible impression of the world we found in America and of the world we came from. As will quickly become clear, we are really and truly an international family with a background and origins in many parts of the world.

Let us go back to the Oil Shock for a moment. It came about when oil-producing countries, mainly those located in the Middle East, believed they had been unfairly exploited by the Western governments and powerful Western oil companies who controlled the price of a resource that was rightfully theirs, gobbled up large quantities of it, and made huge profits from it. They did not want to be rewarded for just the crude oil extracted from their land at prices set by outsiders, they wanted also to participate in the "downstream" profits gained from marketing and refining of petroleum products. They wanted more money and more power. So they formed a cartel to control the supply of oil and therefore its price and thus hoped to raise crude prices significantly. In 1973 this cartel imposed an embargo on oil exports, creating shortages that seriously affected the U.S. economy. However, these shortages were quickly overcome after the industrialized world adapted to them and learned to live with higher energy prices. The world responded with a strong energy conservation movement and a vigorous search for oil in areas where oil exploration had been uneconomical at the lower price levels that prevailed before. So, once again confirming the economic law that greater demand usually brings about an increased supply, the world produced more oil than it needed. After a few years prices went down again, only to rise years later, reflecting growing demand by the rapidly growing Chinese and Indian economies and the wars in the Middle East. Still, we all realized that the cartel, that called itself OPEC (Oil Producing an Exporting Countries), had a point and that the oil "shock" was a warning that someday we might run out of oil again and face another energy crunch. Before too long OPEC may prove to be a toothless tiger since American technical genius has discovered huge reservoirs of untapped energy underneath the continental U.S. These "shale oil reservoirs" are now being tapped with a new technology called "fracking." Future Shock came to us quicker than we had anticipated.

The Schieferdecker connection with the oil industry stems mainly from my father, who spent his entire working career in it. He often said that it would be a very long time before the world would run out of oil. He believed that more oil would be found as exploration technology improved and higher prices made it economical to exploit resources in less accessible places. He usually added that oil was often found in places where you would not want to live if you had a choice. His treks through the jungles of central Mexico and the Pampas of Argentina confirmed this point. My father had the unshakable belief, characteristic of engineers of his generation, that able geologists would always find new oil and that skilled engineers would bring it to the surface and to production. As happened so often during his life, he proved to be right.

Whenever I talked with my father about the days when he grew up I was struck by the immense changes he had seen in his lifetime. When he was born, ships and trains were moved by steam engines. In towns and cities horses provided the most common means of transportation, mostly pulling carriages, wagons and even trams. Electricity was in its infancy and gaslight was only used in urban areas. Outside the cities, kerosene was used as fuel for lamps. Water was drawn everywhere by hand pumps. When my father died he had seen men walking on the moon, owned a television set, and had traveled several times by jet plane to America to see us.

Our parents grew up in a world were people generally lived simple lives. They did not travel very far, they worked hard and their workdays were long. The working class had a much tougher time than the middle class and the aristocracy. The men who worked for my mother's father in his photography business used to irritate their boss, my grandfather, by singing *Wordt het dan nooit geen Zaterdag avond, Zaterdag avond zeven uur."* (Is it ever going to be Saturday night, Saturday night seven o'clock?) They worked a six-day week and each day was about ten hours. Social services were virtually nonexistent and health care was primitive and sometimes not available to all people. Sickness and death were accepted as facts of life and many people died from health problems that are now easily cured or do not even exist anymore. Families were large, but many children died young. Both Netty's parents have genealogies that go back quite far – to the seventeenth century and earlier. Looking at the list of ancestors, their marriages and their children, one can clearly see that many babies did not live much longer than a few days after birth and that many people died young.

Women particularly were at risk when they were having children. Religion played an important part in people's lives. It was very important in domestic politics. Until World War I international politics followed a predictable path in Europe. But after that war, a seemingly unending cycle of upheavals, revolutions, economic disasters, ethnic conflicts, dictatorships and other developments brought violent change to many countries and began to dominate our world. It is remarkable that our family and the countries we were lucky enough to live in survived these upheavals so well and that we ended up quite prosperous.

European colonialism spread to many parts of the world and European countries expanded their territorial claims all over the globe, mostly for selfish and expansionist reasons or to keep other countries out of certain areas they regarded as theirs. It was commonly accepted that colonization and domination of other peoples was beneficial to those being colonized because it brought them the "blessings" of western technology, and European religion and culture. White people in Europe and America did not question their superiority over other races and creeds or their right to control peoples in faraway places. Even at this time, the day to day behavior of people in many non-European countries and certainly their art, opera, music and literature are almost totally dominated by western or European traditions and style, at the expense of their indigenous cultures.

Many members of Netty's family and mine lived in a country that is now called Indonesia and used to be known as the Dutch East Indies. For 400 years it was a rich and–towards the end of the Dutch period–on balance reasonably well-governed colony of Holland that became independent after World War II. People who went there were usually the "risk takers," the more venturesome ones. Serving in the Dutch army I had a personal involvement in the Indonesian struggle for independence and I will write about it.

The country Netty and I grew up in was much less densely populated than it is today. Even in my own lifetime I can see the difference clearly. Yet when I was young, Holland was already one of the most crowded countries in the world. It still has this dubious distinction, but it has managed to become even more crowded. But when I see old photographs of the streets in The Hague through which I bicycled to school, I am startled by their relative emptiness compared with today's overcrowded situation. Much of the clutter in today's Dutch streets is caused by the arrival of the automobile as a common means of transportation in postwar Holland. But the fact remains that the Dutch population has grown by about 65 percent since World War II. The Holland I grew up in was an orderly country where life had an orderly and rather slow pace. I will try to paint a picture of that period and I think back to it with great fondness. But those times are gone and it makes no sense to be overly nostalgic about the past. Our life and our lifestyle in those days had a certain realistic tinge and our values were solid. Nowadays some people try to go back to them. As I write this there is a boom in nostalgia with pictures of the 1930's as a period in which people lived simple decent lives. What is often forgotten is that the thirties started with the worst economic depression the world ever saw and marked the beginning of several decades of frenzied growth, terrible wars and much suffering, all over the world. Not an environment one should think of as particularly pleasant, warm and inviting.

Then there were the wars. Wars have a fascination for us. They bring out the worst and the best in mankind and it is not difficult to understand why wartime disruption and violence have had such an impact on our thinking. It is as if we, who have lived through the horrors of a war, think back to that experience with some measure of nostalgia and pride, as if we are somehow better than those who have missed the experience. In the spring of 1994, we celebrated the 50th anniversary of D-Day. On that day - June 6 1944 - allied forces landed in Normandy, France and subsequently fought their way to Germany, passing through Belgium and Holland. They defeated the German Nazi regime that had dominated Europe for five years and that brought much heartbreak, suffering and damage to our country and our families. During the D-Day celebrations, a few surviving veteran paratroopers, many my age and some even older, jumped again into France and virtually all the publicity about this event underlined that this was probably the last time most of these veterans could participate. This message certainly hit home to me. Much of what I saw on television in old footage about the landing and the campaign that followed brought many good and many sad memories. An important part of our lives passed before our eyes. It was overwhelmingly moving for me to watch it. Equally moving were the scenes we saw a year later when we were in Holland during the time the Dutch celebrated the 50th anniversary of their liberation from the German occupation.

World War II is often called "the last good war." A conflict in which it was clear who was right and who was wrong and in which the Allies were united in a fight against evil. As we get further away from that war and the turbulent years following it, I often wonder if our attitude towards duty, patriotism and the common good has changed. Sadly I think the conclusion has to be that it has. We have become more cynical.

World War II had an immense impact on our lives. It changed our world forever and completely. Unavoidably I will spend a great deal of time describing our experiences in World War II and the years immediately following it. These were years of high drama, intense suffering and much heroism. In times of war, life moves much faster than in times of peace. The rapid changes and often violent events of a war make us live more intensely and create a fascination with war that has been evident throughout history. I have collected a great many books about the war, not because I am a war lover or overly impressed by the military, but because it was such an overpowering dramatic event in my life and for my entire generation and because I am tremendously interested in its history, its significance for mankind and its impact on it. It is perhaps fortuitous that much of the more interesting literature about the war and its aftermath has only recently become available now that I have time to read it. It is as if the world needed about fifty years to really digest the war and see it in its true perspective. Many events and personalities are now seen quite differently than they were immediately after the war. The role certain people and certain countries played in it have been clarified and are now viewed much more objectively and placed against a backdrop of true history without the interference of participants who want to embellish their own actions. Now we also know more about the role of our adversaries, our enemies, and their motivation. Still, there is so much we do not know that we are still far from having a complete picture.

Another and more bothersome side of the development of history is that we now see clear signs of people who try to rewrite it to fit their own perception of the role of their nation in the war and to answer the question who is responsible for it. For instance, there have been startling revelations of the omission in Japanese schoolbooks of the history of Japan's role in the war. Japan's brutal conquest of China in the thirties, the sneak attack on Pearl Harbor that started its war with America and the inhuman way in which it treated its European and Asian prisoners in South East Asia, including many Dutch women and children, are completely ignored or whitewashed. Yet at the same time there are Americans who want to suggest that the use of the atomic bomb against Japan was not only militarily unnecessary but inspired by racist attitudes. The Japanese have picked up on that and voices are raised in Japan to make the Americans apologize for dropping the two nuclear bombs while the Japanese themselves are still stalling on clarifying their own wartime behavior and avoiding any gesture of true repentance.

Since World War II, Holland fought a mini war in Indonesia against Nationalists who wanted to remove the Dutch, their colonial rulers. Much to my chagrin I was called up in the Dutch army and served for almost two years in Indonesia in the tail end of this conflict. Our struggle in Indonesia was not a "good war." It was conflicts that stemmed from the inability of the Dutch to understand that the Indonesians wanted to govern themselves and were even brazen enough to think they could do it as well as the Dutch. In the fifties, North Korea invaded South Korea and America came to the aid of the South. This event was never called a war, but given the name of "Police Action." It is quite possible that this term is a Dutch contribution to the very popular international game of politically correct "double speak" because a few years earlier the Dutch had also called their two major offensives in Indonesia "Police Actions." When the Dutch made their move in Indonesia, their actions were condemned by America and by other members of the United Nations, while the U.S. actions in Korea were seen as righteous and necessary moves against a communist aggressor. Why the difference? Because communist North Korea attacked South Korea, crossing the 38th parallel, an artificial border established after World War II to delineate the limits of Soviet Russia's sphere of influence. So there was a reason to see this conflict as "good." Also, the United Nations had condemned the aggression of the North and supported the American reaction to it. The Peoples Republic of China meanwhile, saw its communist Northern Korean friends badly mauled by the Americans. They felt threatened and intervened massively, rolling the Americans and the South Koreans and their allies right back to the 38th parallel and beyond, thereby becoming an enemy of the U.S. The Korean conflict is now an almost forgotten war although America lost about 50,000 men in it and its final outcome was never resolved. South Korea was devastated and the loss of life among its soldiers and population was tremendous. Today the U.S. and a now- prosperous South Korea are still trying to come to terms with a very xenophobic North Korea that is one of the last bastions of a Soviet-style government. The Dutch military actions in Indonesia are also almost forgotten and are seen for what they were; a futile effort to perpetuate an outdated colonial regime.

For the U.S. the Vietnam War was much more traumatic than the Korean conflict. The American objective in joining it was not clear and it was the first war America lost. This war started as an uprising of the local population against their colonial power, France. The area the French called Indochina included the countries presently called Vietnam, Laos and Cambodia. It is now reasonably well established that the original uprising in Vietnam was not a communist movement, but a nationalistic one, similar to the situation in Indonesia. It was an attempt to gain freedom from France, the colonial power. The French were defeated and thrown out of the country by local troops who received a great deal of support, advice, and equipment from the Soviet Union and were therefore soon branded as communists.

America saw these developments as a threat that could trigger a widening of communist influence in South East Asia. Like Korea, Vietnam was divided in two parts, the communist North and "democratic" South. In reality, both South Korea and South Vietnam became quite undemocratic military dictatorships which were supported by the U.S. because otherwise, it was thought, the "domino theory" would take hold and the Communists would take over, spreading their doctrine over many other countries throughout the South East Asian region. The American assumption that justified the theory was that North Vietnam and the Peoples Republic of China would join forces and roll into South East Asia. This assumption was erroneous because the Chinese and the Vietnamese have been at war with each other for centuries and would never be able to work together although the Chinese found it convenient to help the North Vietnamese. The Vietnam War lasted for many bitter years. President Eisenhower had refused to bail out the embattled French with the nuclear strikes they requested, but later President Kennedy started to bring American troops into Vietnam and his successor, President Johnson escalated American involvement enormously. He started bombing the North and in the process lost his chances for reelection. President Nixon wanted to end the war (at least he said so in his campaign), but once elected escalated the bombing further, claiming that this was the only way to end the conflict. He did manage to end it, but it took him much longer than he had promised the American voters. After Nixon concluded the Vietnam War, he promptly made a dramatic move by using friction between the Soviet Union and Communist China to reestablish diplomatic relationships with the Chinese. This was a first step in what became a gradual opening of China to the West, which weakened the Soviet position significantly and contributed to the ultimate end of the Communist regime in Russia. It was a brilliant move by Nixon, a man who could have been an outstanding president but who had a peculiarly mean streak and who felt he was threatened by plots spawned by his political opponents, the Democrats. Even after he was reelected by a landslide his paranoia returned and he immediately started looking for his enemies. He saw the (mostly young) people who protested the Vietnam War as dangerous agitators undermining the nation. His mindset influenced and attracted people with similar aberrations and his administration foundered with the Watergate break-in scandal and its cover-up which forced Nixon to resign the presidency. If he had not resigned, he would probably have been impeached. After this disaster American politics have never been the same and the quality of political leadership in our country and in many others declined.

Another immensely important event in our lives was the collapse of the Communist regime in the Soviet Union. This country had been America's adversary for almost fifty years. The so-called "cold war" was a fact of life for all of us for such a long time and dominated international relationships with such intensity that it is now almost impossible to see clearly where the world is headed without the threat of war with Russia. The cold war cost America and many other countries enormous amounts of money as it was deemed necessary to keep large armed forces at the ready at all times. It forged strong ties between America and many other countries, especially in Western Europe where the Russians were practically at the doorstep.

The disappearance of the Soviet threat has had a tremendously beneficial effect on peace initiatives in many areas such as the Middle East where opponents were forced to make peace since they no longer had the option of playing U.S. influence off against Soviet support. It will probably have a negative effect on the alliances between the U.S. and European countries that are now beginning to fray at the edges as each country sees its own interests as more important than bonds of friendship with America and its other neighbors.

The cold war impacted our lives in many ways. By sheer coincidence Netty and I were close spectators to several major cold war events. Sometimes we were uncomfortably close.

My first glimpse of the cold war came when I was in the Dutch army, in the summer of 1948. I was in a school for NCOs. We were in Harderwijk, a garrison town in the middle of Holland and every morning we would have a parade. While standing there, waiting for the flag to be raised, we could see the planes go by that participated in the Berlin Air Lift. The Russians had become difficult and were challenging the agreement which gave each of the former World War II allies a sector of Berlin, the German capital. Germany was split in two parts, West Germany became a Federal Republic and a democratic, very prosperous member of the European Common Market. East Germany became a Communist dictatorship, sponsored by the Soviet Union and called the People's Republic of Germany. The entire city of Berlin was in East Germany and could only be reached through a narrow corridor by road or by rail, or through the air. The Soviets decided to shut down the road and rail connection and the allies were forced to either give up their sectors of Berlin or fly supplies in for themselves and the population. They decided that they wouldn't budge and started an air lift which went on for more than a year and became a symbol of Western solidarity against Soviet aggression.

The Dutch problems in Indonesia were seen by some as part of the Cold War but the Dutch never succeeded in convincing the U.S. government that the Indonesian independence movement was Communist influenced. Actually it was not, it was mainly a genuine independence movement. But Netty's uncle Eelco van Kleffens, who was at that time ambassador of the Netherlands in Washington, certainly tried hard to convince the U.S. government of the threat that a weak, strongly left wing government in Indonesia would pose to the western nations if the Dutch would have to leave. He was partly right. After it gained independence, Indonesia had to suffer for many years under the regime of its megalomaniacal president Sukarno who was heavily influenced by Soviet Russia, a country that always tried to undermine western influence wherever it could. Sukarno was ultimately toppled by a military coup, and Indonesia never became a Communist state.

Then in 1956, when Netty and I were debating our (initially vague) plans to emigrate to the U.S. or Canada, the Hungarian people revolted against the Communist regime of their country. This revolt which was brutally suppressed by the Russians became for us a major point in favor of going across the ocean. We said to ourselves that we did not want to live in an occupied country again and hear that knock on the door in the middle of the night.

Later, in the summer of 1961, when Netty was expecting our son Richard, we spent a vacation in Vienna. During our two week stay there, the Russians and their Eastern communist satellites fenced off their territory because too many citizens of their Communist paradise did not seem to like living there and were fleeing to the West. This was the beginning of the famous Berlin Wall, which was actually just the part inside Berlin of a man-made barrier that ran from the Baltic to the Alps and kept the entire population of all these countries prisoner. We drove from Vienna to the Czechoslovakian border and got a glimpse of the Soviet empire when we looked at the watch towers along the border. It took more than twenty years before the wall came down.

When the Cuban missile crisis erupted in 1962, I was again in Europe, this time alone on a business trip. I remember well how I discussed the threat of a nuclear attack on Europe with a German gentleman traveling in a train from Brussels to Frankfort. We quietly talked about the "nuclear threshold" and wondered who would step over it first in case a conflict erupted. It was a tense moment in the history of the cold war and I was not too happy to find myself on the wrong side of the Atlantic.

When the Soviet Union finally collapsed in 1989, the U.S. had spent untold billions of dollars on defense. The American economy experienced great stresses caused by the military spending which triggered huge budget deficits and inflation and deflected resources away from more humane causes. From President Johnson's policy of "guns and butter" to Nixon's bombing of Vietnam and Reagan's spending on defense against what he called "the evil empire," America was spending a good part of its treasure on military projects that now seem useless. It remains an open question why the American intelligence services with their incredibly sophisticated technology were unable to see that the Soviet Union was on the verge of economic collapse. Ironically the cuts in military spending implemented when the cold war was over caused further disruptions as people who had made a living in the defense industry found themselves suddenly out of work. But on balance, we were in my view still not cutting defense spending enough. We did not seem to be able to clearly visualize the role the U.S. has to play in the future, without a Soviet threat that was the major factor in all military and foreign policy decisions for fifty years.

After the Gulf War of 1991 and the terrorist attacks on America in 2001, the U.S. military posture changed again. The need to take military action against rogue regimes in faraway places dictated a revision of its readiness from waging war in large conflicts over large areas of the globe to fighting small wars in remote areas. It certainly made more spending necessary again, and we ended up with a horrendously expensive conflict in Iraq and Afghanistan.

Beyond wars, economic trends had also a great impact on our lives and will most likely continue to do so. The Depression of the thirties hit Holland hard. As a country dependent on world trade and active in the commodities trade to and from Indonesia, the disruption of trade and deflation of currencies brought great misery to the Dutch. Unquestionably, America was hit much harder by the Depression, but then almost all economic events are on a larger scale in the U.S. than in little Holland. Although I do not know this for a fact, my grandfather, who made his career and fortune in Indonesia, most likely went there from Germany where he grew up because Europe had been in an economic depression in 1870. He probably thought it would be better to go to an area where an economic boom was in progress. When the Great Depression hit in the thirties, he sustained severe financial setbacks. At that time my father, who worked at Royal Dutch Shell, was sent to Patagonia, a desolate region of Argentina, with my mother and me. Basically his assignment there was to decide how many people should be let go at several oil fields they were developing there. The Argentine government had reneged on a promise to build a refinery near the oil field Shell was developing. World demand for oil was shrinking rapidly and Royal Dutch had to cut back on its spending on oil field production development. The Great Depression created an atmosphere of fear in the world that remained with us and overshadowed the thinking of several generations for decades. Most people tried to avoid risk, hung on to their jobs and saved their money. Interest rates were low and capital growth through investment in equities was virtually non-existent. This atmosphere was not conducive to entrepreneurial activity and risk taking. It spawned an attitude of fear of change and of new things which put a stamp on the behavior of people all over the world until well after World War II.

World War II created enormous disruptions in the economies of many countries. Holland's economy was seriously affected by the German occupation and the Allied military action to dislodge the Germans that followed. The Germans systematically plundered the country, starting in an organized fashion, and gradually building up to a high level of vicious random destruction. For example, after they were finally gone, every foot of the docks in Rotterdam's harbor was meticulously blown up to make it useless for shipping. All cranes were toppled into the water. The entire railway system in the country was stripped of its brass overhead wires and many miles of track were ripped up. Almost all locomotives were gone or destroyed and there were hardly any railway cars left. There were hardly any bicycles or automobiles left either. Financially the country was in very sad shape and it took almost fifteen years before the Dutch guilder was again freely exchangeable into any other currency. The shops were totally bare and rationing of food, textiles, shoes etc. continued for at least two years. Small wonder that it took so long for people to change their lifestyle from merely trying to survive to recovering a sense of optimism about the future.

When we moved to America in 1958, Holland was well on its way to becoming the prosperous country it now is, but for us it was still quite a quantum leap forward. Eisenhower was president, new technological developments were presented almost on a daily basis, people were confident about the future, families moved to the suburbs, houses were equipped with more convenient appliances than we knew in Holland, the interstate highway network was being built and large cars with lots of chrome and spectacular tail fins rolled along these new roads. People in America had come out of a depression and a war as victors and they were optimistic again, aggressively seeking the good life. Quite a change from postwar Europe. There were problems lurking in the background, but it took almost fifteen years before America began to feel their impact. There were unresolved social and racial problems such as vast differences between rich and poor in many parts of the country and the movement towards racial equality that caused much pain was just beginning in 1958. But still, America had a very low rate of inflation, low interest rates and an extremely strong currency when we came. Worldwide it was an uncontested superpower. Slowly change set in. It became clear that the Europeans and later the Japanese were manufacturing goods that could be sold to the U.S. at very competitive prices. It took decades before American corporations and their managers awakened to the competitive threat and tightened up. The economy was further burdened by the implementation of large social spending programs. Many of these programs fulfilled needs that had been ignored for several decades, but the cost of these programs, in addition to the cost of defense spending, caused large budget deficits that forced the government to borrow more and to raise taxes. Interest rates began to rise and gradually confidence in the future sagged. The Vietnam War and the policy of President Johnson to finance both large expenditures for this war and simultaneously establissh a very ambitious program of social reform put the country in a downward slide which was further aggravated by the policies of the Nixon administration. Nixon had to resign because of the Watergate scandal and was succeeded by Ford who was not elected. Ford tried to win the next election, but lost to Carter and during the Carter administration inflation peaked. Jimmy Carter was only president for one term and his successor, Ronald Reagan, an elderly, somewhat anachronistic president who was a Hollywood movie actor before becoming governor of California, managed to bring inflation under control by implementing draconian measures. Interest rates reached historically very high levels, the dollar lost further ground, but the rate of inflation was significantly reduced. The American economy then entered a period of great prosperity with excellent growth. At the same time government spending continued on an economically unsustainable level because Congress was, ever since the days of the Great Depression, controlled by the Democrats who favored spending programs for social purposes and also because Reagan, a conservative Republican, promoted heavy spending for defense. Reagan's defense build-up is credited for causing the downfall of the Soviet empire. We simply outspent them. But the result was enormous budget deficits that caused heavy government borrowing. This growth period flattened out when Reagan's successor George H. W. Bush was president and at this writing we really do not yet know whether the Reagan-Bush years laid the groundwork for the long period of economic growth that started on their watch. Prosperity continued during the presidency of Bill Clinton who talked well but ran an erratic administration. But he achieved excellent economic growth, and created a budget surplus. Robert Rubin, the Democratic secretary of the treasury in the Clinton administration, did an outstanding job, establishing conservative spending policies and a strong dollar, only to slip seriously after he left government and became part

of the management of City Corp, one of America's largest banks. The bank's policies which he strongly supported contributed greatly to the credit crisis of '08 which
almost brought the American economy to its knees.

The event that overshadowed US diplomacy for years was the terrorist attack
on America on September 11, 2001. President George W. Bush was only in the
eighth month of his administration when this attack hit. Netty and I were home. I
was reading the paper in the morning as is my habit, when Netty told me she had
seen on TV that a plane had hit the World Trade Center. We looked at our TV and
then went outside, it was a crystal clear beautiful fall day, and from the end of our
street, we could see Manhattan. Through our binoculars we could see the towers
burn. This was the first time America was attacked at home and the impact of this
atrocity was and is still felt as an event that changed our world. We went to war, first
in Afghanistan, then in Iraq. The outcome of these actions is still not clear. What
is clear is that it cost many lives and enormous amounts of money. The economy
had already started a mild recession when Bush II was inaugurated. It now went
in further decline and the dollar weakened severely while the national debt rose to
unheard of levels. The boom we had experienced for more than ten years came to an
end and in a complete role reversal the Republicans used their control of Congress
to outspend the Democrats and create huge budget deficits. They were forced to
borrow excessively abroad and put the dollar into a tailspin. America became a
much maligned and resented superpower and terrorism was a factor we probably will
have to live with for many, many years. The question remains whether the boom
period was only a period in which America postponed facing up to its deeper, more
systemic financial problems and a needed restructuring of its society. My conclusion
is that the two or three decades briefly described here brought many positive changes
in the environment in which we lived. The financial and economic disruptions we
lived through made it no longer possible for us to adhere to a traditional code of
economic behavior. What happened in the fall of 2008 changed the playbook drastically. It completely uprooted our economy and our way of looking at things. We
came to the brink of the precipice and almost were thrown into a thirties type depression. Our parents and grandparents could stick to traditional economic behavior.
They knew that if you put money in a savings account or invested it in the shares of
a sound company, capital would inevitably deliver a handsome return if one waited
long enough and did not squander one's savings. They had a good economic compass that had been proven to be right for decades. We had to discard our compass.
Today we must be constantly alert to change, try to understand it and act upon it. It

seems to me that we will unfortunately have to continue to live that way and that our children and grandchildren will face a much tougher challenge. They will have to be constantly alert and aware of the world around them to survive. To say you do not understand what is going on in the economy and therefore do not care is in my view absolutely suicidal. There is no investment without risk and there is no certainty in life. In Holland after four decades in a welfare state the Dutch have strung up so many safety nets that people now expect their government to take care of everything. Despite this we see that the economy of the Netherlands is over all doing well. The Dutch like to govern by consensus and they have recognized that the economic burden of a multitude of social measures has become so great and has spawned so many excesses that the painful process of giving up entitlements had to be started. The country is adjusting as the Dutch always seem to do. They have found a way of life that is financially conservative but socially liberal. Life in America offers more risk but also definitely more opportunity, and in the long run the American system always seems able to find working solutions which justifies an optimistic view of the future, uncertain as it may be. Netty and I prefer to live in this environment and have no desire whatsoever to return to our country of origin

2 : *Holland and the Dutch*

Holland or the Netherlands (both names can be used) is an interesting country with a long, varied and fascinating history. Some basic knowledge of the history of the Netherlands is important to get a flavor of the country and the origins of its people and in my view essential to a clear understanding of our family's history and its mostly Dutch background.

My fascination with history will certainly be quite noticeable in this family story and will here and there result in the linking of major parts of my own story and that of our immediate relatives to what was happening in the world around us in the past eighty years. I am particularly interested in those segments of world history I never learned about in school because they had not yet taken place or occurred too recently to be part of the history curriculum. It is not unusual to expect a change in public opinion about occurrences that took place only a few decades ago. This has happened especially with the tumultuous and complex history of World War II and its aftermath, particularly the Cold War. Many things are only now revealed or discussed in a proper perspective and in recent years drastic changes have often been made in our perception of events that took place in the recent past. Another reason why Dutch schools in my time ignored a good part of world history may stem from a rather provincial attitude that believed that only the history of Europe, the Western world and particularly The Netherlands mattered. What happened in America was unimportant because the U.S. was a young unsophisticated country and had only a short history in the opinion of the Dutch. What happened in the rest of the world outside Europe and its colonies was by definition also unimportant. For instance, I cannot remember ever having heard of the U.S. Civil War while I was in a history class in Holland. These attitudes are still prevalent in Europe and to a large extent also in the U.S. We tend to think our own history is most important and ignore the history of major countries in Asia such as China, Japan and India and we are only just beginning to realize that the European conquest of the rest of the world was in almost all cases a disaster rather than a blessing for the people living in the regions that were being colonized.

We also have the imbedded belief that art, be it music, painting, sculpture or literature, is only valid if it has Western European origins. It is only now, at the beginning of the twenty first century, that these prejudices are slowly being removed. Be that as it may, I can only hope that reading my discussions of history written in a style that reveals lack of writing and literary experience and lack of real in-depth knowledge of history, will not be a tremendous bore for my children, grandchildren and others. Believe me, it has been a great deal of fun for me to put this history together. Let me not forget uttering the hope that what I write will be mostly correct.

If one would want to engage in hair splitting, Holland would be the name originally used for what are now the two provinces of North and South Holland that were usually combined with the province of Zeeland. The official name now used by the Dutch government is "Kingdom of The Netherlands" which consists of twelve provinces, including the three mentioned before. "Netherlands," of course, refers to the low elevation above sea level of the country and the name "Low Countries" sometimes used for both Holland and Belgium is an appropriate derivation from that.

People living in the province of Friesland, who have their own language, history and traditions, are a fiercely independent lot. In tune with moves by ethnic groups that are asserting their independence all over the world, the Friesians are now agitating for more special treatment and for preservation of their ethnic identity, language and history. In Friesland, road signs indicating names of towns and villages are now both in Friesian and Dutch. To this day, Friesians speak of going to "Holland," when they mean leaving their province to go to the wicked strange region comprised of the two provinces on the shore of the North Sea. The Friesians (*Friezen*) are good people. My mother and Netty's father were, at least in part, Friesian. They were born there and spent a good part of their youth in Friesland. They always went to great length to ensure you knew that they were not "Hollanders." Netty's uncle, *Oom* Eelco, gave us his personal memoir in two volumes he published titled *Belevenissen* (Life Experiences). He describes how strange it was for him as a grade school child, to move to Groningen, capital of the adjoining province of the same name. He moved all of fifty miles to the east of Heereveen where he had lived before, and suddenly found himself in a strange new country. His father was newly appointed as district attorney at the court of justice in the city of Groningen. He claims that *Groningers* not only speak differently, which is true, but also look different physically, since they belong to a different race. I think the second point is questionable. There are some other statements in his memoir that are in my opinion not entirely true or somewhat off the mark. But most of what he writes is excellent, very readable and very interesting. I will use the valuable background information Oom Eelco gives us elsewhere when I deal with the world in which Netty's father grew up.

Some four centuries ago, Holland was a world power, regularly waging war with England for control of the oceans and thus protect its trade interests. From that time stem the many mostly derogatory references in the English language to the Dutch. In the Greenwich Library I found two full pages of them in a book called *Wicked Words*. The political entity then known as "Holland," consisted of seven provinces. The city-state of Amsterdam was probably most powerful in Holland, and for quite a while a dominant center of world power. Beyond Holland (North and South), the province of Zeeland was also part of this powerful group. Today Holland is a rather small member of the European Union, but if compared with other smaller member nations, it is in many respects a more significant one. The Dutch always participate much more vigorously than other smaller European countries in international efforts, be they sponsored by the EU or the United Nations or by NATO, the North Atlantic Treaty Organization (originally founded to present a united military alliance to oppose the threat of the Soviet Union). It is a fact of life that Germany and France dominate in today's European Union and that the United Kingdom is a third key player. The rather insignificant role played by the Netherlands in the Union is often a source of irritation for the Dutch. Still, the Dutch tend to be reasonable in international affairs, usually joining the consensus point of view and seldom rocking the boat.

The population of Holland is generally quite well educated and almost everybody speaks some English. In addition, many people have a working knowledge of several other languages. There is, and always has been an attitude of openness to the rest of the world and of tolerance towards other cultures and religions or political attitudes which is further stimulated by the business done by many Dutch companies all over the globe. The country is so small that the home market is negligible and any Dutch business of reasonable size must look abroad to grow. Of the ten or twenty largest companies outside the United States and Japan, there are at least three or four that are Dutch or partly Dutch. Royal Dutch Shell is partly Dutch and partly British and so is Unilever. Large companies such as AKZO (chemicals) and Philips (consumer electronics) are purely Dutch. Heineken is the world's largest exporter of beer and KLM, now part of Air France, is prominent among the world's medium sized airlines. Countries such as Belgium, Norway, Spain or Greece, to name a few other smaller EU members, do not have a comparable international business presence. The Dutch have always viewed the world as their oyster and have never shirked away from moving abroad to work or settle. Characteristically they have usually assimilated themselves into the population of the country where they settled and not made much of an effort to maintain their national identity. This is probably a reflection of their self-assured disposition which makes it unnecessary to be demonstrative about their background or seek support from fellow countrymen.

The Irish, the Italians, Greeks and other ethnic groups living in and around New York City parade down Fifth Avenue to make sure the world knows who they are and where they come from. It is their way of demonstrating how well they did after arriving quite poor. They want to maintain a support network that protects them from those who arrived earlier and may feel superior to them and those who arrived after them and may threaten their newly achieved position. To the best of my knowledge, the Dutch as a group have never paraded in New York City. Historically speaking, they do not need to because they were the ones that originally bought the place. They bought Manhattan (cheaply of course, for a few trinkets) from the Indians (now called Native Americans) who were living there. The coat of arms of Manhattan shows a Dutch windmill and the colors of orange, white and light blue, the original colors of the flag of the Dutch republic. They were there first and since they tend to feel somewhat superior to everybody else anyway, they do not need a parade. But that may not be the only reason. They want to assimilate, yet at the same time feel quite comfortable maintaining some residue of a national identity. So they tend to be quite happy becoming citizens of a new country, without completely rejecting their own background. This is not to say that Dutchmen traveling abroad cannot be as obnoxious as any other group when they try to tell the world how great they are. Dutch crowds attending football (soccer) matches are as bad as any other nationality, if not worse. However, in normal life outside the sports stadium, I believe the Dutch are individualists and internationalists and feel quite capable of handling their own affairs. Since they have no desire to remain Dutchmen at all cost, wherever they are, it is often difficult for them to organize any kind of club or group outside their country. The difficulties the Netherland Club in New York City has had for decades to stay financially viable are an example.

It is also worth noting that most Dutch people living and working in America are well educated and did not come here because the economic situation at home was desperate, or because they were victims of political persecution. They came here to seek a career that was even better than the one they could build at home and/or to benefit from the less confining business climate the US offers. In our case these are certainly the principal reasons why we came here. Once we got here we were anxious to get to know Americans and found them often more interesting than people who like us happened to come from Holland and with whom we had otherwise little in common.

Another factor why Dutchmen mix reluctantly with other Dutchmen abroad is that they are still burdened with the quite pronounced social stratification of society in Holland, which is an almost unavoidable fact of life. The Dutchmen who come to America carry their own social prejudices in their luggage. Consequently, to find Dutch friends abroad, one has to find people who belong to one's own, often quite narrowly defined group. Social stratification in Holland is difficult if not impossible to escape and equally difficult to define. In many respects the situation is similar to that in Britain, but definitely not as pronounced. As a people the Dutch are very tolerant and willing to welcome any foreigner, unknown religion or new political movement, but the stranger who comes to live in Holland will discover that as individuals the Dutch are often hard to approach. As true individualists they carry this characteristic quite far. So even while they like to be their own master and prefer not to be identified as belonging to a certain group, a Dutchman is still very conscious of the pigeonhole he belongs in. If he is looking for a marriage partner or a friend, he still has to apply a number of tests before he can be certain he is associated with the right person. For instance, when Netty and I grew up one of the important divisions in Dutch life was religion. Our families were Protestant and our parents simply did not have any social contact with Catholics. Jews were another matter. They were a more or less floating group that dissected society and that was almost totally destroyed by the German anti-Semitic policies. As it turned out, my best friend Rob Laane is a Catholic and so was my close friend Oc (Octave) van Crugten, with whom I served in the army. Needless to say, while Catholics, they belong to the correct social group and went to the right universities, otherwise we would not have felt comfortable with each other. This is a little tongue in cheek but really quite true. Broadly speaking the religious division of the population has now disappeared, but the social stratification is still very much intact. The sad reason for the disappearance of religious divisions in recent years is that religion itself has virtually disappeared in the Netherlands. Since the government takes care of nearly every facet of life, the threat that something could go drastically wrong in one's life for which divine intervention might be needed is gone and so is the need to contemplate the deeper origins of spiritual life in a society where materialism and the pursuit of comfort has taken the upper hand.

As I mentioned earlier, Holland is somewhat similar to England in the arena of social stratification, although the Dutch nobility is considerably less well established and socially less powerful. There is no House of Lords in Holland. Despite all efforts to level the playing field, there still is a clearly defined upper class, a middle class and a lower class, but the differences are ebbing away. People belonging to these classes behave differently, have different table manners, different hobbies, prefer different sports (for instance, in Holland golf has only recently become a sport for all classes as it is in the U.S.), and most important, speak with a notably different accent. In contrast to the U.S. it is difficult to move from one minutely defined Dutch social layer to another. I believe that social mobility as it is strongly imbedded in US society is a great asset, but as a former Dutchman, when I have social contacts with other Dutch people, I just often feel the old barriers go up again as soon as we start talking. In the 1960s a book called *The Dutch Puzzle* became a best seller in Holland. It was written by a Spanish nobleman, the Duke de Baena, who was for many years Spain's ambassador to the Netherlands. It describes the Dutch in a witty and masterful way. The Duke says, "Never in my long and adventurous life have I known a people so riddled with paradoxes as the Dutch...Each Dutch citizen wants to be free as a person; nothing could be more laudable than his attitude towards life. The laws of the realm provide the Dutch with all the basic freedoms that they could wish for, so they have nothing to worry about here. Freedom of speech, of opinion, of religious practice, of sexual peculiarities, of the rights of minorities, of racial diversity – all these rights are firmly rooted in the Dutch soil and soul, more deeply, perhaps, than in any other country in Europe: but...The application and interpretation of these holy rights to daily life in Holland are not always so easy to follow nor to understand. Along with this great feeling for liberty, there also exists – and here we come to the first paradox – an extraordinary conformism with a real stranglehold of tyrannical conventions that the Dutch dare not break. With the curious result that a great majority of the Dutch are constantly thwarted in their daily freedom by all sorts of conventional habits, habits that are looked upon with great respect by a bourgeois society that does not believe in eccentricity or even in enthusiasm, but which is obsessed by a middle-class idea of respectability. ..." Very well said, I believe. The Dutch are free to do as they like, as long as they stay within the parameters of their group or class. And so it was when I grew up and so it remains.

The Spanish duke visited Holland three times. The first time he came was right after the first World War, when the Dutch were feeling quite superior. They were prosperous, had stayed out of the war and were convinced the Lord had kept them out because they were such good people. The second time he came as ambassador to The Hague was right after the Second World War when Holland was devastated and the Dutch had gone through a terrible experience. He observed that they were still quite religious and showed remarkable resilience and spirit in their effort to recover from the war's impact. The duke wrote in great detail about the religious divisions that ran through Dutch society of that time. He observed that, "Before the Reformation was established, the inhabitants of Flanders and the Delta were perhaps the most licentious people in Europe. Their Roman Catholic faith did not stop or even lessen their natural inclination to indulge their senses, and in the paintings of Jan Steen, one of the last of the great Dutch Roman Catholic painters, we can still witness the manner in which the Dutch could revel in eating, drinking and loving to excess – *La Kermesse Heroique*. Something had to change, and that something became of enormous importance in the Netherlands. To brake their self indulgence, the Calvinists came along with their most rigid form of self denial. This is perhaps the most important paradox of all in the Dutch character. The nature of the Dutch today is still warm-hearted, tender, realistic and full of the urge of the senses. Because of the Protestant and Calvinistic education the Dutch receive, they are taught to be reserved, cautious, calculating, prim, proper and rigidly puritanical in their outlook on life. The result is a constant struggle between their natural urge to satisfy their senses and the principles of their education, a fight between Jan Steen and Calvin." I think this observation is also right on the mark. My parents and also I, myself, have always been burdened by a feeling that being frivolous, "cutting loose" as they say nowadays, was somehow not right. You had to be sober and keep a low profile. *"Dat mag niet"* – that's not allowed – is an expression that has overshadowed our lives and made many pleasures sinful and unacceptable. The third time the Duke de Baena lived in Holland was in the sixties when the Dutch had turned away from religion and had embraced the welfare state. He noticed a certain lack of spine and great complaisance among the Dutch. His book ends in 1968 and with the benefit of hindsight I can add that it got a lot worse. Jan Steen has practically overrun Calvin in Holland. Compared with the postwar period, materialism, sexual indulgence and lack of a moral compass are very much in evidence. Still, in Holland at the turn of this century, family life flourishes and businessmen are successful and very disciplined in their work. So it is not all a Sodom and Gomorrah although you have to wonder when you see whole pages of small ads in Dutch newspapers in which prostitutes offer their services, brothels describe the "relaxation" they offer their visitors and homosexuals display their charms. This has gone on for years and if these advertisers were not making any money with their offerings they would be long gone. So you have to assume that a lot is going on behind the scenes.

As the history of the Netherlands shows, Holland was and remains a country of merchants, businessmen and entrepreneurs. There is an intense interest in the outside world. As the Duke de Baena wrote," The consequence of this is their deep curiosity in the habits, character and social conditions of foreigners; but this does not mean that their interest in the outside world changes anything at all in their national ideas and dogmatic principles, which finally are equivalent to constant sermons. The Dutch do not often realize that when speaking to you they are frequently giving you a lengthy sermon, which can be irritating because it sounds as if they alone among human beings have the privilege of knowing the truth." I often think back to my own pronouncements when I was new in the U.S. and my American friends asked me what I thought of their country and how it compared with Holland. I shudder when I realize how I was preaching and pontificating and suggesting I knew it all. Perhaps, I am still doing it from time to time. Many visitors from the Netherlands are apt to do it here and nobody seems to realize that Americans are taught to be friendly and noncritical in their relationships with others. Certainly less critical. There is a tendency among the Dutch to be outspoken and blunt in discussions and critical in voicing opinions about others.

In the so-called Golden Age, Amsterdam became the richest city in the world. It was populated by businessmen who led a very opulent life and the leading families in that city were not members of the nobility, they were burghers. They were businessmen and rich, and they liked to call themselves "Patricians." The men and women one sees on portraits by Rembrandt, Frans Hals and others belong to that group. How wealthy these burghers were becomes clear when one realizes how many good paintings of artists living in that era presently exist and are displayed in museums and private collections all over the world. These painters must have had patrons and they catered to them. They were free to paint what they liked and what attracted them. In countries like Italy and Spain, most painters catered to their most important client, the church, with the result that their museums are filled with pictures of saints and martyrs with arrows piercing their bodies and other devotional scenes. Much less interesting, in my opinion. The population of Holland during the Golden Age was, of course, considerably smaller than it is now. Thus the people living at that time must have possessed an enormous number of paintings and mountains of furniture, large cabinets *kasten*, tables, chairs, clocks, etc., etc. Today almost all families of some means living in Holland own several antique pieces of furniture which were mostly made during the Golden Age and later. So given the fact that the population must have increased at least tenfold since that time, the Dutch must have been very, very wealthy in the Golden Age and have accumulated enormous quantities of earthly goods.

The form of government of the original seven provinces in the seventeenth century was a republic and a very democratic and orderly one. The head of state was a Prince who had the title of Stadholder, but the real power lay with the patricians. Merchants had the upper hand politically and in wealth. There was no king surrounded by a group of nobles who lorded it over the population and controlled large tracts of land. The Prince ruled a republic, a truly unique construction. Accordingly there never has been as much of a deep divide between a small group of extremely rich and powerful nobles and all the others, as you could see in Britain until very recently and in France before the French revolution. The patricians were a large and growing group. They have always had a dominant position in Dutch society and their roots are mainly in the two main provinces in the western part of Holland. Even today this is the case. The business people are concentrated in the west and the Dutch nobility generally has roots in the eastern part. The Patricians even have a register of their own in which they trace their ancestry, a blue book which is kept up-to-date by an organization specifically entrusted with this task called *Het Nederlands Patriciaat*. When your family is in that book, you have made it. The Schieferdeckers are definitely not in it. They do not have a long enough history in Holland and if they had, it is questionable if they would qualify as they are a family of business people with diverse and ordinary origins. The van Someren Gréve and Hesselink families are in, (despite the very humble background of my grandfather Hesselink). The van Kleffens family is not listed either because as Netty's mother said, "they felt they were too important for that." The nobility, meanwhile, is listed in a red book. They keep to themselves but intermingle with the patricians if they must, and throughout history they had to.

Holland has many universities, but the four more important and oldest ones are Leiden and Amsterdam in the west, Groningen in the north and Utrecht in the middle – towards the east. As could be expected, the nobility has traditionally preferred Utrecht and the patricians Leiden and Amsterdam. The important technical university of Delft is of more recent vintage.

After World War II Holland was governed for a very long time by a coalition of the Socialist and Christian Democrat parties. They made a concerted effort to make the country more egalitarian and to abolish the social stratification described above. They were extraordinarily successful in eliminating financial stratification, but social stratification largely remained. At the outset their policies were very liberal, very much to the left, and they had a profound impact on Dutch society.

The welfare state has penetrated every area of human life in the Netherlands and it has undoubtedly brought tremendous change and vast improvements in the life of many. It has created a social environment that is very different from the one I grew up in. Today it is impossible to list all the entitlements and services the Dutch government offers its citizens. They reach into every nook and cranny of life and sometimes have maddeningly precise and complicated rules. People were given universal health care, everybody got a pension and it became virtually impossible to fire an employee, no matter how bad they performed. Anybody who has to stop working because of illness or job elimination receives 70% of his or her former pay from the government, no questions asked and no time limit. So, many people who wanted to stop working and relax claimed to be unable to work for health reasons. Backaches were and are still popular because they are hard to disprove. Meanwhile, on the positive side, there is now general prosperity, nobody lacks medical care or housing, splendid roads were built and significant public works completed, particularly a huge flood control system built after the disastrous flood of 1953. While generally beneficial, the welfare state has also brought unattractive and unwanted side effects. It has embedded behavior into Dutch society that stems from living for almost five decades in an environment where individual "rights" and "entitlements" are of great importance and come first while citizenship and civic duties such as the requirement to defend one's country or volunteer for charitable work are pushed into the background. The overarching emphasis on fairness and equality for all has reduced the competitive drive in people and in businesses and has, at least in my opinion, diminished commercial risk-taking in a country that has always prided itself on its entrepreneurial spirit. In the armed forces it has eroded discipline and fighting spirit. The level of charitable giving known in the U.S. is totally unknown in Holland. People feel the government should take care of all social ills. Tuition payments which in America are a major financial burden for every parent are equally foreign. A comparatively very modest sum is annually required for university enrollment and recently a small increase in this fee almost triggered student riots. Admission to a university education is open to every high school graduate and not based on academic achievement. That would be undemocratic. For instance, because demand exceeds available space, there was until recently a lottery for those who wished to enter medical school. No matter how gifted you were, if you drew the wrong number you were out of luck. This system has been changed in the last few years and sanity and merit prevails again, luckily.

So in the fifties, sixties and seventies, government policies were structured to create a complete welfare state with "cradle-to-grave" security for everyone. Unavoidably taxes went up to finance these plans, and it soon became clear that the prevailing political doctrine saw taxes not only as a means of covering government expenditures but also as a means of achieving social objectives i.e., an egalitarian society. As time went by, the new system built a large number of entitlements and a great deal of inflexibility into Dutch society and over the years this inflexibility became a huge burden. The end result was that the rich got poorer and the poor got a little more prosperous. However, there was one snag. The rich used to save and now stopped doing so. Capital formation declined and economic activity diminished. The Dutch lower middle class now tends to spend all the money they have because they do not have to worry about building a nest egg for their old age. Polls indicate that a large majority of Dutch people consider themselves as belonging to the middle class. They have a voting majority, and support government give-away programs for their own benefit.

Gradually it became clear that the government was spending too much and even worse, was actually using windfall income received from the discovery of a huge natural gas field in the Northern provinces, to cover budget deficits. It was suddenly realized the gas might run out some day. It also began to sink in that the Dutch population like that of most other industrialized countries was getting older and that there were simply not enough young people born to earn the money the government needed to spend on their parents. While this notion was beginning to work its way into the political thinking process, the economies of many other Western European countries were also beginning to slow down. Not surprisingly, of course, because they had welfare states similar to the Dutch and their demographic trends were the same. There was more and more competition from developing nations, particularly in Asia, that had much lower wage levels. A worldwide squeeze on profitability spawned a movement to slim down payrolls. This hit the Dutch particularly hard because they found themselves frozen into a rigid full-employment system with guaranteed compensation for anybody who was out of work. Initially a particularly Dutch solution was proposed to alleviate the problem of finding jobs for younger people and increasing the number of jobs. It was decided to promote early retirement and force everybody who was working to take more time off. So even the smallest businesses had to close down an extra day a month. Businesses had to grant older employees early retirement. The way they did this was to ask them to agree to leave voluntarily. Those that agreed to leave then got the customary unemployment compensation of

70% of their previously earned salary and their employer contributed the remaining 30% until they reached retirement age and their pension would kick in. Obviously this proved to be a harebrained and extremely costly idea. It increased the cost of doing business for everybody, increased the cost of unemployment payments by the state, ignored the contribution older more skilled people were making and lowered the competitive position of the Dutch economy. The Dutch government realized it was bankrupting itself.

In the mid-nineties the government began discussions with employers, the unions and the political parties. The Dutch realized they really had to tighten their belts and although there is much anguish about the way in which this had to be implemented, it was done. It was an amazing change for an entire nation and a typical example of the Dutch ability to be reasonable and accept a consensus point of view. There were no strikes or riots, everybody seemed to agree that the welfare wagon had rolled on too far and that some of the more extreme entitlements had to be rolled back. With this new social contract agreed upon Holland turned its economy around and in 1996 its currency was among the strongest in the EU, its financial position sound and its methods to repair overspending the envy of its EU partners. Many countries sent delegations to the Netherlands to find out how they had managed to get a social contract accepted by the entire population that initially resulted in the loss of many jobs, a reduction in social spending, a lowering of taxes to promote private enterprise, privatization of several sacred institutions like the postal service and many other measures that were basically capitalist and not socialist in origin. The Dutch solution was called the "Polder Plan" and people started to dig for its origins and for documentation. This lead to a stunning discovery—there was no plan. The Dutch had simply sat down with all parties and reasoned things out. Most important, they had reached a political consensus. The timing was right and the economic pressures of the previous years had made it clear to all that they could not continue to ratchet up the cost of their welfare state forever and at the same time remain competitive. Corporate profitability improved, unemployment went down, inflation was lowered and interest rates could be set at attractively low levels. It was a clear example of the Dutch habit of lengthy discussions with all parties concerned, consensus building and a national characteristic of tolerance.

As a side effect of the fiscal climate in earlier years, people with money voted with their feet and left the country in droves and, thus far, they have not returned.

Water has always played an important role in the history of the Netherlands. The Netherlands is situated in a delta formed by the rivers Rhine (*Rijn*), Meuse (*Maas*) and Scheldt (*Schelde*), and has for thousands of years commanded these major transport routes. Because of its unique strategic position, many attempts were made to dominate the country. The Romans, Franks, Burgundians and Hapsburgs have all left their mark on its culture, and Holland's curiously erratic borders in the east and south are the result of numerous peace treaties.

The landscape of the Netherlands was formed in prehistoric times by several ice ages. Around 3000 BC changes in the sea level formed the dunes along the present North Sea coast. Still, large areas of the country were flooded regularly, making it virtually uninhabitable. The first traces of habitation go back to 150,000 B.C. in the hilly area of Utrecht, but it wasn't until 5000 B.C. that a form of farming was found. In the province of Drenthe there are still impressive grave sites constructed by prehistoric inhabitants. The graves were made of huge boulders left by glaciers that covered the country during the ice age. The graves are called "*Hunnebedden*" in Dutch. They fascinated us as children, and I can well remember building models of them with rocks in sand boxes to be displayed at school to give our parents an impression of what we learned in our history lessons (they dutifully pretended to be interested.) Other traces include utensils made in the Bronze Age (1900-750 B.C.) and later in the Iron Age (750 B.C. and beyond.) The Celts then living in the country were driven out by Germanic tribes such as the Friesians in the north and the Batavians near the great rivers. When I was young, the first history lesson of a Dutch child always began with the statement that the Batavians (*Batavieren*) came to the Netherlands by floating down the Rhine in log canoes. Where they came from and why they did it was usually left to the child's imagination. In 57 B.C. the Romans conquered the Netherlands and Julius Caesar describes his campaign in his "de Bello Gallico." Tacitus, the Roman historian, when talking about the inhabitants of the delta is said to have written about the Batavians: "They form a Germanic group that is extremely civilized but with very rude manners." Little has changed since then.

Although I never studied Latin, I remember that Tacitus also wrote that "Frisia non cantat,", in other words, the Frisians don't sing. This is still a fact and applies to most Dutchmen. There have been several embarrassing moments for Netty and me in America when people asked us to sing a typical Dutch song – we did not know any. There are only a few songs one can call typically Dutch, and many of them have words that are not fit for translation in polite company. There are hymns, of course, after all we started out as religious people and several hymns now found in the church we occasionally go to in Old Greenwich are originally Dutch. The Friesians were never subjected to Roman rule, which may be a reflection of their particularly stubborn nature. Both Netty and I have a touch of this stubbornness, and we are pleased to note our sons and daughter also have a streak of the same disposition. I just have to copy another statement here out of "the Dutch Puzzle" by the Duke de Baena: "The world of hazy beauty in winter and of gleaming sunshine and sparkling clouds in summer is to be found above all in Friesland. The inhabitants of that mysterious region of Holland maintain that they are totally different from the Dutch and all the other peoples of the world, and permit only a certain comparison to be made between themselves and the original Anglo Saxons." My mother, Netty's father and Oom Eelco would have completely agreed.

Under the Romans peace and prosperity prevailed for more than 250 years. The Romans had a profound influence on the native tribes. They built a network of roads and dug canals. The *Vliet,* the canal running along the eastern border of Voorburg, the village where I grew up, was originally dug by the Romans to connect the Rhine with the Maas. It runs from the *Maas* to what is now called the *Oude Rijn* (the Old Rhine) near Leiden and is still in use. Voorburg's history went back to Roman times and the first cub scout troop I belonged to chose as its name "Forum Hadriani" after a Roman market place of which remnants had been found nearby. Later the troop's name became too burdensome and was changed to *Zwarte Panters* (Black Panthers!) because we wore black scarves.

When the Roman Empire began to decline, the Romans withdrew and little was left of their work while Germanic tribes took over. Around A.D. 600 Christianity came to these tribes. Here again the Friesians persisted obstinately in their pagan beliefs. It was only when Anglo-Saxon preachers came from overseas that they were converted. The Friesians then were numerous and reached down to Utrecht. An old monk from Germany, Boniface, wanted to bring the gospel to Friesland but was murdered in 754 in Dokkum, the town near the hamlet where the van Kleffens family originated. Netty's father always insisted that this evil deed was accomplished by poking a spear upwards from under an outhouse where poor Boniface had gone to answer nature's call.

The Roman Empire was replaced by the Frankish empire. The Friesians were defeated by the Franks and pushed back northward and Pepin III, king of the Franks, was anointed by Boniface the missionary, obviously before he made his fatal trip to the outhouse. Pepin was succeeded by Charles who became known as Charlemagne and saw himself as lawful successor to the Roman emperors. For this reason he went to Rome in 800, to be crowned by the Pope. Charlemagne often stayed in the Netherlands at Nijmegen where the ruins of his castle still exist. The Frankish kings developed a feudal system of governance with counts in charge of certain counties, the names of which are still used in Holland, as in Twente, Gooi and Brabant. After the death of Charlemagne, his empire was divided among his three sons and Holland became part of the Holy Roman empire. (It was part of this empire until 1648, when the Eighty Year War was concluded, but actual power lay elsewhere.) Trading flourished and certain cities became important and had to defend themselves against marauding Vikings. Most of the Vikings raiding Holland came from Denmark. They focused their raids on churches and monasteries they were known to be store-houses of wealth. As the Vikings became Christians they gradually lost their zeal for terror and plunder.

The counts administering regions gained power with the count of Holland becoming the more important one. A long list of counts of Holland reigned, and as a school boy I had to memorize their names in the proper order, an example of the futile and "knowledge of facts" orientation of Dutch education in those days. There were many disputes about succession between the counts of Holland and many fights between towns and rulers which also involved the bishops of Utrecht, religious leaders with a different agenda from the counts. Friesland had no dynasty of its own but was fought over by large landowners and feuding monks. In fact, the Frisians did not lose their independence until the end of the fifteenth century. Then the German emperor took over in their region, not the counts of Holland.

The rise of the power of the cities and towns in Holland and the building of dikes and reclamation of land started from the year 1000 onwards. Water Boards - organizations formed to protect the collective interests of people living in low lying areas - were formed. These Water Boards still exist. They supervise maintenance of canals and dikes and charge a tax from all landowners. Near Wassenaar and Leiden is the border between two of these jurisdictions. The level of water maintained in each one is different and connecting canals have locks to keep the water from flooding in or out of the area.

Culture, literature and architecture began to center around cities. Around the tenth to the fourteenth century, regional states were formed which later became the present provinces. The Knight's Hall (*Ridderzaal*) in The Hague, built in the thirteenth century for Floris V, count of Holland, as part of his palace, dates back to that period. (Today this hall is still in use and every third Tuesday in September the queen goes there in her "Golden Carriage," to open parliament for the year with a formal address to both houses, called the "States General," a term used to indicate both houses of parliament that goes back to the fifteenth century. The oration is called *de Troon Rede* (the address from the throne). In it the government outlines its program for the coming year. It is comparable to the State of the Union address in the U.S. Many towns were quite independent and robust little states, minding their own business, but overall sovereignty moved to the family of the Dukes of Burgundy. The authority of Burgundy had deeper roots in the area of what is now Belgium, however. The important cities of Antwerp, Ghent *(Gent)* and Bruges *(Brugge)* were in its grip, but its influence weakened towards the north and the Friesians once again stayed out of reach.

The Burgundian Empire reached from Austria to Spain. Through many well-arranged marriages the house of Burgundy expanded and prospered for two centuries, becoming one of the mightiest dynasties in Europe. Early in the sixteenth century control of the Low Countries moved from the dukes of Burgundy into the hands of the Hapsburg emperor Charles V who was born in Gent in 1500. He was a son of Philip the Fair and Joanna of Castile and was destined to inherit an enormous empire, including what then was named the Netherlands. Charles was declared to be of age in 1515 and became king of Aragon and Castile which included Mexico, Peru and the Philippines. He also inherited the Austrian States and as a result of much intrigue and bribery, became emperor of the Holy Roman Empire. However, the region called Burgundy itself, was part of France and not under his control. Charles appointed a governor to rule over the "Seventeen United Netherlands" from Brussels and organized a civil service that functioned well and was overseen by a chancellor and an advisory council of nobles, professional administrators and lawyers. The States General was one of these councils and later became the governing parliament of the Netherlands. Charles rarely visited the Low Countries, and since the Reformation had started, spent most of his time fighting the Protestants in Germany and in France, and also the Islamic Turks. The fight against Islam stems from the late Middle Ages when Christians slowly reconquered Spain. The *Reconquista* took place from 1085 to 1340. Charles is a key figure in the history of Holland and still has quite a good reputation as a wise and just potentate whose main problem in Holland arose from the increasingly powerful groundswell of the Reformation and its related rebellion against the Catholic Church. Also, his attempts to centralize government ran into opposition from the powerful Dutch cities that began to draw up their own statutes. These two forces, the economic power of the cities and the question of religion, were most likely important sources of friction, causing the rebellion against Spain and the eighty year war that followed after Charles V ceded dominion over the Netherlands to his son Philip II in 1555. As is the case in almost all wars, there also were powerful economic disagreements. The Dutch cities were key transit points in the traffic that moved grain from the Baltic and Eastern Europe up the great rivers. The cities were also important as sources of tax revenue. Dutch harbors were taking trade away from the Hanseatic League and the population of Holland grew and could no longer live off the produce of its own land. As the Dutch cities became more and more prosperous, they did not like to pay taxes to the King of Spain and resented his efforts to control them through a centralized government.

The Renaissance that originated in Italy had an important influence on European society in the fourteenth and fifteenth centuries. Humanism became influential as an expression of the new spirit, which was characterized by great admiration for ancient Greece and Rome. Desiderius Erasmus was a world-famous scholar who lived in Rotterdam and advocated a sober form of religion within the Roman Catholic Church. Education blossomed through Latin schools and the comparatively low percentage of illiterate people in the Netherlands astonished observers from other countries. Well-to-do burghers took up litera-ture after the invention of printing. They also became interested in architecture and sponsored the building of churches. The art of painting developed in the second half of the fifteenth century and Haarlem became a center for painters. Hieronymus Bosch, who worked in's Hertogenbosch, was a painter of that era who showed in his work that the link with the Middle Ages still existed. Over time the Catholic Church became more and more opulent and developed excesses which ultimately led to the Reformation and the proclamation issued by Martin Luther in 1517 who quickly found support in the Netherlands. In Friesland the Baptist faith developed and was preached by Menno Simons. This group became the origin of the *Doopsgezinde Kerk* to which my mother, the van Someren Gréve family and Netty and I belonged when we lived in Holland. The Mennonites in America are descendants of a group, named after Menno Simons that emigrated to America to follow its stricter learning. The American Quakers also have links with our original church in the Netherlands. My mother's sister, Tante (aunt) Jet and her family, who lived in Arnhem and were forced by the Germans to leave their house after the battle of Arnhem, received significant material assis-tance after the liberation from "Quaker Relief," which closely followed the Allied forces and helped people of her church. When we moved to Riverside, we found the Congregational Church and the way in which it worshipped closest in spirit to the church we attended in Holland.

When the teachings of Calvin reached Holland from Geneva around 1550, Calvinism became the foremost Protestant movement in the Netherlands. The Spanish government saw this as a threat and began action against the Protestants. Embracing Calvinism was seen as a gesture of revolt, particularly amongst the lesser nobles who were disparagingly called beggars, or *geux* in French by the Council of State. This word became *geuzen* in Dutch and a badge of honor for a group of raiders who operated from the sea, invading the country from time to time. Some of the leading nobles, who were in the governor's council also were suspected of heresy, among them the counts of Egmont and Hoorne and the Prince of Orange. Meanwhile an economic depression caused by food shortages and a frozen Sound *Sont* near Denmark, which prevented food supplies from coming through, contributed to the fury of the people who started to raid churches, causing irreparable damage and removing all statues to prepare them for Protestant services. To this day visitors to old Dutch churches can see the niches were the statues were ripped out. In 1567 King Philip II reacted. He asked the leading aristocracy to swear an oath of allegiance to him and sent 10,000 men to the Netherlands under the command of the Duke of Alva who began a regime of terror and worse, raised taxes. This caused the population to reject the King's authority and started the war which would last eighty years and became a major event in the history of the Netherlands. Today pilings along canals used to tie up ships are called *ducdalfs* as in Duke d'Alva, a sly way of showing resistance against Spain. As skippers threw a line around a piling and tightened it, like a noose, they were thinking about how much they would like to do the same to Alva. The Prince of Orange fled to Germany with thousands of other rebels. The Counts of Egmont and Hoorne were taken prisoner and executed. Ludwig van Beethoven's Overture Egmont commemorates this event (Beethoven knew about it since his family was Flemish in origin. He was born in Antwerp.) The piece includes a dramatic moment of silence when the executioner's ax comes down on the necks of the poor counts.

William of Orange, who was called William the Silent (*Willem de Zwijger*), raised an army of mercenaries, but he initially lacked popular support and thus was beaten by Alva. Things changed when Alva established a 10% tax on all trans- actions. This touched the Dutch in an extremely sensitive spot and infuriated the merchants and entrepreneurs. It also reduced the States General's ability to collect its own taxes. William of Orange raised another army with financial help from French Protestants, the Huguenots. He attacked but was again unsuccessful. However, the "Sea Beggars," or Geux, did better and captured Brielle in 1572, an event every school child in Holland sings about. *In naam van Oranje doe open de poort, de watergeus ligt voor den Briel.* The rebellion was now in full swing and a number of cities elected William as Stadhouder, which implied that he would still represent the King's authority. Amsterdam did not join for business reasons. A folk song written at that time which became the Dutch National Anthem in the twentieth century, repeats William's own words: "I have always honored the King of Spain." In other words, he was not declaring independence. Meanwhile William lost financial support from the Huguenots in France, as many of them were murdered in Paris in the St. Bartholomew's night massacre. He had to withdraw to the province of Holland. Alva seized the initiative again and sent an army to plunder some of the rebellious towns. Alkmaar defended itself by breaking the dikes around it and flooding the Spaniards out in 1573. So did Leiden in 1574, after a very long siege. The *Geuzen* or Geux came across the flooded polders on flat bottomed boats and the starving population of Leiden saw the Spaniards leave. They rushed out of the city gates and met the Geuzen who presented them with herring and white bread. They also found the food the Spaniards had cooked in their trenches, *hutspot met klapstuk*, a hash of potato's with carrots, onions and sort of a cooked flank steak, tough, awful meat. To this day, the people of Leiden and those who studied there eat herring for lunch and *hutspot* for dinner on October 3rd, the day Leiden was liberated. Netty's father always insisted on these dishes on October 3rd, whether we liked it or not. In thanks to God, the first University of the Northern Provinces was founded in Leiden in 1575. The tide had turned, the Prince of Orange joined the Calvinist church and the States General prohibited Catholic worship.

After the departure of Alva, efforts were made to negotiate an agreement between Spain and the Netherlands' provinces which initially included much of what is now Flanders. There would be religious freedom and the Catholics living in the area would be left alone. Later this proved to be unacceptable and the Northern Provinces made a pact, the Union of Utrecht, which gave them much independence, leaving decisions on war and peace and taxation for unanimous decision. In 1581 the Northern Netherlands finally declared themselves independent from Spain. In 1584 William of Orange was assassinated in Delft by a religious fanatic. He was shot coming down the stairs of the *Prinsenhof* and the bullet hole is preserved in the wall there. In recent years the building was regularly used for the now defunct Antiques Bourse where my father liked to browse and where he acquired several paintings we now have in the family. (Adriaan's Willaert, our Thomas de Keyser and our little Jan van Goyen).

The death of William of Orange confronted the States General with the realization that they needed a leader. They offered sovereignty to the King of France and Queen Elisabeth of England who sent the earl of Leicester as Governor-General. Leicester failed to impress the locals and left after two years. The big threat was the Spanish "Invincible Armada," a huge fleet that was formed in Spain and was sent to teach England a lesson and also to put down the Dutch rebellion. The story of the Armada is interesting. The fleet was poorly organized, poorly commanded and poorly equipped. It included many ships that were unfit for the North Sea. The fleet was beaten by Sir Francis Drake with significant Dutch assistance and subsequently almost completely destroyed by storms off the coast of northern England and Ireland. Some of the Spanish survivors landed in Ireland and settled there.

Prince Maurits succeeded his father. He was assisted by Johan van Oldebarnevelt, the very able senior civil servant of the States of Holland. Maurits was a good soldier and won several decisive battles between 1588 and 1595 while van Oldebarnevelt succeeded in uniting the provinces of the Northern Netherlands with France and England in the Triple Alliance against Spain. Just before he died in 1598, Philip II ignoring reality, had granted the Netherlands to his daughter Isabella.

The climate was ripe for change, but the Dutch were divided. Maurits was for continuing the war, van Oldebarnevelt was for peace and had most of the business people in the important cities on his side. Van Oldebarnevelt negotiated a twelve-year truce. Characteristically, during the truce the Dutch soon got to squabbling among themselves about finer points in their religion. This conflict aggravated the controversy between the Statesman and the Prince. The former joined with the moderate "Remonstrants" and the latter with the more conservative orthodox "Counter Remonstrants." The majority of the provinces sided with the Prince against the powerful provinces of "Holland," and it was decided to convene a national synod at Dordrecht where a new translation of the Bible was authorized. This became the *Staten Bijbel*, the States Bible, which the orthodox Dutch Reformed Church still regards as the only true word of God. The conflict with van Oldebarnevelt later turned ugly and he was imprisoned and executed. At the end of the truce, Maurits continued his successful campaigns and after he died in 1625, his half brother Frederik Hendrik became Stadholder. He also fought skillfully and managed to add parts of Brabant and Limburg to the Republic. After the initial sieges and battles in the earlier part of the war, hostilities moved farther away from the provinces of "Holland." Maurits and Frederik Hendrik campaigned in the eastern and southern parts of what is now the Netherlands, thus allowing the mighty cities, particularly Amsterdam, to gain power. In addition, Admiral Maarten Tromp destroyed a second Armada. However, an outright victory seemed impossible.

In 1640 negotiations were started for a simultaneous peace treaty between Spain and the Republic and between Germany, France and Sweden who had also been at war (and a much bloodier one) for thirty years. It took two years to get all the provinces to agree and then two more years to iron out all difficulties. The treaty was signed in Münster (Germany) in 1648. The United Netherlands became a free and sovereign country that was also acknowledged by the German Emperor, who was in name still sovereign over part of the Northern and Eastern provinces. Spaniards were excluded from trade with areas of the Eastern and West Indies which had been won for the Republic. The position of Amsterdam as an international port was assured at the expense of Antwerp (Holland kept the Scheldt closed to shipping until well into the eighteenth century) and freedom of religion was accepted.

The seventeenth century brought the Golden Age—the most important period in the country's history. Many factors contributed to the economic boom that started in the first two decades, but the most important one was without doubt the absence of protectionism and of a central government that could hamper free trade. Trade with the Baltic in grain and many other commodities flourished. Grain was mainly exported to Spain, a curious fact that highlights the existence of active trade with the enemy throughout the long war. Amsterdam became a major transit port for goods from the Baltic to the Mediterranean and other destinations. This role of Amsterdam and later Rotterdam as important intermediaries in trade, is still a major factor in the Dutch economy. My grandfather who grew up in Germany in the small town of Grimma, near Leipzig, in Saxony, belonged to a family of traders in commodities from the Levant and other places and it was therefore logical for his father, my great grandfather, to send his son to his business friends in Amsterdam for training. My grandfather joined a Dutch firm and eventually went to the East Indies, but that was in 1882.

In the sixteenth century, Holland had not participated in the voyages of discovery that made Spain and Portugal great colonial powers. Both countries were intent on finding new trade routes and on making as much profit as possible out of the areas they conquered. It is worth noting that their policies in administering their colonies differed materially from those followed by the Netherlands, Britain and others. The Spaniards focused on conquest and on exploitation of the land, bringing home all they could get, particularly gold and silver, and on forcing the natives to become Catholics. The Dutch and British were more inclined to establish trading posts. Later when these posts expanded and gradually became colonies, they treated them as profit making enterprises, leaving the population and their religions mostly alone. Traveling east, the Portuguese concentrated on the spice trade. When Philip II captured Lisbon, the European gateway for spices, he closed the port to the Dutch fleet. Only then did the Dutch consider going it alone, which had the added advantage of breaking the Portuguese price monopoly. Later the Dutch also decided to expand in the Americas. Gradually the Dutch became very successful in their voyages of discovery. They prepared thoroughly, had quite well developed cartographers, and above all, had guidance from people who had lived in Spain and Portugal to obtain information. Jan van Linschoten, a famous cartographer, spent 13 years in Spain, Portugal and India and wrote a book that became a source of a great deal of information.

The first voyage, in 1596 during the war with Spain, became one of the most famous ones. Its objective was to find a Northeast passage - the polar route. The expedition stranded at Nova Zembla and was forced to spend the winter there. The stranded crew built a house from the wood of their ship and the remnants of this house are still visited by tourists today. They never made it to the Far East but discovered Spitsbergen which later became a center for the Dutch whaling industry. When I was a young boy, my father was a member of a foundation that published reprints of the old stories of the voyages of those days and I remember vividly how I enjoyed sitting in a big chair with him, listening to him read these stories to me, embellished with asides by him in his customary dry humor. The story of Nova Zembla (now the Russian island of Novaya Zemlya) was our favorite. In the 1970s a Dutch expedition went to Nova Zembla to conduct an archeological search of the remnants of the Dutch settlement there. This expedition was led by a scientist whose name is Haquebord. He is a grandson of tante Gé, my mother's aunt, who lived in Dokkum, Friesland.

Other voyages around the Cape of Good Hope were made in 1596 and 1599. These expeditions were successful and trading posts were established, the first one in the Moluccas. Several trading companies competed with each other, and Prince Maurits and van Oldebarnevelt insisted on establishing a united front against a similar British company. Thus the VOC, or United East India Company was established in 1602. It was given a monopoly and its exploits appealed to the imagination, but it never contributed more than 10% of the total revenue of the Dutch economy. Nevertheless its divi-

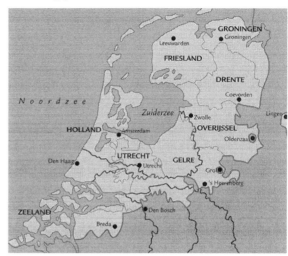

THE NETHERLANDS IN THE GOLDEN AGE.

dends were high and there was active speculation in its shares. The shares were traded on the Amsterdam stock exchange, which was completed in 1611 and is the oldest stock exchange in existence. Its architect was Hendrick de Keyser, the father of Thomas, the painter of our portrait that shows a mother with her two children. On the southern tip of the African continent, the Cape colony was established at what is now Cape Town to serve as a Dutch re-provisioning harbor for East Indiamen.

Beyond going to Asia, the Dutch also went westward. Henry Hudson, an Englishman in their employ, discovered the Hudson Bay and Hudson River. Beyond discovery, sailors going to the Americas operated as privateers against the Spaniards. This business was concealed in the WIC, the West India Company. The greatest success was achieved by Piet Hein who captured an entire Spanish silver fleet. This really struck the imagination of the Dutch and school children are still singing about it *"Piet Hein zijn naam is klein* (his name is short), *zijn daden benne groot* (his deeds are big) *hij heeft gewonnen de zilver vloot* (he has won the silver fleet.) It is interesting to note here that the word "filibuster" or "filibustier" in French stems from the Dutch word *Vrijbuiter* which originally meant freebooter or pirate. Klaas Compaan of Zaandam was an example of a highly successful Dutch pirate. To prove to the world that he meant to do as he pleased, he threw the Bible, his hymnbook and his ship's log overboard. He completed 358 successful piracies, sent lots of his loot home and ended his life peacefully and respectably living in a small house in Oostzaan.

Business activity in the Netherlands flourished in the Golden Age. Industry, especially shipbuilding was important and so was agriculture. The merchant fleet consisted of more than 2,500 vessels. In addition there were more than 2,000 fishing vessels. Polders were created by using windmills to pump out lakes. Ultimately the boom reached its pinnacle and a gradual decline set in around 1650, as England became more powerful, but still, arts and sciences continued to blossom in the Netherlands.

The Republic of the Netherlands was unique in that it was governed not by nobles or clergy but by a burgher elite. The burghers had an important influence on the commissioning of art and the result was many genre pictures showing important people or moralistic subjects. Famous are *the Company of Captain Banning Cocq* by Frans Hals and *The Night Watch* by Rembrandt. Rembrandt (1606-69) painted also for the court and was one of the few who made religious pictures. There also was much activity in literature and architecture. Jacob Cats was a famous writer whose style appealed to the burghers. In 1648 Jacob van Campen designed the Palace on the Dam which was actually originally the Town Hall of Amsterdam. The city of Amsterdam expanded rapidly and its three concentric rings of canals surrounding the old center were developed between 1612 and 1672. Literary circles were formed and continued to exist for decades. Tolerance towards dissenting views was their hallmark and Joost van den Vondel, a catholic, became Holland's most famous poet, who risked his life by writing a classic tragedy with the "legal" murder of van Oldebarnevelt as its subject. He got off with a small fine. Hugo de Groot, a writer and jurist, became known for writing the textbooks that became the foundation for today's Maritime and International Law.

Stadholder Willem (William) II was not a crowned sovereign but the head of the Republic. He was a son of Prince Frederick Hendrik and had to cope with the rising hostility of England. He was married to the daughter of Charles I of England, who had been banished by Oliver Cromwell. The city regents were opposed to intervention on behalf of the Stuarts and further curtailed William by limiting financial support for his army. William died just before his son was born, which marked the beginning of the first "Stadholderless period." The economic success of the Republic, meanwhile, caused further friction with England. England restricted the role Holland could play in trade with its ports. This led to the first Anglo Dutch war which lasted from 1652 to 1654. This war ended badly for Holland and Cromwell demanded guarantees that the House of Orange would never be reinstated in its titles. They were secretly included in the peace treaty by Johan de Witt, who was

Raads Pensionaris, the highest non royal executive of the Republic. When the Stuarts returned to the throne of England, Prince William III was ten years old and the Republic was again at war with England which had taken New Amsterdam in 1664. This time the Dutch won. Admiral Michiel Adriaenszoon de Ruyter sailed up the Thames to Chatham near London and destroyed the British fleet. De Witt was credited for maintaining a strong fleet. However, he had neglected the army and when the French joined up with England, and Münster and Cologne to declare war on the Republic in 1672, the Dutch turned to William III and murdered Johan de Witt. Johan de Witt's statue is in The Hague, in front of the *Gevangen Poort*, the old prison. A large blue stone there in the pavement still marks the spot where he was murdered after a mob dragged him out of the nearby prison. William was appointed Stadhouder and head of the army and navy. De Ruyter was again victorious at sea and England was forced to come to terms with the Dutch in 1674. Münster and Cologne also made peace, leaving France. William wanted to continue fighting to gain a balance of power in Europe, but the States General wanted peace to do business. William then married Mary Stuart and became King of England which enabled him to build a Grand Alliance against France. The war dragged on until 1697 when a peace was signed without victory.

At the beginning of the eighteenth century Holland was still a world power with vast economic interests, but there was now more competition from other countries, Holland turned inward and tried to conserve power and its decline began, but there was still a great deal of wealth and capital markets flourished, financing reclamation of land in North Holland and investments abroad. However, industry declined and high wage levels caused unemployment, widening the gap between rich and poor. Wealthy families made mutual agreements to ensure employment for each other with the exclusion of others. Thus newborn babies of Regent circles were appointed to offices. The job was then actually done by others at lower pay, creating anger among Patricians who were excluded from Regent circles. Interest in foreign affairs waned and when William III died in 1702 without heirs, the last descendant of William the Silent was gone. The title passed to the Frisian line of the Nassau family. The second Stadholder less period started.

When the Republic became involved in the Austrian war of succession in 1747, it turned once again to the house of Orange to provide leadership. The then Prince William IV (of the Friesian line) was invited to become Stadholder. There were wars all over Europe, and France invaded the southern part of Holland, causing political pressures in the country. Non regent burghers joined forces with the House of Orange and agitated for a more democratic form of government. William IV tried to fight corruption and nepotism, but only brought in his own group of friends which led to riots among his supporters. The old regent aristocracy fell from grace and dissatisfaction with the way things went expressed itself in an anti-Orangist or "Patriot" party. This development foreshadowed the situation that developed after the outbreak of the French revolution. Actually, the main aim of the Patriots was constitutional reform. When William IV died his widow governed for a while until his son William V came of age. A struggle ensued between the Stadholder and the cities, with the former favoring a buildup of the army and the latter, particularly Amsterdam, favoring the navy. When England went to war in 1777 against the American colonies, the Dutch supported the new American republic, built up their navy again and started to give convoy protection to the merchant fleet trading with America. This caused the English to declare war, and the Fourth Anglo Dutch war broke out in 1780. The English navy was far superior to the Dutch one and did great damage to Dutch trade. The Patriots blamed the Orangists and the prince for this disaster and political attacks on the prince multiplied. Inspired by the American Declaration of Independence, the Patriots drafted a new constitution, but the prince asked his brother-in-law, the King of Prussia to help him restore order and succeeded to reverse the trend. Many Patriots fled to France and continued to agitate from there. As a consequence of the French Revolution, the tide started to turn in 1795 when French troops invaded a large part of the Dutch Republic and ultimately William V was forced to flee to England where he later died. He left Scheveningen in a fishing boat and it took until 1813 after Napoleon was defeated for his son William VI to return, again at Scheveningen, also with a fishing boat, and be proclaimed King William I of the Netherlands, no longer a Stadholder, therefore.

Culture in Holland in the late seventeenth and eighteenth century represented somewhat of a decline from the flourishing art life in the beginning of the seventeenth century. Wealthy merchants bought country houses and cultural activities moved to a more rural setting. It became fashionable to speak French and French taste reflecting the influence of the court of King Louis XIV became popular. Daniel Marot was a new star, he was an engraver and interior decorator and later became an architect. He designed the Hotel Huegetan on the Korte Voorhout in The Hague which much later became the palace of Queen Emma, the mother of Queen Wilhelmina. It is now a museum. He also designed the interior of the palace Het Loo, now also a museum and has been completely restored. Comprehensive designs of furniture and whole interiors were new in Holland and were imitated on a more mundane level in the beautifully painted interiors of houses in *Hindelopen* (Friesland) and the *Zaan* (North Holland). Paintings began to reflect the more bourgeois complacency of the burghers. Literature became more popular and many literary societies were organized. Several writers emerged who produced important work. One was Hieronymus van Alphen, who is known to most Dutchmen for his simplistic children's rhymes but who also wrote philosophical studies reflecting a rationalistic outlook on life which became part of the philosophy behind the French Revolution.

By the end of the eighteenth century, society in the Dutch Republic had become inflexible and conservative while the gap between rich and poor had again widened considerably. People became more restless and were influenced by the ideologies of the French and American revolutions. It did not come to a real revolution in The Netherlands, but when French troops invaded, the Patriots came with them and seized power. The Batavian Republic was proclaimed and, as we have seen, Stadholder William V fled to England and died there. A new constitution was established and elections for a National Assembly were held for the first time. A more centralized government was created that promoted greater national unity. However, in France Napoleon came to power and he wanted the Netherlands to be linked more closely to France to help in its struggle with England. The Pensionary (*Pensionaris*) in those days was Rutger Jan Schimmelpenninck who had led the revolt against William V. He had to resign in 1806 when Napoleon proclaimed the Batavian Republic which later (when Napoleon appointed himself as emperor) became a kingdom with his brother Louis Napoleon as King. Meanwhile the Dutch economy had declined steadily and the Dutch East India Company suffered great losses. It was liquidated on December 31, 1799, as it was no longer able to meet its obligations. The West India Company had already been disbanded in 1791. The country was forced to participate in France's wars with England and as a result the British occupied the Dutch colonies. Most of them were returned in 1814. Louis Napoleon encouraged important cultural developments and paved the way for what later became the *Rijks Museum*, giving it works from the former Stadholder's collection, including Rembrandt's *The Night Watch*. He unsuccessfully protested his brother's plans to annex the Netherlands and abdicated in 1810. Napoleon introduced military conscription in Holland and nearly 15,000 Dutch soldiers perished in his ill-fated Russian campaign. Anti–French sentiment ran high, and when Napoleon was defeated at Waterloo in 1813, the Dutch once more turned to the house of Orange and William VI returned from England in 1813.

He was inaugurated as King William I in 1814. He also accepted sovereignty over the Southern Netherlands.

King William I reunited the seventeen provinces of the Northern and Southern Netherlands after 225 years of separation. However, political, religious, language and economic differences had grown so great that the new kingdom could not survive for long. After political disturbances and riots in the Southern provinces an independent state called Belgium was established in 1830. An international conference established a separation between the two countries, but first the Belgians and later the Dutch disagreed with the arrangements and William I started a military campaign against Belgium, later known as the ten-day-campaign. At first he was successful, but when the French intervened he had to withdraw. Volunteer units recruited from students participated in this campaign. Ceremonial re-enactment outfits of these student units still exist with old fashioned black uniforms and plumed caps (*chacots*). They march in parades, and when I was a student I joined the one in Leiden and drilled with them until I was called up in the real army, and then it was no longer fun to play soldier. The final treaty, acceptable to both parties, was signed in 1839. It marked the end of the brief reunion of the Northern and Southern Netherlands. Since then the North has been known as the Kingdom of the Netherlands.

William I was blamed for being high-handed, but he was a strong supporter of trade and industry and achieved many successes in this arena. He organized the Netherlands Trading Company which focused mainly on doing business with the East Indies. This company grew into one of the country's largest banks and after numerous mergers after the Second World War became ABN Amro, which until it was split up in 2007 was one of Europe's larger banks. In an attempt to promote trade with the Far East, a system of forced farming was introduced in Indonesia. Native farmers were forced to plant specific crops on one-fifth of their land. The products were shipped to Holland and in return textiles and other goods manufactured in the Netherlands were exported to the Indies. This system which was tantamount to servitude, became a black mark in Dutch colonial history and is still prominently mentioned in today's Indonesia as an example of Dutch oppression. (See Chapter 17.)

William I also promoted transportation in Holland. Canals were dug and the first railway was established. These initiatives and also private enterprise, specifically shipbuilding and several newly established steam ship companies, revived the Dutch economy and made Holland once again a major player in world trade. New polders were established, the large Haarlemmer Meer, a lake near Haarlem was pumped out and became a polder. Amsterdam's Schiphol Airport is located in this polder and is, I believe, the only major airport in the world that lies below sea level. One of the steam-driven pumping stations, the Cruquius still exists and is now a museum. Despite these efforts there was still much rural poverty and many people decided to emigrate, particularly to the U.S. Dutch enclaves in Michigan and areas nearby originated in that period. William I had been extremely successful in promoting prosperity, but when he tried to make the Dutch Reformed Church the national religion, he failed. When he lost his first wife and announced his plans to marry a Roman Catholic Belgian countess, William I was forced to abdicate in 1840.

After Belgium became independent, it was necessary to revise the Dutch constitution. Leading liberals and progressive Roman Catholics seized the opportunity to propose democratic reforms which would curb the political power of the king and introduce ministerial responsibility. The new king, William II opposed the reforms, and only the threat of revolution similar to upheavals that took place in other European countries in 1848 brought him around. The new constitution, proclaimed in 1848, introduced ministerial responsibility to parliament and assumed that the king could do no wrong. The lower house of parliament as well as the provincial states and municipal councils were elected directly by the electorate, and the upper house was elected by the Provincial States. The king had few powers left but could still dissolve parliament. William II could not accept this reduction of his powers, he died in 1849, leaving the unresolved problem of the extent of his powers to his successor.

King William III, who succeeded his father in 1849, also had trouble with the limits of his powers. He dissolved both houses of Parliament in 1866 because he was reluctant to accept the resignation of the Cabinet. He ordered new elections and asked the voters to favor his cabinet choices. This was unacceptable to the Parliament and the Cabinet stayed on. The conflict was resolved only after another Cabinet crisis and another dissolution of both Houses. The new Parliament expressed disapproval of the dissolution and the king had to admit defeat. Since then the Dutch sovereigns have accepted their role as a symbol of the country's unity and stayed out of politics. When William III died in 1890, he was succeeded by his 10 year old daughter Wilhelmina. Her mother, Queen Emma, acted as regent until Wilhelmina became 18 years old.

In the years from 1840 through the end of the First World War, Holland gradually developed from an agricultural society to a modern capitalist economy. The country became more and more industrialized and the generally free-trade attitude of the liberal party fostered a distaste for government intervention and regulation of the workplace. As working conditions worsened, the first labor union movement started in the 1870s which soon split as is usual in the Netherlands, into a Socialist, a Catholic and a Protestant union movement. The system that recognizes these three streams or pillars of Dutch society still prevails. It is called (loosely translated by me) "pillaring" (*verzuiling*.)

In the beginning of the twentieth century, social issues such as the right to strike came to the fore. In 1889 the Factory Act had been passed which prohibited child labor and regulated work conditions for men and women. In the same period the political emancipation, sought by the Catholics who were getting tired of being treated as second-class citizens, created a political problem that caused the fall of several Cabinets. Freedom in the choice of education was a closely related issue as the government only provided nondenominational education, and the Catholics and Protestants wanted to organize their own schools, paid for in part by government subsidies. There was also a new law on secondary education that resulted in the formation of the Higher Burgher School, or HBS, which replaced the old French schools and provided better math and sciences-oriented training for a modern industrial society. These schools together with the old-line Latin School, or Gymnasium, prepared students for a university education. In the 1880s new political parties emerged. There were Protestant, Catholic and Socialist parties and some of these still exist although the political landscape in Holland changed considerably after the Second World War, and issues related to religious convictions faded. Only men of "financial well-being and moral decency" could vote at first and it took until 1917 before there was universal suffrage for men. Women were not included until two years later!

This brief review of Dutch society and history reflects a country with a rather short history as a working democracy that really has no reason to feel superior to so called "young" countries such as the U.S. In fact after Britain, the U.S. is the second oldest democracy. Many Dutchmen do not seem to realize this. They view the "States General" as a parliament, but ignore the fact that the members of this chamber were not elected in open and free elections. They are correct when they see themselves as a country with a much longer history than the U.S. but as a parliamentary democracy they are only a fairly recent phenomenon.

Queen Wilhelmina became a true mother-figure for the Netherlands. She led the country through a period of social upheaval in the early part of the 20th century, World War I and the worldwide depression that followed, and she was a truly beloved symbol of Dutch unity and resistance against the German occupier during World War II. In 1948 she relinquished the throne in favor of her daughter Juliana, forty years after her coronation. She died in 1962, after spending her final years completely removed from public life. Wilhelmina was known to have a somewhat domineering character, a trait that served her well during the last war when she spent years in exile in England with her ministers. Winston Churchill is believed to have said she was the only "man" he really feared. I have seen her often, from a distance of course, before and after the war, riding in the "golden carriage" to open Parliament or just traveling through town in her big limousine, clearly marked by her fairly large orange standard with her personal crest on the front fender. In the thirties, her mother, Queen Emma, could also be seen driving in a big, old, black automobile with just a driver and a footman in front. As she passed us in her car, my father driving the other way in his would lift his hat and bow and she would bow back. No sirens, no security guards, no fear of terrorists or other nonsense. Just a reflection of a quiet time long ago. Netty can remember a time, before the war, when she was walking with her father in the street where she lived and suddenly noticed that her father turned towards an older lady, doffed his hat and bowed. It was Queen Wilhelmina with a lady in waiting, also taking a stroll in Wassenaar.

Queen Wilhelmina had a difficult life. Her father William III was quite old when she was born. He married Queen Emma, a German princess late in life having lost two sons out of an earlier marriage. He is said to have also fathered several children out of wedlock. From early childhood Wilhelmina was groomed to become Queen and never had a true childhood. She was crowned as Queen at age 18 and shortly afterwards married Prince Hendrik von Mecklenburg, a German prince. Hendrik was once described in TIME magazine as "a taxidermist's dream of a German prince-ling." And he was. He was also known to have had several affairs during his life and he lived a life of constant financial need as his wife rigorously controlled the purse strings. Hendrik never learned much Dutch and was generally kept in the background. He served as head of the Dutch Red Cross and fulfilled ceremonial functions such as serving as leader of the boy scouts. He was a very heavy man and when I was a young cub scout I once participated in a parade in which Hendrik marched by in a scout uniform with the then usual wide brimmed ("smoky the bear" type) hat and khaki shorts. I still remember how his fat knees jiggled and how disappointed I was to see a prince look like that. I asked my mother, "Is *that* the prince?"

Queen Wilhelmina and Prince Hendrik, gave their only daughter, Juliana a much freer and more pleasant childhood. Juliana studied in Leiden and lived there with friends like an ordinary student. As a young woman she seemed rather plain looking and it took quite a while before she got married. In 1936 the whole country heaved a collective sigh of relief when she married Prince Bernhard von Lippe Biesterfeld, another German prince, but a very charming and dashing one. Instructed by Wilhelmina, Dutch diplomats had been on a bizarre manhunt all over Europe for a suitable consort for Juliana. The queen thought the Dutch nobility too low for her daughter and wanted to find a prince. Many candidates were tracked down and interviewed. Almost all proved to be unsuitable either because they were not interested or because they had some problem in their own or their family's past. Finally Bernhard appeared on the scene. It seems he presented himself as a prospect and he proved to be a good choice. Juliana underwent an almost immediate dramatic change, noticed by the entire country. She became a happy woman and her outward appearance improved visibly after she got out from under the influence of her mother's severe and dowdy lifestyle. In 1938 the entire country waited breathlessly for the arrival of Juliana's first child. On January 31 her daughter Beatrix, now queen of the Netherlands, was born. This event caused tremendous jubilation and great relief particularly to small manufacturers of commemorative junk, plates, spoons, calendars, etc., who had marked their trinkets with "January 1938" and were facing financial problems if the birth had occurred a day later, in February.

Princess Juliana had three more daughters. Irene was born in Canada, during the war. She married a Spanish prince who was an unsuccessful pretender to the Spanish throne. Irene became a Catholic on his behalf which caused an uproar in Holland. Later she divorced her husband and she now lives in Holland keeping herself totally out of sight. Margriet was born after the war. She married a commoner and is now quite popular. Christina, the youngest, was born with poor eyesight. It was discovered that her handicap was caused by German measles (Rubella) contracted by her mother during pregnancy. This event caused considerable heartbreak for her mother and led to an episode where Juliana came under the influence of a faith healer, a woman who suggested she could improve Christina's eyesight through prayer. There was a period in the 1960's in which the monarchy seemed in danger as rumors were flying around about Queen Juliana's odd behavior and indulgence in strange religious practices. The faith healer lived for a while in the palace and had extraordinary powers over the queen and her retinue. Additional problems arose when it was revealed that Prince Bernhard had accepted money from Lockheed, a U.S. aircraft manufacturer, in exchange for support of airplane orders to be placed by the Dutch air force. These difficulties now seem to be forgotten. Like Queen Wilhelmina who left the throne in 1948 in favor of her daughter, Juliana in her turn, stepped down in 1980. Princess Christina lived an independent life, despite her handicap and went to Canada and later to New York City to study voice and pursue a career as a singer. In those days she became friendly with our good Dutch friend John Hafkemeyer. Christina married a commoner from Cuba, Jorge Guillermo. The couple visited our house when we gave a party in celebration of John's engagement to Isaure de la Barre de Nanteuil, a wonderful lady of a French noble family. During that visit we got the impression that Princess Christina resembled her grandmother in willfulness and general appearance, while her husband struck us as odd and a little of an opportunist. In 1994 Christina announced she was going to divorce Jorge, not to our surprise. Bernhard died in December 2004. At that time it was revealed that he had two more daughters, born out of wedlock with different women. What was known among the cognoscenti was now made public. He had had many extramarital affairs. Juliana died in 2004.

Queen Beatrix, the present sovereign, is an attractive, intelligent and strong person who is now quite popular after several troublesome years following her marriage to a German. Her husband, Claus von Amsberg, had served in the German army during the war and later became a diplomat. Claus was not really a prince, but was given this title by the Dutch government. Their wedding was held in Amsterdam at the insistence of the then Princess Beatrix. Amsterdam has always been a politically leftish and rebellious town and the atrocious behavior of the public during the wedding ceremony was a good example of that characteristic and the Dutch tendency to be rude as observed by Tacitus around A.D. 80. People shouted *"Raus mit Claus"* and threw smoke bombs. It was not a very dignified event and it would have been much better if the wedding had been celebrated in another city. Beatrix gave birth to three sons who are now adults and are quite popular. Prince Claus unfortunately began to suffer from depression attacks and had to stay in the background for several years. Gradually he came more into his own and much of the old acrimony was forgotten, mainly because Queen Beatrix has proven to be an excellent head of state with a high sense of duty and a personality that suggests clearly that she is a woman of great intelligence who makes up her own mind. Claus died in 2002. He became popular as a self-effacing, quiet man who made many positive contributions to his country.

After the peak of Dutch art in the Golden Age, cultural developments in later years seemed unimportant, complacent and uninteresting. However, the nineteenth century is now seen as a much more interesting period. Earlier in the century, historical painting flourished and inspiration seemed to be derived mainly from traditional themes. But around 1870 a group of artists settled in The Hague and formed the

Hague School with work that resembled the French Impressionists without having an actual connection to them. Prominent painters in this group were the Maris brothers, Josef Israels, Breitner and Mesdag. We own a watercolor of a shepherd with his sheep in front of a stable (*schaapskooi*) traditional in the past century in the eastern part of the country, by Jacob Maris and a water color-seascape with a fishing boat by Mesdag. The latter painted the famous *Panorama Mesdag*, an enormous circular painting displayed in the Hague. It shows a 360-degree view from the top of the dunes at Scheveningen of the beach with fishing boats on it (before the Harbor of Scheveningen was dug, the fishing fleet was simply kept on the beach). The picture also shows cavalry exercising on the beach and the city of The Hague in the distance. This museum is probably our greatest favorite in Holland. In 1993 we had occasion to see the entire painting close up and from below the visitors' gallery as guests of a lady we knew, who was working as a restorer on the enormous painting. Another prominent painter in that period was Louis Apol, great-uncle of my old friend Eelco Apol. Apol concentrated on winter scenes and made several expeditions to the Arctic regions. As it turned out, Netty's uncle Eelco van Kleffens owned a very large Apol, a view of the harbor of Rotterdam (this is not a winter scene). Netty's brother Pul inherited it after Tante Margaret died. He had the painting thoroughly restored. It shows a fascinating view of the harbor as it looked a hundred years ago. Vincent van Gogh who lived in the same period, worked in the provinces of Drenthe and Brabant and later in France. He became the best known Dutch artist after Rembrandt.

In architecture, neo gothic buildings came in vogue in the eighteen hundreds. The architect Cuypers designed numerous Catholic churches and the Central Station in Amsterdam as well as the Rijks Museum there. Later Berlage became an innovator among Dutch architects. He built the bourse in Amsterdam which reflected a more modern open style that used no ornaments and basic building materials. His principle was that the interior parts of a building should be visible in its outward appearance.

In literature the Netherlands in the earlier part of the nineteenth century had a period in which most writers were unimaginative, pedestrian and totally complacently bourgeois. However, one writer, Nicolaas Beets wrote an outstanding period piece called "Camera Obscura". This work while reflecting the general complacency of people in the 1830s, offers wonderful cameos of life in those days. Later in the century a movement of the "men of the eighties" came to the fore with several well-known writers who reflected a more romantic impressionistic view of nature and others who wrote about the problems of the new industrialized society.

In the beginning of the twentieth century the Netherlands became one of the most industrialized countries in the world. It was almost swept into World War I, general mobilization was called in 1914, but the country managed to remain neutral. My father joined the army while studying at the Engineering University in Delft. He spent almost four years in the army, but towards the end of the war he was allowed to spend part of the week in Delft to complete his studies. After the Great War, the Netherlands became a faithful member of the League of Nations and pacifist ideals became an important part of political life in Holland. These ideals were only given up a few years before World War II as more and more conflicts threatened in Europe, mostly caused by Nazi Germany. The Dutch National Socialist Party or NSB emerged, but at first it was not stridently pro-German or anti-Semitic. The NSB's greatest election success was in 1935 when it gained almost 8% of the vote. As the Dutch population got a clearer picture of what was happening in Nazi Germany and the NSB drifted more towards a pro-German posture, voters' support dwindled quickly. Holland has always been a country with a large number of political parties, and sometimes their differences in political goals were so subtle that only informed insiders could make a clear distinction. Before the war the three most important parties were: the Socialist Party, the Roman Catholic Party and the Anti Revolutionary Party (orthodox Protestants). These three comprised about 75% of the seats in parliament, and cabinets had to be formed with at least two of these parties well represented. Much political negotiations were needed to establish a working coalition. Today this situation still exists with often months going by before a government can be formed. Dutchmen vote on their party's list of candidates, which leads, in my view, to the unfortunate circumstance that most people do not vote for a certain candidate but only for a party. As a result, people work their way into a party's structure by joining as members and gradually climb to the top without really ever being scrutinized by the electorate or personally tested in the rough and tumble of political campaigns.

The Great Depression that began in 1929 and that had the entire world in its grip also hit The Netherlands. Large numbers of people were jobless and I can well remember making a tour of the harbor of Amsterdam with my grandmother in a sightseeing boat and noticing large numbers of ships, freighters as well as ocean liners, laid up with canvas covers over their funnels, a very depressing sight. The government which had generally followed a "laissez faire" policy was forced to intervene and to promote public works. Unemployment peaked in 1935 with 30% of the work force out of work, fertile ground for radical political movements. The guilder was devalued which gave some relief, but the big political debate was between the conservative Anti

Revolutionary party which wanted to stay on the gold standard and cut government spending to the bone, and the Socialists who wanted to promote government spending for job-creating projects. The biggest project started in those days was the reclamation of the Zuider Zee. This inland sea was closed off in 1930 by the *Afsluit Dijk*, the IJsselmeer Dam. A highway on this dam connected Friesland with the western provinces. It brought us closer to my mother's hometown of Leeuwarden and we frequently drove over it. As business slowly recovered, trade with the Netherlands East Indies picked up and companies like Royal Dutch Petroleum, Unilever and Philips Lamps became more important and grew into true multinationals.

Culturally there were interesting developments between the two wars. A movement called *"De Stijl"* [the Style], named after a periodical in which various art forms were represented, became internationally known. It included architects such as J. J. P. Oud and Gerrit Rietveld as well as painters such as Piet Mondriaan. Literature flourished also with many Dutch writers being widely read in the country and sometimes, in translation, elsewhere. Several composers emerged such as Pijper and Andriessen and the Amsterdam Concertgebouw orchestra became world renowned. Contemporary composers such as Ravel, Stravinski and Mahler were part of the repertoire of Willem Mengelberg, its conductor who was a personal friend of Mahler. My parents often went to The Hague to hear the Concertgebouw orchestra when it played there. They always were in evening dress for the occasion, with my father wearing a dinner jacket (tuxedo) with a stiff shirtfront. Broadcasting became popular with four separate broadcasting companies representing each "pillar" of Dutch society. In science Holland had an important position with several Dutchmen winning Nobel prizes. In physics and astronomy, Kamerlingh Onnes, Lorenz, van der Waals, and Kapteyn had world-wide reputations.

Despite the depression and the threat of another war, the Netherlands was a pleasant, orderly, law abiding and reasonably well governed country. It was perhaps somewhat complacent and self-satisfied and there may have been many social inequities, but there were certainly no deep social rifts and it was a good place to live and grow up in, certainly for Netty and me. We were privileged children who were really not affected by the depression. There are certainly not many people in this world who grew up in a country that changed its topography by conquest of the sea. Elsewhere I will try to describe how we lived before the war and how everything changed when we were invaded by the Germans on May 10, 1940, and what happened after that. Dutch history then becomes part of my own life experience

3 : Ancestors on My Father's Side

The memories I have of my grandparents Schieferdecker are almost as vivid as those I have of my own parents because I saw them often and they both lived a long life. Also, they had every reason to pay much attention to me because I was their only grandchild and they did not live far away. After Netty and I were married a house was being built for us nearby in Heemstede and until it was ready, we lived with them for a few months in their large house in Bloemendaal. When I was a child, we went to see them almost every other Sunday. I have very good memories of those visits, and particularly of Christmas at their house and of visits there during summer vacations when I was allowed to bring a friend. Sometimes the Sunday visits were a bit of a bore for me because I was the only child among a number of adults, and I had to amuse myself, but again, the overall memory is good, warm and pleasant. It is a wonderful gift to have known one's grandparents well.

My grandfather Hermann Max Schieferdecker, who used Max as his first name, was born in Leipzig-Reudnitz, in the Kingdom of Saxony, Germany on April 27, 1860, the same year Abraham Lincoln was elected president. He died in Bloemendaal on October 13, 1955. He was, therefore, 95 years old when he died. During his long life there were three major wars. First there was the Franco-Prussian war of 1870 -71, which took place when he was a young boy and which he remembered vaguely. At the end of that war Bismarck, the "Iron Chancellor" of Prussia success-fully concluded his struggle for the Prussian hegemony of all the German States. With their customary lack of tact, the victorious Germans declared the foundation of their 2nd Reich in France, in the Hall of Mirrors of the palace of Versailles. After that conflict came World War I and finally World War II with the death by a German firing squad of his only son-in-law. In addition, there was the worldwide economic depression in the early thirties, the Russian Revolution, and the end of the Dutch colonial period in what is now Indonesia, a country where he lived for a long time, was married and fathered his two children and in which he made his fortune. He saw his daughter and son and also me, his only grandchild, grow up, attended our wedding and frequently saw his great-grandsons our sons George and Adriaan as little toddlers. I have good background information on him thanks to the efforts of my father, George Schieferdecker (A.A.G.), who in his usual meticulous way prepared, among others, a large file on his father Max Schieferdecker. All this information will be reproduced here, but it should be understood that the quantity and quality of the information on a particular ancestor does not mean we or I loved or admired him or her more than the others. It merely reflects that there is more information on him or her and therefore, more left for us to enjoy and pass on. I can only hope this material will be as interesting to my descendants as it is to me.

The following is a translation of a letter tante Jetje van der Hoop, my father's only sister, wrote me on February 16, 1969. We were then already living in America and I was beginning to collect data on our families. She responded to my request to tell me

CARL AND LOUISE SCHIEFERDECKER.

as much as she could about our ancestors in Germany. Her contribution is valuable because she adds the female touch by describing her grandparents and her father more intimately than my father could or would. This is welcome even if she may be wrong on where slate is found in Germany:

"In response to your request for information on our ancestors, I wrote Ilse Kruschel, hoping she could recover something. Note: Ilse was a distant cousin who lived in the then Communist Peoples Republic of Germany (which called itself the "German Democratic Republic," or in German DDR.) We often called it East Germany. Netty and I met Ilse several times after the war when she visited my grandmother. The response was disappointing. It appears she does not know more than your father and I already knew, or she did not understand that we wanted to go back beyond our grandparents, to your great grandparents. We could, of course, trace back more, by way of marriage certificates, certificates of baptism, birth certificates, but you would need a civil servant for this. Leipzig was not bombed, but it would still be a costly undertaking.

Ilse went to the Johannis Friedhof (cemetery), which will disappear in a few years and will be replaced by a botanical garden, and has copied from the headstones the following information:

Your great grandfather's name was Carl Gottlob Heinrich, born December 20, 1831, he died May 17, 1907. Your great grandmother's name was Louise Günther, born April 25, 1830, she died May 10, 1914 [note: my father recorded her date of death as May 11.] Louise and not Luise as I was erroneously named. He was quiet and intelligent. You can see it from his handwriting and his note books with recipes (if they are still there).I do not know where the family came from. I thought from the Rhine area, where there is much slate and where in Baden the name appears frequently.

Your father says there are more areas in Germany where slate is found. Anyway, they must originally have been slaters in the days of the guilds. Your grandfather wanted to emphasize that by using slate as roof covering for his house in Bloemendaal. Your great grandmother came from Zeitz. In that area the population has strong Slavic features and she had that too. She was the only girl in a family with eleven children. She told me once that until her marriage, she had to knit socks for all those boys and she got really fed up with it. Her father was a cabinetmaker and so were several of the boys. When she married she was equipped with birch furniture (in the Biedermeier style.) I have known that furniture and remember it well. Carl and Louise had four children. A boy Heinrich, who died young, a girl Martha, your grandfather Hermann Max and another boy Arthur. After the war of 1870 [the war between Prussia and France] (I believe), there was an epidemic of typhoid in Leipzig, which almost killed your grandfather and his sister. Martha remained a delicate child and died at the age of 16. There should still exist a sampler from her (indeed, we have it.) Your grandfather has told me that he was never able to forget the feverish dreams he had during that period of sickness. But he came through unscathed.

The youngest son Arthur was a blond promising child until at age eight, he fell down a flight of stairs and landed on his head. He had a big scar on his forehead. After that he could not study anymore and became a bookbinder and stayed with his parents for the rest of his life. In my mind's eye, I still see his quiet pitiful figure. He gave me a book he had bound himself. I do not have it anymore, as so many other things. (She refers to her house being burned down by the German SS during WW II.)

He died just before his parents' fiftieth wedding anniversary, which his father also did not see, anyway. He (the father) died from bronchitis, his wife seven years later from pneumonia.

Of all the Günthers, there is, I believe, only one male descendant left, in Gera. I am still in touch with an aunt of him, the widow of an uncle (Ernst).

After the death of your great grandfather, his widow came once with a girl servant to stay in Bloemendaal as a house guest. (There is a photograph of that visit, which was taken in 1913.) Then I got to know her better. She was a person who did not talk much, but could quite unexpectedly make an interesting comment. She had knowledge of many things that are now lost or outdated. For instance, during a walk I was impressed with her knowledge of the medicinal characteristics of all kinds of plants and knew how they should be prepared for use. She was a simple, very intelligent woman, and in my opinion it cannot have been a total pleasure for her to stay in Bloemendaal. (note: she refers here probably to the difference in social status between her and my grandparents.)

You have known your grandfather yourself and your father can tell you about his life. As a boy he was interested in nature, rocks, butterflies and birds, and it was I believe a source of quiet satisfaction for him that your father became a geologist. He was a really self-assured, unassuming person and that characteristic appears to be hereditary. (She probably refers to my father here.) He was unpretentious, not a show-off, but his knowledge of business was solid and extensive. The family background of your great grandfather and his father, the cabinetmaker is hazy. There is more known of the Stibbe family because they have a family book. Your father should have a copy of that (I have it now).

VISIT GROSZMUTTER, SUMMER 1913.

In any case, you can certainly say that on both sides there were no individuals with strange characteristics, just stability and common sense. They all got quite old and did not die of unpleasant sicknesses. Longevity is also hereditary."

The house with the slate roof, Mollaan 7, Bloemendaal, where my grandfather lived for almost thirty years and where he died was built in 1926, and I laid the "first stone" (corner stone) for it as a very small boy. (We have a video tape, made off an amateur film we made during a party Netty and I gave at this house to say good bye to all our friends before leaving for America. This video gives an impression of the interior of the house.) The house was built on land belonging to my grandparents who originally lived next door in a house they also built and where I was born. My father spent most of his youth in this (first) house. The new house was designed by a well-known Dutch architect, Prof. Slothouwer. Now that I am myself well past my eightieth year, I can only marvel at my grandfather building a new house at age 66. Perhaps the fact that my grandmother was only 56 then and a very energetic woman may explain why they undertook this no doubt quite exhausting project. The economic boom Holland experienced before the crash of 1929 may also have been a factor. The house was large and extremely well built out of what seemed hand-shaped brick. The bricks were not smooth, but still uniform in size, of course. It had a slate roof, as Aunt Jetje mentioned, because in German the name Schieferdecker means "Slater"

MOLLAAN 7, BLOEMENDAAL IN 1950.

(a roofer who specializes in slate roofs). When the house was designed, my grandfather insisted on a slate roof. Upon entering the house there was on the left a formal parlor room which my grandmother used to receive guests. It had mahogany paneling and the desk Netty now has in our guest room was there. On the right was a coat room and toilet. Straight ahead one came into a large hall which served as dining room and also had a sitting area in the front. There were large French doors there that opened up to a terrace that also stretched out to the front of the parlor room. The old oak cabinet now in our sitting room and our large standing clock were in this hall. The larger oak "kast" that was in the living room of my parents in Wassenaar and now is with Adriaan, was also there. Beyond the dining table which was placed in the middle of the hall was a grand piano and beyond that a stairway to the upstairs part of the house. The walls of the hall and the stairway were paneled in oak. In the outer wall of the stairway, facing the old house, was a very large window with colorful stained glass panes framed in lead. They showed the crests of all the cities and towns my grandparents had lived in. In the hall, left of the piano was my grandfather's study which was also quite large and a room where we would often gather. This room had also some paneling, but it was dark-green painted wood. The fact that he did not use expensive woods for his own room reflects his frugality. Equally frugal was the big lamp that hung above the large writing table in the middle of the room. It was a circular brass affair, originally built for gaslight. Since he liked it, he had it modified for use with electricity and moved it to his new house. My grandfather's roll- top desk stood perpendicular to the window and when we drove up the driveway to the house, we could usually see my grandfather sitting behind his rolltop desk. The cabinet now in our dining area was at the other side of the room. There was a narrow area between the roll top desk and the wall where my grandfather had his "letter-press," an installation that made it possible to copy hand-written and typed letters on special thin paper by pressing the original and special copy paper together between blotting paper. The press could be raised and lowered with a heavy, hand-operated screw thread. Writing this I am reminded of a comment Netty made recently when we were reminiscing about our parents and grandparents and asked ourselves how they spent their days. Netty remarked, correctly, that letter writing was an important task and letters were the most important means of communication. We have now almost forgotten that very significant fact. People would sit down and spend a couple of hours a week writing letters, corresponding with friends and relatives, mostly by hand. Mail was quite fast and efficient and "junk mail" which has now become a daily nuisance and has created a paper disposal chore, did not exist. The mailman would deliver mail twice a day and bring one or two letters. The telephone was there but was used sparingly because it was expensive. So my grandfather had a writing table and in addition a roll top desk to handle his correspondence.

I AM LAYING THE CORNERSTONE FOR MOLLAAN 7 IN 1926.

Returning to the house, there was a large landing upstairs and to the right, above the study, a small bedroom and a sitting room where my aunt Jetje lived before she was married. Against the wall of the small hallway leading to her rooms was the bookcase we had in our family room in Riverside. On the same floor there was a large guest room (above the dining room) and a master bedroom and bathroom (above my grandmother's parlor room). The antique samplers we now have and which my grandmother had collected hung in the hallway leading to the master bedroom. Behind a door on the landing there also was a stairway to the huge attic where there was another bedroom. On the ground floor, beyond the dining room, was a separate wing. It contained the pantry and behind that a kitchen. The telephone hung on the wall in the pantry. In those days it was really not nice to have the phone in one's living room. Opa had another phone extension in his study, however. This was for business calls and all outgoing calls were closely monitored and supposed to be brief since they "cost money." Above the kitchen were servants quarters, consisting of a small kitchen, a sitting room and a bedroom and bath. Until shortly before the war my grandparents employed live in couples, usually the husband worked as their chauffeur and also served at the table, while his wife cooked and cleaned. There were also cleaning ladies, a seamstress who came once or twice a week, and a gardener who was an independent contractor and came twice a week. His name was Huib. He became a good friend of mine when I was a boy.

The garden was large. The house was situated against a hill, which actually was a dune and part of the coastal sand dunes that are a major part of the landscape of Bloemendaal. The area where the house was standing and the lawn in front of it were probably somewhat leveled off to enable construction, but there were several very large trees standing in front of the house. Particularly prominent was an enormous linden tree in the middle of the front lawn, near the street. This tree blew down in a storm when my grandmother was still living there. Behind the house was a hill covered with many old trees, part of the back garden. There were two paths going up the hill, one had steps and one, behind the garage just went straight up. The garage was nestled against the foot of the hill. It had a flat roof you could reach with stairs in the back, a favorite spot for me and my friends to play. On top of the hill one could look through the trees and see the city of Haarlem. Other houses abutted this hill/garden and also a small church which was built on land my grandfather had donated for it. You could go to church by walking up the stairs to the top of the hill behind the house, entering the church grounds from the rear. My grandparents did this regularly until they were too old to make the climb. My aunt Jetje (Henriette Luise van der Hoop) was married in that church to my uncle Bernard van der Hoop, a man I became very fond of. At their wedding I was assigned the role of flower boy. During the war Bernard was a member of the Dutch resistance movement and he was executed by the Germans in the final weeks of the occupation. His death was the greatest tragedy our small family had to endure during the war.

My grandfather was a very successful businessman and his career was remarkable, particularly in view of the fact that he was a German from a quite modest background who came to the Netherlands at age 21 without much money. Over the years he became well known in business circles in Amsterdam. I discovered that when I started working there in 1950 and met some of the older gentlemen on the stock exchange, who when introduced to me immediately recognized my name and spoke about him. For me this was a very unusual experience because our name is unique even in Holland and while Dutch people always seem to know each other, our small family was not all that well known. Opa spoke very good Dutch with only a very small trace of an accent and became as much a Dutchman as any other native born one. When I was quite little I called him *Opa dun* (thin Opa) to distinguish him from my other grandfather, my mother's father, who was more rotund and whom I called *Opa dik* (fat or chubby)—but *dik* in Dutch does not sound as derogatory as "fat" often sounds in English. For George and Adriaan he was "*oude Opa*" (old Opa) for obvious reasons. We are fortunate to have a number of documents that bear testimony to his life and his extraordinary career, achieving considerable success from a humble start. Official documentation of his birth on April 27, 1860, appears in a certificate of baptism I have. It is a copy of the original as it is dated "1908" by officials of the Netherlands government. The certificate mentions he was baptized on May 17 1860. It mentions the names of his parents and also the names of the people who acted as witnesses. It also states the profession of the witnesses, confirming they were trades people, who also were *Bürger* (the German indication of a person's status as citizen of a town or a burgher). My grandfather was born in Leipzig – Reudnitz, in the kingdom of Saxony or *Sachsen*. This was more than ten years before Bismarck proclaimed the formation of the German Reich in Versailles.

Among my grandfather's papers are certificates stating that his father, Carl Gottlob Schieferdecker, was officially certified as having become a Bürger of the city of Leipzig, having come from elsewhere, and granting him all the rights of citizenship of that city. The witnesses at the baptism were Amalie Günther, wife of Christian Friedrich Günther, furniture maker, from Camburg, Gotthilf Günther, also furniture maker from Camburg, Eduard Berger, blacksmith from Reudnitz and Karl Baumgarten, house painter from Grimma. The Günthers were probably brothers of my great grandmother. This document is first endorsed in French by the Dutch Consul in Leipzig, who certifies the signature of the pastor and perhaps used French as the then standard language of diplomacy, or more likely, because he was a Frenchman (his name is "de Liagre"). The Consul's signature is legalized by a functionary of the Dutch Ministry of Foreign Affairs. Opa probably needed this document to become a Dutch citizen. He was naturalized in that year (1908). One can only speculate what would have happened if Max Schieferdecker had been tardy and postponed his naturalization. My father might have ended up in the German army in 1914 and since it was such a terrible war, chances are he might not have survived it. Opa was confirmed as a member of the church (it is not clear which one, but most likely the German Evangelische Kirche the Evangelical Lutheran State Church) on March 22, 1875. He graduated from the Real Gymnasium, the

Latin High School, which was probably very similar to the Dutch Gymnasium in curriculum, i.e. a high school with heavy emphasis on the humanities, on Latin and Greek and on a classical, philosophical curriculum. This education may have meant a step-up from the environment of his own parents. On a trip to Dresden in 1998 we bought a print of the Fürsten und Landesschule in Grimma, this may have been Opa's high school. He was excused from serving in the German army for medical reasons. I have the papers confirming this. He must have been happy that he did not have to serve, but the judgment of the doctors turning him down is questionable in view of his long life and the fact that he was always in good health, and to the best of my knowledge, never saw the inside of a hospital. After he graduated from the gymnasium he spent three years, from July 15, 1876 until July 15, 1879 as a trainee with a firm called B. Schindler, Colonial Waaren Geschäft at Leipzig. The name of the firm indicates they were traders in goods from the "colonies," i.e., the Near and Far East. The name Schindler became well known after World War II because a man of that same name managed to employ and thereby save the lives of a number of Jews, who otherwise would have perished in the Holocaust. My grandfather then spent two years with a banking firm called B. Breslauer, Bank und Wechsel Geschäft as a bookkeeper. I have two letters of recommendation from his first two employers stating that he was a good and faithful employee. After these initial years his father, Carl Gottlob Heinrich Schieferdecker, who had a business trading in goods from the Far and Near east, sent him to Amsterdam as his representative. Incidentally, Carl Gottlob was also judged unfit for military service, which most likely enabled him to avoid participating in the war between Prussia and Austria of 1865 and the war between Germany and France of 1870 – 71.

There are a number of documents on Carl Gottlob Schieferdecker's life in our possession. They include:

1. His certificate of baptism.
2. A paper that certifies he is unfit to serve in the army for health reasons.
3. A recommendation after he worked as an apprentice from Easter 1857 until Easter 1861 in the firm of Curt von Schierbrand.
4. A marriage certificate dated January 24, 1858 between him and Henriette Louise Günther.

The certificate mentions his father was a "landowner and millwright" and his wife's father as a cabinetmaker. They married in the Evangelical Lutheran Church.

5. A document showing the formation of his own firm: Carl Schieferdecker.

6. Admission to *Bürger Recht* (rights of a burgher/citizen) of the city of Leipzig. Together with a form stating that he swore an oath that he would faithfully obey the King of Saxony and the laws of the country.

7. Admission to burgher of the city of Grimma (without an oath) where he lived after retirement. September 28, 1892.

8. A handwritten postcard indicating he moved to Leipzig - Gonnewitz on March 13, 1899.

9. A travelogue he wrote on his trip to Holland in his own handwriting (see below).

10. A death certificate dated Leipzig May 18, 1907.

11. There is also an envelope with several quite touching small antique envelopes containing poems and wishes on the occasion of births, baptisms etc. which were kept as souvenirs by my great grandmother Henriette Louise Schieferdecker.

Max Schieferdecker was 21 years old when he started in Amsterdam, representing his father's firm. In one of the rare conversations I had with him about his career when he was very old, I asked him about those days. He told me with a broad smile that his job as youngest apprentice in the office was to sweep the floor first thing in the morning, before the other employees arrived.

Among his papers is a reproduction of an old print he must have cut out of a newspaper or a magazine. It shows the "Nieuwe Zijds Kapel" in Amsterdam in the eighteenth century, a church with a few old buildings in front. He has traced the outline of a third floor window of one of the houses and on the back of the print he wrote with ink pencil, the kind of pencil which is difficult to erase and which he used for most of his notes (ball point pens did not yet exist and fountain pens which had liquid ink inside were difficult to carry in one's pocket as they frequently leaked ink). He wrote: "Here I lived in 1881 – 1882 until my departure to Batavia on the SS (steam ship) *Prins Frederik* of the "Nederland" Shipping Company (*Stoomvaart Maatschappij "Nederland"*) on Sunday, May 21. Its captain was named Merkelbach van der Sprenkel. Arrived Sunday, June 18, 1882 in Batavia". He signed it with his initials, H.M.S., as was his habit.

NIEUWE ZIJDS KAPEL.

He went to the Far East after two years in Amsterdam when he was hired by Alexander Theodoor Krause and Victor August Wellenstein who on June 1, 1882 had organized a firm in Batavia (now Jakarta) to trade in products of the Dutch East Indies (now called Indonesia), mainly sugar. The firm was called Wellenstein & Krause and my grandfather was one of their first two employees. Just reflect for a moment on this and realize how venturesome he was. He had left Germany to settle and work in another country, quite far away for the standards of those days, living and working among people who spoke another language and then a little later, just leaving for a part of the world that was then much much farther away than it is now and doing this for a firm that barely existed. He was definitely a risk taker, an entrepreneur. He must have realized the Far East offered a more interesting career perspective for him. Dutch and German society in those days, and also in my days, was structured and very formal. People without academic degrees normally did not get very far. He had no academic degree, so he ventured out to a less-structured part of the world where personal initiative was valued more than book learning.

The history of Opa's firm is written up in a very interesting small book which was printed in 1932 on the occasion of its 50th anniversary. This booklet is certainly of historical value, but it is also quite amusing as it—unintentionally—reflects the colonial attitudes of people in those days. It mentions that Mr. Krause handled the affairs of the firm in Amsterdam while Mr. Wellenstein worked in Batavia. They had an office in Batavia in an old building where several others also worked and "all used the same Chinese cashier (book keeper)." They soon got a better office and in 1886 the firm moved its headquarters from Amsterdam to London as most of the trade was concentrated there. In the 19th century, there was much trade between Germany and Holland and it seems to me likely that both founders of the firm were also Germans or of German extraction (their names would certainly suggest it). In the years before World War I, people traveled freely throughout Europe, often without passports, did business wherever they liked and transferred money freely. Only recently, with the coming of the European Union and the collapse of the Soviet Union have barriers been lowered again, removing most of the many cumbersome regulations requiring documents such as passports, visas, export and import permits, etc. that were established in the past half century. Wellenstein & Krause had strong links with Britain and as the firm progressed, many English names begin to appear. The sugar exporting business in those days and the risks it faced is described in the booklet in very cryptic language. In the 1880's, most of the sugar was bought from plantations on Java, which milled and refined it in their own factories and then shipped it over to Europe and the U.S. There were strict rules as to quality, consistency and color in addition to many other requirements. Ships sailed to the island of St. Helena or to the Azores or to another convenient harbor like Lisbon "for orders." When the captains reached these ports, they received orders that had been mailed or telegraphed in by the merchants at home, telling them to which port their cargo had to be delivered. Cargoes were usually sold by traders while en route and the exporters had to pray they would eventually obtain good prices as the vessels moved slowly to their destination and much could happen in the interim. This process took some six months and cargoes were financed with bank drafts. The reputation and creditworthiness of the trading firms were the key to obtaining proper financing. The young firm survived a sugar crisis on Java in 1883 in which prices fluctuated drastically and soon it faced competition from sugar beet production in Europe, a crop that was subsidized and encouraged by local governments. The firm became more and more successful in selling sugar to the U.S. shipping to the East Coast as well as the West Coast. The Spanish American war offered an unexpected windfall for business with the U.S. as Cuba was temporarily cut off as a source of sugar and afterwards took quite a while to restore its production. Once a foothold was established in America, it became a major focus of the firm's business in the 1890s. The booklet mentions that the biggest buyer of W&K in America was the American Sugar Refining Company founded by H. O. Havemeyer who structured the large U.S. Sugar-Trust. Its sugar was sold in the U.S. under the brand name "Domino." Mr. Havemeyer did quite well for himself as will be noticed by anybody visiting major museums such as the Metropolitan in New York where numerous paintings can be seen that were donated by him and his family. Australia with its Colonial Sugar Refining Company, now C.S.R., was also developed as a market. The booklet mentions with some disdain that the weight of the bags of sugar they used was too heavy for the backs of the Australian dock workers and had to be brought "down" to 200 lbs.! The book then mentions an amusing event that is described in a somewhat condescending manner. On a certain day the firm was visited by "a little Japanese who called himself Suzuki and who said in broken English that he wanted to try to import Java sugar in Japan." Soon business with Japan flourished as did the business with India and Hong Kong. A small chapter of the booklet discusses personnel, mainly the Dutchmen working for the firm. The name of a Chinese clerk who worked 43 years for the firm is briefly mentioned as well as the names of two Chinese cashiers who each worked more than 25 years at the office. The final sentence states that two Indonesian foremen served the firm each for more than 35 years, but their names are not stated.

Max Schieferdecker traveled to Batavia by way of Marseilles. After the Suez Canal was opened in 1869, it became customary for people traveling from the Netherlands to the Far East to go by train to the Mediterranean and board their ships there, thus considerably shortening the trip. The Wellenstein & Krause firm was actually organized in Batavia on June 1, 1882, less than three weeks before Opa arrived.

THE OFFICE OF WELLENSTEIN & KRAUSE IN THE OLD TOWN
OF BATAVIA.

Among the documents my father collected is a newspaper clipping dated
November 29 1928. It is an article out of *De Indische Mercuur*, a newspaper that
was published in Holland for people who had lived in the Dutch East Indies or were
interested in that country. It is titled "ARRIVAL IN THE INDIES, THEN AND
NOW." Opa wrote a note under it in his precise handwriting saying: "I could have
described my arrival in Java on Sunday June 18, 1882, in exactly the same way". He
again signs the note "H.M.S." The fact that he saved this article and that he added
this note to his papers suggests that he wanted to leave a record of an event that must
have been a very important one in his life.

The following is an excerpt of this article, which as many writings of those
more leisurely days is quite lengthy and written in the then usual flowery language:

"Who arrived about a half century ago from the Netherlands in Indonesia and
many of the older ones among our readers will remember this event can still speak
of the 'forest of masts' on the roadstead of Batavia…Those days are long gone! It
was in the days that the steamship began to replace the sailing ship; although the
latter was far from finished, to the contrary, the number of sailing vessels was still
larger than that of the steam ships who were after all often still sailing ships with
auxiliary steam power. So one could still enjoy the sight of the 'floating forest',

consisting of merchant men of almost all countries. The *blanda baroe* (a Malay term for a white newcomer), the new Hollander, who looked over the roadstead to the land behind it from the upper deck of the ship that brought him there, perceived way in the blue distance the giant mountains *Gedeh* and *Salak* which rose massively and high out of the seemingly flat Indonesian landscape. There was no trace of a city or any inhabited place. Behind him, towards the North, reaching far into the distance, a circle of small islands, the Thousand Islands that constitute the Bay of Batavia and the islands *Onrust* and *Kuiper* which at the far West side are the gate posts. *Onrust*, easily distinguished by the high government buildings and masts and hulls of navy ships under repair. The smaller island of *Kuiper* adds its coaling stations to it.

The moment of debarkation has arrived. Small harbor vessels come alongside to take on passengers and cargo. From the roadstead one was quickly inside the piers which are the beginning of the canalized Batavia River. About halfway one perceives on the left a small lighthouse and looking beyond it one is surprised to see native fishermen tending their nets standing in the water up to half their naked bodies, apparently not worried about the crocodiles who prowl in the rivers and coastal waters.

Thus one approached *de Boom* (the wooden barrier) with the landing dock which impresses the newcomer as looking like a kind of haystack, which is called *Pondok* here, a waiting area consisting of a roof on poles which offers shelter against rain and sun, where also part of the customs formalities take place. One is on Java's soil!

In the mean time one would not linger longer than necessary. There was transportation present and brown skinned coachmen struggled among themselves to offer their services to bring debarking people "uptown". The trip commences; past an old fashioned Dutch draw bridge one was soon in the area which was once the site of the Castle of Batavia, now an open field with high trees, bushes and lawns which do not in any way resemble the old glory, except for the Rotterdam (or Amsterdam) arch gate, a baroque piece of work that withstood the ravages of time well, and that Daendels (a hated pro French Dutch Governor General, installed by the French during the days of Napoleon) left standing, perhaps as a gesture towards the past that may not have been totally insignificant to him.

Still, as a powerful symbol of that past, the warehouses that are still in use and that date back to the period after the days of the *Compagnie* (Dutch word for the

East India Company), a complex of fortresses and then the famous "cannon," with its well known offering place.

❧

Passing through the gate, the Town Hall arises, completely intact, which in the early years of the eighteenth century replaced the older building on the same spot. A large building in the sturdy old Dutch Indies style.

Then one swings through the long and wide *Nieuwpoortstraat* of which the houses, whether shacks or substantial, bring visions of life and business of pre-ceding generations, past the long *Molenvliet* canal to *Weltevreden*, the European residential area, which commences with the *Harmonie Club*, with the neighbor-hood called *Noordwijk* where the traveler finds temporary shelter in one of its hotels.

This is a sketch in broad sweeping terms of arrival in the Indies, 50 years ago. It is not this way anymore! Debarkation now takes place at Tandjong Priok, a modern tropical harbor.

Still, with all its differences, there is a lasting similarity between reaching one's first destination: those who set their first step on firm ground fifty years ago and those who do that today experience the same deep impressions and sensations. It is that mental process that is experienced by all who coming from the northern hemisphere set foot on the southern hemisphere and get in the spell of all those contrasts, especially the visual ones. In the later years of ones life, memories are almost imperceptibly brought back to ones point of departure, the first day of arrival in the Indies..."

❧

DORA STIBBE AND MAX SCHIEFERDECKER WERE MARRIED ON
DECEMBER 12, 1890

The drawbridge is still there. I took pictures of it when Netty and I visited Djakarta (formerly Batavia) in 1988. He married Dora Estella Johanna Stibbe on December 12, 1890. A year later, on December 20, 1891, he became vice consul of Spain in Batavia. In those days it was of interest to business people to serve as consuls for countries that needed representation in important trade centers but were unwilling to go to the expense of having a full time local consular representative. It was certainly not a full-time job and the rewards must have been minimal, but it probably added some prestige and an opportunity for business contacts. As consul he could resign from serving in the *Schutterij*, a semi-voluntary military service in which Europeans served as weekend soldiers. No doubt this service was organized to have an armed militia handy to support the authorities in case of unrest among the native population. He first was a corporal and was later appointed lieutenant. I have a postcard a friend sent him to tell him that he (the friend) had to rush to report him sick and that he really should have been prompter in reporting this so that the captain would not be obliged to ask where he (Schieferdecker) was.

Aunt Jetje and my father were born in Batavia in 1891 and 1893, respectively.

In 1895, Opa moved his family back to Europe. He had spent almost 14 years in the Indies, without interruption. This is a long time by any standards. When I was young, people living in Indonesia would come back to Europe every four years or so for a "home leave" of about six months or more. He resigned as a managing partner of the firm in 1897, but remained a nonmanaging partner (*Commanditair Vennoot*) until 1901. This probably means that he continued to have a financial stake in the firm until 1901. Why he left the firm is not clear, but he was obviously financially able to do this although he was only in his late thirties! It is quite possible that the health of my grandmother was a factor in deciding to go back to Europe. The family moved to Grimma in Saxony, Germany. Opa's parents lived nearby and they stayed there until September 15, 1898, when they moved to Haarlem in Holland. My father told me later that his mother "could not stand" living in Germany. They lived in Haarlem on the Hazepaterslaan no.17, which interestingly was next door to the family of Willem van Someren Greve, the brother of Netty's grandfather, and therefore an uncle of Netty's mother. On April 13, 1899 Opa joined the Nederlands Indische Escompto Maatschappij, a trading bank which was domiciled in Batavia.

He became "*procuratiehouder*" in its Amsterdam office and later a member of its board of directors until he resigned on March 15, 1901. In that year he sold his house in Haarlem and traveled for a year through Europe with his entire family because my grandmother had continuing health problems. These problems were never totally explained to me, but later in her life my grandmother became a vegetarian and remained fit and energetic for almost her entire remaining life. I was told she suffered from heavy migraine headaches for many years and that the vegetarian lifestyle she adopted later helped her overcome this problem. The family

MAX SCHIEFERDECKER AROUND 1900.

visited many European resorts that were well known in those days, including Friedenweiler in the Schwarzwald, Germany, Caux and Lugano, Switzerland. During this trip their first house in Bloemendaal (on the Mollaan no. 5) was being built. I believe that during that trip, my grandparents met Daan and Marie de

Clercq in Switzerland and became friends.

It seems clear my grandfather stayed in touch with his former colleagues because in September 1902 he became manager of the Amsterdam office of J. M. Fraser and W. Suermondt Lzn. The name Fraser suggests a continuing link with the Wellenstein & Krause firm because its history lists the firm of A. C. Fraser & Co as a managing partner since its inception. There also was a Mr. Alistair G. Fraser who was its representative in London. Opa's office was in a building on the Damrak, no. 20-22. This building still exists, I believe. He

became consul of Panama on November 8, 1909; this was in our family a matter of some hilarity, because it was just a small thing for him. Nevertheless, as he would remark with some amusement, the Germans he dealt with immediately started calling him "*Herr Konsul*" and my grandmother "*Frau Konsul*".

Max Schieferdecker arnd 1900.

Carl Gottlob Schieferdecker and his wife Henriette Louise visited the family of their son Max in Bloemendaal in 1905. This was a big journey for the then 74-year-old man who started life as the son of a humble millwright and who now visited his own son who lived in a large imposing villa with lots of personnel and who had achieved a great deal in his life. He would die two years later. He described his trip in a clear handwritten travelogue. (In German, of course):

"...Experiences during our visit with the children in Bloemendaal where we arrived on May 29, 1905, at about midnight and where we left early on July 9 1905:

June 1; A walk with Max and George through the environs of Bloemendaal and the dunes.

June 3; Made a trip with Dora by carriage through the wider beautiful environs of Bloemendaal.

June 4; Sunday, went with Max and the children by train to the sea resort of Zandvoort, saw the sea (probably for the first time in his life), with large sailing vessels and a steamship which had run aground on the beach.

June 6; Dora's parents came here from The Hague to greet us and invite us.

Whitsunday; Carriage trip with Max in a different area of the surroundings of Bloemendaal, saw among other things the old ruin of the Brederode Castle, inside and outside.

Whit Monday; carriage trip through the dunes and forest, many large beech or linden trees along well kept avenues. Then through a beautiful park in Haarlem and through the town.

Whit Tuesday; We went to Haarlem with Jet and George and they showed us all that was worth seeing in the town.

June 19; Went with Dora to her parents and in the afternoon we went with them to the sea resort of Scheveningen with its beautifully furnished hotels and the large pavilion built on a pier in the sea which one can reach on a boardwalk with electric lights on both sides and from which one has a wide view of the sea with its sailing ships, steam ships and fishing boats which offer an overwhelming sight, at least for someone who never saw something like that before.

June 20; I spent the morning alone with Stibbe in the Hague, we saw several beautiful buildings that were worth seeing from the outside and some also from the inside including his distinguished club (probably *de Witte Societeit)* with its many large and small rooms which are all artistically and beautifully finished, then the Government offices and the buildings of the first and second Chamber of Parliament, also the palace of justice and then from the outside the residential palace in which at this time the young Prince was staying. The city is beautifully laid out, particularly the part that joins with Scheveningen which has superb villas with nice gardens belonging mostly to people who got rich overseas or those who were in high government positions on Java and live there now on their large pensions. In the afternoon we made a trip by carriage with Dora and her parents through the *Boschjes* (the small park), interesting ponds and water parties, past the canal, the *Koninginnegracht* to the *Bosch* (the larger park), in which the *Huis ten Bosch* is situated, previously the palace of Queen Sophie, first wife of King William III; it is empty since her death and its large rooms have been used for the peace conference. This large room, the so called *Oranje Zaal* has been beautifully decorated by Rubens and his students. High up in the cupola was the portrait of Amalia van Solms, the Great Grandmother of the Queen. The largest painting showed the entry of Prince Frederik Hendrik into 'sHertogenbosch in 1629. Further there were "Venus and the Graces" and the "God of war" by Rubens and also "Wisdom and Power of Peace" and all the paintings looked so freshly done. The chairs were made of brass and decorated with tortoise shell and in the middle was a beautiful table so highly polished that you saw the whole cupola reflected in it. We also walked through the dining hall with beautiful frescoes by de Wit nice Chinese china and Delft china with the Royal crest on it. Then came the Chinese room with Japanese wallpaper, thick damask curtains and cabinets with gold leaf. Further we saw the living room with furniture embroidered by Dutch ladies as a present for the 25th jubilee. A large chandelier made out of Russian crystal given by Peter the Great, two large porcelain vases from Napoleon III; a portrait of him and his spouse, busts of their sons and a charming marble group showing "a sleeping and a playing child" a bench(?) wonderfully carved out of one piece of wood from British India, a beautiful flower bouquet in mosaic, a gift of the Pope; furthermore the death chamber (of Queen Sophie) and the adjoining writing room in which one could see on a table the bible still open at the last psalm she read before her death. When we came here we saw several Royal draperies in front of the castle which had been brought outside so the young Princes and Princesses could view them. After these dignitaries had left again we were let inside and got our guided tour. Afterwards we drove back to the house of the Stibbe's through the forest and the beautiful streets of the city.

June 21; In the morning I took a walk with Stibbe through the pretty *Boschjes*. We actually wanted to see the new harbor, but had to turn back because it got quite stormy near the sea. In the evening we went with Dora and Mrs. Stibbe to a concert in Scheveningen in the beautiful concert hall of the *Kurhaus* where Salzmann from Haarlem also sang. The electric illumination and the then very turbulent sea offered a wonderful sight.

June 22; Max brought us to Rotterdam where we first saw the so called White House (an early high rise building called *Het Witte Huis* that was famous and still exists) where we climbed its 10 floors by elevator, and from which we could see the entire city and the harbor with its many steamers, sailing vessels and its impressive traffic from above; the railroad is for a long stretch elevated above the city. We boarded a carriage and crossed over one of the large bridges to an island that is also completely built up. We circled the island and returned along the same route as we had come. We walked through wonderful parks to the zoo and palm garden with its great number of animals and many large greenhouses with many beautiful species of palm trees and other rare plants and flowers. Afterwards we traveled back to the Hague from where we left in the evening to go back to Bloemendaal after a four day visit during which Dora's parents went out of their way to please us.

On June 24 we were in Haarlem to hear a concert given by students of a music school for string instruments. After a large number of solo pieces played on the violin with piano, the entire group of about forty boys and girls, in which George also participated, played several pieces really well and received much applause.

On June 25 we received a courtesy visit from Aunt Louise Stibbe (*Reisetante*— "traveling Aunt") with her daughter and another Aunt. (note by my father "this was Aunt Louise Stibbe, the Mother of Anna and Marie Stibbe (pianists) who often traveled abroad.)

June 26; we went with Dora to visit Max in Amsterdam, and with him we first traveled around the entire very large harbor in a small steam boat. On shore we saw huge warehouses where the large ocean steamers were loaded and unloaded with huge steam cranes. There were also two colossal India steamers of which one had recently arrived, while the other one (the Willem III) was being prepared for a trip to Java. Max had obtained permission from the management of the company to visit this steamship the evening before it sailed, and see its interior with its electrical lights. Unfortunately this trip had to be canceled, because an unusually strong thunderstorm hit Bloemendaal which made it impossible for us to go to Amsterdam. Also on the canals in the city there were many small vessels, steam and sail, that transported the cargo of the ships etc.

On June 28 we visited the small, but also nice seaside town Wijk aan Zee with George and Jet.

On June 29 Mother went to a charity concert in Bloemendaal with Max and Dora.

On July 2nd we made a trip with Max and Dora through the environs of Bloemendaal and in the evening visited a spot where one had beautiful view of the dunes..(probably a place called *het Kopje*)

July 4; We were in Haarlem to attend a concert played on the famous and truly beautiful organ in the large main church. Both the church and the organ had been restored.

On July 7 we went together to Amsterdam, on our own. Max took us around there and showed us the stock and commodity exchanges from the inside with its three large halls for trading tobacco, coffee, tea etc. and securities. We also saw the mint, the Royal Palace, the Crystal palace [burnt down later], the museum etc. Afterwards we had lunch in a large hotel (Krasnapolsky) with its winter garden in a large hall lit by overhead glass ceilings which contained beautiful palm trees and other rare plants and flowers which were artistically displayed. One side of the garden had mirrors so one saw everything double. With electric lights this must be even prettier. Afterwards we steamed down the Amstel river on a small steamer for about an hour and returned with Max to Bloemendaal.

On July 7 we had planned farewell visits in Amsterdam, but we had to stay home because I had a bad cough attack and was too tired.

July 8 we prepared for our departure and in the evening we made a farewell visit to the Mullemeisters in beautiful Heemstede. We went there with Max in a carriage*.

On July 9 we left Bloemendaal at 9.30 in the morning to travel home and were happy to arrive in Leipzig around midnight...."

* The Mullemeisters were old friends of my grandparents from Indonesia. They had twin daughters of which one married a Mr. Schuyten who emigrated to the U.S. and settled in Seattle. The other daughter followed her sister and also moved to Seattle where she became a teacher. Mrs. Schuyten had several children among which were Hans and Herbert Schuyten who visited Bloemendaal with their mother and aunt when I was about 10 or 11 years old. Later when Netty and I emigrated to the U.S., Hans and his then-wife Nancy lived in Stamford and welcomed us warmly and helped us settle down in Greenwich. His mother and her twin sister would visit Stamford and also my grandparents in Bloemendaal. When they came to Holland they would travel by ship, bringing their car which they drove across the U.S. from Seattle to New York before boarding.

The Netherlands government official Gazette of July 1, 1909, mentions under law no. 223 that Hermann Max Schieferdecker had been granted Dutch nationality. In 1910 he was a key participant in the formation of the ANIEM (the General Netherlands Indies Electrical Company), the company that became the sole electrical power company for the entire archipelago. Max Schieferdecker was chairman of the board of that company and served in this capacity (incredibly) until 1950 when he was ninety years old! For a long time the shares of ANIEM were among the more actively traded stocks on the Amsterdam Stock Exchange.

An article that appeared in the *Indische Mercuur* of March 26, 1930, written on the occasion of my grandfather's 70th birthday, mentions that he was among the first on Java who was interested in establishing a long distance telephone service. It states that he participated in the founding of the *Intercommunicale Telefoon Maatschappij* of Batavia. It also mentions that this company was later taken over by the government of the Netherlands East Indies.

Other boards he served on were:
Suikercultuur Maatschappij
Cultuur maatschappij Balong Bendo
Suikerfabriek Krian*
Suikerfabriek Bodjong
Cultuur Maatschappij Maswati
Kina cultuur Maatschappij Boemi Kasso
West-Java Kina-cultuur Maatschappij
Cultuur Maatschappij Ardiredjo
* I visited Krian when serving in the Dutch army in Indonesia.

(*Suiker* = sugar; *Cultuur* = cultivation, plantation; *Maatschappij* = company; *fabriek* = factory; *Kina* = quinine)

In 1918 my grandfather resigned from the firm of Fraser & Suermondt that had by then become van Eeghen & Suermondt. There are letters of resignation among his documents. Remarkably, the original contract between him and his partners, drawn up in 1902, is only about half a page long. It simply states that the three men have agreed to start a partnership and will each have a one-third share of the profits and agree not to trade for their own account. Today's American lawyers could learn something from that. Among his papers are also his letter of resignation from the partnership and his draft of this letter in pencil, in his steady, but hard to read handwriting. There are also the responses from his partners who express great regret at his decision. One, Baron Mackay, says he still wants to discuss his decision with Opa, probably to see if he could convince him to stay.

For many years my grandfather used to go regularly to Amsterdam and when he celebrated his seventieth birthday, April 27, 1930, there was a big dinner party in their house with many of his business associates and friends. I recall that my grandmother, who knew how to entertain and give dinner parties, had a carpenter make a large wooden oval which was displayed on the table. It had 70 holes to hold 70 burning candles. At this occasion I had to sing a song specially composed for this event together with my cousin Tineke. Her father, my uncle Otto Jonas, played the piano. Since I was then only five years old, this was quite an ordeal for me. I still remember some of the words.

MANAGEMENT AND BOARD OF DIRECTORS OF ANIEM AT THE
COMPANY'S 25TH ANNIVERSARY, IN 1934. HMS IS SEATED,
SECOND FROM LEFT.

When I was little, I often stayed with my grandparents. At first they would
have a children's bed set up in their bedroom and I would sleep there. Later when
I was older, I was put in a guest room. My grandfather had some interesting old-
fashioned things in his bedroom. He had an old shaving stand, an oval mirror with
a small flat shelf under it that carried porcelain bowls for water and shaving cream.
I guess he always used this mirror in the old house and simply moved it over to the
new one. The stand also had two candle holders because in the old days one did
not have gaslight everywhere. He always used a straight razor to shave until he was
quite old and finally shifted to using a newfangled Gillette safety razor with replace-
able blades. On his night table he had a small stand for his pocket watch. When he
retired he would hang his watch on a little hook on the stand, which had, in front
of the watch, a magnifying glass that allowed him to see easily what time it was
without having to peer closely at his watch. Like my father he always wore a three
piece suit with a vest and a watch chain. I still have two gold watches that belonged
to him. One is quite old and was given to him by his parents. The crown is protected by a gold cover that opens when you push a little button. The back also has

a cover under which is a second gold layer, protecting the works. On this second cover is inscribed in German *Dem braven Sohne 27ten April 1885* (to our stalwart son). It was obviously given to him by his proud parents on his 25th birthday. He was then already three years in the Indies. On the other end of his watch chain he had a little flat gold receptacle that held a special kind of flat pencil that could be pushed out to write with. He also had a small whistle there that he used to use to call his dogs and when he had no dogs anymore, he used it to step outside to warn me and my playmates that it was dinner time when we were playing on the hill in back of the house.

Opa usually wore gray striped pants, similar to the ones that nowadays go with a morning coat, and are only worn at weddings, and a black jacket and vest. This was normal attire for businessmen in his days. In summer, on the rare hot days, he replaced the black jacket with a white linen one and in winter, at home, he sometimes wore a *huis jasje* (a special warm house jacket that resembled a short house coat and was called a "foyer"). He always wore a tie of course and I don't think I ever saw him without a vest or tie. In his final years he often wore a small skull cap on his head. He liked that because it kept his bald head warm. I now have his little black cap at home. I was quite moved when I found it in my father's desk when I cleaned out my mother's house after her death in January 1997. My father had kept this small remembrance of his own father all those years. He took daily walks, moving at a fairly brisk pace, usually carrying a walking stick or an umbrella. He was a lean man with fairly large feet, usually having a serious look on his face and in his later years somewhat stooped. He had a small mustache as long as I knew him. Richard has a portrait of him done in 1935 on the occasion of his 75th birthday, April 27th. Opa and Oma were visiting their daughter at that time. This painting used to hang in Oma's parlor and later in my father's study. I think it is a very good portrait that catches his personality sober and earnest and quite frugal very well. The painter was a Spaniard living in the Canary Islands where Tante Jetje and Oom Bernard lived after they were married in 1930.

When Opa went outside he always wore a gray hat with the rim turned up, and he had provided all his hats with a little bright blue feather in the hat band so he could recognize it in a coat room. He had also marked his umbrellas and walking sticks with a small dab of red lacquer, the kind he used to seal letters with, so they could also be easily recognized. He was a serious man who anticipated life to be full of unexpected pitfalls and problems such as getting one's hat or umbrella swapped for another one in a coat room by a careless attendant. Consequently he documented everything and was meticulous in his personal and business affairs. Most of the time he was calm and composed, but he had a well developed dry sense of humor that came out often. I never saw him become emotional, except on the day when I came with Netty to say good bye before shipping out to Indonesia with the Dutch army. He began to cry. He was then almost ninety years old and may have feared he would never see his only grandson again.

During the war he had to endure quite a lot for an old man (he was eighty when the war came to Holland) and as a man who was born and raised in Germany, the behavior of the Germans in Holland must have bothered him immensely. During the German occupation of the Netherlands his background and that of my grandmother put the elderly couple in a remarkable juxtaposition. Following the Nazi doctrine which blamed the Jews for almost all the problems the Germans had encountered in their economy and history, the Germans began the persecution of the Jews who lived in the countries they occupied during the war. My grandmother was Jewish, but it had never occurred to us that this was unusual or different. As a first step Jews were ordered to register and it was shameful how the well organized and efficient Dutch civil service proceeded to help diligently with the implementation of this new rule and the many others that would follow. Their excuse was that they were in danger themselves if they did not obey orders, but they surely could have been less precise or downright sloppy like the Belgians who lost a considerably lower percentage of their Jewish population as a result of their deliberate lack of administrative precision. My uncle Bernard van der Hoop, who was a man of the world and had lived under various rogue regimes in different countries such as Argentina and in Spain under the fascist dictator General Franco, immediately recommended that Oma should not register herself as she was never a practicing member of the Jewish faith (she was in fact a devout church-going Christian) and neither were her parents who were long dead. In other words how would anybody ever know she was Jewish? Despite this she registered, and I will never forget seeing her in her house, ready to go out with her coat on and for the first time having a big dirty yellow star on her coat with the word "Jew" on it. Since Oma had a mixed marriage, nothing much happened after that.

In 1943 when the Germans began to fear an invasion by the allies, they proceeded to evacuate large segments of the Dutch coast. My grandparents had to leave their house, store all their furniture and moved in with my aunt Jetje and her husband Uncle Bernard. By then, unbeknownst to us, Bernard had joined the resistance in Leersum where they lived. They owned a very nice small country house as a retirement home, on a quiet road. I went there often and stayed there for a few weeks in 1943, when I myself had to disappear for a while. My big old boxer dog "Moro" also stayed there when the Germans began to requisition dogs. Word had it that the dogs were being trained to find land mines and/or were used to run over mine fields to explode them. Uncle Bernard went to register Moro with the Germans, but just before entering the hall where the dogs had to be shown, he temporarily swapped him for a tiny Pekinese dog that a helpful fellow was offering for that purpose. Obviously that dog was deemed too small to serve in the Wehrmacht.

It must have been in the fall of 1943 when Oma and Opa went to Leersum that Uncle Bernard arranged for false identification papers for Oma and the matter of the star and the identification papers with the big black J stamped on them was resolved. This was very fortunate because the SS men who came in September 1944 looking for Oom Bernard did not know she was Jewish. In Chapter 13 I have described the drama that unfolded in Leersum in September 1944 and in the months afterwards. Oom Bernard was shot just before the liberation together with 117 others as a reprisal against an ambush the resistance had set which seriously injured the uppermost SS general in the Netherlands.

There is a small monument in front of the Town Hall of Leersum with Bernard's name on it (B. C. M. van der Hoop) together with the names of several other people of the village who were killed in the resistance. My grandparents found a boarding house near Leersum, in Doorn, where they waited out the last horrible winter of the war. Soon after the liberation they moved back to Bloemendaal and found their house in quite good shape. German soldiers had been in there but had done relatively little damage. Despite the atrocities the Nazis committed, German soldiers were usually well disciplined and orderly. My grandparents continued to live in their house in Bloemendaal until they died. My grandfather died on October 13, 1955, at the age of ninety five. He had been ailing for some time and it had become more and more difficult to move him upstairs, so his bed was placed in my grandmother's parlor. He was taken care off by Freddy Klein, a retired nurse who was the daughter of old friends of my grandmother from her days in Batavia and was part of Oma's extensive entourage.

At the time of Opa's death Netty and I were on vacation, making a trip by car to Portugal and Spain. In Lisbon we stayed with Netty's uncle and aunt van Kleffens. When we came back, my father told us that Opa had died. My father was very distressed and cried when he told me, so I did not ask him why he had not tried to reach me. In truth, it would have been very difficult to find us as we did not have a prepared itinerary and did not know where we would stay as we found our way back from Madrid through France. Making frequent long distance phone calls was in those days not done, if not impossible (Spain was still a fascist military dictatorship with all kinds of difficult rules). Nevertheless it has always bothered Netty and me that no efforts were made to find us and we were unable to pay our last respects to my grandfather, a man we both loved very much. He was cremated and his ashes rest in the cemetery of Westerveld, near Haarlem.

My grandmother, Dora Estella Johanna Stibbe, played a very significant role in my earlier life, mainly because of her distinct personality and the influence she had on me. Oma Schieferdecker was always busy doing meaningful things for herself and for those in her environment. Today she would perhaps be seen as a "do-gooder" or a very active volunteer lady. She was involved in many charities and worthy causes and was an easy mark for people who had schemes for spiritual uplifting or new religious philosophies. She had a great deal of energy despite her very small size. She grew up in the Dutch East Indies where she was born in Palembang on the island of Sumatra on January 13, 1871. I have a handwritten document stating that it is an official copy of her birth certificate. Her father reported her birth to the authorities in Palembang with two witnesses, a Mr. Willem Stort who is an officer with the local military and the Reverend Willem Moulijn, pastor of the local Protestant Congregation.

In her behavior, manner of speech and general life style Oma reflected the time period in which she grew up. She was a true Victorian lady. Her father, Aslomon Stibbe, was a judge and reached in his lifetime the highest position a judge in the Dutch East Indies could achieve, that of president of the High Court of Justice.

Aslomon graduated from the "Gymnasium" in Kampen in 1861. He studied law in Leiden and became a member of the Leiden Student Corps in 1861. I have a copy of his membership certificate of that organization, which was organized in 1839 and which I joined myself in 1945 (I lost my certificate). It is interesting to note that he was apparently welcome to join the student corps despite the fact that he was a Jew. Throughout their history the Dutch have generally been tolerant in religious and racial matters. They are no saints and there certainly is and was some quite nasty anti-Semitism in Holland, but in general the fact that one is Jewish never was a matter of great importance in Dutch society. Aslomon was almost certainly a secular Jew and so were his children. After getting his law degree, he earned his doctorate in law in 1865. I have two copies of the thesis he defended on that occasion. As was customary in those days, he defended 32 points of law for his promotion. These points are neatly printed in a booklet. The statements he makes range from corporate law to criminal law and also include international law. The final one indicates his interest in the law for the East Indies and perhaps his intention to build his career there. He states "It would be desirable for the Netherlands East Indies to have a legal system of its own reflecting the way in which society over there is organized and applicable to Europeans as well as Natives." Much later in his career, after he retired and lived in the Hague, he served for many years as chairman of a government commission, that was writing a new set of laws for the East Indies. From my own studies in that area I know that laws written to govern the Dutch part of society there were almost identical to those used in the homeland while the Indonesian part of the population depended mainly on a legal system based on old traditional Indonesian customs. It is possible he chose a career in the East Indies because he could advance quicker there and would not find entering the judiciary as difficult as it would have been for him at home as a Jew. However, I have never heard anything about this and have absolutely no information on this score. So this statement is pure conjecture on my part.

There is also a copy of the cash account he kept as a student which is quite a curiosity. His room rent was fl.38.75 (about ten dollars) for three months and he spent fl.0.25 for a haircut (about $0.10) and fl. 0.75 for a pair of white leather gloves. Music at the party he gave when he earned his doctorate cost fl. 10.00, or about $4 at the approximate rate of exchange at that time. Aslomon married Henriette Stibbe on March 7, 1867. They were cousins - their fathers were brothers! Aslomon's Father was Lion Stibbe who was the seventh child in a family of 14 children and Henriette's father was Josef Stibbe who was the 13th child of the same parents. Josef died in 1868. Aslomon's mother was Doortje Levie Bendien and Henriette's mother was Antje Tels. Both mothers and Aslomon's father died in 1880. I assume all these ancestors were 100% Jewish as their names indicate except maybe for Antje Tels whose name may not be Jewish. We had some discussions about the background of Antje Tels during the war as the Germans began to harass the Jews and it was important to reduce one's Jewish ancestry as much as possible. However, not much came of it, I think, and since Aslomon's grandfather was even chief rabbi in the town of Zwolle, there was not much question about his origins and therefore that of my grandmother.

Aslomon was born and raised in Kampen, a small town in the province of Overijssel. Netty and I visited Kampen in the fall of 1996, just to get a flavor of the place. It is a delightful, very old town with a long history. It used to be much more important than it is now. In the fourteenth century it was a *Hanzestad*, part of the Hanseatic League, a group of free cities that traded with each other and promoted and protected their economic interests. The most important members of the league were the German cities of Hamburg, Bremen and Lübeck. While walking around Kampen we happened to see a building on a street running along the river IJssel that was a former synagogue, now turned into a small museum to commemorate the Jews that had lived in Kampen and had perished during the war in the Holocaust. I picked up a small brochure describing the history of the Jewish community in Kampen. It states:

"There were already Jewish merchants living in Kampen in the fourteenth century because books dating back to the middle ages mention the first persecution of Jews in the days of the great bubonic plague epidemic. Naturally the Jews were immediately seen as the cause of the epidemic. Towards the end of the fifteenth century Jews were forbidden to live in Kampen. Later when the economy of Kampen declined, the town fathers decided to try to attract Jews to the city again to improve business. In 1661 they invited Portuguese Jewish merchants and Kampen became the oldest Jewish settlement in the province. After 1674 they also invited Jews from Germany and after the Portuguese Jews left town, these German Jews became the founders of the permanent Jewish community that was exterminated by the Germans in the years 1940 – 45. This community which came from Amsterdam and Germany, consisted of merchants, shopkeepers, cattle traders and butchers. In 1748 there were ten families and in 1796 there were 140 people in the community. After 1774 Jews could become full citizens and members of the guilds. The brochure then discusses the history of the synagogue. It states that Salomon David Stibbe (1760 – 1840) was a prominent member of the congregation. He was a shopkeeper and distiller and ran a pawnshop with his wife. He was active in the provincial assembly of his faith and was briefly a member of the Dutch parliament (1813). He was especially interested in education and wanted to modernize the schools so that young people could integrate better into society." Salomon Stibbe was my grandmother's great grandfather. I have a Stibbe family book which lists the first known persons to have been born in 1717. The book was published in 1912 and my father has updated it with notes about people he knew. He wrote down that several of them were murdered in the Auschwitz death camp operated by the Germans in Poland.

It seems reasonable to assume that my ancestors were upper middle class people in Kampen and that Aslomon was an extraordinary successful scion of the family. His marriage to a cousin may well be a reflection of the small Jewish community he grew up in. He may not have had much of an opportunity to find a bride who had the same social background.

Aslomon and Henriette went to Indonesia in 1867, shortly after their marriage and two years after Aslomon earned his doctorate. Their ship still went around the Cape of Good Hope as the Suez Canal only opened in November 1869. In March 1878 they came back home on a two-year leave, this time through the Suez Canal. My father told me his grandfather Stibbe had found the trip around the Cape of Good Hope so uncomfortable and had suffered so much from sea sickness that he swore he would not go back until the Canal was ready. Their mothers and Aslomon's father Lion were still alive in 1878. Among our family papers are three letters Lion Stibbe wrote to his son in 1871. He was then 72 years old. He was a business man and writes that he was quite busy, working in his office most days from 6.30 a.m. until 9 p.m. Lion's handwriting is quite steady and clear and his letters are remarkably brief and quite to the point, despite the enormous distance between him and his children who must have been curious about life at home. He does, however, send them copies of recent newspapers and discusses local elections in Kampen where they lived. He also tells his son that he sent him a number of things he had asked for and states he received payment for them and was returning a receipt for the money with his letter. He congratulates his son on a promotion and a move to Semarang and writes their mother is far too busy to write as she has been more than two months without a maid. Still Lion's wife Doortje adds a few lines to his letters and expresses the hope they will be in good health and protected by the Lord. There is also a small piece of paper in my files on which Lion has calculated what the education of his youngest son, Aslomon, had cost him every year of his 6 year studies in Leiden and how much he spent on outfitting him for the Far East—fl.4,852.50, after an amount of fl.3,600.00 was deducted for a reimbursement. Since he had six children it seems logical and fair to his other offspring that he tried to keep track of what he spent on his youngest son which was probably more than his expenditures on the others. In one of his letters there is also mention of a remittance he received from Aslomon, so it is quite likely that he was repaid, at least in part. The reimbursement of fl.3,600.00 may be what he is talking about and the accounting may have been part of the same letter. In writing to the Indies, he mentions the ships that will carry his letters, so it must have been customary to direct a letter to a specific ship. He writes on September 19, 1871, that he just received a letter dated August 9th. This would suggest that the time the mail took in those days, after the Suez Canal opened, was not all that long and even compares favorably with the time it takes today to write an air mail letter to Europe, which can easily take a week or two.

Aslomon's career path is shown in a handwritten document on which various bureaucrats list his assignments in the Far East and the time he served in each position as well as the salary he earned. This document appears to have been prepared by others and represents a computation of the years he served for the purpose of computing his pension. He started out to be at the "disposal of the governor general" for July and August 1867. He earned fl.150 (about $75) per month at that time. The governor general was the highest government representative of the Kingdom of the Netherlands in Indonesia. He was appointed by the queen and reigned somewhat like a viceroy, although in a much more modest way than the British Viceroys in India. My father told me a story he heard from his grandfather Stibbe about the GG as he was called. This GG liked to take a walk outside the palace in the cool early morning. One morning he did this again, but before he returned the soldiers guarding the gate had changed. So he was challenged by the new guard. The man asked him who he was. He got

ASLOMON STIBBE IN 1895.

the answer "*ik ben de gouverneur generaal*" (I am the GG). The guard responded, "*Ja daar heb je nogal het smoel voor.*" (Sure, you have the mug for that). The GG had several palaces, one in Batavia, and one in Buitenzorg, now Bogor. The latter was in the mountains, a cooler place where he spent time during the hottest part of the year. The Bogor palace still exists and is located in a beautiful park that contains a world famous arboretum and plant collection. Netty and I visited it in 1988 and noticed a graveyard with graves of several GGs and their spouses. Today it still is a truly magnificent park. Under the GG served six Governors who were overseeing large provinces and were assisted by a number of *Residents*, each responsible for the administration of specific areas. A number of *Assistent Residenten* reported to them and they in turn supervised a group of *Controleurs*, young, beginning civil servants who had to cover large areas on horseback and on foot to keep an eye on the population. The judiciary was, of course, independent of these administrative executives. In modern times the Dutch colonial authorities had established lower courts where Indonesians could settle disputes in accordance with their own traditional tribal and religious laws. The word "adat" was used to indicate these laws. If legal disputes (Dutch as well as adat) got more severe, they came before a *Landraad* and the court above that was the *Gerechts Hof.*

The final and highest court was the *Hoog Gerechtshof.* In 1895 Aslomon became a member of this highest court and ended his career as its president. Among his papers is a copy of the speech he made when he assumed this position. Aslomon was decorated as a *Ridder in de Orde van de Nederlandse Leeuw* in 1894. His pension statement shows he made many moves within the judicial hierarchy. As we saw, he was stationed in Palembang, the largest city on the island of Sumatra where my grandmother was born. After his retirement he moved to The Hague where he lived for many years. The Hague is not only the city where the seat of the Dutch government is but was also favored by retirees from the colonies as a place to live in retirement.

My grandmother was the second child in her family. Her older brother was George (Jan. 4, 1868 – Nov. 11, 1941), a man I have known well. Her younger brother was Anton Stibbe (May 24, 1874 – May 6, 1970) who became a businessman but not a very successful one. He was a tall rather dull man without much ambition. Anton married at least twice and lived in French Indo China as well as in Indonesia. He retired in southern France and in 1937 married a much younger French woman at the rather advanced age of sixty-three and to everybody's surprise she bore him a son in 1940 when Anton was sixty-six. After the war Anton spent much time with my grandparents in Bloemendaal, I suspect, because his marriage was not the greatest and he did not have much money and needed a place to stay. Tony, his son, was a rather undisciplined redheaded lad who also spent some time in Bloemendaal. My mother used to call him "Terrible Tony." Anton died in France and we completely lost sight of his wife and of Tony.

My great uncle George Stibbe also became a civil servant in Indonesia. He studied for this profession in Holland, probably in Delft. After George had left for the Indies, the universities of Leiden and Utrecht opened special faculty for people who were preparing for a career as government officials in the colonies. Admission to this faculty was on a selective basis and controlled by the government's expected future manpower demand. After graduation one was assured of a spot in the extensive government apparatus in this large country. Uncle George was a quiet, very precise and self-effacing man who reached the position of Resident, two steps below governor general. He married late in life, at age forty-six. His wife, Louise Hardenberg, was a widow, who was a little older than he (fifty-one when they married) and quite a character. Tante Lous and Oom George lived in the Hague as retired people. As a young boy I frequently visited them with my parents.

Oom George was bald and had a small goatee. He was always meticulously dressed. His wife was a sight to behold. She was quite large with a sharp almost beak like nose and numerous chins. She dressed like Queen Victoria in huge tent like dresses and we suspected her of wearing a wig. She did have a great sense of humor, however, and I liked to visit her because she would kid around with me and always slip me a generous amount of money. She had many mostly imaginary ailments and would call my mother frequently to recite all her troubles on the telephone in a long monotonous drone, interrupting herself sometimes suddenly with the question: "are you still there?". Tante Lous and Oom George preferred to live "en pension," a sort of high class boarding house where they had nice rooms with their own furniture and their own paintings on the wall and where the landlady and her servants took care of the cooking and housekeeping. I do not think Tante Lous ever prepared a meal. Tante Lous was an imperious lady who was very annoyed when she was awakened very early on May 10, 1940 by gunfire and was just about to call the General Staff to complain about the noisy army exercises waking up citizens in the early morning when she heard it was caused by the German attack on Holland. She died early in the war and Oom George died soon after her which in a way was lucky for him because the persecution of the Jews was just starting and as a widower he was no longer protected by his mixed marriage.

DORA STIBBE AS A YOUNG GIRL.

Oom George had a rather pessimistic mind-set and was a shy man who kept to himself. He had a great knowledge of the Far East and I remember him predicting to my parents that the "yellow race" (meaning the Asians) would eventually dominate the world and that their great grandchildren would be their slaves. This did not quite become a reality yet, but the currently quite powerful Japanese economy and the emerging dominance of China and India make one think about the future, especially for the Europeans. As the only heir of Oom George and Tante Lous I received a surprisingly small inheritance from them and some of the paintings we still have such as the Poggenbeek water color George has, the Kuypers landscape and sheaves from the same painter are from their estate. I have fond memories of this interesting couple who strangely enough had not been on speaking terms with my grandparents for several decades, for reasons we all had forgotten.

My grandmother was much more energetic and livelier than her brothers. She ran her big house very capably and entertained in a grand, old-fashioned style. When I was little she would tell me at length about her youth in the Far East, putting everything in a somewhat favorable and romantic light. She always spoke in the soft romantic tone of her generation and often mentioned her great love and admiration for her parents. I have a series of large pictures showing the main rooms of their house in Batavia. She would tell me how she went to school in a carriage with an Indonesian coachman and how she attended balls when she was a young lady. They would have ice blocks stacked in the center of the ballroom with a fan to move the cool air around, an early form of air conditioning. The fan was moved by an Indonesian servant who pulled a rope attached to it. She also told me how one day the skies darkened to the point where the day turned into night and a rain of ashes came down, caused by the eruption of the Krakatau (Krakatoa) volcano, one of the major volcanic eruptions of the century. The eruption took place in the night of August 26 to 27, 1883 when she was eleven. An earthquake in the seabed of the ocean caused tremendous waves (Tsunamis) and thousands of people on Java and Sumatra died as a result of flash floods. Records I have seen report 36,000 deaths. The small island of Krakatoa was 47 sq. miles before the eruption and only 16 sq. miles afterwards.

After my mother's death in 1997, Netty and I cleaned out her house in Wassenaar and among my father's books I found three very interesting items. There was a *Reis Journaal*, a travelogue written by my grandmother during a trip to Europe with her mother in 1889. There were two *Poesie Albums*, one had belonged to my grandmother and the other to my mother. These albums were books kept by young girls in which they asked their friends and relatives to write little poems about their friendship for each other, almost always decorated with glued-in pictures of flowers and other romantic illustrations which were added by the author of the poem to make things look more beautiful. The poetry is invariably sweetly romantic and, in today's standards, incredibly sugary and innocent. The penmanship is of outstanding quality and there are hardly any erasures or mistakes. My scribbles and those of my contemporaries and of today's children are way way below the work of those girls in years gone by. As a time capsule, Oma's album is also interesting in that it presents a picture of a young girl's life in colonial Batavia. The album itself was printed in Holland and sold in Batavia. Among its pages are a few printed quite bombastic poems, all about the beauty of European flowers that were unknown in the Indies and had most likely never been seen by the writers. The contributions by friends and relatives start in 1884, when Oma was thirteen years old, and end in 1887 when she was sixteen. She was married when she was nineteen! Oma attended a small private school for girls in Batavia and never attained any great academic heights. Yet her level of knowledge of languages and of literature and art was very good. There are poems in the album in French, in English and German beyond the ones in Dutch. So these thirteen to fourteen year olds living in a colonial backwater managed to compose poetry in four languages! Perhaps they copied their entries from somewhere else, but still they understood these languages and were sufficiently comfortable in them to use them.

The first poem is by Dora's mother, my great grandmother who writes (translated from Dutch):

Tenderness
Most beautiful trait of pure souls,
Sweetest feature in a sweet face!
Manly pride and passion kneel down
Where you cast your friendly glance.
Tenderness is the power of the weak,
Is their scepter and their sword,
The tiny flower that would break from a sigh,
Trembles and bends and is saved.

Tenderness will lead the tyrant;
 Into the sanctuary of faith.
Rules unobtrusively and modestly

The almighty power of the quiet woman.
Her command rustles as a prayer,
And her gentle hint is a prayer;
Before her feet peace is spread,
And her sons are blessed by God!

As I mentioned, my grandmother always spoke with love and affection about her mother who, according to her, was a quiet woman who had great inner strength. These characteristics seem to be present in her poem.

Dora's brother George also contributes to the album, but he says he cannot produce poetry so he writes prose. He writes in Haarlem on September 25, 1885 on a separate piece of paper. (obviously he was in Holland, probably in school seventeen years old at that time.)

"Dear Dora!
In this album you also want to have a word from your brother. As you know, I am not a poet so please accept this prose.

Even if the form is not beautiful, take my good will for what it is, because the words that flow from the pen flow from my heart.

There has always been a struggle between the good and the beautiful, between appearance and substance, between feelings and reason. May you be spared from these struggles, may you never waver between feelings and reason, between will and passion then my wishes will be fulfilled!

In this world there is a constant battle for survival, may this battle be short and easy for you! Wherever fate locates us and however it will favor us or hurt us, be assured that I will never forget that I am your brother and may you also never forget that you are the sister of your George."

A poem in English by M. Cordes obviously a girlfriend of Oma in Batavia, reflects the flavor of these albums very well:

Remembrance
Forget me not! An echo lives,
In friendship's feeling heart,
Responding sweetest symphonies,
When absence makes it smart.
O, simple words, with love imbued,

How hearts respond to thee!
In cadence soft, through struggling tears,
Farewell! Remember me!

Your Affectionate
M Cordes

The travelogue is on the one hand quite interesting and on the other somewhat boring. Dora Stibbe was 18 years old when she went on that trip with her mother. Little more than a year after this trip she married my grandfather in Batavia. She must have known my grandfather at the time she went away, yet there is not a word about him in the entire story except for many references to the fact that they were longing for mail from the Indies and that this mail was often delivered to hotels where they had just left and then had to be forwarded on to them to the next hotel. Remarkably, after several stops the mail catches up with them in Interlaken. There is a "big package" of mail mainly from "Papa," of course, but still there is reference to a "long desired" letter. Was this from Max? Maybe. It is quite possible that this trip was organized to give her some distance from Max and to see if she was serious about getting married. Oma and her mother first stay in The Hague and later in Kampen with relatives. She mentions going to several concerts and is extremely enthusiastic about the music she hears that is obviously better than what she used to hear in Batavia. They visit Arnhem and see sights that still exist and that Netty and I also visited when we were young, specifically the Bedriegertjes in Roosendaal. This is a garden where people walking through it are constantly surprised by sudden jets of water, little fountains, etc., which can drench you if you are not careful. There is of course a fellow hiding somewhere who surreptitiously controls the water flow. After a tearful goodbye to an aunt, they go to Germany where they visit Frankfort and travel on a boat on the Rhine. From there they travel to Switzerland with many stops there, Schafhausen, Bern, Luzern, Interlaken, etc., etc. Dora is totally overwhelmed by the mountains, the lakes and the sights. They stay in hotels where they can see a waterfall, at night lit up by electric light, a wonderful thing to see! They rent carriages to take them around, but they also hike for hours. All this in a very hot summer and dressed up with gloves and light overcoats (to fend off the dust). They meet many people, some nice, some not so. She thinks the Germans are nice, the English stiff and Americans crazy! Here follows a translated part of the story:

"At this time I am sitting here in the shade of the trees in front of the hotel. It is a little cool today, but otherwise the weather is beautiful. In front of me are the rippling waters of the Vierwaltstätter See and in the background the Alps solemnly rise. Today their mountain peaks are unusually clear, visible on the horizon. From time to time small elegant "saloon" boats loaded with pleasure travelers stir the clear blue water and create some movement in the otherwise calm and peacefully natural scene that stretches out before my eyes. Here and there small rowboats rock like little nutshells on the water and out of the window of the music room comes the lovely familiar Chopin music. One can hardly imagine a more heavenly spot, it offers a singular opportunity to think quietly about so much that appears strange and amazing to our limited human brain. One looks here up to these giants who have watched for many centuries over our futile efforts and who seem to look at us so earnestly and remind us how transitory our existence is and how durable theirs is and sometimes with their grim wild formations they seem to threaten to crush us, to take revenge on us who have disturbed their peace, have tunneled through their insides, have robbed them of their beautiful forests, challenge them by constructing roads and by building houses on the highest and most dangerous places. How small and insignificant is man, if compared with them and yet man is more powerful and can by joining forces accomplish so much that amazes us. But if I go on this way I will never finish! It is ten o'clock already. Time is valuable so let me take advantage of it. I was in Interlaken" Oma shows here that more than a hundred years ago, she and certainly other people like her were aware of the impact human action has on the environment. Not badly written for an eighteen-year-old. There are several segments in Oma's travelogue that are equally interesting and well written, but it would carry me too far to translate them all. May this brief quotation just serve to show what kind of a woman she was and how well educated she was despite the fact that she had grown up in "the colonies," which were regarded as a cultural backwater.

I have a document called *Akte van Bekwaamheid* a certificate that states that on January 25, 1889 Dora Estella Johanna Stibbe passed an exam that qualifies her to teach "the principles of French and English" at grade school levels. So she did achieve some academic excellence.

In retrospect I think there was sometimes friction between my grandmother and my mother who believed her mother-in-law looked down on her because of her more humble family background. This may have been true, but I also think my mother was overly sensitive on that score and should have realized she herself was very well educated (she had a law degree and her mother-in-law had barely finished high school), and with a little flexibility she would have been much more appreciated by my grandparents than she was. *Omatje*, "little Oma" as she was called was extremely energetic and always busy with numerous projects. She had a way of walking through the house with quick steps you could hear from afar. She would make a sort of clip-clop noise as she would put her heel down first, to be followed by the rest of her foot. With parquet floors everywhere in her house, you always knew where she was. As a young woman she must have been quite pretty. We have a portrait of her, a photograph printed on an oval shaped background of porcelain. This portrait was made in Germany probably when they lived there. She looks still very young then. On this picture she wears a small brooch in the shape of a crescent moon. Netty still has that brooch and treasures it. It is now well over a hundred years old.

As I mentioned, Oma, or Dora as she was called, was nineteen years old when she married Max Schieferdecker who was then thirty. In the Batavia of those days young purely Dutch women must have been a rare commodity and Oma must have been quite a catch. Even in my days men often went to Indonesia as bachelors and once settled there, wrote their girlfriends or fiancées to come over after having married them by proxy. In Dutch that is called to marry *met de handschoen* (with the glove). Often a complete wedding ceremony and party was held in Holland without a groom, however. Sometimes men who came from Holland married local girls who had some Indonesian blood. Others, particularly enlisted men serving in the colonial army, took Indonesian mistresses. Many soldiers married their mistresses later after they had several children. These children of soldiers were of mixed blood, of course, and they were the origin of a fairly large segment of the Dutch population in the Indies. They met with little discrimination in the Indies and even in Holland and were Dutch nationals by law. There were when I was in Indonesia many people of mixed blood who formed a strong middle class and considered themselves Dutch, even those who were mostly Indonesian. There was, of course, an endless variety in racial backgrounds and economic status among these people, but the Dutch attitude towards this group has always been very open and welcoming. When Indonesia became a free country the people with a mixed background were facing a terrible dilemma. Many had never been in Holland and felt completely at home in Indonesia. Others felt more Dutch and had no problems leaving. However, the ones that wanted to stay in Indonesia had to choose whether they wanted to become Indonesian citizens or not. If they did, they could stay. If they did not, they usually had to leave and start a new life in a cold wet country they did not know. Many Dutch families have a touch of Indonesian blood.

When I was a little boy, my grandparents had quite a number of personnel in their house. Later, in the late thirties, Oma simplified her life and had a live-in maid and another woman who came in daily. They no longer owned a car. Oma made a great effort to educate me and made it her task to introduce me to the better things in life. She took me to museums and in summer, when my parents went on vacation and I stayed with her, she would take me to the theater and on excursions with tour boats to Amsterdam and other places. I often was allowed to take a friend along when I was there in summer, and Oma would organize activities to keep us busy. One summer she hired a young woman who was skilled in working with cardboard and paper, sort of an arts and crafts teacher. She taught me and my friend to make all kinds of quite useful and nice things such as blotters, photo albums, etc. Oma was interested in volunteer work and charities. During World War I many Belgians fled to then-neutral Holland to escape the German occupation of their country. Germany attacked Belgium without warning in August 1914, in order to outflank France, its enemy. The German occupation of Belgium was tough on the local inhabitants and many towns and villages were destroyed. In Belgium the Germans immediately started to build their reputation as cruel occupiers of innocent people. In several cases civilians were executed for resisting the occupiers. Executions started a few days after they entered the country as if the Belgian villagers had always planned to oppose the Germans. Oma was very actively involved in the Dutch efforts to help the Belgian refugees and she received a decoration from the Queen of Belgium for her work. I still have the medal and a document stating she was awarded *la Medaille de la Reine Elisabeth*. Later on Oma's favorite charity was the *Baby Huis*, the house for babies. This was a place where a small staff cared for a number of young babies, as I learned later, born out of wedlock. I guess they tried to find adoptive parents for children that were not wanted by their mothers, but they also found jobs for the mothers so they could keep their children. It was, of course, not explained to me where these babies came from and why they were staying there and it never occurred to me to ask. Oma would arrange bazaars to raise money for this institution and made all sorts of clever things herself to be sold in the bazaar. She was very skillful in embroidery and kept her hands busy until she reached a very old age. We still have some of the things she made. She also is the one who collected the paintings and antiques we now have. In fact there was much more in her house, but after her death my father and aunt sold many things for which they had no room. She was a favored client of several art dealers.

She was, as I mentioned, a vegetarian and a frequent visitor at a store called *het Reform Huis* that was what now would be called a health food store. In this store you could buy ingredients for müsli, a dish I knew and liked from the thirties on and which has now, sixty years later, become a heavily advertised health food to which the cereal manufacturers have hitched their wagon. Oma became a vegetarian when she was looking for a cure for her migraine headaches and her generally poor health. She was introduced to the vegetarian lifestyle by a German woman, Frau Hinrichs, who lived in Bad Godesberg. Oma would go there for prolonged stays, to take "the cure." It worked wonders for her. Later, Frau Hinrichs turned out to be a fanatical Nazi and great admirer of Adolf Hitler. This did not deter Oma from going there almost every year before the war until my father and my uncle Bernard told her that things in Germany were not going in the right direction and that it was really better to leave Frau Hinrichs alone and let her march around with her brown shirt friends. I am relating this story mainly to illustrate Oma's outlook on life and her somewhat detached and innocent attitude. She had a strong tendency to look only at the good side of people and ignore the negatives or the bad side.

Oma liked to entertain in style. When I was a young boy, she would arrange musical afternoons where my father would play with a trio, consisting of a pianist, a violinist, both friends of my parents, and my father playing the cello. This was a serious hobby of my father's. Although my mother was a reasonably good pianist, I believe she felt she was not quite good enough to participate. Sometimes Oma hired professional artists to perform, usually people who needed some financial help. When my parents celebrated their 25th wedding anniversary Oma gave a fairly big dinner party where several of our relatives were present. I was there also with Netty, then officially my fiancée. This dinner took place just before I left for Indonesia and I think it must have been during my last leave. One of the guests was Eric Cohen Tervaert a son of old friends of Oma's from Indonesia. He had returned from there with his Indonesian wife (who did not attend the party) and was a

MY GRANDARENTS
AROUND 1953.

102

nervous wreck having spent several years in a Japanese concentration camp. Eric was highly emotional and probably suffered from what would now be recognized as post traumatic stress syndrome. The desert was ice cream, a specialty because in those days people did not have freezers and the ice cream had to be delivered at the right time by a man from the pastry shop on a motor cycle. After the desert was served we heard a bustling in the vestibule and a group of ladies came in with a male pianist. They were singers hired by Oma and they proceeded to sing several highly romantic classical pieces in honor of the wedding anniversary of my parents. The music made Eric burst out in tears, and I almost choked from laughter and had to leave the table for a moment because I had drunk a little too much and also because the whole scene was like a situation comedy with the friendly ladies nobody knew nodding at us, and Eric crying and blubbering in his napkin.

As a Victorian lady Oma was extremely straight-laced and prudish. She never swore or used bad language of course. I recall how one day after Netty had become pregnant for the first time and we were proud and happy about this event, we visited Oma and Opa and after dinner I announced with a flourish that I had wonderful news: "Netty was expecting a child." After I had said this, there was total silence and Oma turned the conversation to another subject. My parents who were also there drove us home that evening to Heemstede. We did not yet have a car then. I said to my father I was quite upset about the way Oma had acted. He said he thought the possible explanation was that in Oma's mind pregnancy was a subject ladies only discussed among themselves in a whisper behind the potted palms. As soon as he got home, he wrote a stern note to his parents saying they had really "offended the children" and that he hoped they would make amends. I do not remember how this tempest in a teapot was resolved. We always regarded it as a humorous incident and considered it rather typical for my father to write a note rather than confront his mother directly or by phone. I do remember how delighted Oma was with her first great-grandchild, our son George.

In 1958, when we decided to emigrate to the U.S., I went ahead by plane to find a place to live for our small family. Netty followed me by ship with George and Adriaan. Oma came to see Netty off on the ship, the "Statendam" of the Holland America Line. We have a photograph of that moment. It was the last time she saw her great grandchildren. She died at her house a year later, in September 1959, shortly after my parents had returned from their first visit to us. She was eighty-eight years old. Like her husband she was cremated and her ashes rest beside those of Max Schieferdecker in the Westerveld cemetery near Bloemendaal..

4 : Ancestors on My Mother's Side

My mother's father, Gerrit Hesselink or Opa Dik (fat opa) as I called him, was a rotund jovial and very self- assured man who was full of good humor and zest for life. In contrast to Opa Schieferdecker who was quiet and usually kept himself in the background while still being firmly in control of his family and his affairs, Opa Hesselink was open and talkative and had a knack of getting along with everybody. I knew him well as he visited us frequently, and when I was a small boy we made several trips to Leeuwarden to see him. My mother was extremely fond of him which is understandable since he was the only parent she had ever known. He raised her after his first wife died when my mother was only five months old. Opa Hesselink was born in 1869 and died in 1938 at age sixty-nine, when I was thirteen years old. I remember vividly how quiet and sad my otherwise very vocal and lively mother was when she and my father returned from Opa's funeral. The final years of my grandfather were difficult and quite tragic. He had lost almost all of his money due to the mismanagement of his business by his only son and died of cancer (of the kidneys, I believe). It is also possible he contracted prostate cancer, but I was always told it was his kidneys. However, despite his affliction he remained cheerful and enjoyed his final years in a nice two-room apartment in what now would be called a continuing care facility called *Mooiland* in Heelsum near Arnhem, which had been newly built by the church he belonged to. My parents and Otto and Jet Jonas, my mother's sister and brother-in-law, had arranged for him to stay there after he lost his second wife and needed help. I believe my father paid for Opa's residence there and in exchange for this and other financial assistance he acquired Opa's large house on the Nieuwestad in Leeuwarden, the most important residential and shopping street in town with a canal in the middle, and a property in Heereveen, where a subsidiary of Opa's business was located.

After he settled down in *Mooiland,* Opa immediately made many good friends including a lady, Johanna Cambier van Nooten, an interesting woman who had spent her working life as a singing teacher. She belonged to a quite prominent family of academics and was well to do. She nursed Opa Dik through his final years.

Gerrit Hesselink was born in 1869 in Nordhorn, Germany, a small town just over the Dutch border near Almelo. He was part of a segment of the population that while living in Germany was Dutch, spoke Dutch and went to a Dutch church where the sermons were preached in Dutch.

His father was Hermannus Hesselink who was born in 1827 and died in 1911. Hermannus was a Dutchman who lived and worked in Germany. His occupation is unclear. In the official documents on Gerrit's second marriage, Hermannus is described as a "gardener living in Nordhorn, Prussia." My mother always said he was a *rentmeester* which means in Dutch he was manager or caretaker of estates belonging to others. This is more likely given the way he lived. He was born in Vierakker, a small village near Zutphen in the Netherlands, and grew up either in Lochem or in Varsseveld. Gerrit was the third son out of four who all spelled their family name differently. Son #1 called himself Johan Hendrik Hesling. He lived in Dieren. He had a son named Herman who I knew as a boy. He was an engineer living in The

HERMANNUS HESSELINK

Hague with his family. He was an executive with the PTT (the government postal, telephone and telegraph monopoly). Son no. 2 Derk Wilhelm Heslink lived in Nordhorn. Son no. 3 - was Opa Dik, Gerrit Hesselink. Son no. 4 was Karel A. Heslink who lived and died in Berlin. Why the confusion about the spelling of the name existed is unclear. It may have been the result of errors by German-speaking clerks in Nordhorn. The family was certainly not illiterate, but they were no academics either. The spelling "Hesselink" seems the correct one as there are several families in Holland with the same name. Opa's mother was Everdina Jeannette Jansen, also clearly Dutch, who died in 1879 when Gerrit was ten years old. Hermannus remarried Engelina Berendsen and had one more daughter, Harriette, who married Hermannes Gerardus Engels. Her family had musical talents. My mother said they had a son who was first violinist in the Maastricht Symphony orchestra and a daughter who was a well-known concert singer and performed in radio broadcasts. The violinist was not liked by my mother because he would visit my parents from time to time and displayed bad table manners and "ate too much" as she put it. The singer was nice, according to my mother.

Opa Dik was a great raconteur and told me many stories of his youth of which I remember three. One was how he and his brothers and friends would go swimming in a river on hot summer days. Since they did not know how to swim, they would go to a butcher and ask for pig's bladders. They would tie them shut, blow them up and use them as flotation devices to have a good time. He also told me how he was a good runner as a boy, which surprised me given his rotund appearance. He said he would run for prizes against other boys and once lost because a friend who had promised not to jump over the finish line did it anyway and won. His third story was about making a little money by working on Sundays in their church, pumping the organ. In old churches, the air needed to play the organ was pumped by assistants to the organist, or in this case boys who would stand on two wooden treadles, alternately pushing them down to operate leather bellows. One day he thought the service was over and left, only to discover later that he had ruined the entire end of the service planned by his pastor. Gerrit must have grown up under very modest circumstances. His father sent him out into the world as a very young boy to make a living for himself, telling potential employers that "he was a strong lad despite his young age who could work as good as a grown man." Relating this story my mother always said Opa felt he was being sold like a slave and from then on never cared much for his father and rarely saw him. I don't think Opa had much of an education; he probably did not even finish high school.

Gerrit Hesselink moved to Friesland and settled in Leeuwarden where he first worked in a men's clothing store owned by two brothers, Pier and Oepke Plantenga. My mother said

GERRIT HESSELINK AND JANNIGJE BEETSMA IN 1895.

her father managed the store and Pier and Oepke "did nothing." This comment about two merchants probably quite correctly illustrates life in a small sleepy provincial town in Holland, where life was quiet and orderly and people had plenty of time to enjoy life. My grandfather was a worker who was always busy and had little patience with people who did not do a full days work for a full days pay. Yet there were clearly quite a few people in his environment who were less highly motivated and still lived nicely. His two brothers-in-law were an example of the easy going group.

In Friesland, in 1895 Gerrit met and married Jannegje Annes Beetsma, the middle one of three sisters. The oldest sister was Aaltje whom I have known very well. My mother was named after her. Aaltje married Bastianus Martinus Petrus Deibel, and they had two sons, George and Anne. I also knew them very well. George and Anne each had one son and strangely enough both elected to name their son after their father. So I ended up with two cousins both called Bas (Bastianus Martinus Petrus) Deibel, and both living in Leeuwarden, a stone's-throw away from each other. We always called the older one *"Grote Bas"* (Big Bas) and the younger one *"Kleine Bas"* (Little Bas). My mother said that Aaltje and her husband ran a sort of boarding house or hotel for cattle farmers who came to town for the cattle auctions that were held weekly in Leeuwarden. As in many other smaller Dutch towns, there were not many hotels, perhaps none, and Friday was market day, a busy day with many people coming in from out of town to trade. My mother's aunt Aaltje probably did most of the work running the boarding house. My mother commented that her uncle Martinus was quite "lazy" and preferred to go hunting with his brother-in-law, Tjerk Spriensma, who owned a big farm outside Leeuwarden where he raised cattle. Friesland was and is a world famous cattle producer and Frisian cows are known all over the world as prime quality cattle and big milk producers.

The Spanish nobleman, Duke de Baena, to whom I have referred in previous chapters, writes about the Frisian farmers as follows:"Many of the old traditions and habits of the seventeenth century are still alive today in the northern provinces of Friesland and Groningen which are inhabited almost entirely by farmers and cattle breeders who are not only extremely rich but also very cultured. I have been invited as a guest into many of their homes and though the export of cattle to Spain was the main topic of conversation, much could be discussed in English or German—or even in Spanish, in my case—as regards literature, art and culture in general. Drinking my cup of coffee in the parlor or dining room of one of those spacious farms and looking out the window, I could see endless green pastures on which the famous Frisian cattle were grazing; but if my eyes were directed towards the interior of the home, I would see bookcases filled with books of very fine quality dealing with all sorts of subjects that a civilized man can know and like. I found myself every time in a highly civilized world where culture had come and spread its roots among people who lived in constant touch with nature, and this is I believe the charm which Dutch life has still retained and offers the visitor…" Although her uncle Tjerk was probably not one of those very erudite farmers, my mother always went to great pains to explain to me and others that these "farmers" were not exactly peasants but often very wealthy and well-educated people. She had a level of insecurity about her Frisian background that I believe was entirely unwarranted. My mother said Tjerk also preferred to go hunting and tending to his stable of race horses (probably mostly trotters as harness racing is a popular sport in Friesland), rather than work. Tjerk married the youngest sister of the three, Siebrecht (Tante Siep). I did not know Tante Siep very well, but my mother was very fond of both aunts who acted as surrogate mothers for her and her sister and they visited Siep's farm frequently. Siep had four children—a son Rienk, who was a Nazi sympathizer during the war, a daughter Geertje who married Laurens Haquebord (a Huguenot name) and had seven children and a daughter Jannegje who remained a spinster. My mother explained that Jannegje's brothers "had decided she could not marry, because she had to take care of her aging mother." The fourth was a son, Willem, who became a successful businessman and owned a wire and cable factory in Dokkum. Willem did much resistance work during the war, which illustrates the often agonizing problems families had when one of them ended up on the Nazi side and the other on the patriotic side. I don't think Rienk was a member of the nazi party or an active collaborator, but I do remember his daughter Wieke, an attractive blond girl, was engaged to a German officer. Geertje Haquebord or Gee as she was called was about my mother's age and close to her. When my mother was young she said she often walked on Wednesday and Saturday afternoon when she was free from school to the farm to play with her nephews and nieces there.

There is a photograph of Tante Gee with her offspring which shows, I believe twenty-two people (children, in laws, grandchildren, etc.). One of her sons became a well known historian in Holland and is particularly known for research and excavations at Nova Zembla (Nowaja Zemlja), a Russian island above the polar circle in the Barentz Sea, north of Archangel where the first Dutch attempt to reach the Far East by going the northern route failed. The ships got caught in the ice when winter came and the crew was forced to spend the winter there. They used the timbers of their ships to build a house in which they lived. In spring they built small boats to reach Russia and safety. Laurens Haquebord Jr. is involved in historical digs, looking for the remains of the house and for artifacts. The names of the two Dutch captains in charge of the original expedition were Heemskerk and Barentz, hence the name of the Barentz Sea.

My grandmother Jannegje died on January 21, 1898. I do not know what the cause of her death was but suspect it had to do with her being pregnant with a third child. She was thirty-two years old and left her husband then thirty-one and two daughters, my Aunt Jet (Harrietta Allegonda) three years old and my mother just five months. The death of a young mother was, of course, a calamity, and the two young girls were initially brought to their aunts. Jet went to Aaltje and my mother to Siebrecht.

My mother had no recollection of her own mother or of that period. She grew up without any complexes or other mental problems that could have resulted from her not having had a mother of her own. The Dutch are stoic people who do not show their feelings easily, and the Frisians are considered by the Dutch to be the most reticent and stoic of all. There is a well-known story of a Frisian farmer who was found by a friend while in the process of committing suicide. The friend found him lying on the floor in a pool of blood after he had slashed his wrists. The friend asked him in Frisian: "*Mat dat sa?*" (Is that the way it has to be?). The farmer answered: "*Ja dat mat sa.*" (Yes, that's the way it has to be). The friend departed, leaving the farmer to his own devices.

In hindsight I do believe that the lack of motherly affection my mother experienced had some influence on her. I certainly did not lack any affection from her side when I was young. She was a very warm and open person, but she never cuddled me very much. Or perhaps I should say she had a certain clumsiness in her way of dealing with physical contact with other people and with me as her child, that makes me realize she must often have been left to her own devices when she grew up.

Three years after the death of his first wife, Gerrit Hesselink remarried. His bride was Aaltje de Jong who owned a photography business. Aaltje de Jong was thirty-six years old at that time. I called her "Oma Dik," naturally. This second marriage of Opa Dik may have had some undertones of practicality and business interest. The bride being four years older than the groom and bringing in a business. However there is no doubt in my mind that Opa Dik worked very hard in the business and made it grow substantially. It is unclear how Aaltje de Jong came to own a photography business, an unusual circumstance in that day and age, and where the business was originally established. Most likely her father owned the business before her. Taking pictures of people was a good business in the old days and to have one's picture taken was an event.

I clearly remember the house on Nieuwestad, no. 53, where the family lived and the studio was and where my mother grew up. (In the fall of 1995, I visited my mother who was then ninety-eight years old, very deaf and nearly blind. She could not remember much of what happened the day or week before, but things of her past were still clear. When I asked if she remembered the number of her house on the Nieuwestad, she answered immediately: "Yes 53!") It was a very big house with at least four floors. The photo studio was on the ground floor. The cameras were huge affairs made of beautifully polished wood, on wooden tripods. The photographer would stand behind them, duck under a black cloth and peer through the lens to get the optimum picture. The picture was taken on a glass plate that was developed almost immediately. Prints were made later from the plate.

1901 – MARRIAGE OF GERRIT HESSELINK WITH AALTJE DE JONG.

This system was used all over the world and because the glass plate negatives were more durable than film, many old pictures have been retrieved and are kept in archives. I do not think any negatives of Photo de Jong were saved. Behind the people being photographed was usually a backdrop with various scenes painted on it – mostly nice landscapes in brownish and gray subdued colors. One of the backdrops Opa Dik used showed a rendering of a villa in park-like surroundings near Leeuwarden where the *Commissaris van de Koningin* (queen's commissioner or governor of the province) lived. Many photographs we still have were taken at "Photo de Jong." As I mentioned the business had a subsidiary in Heereveen, and I believe also one in Sneek. I was told his crowning achievement was being asked to make a portrait of Queen Wilhelmina in a Frisian costume when she was visiting the province as a young girl. Opa employed a number of people, including a young boy my mother often mentioned, called Jochem. It was Jochem's task to light the stoves in winter. There were five stoves of which two were left burning through the

MY MOTHER AND HER SISTER JET
(L) AS YOUNG GIRLS.

night. The other three were lit every day. This was done with special kindling wood soaked in resin to make lighting easy. My mother said that Jochem used too much kindling and that her father took over the job for a while. In winter, when the canal in front of my mother's house was frozen, a sled was taken out and my mother and Tante Jet were put in it, while Jochem had to run behind it to push the sled. Later the girls learned to skate on the canal, pushing a chair in front of them to stay on their feet. A common practice in the old days.

Opa Dik was a gregarious, caring and very religious man who knew many people in town and was, I believe, quite popular. He liked to sing and had a good voice. He belonged to a choir that gave performances in town and performed as a soloist. As I mentioned, he left home at a very young age and after working in a clothing store, started working for a small trading business. My mother told the story of how the owner of this business developed cancer and Gerrit had not only to take care of his business but also nurse and feed his boss since nobody else was willing to do it. The man had apparently developed some very unsightly cancerous sores. Opa Dik stuck with him till the end. Opa had many stories about life in Leeuwarden, but unfortunately I have forgotten all of them except one. This was the story of a butcher who had a serious falling out with a skipper of a canal barge. (Transportation by barge through the system of canals and rivers is still a major economic activity in Holland and throughout Europe.) The butcher owned a big dog. Knowing when the skipper would come through the canal in town, the butcher prepared his dog by giving him huge quantities of water to drink. When the skipper's boat came in sight, he took the dog for a walk to the bridge and as the skipper passed under it, the dog lifted his leg and soaked the skipper.

Opa and Oma Dik had a son Hendrik Hans Hesselink who was born in 1902. Oom Henk was 5 years younger than my mother and was spoiled. While my mother and her sister were raised quite strictly and had to toe the line, Henk was allowed much more leeway with the result that he never amounted to much in school and when he was given the business to run, he did a poor job, often coming late to work so in the mornings his employees were seen hanging around on the street before the still-closed door. In my eyes, as a young boy, Henk was a nice man, but my mother

AROUND 1930. STANDING L TO R: OTTO, HENK, MY FATHER. SEATED: JET, ME, OPA, TINEKE, JETJE, OMA, MY MOTHER.

told me later that he was a man about town who was careless and lazy. Henk married a young woman, Jet (Henriette) Ooyman. Later they were divorced and Henk went more or less off the deep end. The firm (or Henk personally, I am not certain) went bankrupt and my father who had supported his father-in-law for many years, was forced to withdraw all financial support from Henk. All contact with Henk was lost over the years, but in the last year of the war my mother got a phone call from people in a state mental institution in the province of Noord Brabant, asking if she was the sister of Hendrik Hesselink. They said Henk was severely disturbed and was dying. He was calling her name and asking for her. My mother did not go to see him, perhaps because it was physically impossible and probably also because she did not want to go, fearing it would be too difficult for her to be confronted with her step brother.

My father became the owner of the houses in Leeuwarden and Heereveen where the business used to be located. The house in Leeuwarden was rented out and became a store for all kinds of things made out of cane, bamboo and rattan. Later on my father sold the building to the owner of that store. The house in Heereveen was also located on a canal, and in 1940, the first year of the war, my friend Eelco Apol and I made a trip to Friesland in a small sailboat. We almost capsized near Heereveen and got a lot of water in our small open boat. As everything, our food, blankets, etc., had gotten wet, we needed some help. We went to the Steensma family, who operated a photography business in my father's house in Heereveen. We tied our boat up in front of their house and asked them for shelter. They were very hospitable and put us up for three days, dried everything and sent us on afterwards. My father later sold the house to Steensma.

My mother frequently told me stories of her life as a young girl in Leeuwarden and gave me a good idea of the situation in her family. I remember visiting Opa and Oma Dik as a very young boy. In those days they lived in a smallish house in the Transvaal Straat, near aunt Aaltje and near everybody else. Leeuwarden is and was a small town and everything was nearby. At the time my Aunt Jet and Uncle Otto also lived in Leeuwarden with my niece Tineke, so there were good reasons to visit. Oma Dik, Aaltje de Jong by birth, was born on a ship as her father was a skipper. The name of the skipper was Hans Hendrik de Jong and he was born in the village of Nijehaske, now part of Heereveen, Friesland. His wife's name was Fokje Hooghiemstra (a very, very Frisian name). The first time I visited Opa and Oma Dik, Fokje was still alive and lived with them. Apparently Oom Henk was already running the business at that time. Fokje was still dressed in the traditional Frisian costume with a white lace headpiece under which she had the traditional golden head cover. This was made of real gold and Fokje, who had gotten a little daffy in her old age, accused Oom Henk of shaving pieces of her golden headpiece to sell for money. I remember being scared of Fokje when she suddenly appeared before me as a large apparition dressed in her black outfit with a white skull cap, offering me a peppermint. I believe that during that same visit my mother and I called on Oom Henk who lived in the old house at Nieuwestad 53. In one of his rooms was a model of a Dutch boeier ship, a "tjalk", as used in the Frisian canal system by skippers who lived on board and carried freight. The Frisians call them "Skutsjes." Some of these ships even went out into the North Sea and traded with the Scandinavian countries around the Baltic. I took a fancy to this model and played with it so Oom Henk packed it up and had it shipped to our house in Voorburg. I still remember it arriving there in a big package, the mast struck down. We have kept this model in our house for many years, and it is now at my son George's house in Mamaroneck, NY. Over the years, the condition of the model began to deteriorate because I played with it as a child and the fabric the sails were made of was torn. I fixed up the rigging with new lines. But the most important job was done by Netty who took the old sails that were totally decayed, copied them with new material and gave the new sails the right brownish color by soaking them in tea! The result was and still is marvelous, at least we think so although antique dealers will tell you the worst thing you can do is repairing an old piece to make it look nice. The story behind the ship model was that during an exceptionally cold winter a skipper who was stuck in the ice in the canal in front of the Nieuwestad house, and who needed money, had built the model. My grandfather bought it from the skipper to help him and kept it ever since. I hope my children will also keep it and will understand its value. Aaltje de Jong, Opa's second wife, died in 1936. After her death Opa moved to Heelsum.

Opa Dik was buried in Heelsum. The cemetery where his grave was located was severely damaged during the battle of Arnhem in 1944, when British paratroopers landed in that area in an attempt to create a bridgehead over the Rhine for the advancing allied armies. The paratroopers were defeated and as a result the war was prolonged for the part of Holland located north of the river and lasted through the following severe and horrible winter. We never found much back of Opa Dik's grave.

5 : *Netty's Ancestors*

N etty's maiden name is van Kleffens; her mother's maiden name is van Someren Gréve. Both families have well-researched genealogies and both are prominent in the Netherlands. To have good genealogical data on one's ancestors is fun and provides an insight in one's background even while information on most individuals is limited to date and place of birth, date of death, marriage partner and date of marriage, and number and date of birth of children. These raw data still come to life, particularly if seen against the background of history. One member of Netty's family, her uncle Eelco, (Eelco Nicolaas van Kleffens), has certainly earned his place in the history of Holland and the world. He was without a doubt our most prominent relative. Shortly before the German invasion in May 1940, he was appointed minister of foreign affairs of the Kingdom of the Netherlands. He and his wife, Tante Margaret (née Horstmann) were flown over to England just before Holland capitulated to the Germans, and in the following war years, he was a key member of the Dutch government in exile in London. After the war he served as ambassador of the Netherlands in Washington, D.C.; and during that time was a member

QUEEN WILHELMINA WITH OOM EELCO
AND HARRY HOPKINS.

of the UN Security Council. In 1954 he served as President of the UN General Assembly for one term. Initially he planned to end his career by serving as minister to Portugal, a quiet post in a country with a pleasant climate he had carefully selected to build a nice retirement house and to accommodate what he thought was his wife's poor health. But later he reactivated his career by serving for a few years as an ambassador representing the European Coal and Steel Community, the body that preceded the European Union, at the Court of St James in London. Netty and I have known him and Tante Margaret very well. He made a big impression on us, perhaps chiefly on me and on numerous other people. So I will discuss him at great length in this memoir.

The van Kleffens family history was traced back to 1622, just eighteen years before the first known van Someren Gréve ancestor was born in 1640, beginning their history. This is impressive particularly if compared with the rather rudimentary information we have about the Schieferdeckers, which starts with some difficulty two hundred years later, in 1831. A major reason for so much information being available is that the ancestors of both of Netty's parents lived in the Netherlands and did not move around too much until Netty's grandfather, Opa van Someren Gréve, usually referred to as Opa Gréve, moved to the Dutch East Indies and married there. In addition, there were people in both families who felt their ancestry was important and should be documented while others may have been less interested in their family background The van Kleffens family originates from the northern part of Friesland. Leeuwarden is the capital of the province of Friesland and Northeast of it is Dokkum, a very small town with a very long history. South- west of Dokkum, close to the Wadden Zee, the sea arm that separates the string of islands called the Wadden Islands from the mainland, lies a tiny village, actually more a hamlet, called Raard. This village consists of a church with a few houses around it, situated on a small hill called a *terp*. *Terpen* are a common sight in that area, built to protect the inhabitants from the frequently occurring floods. They were built by hand and usually formed the center of a village or hamlet with the church on top of it. When there was a storm and it was feared the land would be flooded, the church bell was rung to alert the villagers to the danger. They would leave their usually lower lying farmsteads and seek shelter in the church. Raard is the official cradle of the van Kleffens family and Oom Eelco and Tante Margaret's ashes are buried in the small graveyard of the church. There are several other ancestors buried there and nearby are two large farms, one called *Noord* (North) *Kleffens* and the other *Zuid* (South) *Kleffens*. The family no longer owns the first, but Zuid Kleffens remained in the family until recently. It belonged to Oom Eelco and after his death the younger Eelco van Kleffens, the son of Netty's brother Pul, inherited it. Neither his sister nor Netty's or Tilly's children received an equal inheritance. It was just his name that benefited him, somewhat to the chagrin of his cousins. In 1998 the younger Eelco decided not to keep the property which is understandable.

CHURCH IN RAARD.

Despite its name and its tradition, owning a farm and/or farmland like this is not an attractive investment in today's Holland. Dutch laws strongly favor the tenant at the expense of the owner. Farm rents are government controlled and kept artificially low to enable the tenants to prosper. For the owner, the return on investment is therefore unattractive, and if the owner would wish to sell his property, he cannot do so in an open market. A board of farmers, the same one that controls the rent levels, decides what a fair price is and gives the tenant priority. So even if the owner could get a much better price from an outsider, he is prevented from selling to him. Nobody seems to think this is unfair to the property owners or to have a notion of a conflict of interest within the board.

When one drives around north of Raard, one quickly reaches the Wadden Zee. The road runs towards the great dike built to protect the land and prevent the floods that bothered the population in the old days. At the point where the road crosses the dike, a sign warns that the road beyond it may not be passable when storm floods occur. Beyond the dike the road crosses a marshy area which floods during storms and at its end is a ferry terminal with a big parking lot. Nowadays people going to the islands park there and take the ferry to their vacation destination. It becomes quickly clear to any visitor that in the days before the modern (higher) dikes were built, the land flooded often and that the life of the inhabitants of Raard and other villages was hard. In the past hundred years or so, many *terpen* were dug up or removed and the valuable sand was used elsewhere as building material. Several *terpen* yielded important archeological artifacts and a museum has been started to preserve them. Why did people live and farm in such an inhospitable environment?

Probably because the clay soil is very rich and yields great grazing land for cattle. Frisian cattle are recognized throughout the world as a prime breed with excellent milk production.

Netty's grandfather Henricus Cato van Kleffens was born in Dokkum in 1861. He was the eighth and youngest child of Eelke Nicolaas van Kleffens and Catherina van Slooten. His father was a doctor in Dokkum and lived in a large house that later was visited frequently by Netty's father, a place he became very much emotionally attached to. Why Netty's grandfather had such a peculiar set of given names is a mystery. There are no similar names in the family genealogy, but a look at the list of his siblings reveals a little sister who was born fifteen years earlier, on September 10, 1847, and died twelve days later. Her name was Henrica Catherina. Infant mortality was high in those days, even among people who were well off and had medical schooling. Another sister was born and died in 1850 and a year later, in 1851, a brother had the same fate. Perhaps it was an attempt of his parents to make the mother's name, Catherina, live on in the form of Cato or perhaps his father wanted to express his knowledge of the classics by naming his youngest son after the Roman statesman who lived from 234 – 149 B.C. Whatever the reason, the name Henricus Cato lived on in Netty's brother. He was named after his grandfather because Opa van Kleffens, a very strong-willed man, insisted on it and threatened to disinherit his son and daughter-in-law if they did not comply. At least that is the story we always heard from Netty's mother. So it came to pass that Netty's brother had to live in this modern day and age with a very old fashioned if not impossible name. Netty's father was

THE VAN KLEFFENS FAMILY IN 1900 – CHILDREN
L TO R - EELCO, ADRIAAN, NINI.

named Adrianus, after an older brother of Opa van Kleffens. He was called Pul, the nickname he got as a student in Leiden. Logically his son began to be called "Little Pul" or "Pulletje" and later on that was simplified to also just Pul. The name has no meaning and nobody could have trouble with it or ridicule it. A good solution to an awkward situation created by Opa van Kleffens who was a short man, which may explain, at least partly, his bellicose nature. Tilly and Netty had rejected all other names their parents suggested like Harry or Arry. They wanted Hans, but that was not allowed by Opa van Kleffens because that was the name of Opa van Someren Gréve. A much better description than I can ever give of Netty's grandfather and great grandfather and of life in Friesland in the old days can be found in *"Belevenissen I 1894 – 1940"* (Experiences part I 1894 – 1940) an extremely interesting memoir written by Netty's famous uncle Eelco. Oom Eelco wrote his memoir in Portugal after he had retired there. Part I is well written and deals with his life up to 1940 when he was a quite young (he was 46) minister of foreign affairs in the Dutch government and had to escape to England soon after the Germans invaded the Netherlands. This book was published in 1980 and I believe it sold quite well. There was and still is great interest in Holland for accurate historical information dealing with World War II, and since Oom Eelco played a key role in the Dutch government in those days, his memoir is impor-tant. For us it is even more important because it gives an insight in Oom Eelco's character and career and affords us background information on his grandparents and parents that we would otherwise not have. It is all, of course, seen from Oom Eelco's point of view and therefore not without a certain bias and indulgence in his own importance and that of his genealogy. Still it is so well written that I want to translate at least a section of the first part of his book. This way our children, who unfortunately do not have a complete mastery of the Dutch language, can get a taste of what he had to say and how well he said it. Regretfully he postponed writing the sequel, part II, too long. When he started part II he was weakened by all kinds of health problems. As Tante Margaret confirmed to me when we talked about the second volume, she had helped him write it, as she had done with the first one, but had to do much more work on part II. She ended up being forced to produce more of a "cut and paste job" than a worthy successor to the very good first volume. This is particularly sad because Oom Eelco's memoirs of the war years in London and the trials and tribulations of the Dutch government in that period would have been invaluable for students of Dutch history. However, as a true old-fashioned diplomat Oom Eelco was discreet. He would never have indulged in a "tell all" memoir of the kind that are written more and more by people who cannot wait even a year after leaving office before they start spilling the beans in a book. As it is, part II of Oom Eelco's memoir does not tell us much of real interest. Of great interest to this family history, however, is what he wrote in part I about his childhood, his parents and grandparents and the environment in which he grew up. Oom Eelco was five years older than his brother Adriaan, Netty's father, whom we knew as Opa van Kleffens, but lived about ten years longer. Consequently, his memoirs cover a longer period of time and while Netty's father spoke often and fondly about his childhood and his Frisian background, he did not write it down. Oom Eelco did. So he gave us the window through which we can look into the early days of Netty's father and particularly into the life of their parents. Also, Oom Eelco was fourteen when their mother died so his memories of her are stronger. Netty's father was then only nine and the death of his mother cast a dark shadow over his life and affected his personality. What I find also interesting is the depth of Oom Eelco's research into his background. He makes a great effort to establish quite clearly that the van Kleffens family is (at least in his opinion) of great importance in Friesland and in the Netherlands. This may be seen by some as a sign of arrogance or an attempt to elevate his background to a higher level to match his colleagues at the ministry of foreign affairs, a branch of the Netherlands government that traditionally counted many members of the Dutch nobility among its professional diplomats. My view is that Oom Eelco was of the opinion that he *was* an important man and his family *was more important* than almost any other family and therefore others would be interested in his background. I was very fond of him and agree with him that his background deserves our attention if only because it gives an excellent picture of grandparents van Kleffens and the environment Netty's father grew up in.

"This writer, Eelco Nicolaas van Kleffens, was born on November 17, 1894, in Heerenveen, Friesland. Heerenveen was known in the province as a *flek,* something between a village and a town, developed too late to lay serious claim to the rights a town has and not surrounded by fortifications. However, this did not prevent Heerenveen and several other *"flekken"* to have more inhabitants than many Frisian towns: it had eight thousand souls in my childhood, and now there are almost twice that many. It was a prosperous community.

Heerenveen originated in 1551 when a beginning was made with the digging of peat. (Peat originated in pre-historic bogs. It is partly decayed plant matter that when dried and cut in blocks was used as fuel for stoves.) Heerenveen was located near the area where three *grieternijen* (rural districts called *grieten* under a *grietman*) came together. I was the oldest child. In 1896 a girl arrived; three years later another son.

When I was about two years old, my parents moved to the Haskerland part of Heerenveen, called Nijehaske. This was important for my schooling because it determined where I would eventually go to school and the one in Nijehaske had an excellent reputation. That this school would many years later carry my name has touched me deeply since I was already indebted to it on account of the education received there and now this too!

Nine years later, in 1905 when I was eleven, we moved to Groningen, where my father was appointed as assistant prosecutor. A big change that I experienced very clearly because it meant not only leaving the microcosm of Heerenveen, but also exchanging the limited and very Frisian milieu with a broader and more Saxon environment. In my estimation I came into a foreign country for the first time in my life. I will return to this point.

In the "Frisian Encyclopedia" (1958) Heerenveen is called a "center for administration, education, industry and medical care with an urban character." In the beginning of the twentieth century until 1923 it was also a center for the administration of justice. There was in those days a district court and a lower court, which is still there. That was the reason why I as offspring of a family out of Westdongeradeel was born in Heerenveen, because it was there that my father started his career with the judiciary. He was prosecutor with the lower courts of Heereveen, Beetsterzwaag, Lemmer and Steenwijk with its seat in Heerenveen. The three other seats of the court outside Heereveen caused many tedious trips in winter, to Beetsterzwaag in a steam driven tram, to Lemmer by horse-drawn coach, three hours both ways, to Steenwijk by train in which it was either very hot or very cold. Complaints about rheumatism were soon heard. And all that for a salary of eight hundred guilders a year of which a small amount was deducted for a pension fund that offered a modest pension later on! Such a job was really only an honorary position. Still, there were always people interested in a function with the judiciary. In those days a fairly large portion of the population lived off their own capital; compared with today, taxes were low and a job with the judiciary was seen as a "nobile officium," considerably more so than that of a lawyer.

In what kind of a community did a child grow up in Heerenveen? It was a strongly stratified society. It was divided in two main groups: the "upper ten," and the rest consisting of several sub groups. Those belonging to the "upper ten" were 'university men, namely members of the judiciary, a few lawyers, notaries, and physicians (I was brought into this world by a doctor who had the hardly 'upper ten' name of *Tobbe*), and a few industrialists (however, others were excluded for unfathomable reasons). The few members of the Frisian nobility were not seen much; in those days without automobiles most of them lived too far out of town.

So it transpired that I was a junior member of the "upper ten." Not because of my own efforts of course, but as a son of my father. A thoroughly undemocratic situation, but its validity was not contested by anyone; it was further emphasized by impromptu signs of respect and maintained through mutual Sunday visits by the adults. The sight of all those gentlemen with top hats and their beautifully dressed spouses who all wore the unavoidable little hats made by the *dames Bruggeman*, kept making it hard for me not to laugh. More than half a century later I was assisted at the embassy in Washington by a naval aide who had a very loud voice and kept trying to impress his audience with the correctness of his favorite slogan, "inequality has to be." The people of Heerenveen did not need this kind of reminder. They were used to social inequality from birth and considered this a natural and self-evident institution. Before 1900 it did not occur to them to challenge or question the correctness of this situation. They were not offended by it and enjoyed in those days a large measure of equality before the law. There were no significant tensions among the population of my birthplace and it had a peaceful and happy ambiance, which was beneficial for a child to be raised in.

If this leaves perhaps an undemocratic impression, it was balanced by the total democracy of the school. I shall always be grateful to my parents for deciding not to give me private tutoring but to send me to the public grade school of Nijehaske. This taught me early on and without trouble how to establish an easy rapport with contemporaries from all walks of life, something one cannot easily learn at a later age.

The high educational level there has already been briefly discussed. It was even more remarkable in view of the large number of students in each class, twenty-four in each and with only one teacher for every two classes (when one class had to do written work the other was taught orally). I warmly remember those educators and I admire them. Miss Brandenburg, Master, that's the way he was addressed, Hesselius, Master Nijk and above all the principal Master Dijkstra. I have never forgotten them, and have always gratefully remembered them.

But I am digressing and must return to the really total democracy of the students. All those Ypkes and Lykles and Sybes and whatever their names might be, were my friends. We all liked each other, which did not exclude a healthy brawl from time to time. We were all on the same level of knowledge or lack thereof, all young Frisian boys and girls because they were there too: Baukjes and Froukjes and Wytskes and Sytskes. Young Frisian Cecilia's who sang forcefully with fresh crisp children's voices. That was outside my parental home, my daily environment in those first days of the twentieth century, besides Ru Cleveringa (more about him later) and some of his pals who went to the Schoterland School, however.

There was one exception to this high level of equality: languages. There were only two languages in question: Dutch and Frisian. Children like me who came to school speaking both had an advantage over those who spoke only one. Many children entering school at the age of five, in those days spoke only Frisian. Even in 1955 a poll revealed that 46% of the inhabitants of Heerenveen were used to speaking Frisian. Around the turn of the century, that percentage was much higher, as was the percentage of those whose only language it was. The lower grades of the Nijehaske school were therefore mainly engaged in teaching the children to speak Dutch, which was not easy with these headstrong youngsters. I remember vividly the teacher who had spoken vigorously for half an hour to her little pupils to inform them that the very Frisian combination of the letters *S* and *K* did not occur in the Dutch language. In Dutch it sounds like "sch"as in *"schip"* (ship), when the small son of a barge skipper raised his hand and said with a hint of joy and pride: *"skip Miss."* She could say what she wanted, but she could not touch his father's ship.

In those days the hygiene in school was rudimentary. In winter—and the winters were fierce in those days when the children came into class with their socks wet from the snow (there were racks in the hallway for their wooden shoes), the windows were kept shut as long as possible while the stove was red hot. But then slowly an atmosphere emerged that made one think of the department for small predatory animals in a zoo, and one was forced to let the cold air in. All this was considered quite normal in those days, but it no doubt fostered tuberculosis common in those days. I narrowly escaped it: half a century later, an Italian physician in Rome who gave me a chest x-ray found traces of what he called a *vecchio processo pulminare,* which must have originated in that period.

In addition to the structure of the Heerenveen community there was another issue that had an important impact on my early upbringing. Because of my father's work in the judiciary, my attention was frequently drawn to the notion of 'public authority' and the power of government. It was pointed out to me at an early age, and in a way that was understandable for a child, that the reach and execution of that power are limited by laws in order to leave people as much freedom as possible and also that power has to be applied humanely and intelligently. I gladly accepted that - didn't ponder it too much and thought it was self-evident as I had no knowledge of other countries where all this was not so self-evident. It was part of the daily environment in which it was my privilege to be raised. When I asked my mother why so many people greeted my father on the streets in a manner that indicated appreciation and in typical Frisian fashion had no trace of suspicion or docility, she answered "because he protects people against scoundrels and does that well and you should not think that this is always easy." Not a bad environment to grow up in.

If this were a book about Heerenveen, a good deal more could be said about that town. But it is after all part of a few biographical notes about E. N. van Kleffens, and therefore I should first cover the other side of the axis of his childhood. That other side was Dokkum, in the vicinity of which the origins of our family lie and where my grandfather van Kleffens lived, head of the family we all belonged to. It was together with Stavoren the oldest town in Friesland and in importance it ranked fifth.

There was a great and clear contrast between Heerenveen and Dokkum. Heerenveen was since its inception an energetic town. In contrast to this, Dokkum, which was much older and known by most Dutchmen as the place where around 754 Saint Boniface was killed, had become somewhat static. During my childhood and before it started a planned expansion to attract industry, it looked like an old lady who had experienced much during her life and was inclined to spend her old age in quiet contemplation. During many centuries she had experienced many difficult years: *Schieringers and Vetkopers, Saxons, Geldersen and Bourgundians* had besieged the town in succession and when during the eighty year war with Spain, it became briefly a base for the *Watergeuzen*. The Spaniards came to execute a bloody reprisal that became known as "the Wallonian Fury", *de Waalse Furie*.

After the Spanish war, it experienced better times, unfortunately only briefly. Dokkum had always had an open connection with the sea, and it was the headquarters of the Frisian Admiralty from 1597 until 1648 when it silted in. The closing of the harbor brought Dokkum back to being a trading and distribution center for northeast Friesland and made it more inward looking. In addition, the old lady's income declined seriously as a result of the economic slump experienced by the farmers in the period 1878 – 95. In those days grass was growing between the cobblestones of Dokkum, a situation that was out of the question in Heerenveen.

So Dokkum was around the turn of the century a quiet little town, except for the active market on Wednesday and the equally active Saturday nights when the uniformed *Schutterij* (sort of a home guard) having completed its exercises (and before the liquid pick-me-up that used to follow), made its tour through the narrow streets of the old town, marching with thundering step and preceded by a blaring band. All this noise sounded then as a sharp dissonant to the soft tones of daily life. In contrast to today's often ill-sounding street noises one heard during the rest of the week little else than the rattle of a passing carriage—Rubber tires were still unknown—from time to time the barking of a dog or the singing of schoolchildren in their class and, regularly the tinkling sound of the bell tower in the eighteenth century town hall. Housewives were quietly hanging their laundry on wash lines; little noise came out of stores and workshops. The walls and fortifications that surrounded the old town contributed strongly to the introverted and closed-in ambiance. A railway connection came only in 1901, a superior court wasn't there either, only a very calm lower court, the Dokkumers liked an orderly existence.

But despite the then quite boring background, Dokkum remains a paradise on earth in my oldest memories. That stems from the people as well as material things. The people, first of all our grandfather, were extremely kind and showed a cheerful interest in us as if they wanted to extend, every year, a warm welcome to the younger generation during their summer visits. For children there was an attitude of "everything goes" within certain broad boundaries. Dokkum had additional exciting facets. Behind the house that was built in 1743, there was a large garden where children could safely play and where all kinds of fruit ripened and was available to interested youngsters. It was wonderful to lie under a raspberry bush on a hot August day and to pick the berries warmed by the sun and to eat them immediately after a quick check for a possible worm! On rainy days there always were a few unused rooms where we did not bother anybody and found all kinds of fascinating toys that used to belong to our uncles and aunts.

But the stable was our favorite place; it was the area where my grandfather's devoted and friendly coachman, called Sape, was in charge. Among Sape's many children was a daughter, our dear friend Brechtsje who while herself still a teenager, knew how to keep us gently, but firmly, under control. She knew how to keep us quiet. We were privileged to be read to by Brechtsje, every day after lunch, while sitting in one of the three carriages that were kept in the carriage house. What a dream world for children, so very different from Heerenveen; smelling a little of horses and leather and perhaps a little musty but also of intimacy and familiarity when the doors were closed and Brechtsje was reading with her fresh voice to us out of the fairy tales of the Brothers Grimm! There were unforgettable passages in these stories that made a deep impression on us, heavy with romanticism. As an offset we then took a vigorous walk under the high clouds of Dokkum's extensive surroundings where the slight pitch of the grasslands—to allow the rainwater to drain off - took away all monotony of the flat countryside. A good antidote to a big dose of Grimm.

Those annual visits to Dokkum were always short, much too short to our taste: two weeks. The reason was the coordination of my father's limited summer leaves with what seems now incredibly brief vacation time for the schoolchildren: all of two full weeks of summer vacation! That despite this the quickly gone visits made such a deep impression on us was in my opinion caused by the great difference between daily life in our home - although this was certainly not dull or monotonous and that of us as young guests in the house of our grandfather. No schoolwork, unlimited opportunities for play, being spoiled by relatives and others, great differences with daily life at home. All this favored Dokkum and embellished our memories."

FAMILY BACKGROUND ON MY FATHER'S SIDE

"What was left beyond those precious memories? I never went to school in Dokkum, and our presence there was only two weeks a year, not long enough to find lasting friendships with kids of my own age. I believe that what Dokkum taught me through a sort of unobtrusive osmosis was a sense of family, of family property and for the continuity from one generation to the other. And going a little deeper I find related issues that I could only understand when I was older; the sense of not being alone, neither as an individual nor as a member of a family, but above all as a link in a long chain of ancestors and other relatives, and also with future generations. And after that came a beginning of a feeling for tradition, within the family circle as well as outside it, particularly in the form of tasks one takes on voluntarily for the benefit of the community, jobs that are for the benefit of mankind, sometimes for some remuneration, mostly for nothing. The source of wealth was mainly land, land that one farmed oneself or rented to others: [*footnote in "Belevenissen": For the first time in our family there is proof of this in the middle of the seventeenth century. I have in my possession the minutes of the meeting in 1709 in which Klaas Sydses is appointed tax collector of Raard. There had been a call for the meeting in writing and the church bell had been rung so that everybody knew there would be a meeting and everything was above board. It was due to the stewardship of this Klaas Sydses that 'van Kleffens' became our family name*].

Beyond many functions of local importance or for the benefit of the "county," supervision of the sea dikes or the board of oversight of the county, our family produced two members of the parliament of the province of Friesland, Klaas Sydses (1672 – 1739) as a representative [of the inhabitants with voting rights] of Westdongeradeel and his grandson Reinder Eelkes (1762 – 1838) as a representative of the town meeting of Dokkum which he had joined at age 20; the former therefore before the great revolution of 1795, the latter before, during and after that tumultuous period. Reinder served in several local and national public bodies. He was mayor of Dokkum from 1822 until a year before his death, before him this position was held by his father Eelke (also written as Eelco) in 1776 and the years thereafter; he died in 1771. Reinder was an interesting figure who in 1798 was imprisoned for about five months in The Hague in the "Huis ten Bosch" palace together with several other prominent Frisians.

Why do I relate all this? To make clear that I was brought up in an atmosphere of public service. I also remain especially grateful for that to old Dokkum. Heerenveen alone would not have been able to give me that spirit. It played a real role in my life, particularly much later (in the second half of 1922) when I was confronted with the choice between a promising career with Royal Dutch Shell and an uncertain future in the service of my country.

Without indulging in genealogy, I think there might be readers who are interested in the origins of the name 'van Kleffens'. The answer is simple.

Kleffens in the olden days written as 'Cleffens' - is one of the many names of Frisian localities ending with '-ens' that in the early part of the sixteenth century was located a little to the west of the village of Raard near Dokkum. My ancestors lived in this hamlet until the beginning of the eighteenth century mainly as landowners. For many years they had patronymic names which often became a family name. In our case this did not happen: our name stems from the purchase of three farms respectively in 1719, 1728 and 1738 which together formed a locality called Kleffens and with which the family was not involved before. The right to vote which was an entitlement of one of the farms was achieved only in 1754 and this gave the owner the title of *"eigenerfde"* [landowner] which beyond the right to hunt entitled the owner to participate, actively and passively in the election of a representative for the county to the provincial parliament.

Footnote in Belevenissen: From a contract dated 1770 which is in my possession it appears that there were two more pieces of land with voting rights in the family. It is interesting to note that there was here a curious mix of public and private law as the contract states that the seller the "douariere" (widow of a nobleman) of Ernst Baron van Ayla living in Ternaard, retains ownership of a small piece of land called a "hornleger" [hare's lair] which was deemed to have the right to vote attached to it. The new owner could use the land, but could not exercise his active and passive voting right for the Provincial counsel and was obligated to deliver every year two roosters to the seller to show his recognition of this situation. Those votes were called "rooster votes". This exception was bought out in 1754 for 132 gold-guilders. I have the contract of this purchase too.

Klaas Sydses the energetic and likable fellow who pulled all this together, did not move to Kleffens himself but allowed his two surviving sons, Syds Jr. and Eelke, to settle there to manage two of the three farms. The third was torn down in the beginning of the nineteenth century. Klaas Sydses continued to live in Raard where he died eleven days after his wife and at the end of a complete life.

Since then the family carried the name "van Kleffens" without interruption. As it was recognition of an existing situation, the name seems to have originated out of its own. There is no proof of any effort whatsoever by the interested parties to take a formal step to establish it. It was deemed so self evident that it was never challenged and soon generally adopted by all members of all branches of a not very numerous family.

Our family lived at Kleffens until 1829. However, at that time the only person left there was a mother and guardian of three small children, my great-grandmother Mrs. van Kleffens, née Helder. She moved to Dokkum to facilitate the education of her children. I still own a receipt for fees from the village schoolmaster of Raard who had taught them reading and writing. Her oldest son was my grandfather, after whom I was named. He was born at Kleffens but spent almost his entire life in Dokkum where he died in 1907, eighty-nine years old.

The preceding may also explain why our family crest is older than the family name. (*Footnote in Belevenissen: The origin of the family name is very clear: it is a toponym. However, this does not clarify the origin of the 'word' Kleffens. There are two theories that have been brought forth. According to the first, it is the joining of "Klef(fe)" and "nes" which are part of the old Germanic male name of Klef or Kleffe, and the name of a piece of land jutting out in the water, a "kaap" (cape) or "Klef(fe)'s Kaap." According to the other, the second syllable of Kleffens is derived from "ings or ingen," or the descendants of Klef(fe), so it becomes a patronymic derived from the name of a locality. This issue has not been resolved according to the Encyclopedia for Friesland and a letter from an expert on names, J. Winkler that is printed in the "Stamboek van het Geslacht van Kleffens".*)

Of the two farm houses left at Kleffens after the third one was torn down, one property was transferred to the Fockema family through a marriage and came later in the hands of others. This property was traditionally named *Noord Kleffens* (North Kleffens). The other *Zuid Kleffens* (South Kleffens), which after 1829 was completely used as a farm, now belongs to the writer. In the early part of the twentieth century the farmhouse was rebuilt after a fire damaged it. The corner stone was laid by me, it was the earliest official duty I participated in in my life; a small stone was put in the front wall of the house as a remembrance.

To try to describe all kinds of family members who lived long ago would fail due to lack of sufficient historical material. It would also lead us outside the framework of these notes which are after all intended to give an insight in the life and career of this writer. I will therefore limit myself to those whose character traits are most clearly and often repeated either, singly or together, among members of the family. Klaas Sydses was already mentioned. He was the one who skillfully and purposefully created the basis for a firm family tradition. His son Eelke and grandson Reinder were both mayors of Dokkum and both intimately involved in local and regional politics and government, the latter also on a province and national level. I need to add my grandfather, Eelke Nicolaas (1818 – 1907), mentioned previously, who demonstrated two other characteristics: social involvement and scientific curiosity.

He was not the first university-educated person in the family. Three others belonging to another family branch preceded him in this respect: Gerardus Sydses was entered in the "Album Academicum" of the Groningen University in 1767 as a theology student. His example was followed later by his two surviving sons Paulus Theodorus (1781 – 1840) who was also known as an Orientalist and Syds Gerardus (1795 – 1858). My grandfather also studied in Groningen where he earned his doctorate in 1841—at age twenty three—after submitting a thesis about lung cancer, written in Latin as was customary in those days. He subsequently established his practice in Dokkum. His oldest son Adrianus (1845 – 1892) also became a physician in Dokkum after studying in Groningen and Vienna. His youngest son, my father (1861 – 1942) and both his sons all studied law, my father in Groningen and his two sons in Leiden. Five other members of the family studied in Groningen, three became lawyers, the other two clergymen.

When my grandfather became consciously part of my memories, he was in his eighties and could look back upon an active, useful and varied life albeit largely spent in Dokkum. His medical practice played the most important part in his life, perhaps more as an expression of philanthropy than as a source of income.

After many years, when he had delivered the 3,500th baby in Dokkum, thus renewing the entire population, he thought it was time to retire from his practice although he continued to help old acquaintances in the town and its surroundings. In the 1860s he participated so energetically and actively in the fight against the cholera that had come from Asia that he received a plaque from King William III with an inscription, praising his work. He was short if compared to today's standards, the length of his walking cane confirms it, but he was greatly respected in his town. His religion and his intelligence were important parts of his personality, but he did not actively attend church. He kept up with his medical publications.

He was known as a well-balanced, moderate, wise, and helpful person; he bore the influence he had on his town and his family with a certain grace. He has known much sadness in his family: four of his eight children died young, and he survived two of the others. His wife, Catharina Elisabeth van Slooten, died some twenty years before him. She was also a member of a distinguished family in Dokkum and he had dedicated his dissertation to her with the notation "optima carissima." Small wonder that he had become somewhat quiet when I got to know him. However, this did not impede a lively interest in his grandchildren: my sister, my younger brother and me. Towards the end of his long life when he died in 1907, he was almost ninety years old he had a clear sense that his era had come to an end, which made him somber in his final days. What contributed significantly to his sadness was the death, a few years before his own, of his oldest surviving and only remaining daughter who was born in 1843 and had the pure Friesian name of Rienskje. Beyond being a wonderful companion for him, she managed his household in a friendly and resolute manner: for that she also deserves to receive a honorable mention here. She was a Martha-like figure, very busy with facilitating everything, a somewhat withdrawn but totally unselfish person, quiet in her attitude, in her words and her voice and very well mannered. If she had been a catholic, she would have been a perfect mother superior, very concerned with the troubles of others, tactful but also a "no nonsense" type personality. Her carefulness made my mother's short stays in Dokkum a refreshing experience and under her stewardship there were never any problems with the house personnel."

FAMILY BACKGROUND ON MY MOTHER'S SIDE

"My mother's father, Dr. Johannes Veenhoven was a physician, a native of the province of Groningen and like his "opposite number" an alumnus of the University of Groningen. He practiced in Hogezand. His spouse, Gesina de Boer, came also from that part of the country. Both died before I was born.

Like my mother who died in 1906, this grandfather died relatively young, at an age where most people do not have much time to make notes about their genealogy, even if they would like to do so. There were three sons - one was a notary in Smilde, in the province of Drente; another was a lawyer in Utrecht; and a third who lived off the income of his capital in Dordrecht and got quite old. None of them was married and none left to the best of my knowledge any information about their family. What little I had on that subject was lost during the German occupation. My parents had little contact with other branches of the Veenhoven family who lived scattered all over the country.

I will come back to my mother, Jeannette Frésine Veenhoven, but I wanted to relate the above explanation to make clear why I cannot present more information about her background beyond pointing out one more general detail which is in my opinion a key element in the makeup of her which this writer."

❧

At this point Oom Eelco starts a discussion of the origins of his mother who is not Frisian but came from the province of Groningen. It is almost as if he is apologizing for his mother not being from Friesland. He explains that in the province of Groningen there are some areas that show a strong influence of Frisian elements and others where there is much less of it. He states that his parents' move to Groningen brought a totally new element in the family. He was only ten years old when his father was transferred there, but it immediately became clear to him that he was among different people. He was used to classmates with a more oblong head shape and now he was among boys with more rounded heads. He calls them "brachycephalic" (heads with a width that is more than 80 percent of its length). He thought that was so unusual that he mentioned it to his mother after his first day in school. His mother explained to him why there are different races in this world and cautioned him to be tolerant on that score and suspecting a first germ of a feeling of Friesian superiority told him he should not think he was even the least bit better than those round headed Groningen boys!

Oom Eelco wonders whether the fact that his family was no longer purely Friesian like its preceding generations, would have an impact on its characteristics. He comments that nobody knew about genetics in those days although the laws of Mendel, discovered in 1865 and initially forgotten, were rediscovered only in 1900. He says that even now nobody has an answer to this question although it has been discussed in a symposium about the cultural unity of the northern part of the country. He reproduces a table designed by a Friesian pastor who developed a list of 24 character traits and compares how northern Gorningers stack up against Friesians. It shows that the Friesians have more ambition but are less interested in monetary gains, have more feeling for music but are less tolerant etc., etc. It is a fascinating discussion for someone who lives in America and realizes that the province of Friesland is about 1,300 square miles in size and now has a population of about 600,000. Groningen is about 900 square miles and its population is 560,000. Connecticut, the small state where we live is 5,000 square miles and its population is 3,200,000! It is also useful to point out that today's studies conclude human behavior is the result of a combination of (i) genetics (or family background), (ii) the environment in which one is raised (upbringing), and (iii) the chemicals at work in our body and our DNA.

JEANNETTE FRÉSINE VEENHOVEN.

Oom Eelco comments that there was one characteristic in the family of his mother that was as far as he knows not present in the van Kleffens family: a talent for art and in particular drawing. He states that appreciation for literature and music was often found in his father's family, but there was no aptitude for drawing or painting and certainly not sculpture. This was totally different in Oom Eelco's mother's family. Her two older brothers were reasonably good painters and had a great interest in the art of drawing and painting. The eldest of her brothers owned a respectable collection of paintings and the younger one went to Giethoorn and Kortenhoef in the summer time to paint. (*After the death of Netty's mother, we got a small painting done by one of the brothers Veenhoven, Oom Ger.*) Oom

134

Eelco describes how, on the other hand, he totally lacked any aptitude for drawing. *(His niece, Netty, also offers solid proof of this point.)* In school, the teacher placed a bucket on his table and told the class to draw it. Young Eelco drew an almost perfect circle because this bucket had a circular opening like all other buckets.

The result was wrong, of course, but he says he still cannot understand why.

Oom Eelco then starts to describe how he remembers his mother. He approaches this subject by commenting that he will probably not be the first one to be struck with the notion that many people writing their biography are very brief in their discussions of their parents. This is, in his opinion, odd as most people inherit important character traits from one of their parents. He then mentions a few examples. Little was known about the father of Winston Churchill until he wrote a biography of his father, the Duke of Marlborough. The brevity of Talleyrand's comments about his parents is due to their neglect of their son and total indifference towards him. More than a century later, the German Chancellor Bülow was very brief about his mother as she had a rather colorless personality. He did write extensively about his father, however, who had great influence on his son and a fairly similar career. In the case of Oom Eelco the reason why he can only write briefly about his mother is not due to lack of appreciation, or colorlessness or resentment. His choice of examples of others who were brief in their memoirs about their parents is interesting as it quite clearly reveals Oom Eelco's self-image. Nevertheless, the reason he cannot say much about his mother is that she died too early to leave a clear impression in his memory. Oom Eelco continues,"I am grateful for the memory of her selflessness, how

HENRICUS CATO VAN KLEFFENS IN CEREMONIAL UNIFORM.

no effort or care was too much for her children. However, she would not spoil us through weak indulgence. Later I learned through others that she was very intelligent and sensitive and that she had the gift of making the right decision quickly. *(All these characteristics could equally well describe Netty.)* Her two older brothers, who I met frequently when I was older, told me that among her contemporaries in grade school in Hoogezand she displayed a friendly demeanor and naturally accepted leadership. It remained that way. Later in her life, when she gently laid down a rule in her own family, it was not further questioned. In Heereveen she held regular ladies' visiting days every other week which were well attended. She was devoid of any pretense and her even-tempered and natural disposition were generally much appreciated.

Her death at just forty years old was for us a calamity. She was the kind of mother who is irreplaceable certainly more so for my younger brother *[Netty's father]* who was then six years old and our sister who was three years older. My father remarried twice, first with a cousin of my mother's, Sabine Ilpsema Vinckers who came out of a family from Groningen. We knew her already for many years and we all had a very close relationship with her; we were sorry to lose her also after only a few years when she was stricken by a fast moving illness. [Netty's father was very fond of his "second mother" Ma Bien as he called her and had to suffer another blow when she also died.] After that a few years went by before my father married for the third time, a marriage that quite unexpectedly proved to be such a disaster that it ended soon in a divorce. At that time, I was already a student in Leiden and came infrequently home to my father's house. But for my brother and sister these events were traumatic experiences that cast a shadow over their early years.

While my mother left us when she was still young, we lost my father when he was in his eighties. That was in the middle of World War II. On the last Sunday before the German invasion of the Netherlands in May of 1940, Margaret and I visited him in Arnhem. Five days later, our contact with him was disrupted forever by our hasty and unexpected departure for London as decided by the Dutch cabinet. It would be five years before we returned to the famished and looted Netherlands. My father had died there three years earlier on July 31, 1942. The news of his death reached me on August 6th in Washington D.C. by an unavoidably circuitous route. Queen Wilhelmina had addressed a joint session of Congress on that day.

This message touched me deeply. Despite our very different personalities, my father and I had a very strong and solid relationship based on mutual affection, trust, and respect. I do not think he could always immediately understand why I acted in one way or the other, but he was always convinced that I had thoroughly considered it and that it was well intended. I could always count on his advice and support whenever I needed it. He never tried to influence my career choices although he would have loved to see me become a defender of law and order like him as a prosecuting attorney. However, since the spring of 1902, when I was about seven and a half years old, I felt attracted by an entirely different career path and my father never objected to that, even though neither he nor I knew how that objective could best be achieved. I can never be grateful enough for everything he did for me and for what he meant to me. From the beginning he was very fond of Margaret and that continued to be the case."Oom Eelco continues his description of his father with a review of his various assignments. Opa van Kleffens first served in four lower courts in the Heerenveen area. Then he went to Groningen where he served at a higher court as an assistant prosecutor and after that in The Hague in the same capacity. In 1913 he came back to Heerenveen as prosecutor and after that went on to Zutphen and finally Arnhem in that position."

"The reason why my father decided to resign earlier than necessary was typical. A new penal code would take effect on January 1, 1926. Among other things, this law changed the position of the accused versus the prosecution to the advantage of the former. My father felt that this change was so wrong that he did not want to be associated with enforcement of the new laws and drew his conclusion.

To round out this picture and also to facilitate a proper understanding of what will be discussed in subsequent chapters, a bit more about those that were indicated before with 'us' or 'ours': beyond myself, my brother and sister. I will start with the latter who came first after me in age, two years younger than me and named Gesina Jantina (real Groninger names out of my mother's family), but always called Nini. She had a lively imagination, especially as a child; and beyond that externally as well as within herself had something very distinct, for she did not resemble any of us. Sometimes that placed her in a separate world and made her at times appear somewhat reticent or "brooding." This was caught very well in a picture, painted a few years after they got married by her husband, my very talented friend George Suermondt, who died in 1925 at the young age of thirty-one. *(This is the picture we now have.)* More than two years after her husband's death she remarried the highly principled naval officer D. C. M. Hetterschij who ended his career as vice admiral. Like the life of her first husband, her own life also ended early. She died in 1930 after a brief illness. Her passing was also deeply mourned by all of us. *(Netty believes her aunt Nini died while pregnant. The child she was carrying poisoned her and she was advised to have an abortion. She refused, hoping her child would survive her.)*

Despite our difference in age I had more in common with my brother Adrianus ('Adri') who was born just before the end of the century (1899 – 1973). He was five years younger than I and got married, seven years before me, with Elise van Someren Gréve, a niece once removed of the famous General van Heutsz. I was very close to him, especially in our younger years. As I mentioned already, he did not have a very pleasant childhood due to the early death of our mother at an age where he still needed her very much. Later on, he had a particularly hard time during the German occupation of the Netherlands. Despite all efforts by his wife to gain his release the criminal Nazi government whose authorities also tried to torture him mentally imprisoned him several times [this is incorrect, he was imprisoned only once]. They asked him for instance: 'Sie wissen doch dass Sie Todeskandidat sind?' *(Surely you know you are a candidate for death?)*. A happier period came for him after the war, especially when he stayed with his wife in Luxembourg as a much appreciated member of the Court of Justice of the European Coal and Steel Community, an organization that later came to be called the Common Market. Regretfully, party politics at home brought his mandate to an undeserved and ill-conceived end, which has hurt his feelings despite many expressions of appreciation and sympathy. The warm reception he received at the Court of Justice in Arnhem where he was offered the honorary position of substitute justice, a position our father also had, was a source of great satisfaction for him. His reverence for our family and for historical things found an expression in the interior decorating of his house in De Steeg where he and his wife settled down and which included doors and tiles and other things that came out of our old family house that he had found in Dokkum." *(The house was torn down, but a local contractor saved the doors and tiles and passed them on to Netty's father.)*

Oom Eelco continues his biography with a sketch of his old friend Ru Cleveringa, who was also a good friend of Opa van Kleffens and who in his retirement also moved to De Steeg and lived very near Opa's house. Professor Cleveringa was a famous figure in the Dutch academic resistance against the German occupation. He taught law in Leiden and when the Germans occupied the country, he was dean of the Faculty of Law. On the day the Germans ordered all universities to fire their Jewish professors, including professor Meijers, a world famous jurist and a star member of the faculty, Cleveringa addressed the entire student body in the largest auditorium available to express his strong opposition to this measure. As a result, the University of Leiden was closed and Prof. Cleveringa was imprisoned. The other universities stayed open since they chose to go along with the measure. When I went to Leiden, Prof. Cleveringa had returned there and when I invited Netty for the first time to go with me to a big ball, she stayed with the Cleveringas. I saw Prof. Cleveringa for the last time after the funeral of Opa van Kleffens in De Steeg when I went for a solitary walk in the woods near the family house and met him as he was also taking a walk. I spoke with the old professor and I got the impression that he was a little confused mentally. Unfortunately, this was true and his condition gradually worsened. He died a few years later.

WASSENAAR 1945. L TO R. OMA GRÉVE, PUL, MAMMIE, OPA GRÉVE, LOUS.

Netty has her own impressions of her grandfather van Kleffens. Her father always spoke fondly of his own father although he realized that many others had a less charitable view of the old gentleman. Particularly Netty's mother could become quite upset when she would tell us about the way in which her father-in-law treated her and tried to exert control over her husband. Netty's grandfather died during the war as Oom Eelco mentioned, and Netty's father who was a very sensitive man who had a strong emotional attachment to his youth and his parents, must have felt a great loss. It was probably very similar to my mother's attachment to her father who was the only real parent she had known and whom she adored. As Oom Eelco stated, the early loss of his mother very much affected Netty's father emotionally and the fact that his father was somewhat distant cannot have helped him either.

❧

Netty's grandfather van Someren Gréve (1878 – 1949) was a very different man. I met him once or twice when I came to see Netty at her parent's house in Wassenaar. This was in the early years just after the war and I was certainly not yet a member of the family, just a visiting boyfriend. He was a friendly, gentle man who lived in Switzerland with Netty's grandmother. They had met each other in what now is Indonesia, married there, and lived there for many years. Later they lived in The Hague. When retirement came, they had decided to live in Switzerland, which proved to be a very smart choice as Switzerland remained a neutral country and stayed out of the war. Consequently, Netty did not have much contact with her grandparents during the five war years and only sporadically in the first few years after the war as it was not easy to travel back and forth in those days. After the war Netty and her parents could not go to Switzerland as often as they would have liked. Switzerland was a different world to the Dutch. It had everything Holland lacked in food, clothing and other material things.

Opa van Someren Gréve, or Opa Gréve as we called him died on December 29 1949 in Lutry near Lausanne where they lived. At that time, Netty and I were engaged, but I was in Indonesia in the army. In the interim Netty had visited her grandparents several times in Lutry. Later I got to know Oma Gréve (1882 – 1969), or Omi as she liked to be called much better. I visited her regularly in Lutry when I was staying in Geneva. I was there to get some exposure to the Swiss securities business and later on, she came to visit us in Riverside and was our house guest for a while, alternating between us and her son and daughter-in-law, Erry and Pia who then lived in Greenwich. I liked Omi very much. She was easy to get along with and a great source for stories about life in the Dutch East Indies in the old days. Her maiden name was van Heutsz, and her father's brother was a very famous general in the Dutch colonial army who managed to "pacify" a part of the country now called Aceh (in Dutch *Atjeh*) after a struggle of many years. Aceh is located in the northwestern tip of Sumatra, the island closest to Singapore.

GENERAL VAN HEUTSZ.

140

The population there is known for its strong adherence to Islam and its fiercely independent nature. In later years the war there was seen by some as a cruel expedition against people who were relatively poorly armed and only wanted to be left alone. This assessment was probably totally correct, but in the later part of the nineteenth century, known as the period of colonialism, it was viewed as quite normal to secure the borders of a colonial empire, if only to prevent other European countries from capturing the territory. Many Dutch soldiers died in Aceh in very intense fighting at close range in a densely vegetated jungle-like environment. After many years of inconclusive fighting, van Heutsz put an end to it. He did so with overwhelming force. In 1904 he was appointed governor general, the highest representative of the Dutch government in the Indies. He stepped down in 1909. Accordingly, Omi belonged to the highest level of Dutch society in Indonesia. Like many others in her environment, she had some Indonesian blood. Since General van Heutsz and his brother looked very Dutch and were born in the Netherlands, most likely one of the male ancestors of Omi's mother had married an Indonesian woman as was quite common in that country. It has never been made clear to Netty who her Indonesian ancestor was and where and when she lived. As I stated, many Dutch people have some Indonesian blood, and most people do not think this is much of an issue, but there is still some prejudice on that score and therefore it is not easy to find out who one's Indonesian ancestors were as people tended to cover up the traces. Photographs of Omi's mother suggest that she is the one with the Indonesian ancestry.

In February 1984, Netty and I interviewed Netty's mother, Oma van Kleffens, as part of an oral history project we had started. We made tape recordings of interviews with our parents and others. Most of what follows is based on what she told us. Opa van Someren Gréve's name was Hendrik. He was the son of Willem van Someren Gréve and Rebecca van de Poll. Willem who was a sea captain, was master of a ship called *Postiljon* of which we have a picture. (*We called our first newly built boat, a Seawind Ketch, "Postiljon". We did not continue using this unique name because we discovered that almost all Americans had great trouble with it and could not pronounce it.*) The captain sailed between Holland and Indonesia. His wife often went to sea with him. Opa had five brothers and sisters and he was by far the youngest. His oldest sister was almost an adult when he was born. He was born in Haarlem and went to school there. He went to a "Handelsschool", a secondary school with emphasis on business, accounting and economics. When he was eighteen he went to the Netherlands East Indies to work with his brother who had started a business there called Ruhaak & Co. This company imported all kinds of hard goods into the Indies, from nails to household appliances etc. He spent his entire career with this company, first as director of the office in Surabaya and later of the office in The Hague. In the Indies he met and married Omi, Louise Mathilde van Heutsz, who was the daughter of an army officer Henricus Johannes van Heutsz and his wife Mathilde Kocken. The brother of Omi's father, Henricus van Heutsz, was Johannes Benedictus van Heutsz, the general and later governor general of the Netherlands East Indies. Netty's mother knew him well and remembers vividly how he once presented her with her entire name LIESJE VAN SOMEREN GREVE in chocolate letters. She told us that the general was a "no nonsense" type of governor general and that he abolished the *Pajong*, the ceremonial parasol traditionally held over the heads of sultans and other important persons in Indonesia and initially also adopted by the Dutch for their highest authorities, as a visible sign of their importance. As governor general, van Heutsz strove to improve the attitude of the Dutch civil servants entrusted with the oversight of the interior or *Ambtenaren BB (Binnenlands Bestuur)*—officers of the Department of the Interior—towards local dignitaries. Beyond abolishing the *"pajong"* he also ordered that the local dignitaries would no longer be required to squat on the floor (in the traditional Indonesian manner) while his Dutch supervisor would sit in a chair. Apparently these moves were resented by some in Indonesia. The brothers van Heutsz were Catholics. But when the marriage between Henricus van Heutsz and Mathilde Kocken ended in a divorce this created a tremendous uproar as divorce in those days was not generally accepted and certainly not among Catholics. The treatment of the divorce by the Catholic clergy upset the children of Henricus and also his brother, and as a result the family turned away from the Catholic Church. The governor general retired in Montreux, Switzerland and died there. Although the church made an effort to get him back in the fold, particularly after he became a very famous man, he never went back to his original religion. While living in Montreux he received a letter from Queen Wilhelmina who in her way also wanted him to return to the fold and stated that she felt that famous Dutchmen like him should live in the Netherlands, but he was a rather headstrong man, ignored the message, and did not budge. Netty's mother (Oma van Kleffens) was very fond of her grandmother van Heutsz and remembers that she died in Indonesia when the family was on leave in Holland and how shocking that news was for her. She also told us that her great grandmother's name was Dekens and that her great grandfather Dekens came from Belgium and as she put it: "Oma Dekens was born in the Indies and always lived there." Perhaps this is the grandmother who brought the Indonesian blood into the family.

Omi had two sisters and one brother. The oldest sister was Nien who became a nun. Oma van Kleffens stated that in the old days there were not too many good schools in Indonesia and the Catholic schools were the best ones. Nien went to such a school and developed, a"sympathy" as she put it, for a nun and became one herself. Netty's mother states that she was also very close to this aunt, adding "what a shame she became a Catholic." She lived in an Ursuline convent in Batavia. Omi's other sister was Zus. Her real given name was Virginie. Her husband was a Mr. Enger who was director of a sugar factory called "*Tjebongan*" near Djokjakarta. There was a younger brother Johan, who is described by Netty's mother as a somewhat weak man she knows little of and who worked in the office of Opa Gréve and died in Indonesia. Opa Gréve had four brothers and five sisters. His oldest brother was uncle Willem who married aunt Lucie Lugt and had sons named Willem, Jan , Hans, Anton and Coen and a daughter Lucie. They lived for a while in Haarlem, next door to my grandparents Schieferdecker. Small world—especially in Holland. Lucie married Piet Lefèvre. They had two sons and a daughter also named Lucie who was a good friend of Netty and who married a friend of mine Billy Zeverijn. They have three sons and this family visited us several times in the US. Lucia, as she called herself in later years was a bridesmaid in our wedding. She died in 2003.

In 1916 during World War I, Omi and her children returned to the Netherlands together with her father van Heutsz. They were passengers on the last ship that could get through the British naval blockade of Germany that included Holland although it was neutral in that war. Because of the war, the ship went around the Cape of Good Hope, rather than through the Suez Canal. Oma van Kleffens remembered that trip vividly. They visited Cape Town and also landed in Durban. The ship had to sail without lights and was held in Scotland for six days by the British Navy. In Holland they bought a house in Hilversum and lived there until the end of the war. Opa Gréve stayed in Indonesia until the war was over. Around 1919 he returned and the family moved to The Hague. They lived there on the Schimmelpennincklaan in a very nice area called Sorghvliedt. The large houses in this district are now mostly embassies. There were four children. Netty's mother was the oldest, and then came Oom Wim, Willem Henri van Someren Gréve and Oom Errie, Ernst Hendrik van Someren Gréve. Her sister Lous, Louise Mathilde van Someren Grve was born in 1920, when Oma was 38 years old. [Opa returned from his wartime stay in the Indies in 1919!] During the depression Oma's parents went back to Indonesia to take care of business there, leaving their children in The Hague, except Lous who was taken along. Tante Jo Braat took care of the children.

This was awful Oma said, because she was not allowed to go out and see her boy-friends or do anything else.

I saw a great deal of Omi while staying in Switzerland in 1952 and afterwards in the Netherlands and at our home in Riverside. In Switzerland, she had an apartment in Lutry, very near the house of her youngest daughter Lous who had married a Swiss lawyer, Jean Felix Paschoud. They were an attractive young couple. Lous was only ten years older than Netty and therefore in her early thirties when we got married. She was a very good-looking woman and at our wedding made quite an impression on my friends and she knew it. Jean was partner in his father's law firm in Lausanne. They had at that time two children, a girl Carole was the oldest and Féfé (Felix) her brother. Lous and Jean lived in a beautiful charming old house in the center of Lutry, an old village bordering on Lake Geneva. The main highway that runs from Geneva by way of Lausanne along the lake passes Lutry, but to accommodate heavier traffic, a new road was laid out a little higher on the hillside that is covered with vineyards. Lous' house fronted on what used to be the main road, with a gate on the side to enter the yard. The back of the house overlooked the lake. The old stone house had numerous rooms and a cellar contained a wine press. A horse could be hitched to the press and run it by walking around in a circle. The back yard sloped down to another street where Omi's small apartment house was located. Omi also had a view of the lake from her apartment. I spent about six weeks in Geneva and came almost every weekend to stay with Omi. Since I had come there by car from home, I could offer Omi an opportunity to tour around, which she enjoyed very much. She was a good cook and especially skilled in making Indonesian dishes, which I appreciated. When she stayed with us several years later, she also produced several memorable *nassi gorengs*. I saw quite a bit of Lous and Jean in those days. Their third child Louis was born a year later, in 1953. Carole came to stay with us in Old Greenwich for some time as an "au pair" to help Netty with the care of Richard and Janet. Unfortunately, this visit was not a great success. Carole was a lovely strapping girl, but sadly we found she had some quite severe psychological problems and we were upset that Lous and Jean had not forewarned us at all about their daughter's problems. Thinking she would enjoy going to New York City and to attend some courses in art and English at the New School in Greenwich Village, we had enrolled her there and made arrangements for her to travel once or twice a week to the city. We also got her driving lessons, and getting her U.S. driving license was a great victory for her. We later found out that Carole had just daydreamed through her courses in New York City and had not learned a thing. At home she also daydreamed for long periods of time and seemed detached from reality. Janet who was then quite small called her "Cavolla" and got along well with her. Carole returned home and lived with her parents for a while. In 1972 she got a boyfriend, and we thought she might find a solution for her problems with an understanding and loving husband. Tragically she died a short time later in an automobile accident that her boyfriend survived.

Carole was the fourth of Omi's grandchildren to die young. The first death was Netty's youngest brother Eelke who drowned in the summer of 1945, just after Holland was liberated. Then Omi's youngest son Errie, who lived in the U.S. with his wife Pia, lost both his sons to cancer. Their oldest son Peter Hans died in 1960, when we had only recently arrived here. Netty spent a great deal of time trying to help Pia and Erry while their son was cared for in a veteran's hospital. He had been drafted in the military and got sick while in the service. He was a nice young fellow, slightly built and quite sensitive. I believe that Robert, the second son of Errie and Pia, died in 1974. He had Hodgkin's disease. Jeltje, the second child and only daughter of Wim and Soph, Omi's oldest son, died also in 1974. She suffered from bone cancer and her illness manifested itself in Asia where she was living with her husband and young children. It progressed very quickly and she died shortly after she returned to Europe for treatment. Omi herself died in 1964 in Switzerland so she was spared the knowledge of the death of Robert and Jeltje, but still she had her share of grievous losses during her lifetime. In her final days she was cared for by a Dutch lady, Mrs. Feikema, who took most of the burden upon her shoulders. It was a Godsend that this lady had been found because Omi's children were scattered all over the world except for Lous and Jean and they were not able to do much as Jean had developed a busy law practice. Jean counted many celebrities among his clients. They were people who had descended on Switzerland because of its favorable tax laws, its banks that offered secret (numbered) tax exempt accounts and the pleasant climate and landscape of Lake Geneva. Charlie Chaplin was among his clients. He lived in the neighborhood of Lutry until his death. A criminal gang dug up his remains some years after his death. They called Jean's house and demanded a big ransom in exchange of a return of the body. Lous happened to pick up the phone and calmly told them nobody was interested in Charlie's body. They could keep it. So they abandoned the body and fled. Later on they were apprehended. They were Polish refugees who thought they had found a smart way to make a lot of money quick. In his final years Jean suffered from Alzheimer's disease. He died in 1997. Lous lived on for several years, but became severely depressed in her final years. She died on March 24 2006. We heard about it through Hans van Someren Gréve, Netty's cousin. Her son's, Netty's cousins, had not bothered to inform us of their mother's death.

Unfortunately the settlement of Omi's small estate caused a deep rift between Netty's mother and her siblings. Lous stayed more or less neutral and wisely remained friendly with both sides, but Netty's mother had a major falling out with Erry and Pia, probably caused by both of them as they both had a tendency to fly of the handle quickly and be harsh in their judgment of others. Netty believes her father stoked the fires of her mother's wrath instead of trying to calm things down. Netty's father was a wonderful and pleasant man, but he had an unfortunate tendency to become very inflexible and stubborn in matters concerning legal disputes, particularly those with his in-laws. Wim who tried to mediate also got caught in the crossfire and was put in the doghouse by his older sister. Fortunately, Netty's mother and Wim patched things up much later, but the rift with Pia and Erry stayed until their death, a situation that bothered Netty very much as she remained friendly with all her uncles and aunts. Netty did not see the need to battle so long and hard about a few possessions and some jewelry. What Netty and I learned from this was that it is extremely important to keep all channels of communication open with all members of one's family and to organize the disposition of earthly belongings in such a way that no acrimony can result. In addition, it seems to us that putting too much value on material things is not important in life.

6 : My Parents

My parents, Anton Arthur George Schieferdecker, and Aaltje Hesselink, lived very long and productive lives. I always felt extraordinarily blessed to have them as part of my life for such a long time and to have them play such an important role in it. Still having living parents when I was myself in my sixties, and even in my seventies, was unusual to say the least, and it gave me a better and deeper knowledge of their real personalities and a more complete picture of their lives. Older people usually like to talk more freely about their life, their careers and their younger years while younger and middle aged people tend to be more reticent as they are still busy living and may have less time or desire to talk about their past. After all, they are still building their image and do not want to behave as if everything is already history. On the other hand, it is more difficult to remember one's parents as they were when they were younger because there are so many more recent powerful memories of them in their very old age. Luckily, I had the good sense to talk quite extensively with my parents about their life and to record much of it on tape so I can reach back and still hear their voices.

I will try to give as accurate a description of my parents as they were when they were still younger and vigorous. I will also tell about their final years, since I feel very strongly that they lived not only good, purposeful lives, but that they were perhaps most admirable when they came to the end of their days. When they approached the end of their lives, they mellowed, each in their own way, and they maintained a level of dignity and personal strength that left everybody in their environment in awe. It cannot have been easy for them to go through those final years while I, their only son, lived so far away. But we did come frequently over to Holland. Sometimes I traveled to the Netherlands for business or Netty came with our children when they were still young, and when our sons and our daughter grew older they came over to Holland themselves. Also, my parents visited us here in America several times, but still there must have been many lonely days, certainly in their final years, when they would have loved to see us and were no longer able to travel to America. Yet they never uttered a word of regret about us being far away and they never blamed us for leaving the country, to the contrary, they always supported our decision to go to America and were strong boosters of our new country. Aware of my parents' longing to be part of our life; I wrote them a letter every week and they wrote back weekly.

It is a privilege for me to have had parents that I loved and saw as "good" parents, who gave me a wonderful childhood, coped with me as a teenager and supported me throughout adolescence and young adulthood. They protected me during the war when I was threatened by German efforts to get young men to work in Germany. They were very fond of Netty and gave us financial support and when we married they bought a house for us. When our children were born, they were ecstatic. They loved their grandchildren and never tired of telling anybody willing to listen how wonderful they were. They lived good and straightforward lives without major flaws or dark secrets. They were levelheaded, uncomplicated people who had no serious "hang-ups" or complexes and consequently did not pass any on to me, at least that I know off. They were certainly not dull people, they led interesting lives, and they visited many parts of the world. Overseas they did not just reside as "expatriates" in the many far-flung countries they lived in. They learned the language of the country, were interested in its culture and history, made friends among the locals and traveled around to enjoy it.

As individuals, they were almost total opposites, the embodiment of the French saying "les extrèmes se touchent." There were conflicts, of course. Many conflicts stemmed from this total contrast in character, but they were always amiably resolved and as most members of their generation did, they compromised and did not push their own objectives to the extreme, and they never treated their own agenda as the most important goal in their life. In hindsight, I think there must have been many compromises, and I can only be grateful that my parents had the common sense to work on them and find solutions.

How different were they? My father was quiet and somewhat shy. He was quite tall and, as a younger man, of medium weight. In his very old age, he grew heavier, but he was never overweight. Like his father, he lost most of his hair when he was in his twenties and during the war he grew a mustache because he felt his face showed too many vertical lines and he needed to offset them with something horizontal. He was sometimes a little awkward and shy in his relationships with others and he was not very good at "glad-handing and backslapping," but he could also be quite forceful and cold when dealing with people he did not like or thought to be dishonest or stupid. He had little patience with people like that. When I was still a child, my father was much less involved with my day-to-day life than my mother. He was somewhat distant but certainly not cold. His relationship with me reflected his own upbringing, in the eighteen nineties, when the rule was that children should be seen, not heard, and when adults were not about to be dominated and dictated to by their children as they are now. He often appeared to be unemotional and very controlled, but in reality bottled many things up inside himself. He was not a good public speaker and there were occasions—like funerals where Dutch people traditionally speak to eulogize the deceased—when he was too moved to say much. For instance, at the funeral ceremony of Tante Jetje, his only sister, he asked me to speak because he could not handle it.

My father grew up as the son of wealthy parents who encouraged him to work hard and seek a good education and who had good taste and liked the finer things in life. My grandparents were socially not very prominent in Holland. Their background was too diverse for that, but my grandfather was certainly quite well known in the Amsterdam business world of his time. My mother came from a much more modest social background. She grew up in Leeuwarden, a small town in the northern province of Friesland. She was, however, also an achiever and was very well educated. She was outgoing, talkative and never had a problem approaching other people to state her opinion. My mother did not mind speaking in public, an unusual characteristic for women of her generation. At one point in her life, she even contemplated putting her public speaking abilities to good use by becoming a member of the clergy. When the management of Royal Dutch Shell gave a dinner party to honor my father on his retirement - I believe she was the only woman present - she got up and spoke in praise of her husband. She did not bottle up her feelings and could be embarrassingly frank (and sometimes wrong) in the things she said to others. She could be very warm and trusting with complete strangers and she could be emotional and sometimes quite erratic in her behavior. Netty's Oom Eelco would have described my father as a "Beta" person and my mother as an "Alpha" one. This differentiation makes immediate sense to all Dutch people of my generation who went to high school at age twelve. In the old, now no longer used high school system, one went either to a "Gymnasium," a six-year school where the emphasis was on the humanities, languages, philosophy and history, or to a HBS *(Hogere Burger School)*. The HBS was a five-year school where math and sciences were preeminent, but "modern languages" as the Dutch call them, were also taught. The Gymnasium education involved modern languages—Dutch, German, French and English, and in addition, Latin and ancient Greek. A further differentiation was made after the third year of this six-year school between alpha and beta streams, alpha continuing with the languages and beta dropping ancient Greek for more math and science. And if I have to be totally accurate, I have to add that many people, including me, went to a third type of high school called a "Lyceum." This type of high school offered two years of general education after which one had to choose either the HBS or the Gymnasium side of the same school, the latter including again the alpha vs. beta choice, beginning after the third year. Oom Eelco assuming that like him everyone of his social class went to the Gymnasium used the term to describe his own tendency and that of Netty's father to favor the humanities over math and science. Alpha people were more educated in languages and history while beta people were those who were the more practical ones with a math and science bent. My mother was a strictly Alpha person and my father very much a Beta person. My father was meticulous and orderly. He was a quiet, thoughtful and reserved man who did not talk all that much. He loved music. He was logical and precise in his outlook on life and understood "the way things worked." Pa, as I called him after Papa became too childish, was an engineer with a precise unromantic mind. Ma, whom I called Mama as a child, was a lawyer, a romantic with an interest in words, books and literature and absolutely no interest in or understanding of financial, technical or mechanical things. For instance, referring to the electric wire of a table lamp, she would talk about its *"touw"* (rope). She had a vivid fantasy and was a good story-teller. Ma was not good at working with her hands and never managed to be good at sewing, knitting or crocheting like most of her female contemporaries. She could not draw at all and her handwriting was good but kind of scraggly. Pa had beautiful handwriting until the end of his days and could draw very well. He was handy and as a boy produced beautiful carpentry work, all of which was lost, unfortunately. He was well coordinated and engaged in several sports all his life. When I grew up he played tennis in summer and in winter went horseback riding with a friend. As a geologist he loved the mountains and mountain climbing and took me to the Swiss Alps when I was in my early teens. Pa climbed many of the well-known mountains in Switzerland. He even climbed the Monte Rosa, the highest mountain in Switzerland, twice. [The Mont Blanc is higher, but it is half in France and therefore not considered a Swiss mountain.] Ma tried mountain climbing and liked it as long as she was not in situations where she was overcome by vertigo, thereby eliminating most opportunities for true alpinists. Pa and Ma were once in Chamonix on vacation and Pa tried to get Ma to join him in climbing the Mont Blanc. They had to give up because Ma had trouble jumping over the crevasses in the glaciers. It became a famous story richly embellished by Ma who would imitate the guide yelling *"vous ne pouvez pas rester ici Madame"* (you cannot stay here [on the glacier] madam). Ma played tennis too, but not very well because she had only one good eye and could not judge distances. This was perhaps also a reason for her difficulty with sewing and other needlework. She had tried riding in Mexico when engaged to Pa, but after her first lesson her posterior hurt so badly that she promptly quit riding. Ma loved to read. She read serious fiction in Dutch, Spanish, French, German and English. Pa hardly ever touched fiction. He liked nonfiction, humorous books and books about history, science, particularly geology and mining, and business. He also had a deep interest in the history of the ancient Mexican people, the Incas and Mayas, and had a good library on that subject. When Ma read something that she thought was particularly interesting or beautiful, she liked to read it aloud, to make everybody in the room share the words she enjoyed. When they were older, Ma would read to Pa in the evenings, out of books she liked. Pa enjoyed that tremendously. Pa followed the financial markets carefully and ran our family's finances very astutely. Ma had no interest whatsoever in things financial. She looked down with disdain on "business people" as nonintellectuals engaged in grubby affairs and only out to make money. She thought investing was a form of greed that should be frowned upon. She was lucky to have married a husband who was a good investor and kept an eye on their bank account and always gave her as much spending money as she wanted. Pa was lucky to have a wife who was very frugal in her spending habits and never abused his "open ended" approach to cash management. When I grew up, they had an old beat up metal strongbox filled with cash in their clothes closet. Pa would make sure there always was cash in it and Ma would take out whatever she needed.

But what were their similarities? They both had been good students when they were young and attended high school and universities. They were smart and well educated and knowledgeable about many things. They were reasonably fluent in English, French, German and Spanish. In addition, my father learned some Romanian. They both loved music and were good medium-level musicians. Pa played the cello and Ma the piano. For years Pa had a trio with friends to play classical music. Ma did not play in these ensembles possibly because she felt she did not play well enough or did not want to be told what she did right or wrong by her husband and her friends. My parents often went to concerts in The Hague and continued to do so until they were very old. I remember how they would go to the concerts in the years before the war when people lived in style. Pa would wear his dinner jacket (a tuxedo with a stiff starched shirtfront) and Ma an evening gown. Like most ladies in those more frugal times, she owned just one or two evening gowns and wore them all the time for years. Ma loved the theater and Pa went along. They both liked to travel. Ma enjoyed meeting the people in foreign countries and their culture, Pa the mountains and nature (his photo albums show excellent photography but very few shots of people - he found that a waste of film). They both enjoyed good food but drank little if at all. When they grew up, lower class people in bars consumed hard liquor, others drank wine and cocktail parties had not yet been invented. Pa smoked cigars and pipes when he was in his thirties and early forties but stopped smoking during the war. Ma occasionally puffed on a cigarette after dinner, in a funny clumsy sort of way, because she thought it was elegant and sophisticated and she liked the tobacco aroma, but neither of the two inhaled or smoked heavily. They both liked to take walks and to ride their bicycles and they particularly liked to go for a drive into the countryside in their car.

The strong bond between them stemmed from their great affection for each other and their dependence upon each other. Pa needed Ma for her ability to connect with neighbors and friends and relatives and to make plans

for outings and create a *"gezellig huis,"* a cozy and warm home. The word *"gezellig"* is typically Dutch and cannot be very well translated. It evokes images of warm cozy houses in a clammy and cold climate, of rooms chock-a-block full of comfortable furniture—of a culture that because of the climate is strongly oriented towards being happy and snug at home—indoors. Ma needed Pa to be the strong and responsible one, to keep things going in the house, keep track of the money and be her anchor to windward, support and audience. The strongest bond between them was no doubt their sense of humor and the strong loyalty and love for each other and for Netty and me and our children and also for their other close relatives.

My father, George Schieferdecker was born in 1893 in Batavia (now Jakarta) in the Netherlands East Indies (now Indonesia). He had three first names as he was named after his three uncles - Anton Arthur George. Anton and George Stibbe were my grandmother's brothers and Arthur Schieferdecker was my grandfather's brother. As a youth Arthur fell down a flight of stairs, suffered brain damage and never lived a normal life. He died young. I have known Anton and George Stibbe well. My father was always called George and I was named after him, George Peter, and so was our son George who was named after his grandfather George, his Uncle Bernard who was shot by the Germans, and his great grandfather Max. Our own son George had the good sense to marry Diane Alexander who brought many good things into his

CHANGE OF CLIMATE : GEORGE AND JETJE SCHIEFERDECKER IN
BATAVIA IN 1894 AND LEIPZIG   IN 1898.

life and into ours, including a family name that can also be used as a first name. So
the tradition lives on with our own grandson George Alexander who was named after
not only his own father, grandfather and great grand- father but also his mother's
entire family.

When my father was three years old, his parents left the Far East and moved back
to Europe, settling at first in Germany. They lived for two years in Grimma, my
grandfather's birthplace, to see if they should settle down there. My grandmother
did not like it there and the story was that my father as a small child did not like it
either. My mother claimed she had heard he spoke just a few words in German to
his German playmates. They were: *"lass mir in ruhe"* (leave me alone). My mother
frequently used to bring this up as an early sign of my father's shy and self-effacing
character. This was a big problem in her view. She preferred people who were
extroverts and apt to let their feelings be known to others. In 1900 my grandparents returned to Holland, staying briefly with their parents Stibbe in Hilversum and
buying a house in Haarlem on the Hazepaterslaan 17. When reflecting on these
moves of my grandparents, I often think about the strange quirks of life. I realize
that if my grandparents had decided to stay in Germany, they would probably have
been Germans. My grandfather only got the Dutch nationality in 1908, when my
father was fifteen years old and about twelve years after their foray into Germany.

So if they had stayed in Germany, or kept the German nationality, my father would most likely have been called up to serve in the German army in the First World War. In the unlikely event he would have survived this terrible slaughter; he and his parents would have had all sorts of problems in the period following that war because my grandmother was Jewish. When Hitler came to power in 1933 his regime almost immediately started the persecution of Jews, and the Nazi's were tough on mixed marriages. But this is idle speculation. Luckily, my grandfather was smart enough to apply for Netherlands' citizenship and thus our family avoided a great deal of trouble.

In 1901, the family traveled for a year through Europe. My grandmother did not feel well and this trip was an attempt to seek the fresh mountain air for her. They spent the summer in Friedenweiler, a resort in the Schwartzwald region in Germany where I also spent some time with my mother while my father worked in Rumania. They spent the winter in Caux, Switzerland, and the spring in Lugano. When they returned to the Netherlands, my father spent two years in school in The Hague, living with his grandparents Stibbe in Scheveningen. Why he was sent away by his parents is unclear, but it probably reflects his mother's health problems. My grandparents built a house in Bloemendaal at the Mollaan 5. They moved there in 1904. The Mollaan is a very attractive street with large trees on both sides and the house where my father grew up is still there. It is a big Victorian-style house. I was born in that house in 1925. When entering the street from the side of the village, there are just five big houses on the right hand side. The corner house used to be owned by a doctor, and then there is the house on number 7 that my grandparents built in 1926 next to their old house on land that also belonged to them. Continuing down the street there is the old house and then two other large houses followed by a park with big old trees. At that point the park is on both sides of the street. For the 5th and 6th grade my father went to the *Bloemendaalse Schoolvereniging*, a form of private school founded and controlled by an association of parents, a format for private schools popular in Holland in those days. The school still exists and it still uses the same building. As you pass the house in the Mollaan and keep going, you will see on the left an interesting small, quite old pavilion called *"Het Pannekoeken Huisje,"* the little pancake house, where they are baking and selling pancakes. Next to it, on the left is a street. That is where the school is. Behind the pancake house is a very nice small botanical garden called *"Thysse's Hof"* in honor of Jack P. Thysse, a well-known Dutch naturalist who lived in Bloemendaal. It is worth taking a walk in this small, gated park, but like so many public places in Holland it is often closed.

Bloemendaal was and still is a wealthy leafy village. It is a suburb of Haarlem, but also a place where many people live that commute to work in Amsterdam. It has many parks and well-maintained large houses, which are surrounded by old trees. Across the street from my grandparents, on the left-hand side, was a house, actually more a mansion, belonging to the Stoop (rhymes w. soap) family, friends of my grandparents. Mr. Adriaan Stoop had founded and financed the school. He knew my father as a boy and was the one who suggested to him to become a mining engineer like him. Adriaan Stoop was one of the founders of an oil exploration company that operated in Indonesia, called "*Dortsche Petroleum Maatschappij.*" This company merged into the organization that later grew into the Royal Dutch Shell Company, a Dutch/English enterprise that is now in market capitalization the second largest energy company in the world and markets its products under the brand name "Shell." "Dordtsche" continued to exist as a listed company, holding only Royal Dutch stock. My father spent his entire career with Shell and was very loyal to it and its people. A friend of mine, Mr. Hans Bredius, who also lived in Bloemendaal, showed me a picture of the *"Mollaan"* he had copied out of a booklet called "Bloemendaal as it was." The picture showed a group of children identified as the "Stoop children" and next to them a boy who is a little taller and a little older, leaning nonchalantly against a post is identified as the *"jongen Schieferdecker"* (the Schieferdecker boy).

My father told me little about growing up in Bloemendaal. He was not a great storyteller and probably thought that tales about his younger years were not of great interest to me. My mother was much more apt to launch into interesting stories about her life as a young girl in Leeuwarden. Again, that contrast between my parents. I remember him telling me that as a young boy he had to get up early every day to crank up a weight that, by descending slowly during the day, served to compress gas in a tank. They manufactured their own gas in their backyard by injecting gasoline into air and compressing it. It was, I believe their own private gas plant that provided them with gas to burn in their lamps before town gas was installed. People who did not have an installation like that used kerosene to get light. Kerosene lamps also lighted the streets. In Bloemendaal and in other towns a man would come by every evening with a ladder. He would reach up into the lanterns to light them. I also remember my aunt Jetje, my father's older sister, telling me how he had to study the cello every morning before school. Once she found him crying, not because he was playing a sad piece, but because the room was so cold. In those days it was thought useful for a child's education to learn how to play an instrument and equally useful not to spoil them or make them overly comfortable. Parents simply told their children what they had to do, and they were certainly not inclined to heat their entire house because a separate stove was needed to heat each room. Saying no to a child was regarded as good discipline and negotiating with a child, as is common nowadays, was not done. The music studies paid off, however. In an earlier chapter I described my great grandfather's visit to Bloemendaal and his pleasure at hearing his grandson play in an orchestra. My father became a great music lover and as I mentioned, he did enjoy playing the cello. In 1906 after finishing grade school in Bloemendaal, he went to high school in Haarlem, the *"HBS"* or *"Hogere Burger School,"* which emphasized math and science. His sister, went to the *"Gymnasium."* In 1909 my father made his first visit to London with his sister. This trip came up when we talked about the progress of technology and transportation during his life. He told me how he toured around London in horse-drawn double-decker omnibuses. Little boys would scurry among the traffic to collect the droppings of the horses and there was concern that with the growth of traffic, there might come a time when there would not be enough boys to take care of the mess. But transportation would change rapidly in my father's life. At the "HBS" he had a classmate who never graduated from any university but became world famous. His name was Anthony Fokker. In school, Fokker was somewhat of a hell raiser. He liked cars and motor cycles and one day raced a motorcycle in circles on the roof of a one-story building to see how far he could jump with his bike if he went over the edge at full speed. He was one of the first Dutch aviators. He built his own plane and later on started his own aircraft factory. During the First World War, he designed and built fighter planes in Germany for the Germans, including the famous triple-decker plane flown by Baron Manfred von Richthofen, the German ace known as the "Red Baron." After the war he built commercial planes in Holland and for many years KLM, the Dutch airline, used only Fokker planes. Even American Airlines used the Fokker Tri-Motor, a three-engine plane with a fuselage partly built out of a metal frame covered with stretched fabric and wings made out of thin plywood.

My grandfather bought his first automobile in 1911. It was a Dyon Bouton a French car he bought second hand. Later he bought a Spijker, a car manufactured in Holland. Pa told me he drove both these cars before the Great War started. My father finished high school in the spring of 1911 when he was eighteen and entered the university at Delft. This was the *"Technische Hogeschool,"* which was until shortly after WW II the only university-level engineering school in Holland.

He became a member of the Delft student *"Corps"* and went through the hazing period that all students who wished to join it were required to go through. He had to have his hair shaved off and had to sit on the floor while others poured beer over him. He never told me much about his *"jaar club"* (year club), the group of ten or so friends traditionally formed as a unit within a year. This in contrast to Netty's father who had a very strong bond with his year club, a group of men who with their wives were very close friends of Netty's parents and who Netty and I both knew well. I did meet several friends of my father's from his years at Delft, but I don't know whether they belonged to his club or not. A tragic figure was Professor Mekel, who first lived and worked in Mexico with Pa and later taught at the faculty of mining engineering at Delft. He was one of the first prominent people shot by the Germans early in the

GEORGE SCHIEFERDECKER HIGH
SCHOOL GRADUATE IN 1911

occupation years. Professor Mekel had been a member of a beginning resistance movement, but his group's internal security was much too amateurish to cope with the Germans. A Nazi spy infiltrated them. In the beginning, the Dutch still had to learn cloak and dagger work and were no match for the German secret police, the Gestapo. Another friend of my father's was Henry de Voogd, who became a world famous naval architect. Mr. de Voogd designed the Dutch royal yacht and also a much bigger one for the Shah of Persia.

In discussing Pa's friends, I should mention the long and extensive friendship the Schieferdeckers have with the de Clercq family. This friendship is woven through so many events in my life and that of my parents that it needs to be discussed here. I believe it started when my grandparents spent a summer in Switzerland after they had returned from the Dutch East Indies. They became friends there with Daan and Marie de Clercq and their two sons Wouter and Frans. Wouter and my father also became friends, but unfortunately, Wouter died tragically. He drowned while rowing on the river Rhine in Holland. Frans was younger than Wouter, but after Wouter's death, he and later on his wife Ans also became lifelong friends of my parents. Their friendship carried on to our generation and Netty and I became close friends of their three sons, Lucas, Thys (Matthew) and Jan and their wives. It is a source of great satisfaction for Netty and me that the children of Lucas and his wife Agna have in turn become friendly with our children. It would take another book to do justice to the de Clercq family and it would obviously carry me too far to do so. I remember Daan de Clercq quite well. He was a man who would have fit better in today's world than the Dutch society he lived in. He was what nowadays would be called an "activist." A mover and a shaker, politically a liberal, a vegetarian, a pacifist, lover of animals and nature and involved in many "do-gooder" type movements. Unfortunately, he also died quite young. He was run-over by a bus near his house when he was rushing out to another meeting of a group he belonged to. My parents were very fond of him and were quite used to sudden unannounced visits by him whenever he was near The Hague and needed a meal or wanted to stay overnight. His wife could not have been more different than her husband. Mrs. de Clercq, as I called her in contrast to her husband whom I called Oom Daan, was an aristocratic woman with a rather imperious style who made it quite clear she was not at all interested in her husband's activities. She survived Oom Daan by many years, and I saw her often when my parents visited her with me or at the house of Frans and Ans de Clercq. She was a wonderful lady who always treated me very friendly and showed great interest in my childish stories. There were also many good stories about her.

I was very fond of Tante Ans and Oom Frans. They were in many respects totally different from my parents. Oom Frans was a man who aspired to the life of a country squire, which was not easy in Holland where everybody has smallish houses and little space. He dressed elegantly, was a great raconteur but not exactly an intellectual. He liked to hunt and fish and towards the end of the war illegally kept all sorts of animals in the garden of their villa. He owned a cow that we had to take for walks in the park across the street so it could graze, and he fattened a pig in the garage that was later slaughtered by a black market butcher for food. He never managed to build much of a career for himself but was always optimistic and full of crazy plans to entertain his family and guests. He had a quite explosive temperament that manifested itself in some monumental rows with other people. His personality had a negative effect on his relationship with some people and particularly his son Thys. Tante Ans was a very good-looking woman who was interested in fashions and liked to dress up. She was even-tempered, sweet and soft-spoken. Quite a contrast to Oom Frans who could be loud and volatile. During the war when I was a teenager, I often spent time with their family. Shortly after the war, Oom Frans decided to emigrate with his entire family to South Africa where he thought he could do better because he had connections there. This decision saddened my father very much as he regarded

Frans and Ans as his very best friends. Many years later Frans died in Johannesburg in an automobile accident. The third de Clercq to have a fatal accident. Later, Tante Ans came to see us in Riverside and stayed with us after Richard was born. She was here to spend time with her son Thys who by then had moved to New York City after first living in Montreal. She died several years later in Cape Town. It was Thys who helped our son George start his career as an architect by commissioning him to renovate an old brownstone house he had bought at 50 W.84th Street in New York City. It turned out very well and was mentioned in an architectural magazine, much to the delight and pride of the architect's parents.

In his first years at Delft my father worked as a miner in Germany during his summer vacations to fulfill the practical work experience required by the school (30 shifts, I believe). He worked there in coal and in copper mines. I have seen pictures of Pa as a young man having lunch underground in a German mine with a group of miners. In those days Holland had only a few small coal mines so he had to get his experience abroad. In that period he worked near Leipzig and saw his paternal grandparents often. Normally one would graduate from Delft in five years, but in Pa's case World War I interfered. So he graduated about seven years after he started at the university and just before the end of the war. When the war broke out he had passed his first exam and while in the service he benefited from the smallness of Holland by frequently returning to his rooms in Delft to study in his boarding house (at Koornmarkt 25) where he had lived as a student. He was actually billeted in Utrecht and sometimes was moved near the Belgian border. He lost one year completely, but as the war progressed and it became clear that Holland would probably not be involved and stay neutral, he got more leave, spending long weekends and several longer periods in Delft to prepare for exams. At the outbreak of the war, Pa had joined a large group of engineering students who immediately volunteered for the Dutch Army Corps of Engineers in Utrecht. But their enthusiasm to serve their country as officers was soon significantly diminished as they ran into resistance and envy from career officers who had not attended a university and felt threatened by their presence. So Pa and several others never reached officer rank, preferring the less demanding job of sergeant that enabled them to continue their studies at the same time. I do have a document, however, certifying that Pa had passed the required exams to become an officer. There were pictures of my father in the service, working on the construction of fortresses and with groups of soldiers in their barracks. One of his assignments was to go to the Belgian border near Antwerp whenever there was an alert. He had to guard a bridge there and be prepared to blow it up if the

Germans would come over the border. He said he could hear the artillery on the western front at night. Pa told me how in those days the armies were mostly dependent on horses and steam trains for troop movement. His unit had only one lonely automobile, which served in the early mornings to fetch meat for the regiment from the butcher, driving through town with the carcasses of several cows hanging out of the doors. Later in the morning, the same car came to pick up the colonel from his home.

My father earned his engineering degree in February 1918, nine months before the war ended. He must have been demobilized before that since he immediately joined Royal Dutch Shell and went to Switzerland before war's end. Through my grandfather he had been introduced to Mr. Loudon Sr. who was in the top management of Royal Dutch. Loudon introduced him to the chief geologist, a Mr. van Erp, who hired him for 200 guilders a month and decided to send him to Switzerland for about six months to continue studying geology, a necessary extension for the oil exploration business. In those days geology was not taught as a separate discipline at any Dutch university. So he went to the Swiss University of Lausanne. Apparently it was not a problem for him to attend classes given in French or work with German speaking miners. Dutch high schools gave their students a thorough grounding in French, German and English. They still do, but students now may choose to drop one of the three languages and from my own observation, their knowledge of English is good thanks to American TV, but for the other two it is no longer as good as it was in my days and certainly not as in my parent's days. To get to Switzerland in February 1918 he had to get around the Western Front that ranged from Switzerland into France and through Belgium to the North Sea and travel in stages through wartime Germany by train. Germany was not bombed seriously or attacked by ground forces in World War I so the country came unscathed out of it while Belgium and northern France were devastated. When he passed the German border, he was ordered to strip completely to see if he was hiding anything on his body or if anything was written on it. His fountain pen was opened to see if he had secret messages inside instead of ink. His first stop was Cologne, where he ended up in a blacked-out city and bought a dinner of awful food with a dessert with *"ersatz"* flavoring. The British blockade of Germany had strongly affected the German food supply and the German population experienced food shortages. After the war, the Germans blamed Britain for waging an inhumane war against their civilians. The fact that they themselves devastated most of Belgium and northern France and torpedoed Allied ships regardless of whether they carried civilians or not was overlooked.

Pa spent a summer in Switzerland, a time he enjoyed immensely. I believe that his lifelong friendship with Mr. Tell Bersot—who was named after Wilhelm Tell, the Swiss National Hero—dates from that time. He hiked with his Swiss fellow students and their professors into the mountains near Les Diablerets and drew geological charts of the rock formations there. When we spent a month there in 1973 with our entire family, including Netty's parents and mine, Pa had brought his geological maps from that time and explained to us how the mountains around us were formed. I remember him sitting in our chalet at the dining room table, pushing the tablecloth forward over the surface of the table, to demonstrate to his grandchildren how the earth's crust had rippled in ancient times. I still have the maps. I found them when Netty and I cleaned out the house in Wassenaar after Ma's death and I did not have the heart to throw them away. My father returned from Switzerland in November 1918, just when the war was ending and he saw German troops swarming into the railway stations in a disorganized retreat, tossing their weapons on piles on the platforms. In 1919 he spent a few months in The Hague and was then sent to the US. The plan was that he would go to the US to join the "Roxana" Company in St. Louis, which was the US predecessor of the Shell Oil Company. But he could not get a US entry visa. The US was traditionally difficult about letting people in and more so immediately after the war. A citizen of Holland that had been a neutral country was probably a little suspect. Ma, who always had a more suspicious nature, claimed it was because of our German name, but Pa and I doubted that. There are after all many Americans with German names. It was decided that he should go to Mexico instead. He went to London and from there to Mexico on a tanker. There was apparently a shortage of space on passenger ships and direct connections with Mexico probably did not exist.

What my father never told me, and I discovered only much later when I was already married to Netty, was that around the end of the First World War he had been married and divorced in less than a year. After I heard the story and started putting two and two together, I remembered that my mother had sometimes made a slip of the tongue - she always had great trouble keeping secrets and regularly spilled the beans about birthday presents for me and things like that. But she stopped short from saying more as my father would immediately get extremely angry and agitated. I do not know why Pa did not want me to know about this earlier marriage. I suspect it was because he thought, wrongly, that this was somehow shameful or a situation that would affect my love and respect for him or because he was embarrassed by it and preferred to pretend it had never existed. After Netty and I were married, Ma was no longer able to keep silent. She told Netty, urging her not to tell me. Netty can keep a secret very well so I remained in the dark until a colleague of mine in Amsterdam, Ernest van Panhuys, a man I had known in Leiden and whom I introduced to the firm where I worked, asked me if my father had been married before. Ernest, who was a member of a Dutch noble family, was interested in looking up other people's heritage in the *"Nederlands Patriciaat."* He had stumbled upon Elisabeth Alexandrina van Voss, daughter of an Admiral in the Dutch Navy, born on February 14, 1895, married to my father on March 25, 1918, and divorced from him on February 20, 1919. I told Ernest I did not think this was true and when I came home told Netty what Ernest had said. Netty smiled and revealed to me that it was true and that she had known about it for some time. I felt kind of silly about it but decided to say nothing to Pa, and that is the way it remained until after Pa's death when Netty and I went to the Dutch government office where you can go to trace your ancestry. We went there chiefly to find out more information about Ma's family as we knew so little about them. But we also tried to find out about Pa's first marriage, which took place just before the end of the war and ended when Pa was already in Mexico. Netty found a copy of the *"Patriciaat,"* containing the facts Ernest had spotted first and I now know to be accurate. I am not sure, but I seem to remember that I heard somewhere that Pa's first marriage quickly turned sour because his first wife was unfaithful when he left for Switzerland, but I do not know this for certain. Another strange sequel to this story is that I think I met my father's first wife on a ship going to America. In early 1951, shortly before we were married, I was sent to New York to deliver a large number of stock certificates in General Motors that were owned by my firm. The company had announced a stock split and the certificates had to be physically exchanged for new ones. It was found to be safer and less expensive—the insurance premium was much lower—if the certificates were brought over by ship and somebody would travel with them. So I got a free trip to the U.S., the first one in my life. In those days most people went by ship, and there were not many berths available in the limited number of passenger ships in use after the war. So I was quite fortunate to get a berth on the *Westerdam* a smallish ship, combining passenger accommodation with freight. There were a small number of passengers on board so I got to know all of them. There was one lady, traveling alone, who one morning asked me point blank if I was the son of George Schieferdecker. I said yes and asked if she knew my father. She said, "yes, very well," and that was that. I don't remember if we were interrupted, but later, when I started to run the movie backwards, I remembered this brief conversation. I also remember walking the deck late one night and looking through the window, seeing her sitting at the bar with a man who had his arm around her. So maybe it was she and she was still behaving true to form. There certainly was no reason for Pa to keep this earlier marriage a secret. It never meant anything to me and has not influenced my strong feelings of love and admiration of him one bit.

Pa's employment contract with *De Bataafsche Petroleum Maatschappij (or BPM)*, the production subsidiary of Royal Dutch that still exists under the same name, is dated March 7, 1918. It was signed by my father and by several others, including *H. Colijn – directeur*. Mr. Colijn later on became prime minister of the Netherlands during the depression years. Obviously Pa married shortly after he was hired. He left for Switzerland a few weeks later and upon his return from there must have found that his marriage was in trouble. When he went to London he must have started divorce proceedings, which I assume took a while to get completed.

IN TOPILA FEB. 1920.

After a 19 day crossing on the tanker *San Silvester* of the Mexican Eagle Company, Pa ended up in Tampico, Mexico on July 4, 1919 to start his career there. He joined the geological department of the Compania de Petroleo La Corona. Shell usually operates overseas through locally incorporated companies. Pa spent almost seven years in Mexico, actually two periods of about three years each with a home leave in between in 1922. That year his sister Jetje had come over to see him and the two traveled back from Vera Cruz to Havana, Washington, D.C., and New York City. During his first period in Mexico, he started out supervising drilling in Topila-Panuco.

In the period 1920–22, he worked in oil exploration, traversing the country on horseback with a manservant on a mule, a sort of Don Quixote–Sancho Panza team. Pa explained to me that in those days oil was found by practicing surface geology, looking for the anticlines that often produced oil. Nowadays this has been replaced by geophysics. Everything had to be mapped out so he started in Tampico and worked all over Vera Cruz province along the shore up to Guatemala City and into the very rural and isolated Chiapas province. For sport he climbed Mexico's famous volcano, the Popocatepetl and took photographs of the crater. This was no mean feat as it is a very high (about 18,000 ft.) snow-capped mountain in a tropical country. His group contained another Dutchman, a Mr. De Bruin who did not make it to the top. Mr. de Bruin wrote an article about the climb for a Dutch mountain climbing magazine. In the article he stated that "no one reached the top." We later met this man again when I was in Switzerland with Pa for a mountain climbing vacation. When Ma heard about our meeting, which was quite cordial, she was surprised that Pa had not confronted him with this untruth. I guess she would have done it if she had been there. Pa said it was totally unimportant. Pa never saw the Yucatan Peninsula, and the offshore drilling now done there and almost everywhere else in the Gulf of Mexico was not a known technology then. In those days the major oil fields were near the Panuco River and near Tuxpan and Tamiahua. He told me that he had proposed development of another oilfield that later became important and was called Poza Rica. In 1922 after returning from leave, he was asked to head up a geological search in the area of Teuantepec. He worked there with two Englishmen and a Swiss. In 1923 he opened an office in the isthmus of Teuantepec in Acayucan with a staff of six geologists, a lawyer and a land acquisition man. (I have taken these geographic names from the tape I made, written them down phonetically and subsequently matched them with names I found in my atlas – so I hope they are correct.) He had a stable with 24 horses there. The geologists would go out in the field to map the area. When this task was completed he closed the office and went back to Tampico where he was put in a management-training course. He had to work as an observer in several departments such as finance, tankers and refineries. He then was sent to the US, to St. Louis and Tulsa.

As Pa is telling all this on tape, Ma frequently interrupts with background commentary, saying she also was in Tulsa with him, commenting they were married then "and he forgets that completely." Pa quickly confirms that indeed they were married by then and that the trip through the US was also their honeymoon. They combined business with pleasure and traveled to Santa Fe and the Grand Canyon by train. People were met by guides with horses at the lip of the Canyon and offered a descent into it on horseback. Four hours down and five hours back up and then, like real tourists, they were immediately put back on the train to go on. However, Pa and Ma stayed several days. Their descent into the Canyon became one of my mother's favorite stories, richly embellished as the years went by, but some of it was probably true. Certainly the part where she was told to dismount and help brace the horse as it was coming down an especially steep segment of the trail, all of two-feet wide, with a precipice on one side. There was also a perilous moment when the horse spied a nice tuft of grass just over the edge of the path and bent its head down to get it while Ma was sitting on its back, staring into the abyss. After the Grand Canyon they went on to New York, saw the Niagara Falls and New York City, where they took a tour in one of those old fashioned open tour omnibuses. As they passed through a particularly rough New

MY FAVORITE PICTURE OF MY PARENTS - AT THEIR ENGAGEMENT IN MEXICO CITY IN 1923.

York neighborhood, they were being pelted with tomatoes and fruit by the locals. This prompted the guide to comment: "These people think *we* are the sight.

But I am skipping ahead too fast. My parents were married in Mexico City on February 8th, 1924. They had met in Mexico City where Ma was working at the Dutch legation. Only after World War II were all diplomatic representatives called ambassadors and their offices embassies. In the old days most countries only had a few ambassadors in important nations and ministers (who ranked below ambassadors) in most other countries. Ma worked for the consular general, Mr. de Kanter, who worked for the minister, Baron van Asbeck. The Dutch community in Mexico was very small, but Ma managed to build several lifelong friendships there. Ma came to Mexico about two years after the war. She had a study friend who had moved to Mexico after marrying a man who became vice consul there. This was Annie

MY PARENTS AT THEIR WEDDING
FEB 8, 1924

Schaafsma who married Piet van der Mersch. Annie spent her entire life in Mexico and had many children. They all grew up there and stayed in Mexico or the United States. I remember Annie from visits she made to Holland. A lively, slender woman with a quite complacent, chubby husband. Another woman Ma befriended there was Hilda Bolt, the daughter of a Frisian clergyman who worked as a teacher in Mexico. Hilda came back to The Hague and was a frequent visitor to our house. She taught English at the *Lyceum* (high school) where I went after grade school. Hilda never married. She was thin as a rail and had a somewhat hoarse voice, which caused us boys to call her *"Schuurpapier"* (sand paper). Teenagers can be cruel and often rude. Ma had a very good time in Mexico, went to many parties and Hilda and she were squired around by various bachelors, particularly two men who lived there and were in the tourist business. They were Zimmermann and Hamburger, called Zimmy and Hammy by Ma. I am certain that Ma's relationship with these men and several others was friendly and totally platonic. Ma was quite a prude and in those days people were much less prone to get sexually involved in contrast to today, when people roll into bed on the second or third date. Ma was attractive as a young woman. She had beautiful long dark hair. She cut her hair short after I was born but kept her tresses in a drawer, and after her death we found them and Netty thinks she still has them somewhere, wrapped in a blue checkered cloth. Ma was lively and well educated and must have made a big impression on Pa, a good-looking balding young man who was very shy and not all that outgoing. Since he had been involved in a divorce, he was probably also gun-shy. Anyway, they hit it off very well and when Pa came to stay as a houseguest with the consul general, the same house where Ma was living, he decided to propose. He did that by sending her a letter. This was strange in Ma's eyes, but she accepted his proposal anyway. She told me that Pa had a man move all his belongings out the day before she got the letter and that she had noticed that and wondered what he was up to because she knew he was supposed to stay longer. Obviously, he was afraid he would be rejected and wanted to be out of the house in case that happened!

Opa Schieferdecker, my grandfather, probably felt his son should be protected against another bad marriage and insisted on a prenuptial agreement. It was probably an agreement to marry *"buiten gemeenschap van goederen"* (to marry without sharing assets), a contract many people in Holland would write to save estate taxes in case one of the parties would die young. Netty and I also had one. But despite her knowledge of the law, Ma thought the agreement was insulting and did not grasp that it was understandable in view of Pa's earlier divorce, an event that may have been costly for Opa. I don't know if it was and I don't know for sure if there was a pre-nuptial agreement, if there was one, it was soon forgotten and went the way of so many useless pieces of paper. Baron van Asbeck married them and gave a big dinner party at their wedding. There is a charming engagement picture of them sitting on a stoop outside the consulate. It is my favorite picture of my parents as young people. My father brought his young bride into the bachelor household he was running. He had a string of servants at home, including a Jamaican lady who did not like the arrival of another female in her bailiwick and immediately asked for a raise. Her words were: "I do the cooking, I do the cleaning and the butlering. I want more money." Pa had a cook or major domo who did all the shopping and laundry. He was Chinese. He called Ma "Signolla," but left fairly soon as he was also not used to all the new supervision he had to endure. As I mentioned, my parents went to the US on their honeymoon and from there to the Netherlands to introduce their new spouse to their parents.

Let me now return to my mother's life before her marriage. As I said, I know a great deal more about her life growing up in Leeuwarden than I know about my father's youth. Ma liked to tell me about her childhood and university years. In Pa's case you had to make an effort to draw him out and even then he did not tell you much. My mother was born and raised in Leeuwarden. She had only one first name, Aaltje. She was named after her mother's younger sister. As I mentioned earlier, she never knew her own mother–Jannegje Beetsma–who died at the age of thirty-two when my mother was five months old. Her stepmother came into her life when she was four. Ma never spoke much about her stepmother whom I called "Oma Dik".

AALTJE (L) AND JET CA. 1902.
(THE FUR RUG SHOWS UP OFTEN.)

She must have tried to care for her newly acquired children and done a good job, but it simply was not a very loving relationship, I believe. Since Ma's stepmother had a photography business and her father started running it, there are many photographs of my mother as a child.

She is shown with her sister Tante Jet, with surprisingly short hair, dressed in stiff aprons and buttoned boots. Later on Ma had longer hair and when she went to school she had it in long braids. She told me how the housemaid made braiding her hair a painful experience because she made the braids too tight. She also told me how she would be in school, sitting in the customary wooden benches in straight rows. Each bench usually had two children sitting next to each other and an inkwell on the front edge in the middle to be used by both. Children used to write with steel pens they dipped in ink. A nasty little boy sitting behind her would dip the tips of her braids in his ink well. When she discovered that she started a fight and promptly had to stay in school after hours. Ma was always a good student but also quite feisty as a little girl. She was smart and could remember anything she had seen once. Her sister was a little more than a year older, less interested in learning, and more athletic and often in trouble. Once Tante Jet was again late and told the teacher she had been delayed because "the bridge was open." This was a frequent occurrence in a town with lots of water traffic, bridges and canals. Unfortunately, the teacher had to remind Jet that it was winter, the canals were frozen solid and the bridges had not been opened in weeks.

My mother had many colorful stories about her childhood in Leeuwarden. Her first school was a school for girls where they had to line up on Monday morning to show they had clean hands, carried a clean handkerchief, and wore a freshly starched apron. There was a great deal of noise in the streets as horses were used for all transportation and the steel wheels of the carriages and carts rattled on the cobblestones. When somebody in a family was seriously ill, peat moss was spread on the street to reduce the noise level. This was done for my mother when she suffered from scarlet fever as a young girl. This was a serious health crisis for her and her family. There were no antibiotics or other drugs that could be used to help her, so she was very seriously ill for quite some time and after she recovered, she found she lost most of the sight in one eye.

In those days, public drunkenness was a serious social problem. On payday working men would go to a bar before going home and drink themselves into a stupor. Drinks, *"borreltjes"* or *"jenever,"* shot glasses of Dutch gin, were five cents, so little money was needed to get drunk. Policemen would pick up the drunks with handcarts, tie them down on the cart and trundle them through town to the police station. The little girls of Ma's school thought that was very interesting, but Ma thought it was awful and frightening to see those men roaring drunk. She told me how she would get carried away by her lively imagination and feared she would one day see her father being brought to the police office that way. This was highly unlikely as my grandfather liked an occasional nip but was far from a drunkard. My mother often went to Dokkum to visit her aunt and her family there. She told me she would travel in a tram that ran on steel rails but was drawn by a horse. The horse knew where the conductor lived and when they passed his house, would stop without being prompted so the conductor could go inside and have a cup of coffee with his wife. Unhurried times! She also went by *trekschuit*, an even older form of transportation. This was a small barge, with a large cabin with benches in it to carry passengers. A horse walking on a towpath, built along the canal for that purpose, would pull the barge. This was less expensive than the tram. These barges used in olden days all over Holland. My mother thought going this way was nice as the beautiful countryside glided quietly by. Before people had bicycles, they did a lot of walking. When Ma was in Dokkum on Sundays, her aunt (Tante Gé) and uncle (Oom Tjerk) would walk to church in single file with all the children. Oom Tjerk owned a big farm and had all sorts of carriages and a sled to be drawn by horses when there was snow. But for good Calvinists it was more fitting to walk to church. In church the farm laborers who were used to being outside all day and usually got up very early, often dozed off. But when the pastor noticed he was losing his audience, he would suddenly pound the pulpit with his fist to emphasize a passage in his sermon to awaken his flock. Collections were made by church members passing a long stick with a velvet pouch at its end along the rows of worshippers. People would put their hand in the pouch and release their coins—a typically Dutch system that prevented others from seeing how much was given. It is still in use. No open collection trays as are used in America. At home, my mother and her sister had to go to a church service for children. They were each given two cents so they could contribute one cent at each of the two collections that were held – one for the church and one for the poor. However, on the way to the church the girls would each exchange one penny for two half pennies and buy candy for one penny and use the remaining two half pennies for the church collection.

The relationship with Tante Aaltje Deibel, my mother's surrogate mother, was particularly strong. This aunt of my mother's lived close by in Leeuwarden, and her two sons, George and Anne, were a bit older, but frequently in touch with their cousins, my mother and her sister Jet. They treated them as children, talked down to them and often teased them, but still there was great affection between them and in later years I often visited Oom Anne and his wife Tante Mieke and their son Bas.

The two sisters also had piano lessons. When the piano lessons were about to begin and the teacher arrived at their house, they would hide. Mr. Postma, the teacher, would then ask my grandfather, "Where are they?" The response was, "I don't know, why don't you go and search for them?" Mr. Postma was old and tired and would frequently fall asleep while the girls were playing. He would tap their shoulders to keep time, but when the tapping stopped the girls would know he was fast asleep and scurry away again.

After she finished primary school, my mother went to the Gymnasium and started to use Ali as her name. I believe the old building is still there. She remained a good student and breezed through the six years there, learning French, German, English, Latin and ancient Greek. She also had a smattering of math and science but found those subjects incomprehensible. She would tell me stories that gave a good impression of the way in which high school students were treated in those days. Her French teacher stood out as a prime example of the incredibly cruel and insensitive way some teachers behaved towards their students. He would address his class in French only and would openly and loudly ridicule his students' looks, behavior or stupidity. One poor fellow named Plet had apparently a rosy complexion. His teacher called him *"Plet a la peau delicate"* (Plet with the delicate skin). A nice way to make a kid really like his class and his teacher. He would call others *"crepuscule"* or *"excrément de la terre"* and hand out *"zeros"* with glee.

When the Great War broke out my mother was still in high school. It was still war time when she went to the University of Groningen to study law. She joined the women's student club, which was equivalent to the "corps" for the men. In those days, a female student was still a very rare commodity and her club was small. For Ma and her friends this had the advantage of a very favorable supply-demand situation. She had many male friends and admirers. Shortly before the war she had visited relatives of her father in Germany and met a young German there who was called up in the army when war came. He corresponded with her and kept sending her pictures of himself in uniform as a lieutenant in the German Kaiser's army. We still had some of those pictures at home, and when the Second World War started and we were occupied, I took one of them and put them in my wallet. I figured that if the Germans would arrest me and find this picture on me it might help give me an alibi. Luckily, I never needed to pretend I liked the Germans. As World War I progressed, English servicemen ended up in Holland and were interned in camps. Ma and her friends would work in these camps as volunteers. While she was a stu-

ALI AS A STUDENT
IN GRONINGEN.

dent, my mother was engaged to a fellow Frisian who had the typical name of Piebe Piebenga. However, she chickened out and cancelled the engagement. Why, I do not know. Piebe was a doctor and became a specialist in neurology. He was director of a large mental hospital in Franeker and whenever we drove by that place on our way to our relatives in Leeuwarden we would say: "Wonder what Piebe is doing there today." When I interviewed my mother on tape and asked her why it took her so long to finish her law studies–about six years instead of the four required–she answered, "because I was lazy and I liked to party!"

In her student days my mother took an interest in the then-emerging socialist movement. The leader of the Dutch Socialist Party was another Frisian by the name of Pieter Jelles Troelstra and his party gained a lot of ground. It was an antiwar, anticapitalist, pro-labor and generally idealistic party. I think socialism has a strong appeal to Dutch people because they like fairness and are perfectly willing to submit themselves to intricate systems of regulations and nit picking rules as long as they are convinced it is fair to all concerned. In the period immediately after World War I there was a general trend towards the left and socialism won many supporters all over Europe. It was a logical reaction to the horrible slaughter on the battlefields that was viewed by many as having been organized by pompous royals, the ruling classes and the capitalists. Initially the difference between socialists and communists was hard to discern. Both waved red flags and both followed the theories of Karl Marx and sought to declare republics and to abolish the European monarchies. But the socialists were leaning more towards a modified form of democracy while the communists favored the "dictatorship of the proletariat." In 1917 the Communist party, or Bolsheviks took over in Russia and imprisoned the Czar. He was later murdered with his entire family and the idealism of the Russian Revolution was lost in a wave of terror. After the defeat of Germany, the Kaiser was sent packing. He ended up asking Queen Wilhelmina for asylum in Holland, and he lived there until his death during the German occupation of the Netherlands in the Second World War. Remarkably, the Nazi occupiers never paid much attention to him. They probably did not know what to do with him. As usual, the Dutch political scene was not violent or radical but preoccupied with philosophical issues and debates about social justice. It was the social justice issues that interested my mother. As reported and not forgotten by her cousins Anne and George Deibel, she was even seen marching in a Mayday parade in Leeuwarden, wearing a red tulip, the (very Dutch) symbol of the Dutch socialists. I do not think my mother was ever a radical and she certainly was always a great admirer of our queen. At one point there was a historic confrontation between Troelstra and his socialists and Queen Wilhelmina. Troelstra threatened to declare a republic in Holland. However, the queen thwarted him by making a speech to the a large mass of people in The Hague, who decided to declare their loyalty to her by unhitching the horses of her carriage and pulling it by hand in a triumphant parade. Troelstra caved in and the Netherlands remained a monarchy

Later, Ma was a member of the Dutch Women's Movement for Peace. This was not a socialist movement, but its idealistic bent, against the re-armament that was taking place all over Europe, reflected the socialist slogan *"Vrijheid Arbeid Brood, geen cent voor Leger en voor Vloot"* (Freedom, Work, Bread, not a cent for the army or the navy). The "women for peace" used to march through The Hague, in complete silence, all dressed in white, waving placards with "peace" or "silence" written on them. It was all so wonderfully idealistic, naive and nice. When the German Nazi threat became a reality, Holland had to rebuild its armed forces in a hurry and failed miserably doing so. We were sitting ducks for the well-trained, superbly equipped Germans and so were the French, the Belgians, and the British. After that war, the socialists really hit their stride, moved more to the middle, and created a welfare state in Holland that accomplished many good things but as could be expected, went overboard on entitlements and free handouts. In those days, you could not have found a more vocal and ultra-conservative right-wing person in Holland than my mother. What goes around comes around.

After she got her law degree, my mother wanted to work overseas. The war was over and the opportunity to travel must have been irresistible after living for many years in Friesland and Groningen in the confining environment of small towns. At first she wanted to go to the Dutch East Indies, but when her friend Annie Schaafsma wrote her that the Dutch minister in Mexico City might have an opening for her, she wrote to him and got the job. I guess Ma finished her studies in Groningen around the summer of 1921. She sailed for Mexico on a German ship out of Hamburg. Probably because it was nearby and offered the least expensive fare. By that time, the German economy was beginning to suffer under the burden the foolish peace treaty of Versailles imposed on it. The country was poor, undernourished and—later, in the thirties—subject to violent political upheavals as a result of serious economic problems and rampant inflation. The German currency, the reichsmark, was beginning to loose its value in 1921 and Ma benefited from that because the Dutch guilder was then a very hard currency and worth a lot in Germany. When her ship approached Cuba, it ran aground on a coral reef and the passengers had to abandon ship. Ma's story was that a Turkish gentleman insisted on being put first in a lifeboat, yelling, "I am an American citizen." In the event, the ship was repaired in Cuba and Ma had an unexpected nice vacation of a few days in Havana. When she got to Veracruz, there was a man on the dock yelling "La Senora Gesseling." The Dutch minister had sent him to escort her safely by train to Mexico City. She worked there for several years and had a wonderful time and just as she was beginning to get a little bored and was thinking of going to the Dutch East Indies after all, she met my father, married him on February 8th, 1924, and started her life with him.

After a brief period in Mexico, my parents went on their long honeymoon/business trip through the United States and from there to The Hague in the Netherlands where they lived in rented rooms with a landlady in Scheveningen. The neighborhood where their *pension* was located is called Belgisch Park and still exists. Later in 1925 my father was sent to Venezuela, but my mother stayed behind because she was pregnant. On February 18, 1925, I was born in the house of my grandparents in Bloemendaal where my mother had moved after my father had left for Venezuela. And as they say, the rest is history.

After working for a few months in The Hague, Pa left for Venezuela by way of Curaçao by ship in early January 1925. On the island of Curaçao he worked for a few weeks to investigate the water supply of the refinery there. I was born while he was in Cuaraçao, which was at that time a Dutch colony. He settled in Maracaibo where my mother and I joined him later. We stayed there until September 1926 when we moved back to Holland by way of Caracas. Upon our return to Holland, we settled down in the house in Voorburg on Parkweg 183 where I grew up. My parents moved to Wassenaar in August 1952, after my father retired on July 1 of that year.

In 1926 at the BPM headquarters, Pa was assigned to the newly formed production department where his boss was Mr. B. H. van der Linden, a man who became a good friend of my father's and whom he admired greatly. In 1928 Pa spent ten months alone in Rumania. His assignment there was to reorganize the production department there. I believe my mother had a miscarriage during that period. When she told me about it years later, she claimed I would have had a brother if this misfortune had not occurred. It must have been tough on her to cope with this alone, without her husband, particularly since she was also alone when I was born. Ma, I, and my grandparents Schieferdecker spent some time in the German Schwartzwald in Friedenweiler to give my mother a chance to recover. In 1929 when I was four years old, we left for Argentina where we lived for a year near Comodoro Rivadavia, in Patagonia. There again Pa had to reorganize the production department of an oil field that was being developed and that was to supply a nearby refinery the Argentine government had contracted to build. The refinery never was constructed and when the Great Depression hit, the drilling activity was severely diminished. Pa had to fire many people there, a job he did not relish, but carried out. My earliest memories go back to that period and I will get back to it when I describe my own life.

After returning from Argentina, Pa rejoined the production department in The Hague. He worked there until his retirement in 1952. When I questioned Pa about the corporate structure at their headquarters, he explained they did not have anything similar to a U.S. organizational chart. The company had many separate departments, including geology, finance, law, transportation, etc., but the production activity was, of course, very important since it was their raison d'être. They had a sort of team structure supervising worldwide drilling and production activity under the leadership of Mr. van der Linden with an inner circle consisting of four engineers, each responsible for a part of the world where the company was producing oil. Mr. van Dorsser, another friend of my father's, was in charge of the U.S. Shell Oil Company, Mr. Bloemgarten for the Netherlands East Indies, Mr. Moir for Venezuela, British Borneo (now Serawak), and Pa was responsible for Mexico, Trinidad, Cuba, Argentina and Rumania, and later Germany and Austria also. The

Mexican government nationalized all oil properties in the country in the 1930s. Rumania was lost after World War II. Before the war Pa went frequently to Germany and Austria and at least once more to Rumania. When World War II started in 1939, there was some talk about us going to Argentina. If this had happened I would either have been left behind in Holland to complete my education or I would have gone abroad with my parents. The Lord only knows what would have happened to me in the latter case. Maybe I would have become a pilot in the RAF, which was my great-unfulfilled ambition during the war. It is perhaps better that things worked out the way they did. Being alone in wartime Holland would not have been a picnic either, and I might not have survived a stint as a pilot.

During the first few months of the German occupation, my father continued working in The Hague. Later on, he was given a leave of absence since there was obviously nothing to do as there was no contact at all with the company's activities overseas and there was no great desire to be helpful to the Germans. Like many other Dutch companies, the Germans had appointed, *a Verwalter,* a representative of their government as chief executive of the BPM. This was of course a farce, but this gentleman still enjoyed his job and played oil tycoon. He ordered a world-map for his office with little lights showing all the places where "his" company was working! Towards the end of the war, the Germans started to build up their coastal defenses along the North Sea shore, which included the part of The Hague where the company's offices were located. The whole staff was moved inland to the small town of Doorn where people were pretending to work. Pa went there three days a week, spending most of the time in transit. He rode his bike to the station, parked it there, rode the train to Doorn, and once there picked up another bike to go to his office. In the final year of the war when all train traffic was disrupted, he did not go anymore.

After the war, Pa went for a few months to the U.S. to be reacquainted with new technologies. In Holland he played a major role in the development of the oil and gas fields in the northern part of the country that became a major source of energy and income for the then-war ravaged country. All during the war Pa and his colleagues had known of the possibility that a large field existed there but kept mum, of course.

A final highpoint at the end of Pa's career was his leading role in the organization of the World Oil Congress in Holland. Later on just after his retirement he also participated in a similar congress in Rome where Ma and he had the privilege of meeting the Pope. Pa ended his career quite well of. He had accumulated a solid investment portfolio and enjoyed a nice pension from the Royal Dutch retirement fund. Neither he nor any of his colleagues or superiors would become multi millionaires. He was well rewarded, but not excessively like some American executives are now.

In Wassenaar, my parents settled down quite happily into retirement in the newly built house they had just bought. Pa said he had finally felt he was a free man after "having been confined to a cell for thirty years." He became more active on the boards he served on. He had inherited a number of directorships from my grandfather, mainly old Indonesian sugar factories and quinine plantations and two small investment companies. Most of these Indonesian companies were unable to resume their activities after the war and ended up as corporate shells in the Netherlands trying to liquidate the detritus of our colonial empire. Pa sometimes grumbled that his father had hung on too long to his directorships and had kept the juicy ones until they too were not worth much. Why a son had any rights to his father's board seats was unclear, of course, but it happens all over the world. More importantly, he also served on the board of the Royal Geological and Mining Society of the Netherlands. In 1952 the society asked him to undertake a monumental task that took many years to complete. He was invited to edit a nomenclature for geological terms. The nomenclature defines geological terms in English and provides the translation of each term into Dutch French and German. The book was published in 1959. It contains definitions of almost six thousand words. I remember seeing him work on this, using a card-filing system he had invented himself. He corresponded with hundreds of scientists, engineers and language experts all over the world and was helped by many Shell people, including the office staff at the Bataafse where the final draft of the book was typed. I have a copy of the book, and looking at it from time to time, I am still awestruck by the magnitude and complexity of the job he took on and completed. The energy and perseverance he displayed in doing this was very characteristic of him. He was a man who finished the jobs he decided to do no matter what. It would have been a much easier task if Pa had been able to use a computer, but even with electronic assistance it would have been a big job. Pa was elected an honorary member of the Royal Geological and Mining Society in recognition of this work.

Initially Ma did not like living in Wassenaar. She always objected to change, no matter if it was for the better or not. I think my father correctly judged that the profile of the community in Voorburg was changing and becoming more and more urban and mixed. We had lived there through the depression and the war and life was easier now. When I grew up there, Voorburg was a true village, not a suburb. Wassenaar, on the other hand, has always been mostly a wealthy suburb. In Voorburg there were streets where families of executives like my father lived, but a block or two away would be working-class neighborhoods. We lived next door to a prominent doctor, Dr. Piek. He was a Catholic like most of the working-class population. The Piek family had six children, five daughters and at last followed by a son Fransje. I remember all their names: Elly, Tini, Mimi, Anneke, Loesje and finally Fransje. The houses were close together and in summer, when I stepped out of our kitchen and the windows were open, I could see the Piek family seated at the dinner table, not more than 40 ft. away. The sisters would tease Fransje by singing: *"Fransje Piek is verwend, kan zo vreselijk drenzen."* (Fr. P. is spoiled and can whine terribly). The street was wide with a tramway in the middle on a double track separated from the road by hedges. It was busy, there were more and more people and cars as prosperity improved and my parents wanted to have a more modern house in a more agreeable place with more trees. An added incentive was an ordinance inspired by the severe postwar housing shortage. This rule forced people with houses with extra rooms to take in lodgers. When I went to Leiden and afterwards in the military, the authorities decided Pa and Ma had too much room and a lady came to live with them. When you bought a newly built house, this rule did not apply. Wassenaar was the obvious choice. They had many friends there and as it turned out Ma made many new friends while staying close to her old bridge pals. Pa became much more "domesticated" than before. He did much of the shopping and took a hand in cooking, but he also had several groups of old Shell friends and a *borrel tafel* (group that meets regularly for cocktails), at his club, the *Witte Societeit*, a venerable institution in the heart of The Hague.

Life went on and after we moved away to America, our children would often spend a few weeks in summer with their grandparents, at de Steeg and at Wassenaar. When George and Adriaan came over, Pa and Ma were still quite young. They made a great effort to show the boys Holland, the cities, the countryside, museums, and special places like the *Delta Werken*, the huge system of dikes and locks the Dutch built after the disastrous storm of 1953, which killed about 1,600 people. The system is designed to prevent a reoccurrence of a calamity like that. When Richard and Janet were old enough to come over, their grandparents were well in their seventies and perhaps not such active guides as their brothers had enjoyed but they still saw a lot of the country. Pa and Ma visited us several times in Riverside, and I came often over on business trips while Netty sometimes came with me or stayed longer alone or with some of her children. In the eighties when my company Eberstad

PA AND MA CIRCA 1980.

Asset Management was taken over and liquidated, I had more time to come and gradually it became clear to Netty and me that we had to come at least twice a year to keep an eye on my parents and Netty's mother. Pa and Ma had made the fundamental mistake of staying much too long alone in their house and when old age really caught up with them, the situation became intolerable, but it was too late to make drastic changes.

My mother had a gregarious nature and liked her visits and bridge games with her friends and meetings with members of her church. However, she always was a little suspicious of strangers and had a gradually strengthening aversion from letting outsiders in her house. I guess she sensed that she could not handle her housekeeping chores anymore but resented giving up the reins and did not like outsiders to see how her household had deteriorated. At the same time, my father became more forgetful and had trouble driving his car. I noticed some nicks and dents and sometimes he parked his car with Ma in it while he went shopping and then forgot where he had left it. One day I found out that he had let his driver's license expire. I was happy to discover that, hoping he would fail the medical tests. However, he sailed through the tests without trouble, and we were forced to scramble around to get a new license for him. Also, I learned long after the fact, that he had once forgotten to pay his taxes and as a result a bunch of zealous revenue agents swooped down on the house to take possession of his assets. Pa's tax consultant smoothed it all over, but it was time for me to act. As most people with elderly parents know, it is very painful to force one's parents to give up their privacy and independence. Netty and I were fortunate to hear from our friend Kitty Witteveen that a group of women in Wassenaar had organized a service to help older neighbors by visiting them and attending to their needs such as shopping, etc. We contacted them and arranged for regular visits and in addition contracted for food deliveries by a sort of "meals on wheels" service that would deliver prepared meals. I also decided to remove the car. I gave it to a group of Leiden students. I prevailed on my father to have his bank manage his portfolio. He agreed, but said he feared they would not do a good job with his carefully and patiently built portfolio. Fortunately, the bank did quite well. The visiting women were no great success mainly because Ma dealt with them as if they were servants and had come to help clean the house. There was a housekeeper, but lack of supervision resulted in less and less actual cleaning. On a visit I noticed my parents were looking disheveled and undernourished, needed haircuts and were wearing clothes that needed repair. The house was not clean. So I had to force the issue. I arranged for live-in helpers through another group of women from Wassenaar who specialized in this sort of assistance for the elderly. I also was very fortunate in finding my good old friend Eelco Apol willing to supervise these helpers, pay them, and in general oversee my parents' day-to-day finances. It would take a few weeks to get the team ready, but I felt I could go home thinking I had found a reasonable solution. Unfortunately, that was not the case. My mother rebelled and convinced my father they really did not need these helpers. When the first lady arrived, they refused to let her in. When they called me with this message, I told them to break into the house, but they refused, fearing legal complications. So I had to fly back once again to straighten things out. It was the Fourth of July weekend here and I went back and forth in four days. My parents did not expect me when I returned, and in a painful discussion with them, I had to pretend I was very angry and upset, deeply disappointed and aggravated. Once I had let the first lady in and she cooked a nice meal and straightened out the house, everybody was happy. This arrangement lasted for quite a while. In the winter of 1987–88, Pa slipped in the bathroom at night and broke his femur. He was hospitalized and when he returned home, he could not climb the stairs anymore. We had to recruit nursing help and put Pa in the dining room downstairs. He continued to be in pain, however, and after a severe relapse was given some morphine to ease his pain. He never woke up and on March 10, 1988, he died at home. He was almost 95 years old. Pa was cremated in The Hague, and a surprisingly large number of people showed up for his funeral. As is customary in Holland, I delivered a eulogy, and our son George also spoke. In my eulogy I reviewed Pa's life and career because at his age many in the audience were unfamiliar with it, and I wanted to leave an impression of what kind of a man he was when he was still young and vigorous. I also repeated what he had said to Netty a month before his death, during his last stay in the hospital. He said, "You know, the only thing that is of importance in this world is *Life*, because that is the most beautiful thing there is." My cousin Tineke spoke, praising Pa for all the support he had given her and her family in the difficult years of her divorce. This was a particularly moving tribute. Tineke died herself of a massive heart attack less than a year later. Ma also attended the funeral, but seemed a little detached. No wonder, she was approaching her 90th birthday. Perhaps her growing deafness was also a contributing factor to her attitude.

After my father died, my mother would live for nearly nine more years. Since the battle about who was in charge in the house had been settled long ago, she mellowed and became a favorite patient of the women who took care of her. A routine settled in, with each of three women staying at the house for a week. In the beginning, Ma went downstairs every day to sit in the living room and enjoy the view. The doctor, Dr. van Niekerk, a wonderful man, became her favorite visitor. She had not always liked him. In the earlier part of the eighties, she would accuse him, behind his back, of being a "Communist." The reason was probably that the good doctor dressed casually like most Dutchmen do nowadays and when he came to the door she did not recognize him as her doctor and thought he was a stranger who came to spy on her. Gradually it became impossible to move Ma downstairs. It was just too dangerous as she was quite heavy. The routine was changed to sitting in a chair in her bedroom. Her eyesight got worse and her deafness reached a point where we could not find any hearing aid anymore that was any real help. Despite these handicaps Ma enjoyed life and when asked if she were not tired of getting so old, she would say, "I'd still like to live a little longer." It is amazing how strong the will to live is! Luckily, she remained of sound mind. So we could talk with her although, towards the end, it became very difficult to get a message or a thought across to her because of her deafness.

My father and I had frequently talked about his will. I was his sole heir and we had agreed that Ma would not inherit anything from him. So she was penniless and it was my obligation to finance her household. It was Pa's idea that the revenues from the sale of the house would be ample to take care of Ma. This was true, but Pa never thought about the eventuality that Ma would want to continue to live in the house. She had always proclaimed quite forcefully that she wanted to move into a place nearby where many of her elderly friends were living. A sort of "continuing care facility," but when the point was reached where she could apply for such a place, she was not acceptable because she was no longer able to fend for herself. So for nine years I had to finance Ma's upkeep. This was a burden, not a severe one, but from time to time I had a cash flow problem.

Ma died on January 12, 1997, just eight months before her hundredth birthday. We had received a phone call from the lady who was taking care of her that she had a touch of the flu and had trouble breathing. We said we would come over but could not get everything arranged on one day's notice, so we contacted Jetty and Kees Kraaijeveld, Tineke's eldest daughter and her husband. They are both physicians and they had gone to see Ma from time to time. Unfortunately, Jetty had just hurt herself while ice skating, but Kees came immediately and called us to say Ma had recognized him and may have found his visit comforting, but he advised us to come at once. We did, but as we left our house on the way to the airport we got a call saying Ma had died in her sleep. As fate would have it, it was a cold and nasty January day and when we reached Kennedy Airport our flight was delayed because of mechanical problems. We had to spend a night and part of the following day in an airport hotel, but I was able to reach Eelco Apol and he kindly helped out with the preliminary arrangements for Ma's funeral. Since there were hardly any contemporaries of Ma alive anymore, we decided to have a small funeral service preceding her cremation and to send the announcements out afterwards. We had just a few close family members and many of the people who took care of Ma present. I spoke, and so did Jetty Kraaijeveld, on behalf of her family and her deceased mother. A pastor of Ma's church said a few words and prayed with all of us and we played one or two of Ma's favorite psalms. George was there, but unfortunately he had a bad cold and could not speak. After Ma's funeral, we spent a hectic ten days cleaning out the house, disposing of all the furniture we did not want. We shipped what we wanted to keep to the U.S. and arranged for the sale of the house.

Back in 1988 we had asked the cremation center to save Pa's ashes until Ma's death, so we could scatter both together. Formalistic as always, Dutch rules did not allow the scattering of ashes anywhere else than in a designated wooded area of the cremation center. Just before we left to return home, on a gloomy dark January day, Netty and I went over there and performed the final tribute to my parents by scattering their ashes together in one place.

7 : *Netty's Parents*

I met Netty's parents Adrianus van Kleffens and Elise Johanna van Someren Greve in 1946. In the fall of that year when we were in our second year in Leiden, my friend Rob Laane and I went to the local theatre to see Ruth Draper, an American actress who traveled through Europe giving a "one woman" show. She was alone on stage and kept her audience spellbound for a whole evening while presenting a number of characters with no props whatsoever. I thought it was an outstanding performance. It probably was, but it could also be that we just did not know any better since we had been totally starved of anything cultural during the war and the first year or two immediately after it. During the intermission, Rob introduced me to a young high school girl he knew who was also in the audience and who turned out to be Netty's sister Tilly. Shortly after that evening, Rob received a note from Tilly inviting him for a party at her house in Wassenaar, adding "why don't you also bring your friend along, the fellow who was with you at the theatre." That invitation changed my life. We went to the van Kleffens' family house in Wassenaar at van Calcarlaan 27, where I met Netty and immediately fell for her although she was then still quite young. I was twenty-one and she was sixteen. Netty was a slender pretty girl with reddish brown hair and freckles. She exuded a certain soft but self-assured charm that captivated me then and still holds me in its spell. As was customary in those days, Rob and I introduced ourselves first to Netty's mother who was then a very attractive woman, about forty years of age. I do not know where her father was that evening, in any event I did not meet him. He was probably on a business trip. He traveled a great deal, mostly to Belgium and Luxembourg in those years. As I write this it is a staggering realization for me that Netty's mother, or Mammie as I called her ever since Netty and I were engaged to be married, was then younger than our daughter Janet, our youngest child, is now. After the introductions Netty's mother went upstairs, probably to sit in her husband's study and the party proceeded. As far as Rob and I were concerned, the party was not quite up to our standards. We felt older and much more sophisticated than the group that was present there, and as men in our second year at the *Studenten Corps*, we were rather full of ourselves. However, we were interested in meeting girls. Numerically there were relatively few female students in Leiden and those that were our age tended to favor going out with male students that were more senior to us. Almost all the other boys and girls at the party were members of a neighborhood group of kids who were all still in high school and good friends of Tilly and Netty and therefore we also felt a little out in left field. In those days immediately after the war, young people could not yet travel anywhere and had to find their entertainment nearby, often establishing great friendships in their immediate neighborhoods. Netty has fond memories of being part of this group they called *de Soos* (the word is an abbreviation of the word *Societeit* which means "club"). At the party they played some games and there was a little dancing and unavoidably there was a kissing game, the kind I abhorred and I later heard from

Netty that she did not like the game either. Tilly was in charge of the whole affair

VAN CALCARLAAN 27, THE HOUSE WHERE NETTY GREW UP.

and did some kissing of her own with Rob, on the side in the hallway, having pulled him away from the group. She was always much more sophisticated in that area than Netty.

At the time, I think Rob and I were vaguely aware of the tragedy that had occurred in Netty's family. On June 21, 1945, very shortly after the end of the war, Netty's youngest brother Eelke then just six years old, drowned in a small boat basin adjacent to their house in Warmond, a water sports and sailing resort town near Leiden. In the final year of the war, the Germans had selected the neighborhood in Wassenaar where the van Kleffens family lived as a good site to launch V-2 missiles aimed at London and

Antwerp. The local residents were ordered to leave. The missiles were launched from an open area nearly directly across from Netty's house and not more than 300 yards away from it. These V-2 missiles were the first ballistic missiles the world had seen. The family went to Warmond and spent the last winter of the war there in a house they could rent. It was near a lake and was really a summerhouse, not very well insulated and therefore cold during this last winter of the war, which was one of the coldest in Dutch-recorded history. The loss of Eelke affected Netty's family very much, of course, and I do not think her parents ever got really over it. But I have always thought it was remarkable how they were able to recover from this cruel blow and from other wartime adversities they had to cope with, resume a normal life, and even let their daughters give parties.

During the war Netty's family encountered several other serious problems. Around May 1942, Netty's father was arrested by the Germans and incarcerated as a "hostage."

THIS PICTURE WAS TAKEN FOR NETTY'S FATHER WHEN HE WAS IMPRISONED IN 1942. L TO R NETTY, MAMMIE, EELKE, PUL, TIL.

The Germans had employed this method ever since the early days of World War I when they marched into Belgium and had randomly imprisoned villagers, threatening to execute them whenever they suspected anybody in the region was sabotaging their military. In 1942 they repeated the procedure in the Netherlands. They locked up a large number of prominent and not so prominent Dutchmen from all walks of life in a camp. They were held there partly to keep them from causing trouble and partly to intimidate their families and friends, but above all to have a handy reservoir of people they could execute. When they felt Dutch Resistance activities warranted shooting a few people as a reprisal, they did so, giving wide publicity to their barbaric measures. Their objective was to terrorize the population and prevent more resistance. When I try to describe Netty's father, as I have known him, I will elaborate further on his wartime imprisonment, but it was immediately obvious that the Germans had a good reason to pick him up. He was after all the brother of the minister of foreign affairs in the Dutch government in exile.

Another trauma, which according to Netty took place on the same day her father was taken hostage, was the forceful removal from their house of *Juffie* (a Dutch diminutive meaning "Miss or Missie"). Rosetta Alberg, or *Juffie,* was a young woman who lived with the family as a mother's helper or nanny. She had followed the instructions issued to all Dutch Jews and registered. She was picked up at Netty's house by a Dutch policeman and sent to the Westerbork camp where all Dutch Jews ended up before being transported east. While at the Westerbork camp the Jews had no idea what awaited them. They thought they would have to go to work somewhere in Poland or the Ukraine, that conditions there would be harsh but probably survivable. In reality, this camp was just a staging area for the extermination camps in Germany and Poland that were going full tilt at that time. Netty and I once visited the site of the Westerbork camp and found that the Dutch government operated a small museum there. There also was a room where the records were kept of all the Jews who had passed through the camp. These records would tell you when they arrived and when they were transported east, where they went and what happened to each individual. Remarkably, the Germans kept meticulous records of the people they deported to be slaughtered in the camps and recorded their fate. A form of bureaucratic perfection that is hard to understand. Why they did this we will never know, but it puts the lie to "revisionists" who claim that the Holocaust was just a figment of the imagination of the Jews. We asked a young man who worked there to look for Juffie. He found her very quickly. She had only been in Westerbork for a few weeks and had been sent to Auschwitz in Poland, one of the largest extermination camps, where she was killed on arrival. There we were, sitting in that smallish room and looked at the shelves with rows and rows of books, each about two inches thick. As we took out some of the books, we saw that each line on each page was a person and there were many lines on each page. Once again, the enormity of the crimes committed by the Germans sank in. I say Germans and not Nazis or the Nazi regime, because it is in my opinion a well-established fact that a large majority of the German people were aware of what was happening with the Jews and did nothing. They condoned the persecution of the Jews, or even worse, applauded it. In years past, Mammie would sometimes discuss the fate of *Juffie* with us and say how awful she felt about not having been more resourceful in resisting her removal and about not having had an opportunity to find a hiding place for her. But it is difficult to see how she could have taken the risk of hiding *Juffie* or trusting others to do so. She had many problems to cope with during the war with four children and a husband who was imprisoned and in a very precarious position. When she was much older, Mammie was sometimes a little difficult to deal with, and there were perhaps things she could have done differently, but it is an undeniable fact that she did a fantastic, loving and heroic job in those terrible war years. She held her family together and the many energetic efforts she made to try to win freedom for her husband were extraordinary. She was only thirty-six years old on that day in 1942.

Netty's mother, Elise Johanna van Someren Gréve was born on October 22, 1905, in Surabaya, Indonesia, where her father ran a firm called Ruhaak & co. with his older brother. Ruhaak was a trading firm that imported all kinds of hardware, mainly machinery and household appliances into the country. After completing high school in Holland he had gone to Surabaya at age eighteen to join his brother. At age twenty-four he married Louise Mathilde van Heutsz, Netty's grandmother who was then twenty-two years old. I always felt we were fortunate in getting to know Netty's grand-

mother Gréve very well. We called her Omi, a name she had thought up herself to help prevent our children from getting confused about all the Omas in their extended family. She stayed at our house on Summit Road in Riverside and we were able

to visit her several times in Switzerland where she lived for many years. In Chapter Five I have related the main points of what we know about the family background of Netty's mother and the four children of Opa Gréve and Omi. Netty's mother was the oldest of a family of four. Most people called her Lies, Netty called her Mammie and so did I after I entered the family. So from here on I will call her Mammie. As related in Chapter Five, Mammie lived until age ten or eleven in Surabaya. An interesting photograph we have of that period shows her sitting with her two brothers and an Indonesian chauffeur in an old-fashioned automobile. You can see she is the older sister of the two boys, Wim and Errie. Liesje sits in the back, the two boys strike poses, Wim standing and Errie, sitting next to Amin, the driver. Throughout her life, Mammie had a warm relationship with Wim and a more complex one with Errie and she was always very close to her much younger sister Lous. The siblings quarreled after the death of Omi and the relationship between Mammie and her brothers (not Lous) never really returned to what it was. Netty often said that she felt that her father's stubbornness in sticking to a few minutiae in the settlement of Omi's estate aggravated the feud and made it last much longer than necessary. It was only fairly long after Pa's death that Mammie settled her differences with Wim and started seeing him again. Unfortunately, Erry had died by then. Even when he was dying and in very bad shape, suffering from throat cancer, Mammie would not reconcile with him and his wife Pia. Netty, who was close to Pia and Errie, tried to restore relations, but to no avail.

Life in Surabaya in the beginning of the twentieth century must have been good. Mammie's parents were devoted to each other and to their children. Omi was perhaps a little domineering and demanding as a mother and spouse. Netty thinks I see her as a gentler person than she really was because as she puts it: "She was always nice to you because she liked you." This is true and I liked her too. She had grown up in Indonesia in the same kind of world my own grandmother grew up in. Although she was much younger than my grandmother was, she knew many of the people in the fairly small and close-knit society of "people from the Indies" *(Indische mensen)* my grandmother had talked about. We liked talking about Surabaya and its surroundings, a part of the world I knew well after my army service of almost two years there.

Opa Gréve was a kind and gentle soul who was loved by all his children and their spouses and devoted to them as well as Omi. They had a vacation house in Trètes, a small resort up in the mountains in East Java, where it was cool. I visited Trètes twice when it was used for R & R by the Dutch army and could well imagine how nice it must have been in peacetime. It was a relatively small cluster of bungalows built on a steep slope around a sort of club building, which had a large swimming pool. Compared to the sweltering climate in Surabaya, Trètes was a cool heaven. It had a marvelous view of the plain below and of Modjokerto, a small town halfway down the road to Surabaya. The view was particularly attractive at night when the air was clear and you could see the many lights in the villages below, the *dessa's,* where the native population lived, using kerosene lamps, and torches for lighting and small charcoal fires for cooking. At night the villages, with their small houses made out of rattan and bamboo and surrounded by bamboo hedges and palm trees, with their flickering lights and the smoky fires had a romantic aura that is hard to forget. It was not far to get to Trètes from Surabaya and according to Omi they went there often.

In 1915, the second year of World War I, when Mammie was about eleven years old, Omi and her children went back to the Netherlands. This was the first time Mammie saw Europe. They went on an ocean liner the *Jan Pieterszoon Coen.* The war made travel by ship difficult because of the threat of German U-boats and the British blockade of the continent. In Chapter Five, I described how they went around South Africa and ended up waiting for five days in a Scottish harbor before being cleared for departure to Holland. They settled for two years in Hilversum where Mammie completed grade school. Late in the war, her father joined them. He had come by way of the U.S., according to Mammie. They moved to The Hague where they lived in a large house in a very upscale neighborhood called Sorgvliet. When the war was over, Omi and Opa Gréve returned to Surabaya and the children were left in Holland under the care of an aunt, Tante Jo Braat, a woman Mammie did not like very much. Jo Braat did not allow them much freedom and was assisted in her efforts to control the children by an unmarried daughter who according to Mammie was sour and "disillusioned" in life. Curiously, nobody seems to know where Mammie went to high school and what kind of education she had. She was smart enough. She did speak English, French and German quite well and was generally well informed about the world around her. But she did not attend a university. In those days, it was considered unnecessary for girls to go to a university, a point of view that was still quite prevalent when I grew up. Girls were supposed to become ladies and housewives and learn the skills required for running a household and a family. My own mother was a great exception to that general rule. In those days Mammie often visited friends and relatives (other than Mrs. Braat), especially her aunt Bé (nee Belia Adriana van Someren Gréve) Engelberts, a sister of her father. Tante Bé was sibling number eight in her family and Opa Gréve was number nine. She lived in Arnhem and one winter when Mammie was sixteen she was visiting there and Bé's daughter

Emy, organized a sledding party. An automobile owned by the father of one of the friends of young Bé was used to pull the sleds. As it turned out, this car belonged to Opa van Kleffens, the father of Eelco and Adriaan. At the sledding party Mammie met her future husband Adriaan for the first time who at that occasion spoke the famous words, *"wie is dat sproeten kind?"* ("Who is that freckle faced kid?") Adriaan was five years older than Lies and a student in Leiden. This scene has great similarities with the first meeting between Netty and me. We also are five years apart. Netty was also sixteen, I was also a student, and Netty also had freckles! A few years later Lies and Adriaan met again, this time at the wedding of Emy who married Jan Strootman. As they got to know each other better and were engaged, Mammie met her future sister-in-law, Nini, after whom Netty is named, and her fiancé's older brother Eelco. In the spring of 1919 Nini had married George Suermondt, a gifted amateur painter who made the painting that we now have. It shows Nini as she apparently was–a little shy, introverted and a little sad. George died young, so young that Mammie never met him. A few years after the death of George, Nini met and married Dick (Dirk Christiaan Marie) Hetterschij, an officer in the Royal Dutch Navy. When Nini was about to give birth to her first child, the birth had to be induced and something went wrong. Nini died at age thirty-four, just before Netty was born. Nini became Netty's third name, after the names of her father's mother, Jeannette Fresine. Hetterschij later became quite famous in Holland as captain of a submarine that made a trip around the world, ending up in Indonesia. The voyage of this submarine, the K-XVIII, was described in a book I read with great interest as a boy. The Netherlands Maritime Museum in Amsterdam has a model of the submarine and several interesting photographs showing Dick Hetterschij and his crew.

When Mammie met Oom Eelco, he was still single and working on his career in the Ministry of Foreign Affairs. He became an internationally very-well-known diplomat and served during the war as minister of foreign affairs in the Dutch government in exile.

Mammie also met her future father in law, of course. She describes him as a short man who was the youngest and shortest in a large family. As all his brothers were older and taller than he was, he developed an aggressive demeanor that served him well in his career as prosecutor. People in Arnhem called him "the terrier" she said. She did not like him and he treated her not very well. When I mentioned to Mammie that Oom Eelco wrote very lovingly about his father, she said the relationship between those two was very different from the relationship Nini and her brother Adriaan had with their father. Eelco was five years older than his brother and went his own way and did not let himself be influenced or intimidated by his father. Still, Netty's father, whom I called Pa adored his father and they had a good relationship. He was much more controlled by the old gentleman than his brother, partly because he was younger and partly because he was probably less self-assured. A famous incident was the naming of Pul, Netty's brother. Pul was the first grandson of Opa van Kleffens, and Opa decided that there was no question about the names he should be given. They were going to be his names: Henricus Cato. I have described this situation in greater detail in Chapter Five.

Netty's parents were married on September 22, 1927, in The Hague. The picture shows the bridal pair with Oom Wim as groomsman and Lous as the young bridesmaid next to Mammie. Following Dutch custom, the bridal party sat down for an elaborate dinner after the wedding ceremony and the reception. The menu for this dinner was an abbreviated version of the meal served at the wedding of Mammie's parents. When Netty and I were married, we enjoyed a dinner that was a further abbreviated version of the same menu. As far as I can recall we had quite a meal at our wedding and one can only marvel at the ability people in the old days had to consume large quantities of food.

The young couple settled down in Amsterdam, living in a rented apartment on the Reinier Vinklers Kade. After completing his studies in Leiden and earning his law degree, Netty's father had found a position with one of the big Dutch shipping companies, the KNSM *(Koninklijke Nederlandse Stoomvaart Maatschappij)*. This company focused on trade with South and Central America. Pa was in the legal department there and headed up a section that handled "disputes." In due course Tilly was born in 1928 and Netty in 1930. Fairly soon after Netty's birth the family moved to Baarn, a nice village in the country and Pa started to commute from there to Amsterdam. Six months later Netty's father was offered a job with the Dutch government. Among Oom Eelco's papers was a copy of a dissertation written by two women who earned a doctoral degree in 1989. This dissertation is a biographical sketch of Oom Eelco's life and career. It mentions that Oom Eelco wrote letters to a Dr. Gerretson who later became an enemy of his. In these letters he asks Dr. Gerretson help in finding a job for his brother. However, the year the letter was written does not jibe with Pa's move. So I do not know whether this was an ordinary career move or prompted by the worldwide economic depression that by then had a severe impact on all national economies and hit the Dutch shipping business particularly hard. Pa joined the Department of Economic Affairs in The Hague, where he worked until 1953 when he became a judge in the Court of the European Coal and Steel Community in Luxembourg. Initially Pa worked in the Bureau for Foreign Economic Relationships (*Bureau voor Buitenlandse Economische Betrekkingen* or BEB). He worked there for two people who later on played significant roles in the Dutch government during and after the war. One was Lamping who became minister of economic affairs in one of the postwar cabinets. The other one was Hirschfeld, a man who was during the war the top man in Economic Affairs and responsible for whatever the Germans left for the Dutch to eat, produce and manufacture. Accordingly, his role was controversial because he had to deal with the Germans and obey their decrees which became more and more draconian as the war progressed and the situation of the Germans worsened. After the war, he was in an awkward position because he had been in frequent and close contact with the Germans and collaborated with them, of course. But he was able to prove that he had acted in the best interest of the population and was not blamed for his wartime work. He was a prime example of a civil servant who stayed on in his post and kept the economy or what was left of it going, thus enabling the majority of the population to lead a fairly normal life. He did not resist openly and directly, but he did manage to negotiate many situations in a manner that was favorable for the population. His position was even more curious because he was born in Holland of German/Russian Jewish parents. He was actually three-quarters Jewish! Yet, before the war he had frequently participated in top-level trade negotiations with the Germans and had even received a high decoration from the Nazi government. The series of books I have about The Netherlands during the war describes him as a man who felt he was a Dutchman who just happened to be of Jewish descent, a peculiarity that was of no importance. Many Dutch Jews (including my grandmother) were secular and saw themselves that way, and the agitation by the Nazis against them came as a great shock to them and also to the non-Jewish part of the population. After the Germans imprisoned Pa, Mammie was frequently in touch with Mr. Hirschfeld. She told us he had helped her as much as he could. It was Hirschfeld who told Mammie that he had seen a list with 55 names the Germans had of people who were taken as hostages in the first group. This group included Pa. They were selected for execution because they were seen as being in one way or another closely connected to the court of Queen Wilhelmina or her government in exile. Ultimately, they executed "only" five. Mr. Hirschfeld told Mammie he had not been able to see the names on the longer list, but was certain Pa was among them.

After the war the department where Pa worked was responsible for most of the negotiations with Belgium and Luxembourg that led to the formation of the Benelux, the economic union established between the three nations by a treaty signed in 1948. The Benelux was the forerunner of the European Coal and Steel Community, which was in its turn succeeded by the European Union, now an increasingly important political entity in the world. So Netty's father stood at the cradle of what was often called the European Common Market and subsequently the European Union and played an important role in its formation. Many of the key players in the negotiations on the Dutch side were good friends and close associates of Pa. While many of them benefited from the many new opportunities open to civil servants, moving into lucrative jobs in the new institutions that grew rapidly in power and importance, Pa preferred to stay where he was. Mammie was more ambitious and wanted him to move forward with the others. Pa was a true gentleman, not pushy and loath of self-promotion. In the end, he was appointed to a very significant position in the emerging new Europe that fitted his personality perfectly. He became a judge in the High Court of the Coal and Steel Community. Each member nation of the community had a seat on the court, and Pa represented the Netherlands. This court is now the High Court of the European Union and as such has a position somewhat similar in importance to the U.S. Supreme Court. It can rule on supranational cases that affect all of Western Europe and thus have an impact on the laws that govern the Union. Currently the court has 27 judges, one

NETTY'S FAMILY IN 1949. ONE OF A SERIES OF PICTURES SENT TO ME IN INDONESIA. L TO R. PUL, MAMMIE, TIL, PA, NETTY.

for each member state of the Union. It meets in chambers of three, five or thirteen members. It was in those days in the late forties and early fifties that I became a member of Netty's family and became more familiar with her parents.

Adrianus van Kleffens was born in Heerenveen on October 14, 1899, just before the end of the nineteenth century. Throughout his life, he was always proud to be a man of the nineteenth century and he was clearly most comfortable with the life-styles of that period. He liked to talk about the past and was reluctant to look for-ward. He seemed most comfortable when he could relate stories of his life as a boy to his own children. In this respect and in many other ways he was a complete opposite to his wife. The contrast between Netty's parents as personalities was equally vivid as the difference between my own parents. Netty and I often reflected on that, and we both thought that my father would have been a good match for Netty's mother while my mother would have found a Frisian soul mate with a law degree and an equally conservative thinker in Netty's father. Mammie liked to dress well and be part of the social scene in The Hague. Pa preferred to stay home. He dressed con-servatively in a somewhat rumpled style and whenever he could, deliberately behaved as a throwback to the previous century. Neither Mammie nor Pa had any interest in sports or exercise in general. That they had in common. However, when Netty and Tilly were young, Pa frequently went on long walks with them in the dunes or took them on bicycle expeditions. Netty told me that Pa was very good at reading to his children before bedtime. He would get totally involved in the story and imitate the voices of the characters in the book, often scaring the girls with loud voices or unexpected noises. They loved it, of course. They took bicycle trips, including one through Friesland, sleeping in small hotels. Netty said they cycled so much that the girls had sore buttocks. Pa cured that by rubbing butter on their behinds. His liking for children's books continued throughout his life and even when his daughters were adults and he lived in De Steeg in retirement, he continued to read the books he had read many times before to his children. What kind of an escape mechanism that was for him I do not know, but we sometimes worried about it.

I do not think I ever saw Mammie riding a bicycle, a very common and natural thing to do for people in Holland and I never saw either one of my in-laws swimming or even donning bathing suits either. Their lack of physical exercise caused them to age early and develop all kinds of physical problems, I believe. Pa was quite tall, much taller than his brother Eelco. He was broad shouldered and had

thick, powerful arms and wrists. Our son Richard has inherited his powerful build but luckily makes better use of his physique than his grandfather did. Pa served in the Dutch army and became an officer in the cavalry, but he was drafted shortly after World War I. Since the world was rapidly disarming in those days, he did not serve very long. One of his idiosyncrasies was that he claimed he could not deal with being treated by a dentist. As a result, he never saw a dentist for years and when I met him for the first time I noticed he had blackened rotten teeth which he tended to shield by smiling with a tight mouth. At dinner he would cut his food into very small pieces so he would not have to chew very much. His aversion to dentists was ascribed to an early childhood experience when he was tied down in a dentist's chair

ADRIANUS VAN KLEFFENS IN THE SIXTIES WHEN HE WAS A JUDGE IN LUXEMBOURG.

and totally traumatized. He was blessed by the circumstance that he never had a toothache – at least that is what he claimed. Several other behavioral traits may stem from a difficult childhood. He lost his mother early, when he was five years old. Two years later, in 1908, he got a stepmother, Sabina Johanna Janke Ilpsema Vinckers, his mother's niece, who had taken care of him since the death of his mother and married his father. He called her "Ma Bien," knew her well and loved her, but he lost her also. She died in 1911 when he was twelve years old. After that he was shuttled from one family to another, mostly in The Hague where he went to the *Gymnasium* and became friends with Piet Feith (Jhr. Mr. P. R. Feith). Piet became his best friend and the Feith family opened their house to him and became sort of a second family for him. When Pa went to Leiden, his brother was still there but several years ahead of him. Pa joined a *jaarclub* (a group of friends who form a club within their year). Mr. Feith was also a member of this club and so were many others who stayed close friends throughout their life. Many of them lived in or near The Hague and Netty, and later I, have known them very well. Like my father, Mr. Feith was an executive of the Royal Dutch Shell Company. He was head of the legal department. In the U.S. he would be called chief counsel. At Pa's funeral all his club members were present, and Mr. Feith spoke on their behalf. He was so overcome by the death of his best friend that he could hardly speak. We were all touched by what he said.

During his life Pa received a number of decorations the names of which are hard to translate. *Commandeur in de orde van Oranje Nassau, Ridder in de orde van de Nederlandse Leeuw, Grootofficier in de orde ven de Eikenkroon van Luxemburg, Commandeur in de Kroonorde van België* and several other foreign decorations.

When I first met him, Pa was a vigorous man who enjoyed his job despite the hurdles he had encountered on his career path. After the war he had to endure being passed over for higher functions by people who earlier had reported to him but were now politically active. It was the postwar period and waves of left-wing policies were implemented in the Netherlands.

These new policies carried a different sort of civil servant in their wake, and the more patrician types who had been in charge were left behind. A high point in his life was the period when he became a judge in Luxembourg

. As a family we jointly almost forced him to go see a dentist before he went to this new post. I knew of one in Arnhem who was a friend of my aunt Jet, my mother's sister. My mother had him fit her with dentures, and she convinced Pa that this dentist was extraordinarily gentle and a good practitioner. We had told the poor dentist about Pa's hang-ups and my aunt said he almost did not sleep the night before he started working on Pa. He was successful, removed all the old teeth and fitted Pa with dentures that made him a changed man with a new smile. We just wondered why it had to take so long. In Luxembourg both Mammie and Pa blossomed. They found a beautiful large apartment, had an active social life and forged several new and very close friendships with other judges and their families and staff people. Mammie enjoyed the social whirl, particularly the receptions at the palace of the Grand Duchess, who was at that time the sovereign of this little operetta-like principality. Mammie told us these years in Luxembourg where the best years of her life. They had a more than comfortable income that was tax exempt, a chauffeur-driven car with diplomatic plates and many other perquisites. Netty's parents had kept the house in Wassenaar, perhaps realizing they needed a fall-back position in case the Luxembourg period was ending. They did not own the house in Wassenaar. They had rented it ever since they first lived there. Netty never quite understood why they did not buy it after the war when Pa could afford it. It was perhaps his conservative way of managing his affairs. While in Wassenaar one New Year's Eve, Pa became violently ill. He had had previous bouts with serious intestinal disorders, but his elderly local doctor had let things slide. I decided something had to be done, called the doctor, wished him a happy New Year and told him he really should see my father-in-law at once since he seemed most uncomfortable. He came, and decided to have Pa hospitalized immediately. As it turned out Pa had to be operated on. A piece of his small intestine was removed. Much later Mammie learned that it was cancerous, but she never told Pa since she knew he would have been devastated with this knowledge. Pa recovered quite well and returned to Luxembourg. Unfortunately, Pa's appointment was a political one and he did not have sufficient political backing. After about eight years Pa was forced out by a political maneuver in The Hague. Another Dutch judge who had strong affiliations to one of the large political parties replaced him. Pa did not have any political connections and was defenseless against this type of intrigue. I think it broke his heart and made Mammie very bitter. They retreated to De Steeg where they had bought a house they liked very much and after a period of considerable stress they adjusted to the change and lived there quite happily. He enjoyed serving occasionally as substitute judge in the Arnhem court of justice, but it was clear to us that Pa's spirit was broken and that he was gradually losing interest in most aspects of life. His health was not good. Both Mammie and he had problems with arthritic hips. They walked with increasing difficulty and slowed down considerably, paying the price for years of physical neglect.

Pa was not only physically lazy; he also harmed his physical condition by smoking quite heavily and by happily indulging in his daily *borrel,* a Dutch ritual he never passed up. I spent many wonderful happy hours with him drinking *jenever* out of glasses, the *tonnetjes,* round barrel-shaped glasses we still have at our home. These glasses were quite a bit larger than the ones I was used to and I had to watch myself because it was dangerous for me to try to keep up with my father-in-law who could hold his liquor very well. I do not want to leave the impression that Pa was an alcoholic. He most definitely was not. He just seemed to ignore all health warnings and merrily went on with a lifestyle that brought him to an early death at age seventy-three.

As I got to know my in-laws better, I grew very fond of Pa. I guess he liked me too because we got along as old friends while others often had more trouble in their relationship with him. After I became somewhat knowledgeable in financial affairs, working at Jonas & Kruseman where he was a client, he often discussed his investment portfolio with me and we jointly made investment decisions. Yet he could be very standoffish with people he did not care about. He was an extremely intelligent and very friendly man with a highly developed sense of humor and excellent judgement about people who was very good company for me. We spent many pleasant hours together, talking about all sorts of things, particularly matters concerning my own (beginning) career. After all, he was instrumental in getting me my first job with his old friend Kees Schimmelpenninck van der Oye. He understood the situation I was in there and had a better feel for it than my own father, so I always felt I could talk freely with him about my business life and my plans to emigrate to the U.S. and why. But we never talked very much about his experiences as a hostage *(gijzelaar)* during the German occupation. Like many people who had bad war experiences, he preferred to put it behind him and go on with his life. Still I think this experience created a very difficult watershed in his life. He was detained in a sort of "deluxe" concentration camp with a large number of other prominent Dutchmen. The camp was not like the concentration camps we have heard about. The hostages were treated reasonably well. They were not put in striped prison clothes, their heads were not shaved, they could receive mail. They were allowed to organize all sorts of theater groups, discussion circles, etc. The only thing was that once in a while the guards would come in the middle of the night to take a number of them away to be executed. Nobody was ever told beforehand what would happen and who would be selected. We all believe Pa came very close to being shot with the first group of five. As Oom Eelco related after the war, a member of the German Foreign Service, a Mr.

Behne who was stationed in The Hague, felt this would give too much recognition to the importance of Oom Eelco. Behne managed to convince his bosses in Berlin to get Pa's execution called off and to put a sort of "hold" on him. So in a rather strange way he was victimized and at the same time protected by the position of his brother. The hostages were kept in what was formerly a large Roman Catholic Seminary. The seminary was called Beekvliet and was located in Haren, a small town near 's Hertogenbosch. We have a book, titled *Beekvliet,* commemorating that period in Pa's life and the lives of his fellow prisoners. They were put in large dormitories, initially with a large number of hostages. In the beginning the Germans overreacted, taking in many more people than they "needed" for their draconian scheme. My uncle Otto Jonas, husband of my mother's sister Jet, was among the first (larger) group. Later on Otto was released together with many others. But Netty's father stayed there for a much longer period. Netty believes the pressures of his confinement put a lasting stamp on his personality that was already somewhat fragile. Earlier in his life he had shown signs of depression and of panic attacks. No wonder he was affected. Just imagine lying in bed and trying to sleep and hearing the Germans come down the hall, noisily stomping along with their hobnailed boots on the stone floor to fetch a new batch of hostages to be shot at dawn. This happened several times.

MAMMIE IN THE LATE SEVENTIES.

Meanwhile, immediately after her husband was taken away, Mammie started her efforts to get her husband released. Pa was taken into custody on a Friday and Mammie called his boss Hirschfeld on Saturday. He suggested she come to see him the next Monday, "because he might know more by then." That Monday he said he did not know more and suggested "she should count on him being kept there until the end of the war." Another suggestion came from Mr. Rueb, an old friend of Netty's parents, which led to an interesting anecdote. Mr.

Rueb knew a German officer, a Baron Von Oldershausen. Mammie knew this man, too, because he had lived in The Hague before the war and had been on the verge of becoming a Dutch citizen. Mammie had danced with him at a party. When approached, Von Oldershausen immediately offered help. He said he would go to Haren and get Pa out and since Pa had been an officer, make him a "prisoner of war." Mammie said that might get him in further trouble, as he would be shipped out to Germany and who would know what would happen with him there? Oldershausen once came unexpectedly to see Mammie at her house. He called her later to say her children looked at him as if he were a "rabid dog." Mammie said the children were frightened by his uniform and would not know the difference between him and some Nazi SS man. She added that she could really not receive him at home in his uniform. Netty remembers this episode. So the German came back wearing a sort of floor-length camel hair coat. Once inside, Mammie asked if he would not like to take his coat off. He said he couldn't because he was wearing his uniform under it! His message was not good, however. He said he could not do anything. Still, Pa came home quite soon after that. When I asked Mammie why she thought Pa was freed, she said she had an inkling. Von Oldershausen had asked Mammie if she had any connections in Germany. She said she had none, except for her sister-in-law, Wim's wife Tante Soph. Soph had lived in Germany for a few years and knew many Germans, including a man who became the secretary of Hitler. Von Oldershausen encouraged Soph to write and she did. She wrote *Lieber Walther* a long letter explaining how awful it was that her brother-in-law was taken prisoner etc. Soph never heard a word back, but it may have worked. A few months later, Pa was free. Other attempts were made with the help of Mr. Spierenburg, who worked for Pa at that time and became a high official in the European Economic Community (EEC) after the war. Spierenburg's wife was Yugoslavian but had grown up in Italy. She also offered to compose letters for Mammie to copy and mail out to influential Italians she knew. Mammie balked at first, believing the letters to be so melodramatic and bombastic that she did not want to send them. However, Spierenburg prevailed saying his wife knew how to handle these functionaries. Nothing was ever heard from that side either.

In my taped interview, I asked Mammie if there had also been a connection through Turkey, a country that was neutral during the war where there was a good deal of international intrigue. I thought I had heard either from her or from Pa or Oom Eelco that there were channels to Berlin from there. I had heard Oom Eelco had tried to use these channels to get in touch with his brother's captors. As Oom

Eelco writes in his memoirs, he heard that his father had died in Holland on the very day he was in Washington, D.C., with Queen Wilhelmina preparing for her address to Congress. Opa van Kleffens died on July 31, 1942. Queen Wilhelmina spoke on August 6 1942. So it took only a week for him to get the news! This is remarkable for those days. There were definitely sources through which he could get some signals. Mammie said she knew of a story concerning Turkey; it was interesting, but it was not the one I was looking for. Mammie told me that during the war, the minister of the Netherlands in Turkey (there were no ambassadors in those days), one very early morning saw Von Papen the Nazi German ambassador in Turkey and earlier German minister of foreign affairs, walk back and forth. After a while the gardener arrived to work and was given a note by Von Papen. The note was entitled, *"Beim Anfang des Unterganges Deutschlands"* (at the beginning of the destruction of Germany.) Presumably suggesting he knew the tide had turned and the Germans were losing. The Dutch minister saved this note and Mammie claimed it saved Von Papen's life when he was tried for war crimes with the rest of Hitler's gang in Nuremberg. I am not sure this story is totally correct. Why would Von Papen, one of the German top leaders, wander around in Ankara and why would he risk sending written notes? Also, Mammie claimed the Dutch minister in Turkey during the war was Baron van Harinxma. I have not been able to confirm this either. After the war an American officer came to see Netty's father to get a background check on Von Oldershausen. Pa was happy to confirm that he had been helpful to many Dutch people and that the U.S. Army's plans to expropriate his assets were unfounded. Apparently it helped and Von Oldershausen was cleared of Nazi sympathies.

As a parent, Pa was much stricter with his daughters Tilly and Netty when he was younger than later with his son. For instance, Pul and he went regularly to the movies while Til and Netty had been forbidden to go even to Shirley Temple movies when they were the same age. When George and Adriaan were born he exercised his grandparental rights with gusto and spoiled them rotten. After we emigrated to America Pa and Mammie visited us twice. The first time they came by ship. It was summer and we made a tour through New England, Bear Mountain Park etc. The second time Pa came by ship and Mammie by plane. Pa claimed he could not stand traveling in a plane because he was claustrophobic and would panic in a confined space. It was fall and Pa's trip on the *Nieuw Amsterdam* was a very rough one. I picked him up at dockside in New York and noticed that several windows of the promenade deck, quite high up on the ship, were bashed in and boarded up with plywood. Despite these visible signs of heavy storm damage Pa claimed he had a wonderful trip, but still, he switched his ticket to a plane ride back! During this second visit we had the pleasure of having them with us as our guests for a dance of the Riverside Dance Group, an organization of people who enjoyed ballroom dancing and got together a couple of times each winter. We enjoyed these black-tie affairs very much. For many years, Netty was the big organizer and driving force behind this group. It was fun to have her parents present on such an evening.

The last time we saw Pa was in 1973 in Les Diablerets in Switzerland. Netty and I had rented a chalet there. We spent a month in this wonderful place. The chalet was quite big, and we had all our children and George's then girlfriend Maggie, plus Adriaan and his friend Peter McGee there at various times. Our four parents were all in the hotel nearby, a perfect arrangement because we all could do our own thing and still get together for dinners, etc. We visited Tilly and her first husband, Frans Terwisscha, and their children elsewhere in Switzerland. We also spent an afternoon with my niece Tineke Kort, and her children who were also staying in Switzerland, and we visited with my father's lifelong friend Tell Bersot and his wife and made numerous long hikes through the mountains. We had some memorable evenings with our parents in the hotel. One day Adriaan and Peter had just shown up from their train trip through Europe. That evening we all came to the hotel for dinner and Adriaan told us the story of his adventures. Adriaan can do that quite well and his grandfather van Kleffens was enjoying his

LES DIABLERETS SUMMER 1973. RICH PERFORMS A MAGIC TRICK FOR HIS GRANDFATHER WHO WOULD DIE A FEW WEEKS LATER.

stories tremendously. The boys had traveled to Germany to see such cultural highlights as the Porsche automobile factory and the Nuremberg racecar track. In France, they had stopped in a place where they immediately rolled into the bar across from the station, and asked the guys hanging out there whether there was anything to see in their town. The answer was *rien* (nothing). So they spent the evening enjoying a couple of drinks and watching the tricks the dog of one of the bar patrons could do, including being pulled up by his ears by his master without being hurt. They spent the night in a small hotel there and left the next day by train. The town was Amiens. It has one of the famous cathedrals in France, of course. Netty said she never saw her father laugh as much as that evening. Another memorable evening was when Richard showed his magic tricks, much to the enjoyment of his four grandparents. Richard was then eleven years old and a fervent magician. He always traveled with his tricks and could give quite a performance.

When our vacation was over we all went to the Geneva airport. We saw Pa walk slowly and painfully to his departure gate with his cane. Netty ran up to him to say good-bye and a few days later when we were just home we got a phone call from Pul telling us that Pa had died from a massive aneurysm. This completely unexpected news was a tremendous shock for all of us, but especially for Netty, who loved her father very much. Netty and I went immediately back to Europe for his funeral. George and Adriaan were still there so they could come too. It was a sad ceremony with a large number of people in attendance, including many people from his Luxembourg years who had not forgotten him. There also were many simple folk from the village whom he had befriended or had helped with legal and other problems. As I mentioned before, his old friend Piet Feith gave a moving speech, but was so overcome that he could not finish.

Mammie was holding up well after the loss of her husband of 47 years. At the funeral she had seemed a bit detached, as if she could not quite grasp what was happening to her, but later on she managed well and started to live and enjoy her own life after having catered to her husband and family for so long. Initially Mammie continued to live in De Steeg, but it became soon clear that she could not stay there. The house was much too big for her and she was somewhat isolated because she had not yet started to drive again. She had

increasing problems with her arthritic hip joints and walking became painful.

Pul decided that it would be advantageous for her to move back to the "west" of Holland. She did not like that idea because she had always felt much happier in the more rural "east." Yet it was the most practical solution for several reasons. A new apartment building complex was going up in Wassenaar. It was what was then called a "service flat." Meaning one could buy an apartment there and enjoy meal services from the large kitchen in the building and general janitorial help from the employees who were available. Pul and his (then) wife Evelien lived nearby with their two small children and Tilly and Frans also had built a nice modern house close by in Wassenaar. So the house in de Steeg where all the grandchildren had stayed for many memorable summers was put on the market and Mammie moved to Wassenaar in 1976.

The transition to living alone and in an apartment was not easy, but gradually Mammie regained her old self. She even re-activated her driver's license, which she had obtained decades ago and never was able to use as Pa felt she was not a good driver, and simply would not let her try. Actually, he himself was a somewhat questionable driver. He believed the center stripe on the two-lane country roads near de Steeg were meant to keep a car centered and used to swerve to the right only when a car from the opposite direction approached. DAF, a Dutch factory, had just produced a strange little car that had a "variomatic" gearshift. To go wherever you wanted to go, you only had to shift into forward or reverse, like an American automatic shift. This was exactly what Mammie needed and she took to the roads, gaining a measure of freedom she had not had for decades.

After a few years she also started to see an old friend, Willem Count van Regteren Limpurg, who was a friend from Leiden student days of both Pa and Oom Eelco. As is customary in Holland, we called him Mr. van Regteren because one addresses a member of the nobility not by their title but as "Mr." or "Mrs." One is expected to know the titles of the person addressed but not use them. Mr. van Regteren had lost his wife in an automobile accident that also had damaged his legs and impeded his ability to walk. Despite these handicaps he was full of vim and vigor and keen on making trips abroad by car, mostly to Switzerland where he had an apartment in Gstaad. Mammie and he seemed to have much in common and after a while Mammie moved in with him at Almelo Castle, the count's ancestral home. Mammie was careful, however, not to be at Almelo all the time; she wanted to keep her independence. As the years progressed, Mr. van Regteren and Mammie both developed more mobility problems. Mammie suffered greatly from rheumatism in her hip joints and had received hip replacements on both sides. Unfortunately one of these operations had to be redone after a few years because the metal hip joint became loose. She also aggravated her condition by supporting Mr. van Regteren, who always leaned heavily on her arm. Since the castle had many stairs, which made moving around difficult for both of them, it was decided to convert the Orangerie into a place where they both could live on the ground floor. In a long overdue move, Mr. van Regteren's only son Dolph and his family moved into the castle. For several years Mammie and Mr. van Regteren lived quite contentedly in the Orangerie, attended to by two live-in nurses. Mr. van Regteren died on February 21, 1992, and Mammie moved back to her apartment in Wassenaar. Netty and I had often stayed at her apartment while in Holland to take care of her and my parents. Soon we had to find other places to stay, as Mammie needed live-in helpers. She could only move around in a wheelchair. Pul recruited helpers from the same organization that had been so useful for my parents. After some false starts, Pul found Lena and Meta, two sturdy sisters who were not much younger than Mammie but showed a remarkable stamina in caring for her, alternating from week to week. Lena and Meta were rural types of the old prewar school and sometimes a little hard to take for Mammie's children and grandchildren, but they gave Mammie a great deal of loving care. Gradually Mammie began to lose interest in life, and in her final years, she just sat in her chair which we called "the throne" or the "command center" *(de commando post.)* Mammie enjoyed visits by her children, grandchildren and great grandchildren, but it was clear to us that she was just waiting for the end. She died in 1997, on October 17, just a few days before her ninety-second birthday. Unfortunately, she had to experience the tragic death of cancer of Tilly shortly before her own. When Til's husband Menny and her children saw her end coming, they gathered in hotel *Huis ter Duin* in Noordwijk for a final family reunion. Netty also attended for a few days and

arranged for a visit of Mammie to her daughter. Mammie was transported to the hotel in her wheelchair and she spent some time alone with Tilly. This was a heart-wrenching visit, of course, but Netty felt it was a peaceful and beneficial meeting for both. Mammie's funeral was the third such ceremony Netty and I had to attend that year. It was a simple solemn ceremony in the same crematorium where we had been several times before. Netty had selected the music, Pul spoke and so did George as the oldest grandchild.

8 : *The Early Years*

I was born on Wednesday February 18, 1925, in the house of my grandparents Schieferdecker in Bloemendaal. My mother had been staying there to await my arrival. My father had left for Venezuela before I was born, and the plan was that my mother and I would join him as soon as possible.

When I celebrated my seventieth birthday in 1995, I got a very thoughtful gift from our son George. He gave me an original copy of *The New York Times* of February 18th, 1925. Its paper is very brittle and badly yellowed, but it contains a wealth of interesting information. In those days the paper cost two cents in Greater New York. It states that on March 4, President Coolidge was expected to establish a new record in the brevity of

MOLLAAN 5, THE HOUSE WHERE I WAS BORN.

his inaugural address. Silent Cal evidently was expected to act true to form. The New York City district attorney was expected to take steps toward prosecution of theatrical managers of thirteen plays "which citizens had declared offended their sense of decency." He was going to give a jury a look at the allegedly indecent plays "in camera." A five-passenger Studebaker sedan could be bought for $1,125. The day before I was born, the Dow Jones Stock Average had closed at 107.39. General Billy Mitchell testified before Congress that American air defenses were weak. The airship America was going to carry 200 pounds of mail to Bermuda. It is sobering to see how much the world has changed since then and it is for me a somewhat melancholy experience to see my own life slipping into the folds of history.

My birth and the events surrounding it were recorded by my mother in a book called *Baby's Boek* (Baby's book) a sort of photo album with room for written text and photos and several large colorful illustrations by a well-known Dutch artist, Rie Cramer. My mother made a good start with text and photos, but after a year or so, her desire to write disappears and only photos are left.

We acquired the exact same books for our own children and like all parents we did the first one for our son George quite elaborately with text and photographs. The one for Adriaan is a little less elaborate and from there it's downhill to the sketchy records we have for Richard and Janet.

My arrival was a true family affair. My aunt Jetje, my father's sister, acted as my mother's nurse. She was not a registered nurse so she cannot have been my mother's midwife. In fact there is a photo of a lady with a rather stern no-nonsense appearance in the book who was, I believe, the nurse/midwife handling my birth. I do not know whether a doctor was present, but I would think so.

Here is a translation of what my mother wrote in the first few pages of the book:
"Petertje (she uses the Dutch diminutive for Peter) was born in Bloemendaal in the house of his grandparents. When he was only a few minutes old, he was already sucking his thumb so diligently that it was clearly audible. It was a wonderful yet curious experience to have all of a sudden something in the cradle and to hear a small faintly plaintive noise. P had quite a bit of hair when he was born, but like his father hardly any hair on his forehead. He weighed 3400 grams (7.5 lbs.) and was 53 centimeters (almost 21 in.) long. A sturdy boy, therefore. A tiny nose, tilted upward, is planted defiantly in his little face. He has large blue eyes, which he nearly always kept almost closed during the first few days. As soon as he got into the full light he would keep them extra firmly closed. His little ears are large but well shaped. His little mouth is small, but when he cries he can make it quite large.

Aunt Jetje is his nurse. She is sometimes quite busy with him. However, in the first three weeks he was exceptionally good. Slept almost always, except when he was being fed or bathed. The first time he was breast-fed he immediately understood what was expected of him. That was very clever of Petertje."

&

So, as usual with parents, nature was playing its tricks on my mother. She confirmed the old Dutch saying: *"Een ieder denkt zijn uil een valk te zijn"* (Everybody believes his owl to be a falcon.) In Dutch idiom, the word "owl" means beyond the bird, a somewhat dim- witted person, while the falcon is, of course, an ultra-smart and swift bird. My mother goes on to describe how I liked to be bathed, holding still and closing my eyes as soon as I felt the water around me.

Two basic characteristics come out very early. I always liked to be in the water and I always liked food. These traits have stayed with me throughout my life. Also a tendency to close my eyes is still there. Netty frequently reminds me not to talk to people with my eyes closed. She is trying to teach an old dog new tricks. I don't know why I have this habit. Maybe it is to better concentrate on what I am saying or maybe it is because I am really not interested in the people I am addressing. My mother comments that Tante Jetje is quicker and handier with bathing me while she herself still has to learn how to do it. As I wrote before, my mother was a very bright person but not very dexterous in handling domestic chores. When I was twelve days old, Oma Hesselink, my mother's stepmother, came over from Leeuwarden to see the new arrival. To give Tante Jetje some rest, Oma Hesselink was sleeping with my mother and me in the same room, but she was so worried about my well-being that she left her bed at least twelve times to check on me. To protect her hairdo she had tied a handkerchief on her head with three knots. My mother said, "Watch out you scare the baby."

My other grandparents came upstairs every morning to check on my progress and when I was one month old my grandfather dared to pick me up for the first time and danced around the room with me in his arms. I guess he was happy that there was finally a grandchild in the family. I know the feeling, I also had to wait a long time before I saw my first grandchild. My mother writes that when I was four weeks old I began to show an interest in my surroundings and that I was critically looking at her when I was drinking and would wrinkle my nose when I was done. She adds that I was evidently not satisfied with what I saw. Other delegations from Leeuwarden came. My mother's sister Jet Jonas came and concluded that I looked like a real cherub compared to her daughter Piefke (Tineke's nickname). The photographs taken by Oom Henk, my mother's step-brother, confirm this observation. He came over to take the official photographs. For this purpose I was dressed in a long lacy dress which is a Dutch tradition and is called a *"doopjurk"* (a christening robe). This same robe was used for a formal portrait made of me by Willem Bastiaan Tholen, a well-known Dutch artist my grandparents commissioned for this purpose. This crayon drawing titled, "Petertje," used to hang in my grandparent's bedroom and later moved to my parent's bedroom. Now it is in Janet's house in California. Once Netty and I visited Assen, the capital of the province of Drenthe in Holland. In the local museum was an exhibition of Tholen's works we wanted to see. To our surprise they also had a "Petertje" hanging there. Apparently he made more than one! I was almost ready to rush to the museum's director and present myself as Petertje, but I restrained myself.

Other events of earth-shaking importance were that on March 28 I looked at my mother and laughed for the first time and on April 2nd I went outside also for the first time. My weight kept going up and when my mother and Tante Jetje took me to Leeuwarden from April 28 to May 18, I weighed 11 pounds when I arrived and 12 ½ when I left (12.12 and 13.79 lbs. respectively). The Friesian air must have done wonders again. Tante Aaltje and Old Omoe (Fokje Hooghiemstra) were especially interested in me, according to my mother. On June 11th I was given my first shots for Venezuela, a procedure I did not appreciate.

On June 26th 1925, my mother, Tante Jetje and I boarded the SS *Stuyvesant* (a ship named after another Peter) and sailed for Venezuela. My grandparents must have decided to send their daughter, Tante Jetje, along with my mother and me to help and to give her a trip. I was then four months old. I have a picture postcard of the ship. It is stunning to see how old-fashioned she looks. Another reminder for me that I am entering the realm of history. It must have been a true steamship with stokers firing the boilers with coal. My mother firmly believed that I was the focus of all attention aboard ship and states that even the stokers came out of the engine room in the bowels of the ship to see me and play with me when my mother was in the dining room having lunch. Among the passengers was an old lady who was on her way to Barbados who suggested to my mother to drink stout whenever she could to enhance her breast-feeding. My mother took the advice and she writes it was also well received by me, and I got really fat. Not surprisingly I still like Bass Ale. Ma writes they had a fun trip with a lot of dancing and no time for needlework. I believe her. Later on in her life Ma never did any needlework either. They went on shore in Trinidad and Barbados, leaving me under the care of the stewardess.

In Curaçao my father came on board. My mother wrote he became very quiet and appeared quite moved and somewhat taken aback when he saw his son for the first time. Clearly, he needed a few days to get used to fatherhood. They stayed a few days in Curaçao and then went on to Maracaibo where the oil fields were. I seemed to take well to the tropical climate, grew quickly, got a number of teeth, and smiled at anybody who was black. My mother told me later that she had a maid who took care of me who came from the island of Grenada. This

IN CARACAS. 1926.

lady was so proud to be in charge of a really white child that she would powder my face to make me look even whiter than I already was. In her eyes, this compared favorably with the Venezuelan children who were perhaps a little "café au lait." There are pictures of me with two Venezuelan neighbor children, Luis Eduardo and Beatrice. My parents had excellent relations with their neighbors, probably because they both spoke Spanish and perhaps also because they had absolutely no prejudices towards people of different backgrounds, race or creed. Ma had a good friend there in Maracaibo, Senora Anderson. Despite her Scottish name, she was pure Venezuelan, probably a descendant of some wayward Scot. Later on in Argentina we would meet many people with English names, descendants of the people who built the railroads there. Senora Anderson gave me a true Latin American present, a small hammock. Apparently I slept well in this hammock and when we went back to the Netherlands my father rigged it up in their cabin, providing me with a place to sleep that was unaffected by the ship's motion.

I was almost a year old when we returned to Holland, but shortly before we left I contracted a bad case of dysentery that lasted for three weeks and caused my mother much anxiety. So before leaving, we spent some time in Caracas, where the climate is better than in Maracaibo. Caracas is high and cooler, while Maracaibo is at sea level, hot, humid and swampy. The drilling rigs of the Maracaibo oil fields stand in an inland lagoon. Tante Jetje had already left for Caracas so Mrs. Anderson was a great help with all kinds of native remedies. After arrival in Holland, my grandparents found me quite pale. Apparently the tropics had put their stamp on me. My parents went on a three-week vacation to Switzerland and were happy to find me considerably healthier and chubbier upon their return. I added further luster to the family reunion by uttering the famous words, "Mama, Papa," and with that my mother's narrative ends. In a way that is unfortunate because my mother was the only person who wrote about me and she stopped writing rather early in my life so the rest of this narrative will have to come from me.

The photographs that follow in the baby book include pictures of me laying the cornerstone for my grandparent's new house on September 4, 1926. I went first class, using an engraved silver (cake) trowel. We still have two trowels, and if I am not mistaken, the stone marked with my name is still in the wall of the house. A very nice picture, in my opinion, is one probably taken by a professional while my parents and I are taking a stroll on the walking pier in Scheveningen, the seaside resort of The Hague. We are all dressed to the nines, quite a difference with today's more casual attire for leisure-time activities that I often find unflattering.

In the years following our return from Venezuela in 1926, we lived in Voorburg. My parents bought a house there at Parkweg 183 where I lived on and off until I married Netty in 1951. My parents moved to Wassenaar shortly after our marriage, when my father

BACK HOME, A SUNDAY WALK ON THE PIER IN SCHEVENINGEN.

retired from Royal Dutch. I have little recollection of my early years in Voorburg. I seem to remember a visit by my grandfather Hesselink, "Opa Dik," who liked to take walks with me. I would sit on my little tricycle and pedal and Opa would push the tricycle with his walking stick to speed things up. I remember going into one of the three parks we had nearby and to my delight and astonishment finding some coins that were in a neat row on the ground. Obviously it didn't dawn on me that Opa Dik had dropped them there.

My memories of early childhood begin to become a little clearer around 1929 when we once again embarked on a journey, this time to Argentina. I remember some of the sights we visited on the way down. (It is also possible we saw them on the return trip.) Anyway, we visited the Sugar Loaf Mountain in the harbor of Rio de Janeiro, riding a cable car to the top, and a zoo in Buenos Aires. In the zoo I took a ride in a little gas-engine sdriven racing car with a young boy in a white type of labcoat running beside me to help me steer. This ride was the highlight of my life at that time. In Buenos Aires we transferred to a smaller coastal liner that brought us to our destination, Commodoro Rivadavia, a dusty town in southern Patagonia. Landing there was an adventure. There was no harbor, so the ship unloaded us into a launch, that traveled to the beach where a bunch of sturdy men in hip boots were waiting. They formed a chain and tossed me from one to the next. My parents were also carried to the beach, how I don't know. We ended up in what my parents used to call an "oil camp," a small village built by the company in the hinterlands. We were put up in a guesthouse there. Actually it was called the *Gasthaus,* reflecting the quite extensive presence of German immigrants in the area. A German woman ran it and a German manservant called Hans (what else) served our meals. He would appear every day at the door of our living room, click his heels and announce what we could expect for dinner. It was almost always the same. *Hammelfleisch durch die Machine gedreht* (mutton ground up in the meat grinder). There were lots of sheep in Patagonia and only a few cattle herds. I remember the layout of the "camp" vaguely, but still have a quite clear picture of our rooms at the guesthouse and the general store called the *"Anonima"* where you could buy everything you could conceivably need in a desperate place like that. The Anonima sold a few toys among which a foot-long ship with a wind up motor was prominently displayed. On my birthday I found this ship in my bed and I remember how amused my father looked, seeing my enthusiastic reaction.

The "camp" was really a God forsaken place. Most of Patagonia is totally bare of trees and it gets quite cold in winter and hot in summer. The wind blows constantly and carries dust everywhere. I was equipped with motorcycle goggles and frequently wore them when I went out to play with the other children in the camp. The guesthouse was built out of stone and so were two other houses and the office. Since my father was the boss-man in the camp, we soon ended up in one of the two stone houses. All the other houses were made out of corrugated steel and quite primitive. The people living in the camp came from all sorts of countries, mostly European, and were from all kinds of backgrounds. Many people had hired on with the oil company in postwar Europe, trying to find a better living abroad. Unfortunately, this did not work out for them. The Depression began to take hold and the oil fields that had been discovered nearby were unable to dispose of the oil they produced since the Argentine government had reneged on its commitment to build a refinery. My father traveled several times overland to Buenos Aires to see if he could get the government to move. He would drive for about ten hours to a railhead and from there he traveled by train for more than a day to the capital. Ultimately Pa had to close down the fields and the "camp." I guess most people we lived with there were let go and sent home.

Life in the camp was not unpleasant. The company operated a big garage for all the employees and everybody used the same model company car, a two-seater with a hatch in the back that opened up to provide an extra seat for two in the open air. In those days we called that a "dickey seat" (U.S. – rumble seat), a term that goes back to the days of horse-drawn carriages.

Taking trips by car was one of the few things you could do for recreation. I remember frequently sitting between my parents on the front seat and going for a drive through the countryside, just dusty unpaved gravel roads through wild scrub country. We would have encounters with wild ostriches. They were smaller than the ones in Africa and gray. They would run in front of our car, trying to outrun us, being too dumb to realize all they had to do was step off the road and let us pass. Other animals we often saw were guanacos, a fast animal that looks a little like a llama, but is smaller. I understand the guanaco is a forbear of the Llama. Once we traveled on a road that had developed big muddy sections caused by one of the rare rainfalls. Our car got stuck; the wheels had no traction and slipped in the mud. We were in the middle of nowhere and my mother got quite concerned. As always my father stayed calm. We waited until a group of heavy trucks showed up and pulled us out and drained the muddy areas by driving through them. On weekends, people from the camp would drive out into the bush and start a lamb roast, locally called an *Assado*. An entire lamb, slaughtered and prepared by a butcher, was bought and hooked, spread-eagle style, on a spit that was planted vertically in the ground. A good fire was lit around the spit and after a short time we would have a rich supply of roast lamb. People would take the seats out of their cars to sit on, crank up a spring-driven gramophone for background music and that was the feast.

Of the people who were with us in Argentina at that time I remember a few. There was a Norwegian family with a daughter called Solveig who was selected by my mother as a playmate for me. My mother was always aware of my isolated position as an only child and often made an effort to find other children I could play with. Solveig's father must have been rather low on the pecking order since they lived in a small house made of corrugated steel, not brick as ours was. When Solveig had a meal with us she would get up when the meal was finished, stand behind her chair, and say *takk for maltid* (thanks for the meal). There was a Swiss geologist, a Mr. Weber who was a bachelor with a small Van Dyke beard. I believe he had a crush on my mother. He gave her all sorts of presents that embarrassed my parents, and I remember them discussing what to do with this man who was either a fool or someone who had the idea he could enhance his stature in the company that way.

From time to time we would drive down to Commodoro Rivadavia to shop and meet other people. It was on one of those visits that my mother picked

ON TOP OF THE HUT OF AGGY (L) AND NANNY. NOTE THE SCALP AT RIGHT ON THE POLE NEAR THE DOOR.

up a German maid called Anneliese. My mother who was always a bit of a do-gooder had discovered Anneliese living with her family in a shack they had built for themselves on the beach. They were German immigrants who had left postwar Germany to find a better future overseas. Upon their arrival in Argentina they had been thoroughly shaken down by the locals, authorities as well as private citizens, and been reduced to living a marginal existence in self-built shacks. I think Anneliese's folks were not much more than unskilled laborers with little education. Her father was an alcoholic. Anneliese had very little schooling, and for years my mother would sit down with her at the dining room table and try to teach her the basics of reading and writing. She was a tall, quite unattractive, big-boned redhead, a bit blunt but very friendly. Sometimes we would get a live chicken delivered to our house in a gunnysack. Anneliese would go into the backyard and chop off the chicken's head with a rusty axe, pluck it and cook it for us. Ma offered her a way out of her world, and when we returned to Holland, Anneliese came along. She stayed several years with us in Voorburg as our housemaid. During her vacations she would visit relatives who ran a small café at a rural railway station somewhere in Germany. After her first trip there she came back proudly displaying a pin with a Nazi swastika. My mother paid Anneliese quite well (40 guilders a month – the market was more at 30) and she never spent a penny so after four years or so she had built up a nice savings account. Her relatives became aware of that and persuaded her to come to live with them. We never heard anything from her after she rejoined the Fatherland.

On weekends we would go on small trips into the Patagonian countryside. We visited a site where we found the remnants of a prehistoric petrified forest. Large tree trunks were lying around and there is a photograph of me leaning against one of those fallen trees. I have a piece of petrified wood we found there that looks almost like a small segment of a two-by-four. I also believe my father found the dinosaur vertebra there that he kept in the window of the staircase of his house in Wassenaar. I gave that souvenir to our grandson Alexander when he was six years old and had developed a sudden and intense interest in pre-historic animals. The vertebra made quite a splash at the Mamaroneck NY School where Alexander proudly displayed it. I hope he will keep it as a souvenir of his great-grandfather who also had a keen interest in pre- historic life and possessed a remarkable knack for finding things in the field.

Our camp was located on a dusty plain. In the distance you could see the foot-hills of the Andes. We often visited the de Marez Oyens family, Dutch friends who lived on a sheep ranch out in the hills. Their two daughters, Aggy and Nanny, were a little older than I was and impressed me very much. I thought they were beautiful and told my mother I was going to marry one of them but was not yet sure which one. They had built a wonderful hut in the woods where they played cowboys and Indians. Among their treasures was a piece of hairy stuff. They claimed it was a real scalp. They would sit with me in the hut and frighten me out of my wits with their stories. I kept coming back for more. In the final year of the war one of the Dutch Nazi dominated radio stations started broadcasting American jazz music. This was astonishing because jazz music was considered *verboten* as an expression of the deprived minds of Negroid subhumans whose culture was far below the lofty levels of the German master race, their *Kultur* and their music. A young woman anchored the show and delivered rabid pro-Nazi commentary. It was a clumsy belated attempt to lure young- people into the Nazi tent. As it turned out after the war, the young woman was none other than Nanny de Marez Oyens! She was imprisoned as a collaborator.

We returned home around the summer of 1930 from Buenos Aires on a passenger liner where we occupied one of the two "luxury" staterooms. I vaguely remember driving through dark rainy Holland with my parents and grandparents in my grand-father's car, chauffeured by his driver. A few days later we returned to our house in Voorburg that we had just left unoccupied for more than a year.

I soon started school at the *Montessori School Vreugd en Rust* in Voorburg. My parents chose this private school because it was something new and innovative. It offered a grade-school education based on the principles established by Dr. Maria Montessori, a woman who had revolutionized teaching first in Italy, her native country, and later in other countries. The school was located in a park-like setting in a then somewhat run-down mansion that had belonged to a branch of the house of Orange. The school was named after the mansion *Vreugd en Rust"* (Joy and Rest). It differed greatly from the other schools in town where students sat on wooden benches in rows, with the teacher in front, telling them what to learn, read or write in unison and where nobody was allowed to leave their seats unless permitted to do so. In a Montessori school students had their own tables and chairs that were arranged in random clusters. Teachers would sometimes work with the whole class as a unit, or more often pull smaller groups together to discuss certain subjects while the others did other things. There was far less discipline and children were allowed to roam freely in the classroom. The idea was that children left to work at their own speed would achieve more than they would when forced to follow the tempo of the whole class. This worked well for highly motivated intelligent students who could progress at their own speed and for slow learners who would not feel left behind. The trouble was that middle-of-the-road kids like me who were smart enough to work the system and understand it, could avoid subjects they did not like and loiter and loaf for days without the teacher catching on, ending up with significant gaps in their knowledge. But this only emerged later after I had spent some very happy and carefree years at that school.

On my first day I was put in a kindergarten class that had already been together for some time. My little table and chair were next to a bossy little girl named Hetty Brands who immediately began to establish her authority and placed me at the bottom of the pecking order. She explained that the class was controlled by an important group of robber knights under the leadership of "Chief Janus" (*Hoofdman Janus*) aka Jan Apol, later my friend Eelco Apol. His full name is Eelco Johan and when he was about fifteen he decided he preferred Eelco. Hetty said she was under-chief and I was supposed to obey both of them. She emphasized her points by drumming with her pencil on my head. As soon as it was time to play outside, the Chief and his underlings donned the hooded, dark-blue loden rain capes we were wearing in those days, put the hood over their heads and let the rest of the cape flow freely, and galloped outside, making horse-like noises. They claimed prime spots in the big sandbox, in which we could play and also assumed priority in using the swing set. I don't think I was much impressed by this power play, at least I do not remember any sequel to it. But years later I used this story with some success when Eelco's son Govert contacted me and asked if I could contribute an anecdote to be used during a dinner party his father was giving to celebrate his seventieth birthday.

The schoolroom was a large sunny place with lots of windows. The Montessori system was probably at its best at the kindergarten level. Its innovative approach could push children ahead of their peers in ordinary schools by teaching them the rudiments of the three Rs and in addition things such as how to tie shoelaces and stitch on buttons as well as the beginnings of geography and history. While I was in this class my mother and Tante Jetje went to Spain with a group on a cultural tour. In those days a trip to Spain was a huge undertaking that involved many intermediate stops and train rides that took several days. As it turned out, Tante Jetje met her future husband Bernard van der Hoop on this trip. Ma and Jetje returned very happy from this trip, which in several respects turned out to be much more interesting than they had expected. Not only because of the appearance of Bernard in our family but also because they had witnessed the proclamation of a republic and the removal of King Alfonso of Spain who was tossed out of the country just when they were in Madrid. My mother told me cheerfully that crowds in the streets had chanted *Uno dos tres fuera il rey* (one two three, down with the king) and had a little fellow in their midst who resembled the king and was carrying a suitcase, ready to leave.

The republic that was then established was overthrown in 1936 by a fascist military junta led by General Franco who waged a bloody civil war to conquer Spain. Oddly enough, my mother and I were again on a trip to Spain, going by ship to the Canary Islands, when Franco started his revolution. This war in 1936 signaled the beginning of the dominance by Nazi and fascist forces of Europe that ended only with their defeat in 1945. German Nazi "volunteer" air force units supported Franco and received valuable training by bombing Spanish cities. The bombing of Guernica, a defenseless town full of civilians, is generally seen as the beginning of the strategy of terrorizing civilians through bombardment from the air. Picasso's painting of this atrocity called *Guernica* is one of his most famous works.

Tante Jetje and Oom Bernard were married in the summer of 1931. The wedding ceremony was in the church behind my grandparent's house and the entire wedding procession could just walk up the hill behind the house and enter the church grounds from the back. When the couple left the church, I was positioned in front of the door on one side in a brand new white sailor's suit and Ansje van Ramshorst, the daughter of one of my mother's study friends on the other side. We both had baskets with flowers and were supposed to start our job of scattering the flowers in front of the bridal couple as soon as they emerged from the church. We were at first so much impressed by the whole thing that we forgot to start and Oom Bernard had

to say *strooien!* (scatter!) to get us going. Tante Jetje and Oom Bernard moved to the Canary Islands where Oom Bernard had set up an import/export business. They lived on the island of Gran Canaria for many years and my grandparents would visit them from time to time, traveling there by ship. On one of their visits a local painter made the portrait of my grandfather that used to hang in my study in Riverside. It was made when he was seventy-five years old. I think it is an excellent portrait, but I also think he looks a great deal older than I did at that age. Richard now has it.

In 1932, when I advanced to first grade, I moved to another classroom in the building. I have a photograph of that class. Juffrouw (Miss) Schaap sits in the middle near the big coal-burning stove. It shows a group of children of which I still remember many names. My three best friends are there, Paul Beversen (behind Eelco), Frits Regtdoorzee Greup (to my right) and Eelco Apol (left of the aquarium). The girl with dark hair and glasses standing behind me is Alice Cohen who was killed during the war in Auschwitz). For a long time Paul was my very best friend and our parents were also good friends. Our mothers often saw each other and played bridge together. Paul's father went riding on winter weekends with my father and in summer, they played tennis. They also went mountain climbing together in Switzerland. The Beversen family had a German woman living with them who used to be their housemaid, but was later promoted to some sort of housekeeper. This woman, whose name was Mina Kramer, ran the household and had influenced the family into a pro-German direction. They often vacationed in the area where Mina came from and one spring I was invited to come along. Thus I had an early glimpse of pre–war Nazi Germany. Mina's family lived in an old farmhouse built in the traditional style somewhat reminiscent of what we call Tudor, an exterior with exposed wooden beams and white stucco in between. Hanging around with Paul, we visited a camp of Hitler youths. They were camping on a riverbank, military style. I remember how surprised I was to see a boy standing guard with a rifle as if the forces of evil could overwhelm their camp any minute. As boy scouts we never even dreamed of having an armed guard near our camp. In summer Paul was sent over to spend time with Mina's family. He told me he had to share a bedroom with Heinz, a nasty boy who was a cousin of Mina. Heinz was a little older than we were and would get up in the middle of the night to beat Paul up for no apparent reason. Thus Paul got an early taste of the German mentality of those days. During the war Heinz served on the eastern front with an anti-aircraft artillery outfit and I believe he was killed there.

Unfortunately, Paul's mother became a fervent Nazi. Many years before the war she joined the NSB, the Dutch National Socialist Party. This was unusual but not uncommon in the Netherlands around the mid-thirties. We were in the depression years, many people were unemployed and some Dutchmen felt we needed a stronger government that would put the economy back on its feet. The party that followed the example of the Nazis in Germany, promising job creation and an orderly society, was attractive to many and there were no overt signs yet of the dark side of what was happening over the border. The persecution of the Jews had not yet started, and the concentration camps and the general suppression of democracy were then not clearly perceived. The jackboots and silly uniforms of the Nazis were dismissed as typical German idiosyncrasies. So people tolerated those that joined the NSB. The problem was that some persons who were misguided early on persisted in their loyalty to that party even after the Germans attacked our country and occupied it. They became traitors in our eyes. At that point, it became impossible to sustain friendships. So my parents told Paul's parents that they could unfortunately no longer be friends. The Beversens accepted that and to the best of my knowledge never used their position of being part of the party-in-power against anybody.

Paul's mother was the party member even though she was quite wealthy and had therefore no reason to feel dissatisfied with the existing political economy of the thirties. Paul's father was a real gentleman but rather colorless and without strong opinions. He just went along. So Paul and I began to drift apart. After the war Paul had trouble getting denazified when he wanted to go to our university in Leiden. At that time I began to see him again now and then and I helped him to regain acceptance. In the nineties, when I attended a big reunion in Leiden, a tall slim gray haired man buttonholed me and asked if I did not recognize him. It turned out to be Paul and I was shocked and embarrassed that I had absolutely not recognized him. It turned out he had health problems and lived in Wassenaar in retirement with his family. A few months later, I heard he had been killed in a traffic accident. He was riding his bike around a traffic circle and a car sideswiped him. I have always been sorry that Paul and I had not been able to remain friends, but the political situation made that impossible. I did remain close friends with Frits Greup and Eelco Apol. Both have visited us in America with their wives. When I was in the army and arrived with a troop ship in Tandjong Priok, the port of Batavia, now Jakarta, Frits and Eelco, both lieutenants, were there to greet me–a corporal–to take me for a ride around the town. When Netty and I were married, Frits was a groomsman and Eelco was one of my witnesses. Eelco was married by then, and therefore ineligible to be a groomsman. "Usher" is an unknown function in Holland. A bride chooses a number of bridesmaids (*bruidsmeisjes*) and they in turns are escorted by men chosen by the groom (*bruidsjonkers*) who are also in the wedding party but do not usher. People are just expected to find their own seats in church. Another good friend was Ab Boot. Ab was not a great socializer, and in our adult life we were not very close. But Netty and I did continue to stay in touch with him and his mother and we also became friendly with his younger brother Erik.

My stories may wrongfully suggest that a great many Dutch people became Nazis. That is not the case. It just so happened that my parents and I quite randomly knew several families that chose what we called "the wrong side." Looking at my class photo I also see others, particularly Alice Cohen, a Jewish girl who lived two doors away from us. She and her family moved to The Hague before the war. From a Dutch website listing Holocaust victims I learned that she and her entire family (father, stepmother and brother) were killed on the same day in Auschwitz.

I also notice at least two children who had certain learning disabilities. The Montessori school offered a good refuge for them since everybody could proceed at his or her own pace and children who were a little slow would not stand out as failures.

The *Parkweg* we lived on in Voorburg was a fairly busy street with two traffic lanes that were bisected by the tracks of the "blue" tram that connected us with The Hague and also Leiden. The tram stop was almost in front of our house. Privet hedges enclosed the tram tracks. Incredibly, men trimmed miles and miles of these hedges twice a year with hand shears. The connection with Leiden was with a higher speed express tram that would not make all the stops of the local. These trams were a real lifesaver for us during the war when the Germans confiscated all cars and we ran out of bicycle tires. The trams made a lot of noise of course, but we did not mind. As a village Voorburg is very old and when I grew up it had in many respects still the characteristics of a village. Its origins go back to the times of the Romans and when we lived there it was not yet a real suburb of The Hague. It had its own business center with modest shops, a very old Protestant church, and an old *Walloon* (French) church. This Walloon church *(Waalse kerk)* dates back to the days that French Protestants were driven out of their country and found refuge in Holland. It was at this church that the local members of my mother's and my own Protestant congregation, the *Doopsgezinde Kerk,* found a home and where I went to confirmation classes.

The railway tracks connecting The Hague with Utrecht and the east of the Netherlands formed the southern border of the village. The eastern border was the *Vliet*, a canal that also goes back to Roman days. Beyond the *Vliet* was farmland, mainly pastures. On the western side facing The Hague was another small canal, the Broeksloot that was only two blocks away from our house. The *Broeksloot*, was an important place for me as a boy. I would go there to try to catch fish with a net, I would walk along it to explore the farmlands and later on when I had a dog, I would often walk him there. Between the *Broeksloot* and The Hague were meadows where cows grazed. On the northern side, a smaller rail line connected The Hague with Rotterdam to the southeast and Scheveningen and the North Sea to the west. Our street, the *Parkweg*, was one of the two important streets of the village. The other one was the *Oosteinde*, which had larger houses with larger gardens that backed up to the *Vliet*. The Montessori school was on that street. A fairly respectable park also bordered on the *Vliet* and in which there were several ponds surrounded the school. Very near the school was an especially popular smaller pond. In winter when there was ice on the ponds, we would go there to run back and forth across the ice, hoping it would hold. Sometimes it cracked and one or two boys would have to sit in school with wet shoes and socks. If you walked past the school you soon reached the main shopping street, the *Heren Straat*. It was just a continuation of the *Oosteinde* with a different name. One of the first businesses you would encounter was the blacksmith shop. As boys we would go there to watch the smith put new shoes on horses and make all sorts of fascinating things out of metal in his dark shop in which you could see the coal fire burn brightly. The town hall was near the old church in the center and so was the main post office where people who had no phone at home went to make calls and where you could also send telegrams.

At school I learned about the Dutch *Sinterklaas* tradition. Saint Nicholas was a bishop who is believed to have lived in Turkey and who moved from there to Spain. The legend is that he was a great friend of children and saved several during his life, which earned him his sainthood. In the Dutch tradition, he comes annually to Holland in a steamship with his black servant *Zwartepiet* (Black Peter) and his white horse. The saint rides on his horse over the rooftops and drops presents, originally only candy, down the chimneys for children who have behaved well and have left the appropriate carrot and a little water for the horse. Children who had not behaved well risked receiving nothing or just some coals or even a rod or a switch (a bunch of twigs) with which they could be punished. There is a painting by Jan Steen depicting the Saint Nicholas celebration showing a family (as usual with Steen, a messy group) and a naughty boy crying in the foreground who has received a switch. The ultimate sanction is being put in Black Peter's big sack and carried off to Spain. All this caused considerable anxiety among young children who still believed the story. There is a large collection of songs children sing in front of the chimney or at school when the saint visits. He would come to our school and we were considerably relieved when he left again and nobody was taken away. At home in the evening of December 5th, people gather to give and receive gifts that are often accompanied by poems that are funny or critical of the recipient. There are also "surprise" gifts, which contain all sorts of tricks. It is a fun tradition that is unfortunately on the wane nowadays since the heavily advertised, American-style Christmas is beginning to make inroads. Moreover, it is no longer politically correct to have a Black servant or to scare children. The candy tradition is still strong and Black Peter is supposed to throw hands full of *peper noten,* hard-baked small cubes (nuts) of gingerbread, out to children who dive for them and try to grab as many as they can.

I have a vivid memory of walking down the old shopping street of Voorburg on a dark evening with my mother to see the traditional Saint Nicholas table at the local pastry shop, full of all sorts of goodies, in chocolate and marzipan. The whole shop was warmly lit up and full of colorful displays of the kind of things small boys really like. Since the actual date of Saint Nicholas is December 6th, Americans stubbornly insist that is the correct date. However, the good saint comes the evening before over the Dutch roofs and Dutch people traditionally celebrate *Sinterklaas* on the evening of the 5th. The saint comes to the schools on that same day. We would celebrate *Sinterklaas* with relatives or friends. Usually Tante Jet and Oom Otto Jonas and Tineke would come over or we would go to their house in Arnhem. Our family and theirs were too small to have a fun evening with just three people. Gifts were exchanged with poems and sometimes joke presents. After Netty and I got engaged I discovered her family was also dedicated to having elaborate and serious *Sinterklaas* celebrations. We went several times to Netty's house for a truly memorable evening.

Our house was a "semi detached villa," which meant it was on one side attached to a neighboring house. There was a third house also under the same roof that was a mirror image of ours. We had a smallish front yard and a driveway on the side that led to our garage. Our backyard was deeper than that of our neighbors because they were closer to a corner where houses of a street perpendicular to ours also had backyards. At the bottom of our backyard we had a shed where we kept the coal for our central heating and in another section, our bicycles. In the corner between this shed and the garage was a sandbox where I played for years with my friends.

Our house had the traditional Dutch format. On the ground floor two rooms, a sitting room and a dining rooms *en suite*, which meant they were connected with sliding pocket doors in between and along the side the staircase and a narrow hallway, with the kitchen and toilet on one end and a small room that was really useless on the other end. The front door was on the side of the house. Upstairs we had two larger bedrooms with the stairs to the attic in between and on the street side a bathroom with a tub and opposite it a small bedroom for me. My parents had the front bedroom that had a balcony built over part of the living room. Our maid had a room in the attic, unheated with no plumbing. The three upstairs bedrooms had wash basins with running hot and cold water. A water heater in the bathroom produced the hot water. It used town gas, and every time someone turned on the hot water it would start with a big whoosh and large flames would come out of its bottom. In the kitchen we had a stone counter and sink and no hot water tap. There was a gas stove. The central heating furnace was also in the kitchen and had to be continually fed with coal. There was no refrigerator, of course. We lived in a mild climate and we kept things cool in our small cellar. We had one phone, a wall unit, that hung in the living room.

With our central heating (it was installed after my parents bought the house) and hot and cold running water we had a quite up-to-date house for those days. Still, compared to today's American houses it was very primitive. There was one clothes closet in each of the two larger bedrooms. They were really small and I have no idea how my parents fitted all their clothes in this one closet. But then, people did not own that many clothes. Most people took one tub bath a week and changed their underwear at that time. You would wear the same clothes all week and things like deodorants were unknown. This made for a sometimes sticky atmosphere in the tram, particularly on rainy humid summer days. To indicate the differences in lifestyle between then and now, I have sometimes bored my son Adriaan with a recitation of the number of electric motors we had in our house in Riverside compared to what we had in our house in Voorburg. We had one. It operated the vacuum cleaner. If my count is correct, we had about sixty in and around our Riverside house, counting all appliances, tools and all sorts of gadgets. Today we have lots of machines and lots of tools but no manpower. In the old days we had no gadgets but plenty of manpower. In Voorburg we had a live-in maid, the laundry man picked the laundry up weekly, and the garden work was done every week by a gardener with his helper. The local merchants delivered everything to our door. This was a daily ritual. My mother would sit down at the dining room table and the maid would stand next to her. They would discuss what we were going to eat and what had to be delivered. They had small books for the baker, the butcher (his book was in a metal container because of the grease and the blood), the milkman, the grocery store and the greengrocer. All these people would either stop by or send a boy on a bicycle to pick up the book and then come back with their deliveries. The milkman had a pushcart with big gleaming brass milk containers on top and drawers for cheese and butter beneath them. The greengrocer had a horse-drawn cart on which he displayed all his vegetables and had bins for potatoes and other things. Our maid would come out and negotiate with him about the quality of his merchandise. The boys working for the grocery store, the butcher and the baker would return with their deliveries later in the morning so that at lunch we had everything fresh on the table, another reason why we did not need refrigeration. At the end of the week the books were added up and the bills were settled with cash. This whole system was, of course, extremely time-consuming and labor intensive, but it kept a lot of people at work, and if she did not mind being called about ten times a day to the backdoor, it was convenient for the housewife. You did not have things like strawberries and cherries throughout the year. They only were offered in season and there often were independent merchants who would come through the street with a cart or a heavy three-wheeled bike for merchandise, shouting what they had to offer and what the price was.

Life was simple and unhurried. My father and mother would get up around 8 a.m. and after breakfast my father would drive to his office where he arrived around 9 a.m. and stayed until 12:30 p.m. He then returned home for lunch and went back around 2 p.m. He was usually home by 6:30. I would amble over to school, in the beginning riding on a child's seat behind my mother on her bike and later on foot and finally on my own bike. When I came home I would often find my mother reading a book in front of our gas fireplace. She would tell me what she was reading, sometimes reading passages to me that she thought would be of interest to me. Some evenings after dinner, my father would read with me in the *National Geographic magazine*. For many years he had a subscription. Or he would read stories of old ship voyages to me. My father had a great interest in these stories and belonged to an organization that published these old stories in modern-style books. I remember fondly those evenings with my parents and the warm safe and snug feeling they imparted to me. As a boy I became quite a talker and I remember at dinner how my parents were often encouraging me to tell them of my experiences of the day. I guess I had a very normal, pleasant and uncomplicated childhood. We were quite well-to-do, but not rich. The Great Depression that had most of the world in its grip passed us by. We were not unaware of it, of course, and my father's career definitely stagnated for many years because of the Depression. My parents and grandparents helped many people who were less well-off than we were. We were aware of our good fortune, and like the entire population of Holland, we lived cautiously since we had no idea how long it would take before the economy picked up again.

In those days my father had a Chrysler automobile that used to belong to my grandfather. This was a dark blue four-door sedan with wheels with spokes made out of yellow hickory wood. On the back was a luggage rack on which you could strap suitcases with stout ropes. My grandfather had bought a new Fiat for himself and a smaller one for Tante Jetje and I believe he sold the Chrysler to Pa. We took the Chrysler on a first trip to Friesland to visit my mother's relatives. Anneliese went along too, presumably to take care of me. The big dike that now connects the provinces of North Holland with Friesland had not yet been completed so we had to drive around what was then still called the Zuiderzee, first heading east and then north. I remember us driving through a village called Staphorst where the locals still used dogcarts for transportation. I have always been an animal lover and seeing these fat yokels ride on small carts pulled by one or two dogs made me feel very sorry for the animals. In the same town we got a speeding ticket from a local gendarme who stopped us while riding his bicycle. My father was usually very even tempered and it was therefore for me a great exception to see him get really angry about this insult to his dignity. It was a very long trip because there were no real highways for cars yet and one had to follow old brick-paved roads and weave through one town or village after another. There also were tolls here and there. Old, almost medieval institutions where a community would rent out the right to charge tolls to a family who would usually live in a little house next to their wooden barrier and come out whenever somebody stopped in front of it. They would raise the boom after you had paid.

After arriving in Leeuwarden we stayed with Tante Jet and her husband Oom Otto Jonas. They and their daughter Tineke, the only cousin I ever had, lived next door to Oom Anne and Tante Mieke Deibel with their then very small son Bas. This was little Bas. Their houses were part of a complex of identical homes that were built after the First World War to alleviate the housing shortage. They were small rented houses built in the traditional Dutch style. You entered the front door and on the left faced a hallway with stairs leading to the second floor and on the right the connected living/dining room. Under the stairs was the one and only toilet the house boasted. Upstairs were two larger bedrooms that like the rooms downstairs had mantelpieces and coal-burning stoves. In addition, a small bedroom had the one and only washstand with running water. No bathrooms with a tub or any foolish luxuries like that. Not very extravagant accommodations but, for the then-prevailing standards not bad either. People simply lived differently in those days, and despite their unpretentious houses both the Deibel and the Jonas families had live-in maids and guest rooms where we stayed. How we all fitted in is uncertain; perhaps we were spread over guest rooms in both houses.

To visit our other relatives we walked. The whole clan was nearby. Nobody else had a car and to get anywhere in Leeuwarden you walked or rode a bike. There was no public transportation and taking a taxi was extravagant. Walking down the street towards the center of town we passed the house of Oom Anne's brother George Deibel who lived in a somewhat larger house with his wife Tante Fie and son Bas (*grote Bas*). Uncle George had a company dealing in grain, I believe. A few years after my first visit he went bankrupt because he had speculated in commodities, bet the whole firm on one "can't loose scheme" and lost everything. He and his family then moved in with his mother, Tante Aaltje, which was a good solution. Tante Aaltje lived all alone in a big house, was getting older and could use some help. I remember Tante

Aaltje's house very well. I went there often, particularly during the war when Friesland became my favorite vacation destination. I enjoyed the friendship and warm hospitality of Tante Mieke and Oom Anne and benefited from the excellent food they had there, even in wartime, because they were in the midst of an area with rich farmland. Much better quality food than we had in our part of the country.

My first visits to Tante Aaltjes's house were tantamount to a step back into the 19th century. It was the type of large stately house one can still find in the more provincial Dutch towns. Built around the 1880s, it was located on the *Noorder Singel.* Singel is a word used for a body of water that surrounds an old town and often used to be the moat of the fortified part of town. The house faced a small park laid out along the water and behind the park was the *Oldehove* the landmark structure of Leeuwarden, an enormous ancient tower that is leaning in a quite pronounced way to one side. The tower used to be a lighthouse when Leeuwarden, like Dokkum, was still a North Sea harbor. North of the city, what used to be sea gradually silted in or was made into land by the construction of dikes. The old sea bottom yielded a heavy clay soil that is very fertile and excellent for cattle grazing. This land is one of the principal reasons for the high quality of the cattle bred in Friesland. The house had a large parlor type room with bay windows and also another room that served as a dining room facing the street. Behind the dining room was an interior room in which Oom Anne had his office and behind that what they call in Holland a *"Serre"* (a glass enclosed sun room), looking out into a fairly small back yard. You entered the house on the side and saw a wide hall that lead to the kitchen. Tante Aaltje would come out to greet us. She was also a throwback to the previous century, a short woman quite lean, with gray hair tied in a tight knot on the back of her head and a friendly smile. She moved briskly around on old-fashioned lace-up booties and was always dressed in black because she was a widow. She was quite deaf and used a trumpetlike device that she would put in her ear while her sons roared into the other end. An interesting feature of her house was the toilet. When I first visited, the town had not yet gotten around to connecting Tante Aaltje's house to the sewer system, so the toilet was equipped with a throne under which a tun (I looked it up, that's the word) was placed. On the outside of the house was a small door that could be opened to refresh the tuns. A man working for the town would come by with a special horse-drawn cart with two rows of boxes, each with a separate door that he would open to take an empty one out and put a full one in. This was called *het tonnetjes systeem* (the tun system). A very malodorous system that gave me an idea of one of the disadvantages of the "good old days."

Later on, whenever I visited Tante Aaltje I always went directly to the kitchen to greet Bosco, the fat boxer Oom Anne owned and brought every day to his office. Bosco was not allowed anywhere else in the house. Bosco was extremely friendly to people and like boxers do, squirmed around wagging his little cut-off tail as soon as I entered the kitchen. Bosco was not so friendly disposed to other dogs. He was a fighter and Oom Anne had many richly embellished stories of the fights between Bosco and other dogs he had been forced to break up. Bosco's back showed the many scars he had earned in his fights. My preference for boxers dates back to those days and to Bosco.

Oom Anne was a special character and I have the fondest memories of him. He had a highly developed sense of humor and could entertain his audience for hours with stories, many of which were quite exaggerated, but we knew that. He had a special way of expressing himself and it was almost always humorous. He was a meticulous dresser who took great care to preserve his clothes. When he would sit down he would do so slowly, arranging his jacket carefully in the chair so it would not crumple. When he crossed his legs he would put one of his hands on his knee to prevent his trousers from chafing together and his knees from becoming shiny. From time to time and when the weather was nice, he would carry his suits outside to air them. They would be waving in the wind with clothespins on the plea of his trousers, clamped down with a little piece of foil paper to protect the material. He believed that dry cleaning was ruinous for one's clothes because it would "take the strength out of the material." He had a business, peculiar to Friesland. He was a contractor who drilled fresh water wells mainly for the many dairy factories. Dairy farmers usually collectively own these factories. They process the large quantities of milk produced by the Frisian cattle into milk, butter, and cheese, using lots of water. Oom Anne had several drilling teams working in the Frisian countryside and a work-shop in town where two elderly employees would very slowly and deliberately make the wooden pipes used for the wells. These round pipes had a diameter of about seven inches and were made out of solid oak slats that were formed like barrel staves and were bound together by strips of brass. The objective of using oak was to keep the water odorless, for the same reason that oak water tanks are used on the roofs of New York City buildings. Since the pipes were always used below water level, they did not decay. Oom Anne's daily routine never changed and was a remarkable sight. He would come downstairs in his slippers, meticulously dressed but unshaven. In winter he would place his shoes on their sides in front of the stove to warm them up. After breakfast he would walk to the barbershop with Bosco waddling along. He claimed he had a particularly difficult beard that grew in a chaotic way and therefore required shaving by a barber. The barbershop was a source for local news and provided a willing audience for Oom Anne to tell his stories. During the war, there were occasionally German soldiers having a shave and while in his chair Oom Anne would berate the barbers for not having the guts to slice the German's throats. From the barbershop he would proceed to his office. He had a phone there which was handy for us if we wanted to reach the clan. In the early days, neither the Deibels nor Tante Jet and Oom Otto had a phone at home. After having lunch at home, Oom Anne would ride his bike over to the workshop where the two old fellows were working. They were typical characters, smoking small pipes and wearing skipper's hats with white crowns. Oom Anne would return home around 4:30, exhausted from a long hard day at the office and complain loudly about *mien personeel,* his (slow moving employees) and the men out in the field operating his drilling rigs who were stealing him blind and ruining his equipment. Tante Mieke was a jolly, typical Frisian woman. She was blond, quite good-looking and Rubenesque in appearance. She was a real mother hen for Bas, which probably harmed his ability to gain independence as a young man. Bas never left home and stayed with his mother until the very end. She died in her late nineties. For me it was great fun to be in Leeuwarden with Oom Anne and Tante Mieke. Bas and I became very close during the war, but afterwards I began to outgrow the environment and when I got married and built a career, we had less and less in common. Still, I have very good memories of this warm and hospitable family. Around the end of the century Bas had a heart attack, and the bypass operation was not very successful so he became an invalid and spent his final days in a nursing home. He died in 2009.

As I grew older I went upstairs in the Montessori school where we were at first under the care of Juffrouw (Miss) Peiterse. Early on our new teacher had the unenviable job of explaining the "new spelling" of the Dutch language to us. The Dutch do not seem to have the same passion about their language as other people display, notably the French and the English. The Dutch happily simplify the spelling and grammar of their language as they perceive a need for it. They are also prone to use foreign words in their literature and newspaper articles. Today Dutch newspapers are riddled with English words, particularly in technology, politics and sports. In the past the same was true for French words, since speaking French was seen as an indication of good manners and breeding. There are still many French words used in the Dutch language on a day-to-day basis. The "new spelling" did away with many unnecessary hurdles. The word for forest used to be *bosch,* now it became *bos.* The word for bottle was *flesch,* now *fles.* How so was *zoo* now it became *zo.* We were about nine years old, just learning to spell and now were thoroughly confused. After this change in spelling and grammar, there was another one in the seventies or eighties. This last one attacks among many other things, words with a French origin. A present used to be a *cadeau* now *kado,* a desk or office went from *bureau* to *buro.* In my opinion it's a truly ridiculous effort to bring everything down to the lowest common denominator, it is dumbing down the language, but perhaps I am becoming a grumpy old man. The question is whether it is appropriate to defend the purity of one's language at all cost, realizing that any usage is always a reflection of the times the user lives in, or to do the Dutch thing and just go with the flow and make life simple for everybody. Juffrouw Peiterse did not stay long. A mousy looking man who looked like a ribbon clerk, and probably was, swept her of her feet. Her fiancé worked in the East Indies and had come home on leave desperate to find a wife, and Juffrouw Peiterse was probably desperate to find a husband. At school her farewell party was made into a big production with skits and singing. The highlight was a huge cloth map hung on a frame, on which the route her ship was going to follow to Indonesia was drawn. Each stop the ship would make was marked with a little porthole-like opening out of which the head of a kid would pop when prompted, to recite a little relevant (sort of) rhyme. I had Aden and made up something lame about "*baden in Aden*" (bathing in Aden)—really terrible. The best was Ab Boot who had Port Said and came up with "*O nee maar kijk nu es, daar heb je Port Said aan het kanaal van Suez, en zie je De Lesseps daar staan? Die man gaat nooit weer hier vandaan*" (Oh now, look here, there's Port Said on the Suez Canal and do you see De Lesseps standing there? That man is never going to leave here.) (Actually he did leave, the statue was blown up by the Egyptians in 1952.) I suspect that Ab's father, who was in the publishing business and a good writer probably wrote this clever rhyme. Miss Peiterse settled in Indonesia and had a daughter there. I hope she survived the war and the Japanese occupation during which all Dutch people were put in camps where they were often treated very badly.

Our new teacher was Mr. de Groot. He was my first male teacher and looking back, I think he was an excellent one. He was enthusiastic and very engaged in his work. He built many of the desks, shelves and teaching aids in our classroom himself. Mr. de Groot got us interested in current affairs, which was particularly appropriate since we were in the mid-thirties and he made us aware of the many things that were happening around us. We studied World War I and its aftermath and learned about the Nazis in Germany, the Soviets in Russia, and the Fascists in Italy and tried to understand the frictions between Belgium and our country and between France and England. He also did much to make us understand and like nature, and he organized school outings in which we stayed overnight in youth hostels. He was a great teacher who had a major impact on my life.

In those years I also joined the boy scouts. A new troop had been formed in The Hague and several boys in my school and many others from The Hague joined up. We started as cub scouts, of course. The Dutch boy scouts were a carbon copy of the English version and our uniforms, insignia, etc., all came from England. We had green caps, green sweaters made of a hard kind of wool that was extremely "itchy," short, brown corduroy pants and black, woolen knee-length socks. Our Cub Scout movement was based on Rudyard Kipling's book, "Mowgli and the Wolf Cubs." We were the wolf cubs and the ladies who were in charge of our troop were "Akelas," the den mothers. The Akelas were usually single young women who were specially trained for this volunteer work. They were not, as in America, the mothers of one or more of the cubs. Each troop was divided into dens of eight or so cubs. Each den had a senior cub as leader who had two yellow stripes on the sleeve of his sweater and an assistant with one stripe. I never got further than one stripe. To earn a stripe you had to first earn two stars to be put on your cap. Each star required a certain number

OUR CUB SCOUT PACK ON OUR SECOND CAMP. IT WAS IN OMMEN. I AM IN THE FRONT ROW AT LEFT AND FRITS IS PEAKING OVER MY SHOULDER.

of skill tests that I often found difficult to complete since I was and always have been poorly coordinated. For instance you had to catch a ball thrown at you a certain number of times and you had to be able to run while skipping rope. After all requirements were signed off, you got the star. After the second star you could earn badges for certain specific skills. I got one for swimming, a sport I always liked and had no trouble with and one for woodworking. In those days we boys were always doing jigsaw work, using patterns we bought at handicraft stores. We traced them with carbon paper on to plywood. I would sit at my Frisian table made in Hindelopen and saw away, often frustrated because I would always try to push the thin saw faster through the wood than I should, often breaking it. My father who was very handy would patiently try to explain to me that to cut wood you had to let the saw do the work and you couldn't force it. We had school every day from nine till four with two hours off for lunch, starting at midday. We had Wednesday and Saturday afternoon off. So we did not have two-day weekends and neither did my father or any other working person. On Saturday afternoon I would come home and change into my Cub Scout uniform, which always was torture because of the itchy sweater. Later we got nicer sweaters made out of softer material and as a real innovation, green short-sleeved shirt for summer.

When I was about eight years old, it must have been 1933, we went to our first summer camp. This was a big event. The whole Cub Scout pack went by train to Doetinchem in the eastern part of Holland where we were billeted in the hayloft of a big farmhouse. We had brought special cloth bags that could be filled with straw to become a straw mattress. The trick was to pack the straw in such a way that the surface of the straw mattress was more or less level. I don't think we succeeded with that. At night when we were trying to sleep the older boys would tell spooky stories that made us younger ones quite anxious. We went swimming in a local river and in general had a good time. Nosing around the farm, I discovered a closed dark stable in which a large bull was kept. As an animal lover I was upset that this poor beast was not allowed to frolic in the meadows with the cows and asked one of our female leaders why this was so. I remember she got a little flustered, took me aside and explained this was because the bull was kept to help the cows make calves. I accepted that explanation and went on my way.

When the camp was over I left the train in Arnhem where my mother waited on the station platform with my cousin Tineke to take me to the new house of the Jonas family. Oom Otto had been transferred from Leeuwarden to Arnhem and they had rented a brand new house in a newly developed neighborhood. They lived there until 1951 when Oom Otto died suddenly. By that time Tineke had already married Jaap Kort. This house was a real step-up in comfort for Oom Otto and Tante Jet. They now had a real bathroom, central heating and many other luxuries that Leeuwarden did not offer. I assume the transfer was also a step-up career wise. Oom Otto worked for the government in an organization called *het Kadaster,* they were the surveyors of the entire country and maintained the topographical maps. One of their main tasks was to arrange swaps of land between farmers so they would end up owning larger contiguous pieces of land. In densely populated Holland, farmland is continually carved up in smaller and smaller pieces when the original owner dies and several of his children inherit the farm. To make these swaps acceptable to all parties, many negotiations were needed and to avoid conflicts, very accurate measurements would have to be made. The measurements and the negotiations are a service provided by the government. When I arrived at my relatives, I felt sick. A doctor was summoned and he said I had bronchitis, probably from the drafty hayloft. Since Tante Jet and Oom Otto had just moved to Arnhem, they did not yet have a family physician. The doctor who came to see me was Dr. Jan Zwolle who later became their friend and family doctor. (During the Battle of Arnhem in the fall of 1944 when British Paratroopers landed in and around Arnhem, the Germans picked Dr. Zwolle up. He was accused of being in the resistance, which was true and of helping British wounded which was also true. He was summarily executed on the street with a group of others.) After I recovered somewhat we made bicycle trips through the surroundings. Oom Otto was elated with his new location and kept telling my mother and me that he did not understand why we went abroad to Luxembourg while we could enjoy the same nature and hilly countryside right at home.

We did go to Luxembourg that summer and stayed in a hotel called Bel Air in Echternach (it still exists.) The hotel occasionally served ice cream as dessert, which in those days was a special treat so I checked the dinner menu every day as soon as it was put on the tables, scanning for the word "*glace.*" My grandparents Schieferdecker were there too, and I believe my father came for a shorter period, probably because he did not have all that much vacation. My mother and I went back by train with my grandfather who was in charge of the expedition. I remember how flustered he was when he had to show train tickets and passports to the authorities that boarded the train when we entered and left Belgium. To be safe he carried his papers in a chamois leather bag under his shirt. So whenever he had to produce documents, he had to unbutton first his raincoat, then his jacket, then his vest and finally his shirt to get at his paraphernalia. He was a cautious man and in my eyes very old. Actually he was then just quite a bit younger than I am now as I write this.

When my father had owned the Chrysler for about two years, he traded it in for a new Plymouth. This was a car we had for many years and my parents took it on a vacation to the Tirol area of Austria and to Norway. I was left home with Oom Otto and Tante Jet and Tineke who liked to come to Voorburg in summer because one could easily go to the beach in Scheveningen on the tram that stopped in front of our house.

While we had a car, we had no radio at home, a source of entertainment that was then just beginning to take hold. If you wanted to buy a radio, you called a dealer and he would send you one on a trial basis. We got one and I was just fancying myself able to hear all the shows my friends talked about and listen to stations in faraway countries when I heard my father had given my mother a choice between a fur coat and a radio. One evening when my mother came back from a shopping trip, I was shattered to hear her announce she had ordered a fur coat. What I did not know was that she had made a smart choice. She had picked a fairly inexpensive fur coat and also contracted for a *"radio distribution systeem"* this was in a way similar to the cable TV we have at home today. The phone company piped in radio programs along the phone wires and you bought a speaker and a volume regulator. There were four programs. Two Dutch stations, Hilversum I and II, and two foreign ones. Usually a mix between French, English, Belgian and German broadcasts. This idea was another reflection of my parent's frugal attitude. We were still in the middle of the Depression, and I am certain my father did not make a very big salary but we were still among the more prosperous people with a nice house, a car and frequent vacations abroad. It was just my parent's value system that made a trivial gadget like a radio not very important. Moreover, they thought, probably correctly, that the reception on our piped-in system was better. In those days, people had radio antennas strung out all over their roofs and there were frequent crackles and hissing noises in the air on an ordinary home radio set. We would listen to the concerts, the Mattheus Passion and some of the variety programs all of Holland listened to, including me, but excluding my parents who found the jokes vulgar. The speeches of the queen were reverently listened to. Queen Wilhelmina would speak from time to time about lofty goals such as the Moral Rearmament Movement that was emerging at that time. People who were very concerned about the race to rearm that was starting again tried to get a worldwide movement going that urged people to reverse the trend on moral grounds. A fruitless effort, of course, in light of the plans Hitler was making in Germany and Mussolini in Italy.

Our maid Anneliese had gone to Germany to join her greedy relatives. We replaced her with another German girl, Marie, from a small farming town near the Dutch border. Marie belonged to the German Evangelical Church and on Sundays went to a home in The Hague that was run by Church sisters who organized outings for all the girls and kept them out of trouble. Once when my parents were away for a few days, Marie took me along to the *"Schwester Heim"* (the sister's home). It was a fine day and we marched to a nearby park with the sisters leading the parade in their black dresses and white traditional headgear, playing German marching songs on their guitars. It was an embarrassing moment for me and I was glad I did not see any boys I knew as we marched through the streets. Still these people were definitely not Nazis and were trying to make the best of their lives since their homeland had been ravaged by postwar political upheavals and rampant inflation. Marie was very homesick and did not last long.

Then came Helga Nock, a nice cheerful girl from Gelsenkirchen, a grimy mining town in the heavily industrialized Ruhr area. Helga stayed with us for many years and only left after the Hitler regime ordered all the German girls who served Dutch families to come back home. When my parents were away on Saturday nights, Helga liked to listen to German vaudeville programs that were broadcast out of Cologne. I did not understand much of it, but I guess I picked up some German by simply listening. Helga's father was a miner and her oldest brother had joined the German air force, the Luftwaffe, as a professional NCO, probably to get a steady job.

In 1935 my parents took me to Switzerland on a vacation that started with a trip by car through Belgium and France. As we drove through Eastern France we saw the battlefields of the First World War. I remember that we saw a hill that was completely bare. My father told me it had been fought over so hard and there was so much metal in the ground that nothing would grow there anymore. Many of the fields were still full of undulations, craters made by artillery shells that had rained down for years on end. Here and there the metal rods used for barbed wire were still visible as strangely twisted markers. The war had ended sixteen years ago, had cost millions of lives, but the world had not made much progress towards peace. As we toured along we saw large contingents of the French army on summer maneuvers in their blue gray uniforms. In Switzerland we had a good time, hiking in the mountains, visiting several resorts and driving across a few mountain passes. I got my first pair of mountain-climbing boots there. They were heavy, greased leather affairs with plenty of nails under the soles. In the hotels you would put these boots outside your door and men would come in the early morning to collect them, clean them up and grease them to make them water proof. In Lausanne we visited with my father's old friend Tell Bersot who lived in a nice apartment with his first wife. They treated us to a Swiss fondue dish, which I found extremely tasty, but it caused me some trouble because there was a lot of wine in it and I got a little tipsy.

In school things were not going very well with me. The Montessori system was based on students being self-motivated. I was a free spirit not very motivated or ambitious to learn a lot. The things people were forced to learn by rote in the public school system could easily be avoided in my school by simply keeping busy with other easier tasks. Mr. de Groot just could not keep an eye on every student's individual progress. Eventually he caught on, however, and spoke with my parents. I was a good talker and liked to write stories, but I avoided math and had no great interest in learning the years in which historic events had taken place. For their history lessons, Dutch children in those days had to memorize long lists of events and the years in which they took place. We also had to memorize the names of many towns and cities, rivers and mountains in geography. The worst part for me were the math problems in which you had to analyze a situation described in writing and come up with the right number. Things like "a train leaves Amsterdam at 9 o'clock and travels at a speed of 30 kilometers an hour and at 10 o'clock another train leaves Rotterdam running at 40 kilometers an hour. The distance between the two cities is 80 kilometers. Where do the trains meet, and at what time?" All these subjects were part of the government-prescribed curriculum, and the teachers of the Montessori school could not avoid teaching them although they probably disliked doing so. We had no report cards, just teacher conferences so my parents had no clear measure of my progress or lack of it. My father helped me from time to time with the math problems but mostly kept his distance from my schoolwork. My mother would try to help me by looking over my homework, but she tended to get quite impatient with me and often criticized my lack of ambition and knowledge, which did not help my motivation. My friends Eelco and Frits were learning well and competing with each other. Paul and Ab were as lackadaisical as I was about studying. My parents decided they had made a mistake sending me to a Montessori school, but believed they could not take me out of the school before the exams we all had to pass to enter high school. You could go on to a Montessori Lyceum in Rotterdam without having to pass an exam, but it was decided that was not the right direction for me. Ab and Paul went to Rotterdam and did quite well there. Eventually Ab became a physician and Paul went to law school. So it is not clear to me that all the learning by rote the Dutch schools excelled in was really useful. Frits and Eelco went to school in Leiden. Frits to the Gymnasium and Eelco to the HBS. My parents decided to ask Mr. de Groot to tutor me privately. So in the evenings I bicycled to his house for a session of one-on-one teaching. This did wonders for me and improved my motivation. I was given assignments to complete and the discipline began to help.

In the summer of 1936 when I was eleven, my parents decided that my mother and I would travel to Las Palmas in the Canary Islands to visit Tante Jetje and Oom Bernard. My father preferred to go mountain climbing in Zermatt Switzerland

IN SCHOOL IN 1936.

with Mr. Beversen. This trip is described in a diary I wrote because Mr. de Groot wanted me to do this to improve my writing and spelling skills. I still have this diary with my teacher's corrections in a very neat handwriting. I note there are several days in which I wrote, "absolutely nothing happened today."

Nobody flew in those days certainly not to places like the Canary Islands. It turned out to be a very interesting trip for us, a trip that in several respects confronted us with the gathering political storms that would ultimately lead to World War II. Despite these signs we merrily went on with our vacation, reflecting the prevailing attitude of those days that ignored signs of trouble and just went on with life as it presented itself. We boarded the *Boschfontein* of the Holland Africa Line at IJmuiden, the harbor that is located at the entrance to the Noordzee Canal, the canal that links Amsterdam with the North Sea. There are huge locks at IJmuiden that must be passed by any ship entering the canal. These locks have always been a serious problem for the growth of the Amsterdam harbor and particularly in its competitive position vis-a-vis Rotterdam that has a harbor without locks. Our ship had not gone through the locks. It was anchored in the harbor because it had come from Hamburg and we were ferried over to it. My father and the de Clercq family came to see us off and to get a flavor of the ocean liner we would leave on. Among the passengers were many Jewish people from Germany who had made the sensible decision to emigrate to South Africa in light of the developing anti–Semitic policies of the Nazi regime. Helmuth, a young boy became a playmate of mine on board. Helmuth had been brainwashed in school to admire the German swastika flag, because when he saw one on another ship in one of the harbors where we stopped, he began to exclaim how beautiful it was to see it. His mother pulled him up short and told him he was being an idiot because the people behind that flag were pushing him out of his country of origin.

We stopped at Dover to pick up some freight and a few English passengers and then we went on to the Canary Islands. Underway, I became friendly with an older gentleman who was Dutch but had been born in South Africa and had fought in the Boer War. He told me a literally hair-raising story. He had been on a reconnaissance patrol and had seen English soldiers approaching. He and his buddy crawled under a bush and held still. As the patrol passed them, he could see the back of his buddy's head and noticed that his hair was standing on end like that of a dog who encounters an enemy. Obviously he survived this encounter. It was the first time in my life that I met anybody who had fought in a war.

As we approached our destination, we heard that there had been a military coup in Spain that originated in nearby Spanish Morocco where a military governor, General Franco, had rebelled against the republic's government and proclaimed a right-wing Fascist state. He also had troops loyal to him in the Canary Islands. He flew over to mainland Spain with some troops from Morocco and started a military revolt there. The legal government had its own loyalist troops and a full-fledged civil war was beginning. For us the question was what we should do. Continue our vacation trip or just stay on the ship and go on to the next stop, Dakar. We decided to see what would happen once we got there. The ship was going to Tenerife and when we got there it was evening. To my mother's great relief, Oom Bernard came on board. He had taken a boat from Gran Canaria to Tenerife to meet us. He said we could transfer onto the small ship that would sail overnight to Gran Canaria. As we walked around the harbor of Tenerife, armed soldiers would walk by, moving softly on their rope soled shoes. I found these soldiers unusually shabby and poorly equipped. Particularly their shoes called alpargatas, which were worn by all the local people. We sat briefly in a café for a late cup of coffee and we noticed a bullet hole in its window. Once in a while a truck filled with soldiers roared by and we heard shots in the distance. For people not used to hearing guns being fired nearby, this was rather disconcerting, but Oom Bernard told me a white lie, saying they were just training. Oom Bernard was a real operator. He got us a fairly decent hut and when he discovered he had to share his own hut with two priests, he claimed he was a diplomat and could not accept such poor accommodation. Exclaiming *"Yo soy diplomatico"* (I am a diplomat), he brandished a big document covered with impressive wax seals to prove his point. It was a document that had belonged to his father who used to be in the Dutch Foreign Service and served as minister in South Africa. It did not matter because the Spanish official was illiterate, holding the document upside down anyway. So we came to our destination and I still remember seeing the island of Gran Canaria for the first time through the porthole of our cabin. It was early morning, there was a bluish light on the sea, and behind the nearby shore you could see the sand-colored hills and yellow mountains. The air was fresh and it was my first exposure to a sub tropical climate where the light is bright and the sun nearly always shines.

We drove in Oom Bernard's car to a village on the outskirts of the main town, Las Palmas where they lived in a nice big typical Spanish house. The ground floor was just for storage. A broad exterior stone stairway with tile steps led to the main floor. There was a cool gallery around the main floor and the living, dining room and kitchen opened up to it. There were some bedrooms on the same floor and a few upstairs. There was a flat roof that offered a view of the surrounding hills. From my bedroom I could see the town below, a nice view, particularly at night when you saw the harbor and lights glistening below. All the rooms had tile floors in the tropical fashion. My uncle and aunt had a maid called Soledad who lived in the village nearby and a chauffeur Eladio who lived in the house with his wife. There also was a gardener. So they managed quite well on what I am certain was a very modest income. It was a most enjoyable vacation and we often went to the beach.

We would go downtown to visit a German family who were friends of my uncle and aunt and lived very close to the sea. We would change at their house and stroll down to the beach from there. We also went on long walks in the hills, and drove all over the island. We made visits to the families of Tante Jetje's personnel. This was possible because both my mother and my aunt spoke reasonably good Spanish. The people we visited were extremely pleased that we came. We visited the folks of Eladio's wife, who lived in the country in a farmhouse. They had a large family who proudly showed us their house and particularly the bedroom of the matriarch and patriarch, with its large bed in the center and equally large prints of saints on the walls. When we left, they showered us with fruits from their own land. We also went to Soledad's family, who lived in a hovel nearby. Soledad was not married but was the principal breadwinner of her clan. Her parents lived with her and she also had a sister with her two little boys occupying the house. When we entered the house, chickens, cats and dogs were scurrying around. As was apparently customary we were led into Soledad's bedroom, the best room of the hovel. We sat in front of the window and looking out, I saw the sister rushing outside with her two little boys, carrying their best clothes. They went behind a low wall and as their mother was putting on their Sunday suits, one of the boys peered over the wall at me and stuck out his tongue in our direction. He was not happy with the proceedings.

In town we went to see the principal church where I got a glimpse of Spanish Catholic mysticism. A custodian showed us around and among large closets with vestments for priests and cabinets with golden and silver treasures was a glass display case containing, among many other things, a glass jar with the heart of a bishop who had gone to Peru and was martyred there. They only could salvage his heart apparently.

The Canary Islands fell almost immediately into the hands of the Franco regime so there were no military actions when we were there. A large British cruiser came to show the flag in the harbor and the officers were entertained at the English Club in town. My uncle and aunt belonged to this club. It was in those days normal to have such a club in almost any outpost where English people lived. The British Empire was then still very much in evidence but it would soon prove to have lost much of its power. During our voyage the currency aboard ship was sterling, and when I looked at the map of the world in school there was a lot of red all over. Canada, Australia, India, South Africa, everything was colored red, indicating these lands were part of the British Empire.

When it was time to go back we boarded the *Maaskerk*, a much smaller ship, which came to Las Palmas. The trip on this ship was a wonderful experience for me since I was the only kid on board and could go wherever I wanted. I regularly went to the bridge, steered the ship, visited with the radio operator and when we entered Le Havre for a stop, I was shown the engine room in the bowels of the ship which was interesting since they were maneuvering around and there was much activity down below.

I turned twelve when I was in my last year in grade school. That year I spent much time preparing for the exam I had to pass to be allowed to enter a Lyceum – a high school. In spring when the day of the exam came near, I went several times to Mr. de Groot's house to be coached. My parents had chosen the Haags Lyceum for me, a school where Ma's friend Hilda Bolt taught English. It was a private school with smaller classes that was deemed to be better for me because they thought, probably correctly, that I needed a lot of supervision. I also graduated from cub scout to boy scout in that year. I passed the school exam without too much trouble but not with flying colors. As a reward, my father bought a new bike for me.

9 : *From age Twelve*

In the early summer of 1937 I put on my brand new boy scout uniform and left my grandparents' house in Bloemendaal on my brand new bike to participate in the first World Jamboree to be held in the Netherlands. Like all Dutchmen of that time I went everywhere on my bike and having a new one was important to me not only because of the prestige it gave me but also because it would provide me with

adequate transportation to go to high school in The Hague. My parents had given me a bike without a three-speed, a gadget most of my friends had. A three-speed gave you the opportunity to pedal slowly but at greater speed down wind and down hill or on level ground. Going uphill (unusual in Holland) or against a strong wind (very common in Holland) was made lighter because you could switch to a lower gear. My parents thought a three-speed was an unnecessary luxury for me because I was an only child and they realized we were quite well-off compared with many others, so they were convinced I was in constant danger of being spoiled. Therefore, I had to be taught to be frugal. They had also denied me an electric train while all my friends had one. I had only a small Meccano set, which was

an English version of what Americans call an Erector Set. Dutch boys used to build all kinds of machinery like bridges and cranes with their Meccano sets. The only big toy I had was a steam engine. I brought it along to America and gave it to grandson Alexander. I do not think this enforced deprivation of expensive toys had any lasting impact on me; I am just recording it here to give an insight in my parent's efforts to teach me that life is full of disappointments. Let's not forget that we were living in a world scarred by the Great Depression. My parents saw evidence of it everywhere. Many of their friends and acquaintances were fired from their jobs and had to adjust to a life of belt-tightening and scarcity. My father's career and compensation was certainly stalled in those days because his company had to cope with shrinking markets and negative growth, but I think he was reasonably secure in his job. He was a smart and capable executive. So I grew up in a quite privileged environment.

Although our lifestyle was definitely "upper class" in a materialistic sense, it was certainly not too high-brow in a social sense. I certainly do not hold a lasting grudge against my parents for keeping me, materialistically, on a short leash. I remember my parents as caring and loving people who were quite strict with me when I was young but became very generous when I was older. Like my cub scout outfit, my boy scout uniform was made in England. We had large Smokey the Bear hats that were really cumbersome while riding a bike in windy Holland. In addition we carried long sticks that would stick out above our heads when we walked. These sticks were carried like a rifle with a sling, but the idea was not militaristic or intended to give us substitute rifles. It was just that Lord Baden Powell, the chief scout, felt we should carry a stick. He always had a long stick handy when he was serving in the British army and was exploring the bush country in South Africa. When we asked why we had to bother with these sticks, we were told they were useful in case we encountered a rabid dog or a snake. We simply had to poke the stick into the dog's mouth and thus subdue it or use it to clobber the snake into submission. The fact that a rabid dog had not been seen in Holland for more than fifty years, and snakes were exceedingly rare, was a mere detail. We carried the stick lashed horizontally to the frame of our bikes, another cumbersome thing to cope with.

Although I did not realize it at the time, the Jamboree was in many respects a milestone in my life. I was twelve years old, had completed grade school, and was totally on my own for the first time, cycling some twenty miles to a destination I was a little apprehensive about. Luckily we do not know what is beyond our horizon. Had I known that another world war was about to begin in two years, a war that would involve many thousands of the boys that had gathered innocently in

Holland, I would not only have been apprehensive, I would have been very sad. In 1938 Hitler would annex Austria as a first step in a chain of aggressive moves that would trigger the war. I had personally witnessed the beginning of the Spanish Civil War. The first clouds of the gathering storm were visible, but most of us, certainly the people in my environment in the Netherlands underestimated the magnitude of the threat and overestimated the ability of our country and of the other Western European nations to deal with it. All I knew at that moment was that I would meet boy scouts from all over the world and would have to find my way in a huge organization. The Jamboree was held in a place called Vogelenzang and spread over several large country estates. I would join our troop there. Our troop was called the *Zwarte Panters* (Black Panthers) and was assigned a camping site on a plot of land within a large camping area called *Woestduin* that was once a racetrack. It was sort of a side-show to the really big encampment on the other side of the main road where all the foreign visitors had pitched their tents. There were a great number of other Dutch scouts in our area. We camped there for two weeks and enjoyed splendid weather, a very unusual thing for rainy and cool Holland. It was also abnormally warm which was in a way a problem since we had only one uniform shirt. So we became rather smelly and grimy. We participated in numerous events with big rallies and parades in the blazing sun, which did not make us smell any fresher. Our troop consisted of mostly twelve-year-olds and nobody knew how to cook a decent meal. We were cooking on wood fires and since the camp was open to the public, people would stand near our kitchen and watch our feeble efforts to prepare a meal. Women visitors were often unable to restrain themselves and offered to help when they saw us struggle with poorly burning wet wood that produced lots of smoke but no heat and dropping pancakes in the dirt. We did not turn them away. There were many opportunities to get to know scouts from other countries. We all thought it was normal that Germans and Italians did not participate. They lived in dictatorships that had outlawed scouting and had their paramilitary youth organizations, the Hitler Jugend in Germany and the Balilla in Italy. For our troop, the Americans and the Poles were the favorites among the foreigners.

The Americans had a huge camp with comfortable tents. The American boys slept two to a tent on nice field cots. So they would not get wet feet in damp Holland they had a local carpenter make wooden floor grates for them, which they put between the two beds. These accommodations contrasted sharply with ours and we looked at the American encampment with open-mouthed awe. We were sleeping packed in like cordwood on the hard ground with six or seven to a tent of the same size as the Americans. We were not allowed to have straw mattresses because of the mess and the fire hazard. The Americans had a large dining room tent with professional (adult) cooks and nice tables and benches. We ate outside, sitting on the grass. Every country had a show to be presented to the Dutch public in a large arena. The Americans did Indian dances. They had a large tent full of beautiful Indian costumes and a professional stage manager to take care of the make-up of the scouts and to direct the Indian dances. Nobody thought it strange that the American scouts were all white. There were, of course, no real Indians or blacks among them. It was 1937 after all, and they were still regularly lynching black people in the Deep South, and the Bureau of Indian Affairs kept the Indians on a short leash while living on their reservations in abject poverty. We had in our troop a boy who spoke reasonable English since he had relatives in the U.S. His name was Bertie Da Silva, probably a member of the small community of Portuguese Jews who lived in Holland ever since the Spanish Inquisition drove them out of their country. Bertie was a good talker and he managed to talk two Americans into putting on their Indian costumes and walk all the way over to our camp for lunch. This caused quite a sensation in our section. I doubt the Americans enjoyed the meal we prepared for them. We had our regular Dutch open-faced sandwiches with jam or cheese. I was deeply impressed by the American boys who had nice uniforms and had a very self-assured yet casual demeanor.

The military-style, field-green uniforms of the Poles reflected the situation their country was in. They looked like soldiers, and were equipped like a semi-military organization. They did not have Smokey the Bear hats like most of us. They wore caps with squared tops like Polish soldiers and had large capes like the Polish cavalry. Word had it that they would smuggle Dutch girl scouts into their tents, hiding them in their capes. I saw a cartoon in a local paper suggesting this but did not understand the implication of the suggestion. We were living in innocent times. The Poles had an aviation contingent that flew in with their own planes towing gliders. Poland in those days felt the pressure of the Communist Soviet Union in the east and Nazi Germany in the west. Their government obviously saw their boy scouts as a useful training ground for the military. This was, of course, totally in conflict with the spirit of scouting, but we did not notice it and were impressed by their organization and behavior. We also got two Poles to visit us. Like most elderly people who cannot remember the names of people they have met five minutes ago but know many facts and names out of their younger years, I can still remember the names of those two Poles. Tadek Orzanowski and Tachek Urbanec. I often wondered what became of them. Two years later, in August 1939, Germany invaded Poland from the west, destroyed the inadequately equipped Polish army and started a regime of terror and intimidation of the local population, killing a large number of Poles and almost totally exterminating the millions of Polish Jews that had lived in that country for centuries. The Soviet Union helped by invading Poland from the east. They had signed a friendship treaty with the Germans and wanted their part of the spoils.

Towards the end of the Jamboree, when most of the foreigners were leaving, my grandparents invited our troop to their house for an afternoon visit. We all bicycled over to Bloemendaal and entertained my grandparents with skits and scout games we performed in the garden while enjoying cookies and lemonade. During that brief visit I saw my little dog Duco, who had suddenly become very ill and was obviously near death. My parents were away on vacation and my grandparents were taking care of Duco who was then quite old. Duco was a tiny dog, a Miniature Pinscher that Oom Daan de Clercq had given me. I do not remember why. We had Duco for many years. He went everywhere with us, which was easy because he was so small. He was a lively active little fellow who amused us by his antics. He was very clever, particularly in finding his ball. We had a small black rubber ball that he would retrieve if you threw it out. What he especially liked to do was find his ball. He would get extremely agitated and yapped loudly in anticipation when we would put him outside the room to hide the ball. Once you let him in he would race around the room and try to find his ball. He was usually successful. On the day I returned from the Jamboree, the vet was called and he put Duco to sleep. We buried him on the hill behind my grandparent's house. This was a grievous loss for me.

In September of 1937 I started going to the Haags Lyceum. Voorburghad no high school so we had to go either to The Hague or Leiden. The old group of Montessori School kids dispersed to all kinds of schools and I had to make new friends. I did stay in touch very regularly with Paul, Eelco and Frits and also with Erik van't Groenewoud, a boy I had met through our tennis group. Erik and I became close friends for several years, particularly in the period just before and during the war. While Frits and Eelco commuted to Leiden for their schools, and Paul and Ab to Rotterdam, Erik and I went to The Hague, and since our schools were close to each other we often traveled together. Erik's father owned a printing business in Rotterdam. He was a recreational pilot and flew with a flying club nearby at a small local airport called Ypenburg. This fascinated and impressed me very much, and Erik and I often went to the airport with his parents to wander among the hangars and look at the planes. Erik's father was a good schmoozer and when I was in my teens I enjoyed his company, but he was also a man-about-town who during the war got involved with people with Nazi sympathies. This cost him dearly after the war. He was arrested and, I believe, tried. I don't think he did anything really wrong, he was just unprincipled and out for a good time. Many people were concerned about him because he presented a danger since he was never openly pro–German. Erik's mother was a quite attractive and very energetic woman who organized our tennis group and often played with us. She was clearly disappointed in the behavior of her husband and their relationship deteriorated during the war years. I believe they got divorced soon after the war. I was quite fond of her in the years Erik and I were friends, but after the war when I went to Leiden University, Erik and I drifted apart. I never heard from him and do not know what became of him.

The Haags Lyceum was located in what was once a large private house. Classes were held in various rooms and the old stable served as a gym. It was a coed school, but boys outnumbered girls by a large margin. It catered to students of mostly well-off families who needed some extra attention. Since I had been displaying a lack of motivation, my parents thought this school was just the ticket for me. The classes were small so that the teachers could spend more time on each student. Some of the teachers were excellent, but there were also several that were below par. All in all I had a good time in that school and in the first four years I did very well and made good progress. The greater discipline helped. It was definitely no Montessori school. We sat on wooden benches all in rows, looking at our teacher. Every hour a bell rang and another teacher would enter the room to teach another subject.

We had school from 8:30 until 12 in the morning and from 2 until 4 or 4:30 in the afternoon. On Wednesdays and Saturdays we had the afternoon off and were in class from 8:30 till 1. I would go there by tram or ride my bike. During the lunch break, I would usually walk over to my father's office and drive home with him to have lunch. After lunch he would swing by the school to drop me off again. We had seven weeks of summer vacation and a week in October, two weeks for Christmas and Easter, and a few days in between for special holidays. All together we spent considerably more time in school than today's American high school kids. In addition, we spent much less time on sports and extracurricular activities because we were kept busy with loads of homework. Comparing two vastly different educational systems is very tricky, but without claiming to be an expert educator, I think the following is in general correct:

The Dutch school system has materially changed in the past decades, but I believe that in terms of curriculum it is still organized in the same way as it was in our days. To complete high school, Dutch students have to pass an exam that is the same countrywide and government controlled. Those who complete high school usually have a higher level of factual knowledge than their American peers do. However, their knowledge is apt to be more the type one gains from learning things by rote and may not be useful in making a student a well-rounded and motivated individual. American students usually are better writers and public speakers and while they may know fewer facts, they are trained to think for themselves, do their own research and find the information they need. Consequently, Americans usually have a lower level of general knowledge than Dutch high-school graduates do when they enter college. Dutch freshman college students are often at the same level as Americans are after one or two years of college. However, once they are college graduates, I think Americans are often much better equipped for life than their Dutch brethren. They are more specialized, they have better communication skills, and while they may still know fewer facts, they know how to find the information they need to complete a complicated job. The curriculum in American colleges is considerably more rigorous and much more tightly controlled. It requires students to work harder and longer hours than Dutch university students who tend to relax and take things easy once they have completed high school and are released from the pressure of their demanding high school curriculum. Moreover, the better American colleges and universities offer, in my opinion, considerably more depth of academic pursuit. There is more freedom to select interesting classes and the level of contact with faculty members is much more intense than in Dutch universities. Dutch people are used to having universities that offer basically the same curriculum with the same level of intellectual challenge. One university is not regarded as better or academically more elevated than the other. It is often hard to explain to the Dutch that there is a great variety in the quality of American institutions of higher learning.

In the first grade (seventh grade U.S. style), we were taught French and German in addition to Dutch. Most of us had learned some French in grade school. English was considered an easier language for us so we only got that in the second year. We had algebra and geometry, natural history, geography and history, chemistry and physics. We also had courses in government, economics and art history. In addition, we had art lessons, mostly drawing, and we had gymnastics. So we had to absorb about eleven or twelve separate subjects. At the beginning of the school year we would receive a roster of our weekly schedule, listing the subjects and times at which they would be taught. We would also get a list of all the books we were required to buy. The school did not provide us with textbooks. Being frugal Dutch, we would often not buy new books but buy books used by our predecessors, who would sell them in an annual book fair. We had to protect our books with paper covers, which we made ourselves. You would buy a roll of paper in a distinctive color and start folding and cutting. You would stick a label on the cover with your name and the title of the book. The objective of this exercise was to protect the books from wear and tear so you would be better able to sell them to others. We had diaries in which we wrote our homework assignment for every day. These diaries would be personalized with pictures of airplanes or cars and (later) girls. Our classroom was fairly small with about fifteen students.

There were one or two students in our class who had been held back from the previous year. These boys acted like senior citizens and taught us the ropes. They told us which teachers to look out for and which were easygoing. Boys mostly wore "plus fours" pants, with jackets or sweaters. We all wore shirts and ties. I remember I had two pairs of plus fours, that I wore the whole year. I think I was the only boy who came from Voorburg. There were one or two from Wassenaar and all the others came from The Hague. Most of us were strangers to each other, which made it easier for all of us to fit in and build new friendships.

There were two girls in the class. They both worked harder than the boys and were most likely smarter too.

There were several boys in my class that had parents living in the Dutch East Indies. This was typical for The Hague, where many people lived who had connections with the colonies. After a few months the class began to develop its persona. We found out who was a hell raiser, who was smart and who was good at cheating. We sat in benches with a flat top and a shelf under it where you could store books. We often had tests, sometimes unexpectedly and some guys were very good at peeking in books they had opened half on the shelf and half on their laps. If you got caught you got automatically a 1. Our marks went from 1 as lowest to 10 as highest. Nobody ever got a 10. Several of our teachers had retired from teaching in Indonesia. Some had been let go early since the Depression hit the colonies hard, as they were dependent on producing raw materials such as oil, rubber and tin and consumable commodities like tea coffee and sugar. Others had simply reached retirement age, which was quite early in the tropics. Our headmaster called *Rector* was a tough man also from the Far East. He was short, rotund, had a commanding presence, a loud voice and incessantly smoked cigars. In winter when we had all the windows in the classroom closed and the teachers were puffing away on a cigar, cigarette or pipe, the atmosphere inside was often hard to take. Our German teacher was

Swaantje Huisman, a youngish woman who was a friend of Ma's friend Hilda Bolt and a tough cookie. It is amazing how some people have a great deal of authority over a class of young unruly teenagers and others completely fail to keep order. One day I was sitting in the tram on my way to school when I suddenly discovered I had forgotten to memorize a German poem that Swaantje had given us as a homework assignment. The poem was more than a page long, but I was so scared of Swaantje that I memorized the whole thing in the fifteen-minute tram ride. I was a very easy-going student and often had trouble concentrating on my homework, but this time I got the message.

In 1937 my Aunt Jetje and Uncle Bernard left the Canary Islands and came home. It had become impossible for Uncle Bernard to continue his business there. The Spanish Civil War was continuing and the League of Nations, a toothless organization of which most western nations except Nazi Germany and Fascist Italy were members had decided to subject Spain to a trade embargo in an attempt to curb the Franco regime. The League of Nations was organized after World War I and was an initiative of the U.S. President Wilson was its great proponent, but the U.S. Congress, in a postwar isolationist mood, embarrassed its president and voted against joining which made the institution completely toothless. The embargo had little effect on the war in Spain, but it ruined people like Uncle Bernard who was in the export/import business. My uncle and aunt lived temporarily with my grandparents before moving to Amsterdam where Bernard tried to get back in business without much success. In late 1938 they bought their house *De Meezenhof* in Leersum which became their retirement home. I assume my grandfather helped them with this purchase. It was located in a very nice, but very rural area in the province of Utrecht. I loved to go there and stay for a few days. During the war this house would be the place where I found refuge for a short time and where my dog Moro stayed to avoid being drafted into the German army. Later it became the place where the most serious drama took place that our family experienced during the war.

That year my mother and Mrs. Beversen decided Paul and I needed dancing lessons. We were enrolled at a dancing school run by Mrs. Gaillard in The Hague. My mother and I went out to buy a dancing school suit. All the boys had dark blue serge suits with jackets and long pants. My mother decided to buy a somewhat lighter blue woolen suit for me that also had a pair of plus fours. Being slightly different from all the others was deeply embarrassing for me, but during the war when clothing was rationed and very scarce, I benefited because I could wear the plus fours with the jacket to school. To get up to speed with the class we were going to join, we got a few private lessons which confronted me with the (for a twelve-year-old boy) frightening prospect of having to hold a young female dancing teacher in my arms. Later we got into a large group with many girls I thought were attractive and the shyness disappeared. We did stick to the universal dancing school rule of behavior, however, with all the boys gathering at one side of the hall and the girls on the opposite side. When the music started we raced over to bow to the girls we liked and asked them to dance.

As usual we celebrated Christmas, 1937, at my grandparents in Bloemendaal. My great wish at that time was to have a dog of my own again. My grandmother suggested I go with Uncle Bernard to the Haarlem dog pound and see if I could find a dog to my liking. My uncle was knowledgeable about dogs, horses, hunting and fishing. He and I looked at the cages and saw a friendly, fairly young (about two-years- old) boxer. Although we had not named him yet, this was Moro, a dog who stayed with us for many years and survived the war despite the almost total absence of food in the last winter. He became my very best friend and I really loved him. Moro was dark-brown brindled and had a completely black face. This black face prompted my mother to come up with the name "Moro" as in Moor or in *Il Moro di Venezia*. We soon made it a Dutch name, however and usually we called him *Moortje*. Moro was very friendly and always happy to see us. He did not mind staying home alone for long periods of time. Whenever we came back or when we got him out of the bathroom where he used to spend the night, he would pick up something, his rug or a piece of paper out of the wastepaper basket or whatever else he could find, and parade around with it making happy, growling noises. When I would come home from school and put my bike in the shed in the rear of our backyard, I could see my dog looking out the window at me. He would climb on a chair to be able to look out and see me and always had something in his mouth. I could see his head wiggle because he would be wagging his stumpy little tail so much. The day after Christmas, his second day with us, Moro caused some consternation because he deposited a huge turd under the Christmas tree. This proved to be an aberration caused by his sudden change of environment, but initially it gave us some food for thought. Luckily he proved to be completely housebroken and never repeated the trick.

Our German maid, Helga Nock had been forced to go back home by her government. The German Consulate in the Netherlands simply wrote all the German girls working happily in Holland that the Führer wanted them to come back to the Fatherland and off they went. She was replaced by Jo Buunk, a sturdy farm girl from

Zelhem, a small village in the eastern part of the province of Gelderland. When my friend Frits Rechtdoorzee Greup, suggested we go camping with his sister Joke and one of her friends, we asked Jo Buunk if there was a place near her home where we could camp. She said there was a nice woodsy area almost next to her parent's farmhouse. The woods belonged to two spinster sisters in the village, and I wrote them a nice letter asking permission to camp on their property. Permission was granted and in the summer of 1938 we took the train to Doetinchem, where we picked up our bicycles that we had shipped ahead and pedaled to our destination. The Dutch railways operated a very efficient bicycle transportation system. People who went on vacation could ship their bikes to their destination and pick them up after arrival. In some popular vacation areas hundreds of bikes were shipped to their owners without any problems. This system is probably still functioning. We had shipped our gear to Jo's farm. Frits owned two very nice tents and we had all the gear for a good camp. Our experience as boy scouts paid off and the girls knew how to cook. Joke was an attractive brunette and her friend was also quite good looking. They were about two years older than we, but they treated us nicely and did not act as if they felt they were far superior to us. We had a really good time and had an opportunity to get a close-up view of the life of a typical farming family. Jo had a number of brothers and the youngest one often came over to see us. He was obviously very much taken by the girls. The family lived in a traditional small thatched farmhouse where the living quarters were in the front of the house and the back of the same structure consisted of a large barn that housed stables for their horse and some farm machinery. They had no running water, just a well, and used kerosene lamps for lighting. They had some cows but mainly grew wheat. Much of the work was done by hand or by machines driven by the horse. The Buunks were solid upstanding people, very religious and well-regarded in the village. The pride of the family was an older brother who was a schoolteacher. We made excursions on our bikes, swam in nearby lakes and in the evenings went into the village to hear the local marching band play in the bandstand. A picture of a way of life in a peaceful prewar Dutch village that does not exist anymore.

That same summer my father took me mountain climbing in Zermatt, Switzerland. He obviously took pleasure in introducing me to his lifelong passion for the Alps and in taking me along to that village he knew so well and was a Mecca for mountain climbers. My mother preferred to stay in Holland and visit with her friends in Friesland. This was my second trip to Switzerland, but the first one by train. We went to the station in The Hague where the train was waiting. We had reserved a compartment in a sleeper. It was a train that would go through Belgium and France to Basel. The sleeper carriage belonged to the Wagons Lits company. It was the same company that ran the Orient Express before the war. The interior was beautifully finished in glossy woodwork with inlaid motifs depicting vases with flowers etc. On the outside the carriage was dark blue and had signage that said in golden letters, *Compagnie des Wagons Lits et des Grandes Expresses Europeens.* Great fun and very romantic. A French attendant made the beds in our small compartment by flipping up the backrest of our seat and putting on clean sheets. Et voila! The train was pulled by steam locomotives and during the night made numerous stops at dark and deserted French stations where the few people on the platform would converse at the top of their voices to make sure we would not sleep too soundly. We had breakfast in Basel and transferred to a Swiss train that brought us to Brig and from there we went in a small mountain train up to Zermatt where the porters of the hotels were waiting for their guests with handcarts and horse-drawn coaches. Cars were not allowed in the village and I believe and hope this is still the case.

We stayed in the Hotel Monte Rosa, one of the four Seiler hotels that dominated the village hostelry scene. My father said that this was the hotel where the true alpinists stayed. However, I suspect he had chosen it also because it was a more frugal place. It had no running water; you washed in old fashioned wash basins with water supplied out of large pitchers. Employees would bring hot water in buckets when you came back from a day in the mountains and needed a relaxing foot bath. I got a new pair of mountain boots and an ice axe, which made me feel like a real mountaineer. My father wisely prepared me for the mountains by breaking me in slowly, taking me gradually on longer and more demanding hikes. We would wear plus four pants, long-sleeved shirts and hats to protect ourselves against the very strong mountain sun. I loved the mountains, the fresh air and the clear skies over the alpine landscape. As we would climb higher, we would leave the meadows with the brown cows and their pleasantly sounding cow bells behind, pass the tree line and emerge into the world of rocks, boulders and glaciers. We traversed several glaciers and gradually I became quite good at climbing and certainly at descending. My dad had older knees than I and sometimes had problems keeping up with me as I bounded downhill.

We had a grand old time and it was a wonderful experience for me. In the evenings when we were tired and had washed up, we would sit on a row of chairs in front of the hotel, right at the edge of the main street of the village. This offered an opportunity to watch the other climbers come back, some more graceful than others. I remember sitting next to a prim English lady who looked disapprovingly at two large, amply-endowed women who came marching down the street with their sweaty blouses in disarray and their big bosoms jiggling. "Shocking, those women," she said. Listening to the women's conversation, I noticed they were Dutch. Towards evening the parade of tourists would peter out and the village goats would fill the street, returning from their day of mountain grazing. They all had bells that were much smaller than the cowbells and made a higher-pitched tinkling noise. Their goatherd was the village idiot who made himself useful that way. He did not have to provide too much leadership. The goats all knew where they lived and without fail swung into the right alley to find the house of their owners. They would disappear into the dark little stables that most of the traditional wooden chalet-type houses had underneath the ground floor. The parade of goats would be followed by a man with a big broom who swept the goat droppings into the gutter, and that was the end of another day.

I had advanced without difficulty to the second grade of the Haags Lyceum. To everybody's amazement my grades were quite good. The second year that started in the fall of 1938 was going to be important because at its end one had to decide whether to go to the third grade on the HBS or math and science side or on the humanities, Latin and Greek side called Gymnasium. When the school year came to an end my parents and I decided that I was better suited for the math and science side. This was a very serious mistake, but understandable in light of my report card. I had reasonably good marks for algebra and geometry while my marks for French were just average. Also, I had participated in a voluntary Latin class for one or two hours a week in which a totally uninspiring teacher tried to teach us the basic fundamentals of Latin. Since I was still the same easygoing student who was not going to make a serious effort for anything that was not absolutely required, my grades for that little course were poor. So the decision seemed straightforward. That was unfortunate, because I still think I would have done a lot better on the Gymnasium side and would probably also have been much happier there.

But in 1938 many other things began to concern us in Holland. In the fall of that same year, the Nazis in Germany organized the *Kristall Nacht*, a night in which anti–Semitism broke loose and shops and houses owned by Jews were thrashed by mobs of brown shirts and ordinary citizens. Jews saw their property confiscated and many were transported to concentration camps. A large number of German Jews understood that they should leave their country and quite a few ended up in the Netherlands. We were witnessing the beginning of the Holocaust, the organized effort by the Germans to completely exterminate an entire people. I was vaguely aware of the *"Kristall Nacht"* outrage and remember how one of the girls in my class mentioned it to me, saying how upset she and her family were about it. I paid little attention to it. We also took the arrival of a refugee girl in our school in stride. This girl was Gladys Stückmann, the daughter of a wealthy German–Jewish entrepreneur who managed to get his family out and continued to live in style in The Hague. A chauffeur drove Gladys to school in a large German automobile. When she came she did not speak a word of Dutch, but she was a very smart girl and started right away in the third grade Gymnasium. Luckily Gladys survived the war. I do not know if her parents did but believe so. After the war she went to Leiden, got a law degree and married Bas van de Graaff, a friend of Rob Laane. When we were newly married Netty and I became good friends with this couple. Sadly Gladys died very young of cancer. When Netty's nephew Auke married, there were two attractive young men in the wedding party who turned out to be Gladys's sons. I was glad to have the opportunity to tell them I remembered their mother fondly.

In that period it also became more and more clear that there was a threat of another war in Europe and several of our teachers who were in the Dutch army reserve were called up. Ever since World War I and especially since the worldwide Depression started, the Dutch government had squeezed its defense budget down to the point where the Dutch army was in no shape to defend the country. Most people in Europe underestimated the power of the German military and overestimated the French and British readiness to defend their country, or at least act as a counter-balancing deterrent to the Germans. The Dutch hoped to be able to remain neutral again as they had during the previous war. They were innocent and naïve about the threat posed by the Germans and diplomatic courtesy required that Germany be treated as a friendly neighbor. Still, some people made an effort to improve the readiness of the Dutch army. My father belonged to a newly formed political party called *Verbond voor Nationaal Herstel* (League for National Reconstruction). This party was right wing, but its program was mainly directed towards improving the nation's defenses. He was also active in an organization that raised private funds to support the training of young pilots for the air force and collected private and corporate funds for the purchase of antiaircraft guns. They bought a number of 2 cm. Swiss Oerlikon guns of a type that later became a standard Allied and German antiaircraft weapon. Here we had private citizens trying to collect money to train pilots and buy guns to protect their own country. A bizarre situation! The Dutch general staff started to make plans for the defense of the country, building defensive perimeters in the province of North Brabant and on the eastern border of Utrecht.

The Fokker Aircraft Company designed fighters and bombers made out of wood that were at least a little better and more modern than the biplanes the Dutch air force had but no match for the planes the Germans were developing. But it all sounded good and people felt we were now able to defend ourselves. The Dutch navy built several new ships, including a light cruiser the *de Ruyter*. My father went to see the new ship after it was launched and told me how wonderfully modern it was. This ship became the flagship of the Dutch Admiral Karel Doorman who led an Allied fleet into battle against the Japanese in the Java Sea. He was defeated and blown out of the water together with the British cruiser *Exeter*, the American cruiser *Houston* and the Australian cruiser *Perth*.

The Depression-era frugality and the general antiwar sentiment that prevailed among many Dutch politicians, certainly the Socialists, negatively affected military preparedness. Similar attitudes prevailed in other European countries. The exceptions were Germany, Italy, Russia and in Asia, Japan, all three countries with authoritarian governments. Depression induced savings and disarmament had been carried too far and had allowed the axis countries—as the coalition of Germany, Italy and Japan was called—to gain military superiority and do a lot of damage before they were stopped and turned back.

The Axis countries had not exactly been hiding their intentions. Mussolini's Fascist party had ruled Italy since the late 1920s. Italy had attacked Ethiopia, an independent empire in northeast Africa, which we called Abyssinia at the time. Its pathetic emperor, Haile Selassie, appealed in vain for support from the League of Nations, which had become a toothless multinational organization located in Geneva. Some ineffective trading sanctions were imposed on Italy. In Germany, Hitler came to power in 1933 and started a militaristic dictatorship. Concentration camps were built and the persecution of Jews started. Hitler's first move was the occupation of the German Rhineland. The river Rhine was close to the border between France and Germany and the Treaty of Versailles prevented Germany from stationing troops in the Rhineland, the area bordering the German side of the river. In 1935 Germany publicly renounced the Treaty of Versailles and German troops marched into it. France and Britain did nothing. Hitler had been building submarines and airplanes on the sly in violation of the treaty, but his military power was still very limited at that time. He later declared that he would have been forced to call his troops back if France had opposed his entry into the Rhineland.

During the Spanish Civil War Germany and Italy openly and actively supported the Fascist rebels in Spain. German bombers bombed defenseless Spanish cities, gaining experience for the action to come. France and Britain sat on their hands, hoping they could contain the new threat by making deals with Hitler. The League of Nations had no clout and the U.S. was not even a member. Many U.S. citizens were still strongly isolationist and wanted to avoid foreign entanglements.

In 1938 Hitler also completed the annexation of Austria, the country of his birth, without a hitch. Tens of thousands of deliriously happy Austrians thronged the streets of Vienna to welcome their new master. They learned to regret their enthusiasm and after the war it was impossible to find anybody in Austria who had agreed with the so-called *Anschluss*.

Encouraged by the lack of opposition he encountered, Hitler's next move was the annexation of the Sudetenland, a part of Czechoslovakia that bordered on Germany and was heavily populated with people of German descent. Britain and France rushed in to contain Hitler and struck a deal with him in Munich. They would allow occupation of the Sudetenland and France and Britain guaranteed the independence of the remaining part of Czechoslovakia. British Prime Minister Chamberlain arrived back in London triumphantly waving a piece of paper and announcing there would be "peace in our time." That was in 1938. Many people were happy with this outcome and in Holland citizens put out their flags to celebrate the occasion as if an act of capitulation to an aggressor was anything to celebrate. As could be expected, the flag waving proved to be premature. Shortly afterwards the Germans claimed they had been "provoked" by the Czechs and were therefore forced to march into Czechoslovakia. When that happened, the Allies realized they had a major threat of aggression and ultimately war on their hands. The treaty Chamberlain had waved around that provided for a German occupation of the Sudetenland had been tossed aside like a scrap of paper. The Allies were too weak or too indecisive to do anything. They left the poor Czechs in the lurch and started to prepare for war. But life went on. Most Europeans acted as if nothing had happened.

At the end of the 1938–39 schoolyear, I advanced without any trouble to the third grade in the HBS section. That summer we went again on vacation to Zermatt in Switzerland, this time my mother went with us and we were joined by the Deibel family, Uncle Anne, Aunt Mieke and Bas. We had very good weather and made a number of good hikes although not as demanding as the ones my father and I had done the year before. This was the summer of 1939, just a few weeks before the German attack on Poland triggered World War II. In hindsight, it is difficult to understand that we just went on vacation abroad, as if there was no threat at all. It all seems terribly naïve or even foolish. But there was no feeling of having a last fling, of going to the mountains for the last time, as long as this was still possible. It was pure innocence and lack of understanding of the magnitude of what was to come.

In August of that year, just after we got back home, the war started. Hitler invaded Poland and Great Britain and France were obligated to declare war with Germany under their treaty with Poland. The Dutch began a general mobilization. Poland was quickly overwhelmed after German bombers flattened part of Warsaw. The Germans and the Soviets concluded a treaty of "friendship" which resulted in the two nations carving up Poland. The Russians got the eastern half and the Germans the western portion. It seems strange to have the National Socialist, strongly anti–Communist Germans concluding a treaty with the Soviets, but there have been several instances in the past, particularly in the days of Peter the Great when Poland was seen as a threat to Russia and Germany and both sides decided to join forces against the Poles. The Poles fought heroically and were said to have used cavalry charges against German tanks but they were overwhelmed. The declaration of war by France and Great Britain was an unexpected development for the German leader or *der Fürher* – Adolf Hitler. He had gambled that the British and the French would again cave in like they had done in Munich. Hitler reckoned he could deal with the French later and then make peace with England, thus expanding his sphere of influence in the large areas all over the world controlled by Britain. It did not work out that way. The French and Germans dug in along their mutual border; the French sheltered behind their Maginot Line, a huge chain of fortifications that stretched from the Swiss border to the French-Belgian border. In the fall of 1939 and the following winter the opposing armies did not move and what transpired was called the "*Sitz Krieg*" as opposed to the "*Blitz Krieg*" that would follow and that had been perfected by the Germans in Poland.

Meanwhile the Russians, who felt the Germans had given them a free hand, attacked Finland. Again, a move that had deep roots in history. In the past Russia controlled Finland and especially Karelia, the area abutting the harbor of Leningrad (now St. Petersburg). The Finns resisted and fought bravely, using their ski patrols of hardened countrymen against the masses of under-motivated Russian troops who were ill equipped to fight in the snow. The Finns were very popular in Holland, and their spirited defense spoke to the imagination of the people. Collections of skis and ski equipment were held in Holland and many people gave money for the Finnish cause. The Russians were seen as Communist aggressors. The huge Russian bear was attacking the small Finish nation and getting a bloody nose in the process. Two years later, in 1941, when the Germans turned against the Soviet Union and attacked it, the Finns became allies of Germany and the Russians became allies of us since we also had been attacked by the Germans. But that was still in the future.

The winter of 1939–40 was an unusually cold one. Dutch women were urged to start knitting gloves for their soldiers and even my mother, who had great difficulty doing a decent knitting job, did her best. I pity the soldier who ended up getting the mitten-like things she created with the prescribed exposed trigger finger. The traditional defense system the Dutch had was the *Waterlinie*, a contiguous belt of flooded polders that made large areas of the country impassable. As the system froze over it lost its effectiveness, of course, and trucks with big circular saws were brought into action to cut the ice and open up the water defense.

I enjoyed the class I was in, the third class HBS. It was an all-boys class and I was the youngest. Several older guys had joined the school from other institutions and I felt like a big shot. I had moved through the first two and a half years of high school without any trouble and had become quite complacent. I had resigned from the boy scouts and started playing field hockey, a sport that was and still is very popular among Dutch girls and boys. It was a little elitist because working class people were more interested in soccer, but for me it was another step up towards becoming a big guy. I belonged to a "junior" team of TOGO, a hockey club in The Hague. I was not very good at running or dribbling with the ball—still poorly coordinated and certainly not fleet of foot. But I did manage to learn how to hit the ball well, which gave me a role in defense. Playing that winter on the often frozen ground was not easy. The ball would move unusually fast. But as spring approached the game became normal again.

In April the Germans called an end to the *"Sitzkrieg"* and attacked Denmark and Norway. The Danes folded immediately, but the Norwegians fought back long and hard. British and French troops landed in Norway to help, but after about a month it was all over. The Norwegians were occupied. Almost all Norwegians resisted the German occupation, but one of them, a third-rate politician with Nazi sympathies by the name of Vidkun Quisling, was installed as ruler of his country. Since he was the first well-known collaborator and Nazi puppet, his name became synonymous for "traitor" all over the world. A "Quisling" was a traitor.

Still not expecting any harm would come to us, we went to bed on the evening of May 9, 1940. We anticipated little else than the beginning of the Whitsunday holiday, a three-day weekend in Holland celebrated like Easter and Christmas by adding a free Monday to the Sunday on which the religious holiday is officially set. The next day would be a rude awakening.

IO : *Five Days of War That Changed Holland*

In late spring and early summer, daylight comes early in Holland. So in the morning of May 10, 1940, first light came around four o'clock, but to me it seemed still dark when I was awakened by loud totally unfamiliar and terrifying noises. What I heard was the sound of Dutch anti aircraft guns and the drone of planes. I went to my parents' bedroom and found they also were awake. When we opened the curtains in their bedroom and went out on the balcony, we saw swarms of airplanes in the gray early morning sky and the puffs of anti aircraft fire near them. Some of our neighbors also were outside in bathrobes and other improvised cover. Being knowledgeable about planes and aviation, I told my parents the planes were German and that they followed a flight pattern I had read about in the aviation magazine *de Vliegwereld* I subscribed to and always read with great interest. I had seen an article about the German attack on Poland in which the planes had formed up in large circles above their targets, thus covering each other's back.

At that instant we realized that war had come to us, and that our world had changed. A few moments later, just after my parents had gone back inside, I looked out the window again and saw a German bomber flying by at a very low level, dropping three bombs that looked huge to me. I rushed back inside, crying, and yelling at my parents to take cover just as the bombs exploded. They shook the house, but luckily, this did not turn out to be the beginning of a sustained bombardment of our village. We all got dressed and soon afterwards, when we had gone downstairs and were looking out of our dining room window, we saw a German Junkers 52 paratrooper plane come over low, under heavy antiaircraft fire. The plane was hit, broke up and plunged down. Now completely involved in the war, I cheered. My mother rebuked me. I guess she thought I behaved unseemly in the face of death and destruction.

From our point of view, and in reality, that first day of war in the Netherlands was chaotic. By radio and word of mouth we learned that German paratroopers had landed around The Hague. Rumors began flying. We were told that there were Germans around dressed in Dutch uniforms or disguised as nuns and Catholic

priests. Actually there was a grain of truth in these stories, at least the one about the uniforms. That same day the Germans had tricked Dutch border guards with operatives wearing Dutch uniforms. Dutch troops began racing around town since the small airport Ypenburg that was located very close to Voorburg was under attack. It was the one where I used to go with my friend Erik van 't Groenewoud to watch his father fly and where we attended air shows. The Dutch were not totally unprepared. They had learned that the Germans had used similar airborne landing tactics in April during their invasion of Norway and had deployed extra troops, antiaircraft guns and a few armored cars around the airfields. They had scattered automobile wrecks and other obstacles around to prevent easy landings by enemy aircraft. Also some of the antiaircraft fire was effective. The plane I had seen dropping bombs tried to attack an antiaircraft position on the other side of the Vliet canal, at the eastern outskirts of Voorburg. The bombs had no effect and dropped harmlessly in the fields, but the men manning the guns fled in panic and did not return to their battle stations for quite a while. They had a good reason to run. Their guns had been placed out in the open without any protection against bombs or strafing fighters. The plane I had seen being shot down was probably already damaged and crashed in the Haagse Bos, a park nearby in The Hague. As it turned out, there was an officer aboard this plane who had disobeyed his instructions and carried a complete detailed plan of the attack on The Hague. That was helpful.

Despite some panic among them and severe lack of coordination, the Dutch troops deployed in and around these airfields, which were mostly part of reserve battalions, did a good job eliminating or at least neutralizing the heavily armed and very well-trained and aggressive paratroopers. Their initially panicky reaction and, in some cases, lack of fighting spirit described in the history of the May 10th events, reflects the poor training poor equipment and low level of morale and

BURNING GERMAN PLANES AT ROTTERDAM AIRPORT.

battle readiness of the Dutch army in 1940. The army had been starved of funding for decades, its equipment was in many cases outdated, uniforms were old-fashioned, and public opinion had only recently become more positive towards the army and its mission. On May 10, the soldiers stationed at the airfields around The Hague were suddenly thrown into combat with German elite troops without any warning or preparation. That was not an easy thing for them to cope with. The father of my friend Ab Boot was a captain in the reserves and commanded a company near Ockenburg, a small auxiliary airfield. He conducted himself bravely, rallying his soldiers and mounting a counter attack. Sadly, he was killed very early in the actions that followed the paratroop landings there, but that morning we had no idea of what was going on.

I own a large number of books about World War II. Many of these books relate personal experiences or deal with the history of specific·battles or theaters of war. Curiously I have found that many of the books written in the two or three decades immediately following the war have over time proven to be less thoughtful and lacking in accuracy and objectivity. An excellent overview of the entire war, its origins and all military actions on land, sea and in the air is in my opinion a book titled *A War to be Won* that came out in 2000, fifty-five years after the war ended. Its authors, Williamson Murray and Allan R. Millet are scholars and military historians. They have done a superb job in *one* volume. This contrasts with an interesting *thirteen*-volume series of books I also have, covering the history of the Netherlands in the Second World War, written by a historian, Dr. L. D. de Jong, and his staff. The Dutch government invited De Jong to serve as the official chronicler of the war as it affected Holland. He completed this series in the 1970s. Netty gave me these books and over the years, as one volume after another was finished and shipped over to me, I had the pleasure of receiving unexpected presents from Holland. De Jong and his staff performed this assignment with intense attention to detail and produced what is now regarded as the most complete and authentic history of the period. I think this work will stand the test of time. It is an exception to my comment about the value of publications of earlier vintage. In the beginning, de Jong was criticized. The Dutch are quick to criticize almost anybody and anything that stands out from the crowd or claims to know anything better than they do. Dr de Jong is Jewish and managed to escape to London in the first days of the war. In London he worked for the Dutch government in the radio section of the BBC, the British Broadcasting Corporation, and broadcasted to the occupied Netherlands in Dutch. Among many things he was accused of focusing too much on the suffering of the Jews and not enough on the sacrifices of others. It was also said that it was easy for him to make judgements about the behavior of people under stress in an occupied country while he was safely in London. There may be some truth in these complaints, but in general, the immense task he performed is admirable. He may have been absent, but most people who were on the spot, including myself, had no way of getting an overview of the entire situation and only knew what they observed in their immediate environment and what they lived through personally.

I have always enjoyed being an observer of people and events, but I can certainly not claim to know more about the war in the Netherlands than what happened within my own small world. During the war years I saw a lot and covered a great deal of ground in and around The Hague on my bicycle until this was no longer possible because the Germans either wanted to grab me or my bike or both. I will try to give a flavor of what life was like and how our family experienced it during the war years. I shall not be able to give a complete and accurate history of the war, but I will try to link some of our experiences to the greater picture wherever this is possible.

In the war years, our press was totally German controlled, and our radio gave us only German propaganda. The only sources of good information we had were the broadcasts from London and the underground press, which occasionally distributed news and commentary using hand-stenciled sheets. Oom Eelco who served as minister of foreign affairs during the entire war period and who had intimate knowledge of most of what went on in the Dutch Cabinet, was part of a select group of people invited to proofread de Jong's volumes and comment on them. He told Netty and me he had found some areas he would have wanted to describe differently, but in general he said the books were accurate to a fault and well written. A good part of this early criticism of historically correct World War II reports may stem from attitudes prevalent in Holland in the years immediately following the war. People tended to overstate the extent of their resistance to the Germans and felt deep embarrassment over the lack of help they had offered to the Dutch Jews and the extent of their cooperation with the occupier. Those who lived through the occupation felt they had gone through a lot and were not readily prepared to accept an objective analysis of their behavior, certainly not by somebody who had not been there. I believe the Dutch are now more realistic about their wartime activities and have recognized their shameful lack of compassion and support for the Jews. Overstating one's own contribution to the war effort is natural.

Looking at American TV, movies, or sampling books written here in the U.S. about the war, one could easily get the impression that the war in Europe was mainly fought and won by Americans. The part played by the Russians is often overlooked in America and Europe. The Russians fought the Germans in a large number of huge and ferocious battles involving hundreds of thousands of men. They and the Germans suffered enormous losses in these battles. German losses on the eastern front are believed to be around two million men. Their losses on the western front were around two hundred thousand. Ten percent of the Russian population died in World War II. In my view, it would have been impossible for the Anglo-American forces to beat the Germans without the "help" of the slaughter on the eastern front. Also, Americans often overlook the fact that Great Britain fought the Germans alone for almost two years after the capitulation of France in the summer of 1940. The American participation in the war in Europe was significant and decisive for its outcome, but it did not really get going until the middle of 1943.

The first volume of de Jong's works deals with the situation in Holland in the thirties. It relates the impact of widespread unemployment on the population, the lack of funding for defense, the complicated politics of Dutch society, divided as it was socially and politically between Protestants, orthodox Protestants, Catholics, Socialists, and conservatives. This first volume is now considered to be one of the best descriptions of the situation in Holland before the war. The first eight months of the war when Holland was neutral – the days preceding the German attack—are described in detail in volume two, and the third volume covers just the five days of war following the German attack. These books offer the first complete overview of what really happened in those crucial years preceding the war and more important, what happened during the five years of German occupation, in Holland as well as in the free world. Additional volumes deal with the Dutch East Indies and the Japanese occupation of them. What happened in Asia was completely unknown to us in occupied Holland. Only after the German capitulation when we had access to Allied newspapers and magazines, did we hear about the internment of all Dutch men, women and children in Japanese camps and the terrible conditions under which they were forced to live for more than three years.

Covering the days just before the German attack on Holland, de Jong's book investigates to what extent the Dutch were expecting a German attack and were ready for it. Obviously I cannot deal with all the details, I am trying to write a personal memoir, but the role of the Dutch military attaché at the Dutch Embassy in Berlin is particularly interesting and should be mentioned here. The attaché was a Major Sas who had excellent connections with several German officers. One of his German contacts was a Colonel Oster, who was a close friend. Oster had been warning him repeatedly (at considerable risk to himself) that an attack on Holland was imminent. As we now know, the Germans were planning a massive attack on a broad front against France, Belgium and Holland. The logistics were complicated, and they postponed their start-off date several times. So in April and May, the Dutch attaché's warnings had to be cancelled and revised several times and were taken less and less seriously by his lackadaisical superiors in The Hague. In the evening of May 9th Sas had dinner with Oster and afterwards walked over to the German War Department with him. Oster went inside and Sas waited in the street. Oster came out and gave the word: an attack was imminent. The Dutch embassy in Berlin had a code system, but coding a message took a long time so the attaché decided to make a phone call in plain language in which he tried to warn without being too specific. But he did say "tomorrow morning early." This message was, of course, overheard by the elaborate German spy system that was tapping all phones, and because of this indiscretion Colonel Oster almost lost his life. Some of the Dutch forces were put on alert, but drastic measures like blowing up important bridges in anticipation of an attack were not taken. The Dutch air force was alerted and before dawn the engines of all fighter planes were warmed up. Most Dutch fighters took to the air at day-break, but for some it was too late since the Germans bombed the airfields where the

Dutch planes stood lined up in neat rows. During the night the German bombers had flown from east to west over the Netherlands at night, as if they were going to attack England. They then turned around over the North Sea and returned to the Dutch shore at a lower altitude, coming from the west. When they hit the Dutch airfields at dawn, German fighters who had flown in directly from Germany joined them. The Dutch had noticed the fly-over of the bombers, of course, but they did not have the means to do much about the threat beyond using searchlights and firing anti aircraft guns. In the morning, the Dutch pilots fought bravely and scored some success, shooting down fighters, bombers and transport planes, but by the end of the first day they were overwhelmed. Most of our planes were destroyed on the ground or shot down on that first day.

On the ground there was much unusual activity during the night of May 9th along the Dutch eastern border. Dutch sentries heard a great deal of noise, shouted commands and roaring engines. On several spots on the border between Germany and the province of Limburg, German and Dutch civilians who lived in Germany, dressed in stolen and fake Dutch uniforms began to infiltrate the area. Their objective was to secure the many bridges that crossed the Maas and Roer rivers that were essential for the German forces to carry out their offensive into Belgium. Most of these sneak attacks did not succeed, but a few were successful. Dutch sentries were overpowered or confused with stealthy tactics and, in one case, a bridge was even cleared of obstacles to allow an armored train to pass and roll into Holland.

For me going to school that Friday morning was, of course, out of the question, and my father did not go to his office either. He started driving our Packard car for a civil defense outfit he belonged to. As the day progressed, we saw Dutch military trucks go by filled with Dutch civilians under guard. They were members of the NSB, the Dutch National Socialist Party. The parents of my friend Paul Beversen belonged to that party and his father was picked up. Ironically, Paul's father was not a member of the party and not really interested in it. It was his mother who was a fanatic Nazi. But in those days, it was simply assumed that the men made the decisions and the women followed. We had a small military garrison in Voorburg, which consisted of field hospital troops. They used requisitioned moving vans as improvised ambulances they had painted military green with big red crosses. In general, the Dutch army had very few vehicles that were designed for military duty. Most of what they had were civilian vehicles that had been requisitioned or bought new. The moving vans the men in Voorburg used were typical. As was usual in those days, moving vans were built out of wood on a truck chassis. They were large creaky contraptions that in a way resembled covered wagons. Wooden racks were built inside the vans to receive the stretchers with the wounded.

The air raid sirens would howl ceaselessly and every time there was an alarm the streets had to be cleared. Newspapers came out, filled with panicky stories and unconfirmed rumors. It all was an illustration of the dismally poor condition of the Dutch armed forces and the lack of good information, leadership and control of the government. We were total innocents. Suddenly that evening we had to practice "black out." We were not allowed to show any lights outside our houses. This was a difficult thing because nobody was prepared for this drill. As the sun was setting, a large convoy of army trucks arrived in our street and prepared to spend the night. We had fairly large linden trees lining the street on both sides, so the trucks were nicely camouflaged beneath them. The soldiers mingled with the civilians milling around and people came out to offer them chocolates, lemonade, cookies etc. The captain in charge used our phone to make a few calls to find out where he was supposed to go. The Dutch military simply had no decent communications system. Nobody seemed to realize that our street was now a prime target for an air attack.

The next few days went by in a blur. Unbeknownst to me, a little girl living in Wassenaar had been looking forward to her birthday party on May 11. This was Netty van Kleffens, who much later would become my wife. She was sorely disappointed that the Germans spoiled her tenth birthday. In the coming years, they would spoil a lot more for her and for all of us. The Dutch government and armed forces gradually regained a form of order and control in those first few days. At home we set up some garden furniture in our garage and retreated there when the air raid sirens wailed. The Wachters, a young dentist and his wife with their two-year-old son Willem, joined us there. They lived in the third house that shared our roof. They had no garage and felt safer in our improvised air raid shelter. The garage stood in the back of our property and had only a very small window. Its doors were made out of quite solid wood so we reasoned that if we would get hit, and our house would collapse, chances were that the garage would remain standing. If it collapsed too, its flat roof would not be hard to climb out from under. Not a bad idea, but soon we discovered that the frequent alarms were more a reflection of nervousness rather than real danger, so we began to ignore them and stayed in the house.

Throughout the next five years of war, we had many air raid warnings, but we never went back into the garage. We listened often to the radio, virtually the only way in which we could find out what was going on. The Germans attacked on a Friday. The following Sunday was Whitsunday and the churches were overflowing.

People felt helpless and confused and naturally turned to their churches for support. I remember going over to see Ab Boot to play with him in his kayak. Ab and I paddled around in the small canal behind his house and I remember asking him if he had heard from his father. He said he had not. Their phone had been ringing several times, but after they had picked up there was no answer. This was, he thought, a sign that his father was all right and trying to get in touch with them. Unfortunately, he was terribly wrong.

The early morning attack with airborne troops was part of a large scale operation that the Dutch would later call the "Battle for The Hague." The Germans never called it a battle and even years after the war, tried to diminish the serious defeat they suffered by saying the Dutch were forewarned and put obstacles on their airfields. More than an entire *Luftlande Division,* an airborne division with paratroopers, was committed to capture The Hague quickly and put the Dutch government out of business before it could activate its defense system of fortifications behind flooded polders. The Germans landed on three airfields around The Hague and also on the beach in several spots and on highways. The largest landing was right near our home in Voorburg on the small airport of Ypenburg. A large number of transport planes were destroyed there by the small Dutch defense forces and by artillery that was used later in the day. The Germans suffered heavy losses in men killed and taken prisoner and only a small segment managed to dislodge itself and retreat towards the area of Rotterdam, where they eventually linked up with the units that had landed near that city. Other airborne troops landed on Valkenburg airfield, near Netty's home, and a third unit attacked Ockenburg, a very small auxiliary field where Mr. Boot commanded a company of depot troops–reservists who had just been called up and had not yet been trained. His company suffered heavy losses, and he himself was killed after he tried to launch a counterattack with his men, who were severely handicapped by lack of training and equipment. He was posthumously awarded the Bronze Cross, the second highest Dutch decoration for bravery. A Dutch book about the "Battle for The Hague" describes the death of Captain Boot and quotes a sergeant who was present when his men buried him with his sword and "a handkerchief over his face." An untimely end for a very brave man I had known well as the friendly father of my friend.

The news we received on the radio was optimistic, but reading between the lines we understood that the situation was, on the whole, not good. German troops had landed on Waalhaven airport in Rotterdam and managed to penetrate into the harbor area. Dutch marines, a force made up of professional soldiers garrisoned

GERMAN INFANTRY ENTERING ROTTERDAM.

in Rotterdam, had managed to stop them at a bridge leading to the center of the city and were fighting hard to drive them back. Very worrisome was the successful paratrooper attack south of Rotterdam on the bridge over the Moerdijk and another bridge over a large body of water, allowing a German penetration towards Dordrecht and Rotterdam from these bridges. The bridges were seized undamaged. The Dutch troops guarding them were too late installing the detonation charges. They were ready to blow them up but were not allowed to put the charges in place before they received definite orders. These orders never came. Thus, the Germans controlled a narrow salient pointing at Rotterdam but were unable to move further forward or widen their penetration. At the Grebbeberg in the center of the country, a fortified ridge of sandy hills near Rhenen, the line was holding, but that meant that most of eastern Holland was already occupied together with a good part of the south, bordering on Belgium. The Dutch army had built a defensive complex in an area called de Peel, near Eindhoven where some resistance was planned. I remember seeing pictures of the artillery pieces used in this area that dated back to the late nineteenth century, long before World War I!

After three or four days, it became clear to the Germans that their plan to neutralize Holland needed an extra push to stay on schedule. To force the situation in Rotterdam and relieve the paratroopers who were under pressure there, the city was bombed.

The Dutch air force had been wiped out in the first day and the antiaircraft guns surrounding Rotterdam were either inoperable or had in an incomprehensible decision been moved away, thus leaving the city without any antiaircraft defense. It was a totally open city and not very difficult to flatten. Compared to the German bombing of cities like Coventry and London and the allied raids on Germany later in the war, this bombardment was relatively small in terms of total acreage

ruined and number of people killed. Still it was, after the bombing of Warsaw in the fall of 1939, the second attack on a completely undefended city without any important military targets. Thus, this bombardment lives on in history as one of the first two unprovoked gross atrocities, proof of the barbaric mentality of the German military and its Nazi masters. Meanwhile, the Dutch government had decided that it had important reasons not to become captives of the Germans. We had a good-size merchant fleet at sea, ready to join the Allied cause, we had large overseas colonies in the East Indies, and in the Caribbean we had Surinam and Curaçao. At that time the first sentence of Article One of the Dutch Constitution read: "The Kingdom of the Netherlands consists of the Netherlands, the Netherlands East Indies, Surinam and Curaçao." So the decision was made to move the royal family and the cabinet to England where the government could continue to function. Oom Eelco, who had recently become minister of foreign affairs, had gone to London several days before the rest of the cabinet came. His trip was prompted by the desire to establish contact with the British government as soon as we had become their allies.

The Germans did not only attack the Netherlands. The war with Holland was just a sideshow. Their attack was conducted on a broad front, which included Belgium and northern France. They maneuvered successfully around the Maginot Line, the heavily fortified defense system that sealed off the border between France and Germany. The French built the Maginot Line in the thirties at tremendous expense. Curiously, the fortifications only ran north/south, along the border from Luxembourg to Switzerland. The northern border of France, which runs east/west between Belgium and France up to the Channel, was not as well protected. The reasoning was that the Belgians, who had also been devastated by the Germans in the World War I, would build their own fortifications. They did but on a much smaller scale than their neighbors. In the first war the Germans had attacked France from the east and from the north, through Belgium, following the so-called *Schliefen Plan*. Amazingly, it did not occur to the French that the same situation might occur again in the second war. In the first war, the Germans had left the Netherlands untouched although it had a narrow escape. The Dutch province of Limburg forms a panhandle-like protrusion that sticks out into Belgium in a southward direction. The Germans had to deploy themselves on a narrower front to get by Limburg without violating Dutch neutrality. In 1940 they plowed right through Limburg and the Ardennes into Belgium. Near Liege, or Luik as we call the city that lies very close to the Dutch city of Maastricht in Limburg, the Belgians had built a monster fort, which was the key to their defense called Eben Emael, located at a strategic section of the Meuse or Maas River. This fortification was considered impenetrable and held the key to further entry into Belgium. The Germans stormed the fort with small boats and paratroopers who landed literally on top of it in their gliders, using flamethrowers on the bunkers and gun positions. They quickly conquered the fort, demonstrating an incredibly high level of fighting spirit, motivation and willingness to absorb heavy losses. In postwar analysis, the fanaticism shown by German troops is often described as one of the big surprises of the war. In prewar Europe, the armies of France and Britain were considered to be strong, well-trained and well lead. This turned out to be quite untrue. The French army fought bravely in certain spots but showed much less élan in many other places. Their officers were generally not highly motivated, their generals were older men whose military knowledge was based on experiences gained in the previous war and who were not able to cope with the German Blitzkrieg tactics. Most people in Holland and other countries outside Germany believed the Germans to be less enthusiastic about their Nazi party, its doctrine and their Führer, Adolf Hitler, than they proved to be. Until the very last battles they showed a high level of dedication to their Nazi regime and a strong motivation that was often lacking in their opponents. As the Germans swept into Belgium and from there into northern France, the French army began to collapse. The British army was supposed to defend the left wing of the front—the north-west corner. Communications between the British and the French were poor and equipment non-compatible. There was also a level of distrust between the two allies, and there was no consensus about the strategy that had to be followed to stop the Germans. The Germans drove a wedge between the two allies and started to roll the British army towards the sea and the French towards Paris.

At home, meanwhile, we had seen an enormous column of black smoke in the air, which turned out to be the burning city of Rotterdam. Voorburg is about 20 miles away from Rotterdam, as the crow flies. Burned pieces of paper began to float down in our front yard. Looking at them, I could see they were pages from schoolbooks. It was May 14, the fifth and as it turned out final day of our "war." Soon after the bombardment of Rotterdam, the commander of the Dutch forces capitulated.

The Germans had notified him that they would bomb Utrecht, Amsterdam and several other cities if Dutch resistance continued. I clearly remember where I was sitting, near the front window of our house, listening with my parents to the news broadcast. It was in the middle of the afternoon and the announcer, a man whose voice we had become very familiar with, announced that the Dutch army had given up all resistance and that the queen had left the country and was now in England. The announcer was obviously very distressed and deeply moved. His voice broke and he had to stop several times. We all felt a tremendous emptiness in our hearts and a great deal of apprehension about the future. Some Dutchmen felt betrayed and abandoned by their government. As far as I can remember, my parents and I did not share those feelings. We had a sense that the queen did the right thing and that the fight continued overseas. In the coming months, there was hardly anybody in Holland, except for the pro–German group of course, who felt the Queen should have stayed. Shortly after the radio announcement, a man raced by on his bicycle, yelling "*valse geruchten niets van waar*—false rumors all lies!" It was still very nice weather; Hitler really lucked out on that score. We had the doors to our small front yard open and many people were wandering around on the street, to see what was going on. The man on the bike was an illustration of the village atmosphere in which we experienced the beginning of the war and the chaos that prevailed almost everywhere in Holland in those days. We decided not to believe the cyclist. That same afternoon a British "Blenheim" light bomber passed over our house at roof-top level. The plane was burning and a German Messerschmit ME 109 was pursuing it firing into it. The bomber crashed nearby and one of the surviving crew members was taken to our local hospital where he became quite a celebrity with many schoolboys and girls visiting him until the Germans took him away. A bullet fired during this engagement lodged in our garage roof. It was the only damage our house suffered in five years of war. We were very lucky.

In 1939 Oom Eelco had become minister of foreign affairs in the Cabinet formed by Jhr. (*Jhr* stands for *Jonkheer*, a member of the Dutch nobility) de Geer. De Jong's war history books describe the Cabinet and its decision-making process in May 1940 in intimate detail. What follows is a very brief summary of what seems useful to include in this narrative as it involves a member of our family, Netty's uncle – her father's only brother. Prime Minister de Geer was an older man, and definitely a man of the nineteenth century who had spent a lifetime in politics, and was known for his intimate knowledge and interest in the administrative intricacies of the Dutch Civil Service. He was an extremely hard worker who would send his personal attendant home when he wanted to work in his office until very late at night. When finished, he would lock up the ministry building, toss the key in the mail slot and bicycle home. Strangely for a Dutchman, he was absolutely uninterested in foreign affairs and spoke no foreign languages. In the thirties he had been a strong supporter of the fiscal policies followed by then–Prime Minister Dr. Colijn. It was Colijn who guided the country through the Great Depression by cutting government expenses to the bone, hanging on to the gold standard and doing everything Keynes would prove was completely counterproductive to getting the economy going again. De Geer was a pacifist who abhorred war and thought that Neville Chamberlain's cave-in to Hitler in Munich was a brilliant move that had saved the world. He had been prime minister before and his return to government was the result of typical Dutch maneuvering between too many parties, all struggling to remain valid political enti-ties. A year later, in London, he had a nervous breakdown and stepped down.

In one of the most bizarre episodes of the Dutch government's period in London, he slipped away and managed to return to the Netherlands via Lisbon, thus becoming a traitor. He was tried after the war and ended his life in disgrace. De Geer was obvi-ously not fit to be in charge of a government in wartime. Several other ministers in the cabinet were not either and had also been selected for political reasons or because they were harmless figureheads. De Jong states that Queen Wilhelmina was not impressed with the quality of her cabinet. She considered Oom Eelco as one of the two or three she could rely upon. From her rather old-fashioned autocratic point of view, she saw herself as representing the people and the ministers as politicians who were just there to run the government. The average age of the cabinet was about fifty-five and most members were inclined to think in World War I terms. Many of them were either mediocrities or people who simply did not have the required leadership capabilities. The Dutch government foresaw the possibility of a German attack, but thought the Dutch army would be able to hold out for a few weeks until help from the allies would arrive. They thought the Dutch system of fortifications surrounded by inundated land would be effective and would stop the initial German thrust and they expected the French army to lend powerful assistance afterwards. There was a general belief that France had a strong and well-disciplined army that would be able to hold out against a massive German attack and there was a similar exaggerated belief in the strength of the British armed forces.

Nobody reckoned an airborne attack was possible and nobody had prepared for an all-out air war with terror bombing. While the paratroopers started coming down and the antiaircraft guns opened up, Oom Eelco and one of his colleagues called the Prime Minister at his home. They told him that he should send out previously prepared messages to their ambassadors in London and Paris stating that the country was in a state of war with Germany. De Geer initially wanted to postpone such a declaration of war, saying it might just be a German show of force that would blow over. He was still intent on staying neutral. He was a great admirer of the Dutch prime minister who served during World War I and believed this functionary had kept the country out of the war by being flexible and diplomatic. One vignette of his mentality is perhaps useful. The Dutch army had several lines of defense planned. The first one ran along the IJssel River. The second and most serious one was the *Grebbe Linie*, a line of fortifications along a ridge of hills that ran north-south through the center of the country.

Commanding officers had been urging the government to allow them to cut down trees and shrubbery in front of the fortifications so they would have a better field of fire and there would be no cover for an attacking force. The request was denied on the grounds that it cost too much and was a provocation. A day before the attack, the officers proceeded to cut down trees anyway, but it was too late. There had been no time to remove the trunks and they provided excellent cover for the attacking Germans. On top of the hill called the *Grebbeberg* was an amusement park and zoo. It had an observation tower. A relative of de Geer had urged him to have the tower torn down. De Geer, who was in a state of complete denial about the threat of a German attack, refused. Too expensive, and wasn't it a shame for such a nice monument to be torn down. A month before the attack, German officers had toured Holland in civilian clothes. They had wandered around the *Grebbeberg* and climbed the tower to take photographs and get a better view of the fortifications.

De Jong wrote that Oom Eelco stood out as an extremely capable, intelligent and knowledgeable diplomat and leader in the somewhat odd Cabinet of de Geer. He was only forty-five years old when he joined the cabinet, but he had almost twenty years of experience in the Department of Foreign Affairs. When the German attack came, Oom Eelco and his staff had spent the entire night at his official residence, waiting for the war to begin. They called Premier de Geer, who as mentioned above hesitated but later came over with the other ministers when it was made clear to him that a shooting war had really begun. They prepared a declaration to the Dutch people on behalf of Queen Wilhelmina. Later in the morning, Oom Eelco got word that the German Ambassador Graf (Count) Zech wanted to see him. So he had to go to his ministry in the center of The Hague. He tried to drive over, but was stopped several times by troops who were not immediately prepared to accept his statement that he was the minister of foreign affairs. At his office, he met the German ambassador who had a prepared statement that was a recitation of the lies Germany used to justify its invasion. It stated that Germany had been forced to attack because Holland was cooperating with England and was in the middle of preparing a sneak attack on German soil, etc.. etc. The ambassador, who knew Oom Eelco well and had lived for twelve years in Holland, was obviously fully aware that he was delivering a pack of lies. He was crying and so emotional that he could not read his statement so Oom Eelco offered to read it himself. Oom Eelco then wrote a response in Blue pencil, stating that the Dutch government rejected with indignation the German statement and that a state of war now existed between the countries. Oom Eelco shook Graf Zech's hand, a gesture that the two Dutch officers who had brought the German ambassador over found completely unwarranted. Graf Zech was escorted back to the hotel "Des Indes" where he was interned. Oom Eelco wrote later that at that moment he got the idea that he should try to go over to London to plead the Dutch cause with the Allies. He felt that it was essential to have better communications with France and England. At that time there were virtually no channels of communication.

In the following days, French troops would enter the southern part of Holland. They were briefly present in Breda, but they were uncertain about their mission and were later cut off by the advancing Germans. Oom Eelco felt that the French political situation in recent years had worsened and that the stability of the French wartime government was uncertain. So he preferred to go to London. This was easier said than done. It was the first day of war and British destroyers were not yet available. They would later come to Dutch ports to bring demolition teams and pick up the queen and other dignitaries. The air was full of German planes so an escape by air would be hazardous. Still Oom Eelco proposed to the cabinet to fly over to England and found immediate support. It was decided that minister Welter of Colonial Affairs would also go so that he could restore contact with the governor general of the Dutch East Indies, and the governors of Surinam and Curaçao. Oom Eelco knew that the Dutch navy had hidden a couple of seaplanes on the Brasemer Lake, near Leiden. He called the navy staff and asked for permission to use these planes to go to England. He had seen that the wind was calm and asked the planes to land in the sea near the beach in Scheveningen. He said good bye to his staff and so did Mr. Welter. Oom Eelco had been unable to reach Tante Margaret by phone to tell her he was leaving, but when he was being driven to the beach he passed his house and saw her walking in the street. He stopped and asked her if she would come with him if this were possible. She was twenty-eight years old at the time. She immediately agreed, and they drove to the beach where several planes were already bobbing in the sea. German fighters soon spotted them and started strafing them, causing some damage, but they veered away and Oom Eelco, Mr. Welter and Tante Margaret were carried to a twin-engine Fokker T8W seaplane. It had a bullet hole in one of its floats, but the pilot assured them the water would drain out once they were airborne. They took off. Strangely enough, the German fighters had gone to other targets and did not return. They flew along the coastline towards Belgium and France because the pilot had no maps to navigate with. Near Boulogne they decided to cross the Channel and as they approached England they planned to go to a British seaplane base near the Isle of Wight. Suddenly and unexpectedly the plane seemed to be getting low on fuel so Oom Eelco decided they should cut their flight short and try to go to Brighton where he knew he could catch a train to London.

In de Jong's books are copies of the notes Oom Eelco and his party exchanged during the flight. They had to communicate in writing because of the noise inside the cockpit. They landed near the beach in Brighton, and a sergeant climbed on the wing and waved a white handkerchief so as not to be shot at. The local police constable immediately arrested them with the comment that they were using a "peculiar method to go to England." Brought over to the police office, they could call the Dutch ambassador in London who confirmed that their claim that they were two Dutch ministers was correct. They had no English money, but the chief constable lent them a few pounds and even held up the train to London so they could immediately go on their way. When their train arrived in London, the Dutch ambassador was there and they went immediately to the British Foreign Office where they met with Lord Halifax, the foreign secretary.

They arranged to send orders to all Dutch merchant ships out on the high seas to report only to London and allowed a British military force to land on Curaçao and Aruba to protect the local oil refineries and secure fuel for the British forces in the region. After this meeting which ended in the early evening they went to see Winston Churchill who was at that time first lord of the admiralty. Their conversation did not last long since Churchill was summoned to Buckingham Palace to become prime minister. Neville Chamberlain had stepped down the previous day under heavy pressure. His policies of appeasement followed by halfhearted warfare had failed miserably.

Meanwhile, the Dutch Cabinet in The Hague realized it was in a city under attack and decided that all the ministers would gather in one building, a fairly modern structure housing the Department of Trade that had a good bomb shelter. There were telephone connections, but a plan to deal with a situation like this had never been made, so communications with the respective government departments were practically nonexistent. Consequently, the Cabinet was assembled in one place but could not really act. The ministers were removed from their departments and their staffs. A nation in distress was left without leadership. Earlier the secretary general of defense (the highest functionary under the minister) had bicycled over to his department. It was still very early in the morning, but his janitor was already there. The janitor said he had come in early to put a tarpaulin over the carpet in the minister's room because he expected "you would have a very busy day" with many people walking in and out of the office, perhaps without wiping their feet properly and possibly damaging the beautiful, expensive carpet. The Cabinet seemed more or less paralyzed. The real leadership in those dramatic days came from the commander in chief of the Dutch forces, General Winkelman, an older professional military man whose actions have been criticized by Monday morning quarterbacks but are now generally believed to have been beyond reproach. He bravely tried to rally his forces against an overwhelming opponent, stayed calm and demonstrated excellent leadership. In some instances his troops failed to fight with the determination expected of them, but there were also many examples of outstanding courage displayed by people who had been plunged overnight into a war situation without any real preparation. The queen and her daughter Princess Juliana with her husband Prince Bernhard and their two small daughters left the country for England on May 13. The Cabinet followed on the 14th and on that day General Winkelman capitulated, having been threatened with a bombardment of several other cities of the same ferocity as the one that had devastated Rotterdam. The Cabinet came over by ship to Folkestone. Several ministers had no experience dealing with foreigners and quite a few spoke no English. The size and intensity of life in wartime London overwhelmed them. They wondered whether they should issue a statement of their own acknowledging Winkelman's action. They sensed they were forced to make a real big decision, and like true civil servants, their instinct was to duck it. They preferred to leave the responsibility for a capitulation in the hands of Winkelman. Winkelman had negotiated a cease-fire and surrender of all Dutch forces except the navy and the forces in the province of Zeeland.

The Cabinet came out with a mealy-mouthed message that merely confirmed what Winkelman had announced. Oom Eelco was not part of this decision. He had left for Paris with the minister of defense to seek support from the French for the Dutch forces in Zeeland. French troops did come to Zeeland, but they fought almost as poorly as the Dutch. When the Germans started an aggressive attack, they fled together with their Dutch comrades-in- arms. In this action *eleven* French and Dutch battalions were overrun by *three* German Waffen SS battalions! The Germans broke whatever resistance remained with their time-tested method. They flattened Middelburg, the capital of Zeeland, seriously damaging the beautiful town hall and the old abbey, two priceless buildings that dated back to the Middle Ages. On May 17th all resistance in Zeeland ended, and by that time the Germans were well on their way to roll up the British and French armies in Northern France. The Germans separated the British forces from the French and surrounded them, pushing the British back to the channel port of Dunkirk where they were evacuated by a fleet of navy ships, commercial vessels, fisherman and private yachts. It remains a mystery why the Germans allowed the British expeditionary forces to escape albeit without their equipment. In all likelihood, the German supply lines were stretched to the limit and the panzer forces were running out of fuel. Hitler had set his mind on destroying France so he left the British forces for what they were for a few days and continued to march south into France. Soon afterwards, France also capitulated and was humiliated by Hitler, who insisted on signing the armistice in the same old railway carriage that was used in 1918 to end World War I and that had been kept in a museum by the French.

With the capitulation of France, the people of Western Europe faced a frighteningly threatening and uncertain future under the German heel. It seemed the Germans were unstoppable. All hopes and expectations of the military power of the Allies had been dashed, and our life in Holland would very quickly be brought down to one of food shortages, scarcity of almost everything and above all, fear.

Soon after the capitulation of the Dutch army, I started looking around on my bike. I went to The Hague where I saw the German plane I had watched as it was shot down. It had crashed in the *Haagse Bos,* a park. Boys were crawling all over the wreckage and one picked up a boot he found nearby. When he saw that there was still a part of a leg inside, he threw it away. On the beach in Scheveningen, I saw the wreckage of a Dutch Fokker D-21 fighter plane and two other German Junkers JU 52 paratrooper transport planes. Again boys and men were climbing all over the wreckage. In the sand I found a German "potato masher" hand grenade. I tied it on the luggage rack on the back of my bike and went home, with the hand grenade securely tied down but rattling along with my bike's movements. When my father saw what I had found he got very upset and immediately brought this trophy I had so

GERMANS ENTERING AMSTERDAM.

proudly collected very gently and carefully to the police.

The first German soldiers I saw in the first day after the capitulation were paratroopers who had been taken prisoner during the action nearby at Ypenburg and were kept in a school building in our village. They were quite cocky and very fit and young. Soon I saw many more Germans. In those days the main highway going east from The Hague ran through Voorburg. After Voorburg it became a true highway going east to Utrecht with two lanes each way. It was the first one of a system of major highways built in Holland in the thirties as an employment project. Standing on the side of this road where it crossed the bridge over the Vliet canal, I could see the German trucks loaded with soldiers, staff cars and artillery pieces roll by. They had festooned their trucks with Dutch helmets as hood ornaments like scalps. A large number of people stood by silently looking at this show of force going into The Hague. It became very obvious why the poorly equipped Dutch army did not have a chance. The next day I witnessed a small first sign of the new Dutch attitude towards its occupiers. I was standing around with a group of people near one of the bridges over the Vliet canal. A German soldier on a motorbike came roaring up, asking for the direction to Delft. We all pointed in the opposite direction. It is difficult to describe how we felt, being confronted by strange men in strange uniforms who took possession of our country. We all had terrible misgivings, but luckily nobody ever knows what the future has in store

Total losses of the Dutch army in May 1940 amounted to 2,067 killed and 2,700, more or less, seriously wounded. The army's officer's corps represented 4% of its total strength. Of the total men killed, 6% were officers. More than a quarter of the officers of the Dutch air force were killed. The Dutch navy lost 125 men. The total number of civilians killed was 2,159. It is not known what the German losses were. However, it is certainly true that the losses the Dutch inflicted on the German airborne troops and planes were extremely severe. The Germans have stated after the war that they lost one-third of all the planes sent into action in the Netherlands and that one half of all the transport planes they used were lost. These losses were particularly serious since the Germans had a shortage of qualified pilots and many instructors of the German air force flight schools had been ordered to fly these transport planes. Consequently, these losses had a severe impact on the Luftwaffe's performance for several years. An extra loss for the Germans was 1,200 prisoners of war, mostly Lufwaffe people, the Dutch managed to ship over to England.

Criticism of the performance of the Dutch, Belgian, French and English troops in the May 1940 period is easy. Much later, when I was in Indonesia I witnessed myself how soldiers behave when first exposed to enemy fire. Fear and panic are natural reactions under those circumstances, and in 1940 the feeling that the enemy is much better equipped and much better trained contributed significantly to the sense of powerlessness and stress exhibited by the Dutch troops. Good leadership, discipline and training will quickly overcome these emotions and most soldiers, once they have conquered their initial fears, will function perfectly normally. It is a well-known fact that soldiers fight for their unit, for their buddies, not for their country or other lofty principles (although the Germans seemed to be inspired by Nazi ideals.) If the unit is in a strange country like Indonesia where it is impossible to go back home by simply walking away, an additional factor that says "we are all in this together" is added to the knowledge that we were much better equipped and trained than the Indonesians. The Dutch army in 1940 simply did not have time to regain discipline, to let initial fear and emotions calm down and let the sense of belonging to a unit of comrades jell. Officers who had survived the first battle test were unable to reestablish leadership. The Germans came on much too strong and too quickly. They were well trained, highly motivated and well aware of the fact that they were on the winning side. The German army used the same theory now part of the dogma of the U.S. army; "when forced to fight only do so when you can apply overwhelming force."

II : *The First Three Years Of War*

After the capitulation of the Dutch armed forces and the entry of German troops into our country, life resumed an almost normal pace. The Germans appeared to have their plans and organization for the occupation of our country extremely well prepared despite their claim that their attack on Holland was a sudden reaction needed to counter a planned British/Dutch move against them. But before they got their operation in gear there were still a few days of respite in which we could come to our senses. The Germans decided to treat the Dutch magnanimously since their long-range plan was to incorporate Holland, Norway and Denmark in the "Great Germanic Reich." They returned all Dutch prisoners of war to civilian life and did not bother those who had faded back into civilian life on their own initiative. I recall that my father went over to Mrs. Boot's house to tell her what he had heard from one of his assistants who had served in Mr. Boot's unit and who had told my father what had happened in the morning of May 10th when Mr. Boot was killed.

My friend Eelco Apol's family was also directly affected by the war. Eelco's brother Govert attended the Dutch Naval Academy in Den Helder. I had seen him once when he was home on leave and had looked in awe at this older brother in his snappy uniform. The entire Naval Academy had been moved over to England and Govert was gone "for the duration." Luckily he returned safely after the war, no longer a midshipman, of course, but a seasoned officer who had served with distinction on several ships for five years. Eelco's father had been a professional officer in the Dutch army in earlier years. He was recalled when the Dutch army mobilized its reserves in 1939 and served as a lieutenant colonel, the rank he had when he retired. If my recollection is correct, I believe he did not see action as he was in command of a regiment held in reserve in the province of North Holland. Eric van 't Groenewoud's father served as a captain with the Dutch air force. He also returned. Paul Beversen's father came back from captivity as a Nazi sympathizer, which he really wasn't at that time.

I went back to school and naturally we spent a lot of time relating to each other our experiences during those five days. My father went back to his office, using public transportation. His car was now on wooden blocks in the garage. In his office nothing much would transpire there for the next five years. As soon as the Germans invaded Holland, the Royal Dutch Petroleum Company had executed a plan that had been carefully prepared in advance that involved moving its legal domicile from The Hague to Curaçao in the Dutch West Indies. All contacts with the head office were severed, and Pa spent his time working with a few oil fields they had in Austria, Germany and in the Netherlands.

Several of my classmates had parents living in the Dutch East Indies and were suddenly confronted with the reality that they were now cut off from their parents' moral and financial support. Most of them were able to find a home with relatives.

Initially the Netherlands was put under a military regime, as planned by the Wehrmacht. An old war-horse, a General von Falkenhausen, was appointed as the highest German authority. Reflecting the often chaotic relationships in the German top leadership and the underlying conflicts between the Nazi party and the armed forces, he was soon replaced by a Nazi *Reichscommissar*. This was Dr. Arthur Seyss-Inquart, a fanatical Austrian Nazi who was a high party official and an officer in the Waffen SS. In 1938 Seyss-Inquart had been instrumental in the overturn of the legal Austrian government and its surrender to German annexation. He had been rewarded for selling out Austria with a sort of governor position in occupied Poland where he lorded it over the Krakow region. He had never been in Holland and knew nothing about it. He had to make a drastic adjustment from brutal repression and terror in Poland where the Germans deliberately brutalized the Polish population and relentlessly persecuted the Jews among them, to a sort of velvet glove approach in the Netherlands. The Poles and Jews were regarded as being of an inferior race while the Dutch were seen as pure Aryans. He surrounded himself with a group of mostly Austrian cronies of which only one knew something about Holland. His police "enforcer" was Hanns Albin Rauter who was appointed by Himmler, the *Reichsführer SS*. Rauter was a ruthless career soldier and a fanatical officer in the Waffen SS who was also an Austrian and who would, over the years, become the real villain of the occupation regime. It was the shooting and wounding of Rauter by Dutch Resistance people, just before the end of the war that led to the execution of 263 Dutch patriots including my Uncle Bernard van der Hoop. Ironically, during the war and also after it, the Dutch regarded the Austrians as friendlier, more easy-going and less fanatical Nazis than the Germans. This was incorrect in my view. The Austrians were elated when the Germans marched in in 1938, and as we saw in Holland and elsewhere, many of them were dedicated Nazis who were strong supporters of the German cause. Von Falkenhausen remained as the Wehrmacht's commandant of occupied Belgium and France. Only the Netherlands were "honored" with the presence of a *Reichscommisar*.

Seyss-Inquart started his regime with a sort of installation ceremony in the medieval *Ridderzaal,* the Knights Hall in The Hague, the same place where the queen opens the new session of parliament every year with an official speech outlining government policies for the coming year. Seyss filled the audience with Nazis in fancy uniforms, he also invited the Dutch secretaries general, the top civil servants who, in the absence of their ministers, ran the various government departments. The Secretaries General agreed to come to the ceremony but declined Seyss' invitation to lunch. A group of musicians from a German radio symphony orchestra provided classical background music. I guess the Germans were trying to give their presence in Holland an official veneer and legitimacy and wanted us to see them as cultured, well-educated people who could run an installation ceremony in good style. Seyss' "inaugural address" sounded quite reasonable. He said something to the effect that nobody would be harmed as long as no actions against the German authorities were taken. Many Dutchmen received speeches like this and other actions with a great deal of relief. They saw the Germans as basically well intended towards them and a degree of complacency set in. They hoped that we would be left alone and would be able to continue our lives as before. This attitude reflected, of course, a good dose of wishful thinking. There also was a growing conviction that the Germans could not be beat, that they would conquer all of Europe and would dominate the entire world in due course. This defeatist attitude was, according to de Jong's postwar reports, not only prevalent among the secretaries general and other high Dutch civil servants but had also taken hold of several ministers in the Dutch Cabinet of the government in exile in London. Among the bureaucrats in Holland the initial attitude was one of flexible cooperation, no resistance and by all means "don't rock the boat." Holland remained the peaceful, self-satisfied country it had been ever since the fall of Napoleon more than a century ago, when it had been at war for the last time.

In those days religion still played a major role in Dutch society and political opinions were divided among a handful of separate groups and parties, many based on religious convictions. Most Dutchmen wanted to return to their prewar life style and hoped the Germans would permit them to do so. The Germans were aware of these sentiments in Holland and made use of them in establishing themselves as masters of the country. As the war progressed and things got a great deal tougher for Germany, the attitudes of the Germans towards Holland and the Dutch changed drastically. They gradually tightened the screws on the Dutch people, issued more and more draconian measures, and stole everything they could move to Germany. Over time, they reverted more and more to a regime of general terror and repression, leaving behind all pretense of running a government based on laws. In reaction to this the resistance among the Dutch grew rapidly and by the end of the war almost all Dutchmen actively or passively resisted the occupier, and the hate of the Germans and all that is German is even now not entirely gone. But a great deal had to happen before we reached that point. In my estimation, the spirit of resistance was stronger among the average ordinary Dutchmen than among their bureaucrats. The Dutch public showed a massive display of loyalty towards the House of Orange on June 29. This was Prince Bernhard's birthday. It was seized upon by thousands of people to wear white carnations, as the prince was known to do, and to bring mountains of flowers to the Royal Palace in The Hague and other monuments of the royal family throughout the country.

The beginnings of German oppression began to manifest themselves in the summer of 1940. Bread and flour were rationed. Only a month before food had been abundant in our country. Now scarcity was beginning to be noticed. The reasons were obvious. The Germans, who had lived for many years under a regime that invented the slogan: "We will rather have guns than butter," immediately started removing food supplies from Holland. Using gasoline-driven vehicles was prohibited immediately after the capitulation and listening to non–German broadcasts was also forbidden. All newspapers were put under heavy censorship. In August all textiles were rationed. The RAF started bombing targets in Holland and the Germans began their air offensive against Britain, bombing many larger population centers, which would later be called "the Blitz" or more appropriately the Battle of Britain.

In the midst of this beginning warlike environment Eelco Apol and I decided to go sailing in Friesland with Eelco's boat. Eelco had just bought a nice small (about 15 ft.) lapstrake-built wooden sloop and we had sailed it a couple of times on the *Kager Plassen*, a complex of lakes near Leiden, a popular sailing area for people living in and near The Hague. Eelco kept his boat there. For a long time I had been interested in sailing and to have a friend with a boat was a unique opportunity to get on the water. So it was Eelco who taught me the beginnings of sailing, a sport I have enjoyed immensely for more than fifty years. Years later when Eelco joined Netty and me on a New York Yacht Club cruise to Maine, we reminisced about those days of wooden boats with Egyptian cotton sails in wartime Holland.

To go sailing in Friesland one had to cross the *IJsselmeer*, a body of water that used to be called *Zuiderzee* before it was cut off from the North Sea by a big dam. This was too much open water for Eelco's small boat and we planned to go to Amsterdam and from there put our boat on a daily ferry from there to Lemmer, a small harbor in Friesland. This method was well known and followed by many yachtsmen who wanted to go to Friesland. But it is still hard to understand why our parents let us go. It was wartime and we were only fifteen years old! Perhaps our parents were naïve about the potential dangers we could be facing and had just not adjusted to the much harsher environment we would soon be living in. We had no outboard motor – using gasoline was *verboten* – so we only had our sails to move us forward and a paddle if the wind died, which promptly happened on the day we set out. Towards noon of our first day we found ourselves in the canal that leads from our lake to an area near Haarlem and from there to Amsterdam. In Dutch fashion we started to move our boat by having one of us tow it with a long line by walking along the bank of the canal. This is called *jagen* and most canals had a tow path, a *jaagpad*. Before the war, during the depression years, you could see skippers towing their boats loaded with freight, along a *jaagpad,* to save fuel. Sometimes whole families would be pulling, using special slings around their chests to make this hard job a little easier.

We did not make much progress and were relieved when a small commercial skipper came along. He had a boat driven by a diesel engine. Up till the last few months of the war Dutch canal skippers were allowed to ply their trade and use scarce fuel since they were (and still are) an important part of the transportation system. Our skipper and his mate were willing to give us a tow to Amsterdam and off we went. Once we were in Amsterdam it was agreed that the skipper would bring Eelco's boat to the Lemmer ferry the next morning, and we would take the tram to Haarlem to spend the night with my grandparents in Bloemendaal. This was, of course, a cumbersome arrangement, but we were too young to consider going to a hotel and besides we did not know anything about Amsterdam, which was to us a big wicked city. When our tram arrived in Haarlem it was dark—a pitch black blackout night. It was too late to get a connection with a bus or tram to Bloemendaal so we walked, stumbling through the dark for about an hour. My grandmother, who was already in bed when we arrived, received us kindly.

The next morning we left very early to get back to Amsterdam to find our boat. When we got to the ferry we were distressed to see that our boat was not there, so we started wandering about the city to find our skipper. After an hour or two of searching among all the small canal shipping firms who had assigned loading places in Amsterdam, we saw by some incredible miracle our man coming down a canal. He yelled to us that he had just left our boat, "neatly tucked in", near the ferry. When we got back there our boat was indeed there, with all our gear in it, with its wooden deck banging against the steel beams of a dock.

The morning ferry had left so we had to take the afternoon one and found ourselves in Lemmer in the evening. We slept in the saloon of the ferry and the next morning we were on our way, sailing through Friesland. As is usual on a nice summer day in Holland, it was cloudy and very windy. When we had successfully crossed the first Frisian lake we entered a canal where we caught a heavy puff between two farm houses. Our boat heeled over, scooped some water into its cockpit and when the boat righted itself we realized that all our gear and much of our food was sopping wet. Particularly our wet woolen blankets were a problem.

That's how we ended up in Heerenveen with the Steensma family, a photographer who used to work for my Grandfather Hesselink and had his house and business in a property then owned by my father that was located right on the canal where we tied our boat up. This family helped us dry out and we had a very good time with them. Friends of my parents, the Hooghout's who also lived in Heerenveen, helped us, too, and took us under their wing when we went further. They owned a beautiful sailboat a Swedish *Scheren Kruiser*, a nice sleek cruising boat. We sailed with them "in company" to Grouw, a wonderful small town on a lake in the middle of the great Frisian sailing scene. We stayed there for a few days and then had to go back, reversing the whole procedure with the ferry. This time we took the morning ferry and came back in Amsterdam in time to sail down the big North Sea Canal to the Haarlem area and from there we reached the boatyard where Eelco kept his boat. At our destination my parents and Oom Frans de Clercq and his sons were waiting for us. They had all bicycled over. We had been on an interesting summer sailing adventure as if there was no world war going on and no German occupation of our country.

That fall I went back to school and found myself as the youngest and smallest guy in an all-boy class. Like our own son George much later, it took me a while to start growing. Nowadays papers here are full of stories of kids being picked on in class for being short, small, dark or light or whatever is different from the norm. I guess this did not happen in my time in The Hague or maybe it was because I have always been quite self-confident, and when they were teasing me, it did not affect me. We played a lot of field hockey in those days at school and at the hockey club I belonged to. The guys in my class were mostly very good at it. I wasn't. I was and still am poorly coordinated and not good at ball games. When we would be starting a game and the captains were choosing sides, I was often the last one picked. That bothered me, of course, but I did not lose any sleep over it. In class everything went still quite well academically.

The Germans began to tighten the noose step by step. Particularly, regulatory steps taken against Dutch Jews began to be more frequent. Jews were required to carry special identification cards and were banned from restaurants, theatres, etc. The Dutch continued to comply with all the rules that the Germans forced them to implement. In January 1941, the registration of all Jews was ordered. This meant that many people had to decide whether they should report themselves as Jews or not. Not every Jewish person considered him or herself 100% Jewish. For secular Jews like my grandmother, that was an enormous problem. Chances were that nobody would notice if you would not register. After considerable debate within our family, it was decided that she should register. We caved in like almost all Dutchmen caved in to almost all German decrees. The belief that one should obey government rules and regulations was so deeply ingrained in most people's minds that almost all Jews registered themselves, thereby inadvertently taking the first step towards their own death sentence.

A similar but much less serious situation occurred with the ownership of radios. All owners of radios were ordered to pay for a "listening permit" to the government, thereby automatically getting their sets registered, so that much later when the Germans decided to confiscate all radios, it was much harder to disobey their order and keep a radio. Big Brother knew who owned a radio. A small minority decided not to register their radios, thinking that nobody among the authorities knew whether they owned a radio or not. Another trick was to find an old set and register that while keeping a good one hidden. However, here again most people obeyed the rules. They feared they could be betrayed by others or by loose talk. There were, after all, a fairly large number of Nazi sympathizers in Holland, and there were also many people who were fence sitters, sort of neutral and prepared to go either way. We called them *EKWW'ers* which stood for *Eerst kijken wie wint* or let's see first who wins. In our family we were unexpectedly at an advantage in the radio dilemma. Our radio "distribution" system at home was connected by wire to the

German-controlled broadcasts, so we did not officially own a radio. Actually we did own one which we obtained from Mrs. Cambier van Nooten, my late Grandfather Hesselink's friend and companion. She gave it to us when she moved to smaller quarters. We set it up in my room, and every evening we listened to the BBC Home Service, a broadcast that was in English and therefore not jammed by the Germans. Later my parents found this radio set too large and therefore too visible, so I asked a friend to "borrow" it. He later converted it into an amplifier for my record player. Meanwhile, my father acquired a small American-made table radio that he bought from a young man who lived in our neighborhood. This chap was an amateur radio enthusiast and knew people in The Hague who had several of these very small radios for sale. My father had the radio hidden in a shoebox and pulled it out every morning to plug it in and listen to London in his bedroom. I believe that listening to the BBC for several years gave me a good understanding of the English language. We had to play that radio softly because we did not trust the son of our neighbors who was believed to have Nazi sympathies. Since his bedroom adjoined the wall of my parent's bedroom, we had to be careful.

Gradually the Resistance movement began to emerge. In February 1941 the Dutch labor unions and other organizations called a general strike in protest of the persecution of the Jews. This strike started in Amsterdam among longshoremen and spread to many cities in the country. It also reached Friesland where workers in the dairy industry struck and destroyed large quantities of milk and butter. The Germans sent in their *Grüne Polizei*, police units of the SS-controlled security forces. These troops fired point blank at strikers who were picketing at their place of work and brutally repressed the whole movement. It lasted only a day or so, but it was a first big gesture of discontent. Right after the strike, Himmler reacted and ordered the first roundup of Jews in Amsterdam and about 400 were deported. In the meantime, several smaller and larger Resistance groups were established. The Germans rolled up many, often because they operated in an amateurish fashion and were too visible or because they were betrayed by the German *Abwehr*, the counter espionage service that was well organized and very active in Holland right from the start of the occupation. Still the Resistance movement grew, although most Dutchmen did not participate actively.

In the spring of 1941 milk and potatoes were rationed. Dutch farmers were known to produce great quantities of these products. In fact, during the Depression just a few years ago, the government had gone to great length to encourage greater consumption of dairy products. So there could have hardly been a sudden scarcity.

The rationing was a clear illustration of the extent of the German demands on Dutch food production.

Then on May 11, 1941, Rudolf Hess, Hitler's right hand man and one of the most prominent thugs in his entourage, flew to England and bailed out of his plane over Scotland. It never became clear why Hess did this and if he was crazy or managed to get a hearing with the British government. He was locked up and after the war became the last Nazi war criminal to die in prison. He hanged himself in 1987. We enjoyed this sign of weakness and disorganization in the Nazi top and would greet each other with the cry, *Hi Ha, Hi Ha Hess is weg* – Hi Ha Hi Ha Hess is gone. It was one of these strange events that made us hope there would be a quick turn in the fortunes of war, but sadly we soon discovered Hitler kept going, with or without his buddy Hess. After the war a group of conspiracy theorists developed a story that claimed Hess came over to make peace with Britain. He landed near the estate of the Duke of Hamilton with whom he had been briefly in contact before the war. The British determined he was mentally unstable. Also that spring the Germans moved into the Balkans and the Battle of Britain moved into full swing. We were visiting with Oom Anne and Tante Mieke in Leeuwarden for the Easter holidays. The Germans had built a large air base in Leeuwarden from where bombers would take off in the evening to bomb Britain. When they returned in the middle of the night, they would come in at roof-top level, making an awful racket. The next morning Oom Anne would go to the barbershop for his daily shave. Upon returning he would tell us with relish how many returning German bombers had crashed in the fields around town, according to the barbers who knew every rumor in town. In Leeuwarden we heard the German radio announce pompously that they had bombed and conquered the *Festung Belgrad* – "fortress" Belgrade, doublespeak for their attack on another population center that happened to be in their way. A few weeks later Athens fell and after that German paratroopers conquered Crete, which was a British stronghold. This was the last big airborne action the Germans undertook in the war. Their losses in Crete were so heavy that they lost the taste for this kind of attack. These actions and the successes the Germans had in North Africa against the British forces there, almost getting to the outskirts of Cairo, strengthened the feeling among many Dutchmen that the Germans were winning the war and could not be stopped.

These sentiments prevailed among the secretaries general, the caretaker government in Holland, so much so that they even tried to broker a deal between the Germans and the English with the help of the founder and CEO of KLM, Albert Plesman. Plesman had a Swedish pilot in his employ who could travel freely between Sweden and Germany. This man whose name was von Rosen was a relative of Hermann Goering's first (deceased) wife Karin, who was Swedish.   Plesman thinking that as a successful businessman he could quickly structure a deal and do it better than the diplomats, managed to set up a meeting with Goering and proposed an arrangement between Germany and England. Plesman thought he could offer Germany a free hand in continental Europe, the return of its former colonies in Africa and many other concessions based on the thought that Germany had practically won the war. There was some support for this plan because Hitler had stated in a speech in Berlin that he was willing to negotiate. What prompted the secretaries general to go along with this plan was that they were worried that in the event of a German victory the Dutch sovereignty over the Dutch East Indies would be in jeopardy. They wanted to have the Germans on their side in case a conflict arose in the Far East. It was another example of the Dutch over-estimating their importance in world affairs. Neither Plesman, an aggressive and highly successful businessman who saw himself as head of a postwar Lufthansa/KLM collaboration, nor the secretaries general nor the Germans understood the British government's determination to carry on under Churchill. They also misunderstood the growing involvement of the U.S. in the war and its interest in the region of the Pacific Ocean. They were quite disappointed when they heard from Oom Eelco through the Dutch Embassy in Stockholm that there was no interest in this foolish proposal. The reason the Dutch colonies came to the fore in this scheme was that immediately after the May 1940 attack, the authorities in the East Indies had interned a great number of German citizens. It became known that these people had not been treated very well. The German government in Holland decided to retaliate by imprisoning a large number of Dutchmen who had connections with Indonesia, mainly business people and people who happened to be stranded in Holland on leave from their jobs overseas. Initially Hitler's order was to imprison ten times more Dutchmen than there were Germans taken in the Far East. Seyss-Inquart deflected this plan because it was hardly helpful in his effort to mollify the Dutch and prepare them for postwar inclusion in the German Reich.

In my class in school there was a great interest in jazz and swing music, and I was also beginning to get really interested in it. Partly because I liked it a lot and also because the Germans tried to outlaw it as "degenerate" music unworthy of true Aryans. My parents did not like this music either, but for different, not racial reasons. My father called it *ketelmuziek* – music produced by beating on pots and pans. Stores still had American and English records and we spent our savings on acquiring whatever we could get out of the dwindling supplies. For my birthday my grandparents had given me money towards a gramophone. This was a portable windup instrument where you played records with a needle. This was a very proud possession for me and I played the few records I had incessantly. In the spring of that year a major event that gave us joy in school and made us think, again prematurely, that the tide was finally turning in our favor was the sinking of the German battleship *Bismarck* by the British Navy. Unfortunately the *Hood*, the pride of the Royal Navy, was also sunk in that battle, with the tragic loss of all but three of its crew of several hundred. Ignoring the loss of Allied lives, we celebrated the sinking of the Bismarck at school, almost as soon as it happened. I still remember how a boy by the name of Bill Rozenburg, who owned a peculiar bike on which you pedaled lying down, came careering into the schoolyard, lying on his machine, bellowing: "we got him." Obviously he had gotten that information by listening to the BBC, but that was an accepted fact.

In June we were ordered to turn in all copper, brass, lead, tin and nickel materials to help the German war effort. Pa hid our antique brass pots and tin plates somewhere in the attic of our house but turned in some other things. In the same week the Germans attacked the Soviet Union. They must have felt they needed to stock up on metal for the coming battle. Hitler counted on a quick victory over the Soviet forces and hoped they would capitulate and collapse because of poor organization and leadership, in the same manner as the Czarist army had capitulated in World War I. The German army was so convinced that they would achieve a quick victory that they did not supply their troops with winter clothing until it was almost too late. Historians now say Hitler attacked Russia because he was much more focused on getting *Lebensraum*—room to live for his Germans—in the east than on beating Britain in the west. He thought he could later on always make some kind of arrangement with a weakened Britain and believed he would be able to expand eastward by occupying huge areas of fertile Russian soil and oil wells as well. He would enslave or eliminate the local population, which he regarded as inferior human beings. At first it seemed Hitler was succeeding and winning an easy victory. He sliced into Russia like a hot knife through butter. Stalin, who had believed the German–Russian friendship pact was a valid document, had kept his army away from the border so as not to excite the Germans. Also, he had in the thirties systematically executed many leading officers in his army, thereby weakening its staff and leadership and leaving the remaining officers afraid of taking any initiatives. The Soviet air force, using inferior, older planes, was almost immediately eliminated and the army seemed powerless to stop the Germans. They just kept withdrawing into the endless Russian land, lengthening the German supply lines. When winter came, the Germans found themselves unprepared for the terrible cold and were forced to halt their advance, and in November the Soviet army forced the first German retreat at Rostov. The similarities with Napoleon's Russian campaign were obvious, and one wonders what Hitler was thinking, given his dominant position in Europe before he started his eastward move.

The persecution of the Jews in Holland went relentlessly forward with confiscation of their possessions, real estate as well as financial assets. Jewish children were banned from all public schools and roundups of Jews in certain towns started. There was little or no opposition from the Dutch authorities or population against these measures. Several Jewish students disappeared from my school, the Haags Lyceum. Amazingly, we just accepted that as a fact and felt they would somehow find a place to study elsewhere. A Dutch legion to fight the "Bolsheviks" was formed. A Dutch General Seyffard was found willing to act as its token commander. The Resistance later liquidated him. The Dutch legion was later merged into the Waffen SS. It never got enough men to serve, and when parades were held to show the volunteers marching to the front, their ranks were temporarily filled with Dutch Nazis who pretended they were joining.

On December 7th 1941, the Japanese navy executed its enormously successful sneak attack on Pearl Harbor. America was in the war! It was one of these moments where you remember where you were when the news reached you. I remember standing in the backyard of the Deibel family in Leeuwraden when we heard the news. Oom Anne had his very big radio hidden in his attic and was listening regularly to London. What we were doing in Leeuwarden is not clear to me anymore. Perhaps we were there to celebrate St. Nicholas eve with the Deibels on December 5th. As we all know, the attack came on a Sunday and maybe we had planned to spend a long weekend in Friesland for the Sinterklaas holiday. What is still very clear in my mind is what my father said to me that day. He said: "Now it's over for the Germans and the Japanese. The Americans know how to produce and how to organize." They work efficiently and fast, Pa said. He added, "the Americans can out-produce anybody in the world." It is amazing that neither Hitler nor the Japanese leadership understood this point that was so obvious to my father who had been several times to the U.S. The story goes, however, that Admiral Yamamoto, who led the Japanese attack on Pearl Harbor and who had lived in America, had said, "We have awakened a giant." Hitler even made Roosevelt's domestic political task easier by unilaterally declaring war on the U.S. Roosevelt had tried to help the

English war effort by making various arrangements to send them war materiel. The Americans did not have much equipment themselves in those days, and there was a strong isolationist group in Congress that did not want any involvement in "foreign" wars. When the Japanese unexpectedly attacked American soil, the isolationist movement was eliminated, but it was not yet immediately clear that Germany was also going to fight the U.S. Hitler's declaration of war smoothed the path for the start of the enormous American war effort that next to the overwhelming masses of the Russian army would decide the war. That Winston Churchill understood what the U.S. participation in the war meant was very clear. Before the attack on Pearl Harbor, when a German invasion of England was a real possibility, he had uttered the now famous words telling the British people: "I have nothing to offer but blood, toil, tears and sweat." And, "We shall not flag or fail. We shall fight on the seas and oceans. We shall fight on the landing grounds, we shall fight in the fields and on the streets, we shall fight in the hills, we shall never surrender." In his book *The Grand Alliance* Churchill wrote that he had telephoned Roosevelt right after the first news of the Japanese attack broke. Churchill had asked, "Mr. President, what's this about Japan?" Roosevelt had replied, "It's quite true. They have attacked us at Pearl Harbor. We're in the same boat now." Churchill was ecstatic. He now had the manpower, the resources and the fighting spirit of the Americans on his side. He wrote, "So we had won after all." But before we in Holland would feel the impact of the US war effort, we would have to suffer through almost three more years of gradually increasing oppression and bad news. We did not know much about what was going on in the outside world, of course, and there was a tendency to be overoptimistic and to expect an immediate impact of the American participation in the war. In fact, things got much worse and the German propaganda machine did not fail to let us know every detail of the victories of the Germans and the Japanese.

On December 10 Japanese aircraft sank two British battle ships, the *Prince of Wales* and the *Repulse*. They were in the Indian Ocean, on their way to support the defense of Singapore, without proper air cover and they paid the price. There were no aircraft available anywhere to stop the Japanese onslaught. In quick succession the Japanese attacked the Philippines, Hong Kong, Singapore and Malaysia, and by January 1942, they were close to invading the Dutch East Indies. On February 27th the battle of the Java Sea took place. Virtually the entire Dutch navy went out to meet a Japanese invasion force that was approaching Java. During the night they attacked the Japanese warships that were acting as a screen for the merchant ships that carried the troops. The Dutch ships, two light cruisers, the *De Ruyter* and the *Java* and several destroyers, were supported by the American heavy cruiser *Houston*, the British cruiser *Exeter* and the Australian *Perth*. A Dutch admiral, Karel Doorman, was in command. He attacked despite the fact that he had no air support and had little knowledge of the strength and size of the Japanese fleet. His now famous order was, *"Ik val aan volg mij"* – "I am attacking, follow me." Historians have determined that he did not utter these heroic words but signaled "All ships follow me." In a fairly brief night battle all five cruisers were sunk and the island of Java, the most heavily populated and economically most important part of the colony, lay open for a Japanese invasion. There were very few survivors of this naval engagement. It is described in *A war to be won* as follows, "ABDA [American, British, Dutch, Australian] forces gathered their scarce air and naval forces in an attempt to hold Java and thus keep the lines to Australia open and to support the defense of Singapore. This defense failed also when Japanese naval aircraft destroyed most of the Allied air forces in February. On February 27 the ABDA fleet of five cruisers and nine destroyers met a similar force from the Imperial Japanese Navy and learned a costly lesson in naval gunnery, the use of long-range torpedoes, and the importance of reconnaissance and coordination. In a battle in which naval air played no role, the IJN ruined the ABDA fleet, eventually sinking all five cruisers and all but four destroyers." In Dutch literature the battle in the Java Sea is usually described in more heroic terms. It was clearly a valiant but desperate attempt to prevent the inevitable. True to its traditions, the Dutch navy fought heroically. The Dutch air force pilots had also shown élan and aggressiveness. Unfortunately, the Dutch army performed less spectacularly. Their resistance collapsed quickly although the Japanese forces were numerically not overwhelming. Batavia fell on March 5th and on March 9th the Dutch East Indies surrendered, less than two weeks after the battle in the Java Sea.

Reports covering the fighting on Java and other islands of the Indonesian archipelago describe a generally low level of resistance to the Japanese invaders. On Java Dutch forces sometimes retreated from coastal positions *before* the Japanese forces landed. Troops then retreated to previously prepared secondary defense lines, only to find them inadequate, which led to disorganization and panic. Similar stories are related about Dutch army activities in the Netherlands during the five days of fighting against the Germans. At the Grebbeberg defense line, troops would flee in panic before any serious action took place and officers had a hard time rallying them behind the lines, often having to resort to threats of the firing squad if they would not fall in line. There was the story of the Dutch sergeant who jumped in his artillery tractor, driving far away from the fighting, while pulling an antitank gun and picking up another gun along the way. Many fought bravely, but the efforts of those who did were severely hampered by the lack of fighting spirit of their comrades. Dutch soldiers in Holland and in the Far East were the product of a penny-pinching regime that instilled in them the feeling that the army was a joke and that its equipment was inferior. The political leadership was dedicated to saving money on defense and had little regard for the well-being or fighting ability of its soldiers. They were convinced that in Europe the Germans could not be beaten and that in the Far East the Japanese were equally invincible.

The performance of the army during the first few years of the war stands in sharp contrast to the heroism of the Dutch navy and air force. The negative stories about the Dutch army always bothered me, partly because I served in it for three years and participated in some real action in Indonesia and also partly because I felt there was more to it than could be discerned on the surface. In Indonesia I had been among Dutch troops in action and found them just as calm and professional as any other army unit exposed to enemy fire could be. I think that a good part of the bad name the pre–World War II army got was due to poor leadership poor financial support and poor preparation. There were only a few really professional officers in the army who were trained to fight and not to behave as administrators of an organization that emphasized saving money. Professional soldiers, particularly the so-called "colonials" were not held in high esteem in Dutch society. Many young men who could not make it in ordinary jobs in Holland or who had something to hide would sign up to serve with the KNIL, the Royal Netherlands Indies Army. The main force of the KNIL consisted of Dutch professional soldiers, who were out to serve their contract time out in the Indies and earn a pension, and Indonesian volunteers recruited locally. Only at the last moment in 1941 did the government of the Dutch East Indies start with a conscription program so that the men who faced the Japanese were poorly trained and poorly motivated. The unit in which I served in Indonesia consisted mainly of conscripts and the quality of the officers who were leading us was below par. Yet once we were over the initial shock of combat, or rather after "being shot at," our battalion fought well, was quite highly motivated and did its job. I believe every normal person has to overcome fear when confronted with a shooting war for the first time. However, very few soldiers continue to live with a paralyzing fear of action. And while they may not like to be put in harm's way, most people get used to it and are able to function well after the initial shock.

The Dutch soldiers who served during the first wave of attacks by the Germans and Japanese really had no time to get used to action. Their war was over before they could come to their senses. I think there were several reasons for the quite satisfactory performance record of the unit I served in. In 1950 we were in general better trained than the soldiers of 1940/41. We were also better equipped. Most important, we knew that our Indonesian opponents were badly equipped, poorly led and often inclined to run rather than fight. So we felt superior to our enemies. Finally, we had no way out. We could not go home. We were in it together for the duration and had to rely on each other.

When the Dutch East Indies capitulated, we got the news, of course. At that time I experienced a dramatic visit with Pa at the home of Jaap van der Bel, a friend of my parents who had a powerful radio set that could receive the broadcasts that were beamed at the homeland from the East Indies. We listened to one of the last broadcasts and heard that the governor general had just made a radio address telling the population that he had capitulated and ending with the statement: *"Vaarwel tot betere tijden"* (farewell until better times). Mr. van der Bel, who was a retired naval officer and had served in the Far East for several years, was visibly moved and could barely contain himself. It was a bad moment. The news from North Africa was not good either, and the Germans were resuming their march into the Soviet Union while the Japanese seemed unstoppable and people feared they would keep moving from Malaya into Burma and from there into India.

Large numbers of Dutch Resistance people were arrested and executed. The first victims of the *"England Spiel"* were caught and executed. Dutch agents, trained in England were dropped by parachute into Holland with radios and weapons, intended for the Dutch Resistance. These agents were caught by the Germans and forced to use their radios to send messages back to England as if they were still operating freely. They had a coded "fail safe" message system that would alert their handlers in London to the fact that they were captured and were sending messages under duress. These coded messages were sent by the agents but ignored in London with the results that more and more agents were dropped into the waiting arms of the Germans. It has never been made clear how these terrible errors that cost the lives of a number of very brave men could have been made. The best explanation is probably ineptitude and lack of attention to detail on the part of the British/Dutch intelligence service. At home in Voorburg we did not know anything about these matters of course. All we knew was that the war was not going well and that there were a growing number of terse announcement in our German-controlled papers listing the names of people executed for acts of "sabotage" or resistance.

Several acts of sabotage against the Dutch railway system, some quite clumsy and of little effect nevertheless caused the Germans to take drastic action. In May 1942 they detained 460 prominent Dutchmen as "hostages" and incarcerated them in a Catholic seminar near 's Hertogenbosch. Netty's father was one of them. He was arrested on August 18, 1942; several months after the main roundup of hostages took place. The hostages were not treated as badly as the prisoners sent to concentration camps. They could move freely through the complex of several buildings, go outside into a fenced-off garden area and socialize with each other as much as they liked. They could watch movies and organize lectures and plays. But there was a constantly present, terrifying threat. On certain days in the very early morning hours the Germans would suddenly enter the building and select a number of hostages, seemingly at random, and take them outside to a deserted place and shoot them. This happened several times. After the execution all the hostages were called together for a roll call and after letting them stand there for an interminable time, a group of officers would appear and solemnly announce the names of the people that had been executed. They would pretend to be very sorry this action had to be taken but explained that sabotage had taken place and although they had asked the culprits to make themselves known, nobody had come forward so they were unfortunately obligated to act. This twisted logic was a typical example of the German mentality of that time and it increasingly became the rule by which the Germans governed. The names of the people who were executed were widely published in the Dutch press. In those years many horrors against innocent people were committed under the excuse that it "had to be done." The Germans always claimed that they were only trying to do the right thing and were constantly thwarted in their noble efforts to save the world from dominance by Jews and British plutocrats and by evil people who were lackeys of London. Eventually, after about a year the Germans began to release hostages, probably because they concluded that the idea of intimidating the Dutch population by killing hostages did not work. On September 20th 1943, more than a year after he was taken prisoner, Netty's father was released. After the war a book with remembrances of the hostages was published. Netty's father gave each of his children a copy and wrote in it "For Netty to be remembered–A van Kleffens, hostage." The book is called *Beekvliet*, which is the name of the seminary where the hostages were imprisoned. Another book we have is "*Gijzelaar in Gestel*" by Robert Peereboom.

Oom Otto Jonas, husband of my mother's sister Jet was also arrested as a hostage. He was released quite early, probably in September 1942; right after the first group of hostages was shot. The Germans must have decided they had captured too many men. I vividly remember his stories of the hostage camp, particularly the story of the two well-known Dutch comedians who were among the people locked up. The comedians turned out to be more afraid and more nervous and high-strung than almost all the others. Oom Otto told us particularly about his conversations with a colleague of his, a Prof. Schermerhorn a man he knew very well because they worked in the same branch of the government. Schermerhorn became a leader of the hostages and after the war served for many years as prime minister. He belonged to the Socialist party, which was hardly Oom Otto's political persuasion. Sometime later Oom Otto had a much less pleasant experience when he was locked up in the notorious Vught concentration camp. I saw him after he came back from about six month in that camp. He was very thin, his hair had been shaved off and he had a big nasty open sore on his foot where a guard had deliberately stomped on his foot with his hob-nailed boot. Oom Otto had worn wooden shoes like all other prisoners and the wound had started to fester as he was forced to walk around with his wound chafing against the edge. We always wondered why Oom Otto had been arrested twice. He was very anti–German, but he was not actively involved in the resistance. But he did not hide his feelings and Tante Jet was certainly no shrinking violet either if it came to speaking out. They lived in a small, quiet side-street in a residential neighborhood in Arnhem. Their house was not very big and it was like most other Dutch houses in an urban setting, close to the street, so that you could easily see who was passing by. Nearby lived a man who was a typical example of the frustrated little functionary who felt thwarted by his boss. He had to pass Oom Otto and Tante Jet's house on his way to the bus stop. He was a Nazi and worked for Oom Otto. This man, whose name was Drewes, I believe, complained to Oom Otto that he felt every-body was gathering behind the windows to see him pass, ridiculing him. We always felt Drewes had turned Oom Otto in to the Gestapo, but we could not prove it.

All Dutch beaches were declared "off limits" to civilians in April of 1942. This was a blow in many respects. The long, sandy Dutch beaches served as escape routes for several people who managed to go to England with small boats, kayaks, etc. In summer the beaches offered a place to enjoy the sea and the sun and to feel less "closed in." In the previous summer, before Hitler decided to focus on Soviet Russia, we would sit on the beach and see the Germans practice with Dutch canal barges they had requisitioned and modified to act as landing craft. A few of these barges were concentrated in the harbor of Scheveningen and when the weather was nice they would venture out and we would hope they would go over to England as we were certain they would either not make it or be sunk when they got there. In the early war years the Germans had a marching song titled *Wir fahren gegen Engeland* (We are moving against England) the song ended with its title being sung followed in typical German fashion with three thumps on the drums and cymbals. The Dutch translated the three thumps as *plons plons plons* (plunk plunk plunk), as an imitation of the noise made by somebody or something heavy falling in the water. Unfortunately for us the Germans never seriously tried to invade England.

That spring and summer of 1942 the news about the war was almost universally bad. In April the Japanese started putting all European civilians in Indonesia in "protective custody," a move we did not hear about for quite a while, and after we heard rumors about it we had no idea how bad it was. All Dutch men were put in work camps; many were transported to Burma to work on the infamous Burma railroad. The women and children were put in separate concentration camps where they stayed until the end of the war under atrocious circumstances. In Holland all the Dutch Jews were forced to start wearing yellow stars with the word "Jew" on it. As I mentioned, it was a great shock for me to see my own grandmother with such a star on her coat. In June the German/Italian forces in North Africa reached the Egyptian border. All Dutch regular army officers who had been let go in 1940 were ordered to report back to go to Germany as prisoners of war. The Germans started to seize bicycles on the streets in the bigger cities. This started a move to hide men's bikes and ride around on women's bikes. In those days we had different bikes for men and for women. This thirst for bikes on the part of the Germans subsided for a while, but towards the end of the war they would grab any bike they could get. So we started riding around without tires, just using the rims or using ersatz tires made out of strips of rubber.

The hostages, including Netty's father, were taken that summer and the first five were executed in August as a "punishment" for sabotage to a railway line near Rotterdam. In Russia the Germans captured Sevastopol in the Crimea and reached Stalingrad. It was just a terrible time. One day in the early summer of 1942 I was eating my lunch at school. The news about the war was bad. The Germans and Japanese seemed to be unbeatable, scoring successes wherever they went. Like many other students who lived fairly far away from school I did not go home for lunch anymore. I ate sandwiches I had brought from home, saving the paper bags for the next day, and drank some skimmed milk with it. Real milk was no longer available. I was speaking with my French teacher, a small precise man called Mr. Miserus. I liked him because he had a dry sense of humor and we got along very well. He was always impeccably dressed. In class we used a lot of chalk on our black board and the table used by the teacher was often covered with it. Mr. Miserus did not like to have chalk on his clothes or his briefcase so when he came into our classroom to teach his French class, he would first bend over the teachers table and blow the chalk away as hard as he could. We had noticed that, of course, and sometimes we put an extra layer of chalk on the table and enjoyed seeing the large cloud of chalk come up as he did his blowing routine. That day Mr. Miserus was in a very pessimistic mood and told me he thought the Germans would march through Egypt to India and join up with the Japanese. They were already beating the Soviet Russian armies back to the Ural Mountains and could move into Mesopotamia from there. I don't know why I still remember this conversation, but it sticks in my mind as taking place just about when the tide started finally to turn. In August Allied forces tried landing in France. When we heard about this we were elated. We thought it was the first sign of a coming invasion of the continent by Allied forces. Unfortunately, it was a disaster. A mostly Canadian force landed near Dieppe in France. They made an incredible heroic attempt to get a foothold and try out invasion tactics. They got badly beaten and only a few Canadians returned to England. It was never made entirely clear why this attack was made. Maybe it was just a probe, an attempt to give the Germans a message. The message was "we're coming." The first real Allied victory came in November, it was the battle of El Alamein where the British army led by General Montgomery beat the Germans decisively and started rolling them back along the shores of North Africa. Then came the Allied landing in North Africa with American and British troops landing in Oran, Casablanca and Algiers, encountering little resistance from the French forces there who were still controlled by the French puppet government in unoccupied "Vichy" France. The Americans were also beginning an offensive in the Pacific, landing on Guadalcanal and other islands and winning naval battles. In Russia the winter set in again and the battle of Stalingrad began. In the rubble of that city an entire German army corps was encircled and it ultimately surrendered on February 3, 1943. This battle was the turning point in the war on the eastern front. So by the end of that year, things began to look better. We were still a long way from being liberated, however.

12 : *Daily Life During The Occupation*

When the fighting during the five days of May 1940 was over, many Dutchmen decided that resistance was dangerous and useless and that reluctant cooperation with the Germans was the best thing to do. The Dutch authorities, the ones that stayed behind as well as the Dutch Cabinet in exile in London, advised the citizenry to cooperate with reasonable requests and avoid provoking the Germans. In 1940, the year the war started for us, Holland was a rather self-satisfied country that took itself very seriously. It still does. We thought that the German occupier would be fair in dealing with us and keep his word, and that he would, like us, adhere to the Geneva Convention and the rules of laws under which we had lived for centuries. It did not quite work out that way. The Germans broke many rules, had no respect for our system of laws, and by allowing a level of anarchy to take hold, did a great deal of damage to the nation. At war's end, our country was in ruins and in need of decades of repair work and a long economic recovery. Many people lost their moral rudder during the war and much permanent damage was done to the general structure of our society as it had existed before the war. The world changed during the war and Holland had to change with it. After war's end, it took years before we had recovered a sense of societal balance and digested the many changes that were partly forced on us and partly self-imposed because we wanted to start with a clean slate and build a new and more just society.

When the attack came, our country's leadership was weak. But we were blessed with a queen, who was constitutionally only a symbolic head of state but turned out to be one of those strong leaders a country rallies around in time of need. Our queen had a spine of steel and proved in many respects to be a more determined and unyielding leader than most of her cabinet ministers. Queen Wilhelmina, who stepped down from the throne fairly soon after the war to turn the reins over to her daughter Juliana, was the symbol we rallied around during and immediately after the war. She was a true head of state and offered us much hope and support. But when peace came, she suddenly seemed old, tired and terribly old-fashioned in her manner of speech, in the way she dressed and in the general image she projected. She appeared to be almost a throwback to the nineteenth century. That was unfortunate but not very important because after the war the bureaucrats recovered quickly and were ready to take over and pontificate in the usual narrow-minded Dutch way. Queen Wilhelmina is now almost forgotten in Holland. She withdrew totally from public life and after she abdicated, she insisted on total privacy and did not participate in any public functions anymore.

A few years ago a book about her life was published that was unexpectedly well received and met with a warm response. From her letters to her daughter Juliana, which were made available to the author, the book reveals for the first time what she really thought about many people and things. Unfortunately, Juliana destroyed the letters she wrote to Wilhelmina in response. Despite the fact that she was the daughter of a German princess and like her daughter had married a German prince, Wilhelmina became fiercely anti– German during and after the war. She wanted to fight the Germans until they were defeated and had only disdain for the cabinet ministers who initially wanted to negotiate a compromise with the enemy. She also criticized Oom Eelco. Before the Japanese attack on Pearl Harbor, he apparently wanted to make concessions to the Japanese in an effort to save the Dutch East Indies from an attack. Wilhelmina opposed that idea and dismissed it out of hand. During her exile in England, Wilhelmina became more and more autocratic and isolated. She felt she understood the problems of the Dutch people better than her ministers and wanted to curb their powers after the war. This was impossible, of course, since the Dutch Constitution drastically limits the powers of the Crown and states that the sovereign is the head of state but that the ministers are responsible for all government actions. Legally the position of the Cabinet in London was tenuous, however, since the Dutch parliament in The Hague was disbanded so there were no "checks and balances" and it was questionable if the laws passed by the Dutch Government in exile could really be enforced.

The war went on and daily life became gradually more and more difficult. The Germans tightened the noose step by step. Hardly a day went by without a public announcement of some new measure that curbed our freedom of movement or affected our supply of food or consumer goods. Bread and flour were rationed in June 1940. That measure signaled the beginning of a systematic plundering of our reserves of food and raw materials, which were substantial at the beginning of the war. Gradually we became more preoccupied with day-to-day survival rather than lofty ideas about the future of our country and its culture or what would become of our colonial empire. In this age of satellite communication links, cell phones and Internet, it is useful to remember that in the grim years of the occupation we had very little contact with the outside world. Our newspapers were heavily censored and brought us only German Nazi propaganda. They also got smaller and smaller as paper became scarce. But you could not do without a daily newspaper because several times a week they carried the announcements of what rationing coupons would be valid for food items or clothing (textiles) or shoes. There also would be announcements of political or local importance, and when the Germans chose to execute Dutch citizens as a reprisal for real or perceived acts of resistance, they published the names of the victims in the papers for extra effect. You had to be plugged in to the lingo to discover from time to time how journalists managed to put a hint of sarcasm or opposition in an article. For instance, there was a front-page article about the marriage of Rost van Tonningen, a prominent Dutch Nazi and leader of the NSB, who married in a Nazi-type ceremony, described in a rave review in the paper. The article stated "in this Germanic marriage the bride wore a necklace adorned with the SS rune symbol." The inside joke known to many was that the groom had some Indonesian blood in his veins and was therefore not a pure Germanic specimen.

There was no TV, of course, and our radio only produced music and commentary agreeable to the Germans. There were a few entertainment programs, however, and I listened religiously to them. The Dutch version of the Big Band era was an orchestra called "the Ramblers." They had to drop their English name and were henceforth called the "Radio Broadcasting Entertainment Orchestra." In the beginning of the occupation this band often played American or English numbers with a name that in translation often sounded deliberately ridiculous. When things began to go seriously downhill for the Germans, they got nastier and forbade dancing in public places as well as in private parties. This was because dancing was considered frivolous and reflective of a lack of respect for "the heroic struggle of the great Germanic forces against Bolshevism on the eastern front."

We had a particularly venomous pro-Nazi radio commentator, Max Blokzeil, who was before the war a fairly well-known journalist and who was a master in what now would be called "spin," twisting stories around so they would fit his point of view. In his commentary he would often critique local Dutch dignitaries who had not exactly done what the Nazis required. Max was executed after the war, but his voice lives on through a CD I have of "War and Occupation – authentic sound recordings."

Radio broadcasts would be interrupted from time to time with announcements from the German military. They were preceded by drum rolls and booming German marching music. The announcer would come on (in German, of course,) and would say "*Das Führrer Hauptquartier gibt bekannt*" (The Führer's Headquarters announces). It always was a victory, never a loss. In the first few years there were victories galore and the Germans wallowed in them. Beyond the victories on land, mainly against the Russians, there were the successes of the German U Boats. Thousands and thousands of *Bruto Register Tonnen* were sunk. Post-war studies reveal that these numbers of tonnage sunk were grossly overstated. The U Boat commanders were under tremendous pressure to perform and to sink more and more ships, so they tended to inflate their numbers, calling a trawler a freighter, a small tramp freighter a large one etc. When they missed a target, they figured nobody would know whether they hit it or not. When the tide of the war started to turn, the Germans developed an art form of making victories out of large defeats. They would talk about an *Abwehr Schlagt* a defensive battle and say that after winning the battle their troops had withdrawn onto better and improved positions. They would call fortified cities *Egel Stellungen* – porcupine fortresses, and claim huge gains in Russian tanks and divisions destroyed during the German withdrawal. We all knew what was going on of course and were hugely amused by these announcements.

As the war progressed and the Dutch got more adept at resistance, numerous illegal underground newsletters appeared. These periodicals were usually stenciled on both sides of one page and contained information on the war and often very well written articles about the occupation and its impact on us. Names of traitors would be revealed and citizens were warned against them. The origins of these underground newsletters reflected the prewar divisions and segmentations of the Dutch population. There would be a Dutch Reformed one, a Catholic one, a Socialist publication and a middle-of-the road "liberal" one, etc. Several Dutch postwar newspapers found their origin in these underground periodicals. A major present-day Dutch newspaper *Trouw (Fidelity),* originated from a Dutch Reformed newsletter with the same name. The Dutch Communist party was also in evidence with their own newsletter called *"De Waarheid" – The Truth* in Dutch or *Pravda* in Russian, which was the name of the newspaper of record in Soviet Russia, thus leaving no question of who the true master of our Communist party was. Most newsletters were part of larger Resistance organizations that had their own armed underground groups. Interestingly, the

Dutch Reformed (protestant fundamentalist) resistance groups and the Communist ones proved to be the most disciplined and effective resistance organizations. They had strong beliefs and were willing to fight and die for them. Groups representing more middle-of-the-road political and spiritual philosophies tended to be less aggressive in their resistance activities. Writing, printing and distributing these newsletters was a very risky business and many people were shot for being involved in the underground press. Having a copy in one's possession when arrested was, of course, also a very bad thing. It was customary to pass these newsletters along to friends that could be trusted, in order to enlarge their circulation. Other documents were passed on too. Shortly after the capitulation, the Dutch government in exile published a "white paper" that outlined its position in the period of neutrality and explained the reasons for moving the seat of government to London and the policies it wanted to pursue to achieve the liberation of our country. This document found its way into Holland and was reprinted and widely distributed. I remember visiting my grandmother and seeing her old friend Mrs. Esser, there, a wonderful woman with a very strong personality. Mrs. Esser vigorously discussed the white paper and to my horror, I noticed she was carrying it in an open shopping bag. She claimed that she would tell any German trying to grab it that she was just an old lady carrying some papers. That was in the first few months of the occupation and attitudes like that were then quite common. It would get much rougher. We prepared our houses for possible search by Germans or Dutch police in their employ. We removed all pictures of the royal family, eliminated books from our shelves that might be considered offensive to Nazi ideologues (this included novels by the German writer Thomas Mann and others,) made sure underground newsletters were always carefully hidden and we hid illegal radios very carefully too, of course.

The supply of food and clothing diminished as the years went by. The Dutch rationing system was frighteningly well organized and based on a so-called *stamkaart,* the basic document that had your name, age and address on it. This was the key document needed to be eligible for all rationing coupons. You went to the town *distributie kantoor* where sheets with coupons for bread, milk or cheese, eggs, meat and tobacco—or for non-smokers candy—were passed out. The problem for people with new (false) identities was that it was not sufficient to have new identity papers. You also needed a *stamkaart* in order to be able to eat. In addition to food rationing, we also had rationing of clothing and shoes and bicycle tires. You got a certain number of "points" per person per year. Accordingly, you might discover that it took all your points to buy a suit with nothing left for underwear or socks or shirts.

For several years, we were allowed to buy one pair of shoes per year. There was a lively black market in coupons for food as well as clothing. Some people who were too poor to buy their ration of clothes or food sold their coupons. Others were in a position where they did not need everything allowed them. Sick people might not need clothes, farmers with a stable full of cows and a number of chickens running around did not need coupons for milk and eggs, etc. Still, I believe that most of the coupons we could buy on the black market were stolen from the offices where they were handed out or from the print shops that produced them. The underground needed many food stamps to take care of people in hiding, Jews, Allied pilots, resistance people and people who simply refused to go to Germany to work. So they had a whole system of helpers who worked at the food stamp distribution centers and would steal sheets of coupons for them.

For people my age, the scarcity of textiles and shoes presented a real problem. I was growing and wearing out many of my clothes. My mother bought second-hand shoes for me at the shoemaker's and towards the end of the war I was tall enough to wear my father's old suits. So I would show up in school in a double-breasted, pin-striped business suit. To get some more mileage out of old suits, we would bring them to a tailor who would "turn them inside out." This meant that the material that had been inside was now outside and far less worn and shiny than the old stuff. The only problem was that the breast pocket of a suit jacket ended up on the right side instead of left and that a double-breasted suit would button left over right instead of the normal right over left. Nobody cared about these things towards the end of the war. Everybody looked shabby and many people wore the most outlandish combinations. In the final winter, my mother would wear her

SELF PORTRAIT MADE AROUND 1942.

skating boots to keep warm and dry. We all had good old Dutch wooden skates that you had to bind on with leather straps. You needed stout boots to skate in, to keep warm and give your ankles support. So these boots were fine for walking in the snow.

Soap and most other toiletries were in short supply too. Soap was rationed and its quality went down hill fast. The soap bars we got felt more and more like pieces of clay. There was not much soap for doing the laundry either, so people were often quite smelly. When I traveled in the tram to The Hague that was always jammed since the frequency of the service was reduced more and more, you got a good whiff of your fellow human beings. When people cannot buy nice clothes and cannot groom themselves properly, they begin to look unattractive. You see that nowadays in pictures of people living in economically disadvantaged countries. The people look gray, disheveled and slovenly. We did too. Men could often not shave properly because razor blades were extremely hard to get and you used old ones that you tried to sharpen with the help of a special sharpening gadget. Looking at a photograph taken of him for his identification papers, my father decided that he was looking wan (he was probably beginning to lose weight) with too many vertical lines in his face so he created a horizontal line by growing a mustache, which he kept until his death. Many kids, including myself had a great deal of trouble with acne and dandruff. Towards the end of the war, I developed a bad case of boils that popped up all over my face and body as a result of an infection I picked up somewhere.

Lack of hygiene also resulted in a plague of fleas, which infested trains and other public places like movie houses. My dog Moortje was covered with fleas

in summer. I would take him outside and bathe him in flea soap and used a fine-tooth comb to catch literally hundreds of fleas. Women had hairy legs because they did not shave them. Because there were no silk stockings and nylons did not yet exist, girls had trouble looking nice at parties. They often wore socks like American "bobby-soxers" in the forties. We used our bicycles all the time and went everywhere on them. In the early years you could still get coupons for bicycle tires. Later they were not available anymore and a bike became a very valuable possession you had to guard all the time because bicycle thefts skyrocketed and on top of that, the Germans started to requisition bikes.

Since dancing in public places was *verboten*, but dancing lessons were not, lessons were very popular for people my age. It was one of the few ways for us to party, have some fun, and meet girls. Before the war I had been going to lessons in The Hague, but now we had them in Voorburg, which was safer for us. We were taught some rudimentary folk dancing steps so that we could launch into folk dancing if the Germans or the Dutch police visited us. For music, we had a pianist and sometimes a record player. In several years of dancing lessons, young cops who were curious when they heard the music and noticed a party atmosphere only investigated us once or twice. We did a lot of dancing and learned all the "proper" steps from Viennese waltz to tango and foxtrot. What we did not learn, because nobody had any idea about its existence, was the jitterbug or lindy, the dancing style that became popular in the U.S. and Britain during the war. When we were liberated, all the Canadian soldiers wanted to jitterbug with the local girls but nobody knew how to do it. The girls learned quickly, however, and we boys stood on the sidelines looking sheepish and out of place. But that was much later.

My first girl friend goes back to those dancing classes in Voorburg. Hanneke van Dorsten was the daughter of a local doctor, a general practitioner who lived nearby. From our living room I could see Hanneke come out of the tram when she returned from the high school in Leiden she attended. I would wave and she would wave back and my day was made! We had a purely platonic relationship, wrote each other letters and went to dancing classes together. Once in a while we would take a walk with our dogs and that was that. What a difference with today's high school kids who claim to be in urgent need of sex and are supplied with free contraceptives to avoid accidents. Some restraint is impossible of course. I don't recall how my relationship with Hanneke ended, but it did. After a few months, it must have been in 1943, I started seeing Yvonne van der Kuyll. Yvonne went to the same school I did and took the same tram. Yvonne and I went "steady" for quite a while. We would take walks or bike rides and we went to the movies where we did some necking. Again, nothing compared with today's much steamier teenagers' lifestyle. Yvonne lived in Leidschendam, a village just over the border of Voorburg. I would visit with her parents and she would come to see my parents and me.

My mother was a bridge fanatic ever since the game had been invented and became popular. Having two extra people around that could be taught the elementary beginnings of bridge, and thus with Pa form a foursome, was heaven for Ma, and we spent many hours working our way through bridge games. Playing bridge with Ma had a very predictable pattern. Ma would often bid too high and get shot down by Pa who had a keen mathematical brain and knew the game as well as she, if not better. Ma would get upset about that and claim Pa was purposely bidding too low to trap her. It was all done in good humor, however, and actually a lot of fun. At some point in time, it must have been in early 1944, I decided I had to tell Yvonne I really did not care all that much for her while I thought she cared very much for me. She was the possessive type who wanted to build a lasting relationship and probably had adolescent fantasies about being married to me. I was not prepared to being tied down into any long-term relationships and I told her that. She got quite emotional but eventually understood that I had been fair and open with her. "We parted as friends," as the old saw goes, after the usual ritual of returning the photographs we had of each other.

Thinking back to the war years with all its tragedies and problems, there was one aspect of life for me as a teenager that was positive. I had much more contact with the parents and older siblings of my friends than I would have had in more normal times. I remember having had many good conversations with my parents and their friends and with our relatives and the parents of my friends. I think these contacts were very valuable for me as a learning experience. Dutch houses are generally smaller than present-day American ones so one is more apt to gather in a living room rather than roam all over the house. There simply are not that many other rooms and young people coming to visit their friends are used to meeting with them in the living room of their parents with everybody else present. This is still the case in Holland, and in my view an arrangement that is of value to both the younger and the older generation. Another powerful force bringing people together in one room was the cold in winter. We had some pretty cold winters during the war and people who had central heating could not use it since coal was rationed and oil was not available. Usually families had one stove going in the living room and that was often the only warm place in the house. Almost all houses, including newer ones that had been built with central heating, had a fireplace with a chimney that could be used for an old-fashioned potbellied stove or similar contraption.. Like most of our friends we had a small potbellied stove or *potkachel* in our living room, and we arranged our furniture around it to get maximum benefit of its warmth. Many people were forced to take in boarders or did so to help out a friend who had lost his or her home for one reason or another. So you often would find not just the family around the stove, but one or two guests too.

The blackout made it difficult to roam very far at night and rationing of electricity also helped pulling people together around one or two lamps. People would read a great deal, mostly old prewar books because not much of any value was published during the war. An exception was the writer Jan de Hartog who after the war wrote in English as well as in Dutch with considerable success. During the war he wrote a book called *Hollands Glorie* that became a huge best seller. It was a novel telling the story of the Dutch high sea tugs that roamed and still roam all over the world, salvaging wrecks, and moving oil rigs and dry docks. The title referred to the glory of Holland on the high seas and the book stirred nationalistic feelings among us in a period in which we had little to celebrate or be proud of. The Germans did not forbid the book, which had no anti–German or pro–Allied language in it anyway.

There was little entertainment. We had a radio broadcasting system that nobody listened to (except for classical concerts, etc.). The movies were German and most people did not want to see them. Occasionally we could see a French or Italian movie and several of them were excellent. Notably *"Les Enfants du Paradis",* now regarded as one of the all-time French classics. Occasionally we saw some pretty good Dutch plays. Actually, the Dutch theater enjoyed an attendance boom during the war. So beyond these few entertainment opportunities there was little else to do than stay home and read or enjoy conversation. Among my parent's friends in Voorburg, there were successful efforts to organize book clubs, foreign language conversation groups and private lectures with good speakers. Then there were always the bridge games my mother loved so dearly.

Our vacations were usually spent with relatives. We went often to Leersum where Tante Jetje and Oom Bernard had their charming country house, called *de Meezenhof.* In the early years of the war, we went there several times on our bikes. We would strap our small suitcases on our luggage racks and pedal away in the early morning, reaching our destination in the late afternoon. About a five-hour bike ride. In Leersum we would enjoy helping Oom Bernard with his efforts to grow vegetables in his garden and go into the woods to gather edible mushrooms. My aunt and uncle were also canning their vegetables on a large scale for winter use. We enjoyed the good meals there, as there was an abundance of meat and eggs available on the black market in that rural area. Most farmers preferred to sell as many of their products as they could on the black market rather than in the highly regulated official market that benefited the Germans.

Long before the war, the parents of my friend Frits Regtdoorzee Greup had built a summer house on a property they owned in the village of Vierhouten. This house, which belonged to Frits after his parent's death, was located in the center of the Veluwe, a very attractive area in the province of Gelderland, which was completely rural in the old days. It has many forests, large tracts of heather, lots of small farms and attractive small villages. It still is one of the preferred regions for summer vacations in Holland. The Greup family would spend a good part of the summer there and invite their friends and the friends of their children there throughout the summer holidays. I was fortunate to be among those invited there and I have wonderful memories of my stays in Vierhouten. Frits' parents invited people for weeklong visits and organized bicycle trips in the surroundings, visits to swimming pools and memorable bicycle rides in the evenings to watch the wildlife in the woods. Much of the wildlife, deer and wild boar were concentrated in the nearby hunting preserves of the royal family that continued to be preserved during the war, mainly to serve as hunting grounds for people like Hermann Goering, the fat German commander of the Luftwaffe. Here in Greenwich we now have a problem with too many deer that infest our gardens. In Holland wildlife is rare and observing it is a pastime cherished by virtually everybody.

Another vacation destination for me was Friesland. Compared to our fare at home, the food there was superb. I enjoyed staying with Tante Mieke and Oom Anne in Leeuwarden. It was on one of those trips to Leeuwarden that I saw a train-load of Dutch Jews on their way to the Dutch concentration camp Westerbork. Like all trains during the war, it was an old-fashioned one with compartments that each had their own doors and was pulled by a steam engine. There were only one or two Dutch policemen guarding it. The Dutch police generally cooperated with the Germans, claiming they had no choice but to obey the orders of the occupier. Dutch

WELL DRESSED DUTCH JEWS HAVE GATHERED VOLUNTARILY
TO AWAIT TRANSPORTATION.

315

railway employees had a similar rationale for keeping the trains with Jews rolling, including the ones that went from Westerbork to Auschwitz and other death camps. The train that I saw with the Jews was on the other side of the platform in Zwolle, the town where I had to wait to change trains. I wandered over and spoke with a man who gave me some money and asked me to fetch a cup of *ersatz* coffee for him, which I did. I asked him why he did not just sneak off. There was hardly any super-vision and he could easily have blended in with the other travelers on the platform. He said he could not do that. He seemed to be in reasonably good spirits, and like his companions smiled a lot as if to put up a brave face. In hindsight, it all seemed so bizarre because it was so orderly and calm, and it was difficult to fathom that this whole train was full of people heading to their death. The system in Holland was to first isolate the Jews in a Jewish quarter in Amsterdam, then concentrate them in the Westerbork camp from where the cattle trains to Auschwitz and other death camps left later. We did not know this, of course, and neither did the victims. That was the devilishly clever part of the arrangement. Most knew they would be transported to the "east," but thought they would be put to work there and would have to live under rough but survivable conditions. They became suspicious, however, when they real-ized they never heard any news and received no letters from any of the people who were put on the trains. The idea that every day trainloads with hundreds of people would be systematically put to death was so farfetched and outlandish that it simply never occurred to us.

Despite their mostly German content, the movies were a major attraction to me and not only because I could sit in the back with Yvonne or some other girl. The newsreels preceding each show were usually heavy with German propaganda, but for me as a youngster interested in the war's development and particularly in aviation, there was always something to see between the lines. Certainly, the pictures of the eastern front with the ice and snow and horrendously low temperatures gave a very good impression of the problems the Germans were facing there and in my opinion did not show anything resembling German victories. Rather they showed the begin-nings of defeat. A few times when I was bored with school I played hooky by going to the movies. Those excursions were not as much fun as I anticipated because I was constantly afraid of being seen by somebody who knew me or worse, being picked up by the Germans who would occasionally sweep the theaters to catch guys that were avoiding orders to go to Germany for war production work.

German wartime movies almost never dealt with war or military-action-related themes. There were many musical type shows with dancing and singing and many sentimental movies of folks wandering about the Alps in peaceful sunny scenes. There obviously was an effort directed by Goebbels's propaganda ministry to show life in Germany at home as normal as possible and make the German soldiers out in the field feel good about their country. Actually, in the first three years of the war, life in Germany itself, the German home front, was generally quite normal. Most women were not required to work in war production, food and clothing were plentiful, mainly as a result of the systematic plundering of the occupied countries and the RAF night bombing raids were not yet very effective. Much of the hard work was done by prisoners of war (unlike the Dutch, the French POWs were not permitted to go back home after the defeat of France in 1940) and by civilians recruited in the occupied countries by force or by coercion. Only in 1943/44 when the daytime bombing by the Americans and the nighttime attacks by the RAF began to hit home, did the quality of life in Germany really go downhill fast.

The Dutch beaches were closed. The Germans did not want Dutchmen to try escaping to England in small boats and also started to fortify the entire Dutch coastline when the threat of an Allied invasion became real. So for us as teenagers the beach was no longer a recreation opportunity. Sailing on the many lakes was popular and became more so as we were limited in our recreational opportunities. When I received a small inheritance as the sole heir of Oom George, the older brother of my grandmother Stibbe, I asked my father if I could spend some of it on a sailboat. That idea was approved. Oom George died in November 1941. As I mentioned earlier, he lost Tante Lous in January of that year and through her death also lost the protection their racially mixed marriage gave him. The prospect of increasing harassment by the Germans and a delicate health contributed to his death. He was a very unassuming man who lived on his pension as a retired officer of the Dutch colonial system in Indonesia.

This purchase of my first sailboat started a long line of boat ownership for me with its attendant joys and frustrations. Unfortunately I did not have enough money to buy the boat I wanted, a *Vergrote BM*, which was a popular sailboat in those days. I found an ad in a sailing magazine for a boat that was a copy of an American design, probably taken out of an old US sailing magazine and enlarged to get working drawings. Pa and I went to Spaarndam, a village north of Haarlem where the owners, a local butcher, and his friend, a baker, demonstrated the boat for us. It was a hard-chine mahogany sloop with nice lines, a bit chubby for Dutch standards, but we thought that added stability. We bought the boat and asked them to alter the mast so it could be lowered, a normal practice with Dutch boats that have to pass through a lot of canals with bridges that do not always open or are just fixed. The mast would be cut at deck level and at both sides of the cut stout vertical boards were placed supporting the mast. A pin was run through the mast and both boards so the mast could swivel down. The forestay would be equipped with a block and tackle arrangement, and when the mast had to be lowered, the forestay would be detached and using a pole positioned perpendicular to the mast to get leverage, the mast could be lowered easily.

I called the boat *Skua*, after an aggressive sea bird living in polar regions. I had picked that name because it was also the name of the Blackburn Skua, a British dive bomber I had seen pictures of. This way I could express my admiration for the RAF and when questioned say that I picked the name of a bird. Eelco Apol and I traveled to Spaarndam to pick *Skua* up. We spent the night as guests of the butcher's family, bought some smoked eel for our families and left the next day. We paddled through Haarlem with the mast lowered and set sail in the river Spaarne that leads by way of a canal to the Kaag Lake where we wanted to go. We had traveled that route the previous year when we made our trip to Friesland and back. When we were almost at the Kaag, we passed a windmill, and in almost a repeat of our problem in Friesland with Eelco's boat, we caught a heavy puff, heeled over and scooped up so much water that our boat could not right itself. The miller's family spotted us immediately. Their daughter, a very husky girl, quickly grabbed a rowboat and rowed over to us. She picked us up and later also towed our capsized boat to the shore. The family received us very kindly. They warmed us up and after a while we went outside to right the sailboat. It was then that we noticed a group of people who apparently lived with the family in an adjoining small storage shed. They were smallish people with dark hair who were not at all as husky blond and big boned as Dutch rural people usually are, and I immediately understood that they were Jews hiding there. The Jews made the mistake of showing up and eating our smoked eel they found in the boat. They should not have done that because they did not know we were not Nazis or pro–German. Unfortunately, many people hiding from the Germans with host families endangered their hosts in this manner by allowing themselves to be seen by others. In several cases this ended up in terrible tragedies for both the people hiding and for their hosts as they were all carted off to a concentration camp where most of them perished. We did not say anything and went home by tram, a little bedraggled.

The next day I returned with Pa to sail the boat to its berth. We used the jib only because it was still blowing quite hard. *Skua* was clearly not very stable. After this adventure my parents decided we had to go sailing with "Uncle" Steven van

Ramshorst, the husband of one of my mother's closest friends who was supposed to know how to sail because he was a retired officer of the Dutch navy. He was to teach us how to really sail. We soon discovered that his level of expertise was limited. We went out with him on a typical Dutch cold summer day with gray skies and a very stiff breeze. Uncle Steven sailed out on the lake and everything went fine although my mother was perched on the windward rail, constantly warning us of *vlagen* (puffs). Steven made the same mistake Eelco had made at the windmill, he tied the mainsheet down when we were sailing close to the wind and when we caught a strong puff, he could not ease the mainsheet quickly enough, and the boat capsized again. Uncle Steven, Pa and I managed to get on the windward side of the boat and stay dry. Ma plunged into the water and had to be hauled out by us. People in other boats rushed to our assistance, and when they got close by, Uncle Steven true to his naval traditions bellowed "women and children first". We were rowed over to a small soggy island where we tried to dry out. I still see in my mind's eye Pa standing in the wind holding Ma's bloomers up to dry. They resembled two pink windsocks at an airport. We got the boat alongside another yacht and the skipper of that boat helped us right my boat with the help of his main halyard. We struggled back to our marina with jib only, now thoroughly disappointed in my boat and its stability. After a few days, Pa called his friend Henry de Voogd, a famous yacht designer who had designed the queen's yacht. We hauled my boat out and Mr. de Voogd came over. He suggested a bulb be attached to the existing keel, which was just a sheet of metal with no ballast. Since metal was scare, the boatyard made a cigar shape out of concrete, reinforced by some metal rods. This solution slowed the boat down somewhat, but it solved the problem.

That summer and the following one we had a lot of fun sailing on the lake. Pa went often with me or with a friend. He had now plenty of spare time because his company had put him on leave of absence. It was quite an expedition to go sailing. You had to take the tram to the station and from there the train to Warmond, a village just beyond Leiden where the boatyard was. At the end of the day you had to reverse the procedure. When the Germans started to requisition sailboats for the entertainment of their troops and it also became dangerous for me to be seen enjoying myself on the water while I was supposed to assist the German war effort, we decided to sell *Skua*. That was a very easy and quick transaction. We sold her to a black marketeer who paid with a fistful of cash. People active in the black market always ran a cash-only business and needed assets to invest their profits in. So they were eager to buy things like boats that had some value and were not easily detected.

The sale of *Skua* ended my yacht ownership, and I would not own another boat until we moved to America and I bought a 15 ft. Mercury sailboat in Old Greenwich.

Our maid Jo Buunk had gone back home in early 1942. Life on the family farm was better than with us and food was much more plentiful there. She would send us some care packages from time to time, however. Jo's departure confronted Ma with a crisis. She had always been very good at telling our maids how she wanted them to prepare our meals but doing the cooking herself was another story. We went through a couple of very rough weeks as Ma went up the gastronomic learning curve. Having to eat burned potatoes or overdone meat is never pleasant, but in a situation of food scarcity it is extra difficult because you cannot let the food go to waste and you have to make the best of it and eat it. We tried a few daytime helpers, but they proved to be disasters. So Ma fell back on Anna Driessen, a woman who had been our cleaning lady (backing up our live-in maid) in years past. Anna and her family became fixtures in our life during the war and in the years immediately afterwards. Anna's husband developed mental problems and was institutionalized for years. Anna herself was a hard-working skinny woman who was quite deaf but did her best for her family. Anna's brood of three children did not amount to much, unfortunately. Hers was a somewhat dysfunctional family that was doomed to remain at the bottom of society because of the father's problems.

Anna was a devout Catholic and went regularly to church as was customary among Dutch working-class people in those days. Through her we would hear what the priest had said during the service. The Dutch Catholic Church, and particularly its Archdiocese, proved to be strong centers of resistance to the inroads the Nazis were trying to make into Dutch society and the waves of propaganda they were unleashing over us. Priests would speak up against the Nazi oppressors from the pulpit and the church leadership would from time to time issue a pastoral letter to be read to all Dutch Catholic congregations in which measures taken by the Germans were condemned. The Protestant churches, though by nature less centrally controlled and more diverse, were also strongly in the opposition. The Synod of Protestant Churches, representing some half-dozen different denominations, also issued letters to its respective congregations that encouraged people to resist the Nazi influence. Many priests and clergymen were arrested and put in concentration camps, and many died there. Oom Otto, who spent time in the Vught concentration camp, told us that he witnessed a particularly revolting episode when SS camp guards forced a group of Roman Catholic priests to march around naked in a mock procession. They were forced to carry imitation crosses and statues etc. in an attempt to ridicule their religion. The effect was the opposite, of course; the inmates gained more respect for the priests involved.

My father was less and less inclined to go to his office as the war progressed, and his staff disappeared while the actual business of the company was conducted elsewhere in the free world. The Royal Dutch Shell Company was domiciled in The Hague and like many other larger Dutch companies it was saddled with a German *Verwalter,* a caretaker who was supposed to keep an eye on the company on behalf of the Nazi government. What the occupier had in mind with this move was clearly to have control over this large multinational company in the event they won the war. At one point Pa was fired. I do not know for what reason. In fact I do not recall him being fired. But I have found a letter among his papers stating he was rehired. So he must have been fired before.

When the Germans started worrying about an Allied invasion, they evacuated large parts of The Hague, mainly neighborhoods near the shore. Several companies were moved inland, including Royal Dutch. The entire office moved to Zeist where they took space in a large country estate. Pa commuted to Zeist for a while, taking his bike to the station and taking another bike from the Zeist station to his office. They were not doing much there so eventually Pa stayed home and began all sorts of projects to keep his mind busy. He bought a German book about precious stones, one of those German tomes called *Handbuch,* a handbook about six inches thick and hard to lift. It was called *Edelsteinkunde* and every day Pa diligently studied the geology and origin of precious stone for a couple of hours. He also "modernized" and repaired furniture. We had a writing desk in our living room that was used for all letter writing, bill paying and (for me) homework. It was a Victorian piece, showing many unnecessary embellishments in the woodwork. Pa decided to plane the legs of the bureau down and to remove the ornaments from the door of the filing cabinet by turning the ornaments inside out. Our son Richard now has this desk and you can see how Pa successfully streamlined its design. I always admired Pa for doing things like that so skillfully and for having the get up and go to do some studying during the war. As food became more and more scarce, Pa started helping out by foraging in the countryside, visiting farmers and trying to buy food. He could do that because he was too old to be picked up for work in Germany and besides, getting skinnier, he looked old. I could not go out too much beyond going to school because there was always a risk of being picked up. Although I had "student" status, we knew it was quite possible that some German would get it into his head that I should be helping the war effort and once they had grabbed you it was always very tough to get out again.

So I carried on, played tennis with three year old balls, went to dancing classes in Voorburg and walked home in the dark blacked-out streets, and went to school every weekday. I sometimes went to school by bike and would roam around a little in the city of The Hague after school hours. I would watch the German Waffen SS troops exercise in the barracks close to our school and marveled at the rough way the soldiers were treated by their officers. Once I saw a company-size, machine-gun unit train, and I will never forget how loud the officer in charge screamed at his men. When things did not go to his liking he started yelling, hurling insults at the poor bastards as if the world was coming to an end. It was a picture of the German *Kadaver Diziplin,* the discipline and obedience of dead bodies that was part of the German army tradition.

On another day I was walking to the tram to go home when I saw a commotion near the bridge over a canal, the *Java Brug,* where the tram stop was. Two young men were standing against the railing of the bridge with their arms in the air, one with a Star of David, the other without. A German in the uniform of one of the security services was hitting and punching them and the hat of one of them flew off and floated in the water. It appeared the man who was a non–Jew had tried to defend the Jew when the German had taken some action against the Jew, and after that the German had arrested both. He stood there screaming at his two prisoners, marching around them with his pistol drawn. His problem was that he had no help from anybody and he must have felt uneasy with a large crowd of Dutchmen just standing around and watching. A Dutch policeman came by and tried to disperse the crowd, saying, "don't look at the misery of others," but he had little success. I was amazed by the way this German behaved, carrying on like a madman all alone in a crowded street, probably feeling he was doing the right thing for the Fatherland. What happened afterwards I do not know, I guess my tram came by and I had to get on, but this episode was just one of many similar events I witnessed on the streets.

I have always wondered about the motivation of the Germans. They must have known the people in the countries they occupied hated them. They must have known they were serving a regime run by crooks who forced them to adhere to a totally flawed political doctrine. They must have known their *Fürher* Adolf Hitler was a maniac with a funny mustache and a strange lock of hair hanging over his forehead. By the beginning of 1943 they must have understood they were losing the war. Still they persisted in doing their duty as soldiers and as agents of the Nazi regime, fighting hard and well and never giving up. As they were losing the war, their hate for the Jews grew and they did not seem to be aware that they were spoon-fed this hate by the Nazi propaganda machine.

The Allied Air Forces gained strength and were preparing for the invasion of the European continent; bombing raids on Germany grew more and more common. For us there also was the risk of getting caught in a bombing raid aimed at the Germans in Holland or being strafed by fighter planes while traveling in a passenger train. We frequently heard flights of British RAF night bombers on their way to targets in Germany. You could clearly hear the undulating sound of their engines and you could see the German searchlights crisscrossing the sky in search of their targets. Sometimes two searchlights would catch a bomber in their crossed beams and antiaircraft fire was directed at the target. The Germans called anti-aircraft guns Flak, or *Flieger Abwehr Kanone.* The term stuck and today Americans use it referring to strong opposition or, as Webster says, "clamorous criticism." I never saw the Germans hit a bomber, but they were often successful in Germany, when the bombers had to fly in a straight line to make their bombing run. Also, considerably more bombers were shot down and their wrecks were found in the fields near Leeuwarden, where my cousin Bas Deibel lived. Bas would go to the wrecks and collect memorabilia. There was a big air base in Leeuwarden and when I was visiting there during the battle of Britain days we were kept awake during the night by the German bombers returning from raids on England. One clear night I was bicycling home through the open area that then existed between Voorburg and The Hague. I was with my other cousin Bas Deibel, *Grote Bas,* (big Bas) and we heard the RAF coming over. "Heavenly music," Bas said. The day raids by the American air force became quite common in the summer of 1943. Before that time the RAF night bombing had been the only real threat for the German population. The American planes came over in enormous dense formations of either B-17 Flying Fortresses or B-24 Liberators. These formations were an incredibly impressive sight and must have been a frightening reminder of America's power for the German population. We cheered them on and saw them as visible evidence of our approaching liberation. For us oppressed souls in occupied Holland there was little compassion for our German tormentors. I believe the people in Rotterdam, London and Coventry in particular also did not feel very sorry for the German civilians that were being hit. We all felt it was their turn. It is easy to practice Monday morning quarterbacking, but as they say, "life is not fair and war is hell." After the Allies had successfully landed in France and established airfields there, activity by low-flying fighters against trucks and trains intensified. Steam locomotives were particularly welcome targets.

Most trains were the old-fashioned kind with steam engines. The more modern Dutch streamlined electric trains were not often used, probably because of lack of electric power. Our trains were always packed with people, except for the compartments reserved for the German Wehrmacht. There would be signs on the windows saying *Nur für Wehrmacht,* (wehrmacht only) and there would be a few German military personnel lounging in them while the rest of the train was totally packed with Dutch people. The steam engines had small concrete bunkers on the back of their tenders. These were used as cover for the fireman and engineer who would stop the train and dive into their little bunker when a fighter was seen making a strafing run. As the train stopped the passengers would run out into the fields, trying to take cover. Luckily I never was in a train that was attacked, but I did not let this risk prevent me from going on vacation by train to see my relatives. We just lived with the day-to-day risks wartime presented us with.

In 1944 when the Allied forces penetrated into Holland after a successful landing in Normandy, life in our area got a great deal grimmer. The last winter of the war was the worst period of my life and the life of almost all other Dutchmen residing in the western part of the country.

13 : The Final Two Years of The War

In 1943 the tide finally began to turn. Unquestionably, the most significant historical turning point that year was the fall of Stalingrad on February 3rd. This debacle, in which an entire German Army Group (the sixth) was destroyed, followed the first massive counterattack launched by the Red Army on January 1, 1943. While the Russians tightened the noose around Stalingrad in February, the Germans did the same in occupied Holland. Gradually all pretense of wanting to include us as fellow Arians in the Great German Reich disappeared and the realization by the Germans that the war was not going well made them angrier and more vengeful towards us. February was a month with many important developments in the Netherlands. The Resistance executed the self-appointed "commander" of the Dutch volunteer legion that was recruited to fight against the Soviets. He was shot while answering the front door at his home. In addition, another high-level bureaucrat was shot. At first a decision was made to execute fifty hostages in retaliation for these assassinations. At the time we did not know that, but after the war, we learned from German documents that these executions were intensely debated among the authorities. After much discussion, it was decided that such a mass execution would backfire badly on the Dutch Nazi party, the NSB, because the Dutch population would see the NSB as responsible. The NSB was still trying to project itself as a party representing the Dutch people. Shooting of hostages by the German occupier in retaliation for murders of NSB members would damage its public image it was thought.

The Dutch churches collectively sent Seyss-Inquart a letter of protest against persecution of fellow citizens, the lawlessness of society and the drive for Nazification of the country. This letter was read in every Dutch church. As so many brave attempts to protest the German policies, it was ignored. The Germans started a roundup of students at the universities of Amsterdam, Utrecht, Delft, and Wageningen. The universities were closed and many students went into hiding. The reason for these actions seemed to be, on the one hand, a belief that many people had signed up as students just to get a deferment from having to work in Germany. On the other hand, universities were seen as gathering places of elitist anti–German agitation. The odd idea was that people's minds could be changed by arresting them and or dispersing them. At the same time there was also an action planned to arrest so-called Plutocratensöhne – the sons of plutocrats, i.e. schoolboys who were seen as enjoying the soft and easy life, loafing around at school while German soldiers of the same age fought at the front. According to documents found after the war, this action was also discussed by leading German SS functionaries and Dutch NSB people and even cleared with Himmler in Berlin.

So on February 9, a roundup–using an Italian term we called them razzia's–of schoolboys was organized. Targets were those who were seen as rich kids who were anti German. I was among the people who fit this description. You wonder how they arrived at picking my name and why. As was revealed after the war, mayors who were known to be Nazis were asked to provide lists of wealthy people with sons. We had a Nazi mayor in Voorburg, but I do not think he was aware of my existence. So somebody must have put me on the list. The lists were combed over by local Nazis and given to the German police for action. The plan was to arrest 5,000 boys, bring them to the Vught concentration camp and from there to the Sachsenhausen camp in Germany and then on to work. Like so many other sweeps that would take place in later years, this one required the help of the local police. There were just too many people to be arrested to use only the reliable Grüne Polizei, the uniformed police force of the Gestapo, the German secret police. Luckily there were still more than enough men in the Dutch police force who were willing and able to spill the beans, so almost everybody knew a day ahead of time what was to be expected. The sweeps turned into a fiasco as only about 1,200 boys were arrested. Realizing they were not succeeding, the German police began to randomly arrest young men on the streets and combing through government offices, schools etc. wherever they thought they would find young men. Because of these actions, a high level of anxiety gripped the Dutch population. They saw the Germans randomly arresting innocent civilians just because of their age and feared a wave of arbitrary arrests.

In anticipation of the sweep I had left home and was a guest of my friend Erik van't Groenewoud. At that time we had no clue that his father was really not on the right side. Erik was a year younger than I and therefore presumed not to be

among the "chosen" boys. He had a younger sister, Tineke, who was good protection because she could come to the door, if needed, and pretend to understand
nothing. Tineke was quite young but smart enough to do this. I do not know what
became of her, but I hope she had a nice life. She was a nice young girl and fun to
be with. One of Erik's cousins came too and shared the guestroom with me. Proof
that the rumors were correct came early the next morning. We heard by phone from
my parents who told us in veiled terms that "people had come to call to see me."
Looking out the window we could see a large truck of the Grüne Polizei enter the
driveway of a house across the street. In that house lived the Kouwenhoven family,
strict orthodox Protestants. They followed the rules their church prescribed and as
a consequence had a large number of children among which were several boys of
the age desired by the Germans. I noticed that the German cops were all walking
towards the house and not looking back, so I decided to jump on my bike and race
away. Much to the distress of Erik's mother who wanted me to stay put, which was
obviously a much safer tactic. I was afraid they would come across the street and find
us, so I took the risk. I rode over into the countryside to a small rural train station
about an hour away and bought a ticket there for Maarn, the station closest to my
Aunt Jetje and Uncle Bernard. In those days you could buy a ticket for yourself and
for your bike and you could move your bike yourself from one train to another if
you had to change. Once I got to Maarn I rode my bike to their country house, the
"Meezenhof." They were surprised to see me and asked me why I had come. Rather
melodramatically, I answered *uit lijfsbehoud*, to save my skin. I stayed for a week or
two, I think, and when I heard that the threat was over, I returned home. It was
an eerie feeling to think that the Dutch Nazis had my name and came to arrest me.
My father told me that two of them came to the house looking for me. They went
upstairs to the room where I slept and found nobody there, of course, and my bed
cold and unused. My mother's linen closet was in that room and one of the fellows
opened it and started looking between the stacks of sheets, etc. My father told him,
"I am sure he is not there, young man."

   Back in school I was proud to be among the relatively few selected for arrest
by the Germans, but this kind of absence and distraction was not conducive to my
studies, of course. I had already become a rather indifferent student goofing off a lot
and much more interested in what went on around me than in studying chemistry
and math for which I had no talent anyway. Our teachers had no sympathy at all
for our absences and I remember our Rector, or Headmaster commenting that we
had "no guts" hiding and staying away so long. That was easy for him to say; he was

not in jeopardy. His comment illustrates the strange attitude of our teachers, who went on sticking to their prewar, very Dutch and very thorough and concentrated curriculum. Only one of my friends got caught in these February sweeps. That was Eelco Apol. He had also left his house the night before but had gone on some kind of errand, I believe, and ran into a group of Germans picking up people on the street. Eelco went to the concentration camp Vught, where he was locked up together with a large group of students. He was not treated very badly and as the whole project became a huge failure, they were all let go after a few weeks.

When I came back to school I learned that the Germans had killed a classmate of mine, Jaap Vrede. He tried to escape, running down a narrow alley during one of the sweeps. In that year we also lost three other schoolmates. They had tried to get to Spain to join the Allied forces. They planned to follow an existing route through Belgium and France and across the Pyrenees into Spain. This route was frequently used to help downed Allied airmen get back. About 2000 airmen were assisted by the Dutch Resistance in this manner and there was a well-organized international group that operated this so called "line." Usually the trip was made mainly by rail. To cross the Pyrenees, the help of local shepherds and other mountain folk was needed. Many of these were patriots risking their own lives time and again to get people across into freedom. Unfortunately there were also a few bad apples among them who betrayed their charges to the Gestapo. I heard our school friends were arrested while traveling in a train through France. This was always a risk. The German police would often search trains and our friends fell victim to such a sweep. One of them, a classmate of mine, Dennis Luyt, managed to convince his captors that he only wanted to get to his parents in the Dutch East Indies. They bought his story and let him go and he came back to The Hague. The other three were executed in France. I suspect their contacts en route were not strong or sophisticated enough and they must have stood out in the crowd, dressed differently and probably taller than most Frenchmen. Once in Spain, fugitives who made it that far were not completely out of the woods. The fascist Spanish government was pro–German and passed fugitives only reluctantly on to the Allies. Moreover, the Dutch diplomats in Spain seemed to be less cooperative than could be expected when people knocked on their door, at least according to postwar reports. In one famous exchange a fellow who finally made it to Madrid and joyfully reported to the Dutch Embassy there, was asked, "Sir why are you here?" and "What are you trying to achieve by escaping?" I believe the idiots who were in charge at that embassy at the beginning of the war were quickly replaced.

In 1943 the activities of the Dutch Resistance increased significantly and hardened noticeably. People became more skilled in underground work. We used the term "illegal" or *"illegaal"* in Dutch to indicate resistance work. There also was more paramilitary activity as more weapons became available. We only learned details of much of this work after the war or in a fragmented fashion via the underground press. Still, the Germans rolled up most underground organizations and the number of people executed for Resistance work grew rapidly. A very effective traitor, Anton van der Waals, managed to infiltrate several Resistance groups and was instrumental in their elimination. Shootings of Dutch Nazis increased too and this lead to a most welcome uneasiness among them. The Dutch Nazi party, the NSB, formed its own armed guard service called the *Landwacht*. These were mainly people armed with shotguns who were supposed to keep order among the civilian population. Tightening the screws further, the German military commander General Christiansen ordered all former Dutch POWs to return to POW camps. This order was mostly ignored and resulted in a spontaneous strike that became a countrywide event and was repressed with extreme force by the Germans. More than 200 strikers were executed. The railroads kept running and the strike soon fizzled out.

At the same time the final phase of the deportation of the Dutch Jews was ordered and in May 1943, there were large-scale roundups of Jews in Amsterdam.

Also in May, all men between the ages of 18 and 35 were ordered to report for work in Germany. This latest order made me more than ever reluctant to finish school because you could still get an exemption if you were a student. The earlier idea of picking up the sons of plutocrats was apparently forgotten.

Furthermore, also in May, the Dutch we were ordered to turn in all radios. Most people obeyed and brought their radios to the police. Radio sets in those days were often quite large pieces of furniture cherished by their owners. They were encased in gleaming wooden cabinets that used to be placed in a prominent spot in the family living room so everybody could gather around it and enjoy the broadcast. For ordinary people a beautiful radio was a prized possession and having to cart it away was another blow and an infringement on one's personal freedom. Many people had expected this move by the Germans and had bought extra radios or simply not registered their sets. Still, it was more and more difficult to get good and reliable news about the war, but it was not impossible.

In early summer I sat for the final high school exam and found it very tough going. I did not pass it, and although I was better off staying in school, I still felt bad about flunking. It was remarkable how tough the exam was. The exam is always the same for the entire country. Even my teachers thought some parts of it were absurdly difficult given the circumstances we were living under. I remember Mr. Miserus, the French teacher, being stunned by the French translation piece that dealt with a detailed description of a farmhouse, complete with all the words for farm implements we did not know and would never have to use. The bureaucracy of the Department of Education seemed to feel it was necessary to justify its existence by submitting students to tough exams. At our school we saw it as another example of an out-of-touch civil service that was more inclined to do its best to keep everything going at prewar or better levels and to do the bidding of the Germans. In truth, I failed my final exam as a result of my general lack of interest in my studies and had to repeat the class the next year. This was no great loss for me since I would have had a real problem if I had passed and would have been available for work in Germany. There still were ways around this, you could enlist in a school for further studies, but it was never a certainty that you would be accepted in the next school. Going to a university was no longer possible at that time since all universities were closed because 85% of all students had refused to sign a declaration pledging loyalty to the Germans.

That summer I was also called up for service in the *Arbeids Dienst*, a paramilitary organization in which young Dutch men had to serve for six months. These men were kept in old Dutch army barracks and given old Dutch army uniforms. They had to work with spades and drill with these spades as if they were rifles. This service was a carbon copy of a German institution of the same name that trained their young men in military drill before they entered the Wehrmacht. In the 1930s, the Germans were building up their armed forces but were reluctant to do this too openly since the Treaty of Versailles forbade them from having a large army. So they organized the Arbeits Dienst to train men without making them exactly soldiers. Why the Dutch wanted to do the same is not quite clear, it was probably an effort to keep young men under control and submit them to discipline so they could be easily called up. I had to report for a medical test and when I was questioned about my family background reported that I had a Jewish grandmother. This statement immediately sidetracked the whole procedure for me and without any further checks on the truthfulness of my statement, I was told I could leave. The man who dealt with me was very nice and probably was glad he had a good case for another rejection. So this was at least one situation where Oma's background helped me.

As the number of people hiding from the occupier increased rapidly, the Resistance had to raid distribution offices wherever they could to steal rationing cards. Several of these raids were successful and there were also a number of successful attacks on offices where the civilian population was registered and where identity cards were being issued. In 1943 the Allies cleared all Axis forces out of North Africa, taking a large number of prisoners (about as many men as the Wehrmacht lost in Stalingrad) and subsequently landed in Sicily. Also the bombing of Germany was stepped up. In August the first massive nighttime raid on Berlin was made. That summer we also began to see the USAF in action. On clear days you could see huge swarms of American bombers fly over on their way to Germany. Oom Frans de Clercq, who always had special and quite original ideas, invited me to join him and his sons Lucas and Thys for a rowing trip from Haarlem to Nieuwkoop, a small village nestled along the Nieuwkoopse plassen, a group of lakes. At the Spaarne rowing club in Haarlem we got a "wherry," a rather heavy and beamy lapstrake built rowing boat with sliding seats for two rowers and a steering seat for two in the stern from where the rudder could be controlled with two lines running aft. Nieuwkoop was not all that far away, but it was hard to reach because it was part of another polder system with a different water level than the one in Haarlem. So we had to find a spot where a small canal stopped at a dike that formed the partition between the two systems and where we could carry or rather drag the wherry across. All this succeeded and we got to Nieuwkoop in good time. Oom Frans had found a house where we could stay for a few nights and eat the good black-market food folks in those rural areas enjoyed. He left me in charge of Lucas and Thys and returned a few days later with his youngest son Jan. I remember that day clearly because it was the day we saw the first big flight of American bombers come over. I believe they were B-24 Liberators, and they flew in a tight formation because they did not yet have fighter escorts. U.S. fighters in those days did not have sufficient range to escort bombers over Germany and back. The bombers had to fly close together so the gunners could cover each other's blind angles. The bombers dropped bushels of strips of tinfoil to confuse the German radar and Jan was rushing around in the fields trying to catch as many of these strips as he could. It was an overwhelming and incredibly encouraging sight for us to see so much air power displayed while standing in a field in the Dutch countryside.

In the fall of 1943, further killings of Dutch Nazis by the Resistance led to counteraction from the Nazis. They started a regime of terror murders in which Dutchmen who were known to be anti–German became victims. These actions were called the Silbertanne (silver fir) murders. One of the first victims was the well-known Dutch author A. M. de Jong. My mother had many of his books and I enjoyed reading them when I was a teenager. They were mostly stories of rural life in the beginning of the century when people were devout and poor and lived simple lives. Today his books would probably be judged as too simplistic and sweet, but they were popular in the mid 1900s, certainly during the war when we all longed for normal times and liked to lose ourselves in books that told us about the simple life in the good old days and took us away from the horrors around us.

In late September the final large roundup of Jews in Amsterdam took place. More than 10,000 were caught and deported to the Westerbork camp. This final group included the members of the Jewish Council, a group of prominent Jews who had been appointed by the Germans to keep order among their fellow victims and organize their deportation. This council was organized within the scope of a diabolical system whereby Jews were forced to obey rules promulgated by their own people and submit to orders from their own people when they were selected for transportation. After the war the few surviving members of the Jewish Council were subjected to criticism for their actions. They were mostly well-meaning people with distinguished backgrounds – lawyers, doctors and prominent business people. They were Dutchmen and therefore inclined to follow orders with great precision. From time to time, they objected to certain measures by the Germans, but they were always overruled and yet they did not resign. The obvious suspicion among the other Jews was that they stayed in office to safeguard their own lives or at least prolong them. There was some truth to this as there was always hope, and many Jews thought that Holland would soon be liberated so it always made sense to hang on as long as possible.

On September 8,1943, Italy surrendered and in October the Italian army started to fight the Germans on the side of the Allies. The Germans in the Netherlands heard about the capitulation of Italy through radio broadcasts from London. The Germans, ignorant of the event, wondered what was going on when they saw Dutchmen openly celebrating in the streets.

My father decided in the summer of 1943 that I had to go to another school to get what he thought was a better and more disciplined preparation for a second try at the final exams. I was transferred to the Gemeente HBS 1e van den Boschstraat. This was a school closer to my home so it was easier for me to bicycle back and forth, at least as long as I could still use my bike without it being at risk of confiscation by the Germans. This school was operated by the city of The Hague and had existed for a long time. Most teachers were older "lifers" who were straight out of central casting. The principal and several older teachers were stern old-fashioned men who wore dark suits and white shirts with stand-up wing collars. My classmates were mostly younger than I was and of a somewhat more "petit bourgeois" background. They were also better prepared for their final year in high school because they had all worked much harder than I had in the preceding years. The school building was a dark, grim affair built out of gray stone with all classrooms facing on an inner courtyard and all hallways on the outside where the sun came in. I made very few friends there. It was a miserable year for me; I felt out of place, missed the guys I had been together with for five years and was quite affected by the depressing environment we continued to live in. I was growing so much that I had hardly any clothes left that fitted. It did not really matter because all the others were dressed in similar strange outfits.

By that time my father had simply stopped going to the office. He obviously was not doing much at the provisional office the company had moved to. So he stayed home and spent much time on a few hobby projects I mentioned in the previous chapter, such as preparing the Geological Nomenclature he finished much later after his retirement.

So we entered the winter of 1943-44, still waiting for the invasion of the European continent and the liberation of our country. We had all expected our liberation much earlier and could not quite understand why it all took so long. We always underestimated the military staying power of the Germans and over- estimated the ability of the Allies to fight them successfully. But it became a hard slog as another winter came upon us. It was a pretty cold winter with lots of snow and ice, which tested our ability to keep our houses warm. We all retreated to one room where our pot-bellied stove was the only warm place in the house. Almost all houses, including those that had central heating like ours, had chimneys where a stove could be attached. The central heating in our house had been installed later and there were mantelpieces for coal-fired stoves in each room. Electricity and gas were heavily rationed and we did the laundry in a big pan that was placed on the gas stove. To save on gas and soap, we sent out most of our laundry to a commercial laundry in Gouda. The man who came weekly to fetch our dirty laundry and return the clean stuff became a major source for black market deliveries for us. He would deliver our things in a big square basket with a lid on top and under our clothes he would have put a big wheel of Gouda cheese or some meat or butter. I still see him in my mind's eye, lifting the heavy basket and sweating partly because of exertion and partly because he was nervous and afraid of getting caught. His truck ran on gas generated from wood that burned in a contraption attached to the back. Most commercial vehicles used these devices. In the earlier years some cars had gas cylinders on top or even large gas bags, but eventually the gas was rationed too, and most trucks used the so called houtgasgenerators (wood-gas generators). These were large vertical cylinders in which a load of small wooden blocks was kept slowly burning under pressure so they produced a gas that could be used to fuel the internal combustion engine. It took a long time in the morning to get these generators fired up and starting to produce gas, but eventually they would work and produce the desired result. We were eating less and less meat, had a ration of one egg per month and drank ersatz coffee and tea. I had started to smoke and would get a ration of one or two packs of cigarettes a week. My mother who did not smoke had chosen the alternative of a ration of candy. This candy was nothing to write home about either, but she enjoyed it and regularly took to her bed with what she called an attack of bile or liver problems that curiously always coincided with the issuance of the candy ration.

We became more and more used to overhead flights of bombers and Allied bombing attacks on Dutch targets. The Allies bombed several Dutch cities, sometimes by mistake. In October 1943, the U.S. Airforce bombed Enschede, killing 151 people, and in February 1944 they bombed Nijmegen killing 880. Both attacks were mistakes probably caused by bad navigation. Remarkably none of these attacks caused any resentment among the Dutch people. They were accepted as necessary and unavoidable acts of war.

A more successful attack took place in April 1944 when the RAF bombed a building in The Hague that contained the country's complete population archive. This was the central population registry where duplicates of all identification cards were kept. By destroying a good part of these archives, it became much easier for the resistance to issue bogus or false identification papers. With the central filing system gone, they could no longer be cross-checked against it. The RAF executed this attack at the request of the Dutch Resistance and carefully trained for it by practicing with a mockup of the building in England. They used small very fast twin-engine bombers called Mosquitoes that came in at rooftop level and shoved their bombs into the building, leveling it in seconds. About 110 employees working inside were killed. Some said the raid should have been planned for a Sunday when the building would have been empty. But most people agreed a working day was better because then the filing cabinets would be open and burn better and who cared about employees who were working in a place that served the Germans anyway? Unfortunately, not all the files were destroyed and the bureaucrats who had designed the foolproof Dutch identity card system rushed in to save their "life's work." Still it was a spectacular raid and I remember Frits Greup's father telling us about it with great enthusiasm. His office was very near the building that was attacked and he was bicycling by when the bombers came in.

In 1944 daily raids conducted by the U.S. Air Force became an almost normal thing in our school program. When the weather was clear we could almost count on the bombers flying over. The air raid alarm went off and we had to evacuate our classrooms to gather in the gym and hang around there until the all clear sounded. Shrapnel from exploding AA grenades could rain down on us, presenting a very clear danger. So we stayed indoors, flirting with the girls of other classes and doing homework. The certainty of air raid alarms even made it possible to schedule one's homework routine around them. If you were certain there would be an alarm at around 10 a.m., you would not do your homework for the class of that hour and the two subsequent ones and count on doing some work for the other classes while sitting out the alarm.

The school had its own in-house fire brigade consisting of students who had volunteered for the job and had to supervise the evacuation of classrooms and stay back in the main building to report whatever damage they detected. Strangely, this group became somewhat of a mini fascist operation. They dressed in militaristic style and imitated the heel clicking and jackboot stomping behavior of the Germans. Once I walked past the office of the principal and saw him talking to one of the leading characters of this group. This slight, pimply boy was standing ramrod stiff at attention in front of the principal's desk, probably getting instructions for his fire brigade. I wondered why the principal did not tell the fellow to relax and behave like a normal school boy. I guess he was too much of a martinet himself and perhaps afraid of criticizing German-style militaristic behavior. Later I heard from other boys that the student in question dropped out of school at the end of the school year, joined the SS, and was sent to a unit in France fighting the Allied forces that had invaded Europe. Two weeks later he was killed. He was an example of the young men who were not necessarily fanatical Nazis, but were impressed by the German military and craved a life of discipline and camaraderie they thought they could find there. They were blind to the obvious signs of the impending defeat of the German war machine.

What about the bombing, to what extent was it effective in hurting the German war production, transportation system and the morale of its citizens? In the years since the end of World War II much information has become available suggesting that the impact of the bombing on the German ability to produce planes and weapons was negligible if not totally nonexistent. We loved to hear the RAF bombers come over at night and we loved to see the squadrons of American bombers fill the air with hundreds of white contrails. We felt they were going over to Germany to pay the Germans back for what they had done to our cities and we believed they were devastating their industrial plant. The RAF would apply so-called "carpet bombing" tactics at night, using a lot of incendiary ordnance. The effect of the RAF raids on cities like Hamburg and Berlin was devastating. The incendiary bombs caused firestorms that engulfed whole neighborhoods in enormous fires that would suck up all oxygen and leave very little standing. The added use of very large high explosive bombs would do the rest. Tens of thousands of civilians died in these raids. The crude navigation equipment and bombsights used in those days did not always enable the bombers to find their targets with precision. Many factories and military targets were missed and many civilian neighborhoods were hit because of improper targeting. Sometimes bombs would even rain down on farmland. Clouds and the smoke of fires lit by preceding squadrons further hampered the bombardiers from aiming correctly so the RAF adopted a strategy of just covering large areas with bombs in the hope that the real target would be in there somewhere.

The chief proponent of RAF bomber command was Air Marshall Arthur T. Harris. He was a stern commander who was mainly responsible for building up his fleet of bombers to the enormous capacity it had towards the end of the war. Losses among his bomber crews were heavy, but most people in England and certainly in Holland felt the bombing was a necessary evil, that it was successful in undermining German morale, and that without it the war could not have been won. As I mentioned in the previous chapter, the U.S. Air Force became a factor around 1943 when it started regular daytime bombing of German targets. The U.S. raids were directed more at industrial and military targets, but they also resulted in heavy civilian casualties. American raids such as the one on the oil refineries in Ploesti in Rumania were really heroic. The bombers had to fly a very long distance over enemy territory. They took off from Italy and flew at very low altitude to disguise their presence and intentions. Once over the target, they found themselves engulfed in a storm of antiaircraft fire. Losses were heavy, but the Americans achieved what they came for, they crippled the major source of fuel for the German war machine. Subsequent raids aimed at Ploesti and German synthetic-fuel production facilities were a smart pinpoint attack on German fuel supplies.

These raids were supported by intelligence gleaned from a large British code-breaking operation that had been able to decipher German military radio traffic that was sent with the help of "enigma" machines. These machines scrambled all messages in daily varying patterns. A machine was captured from a German submarine and subsequent work allowed the Allies to have word-for-word access to all German radio traffic. The Germans were so convinced of the infallibility of their system that they refused to consider the possibility it had been corrupted.

Among air raids, a very controversial one was the raid the RAF and the American Air Force carried out jointly against Dresden in the waning days of the war. Dresden was far beyond the area the Allies planned to occupy. It was a city that lay squarely in the path of the Soviet army and it was filled with refugees who had fled in advance of the Russian troops. Dresden was basically undefended and a world-renowned gem of baroque architecture. The sustained raids on this city leveled most of its center and almost all of its historic monuments. There was really no excuse for it and after the war most people on the Allied side felt ashamed of it.

Air Marshall Harris, was revered during the war and in the years immediately following it, was honored with a statue in London. Later on, opinions about the bombing and its effect began to change and many voices were raised in England and Germany to give him a less honorable place in history. It seems to me it is always easy to rewrite history and to second-guess actions taken during wars. There is no question in my mind that Harris did what he was told to do, executed his orders brilliantly and should not be blamed for making a supreme effort to win the war. We have much better bombing technology now, but he did not have anything better than the bombers he had and was obligated to send them out at night because they lacked fighter escort protection and had less than perfect navigation and bombing equipment. The crews certainly were a group of very heroic young men many of whom sacrificed their lives.

After the war we saw statistics that proved that despite the bombing the Germans continued to build planes, tanks and artillery pieces at a fast clip. In 1944, they produced more than in any year before. The German Tiger and Panther tanks were vastly superior to the U.S. Sherman tank and the German fighters were deemed to be equal to if not better than any planes the Allies had. In 1944 they even had a jet fighter that could have done real damage to the Allies were it not for Hitler's order to convert it into a bomber. Allied air supremacy stemmed basically from over-whelming numerical superiority and better pilot training. The Germans had a great shortage of pilots towards the end of the war because they had neglected training and lacked experienced instructors. In later years, lack of fuel forced the Luftwaffe to put pilots in action before they had accumulated sufficient flying time. Thus, they became easy prey for better-trained RAF and American fighter pilots.

German production faltered in 1945 while the Allies throttled down in 1944 because they were preparing for peace. The Russian ability to build massive numbers of tanks and artillery pieces (their favorite weapon) is a stunning achievement in view of the devastation of their industrial capacity in the western part of the country and the move of much of their factories to locations east of the Ural Mountains.

In the first five months of 1944, we had more bombing raids and much more activity by armed Dutch Resistance groups. There was more and more good news from the eastern front where the Russians had relieved the two-year siege of Leningrad (now again St. Petersburg) and equally good news from the Allied front in Italy. The Dutch Resistance executed several spectacular raids on printing businesses to capture rationing coupons, and on distribution offices to do the same and on prisons to liberate resistance fighters. Unfortunately, there were also again many failed raids and arrests of Resistance people through betrayal or unsuccessful operations. I am still in awe of the actions of the Resistance people. Just imagine the guts it takes to move either by car with a wood-burning generator or on bicycles through the streets with German military all over the place, to have weapons hidden under one's clothes and then break into a well-guarded prison. After the operation you had to escape and find a place to hide whatever was retrieved, prisoners or stacks of food coupons. The Germans were very serious opponents, well trained and highly motivated. They were far from the dim-witted, overweight buffoons one could see in the sixties on American TV in quasi-humorous sitcoms about prisoner of war camps etc. The Germans our Resistance people fought were young, ruthless, well trained and dedicated members of the SS and Gestapo police.

In June we were desperately waiting for the Allied invasion to start. That it was coming was no longer a secret. The only question was when and where. In 1942 and 1943 large parts of The Hague had been evacuated and turned into a fortress. The city is very close to the coast and in the eyes of the Germans, it was not inconceivable that a landing would be tried on the nice sandy beaches of the Netherlands. So they evacuated everybody who lived in beach resorts like Scheveningen near The Hague and Zandvoort near Haarlem and Bloemendaal. Part of The Hague was even surrounded by a deep canal that served as a tank ditch and was dug in the past few years with the help of hundreds of Dutch workers. This ditch traversed several neighborhoods, and numerous houses were torn down to make room for it. All along the Dutch shoreline, concrete bunkers were built, again with the help of Dutch contractors and their workers, and several people were accused after the war to have profited hugely from this kind of contracting work. It is a question, of course, if they had a choice. The evacuation of the coastal areas caused massive disruptions of people and families. My grandparents were also forced to leave their house in Bloemendaal.

They moved to Tante Jetje and Oom Bernard's house in Leersum. In a way this was a good solution for my grandmother because she could disappear, get false papers and change her identity in an area where nobody knew her.

On June 4, 1944, we learned that Rome had fallen. The Allied offensive in Italy had finally gained momentum and broken out of a stalemate halfway up the Italian boot. There had been a struggle between Churchill and the American military commanders, especially General Eisenhower, as Churchill was constantly pressing for an attack into Europe's "soft underbelly," i.e. Italy, Greece and Southern France, while the Americans were arguing in favor of an invasion across the Channel, code named "Anvil." Among the Americans there was a feeling that the British were reluctant to chance an invasion with the attendant risk of failure and/or heavy losses. The enormous losses Britain suffered in the trench warfare in World War I, where a whole generation perished for minimal territorial gain, was still an important part of British collective memory. The Americans thought, probably correctly, that the "soft underbelly" theory was not really valid since it would still require passing the Alps to get into Germany. Ultimately Eisenhower settled the debate and the invasion was planned and set in motion. It was an enormous logistical and tactical effort that involved hundreds of thousands of men, ships by the thousands and elaborate camouflage and deception measures in England aimed at making the Germans believe the attack would come across the Channel near Calais and not in Normandy. The most important factor was certainly that the Allies had established air superiority and maintained it from then on until the end of the war.

Then, on June 6, we heard that the invasion had started. We did not know the term "D-Day" yet. All we knew was that the Allies had landed, that they were fighting hard and that they had managed to get a firm foothold on the European continent in Normandy. We were elated and overjoyed. We knew that this time the Allies would stay and we were convinced they would win. At last we could see a glimmer of hope that our ordeal would soon be over. Strangely, I cannot recall where I was and what I was doing on June 6. I think I may have been home, preparing for my second try at the final high school exam. We had a clear sense that we were witnessing an incredibly important event of major historical significance, yet we were just plugging along, doing our exams, invasion or no invasion.

The invasion almost became a fiasco because the weather turned unusually bad. On June 5, Eisenhower had to postpone the landing for one day and then decided to go ahead the next day despite the bad weather in Normandy. His principal weather consultant had predicted that if he attacked the next day he would have a window of a day or two, so he gave the order to "GO." An incredibly difficult decision that could easily have turned out very badly. The Allies needed a few days with relatively calm seas to get enough people and equipment on land. The landing beaches that had been selected had no harbors nearby, so artificial harbors were built and old ships were sunk in place to act as breakwaters. These breakwaters protected docking piers built out of pre-constructed concrete caissons that were floated in, linked together and sunk. Getting troops, tanks and artillery pieces on land was one thing getting enough supplies, particularly fuel, was another. The invasion was preceded by a heavy bombardment of the area chosen for the landings, followed by a massive drop of paratroopers and airborne troops in gliders. Many of the paratroopers landed too far away from their targets and were widely dispersed. Still they managed to join up in sufficient numbers to create confusion among the Germans. They suffered heavy losses. The glider people achieved several preset targets but also missed many others and also suffered heavy losses in part through enemy fire and in part through crash landings.

It appeared the countryside in Normandy was full of hedgerows, which had been growing for centuries along the roads and formed the boundaries of farmer's properties. These hedgerows consisted of extremely heavy and tough wood and presented a major obstacle for gliders crashing into them and for tanks trying to go across roads flanked by them. Amazingly, the Allied intelligence people had not been sufficiently aware of this obstacle. Later the troops constructed large hedge clipper-like contraptions that were welded to the front of tanks, enabling them to cut through the hedgerows.

Five beachheads were established. Two American, two British and one Canadian. One of the two American beachheads turned out to be the toughest. This was "Omaha" beach. The other U.S. beachhead was "Utah" while the British landed on "Gold" and "Sword" and the Canadians on "Juno." British paratroopers landed near a bridge that was key for the ultimate taking of the French town of Caen. This bridge was later called "Pegasus" bridge to honor the soldiers who landed there in a flawless operation and held it despite extremely strong German counterattacks. The emblem of the British Parachute Regiment is a Pegasus. American paratroopers landed more inland near the U.S. beachheads.

The weather had fooled the Germans. They were not aware there would be a break in the weather as the Allied weatherman had detected and figured the invasion would not come for a while. The renowned German General Rommel who was in charge had gone home to Germany to see his wife. Rommel had achieved considerable successes in North Africa against the British and American forces and was now in charge of the defense of Western Europe. When he took command, he immediately ordered extensive improvements in the fortifications along the Channel coast and prepared his troops to meet the invasion head on and immediately wherever it would take place. It was his opinion that once a successful landing was achieved, it would be impossible to throw the Allies back into the sea. His colleagues, however, felt they should allow the Allies to land, and keep troops in reserve to fight them once they were on land and it was clear they were dealing with the main force. There was a strong body of opinion among the Germans that the real Allied landing would be made across the Channel, in the area where it was the narrowest. The Allies had gotten wind of these German suspicions and reinforced them by displaying a mock army near the Channel. They allowed German air reconnaissance to detect this army, which was made up of rubber blow-up decoys that from the air looked like tanks, trucks and artillery pieces, etc.

Early in the morning of the first day, all beachheads except Omaha were secure and troops moved inland. But at Omaha beach almost everything went wrong. Bombers dropped their loads in the wrong places and inflicted no damage on the German defenders. The navy landed an entire division too far north, in the wrong spot. Amphibian vehicles were caught in the surf and swamped. A sheer cliff confronted the men who did land on the beach. There were Germans on top, firing down on them. They were trapped and became demoralized. U.S. Army Rangers climbed the cliff using ladders that were anchored at the top with grappling hooks shot up to the rim, and in a display of extraordinary bravery managed to subdue the people on top. The Germans had already reported that the attack at Omaha Beach had been repulsed and the U.S. command was likewise considering withdrawal of the people trapped below the cliffs. But the soldiers on the beach decided to take the initiative and attacked. After a fierce and close fight they gained the upper hand and achieved a victory at a terrible cost of lives. More than 2,500 Americans were killed on that beach that day. This battle and many others involving unseasoned "green" American soldiers fills me with awe. These boys from Kansas and Missouri or other places thousands of miles away found themselves flung on to this beach under heavy fire. Many of them had no battle experience whatsoever yet they fought like hell. They were fighting experienced German soldiers who were motivated by a Nazi philosophy they did not understand. They knew they were fighting to liberate Europe from oppression and they were willing to lay their lives on the line. Many of them were buried in a large cemetery near Omaha beachhead.

In recent years Europeans have often criticized actions taken by the U.S. government and its military in armed conflicts all over the world. They forget that it is impossible to plan military actions by committee and that the European tendency to soft pedal aggression by tin pot dictators and terrorists leads to inaction and to more trouble. Americans, including myself tend to resent these criticisms and the meddling by Monday morning quarterbacks. They feel the Europeans have no stomach to defend their democratic ideals and would rather resign themselves to being intimidated than take action. Some of these European attitudes stem from a feeling of powerlessness against the overwhelming strength of the U.S. military. That is understandable, but it should not be assumed that the U.S. government has become an out-of-control policeman of the world. Many Americans feel it is useful to remind the Europeans of the sacrifices U.S. soldiers made twice during the twentieth century to resolve European wars and add that it is unlikely they will do so again after having been criticized so often and so unfairly. The cemetery at Omaha beachhead is often mentioned in this respect as an example of unselfish sacrifices made by Americans to rescue Europe.

The initial German response to the invasion was surprisingly hesitant. They waited for orders from Adolf Hitler, who at first could not be awakened, and later in the day the response was spotty. The next day the especially fanatical SS division "Hitlerjugend," named after the youth movement of the German Nazi party, arrived. The SS Panzer troops used the superior Tiger tank that had little trouble with the American built Shermans. The objective of the British and Canadians troops was the town of Caen. As it turned out, it was going to be a battle of almost six weeks before Caen was liberated. In one incident several hundred Canadians surrendered to the members of the "Hitlerjugend" division and were murdered by the Germans who were really mere teenagers. Some Canadian prisoners were machine-gunned and after that the SS men drove their tanks over their bodies. In June and July the invasion proceeded, but not without considerable difficulty. The British and Canadian forces faced extremely tough resistance around Caen and nearby towns. The slowness of the progress of the British/Canadian sector was severely criticized during and after the war. There seems to be more than enough justification for this criticism, but it should also be understood that the Brits and Canadians were facing extremely tough resistance by battle-hardened German elite units. The Germans continued to be able to prevent a breakout. The Americans, meanwhile, also had their problems with tenacious German resistance, but they did manage to cut off the Cotentin peninsula. The important harbor of Cherbourg is situated at the western end of this peninsula and by June 27, Cherbourg was occupied.

Incredible as it may sound, we were having our final high school exam while the invasion was in full swing. Large numbers of warplanes roared overhead, the news was more and more optimistic. The front was approaching Paris, and there we were wrestling with all kinds of problems in chemistry, physics and math. This time I did better although I was certainly not among the best finishers. I did well with my languages, history, natural history and geography, but so-so with math, etc. If you scored high with the written exam, you were excused from the oral exam for math, chemistry and physics. As could be expected, I had to sweat through oral exams for all of those. For languages, the oral exam was mandatory and there I enjoyed myself. The *Direkteur*, headmaster, handed me my diploma with the words: "I did not think you would make it, Schieferdecker." What a nice encouraging statement from a teacher of the old school to a student who was beginning a very uncertain new period of his life. We had a bit of an awkward celebration at the school. Parties were not held because the danger of being picked up was too great. So we dispersed and, except for one fellow with whom I stayed in touch for some time, I never saw this high school class again.

I do not remember what I did that summer beyond following the war and staying out of trouble. It cannot have been much since young men were so restricted in their movements. There was always a chance of being arrested for something and it was not advisable to stray too far away from home. Visits to the center of The Hague, for instance were not good for one's health. My friend Eelco Apol seemed to have developed a knack for getting arrested. At some point between February 1943 and the summer of 1944, he was arrested again, this time it was more serious. I cannot remember why he was picked up and where. He spent a couple of very unpleasant months in the Amersfoort concentration camp. When he came back his head was shaved and he had lost a lot of weight. I visited him at home as soon as he was free and saw how thin he looked. He told me calmly and dispassionately, but in great detail about the atrocious way in which he and his fellow prisoners were treated by the SS and also by the so-called Kapos, older long-term prisoners who stayed alive by beating up on their fellow inmates.

In July, there was news of an attempt on the life of Hitler. A staff officer by the name of von Stauffenberg entered the Führer's headquarters with a bomb concealed in his briefcase. He placed the bomb under the chart table. When it went off it did not kill Hitler—it only wounded him. The top of the table proved to be too thick and sturdy. Stauffenberg belonged to a widespread conspiracy of officers who were mostly members of the German upper class and nobility, traditionally the core of the German professional officers corps. They had belatedly decided that they had to act against their monstrous regime. The revenge and punishment was swift and horrible. Members of the group were tortured and many were executed by hanging. Not normal hanging with a rope, no—by strangulation by piano wire and suspension on meat hooks in a dungeon. There is a film clip of their appearance in a "court." You see the Nazi judge enter in his toga adorned with an eagle and a swastika. He brings the Nazi salute. The accused enter, middle-aged men who look bewildered in civilian clothes holding their pants up by hand because they do not have belts or suspenders. The judge starts screaming at them without giving anybody a chance to say anything and that's the trial. This film has of course been made available by the Nazis because it served their by then almost lost cause. But it gives an impression of the atmosphere and the way in which the Nazis treated their prisoners. These were their own staff officers, no need to imagine how they treated people who had served in the resistance in the occupied countries. As a result of the assassination attempt, Hitler became a more and more reclusive man, suspicious of his army officers and particularly suspicious of members of the upper classes of German society. He personally assumed command of the German army. It remains a mystery why thousands of professional military men, mostly members of Germany's prominent and/or noble families whose fathers and grandfathers had served their country ably and bravely, could serve a regime of low-life scoundrels so well for so many years. These officers were extremely skillful military men who were responsible for most of Hitler's victories. They turned their backs on all the atrocities they must have witnessed, and after the war they wrote books in which they explained their unquestioning and faithful service as the logical consequence of the oath of allegiance they swore to their country and their Führer, an oath they could not break, in their opinion.

On August 1, the Jews remaining in the Warsaw ghetto revolted and started an armed uprising. They fought heroically for several weeks, hoping the approaching Soviet army would liberate them. The Russians did not come. Actually, they stopped their advance and let the Germans bomb the ghetto for days on end. After bombing it, the Germans stormed it killing all the men women and children they could find that were still alive in the ghetto. After the war, many accusations and theories have been heard suggesting that Stalin, the Soviet dictator, purposely lingered outside Warsaw to allow the Germans to eliminate a large number of Jews. There have also been questions about the Allied indifference and inactivity in this area. The Allies had the capability to send strategic bombers to Poland. They chose not to bomb the Germans who were at work destroying the ghetto and who had at that time virtually no fighter planes left. The Allies also avoided bombing the large and from the air very visible concentration camps. The claim that they did not know what was going on in the extermination camps sounds hollow. They did know, but they chose not to interfere. Why?

The Germans had boasted for some time that they possessed "secret weapons" that would have a devastating effect on their enemies and would turn the course of the war in their favor. These so called "V" weapons turned out to be the V-1 or "buzz bomb," a large bomb with wings and a jet engine that propelled it in flight, and the V-2, the first long-range ballistic missile used as a weapon in wartime. The V stood for *Vergeltung,* (revenge). In the event, both these weapons turned out to have little effect on the Allied war effort, but regardless of their effect, they displayed an unexpectedly high level of technological ability. The Allies knew about the V-2 proving grounds in Peenemünde in eastern Germany and attacked them repeatedly with heavy bombing raids, but as with many other attempts to take out German industrial capacity, the raids failed to prevent the completion of the project. The V-1 was launched mainly from northern France when the Germans still controlled that area. The projectile was a cigar-shaped bomb that was the fuselage of a small pilot-less aircraft with short stubby wings and a tail section with horizontal and vertical stabilizers. A small jet engine mounted like a big long stovepipe on top of its fuselage propelled it. It became the first mass produced working jet engine. The V-1 was placed on a track on a specially built launching site with an upward sloping ramp and was launched by activating its engine. These "buzz bombs" would fly at a relatively

V 2 TAKING OFF.

low altitude towards England and made a sort of "pockety-pockety" noise like an old anemic motorcycle. When they ran out of fuel, they would stop flying, dive down and explode. They were huge bombs that did a lot of damage in London. But they had no targeting or navigation devices whatsoever except for an autopilot controlled by a directional gyro compass. So they represented just terror attacks on the civilian population of big cities. People in London would listen to the noise of the buzz bombs and when it stopped would dive for cover. The V-1 killed 22,892 people. The RAF planes took off to shoot the bombs down and one pilot developed a handy method of deflecting them by flying very close and tipping the bomb's wing over with his own wing tip. This disturbed the bomb's compass and made it crash into the sea. The Germans launched 2,448 of these bombs. I did not see many V-1s but I do remember hearing several going over, probably in the direction of Antwerp after the Allies had occupied that city. The V-2 was a much more fearful weapon. One day in the later part of summer, I was standing on the street in front of our house when I heard a tremendously loud rumbling noise. I looked up in the air and saw two huge rockets rise slowly in the air, emitting a loud deep rumble combined with a violent tearing ripping noise. In the coming months we would become very familiar with this noise. The rockets rose really agonizingly slowly, wobbling a bit as they went up. They left a clear white contrail in the air as they slowly arched overhead and disappeared from view. As the rockets disappeared, the contrail stayed aloft for quite a while and curled up into a loop in the middle. I did, of course, not know what I saw but realized I was looking at rockets. Soon the news came out that beyond the V-1 the Germans now had a weapon that would really hit the English where it hurt. Not exactly. Here again the effect on the Allied war effort was negligible, but the V-2 did have a much more severe terror impact on the population because they would hit totally unexpectedly. The V-2s would rain down on London and Antwerp for months to come, slamming down without any forewarning and exploding with considerably more force than the V-1. As the Allies moved through France and Belgium, Holland became the only place where these missiles could be fired off from and with the southern part of the country liberated, The Hague became the prime launching pad. The Allies responded with fighter-bombers patrolling the country trying to find the V-1 installations and the moveable V-2 convoys. They would shoot at anything that moved and attacked more trains, which made travel really hazardous. The problem with the V-2s was that they often did not lift off properly. They would try to get off the ground, wobble a bit and fall back exploding on impact. In many areas in The Hague huge craters were seen where V-2's had crashed in among houses.

A schoolmate of mine who lived near an area where launchings would frequently take place had the whole routine down pat. The Germans would usually launch at night to avoid Allied air strikes. Being German they would always arrive exactly at the same time. So this fellow would set his alarm clock for that time and would hear the trucks go by. He then knew how long it would take to set up the launch and would set his alarm for that. As the launch took place, he would be awake and listening. If the launch succeeded he did nothing. If it did not, he would hear the rocket blast off and suddenly stop. He would then blow loudly on a whistle, which woke up his entire (large) family, and they would all dive under their beds awaiting the blast, which would frequently cause windows to shatter. More than 3,000 V 2s were fired at London, Antwerp and other cities, including Maastricht. They killed an estimated 7,250 people, again mostly civilians and more than 12,000 prisoners used as forced labor died building them. It was the first ballistic missile and the first weapon that cost more lives to build than it killed.

In August, the Allies liberated Paris and also landed in southern France. The French had a division of troops, the "Free French" under General de Gaulle, who participated in the invasion and were given the honor of entering Paris. So the Americans stopped near Paris and the French drove up, suggesting to the Parisians that they were doing all the heavy lifting. There was a grand parade down the Champs Élisées in which many American troops participated, but General de Gaulle marched in front, a very tall man with a big nose and arrogant demeanor. He was the savior of France and deserves to go down in history as a unique man who put France back on

THIS IS THE WAY THE GERMANS TRUNDLED THE V2'S THROUGH THE STREETS AND INTO POSITION. ONE SITE WAS 500 YARDS AWAY FROM NETTY'S HOME.

the map after it was totally defeated and demoralized in 1940. He restored France's self-respect and in the process became a huge irritant for Churchill and Roosevelt.

After the defeat of France in 1940, the Germans initially only occupied part of France, leaving a large segment in the central and southeastern part unoccupied. The government established there took the city of Vichy as its seat and became known as "Vichy France." The head of state was General Pétain, an elderly, somewhat senile man who was one of France's WW I heroes. Obviously Pétain had to collaborate with the Germans and as time passed his regime became almost a Nazi satellite. The French forces in North Africa had mostly stayed loyal to Vichy and when the Allies landed there, some units put up a fight. Thus the British navy was forced to attack and sink almost the entire French navy in the port of Oran (they refused to join the Allies) and General Eisenhower had to navigate between competing French generals with uncertain loyalties. The Allies had hoped to find General Giraud who was in charge in North Africa or his opponent Admiral Darlan ready to take charge of a French government in exile. They were trying to work around de Gaulle who had ruffled many feathers in London. In the event, it was really only de Gaulle who had a totally clean and unblemished reputation and could rally the free French around him. In later years after the war, de Gaulle formed a strongly nationalist and conservative party and became president of France for several terms. He was an arrogant and difficult man, but he understood what it took to bring France back to a respected nation with its own distinct identity. He had a great sense of history and by sheer willpower almost single handedly restored the French nation to its present position among the leaders of the world, a nation that somehow manages to consistently punch above its weight.

As the Allies swept through northern France and into Belgium, we in Holland began to anticipate our liberation. Our liberators seemed unstoppable and were gaining more and more momentum. On September 4th Antwerp was occupied, a very important event because the Allies needed a big port and Antwerp was to become a key factor in supplying the enormous quantities of food and materials the troops needed. However, it took almost three months before the British army, which took Antwerp, was able to force open the entry to its harbor and actually use it. Historians say the English General Montgomery, the hero of North Africa, was more interested in pushing rapidly into Germany and neglected Antwerp. He was the main proponent of the airborne landings near Arnhem and Nijmegen in eastern Holland. The objective of these landings was to quickly capture two major bridges over major rivers that cut through the middle of the Netherlands.

American airborne troops took the bridge over the Waal near Nijmegen, but British paratroopers failed to capture the second one over the Rhine near Arnhem. As we learned later to our chagrin their failure to take the last bridge near Arnhem kept the Allies south of the big rivers for the entire winter and consequently prevented us from being liberated. But these airborne landings were made on September 17th and on Tuesday September 5th, the day after Antwerp fell, we had no idea of what was in store for us. What we did know on that day was that Allied forces were rapidly approaching the Dutch border and the Nazis knew it too. That day became known as *dolle Dinsdag*, (mad Tuesday). It was the day the Nazis and their collaborators as well as the German military panicked. We saw scores of Dutch Nazis pack up and leave in cars with wood gas generators, horse-drawn carts, hearses and anything else that moved. The Germans also appeared to be packing up, truckloads of administrative people were rolling eastward. Anton Mussert, the Dutch Nazi leader relocated to Almelo, a city very close to the German border. Wild rumors were flying. We heard that the British army was in Breda, then Dordrecht, then Rotterdam. Citizens were getting ready to cheer the Allied troops at points near highways to the south that were open and were waiting at places where the victorious Allies were expected to show up any minute. Unfortunately, nothing happened. The rumors proved to be false. The Allied advance had slowed down and almost come to a stop. For a moment, there had been a tremendous sense of euphoria and many people were getting ready to settle scores with local Nazis. It was hard to swallow the disappointment. We had to face a very harsh miserable winter that brought large segments of the population of western Holland to the brink of death from starvation.

In our family the euphoria of that period led to a series of events involving my Uncle Bernard and Tante Jetje as well as my grandparents. It ended about seven months later, just before the liberation, with the tragic death of Uncle Bernard in front of a German firing squad. Oom Bernard and Tante Jetje lived in Leersum, a rural village in the province of Utrecht. Their house, *de Meezenhof*, was a small country house that was pleasing to the eye, with a large thatched roof that covered the entire second floor. The house had a square footprint and brick walls that were plastered white. It had a detached one-car garage. It stood in the woods and when you came to the property, you could not see it behind the trees. Oom Bernard became an active gardener and had an elaborate vegetable garden in a corner of the property. He had a knack of getting along with the locals and although my uncle and aunt had only moved into the community in 1939, just before the war, they had excellent contacts and good friendships with many prominent and also many more humble local people. Around 1943 my grandparents moved to Leersum to stay with their daughter and son in law. Given Oom Bernard's close relationship with many people in the village, his adventurous and energetic personality and his dislike of the Germans, it was almost inevitable that he would end up in the inner circles of the local Resistance movement. I believe my aunt was also active in the Resistance, but neither she nor her husband had ever given us an inkling of what they were doing. I also believe that my grandparents were completely ignorant of these activities.

In early September, either shortly after "Mad Tuesday" or ten days later when the allied airborne attack on Arnhem and Nijmegen had started, Oom Bernard's resistance group decided to act in anticipation of the arrival of the Allied forces. They imprisoned the Nazi mayor of Leersum and locked him up in a cell in the correction section of a nearby institution for wayward boys. When the Allies did not come and the disappearance of the mayor was noted, the SS came after Oom Bernard. We never learned how they knew he was involved and how they got his address. When the Germans arrived, Oom Bernard had just come home too. He carried a gun and when he saw the Germans come he hid the gun in the hallway. They had a wooden bench in the hallway of which the seat covered a storage bin for cushions for garden chairs, etc. He tossed the gun in this bin, probably to avoid having it on his person if he got caught. He ran out of the back door into the woods and hid there. The Germans started rampaging through the house and found the gun. They arrested my aunt and put my grandparents against the wall of the house with their hands up in the air. They were then seventy-four and eighty-four years old.

Tante Jetje was taken away to the concentration camp Amersfoort where she was severely interrogated. She never told me this, but my grandmother told me after the war that she caved in under the pressure and stress of the interrogation and told the man who was grilling her that she would reveal where the mayor of Leersum was kept if he would give his "word of honor as an officer" that he would not take any reprisals against the people who were keeping him there. This *Ehrenwort*, (word of honor), was, of course, given immediately. My aunt often had a somewhat naïve and trusting attitude towards other people and even after five years of war, she still thought that German SS officers knew what the word "honor" meant. I do not know how long she was kept in the concentration camp. I also do not know what happened with the people who had imprisoned the mayor. From a press clipping I found in my father's files after his death I learned that the director of the correctional facility where the mayor was kept was shot in front of his house.

After the war, I always felt it would be too painful for her to tell me about those days so I never asked her. Later – I do not know if it was a few hours later or the next day – the Germans returned to the house and ordered my grand-parents out, threw hand grenades through the windows and torched it.

RAUTER'S CAR WITH DEAD DRIVER AFTER THE ATTACK.

Opa and Oma were brought to the nearby town of Doorn where they found a *pension,* rooming house where they stayed until the end of the war. During that period we corresponded regularly with them and heard they were O.K. It appears the local Resistance people had taken care of them and of their needs for food and clothing.

Tante Jetje left almost immediately after she was released and moved to the eastern part of the country where she went underground with the local Resistance people. After the Germans had left the house for the first time, Oom Bernard came back out of the woods for just a few minutes, collected some of his things and left. He also went to the eastern part of the country to join the Resistance there. In early 1945, he was arrested and imprisoned by the Germans. They did not know his real identity because he had false identification papers. He was in prison when the final crunch came and the Allies were approaching Holland. In March 1945, just before the liberation, Dutch Resistance men in German uniforms ambushed Rauter, the top SS and Gestapo general in the Netherlands. They stopped his car and shot him, severely wounding him. We learned after the war that it was all a big mistake. The Resistance people had heard that a large quantity of fresh meat was ready to be picked up by the Wehrmacht at a warehouse. They planned to capture a German truck and go with it to pick up the meat just before the real recipients would show up. So they tried to ambush a truck during the dark night and when they heard engine noise they thought it was a truck. It was a BMW convertible with the top down. Rauter was severely wounded but not killed. He recovered and was executed after the war. The Germans immediately retaliated by shooting 263 hostages throughout the country.

A group of 117 was shot at the Woeste Hoeve, the spot where the attack on Rauter had taken place. Oom Bernard was among the people killed there. He had been transported out of prison to that place. I have often wondered how Oom Bernard must have felt standing there before dawn in front of a firing squad. As I mentioned in a previous chapter, this was really a senseless action. The Germans kept the executions quiet because the ambush could have suggested that they had little control over the countryside and could not protect their key people. It was just a show of force against the Dutch Resistance.

We did not learn about Oom Bernard's death until a few days after the liberation. Late one morning I came home and found my mother in the kitchen. She told me to go into the garage where my father was cutting wood for our small stove. We were free, but we had no utilities or fuel yet. I entered the garage and found my father in tears. He told me what had happened. There never was a funeral. Oom Bernard's remains ended up in the cemetary of Leersum and were later on removed to an official cemetery for war heroes, the *Ereveld Loenen.* It is near the Woeste Hoeve about 2 km south on the Groenendaalse weg. He rests in section E, grave # 993. I discovered this information only in October 2003 when I went through a file my father had kept on Tante Jetje. In the file is a letter from her in which she tells Pa that she has given permission to remove Oom Bernard's remains because she could no longer properly maintain the grave. Strangely, my father never told me this and claimed Oom Bernard's grave had been cleared, as is often done in Holland.

Today a monument at the *Woeste Hoeve* carries Oom Bernard's name together with the names of the 117 other people shot there that day, March 8, 1945, only two months before the Germans capitulated. In August 1995 I saw a picture in the

OOM BERNARD CA. 1943.

Dutch weekly paper I got here at home in America, showing damage inflicted by vandals on the monument. The monument had a heavy glass plate with all the names engraved on it. Oom Bernard's name was visible on the picture just besides a big hole in the glass. I was totally sickened by that picture which reflected the lack of respect younger Dutch people born after the war have for those who sacrificed their lives so they could live in freedom.

The airborne landings in the eastern part of Holland also affected our family and all of us. It affected us because the failure of the landings north of the Rhine River prolonged the war for another eight, very tough months. It affected our family because Oom Otto and Tante Jet and their daughter Tineke, were forced to leave their house in Arnhem and evacuate together with the entire population of the city. They spent a miserable winter in the country, North West of the city, and came back to a looted and devastated city after the liberation. Amazingly, the Dutch postal service kept functioning quite well throughout the final winter of the war when almost nothing else was working anymore. So we were able to keep up with my grandparents and also Tante Jet, and Oom Otto. I wish we had saved those letters. They would have been wonderful time capsules of a very difficult period in our lives. Operation "Market Garden," as it was code-named, was an effort to speed up the war on the western front by making a bold move across the Rhine river and its tributaries and rush quickly into Germany before winter would set in. Things did move fast in September. On the 12th American troops crossed the Dutch-Belgian border into the province of Limburg. The next day, the 13th, they moved into Germany. On that same day, the 67th and last train with Jews from Westerbork, left for Auschwitz. Incredible as it seems, the Germans were continuing their efforts to achieve the "final solution" of what they called the "Jewish problem." Nothing, not even the presence of Russian troops in the east and Allied troops in the west of their homeland, could stop them. The city of Maastricht was liberated on the 14th. And Market Garden was launched on the 17th when two American airborne divisions landed near and around Eindhoven and a British paratroop division west of Arnhem in Oosterbeek and Wolfheze. To assist with this effort and make it tougher for the Germans to move troops around, the Dutch government-in-exile ordered a nationwide railway strike. This strike succeeded and lasted until the liberation. It not only impeded German troop movements; it also stopped all movement of food and supplies to the densely populated western half of Holland. Thus it was the opening salvo for our "hunger winter." Market Garden started with a great deal of élan as thousands of paratroopers descended on the Dutch countryside. Infantry and tanks rolled in from Belgium and the city of Nijmegen was quickly liberated. Nijmegen lies at a crucial fork in the great rivers that enter Holland there from Germany. It has been a key strategic location for centuries. There is a ruin there that was the castle of Charlemagne around the year 800. From Nijmegen a bridge crosses the Waal River into an area called the Betuwe, a low-lying farm area known for its extensive fruit orchards that often flood in spring when the big rivers cannot handle all the water coming down from the Alps. This bridge was captured undamaged by American forces. To get from the Betuwe to Arnhem one had to cross another bridge over the Rhine, leading directly into the city of Arnhem. The British airborne troops who landed in Arnhem by parachute and gliders planned to force their way into the city and capture that bridge over the Rhine, which would have opened all of western Germany to the Allied forces. They landed successfully, albeit too far away from the bridge, and managed to enter the city and came very close to the bridge. Their misfortune was that German resistance was much heavier than their intelligence had anticipated. Two SS panzer divisions had been pulled out of the front lines and moved to an area north of Arnhem for rest and refitting. The lightly armed airborne division fell into their arms and was soon confronted with an overwhelmingly powerful opponent. They fought like lions and the Dutch people who lived in that area will always remember their sublime effort. They suffered heavy losses, but after ten days of incredibly intense fighting, they had to be withdrawn. Whatever was left of them retreated on September 27 across the river in rubber boats in the dark of the night. A well-known book was written about this episode called "A Bridge Too Far," and a movie of the same name became a classic. It will always be a mystery why the staff of General Montgomery did not know about the presence of the German divisions north of the city. The Allies had total air supremacy after all and the weather was not bad. For decades, the gossip has been that Montgomery was frustrated because he had not been given command of the Allied forces in Europe and had to accept the American General Eisenhower as his superior. The Americans accused Monty (as he was called) of being overly cautious and slow in moving out from the landing area in France in June and of not opening the entrance of the harbor of Antwerp. Rather than opening Antwerp, Monty wanted to show he could move fast and insisted that the full force of the troops under his command had to be used to launch a forceful and deep thrust into Germany along a relatively narrow front. A sort of dagger thrust to force a quick end to the war. Having focused so hard on this goal, he is thought to have deliberately ignored intelligence he had of the presence of extra German troops. He almost succeeded but not quite. So Nijmegen and the southern part of Holland south of the rivers were liberated, while the center of Arnhem lay in ruins and the population of that city was cast adrift.

Of course we did not know all these details at the time. We did know that the battle of Arnhem was lost but thought the Allies could cross the rivers anytime somewhere else and come liberate us. Unfortunately, this did not happen. We again overestimated the abilities of the Allied forces and had no idea of the difficulty of supplying a huge army over a very long distance. We had to learn the hard way that there were other priorities before we would get liberated. We simply were not that important. Only the harbor of Cherbourg was available at that time and getting Antwerp open became crucial. Finally, Monty understood what he had to do and a bitter battle for the entrance of the harbor of Antwerp started. This harbor is located on the Schelde River (*Escaut* in French). The Schelde runs into the Dutch province of Zeeland past the islands of Zuid Beveland and Walcheren. Walcheren was the key. It controls the entry to Antwerp.

The Germans had built enormously strong fortifications near the harbor town of Vlissingen (*Flushing* in English.) Walcheren is a beautiful island with several historical towns on it. Middelburg and Veere are well known. The island resembles a bowl as its dikes are built around its perimeter only so that a breach in the outside dikes floods the entire island. The British commandos who landed on the island used that tactic. Queen Wilhelmina was asked for and gave permission to flood the island. A heavy bombardment by air and sea broke the dikes and the commandos sluiced through the openings, thus gaining a foothold in the rear of the German fortifications. It still took until November 8 before Vlissingen was liberated and the harbor could be used. The local population suffered terribly while this battle was going on. There was not much land to live on after the dikes broke and the weather had turned very bad with frequent autumn storms. In the same period, all remaining German resistance in southern Holland was eliminated. We in the north started to feel the pressure of lack of food, an eight o'clock curfew and regular sweeps to arrest men for work in Germany.

Oom Otto, Tante Jet Jonas and Tineke were wandering in the countryside outside Arnhem. When the airborne attack had failed, the Germans decided that all of Arnhem had to be evacuated. Whether this was done as a form of reprisal or because it was a strategic necessity was never made clear. There was much damage in the city of course, but large parts of the outskirts were untouched. The neighborhood where the Jonas family lived was not damaged. While most of Holland is as flat as a pancake, Arnhem is built on several steep hills. The center is low and flat, along the river, but the nicer houses are in the hilly areas. Perhaps the Germans thought these hills full of civilian houses would be too difficult to control with the Allies dug in just across the river. People were told to get out and move quickly, without taking anything beyond the bare necessities. Oom Otto and Tante Jet had bicycles and the Germans apparently did not take these. They cycled into the countryside, which is beautiful, but soon gets quite rural. The sandy soil there is not as rich as in most other parts of the Netherlands and consequently the farmers who live there are not as well off as those in other parts of the country. I do not know if there was any organized effort by whatever authorities remained in office, but it seems likely that the local farmers were ordered to take in refugees. They would most certainly not have done so out of their free will. There was just too much of a social gap between them and the people who suddenly appeared on their roads in large numbers. The Jonas family ended up with a very rural family in a very small farm. This soon became an impossible situation. The farmer and his wife were primitive types, who bossed them around and their small kid would yell at them, using their first names, a highly unusual situation in Holland in those days. The kid would bellow "Jet get out of my chair," and similar pleasantries. They started looking for better quarters and visited friends who owned and ran a well-known resort hotel out in the countryside called *"de Zilven."* I believe the family's name was Peters. Their hotel was also packed with refugees, but their friends could make room and after a while, they could move there. It was not ideal without any electricity or heat, but a lot better. As far as I know they stayed in the hotel until shortly after the liberation when Arnhem was opened up again for residents and they could return to their house. In the hotel, the food was reasonably good since they were in a farming area and things like potatoes, a commodity we would pay a fortune for in The Hague, were available. Oom Otto became one of the leaders of the refugees in the hotel. It was necessary to have some order and a set of rules to keep people in line. Oom Otto was good at that sort of thing. Shortly after they had to evacuate, Oom Otto pulled off a stunt that was quite daring and risky. He went back to his house on his bicycle. This was *verboten*, but he went anyway. He entered the front door using his key and found a group of German soldiers sitting around his dining room table, having dinner. He said, "Excuse me, but I used to live here, this is my house and I wanted to fetch something that belongs to me." He went to the living room where they had a small piano that Oom Otto used to play on. (He played quite well.) The piano stood in a corner, diagonally, so there was room behind it to put things. He had put a big box with their sterling silverware there. Oom Otto reached over the piano, got the box, and walked out with it while the Germans looked on slightly overwhelmed.

Tante Jet was involved in the operation and organization of the kitchen in the hotel and had many rich stories after the war about the fights among the women in the kitchen. It was during this period that Tineke met Jaap Kort, a young man who was hiding out in the area, trying to stay away from being sent to Germany for work. Jaap's name was Kort, which means "short" in Dutch, an odd coincidence for a very tall man. At one point before the liberation, the Germans had seized Jaap and put him to work cutting wood. With an unexpected sense of humor, they paired him with a fellow called Klein (short) and called them *Holzcommando Kurz und Klein* – wood commando Kort and Klein – a term that in German and Dutch refers to smashing something to pieces – *kort en klein slaan.*

In October the Allies started to broaden their grip on the southern part of Holland. Den Bosch and Tilburg were liberated and in Limburg a tank battle near Overloon raged for weeks and destroyed Overloon and Venraay, two small towns. By early November, the central and western parts of the province of Noord Brabant were cleared of Germans. North of the rivers the first signs of serious starvation began to be noticed in the big cities. To retaliate against the railway strike the German authorities, specifically Seyss Inquard, the Reichscommisar, had cut of all food deliveries to the western part of the country. Our daily rations were down to very little and we were living in a society where everybody fended for themselves. By November the first food transports, by barge from Friesland to Amsterdam and along the canals to Rotterdam and The Hague were allowed.

Around November 21, the Wehrmacht began a citywide sweep in the city of The Hague and its suburbs, hunting men for work in Germany. It was significant that the regular German army executed this manhunt. Up until then the army had not participated in direct actions of this kind against civilians. Naturally it also involved me. Along the grapevine I had heard that widespread action was coming. Across from us lived a family named Prinsen. Mr. Prinsen was high up in the Dutch civil service. He worked for Mr. Frederiks, the secretary general of the Department of the Interior. Each government department had a secretary general, a career civil servant who managed the department while the ministers who were political appointees were politically responsible for its actions. The ministers came and went with the various cabinets while the secretaries general stayed. When the queen left with her Cabinet, the secretaries general were left to run the country. Obviously, they had to toe the line with the Germans and in several departments Dutch Nazis were appointed as secretary general, but many others stayed on and did their best to save what they could. As could be expected, these functionaries were in a very difficult position. They could very easily be accused of being collaborators and in certain cases they did execute orders they should have refused. After the war I became good friends with Jan Frederiks, son of the secretary general of the interior who was forced into retirement. His position had been particularly difficult since his department was supervising all mayors of all the towns and villages, and these mayors had to execute numerous German ordinances that were onerous such as reporting all Jewish citizens, etc. I got to know Mr. Frederiks as a very likeable, quite formal gentleman who had obviously not been a willing collaborator. Ma knew Mrs. Prinsen since she came from Leeuwarden and therefore could be implicitly trusted. Her maiden name was Janke de Jong. Her first name was very Frisian, but in Dutch the verb *"janken"* sounds odd. It means whining or squealing like a young dog does. Obviously among ourselves we always called her Janke de Jong and not Mrs. Prinsen. Prinsen proved a reliable source of information for us. When Janke came across the street to warn us that meant she had reliable information. This time she warned that huge "razzias" were planned, and said I had better go somewhere else. Again I had to find a family with either small children or daughters who would be willing to take me in. This was not as easy as it sounded because the people who took you in were definitely running a large risk. We feared the Germans would come door to door with specific information about the whereabouts of young men. Luckily, this proved not to be the case. The soldiers just came door-to-door asking if there were any men. So after all I did not have to move away, but again we did not know this beforehand.

Eelco Apol came to the rescue. Eelco had very recently become engaged to a girl who lived in Leidschendam, a village next to Voorburg. I was somewhat stunned by having a friend who was engaged. At nineteen years old, we were not all that mature in those days. Eelco's fiancée was Ellen Schlagwein, a very attractive slender girl with jet-black hair and beautiful big, almost black, eyes. She was quite mature for her age, very articulate and fun to be with. What made her even more attractive to us was that she had lived in England for a number of years and spoke beautiful English. Ellen had a much younger sister called Ansje who was a scrawny little girl. Ellen's parents were a different cattle of fish. Her father was a businessman who would be called a "smoothy" in this country. He had a round bald head and almost always a twinkle in his eyes and a sly grin. He ran a paint distributing business that belonged to a friend of his, a Mr. van Someren, no relation to Netty's mother. Van Someren was an Englishman who had been interned by the Germans when they found him in Holland. His wife and daughter Doreen were not interned, I believe because they claimed to be Dutch. Doreen was a very pretty girl with slightly Asian features which made her even more attractive. Her mother was one of those people who lean on others for everything, seem incapable of managing their own affairs, and still get away with making a general nuisance of themselves.

Ellen's mother was a friendly housewifely soul who was quite overweight and wrestled with the problem that everybody knew that her husband had a girlfriend and that he visited her regularly. Mr. Schlagwein made good money on the side, probably by selling paint in the black market. He had all sorts of contacts among the local black market people, and as a result, there was plenty good food in their house. The family lived in a quite small house and it was unbelievably generous of the Schlagweins that they were willing to take

RAZZIA IN ROTTERDAM WINTER 1944.

Eelco and me in, feed us and also take the risk of hiding us. It was the kind of family where "anything goes." There was father, mother, the two daughters and a live-in maid, Marie who was a slightly retarded woman. There also were two totally undisciplined dogs who would climb on the kitchen counter and eat our food if nobody was watching. All in all, a quite chaotic household but a fun place to be and an ideal wartime hiding place. Anybody searching this smallish house would see so many people, mostly women, running around and so many messy rooms full of clothes and other things that he would get quickly confused.

On the third (attic) floor of the house were three small bedrooms where Ellen and her sister slept. Two of these rooms had windows set in dormers, as is customary in most Dutch houses. These windows looked out over a nursery garden where vegetables were grown. The third room had no windows. That was where Marie slept in sort of a double bed. Eelco and I were given Marie's bed and Marie was sent to the couch in the living room. Everybody washed in the sink in the one bathroom on the second floor. The Germans came almost immediately after we arrived. It was very early in the morning and Mrs. Schlagwein raised the alarm.

Mr. Schlagwein was not home, probably visiting his girlfriend. Looking out of the windows in the very early morning light we could see the German soldiers in the nursery walking in a line formation and firing a couple of shots at men running away. We decided to climb out the window of Ellen's room and hide by lying down on top of the two dormers. We were in our pajama's and it was November and brisk outside. Also, the dormers were covered with gravel and the gravel was wet. We lay there for about an hour until the women in the house had calmed down and gotten themselves together and Ellen appeared at the window. Pretending she was looking out, she softly told us to come down when she would give us a signal and hide inside the house. A most welcome proposition!

Soon we came back inside, got quickly dressed, and went downstairs where they had a big heavy, high bookcase in the living room that stood against a niche in the wall. The bookcase was much wider than the niche so we could climb over the book case and lower ourselves into the niche, which was just wide enough for us to sit in on a few cushions. From inside the room you had to be told there was an indentation in the wall to realize someone could be hiding there. As the day went by, people came to visit and we had to keep very quiet. Late in the morning we heard several loud knocks on the front door (there was no more power so doorbells did not work) and two German soldiers stepped inside. Mrs. Schlagwein accosted them in a friendly way and explained there were no men in the house, pointing at all the women and girls crowding around her. The two soldiers did not even make an effort to look upstairs or inside. They just left. Later we heard that their unit had come by bicycle from the northern part of Holland and had been riding all night. They were dog-tired and lacked sleep. Since there were still plenty of Germans around, it was not safe for us to emerge from our hiding place. Also, it just happened to be Ansje's birthday that day and in the afternoon a number of little girls arrived who were entertained and fed whatever was still available in those days. Eelco and I had to sit there behind the bookcase and keep very quiet.

Towards the end of the afternoon, there was a great hullabaloo when Dorien van Someren arrived in tears to tell us that her boyfriend Rob Hartog had been picked up by the Germans in a sweep and was being transported to Delft where all the men were concentrated while awaiting transport to Germany. After Mrs. Schlagwein had cleared the house of miscellaneous stray strangers, she gave Eelco and me permission to climb out of our hiding place and join the crowd. Eelco's first words were: "I am going to the bathroom because I've had to hold in a poop all day!" *Ik heb de hele dag een keutel onderdrukt!* Dorien had a miserable evening and night, but the next day Rob showed up. He had managed to escape. As the men were marched through the narrow streets of Delft, housewives had left their front doors open and urged men to slip inside their houses. As in many smaller Dutch towns the houses fronted directly on the street there. Rob had seized such an opportunity and simply walked away. The Germans had no real control over the number of people they had picked up so they were unable to check how many they had exactly lost in the shuffle. Also, that first night after the sweep, there was a knock on the door late at night. We all scurried away again to our hiding places and Mrs. Schlagwein opened the door carefully. There was blackout, of course, and no electricity. It appeared the two German soldiers who had been at the door that morning had returned and asked if they could stay with us, become deserters in other words. This was of course impossible, and it was a sign of the deterioration of the German army that these fellows were trying to get out in a foreign country and risk their lives doing it. It also meant in my view, that they had a hunch there were more people in the house than just the women who came to the door.

During the following days, we had quite a good time at the Schlagweins. The house was very crowded, but we could get along well and we played games. Rob played the piano quite well. How we got into this I don't know, but we started doing spiritualist seances, half in jest and half seriously. We would sit in a circle around a small table with our hands flat on the surface. Our hands would touch. All of a sudden the table would start making jerky moves up and down. We would ask a question and the table would spell out an answer by letting us recite the alphabet and jumping up when we got to the right letter. We would form words. Rob, whose parents were in Indonesia, asked where they were and got as answer the name of a village in the mountains where they had a vacation home. I still remember the name of the village, Tjepiring Koppeng. This was a source of great satisfaction for Rob and for us it was a sign that there was some merit in the experiment because surely nobody in the room knew the name of that place. Occasionally I quickly glanced under the table because I suspected that Mr. Schlagwein was fooling us. He was certainly the type of man who could successfully pull something like that off. I never caught him or anybody else. Rob's parents were probably not in the vacation house but in a Japanese concentration camp, but at that time we believed the ghosts!

After a few days the Schlagweins decided we had to move. It was too obvious that there were a large number of people in their house. We found a new address nearby with a family that had a warehouse connected to their house and a large attic in the warehouse that had a false ceiling and provided an excellent hiding place for several men. Eelco and I went over to the new address and met with our host and hostess, Mr. and Mrs. Schulte Nordholt. They had married a little late but still had a baby boy. They had a big house and let us sit in the living room during the daytime and early evening. At night we were locked in the hidden attic and in the morning we were released again. I don't recall what business our host was in, it was some kind of wholesale business, which like all economic activity in those times, was dormant. There were two other men who joined us in the attic, one was a fairly nervous fellow who was married and had two small daughters. When his family came to visit him he burst out in tears. Not exactly the kind of man you wanted to be with in stressful times. The other fellow was calmer, also married and quite a humorist. He told us a series of jokes as we were trying to get to sleep in the evening. There also was an au pair living with the family, a sturdy very Dutch girl from the country somewhere. She told Eelco and me in confidence that she had her bedroom door locked all night because our host had tried several times to visit, pleading for understanding and friendship. We did not stay there very long since the risk of further razzias was diminished. One evening in the darkness of the blackout I went back home. I would stay there "for the duration." I did build a hiding place in our own house just in case, but I spent only one night there. It was in our attic, next to the maid's room where I slept during the last months of the war.

Electricity and gas service had been cut off in the entire western Netherlands. This brought new challenges. Our neighbor Mr. Wachter, the young dentist, still had power because of his profession. Recall that we had a house that was in a three-under-one-roof configuration. Our house and the Wachters were on the outside, the older couple with the son who was accused of Nazi sympathies were in the middle. Mr. Wachter got a transformer and a long piece of wire and tossed the wire from his front balcony, past our in- between-neighbors porch over to ours. We brought the wire inside to our living room downstairs where we had a small reflector with a light bulb from an automobile headlight. Thanks to our neighbor and using very little of his precious power, we still had some light at night that way. We had to keep this light connection secret so we told my parent's friends who came to play bridge that we had a car battery.

As winter came, it got progressively colder. Later we learned that by some diabolically cruel quirk the winter of 1944-45 was one of the coldest on record for Western Europe. My parents played bridge with an older couple, Mr. and Mrs. Zeylstra, who were evacuees from Arnhem and were friends of Oom Otto and Tante Jet. They had a son who lived with his family in the street that was perpendicular to ours. There were tensions in the family of Zeylstra jr. because the son had started an affair with a lady who lived in the same street, so the parents asked us if they could stay with us. My parents agreed, which was quite a decision since these people had to share all the food with us and there was not much. The Zeylstras were not entirely helpless in the food department, however. Their son, a lawyer, worked in the government department that was responsible for all food supplies and therefore had the inside track in getting some extras. We spent the entire winter with the Zeylstras and had remarkably little friction with them. Our real salvation was a very big, extremely heavy wooden crate that arrived one night in the darkness. It was a box Oom Anne in Friesland used to ship spare parts to his drilling rigs in the countryside. It came by way of a small canal skipper who delivered it to our door. When we opened it, it was filled with potatoes. This one shipment put us in a very advantageous position. We could even afford to give some of our potatoes to others; Anna our cleaning lady got quite a few, and we also invited a small boy who was referred to us by a church-related social service for a meal once a week.

Food supplies diminished rapidly and we also had a great scarcity of coal and wood to burn in our stoves. Every day large numbers of people passed our house on their way from the city to the countryside. They were all looking for food, trying to buy whatever they could get from farmers, paying for their supplies with money, silverware, fur coats and whatever they could find that might provoke the farmer's interest. Everybody knew that the people in the small farms that dotted the Dutch countryside had held back potatoes, vegetables, milk, butter, cheese and meat from the authorities. They did very well selling their products on the black market. Who could blame them? Getting firewood also became a real problem. There were no woods in our area and the police guarded the parks. The park surrounding the Montessori school was inaccessible because there were German troops billeted in the school. People started to burn up surplus wood they had in their houses, garage doors, attic floors, etc. All this wood was needed to operate the small cooking stoves everybody had. They were small cylindrical affairs, about a foot high made out of stovepipe metal. They had two openings to allow air to circulate inside. In the interior of the stovepipe was an even smaller vessel made out of cast iron in which one could burn small blocks of wood. The whole contraption was placed on the open top of the larger pot bellied stove in the living room and the necessary draft was provided through the larger stove. Once the wood was ignited, it burned fast and frequently needed to be replenished, but it burned very hot and provided efficient heat to cook on.

It was my task to go into the garage every day and saw wood into small blocks, small enough to fit in the small stove. I also had to grind wheat we had obtained on the black market or through Pa's company. Royal Dutch Shell made quite an effort to provide its employees with extra food. Every once in awhile we would receive word by mail, or through the grapevine, that there was something to be distributed to employees. Once they had wheat and another time they had pure cooking fat made from seals that were hunted in the tidal flats north of Friesland. Apparently, the company had gotten permission for a professional hunter to go out and shoot seals. The fat derived from these animals was refined in the company's lab in Amsterdam and transported with canal boats that used diesel fuel the company still was allowed to use.

When we had wheat, we baked bread at home. Pa was good at that. After a few false starts, Ma had given up and yielded the baking department to my father. The trick was to get yeast to leaven the bread. I think we got it from a bakery. We had a small coffee grinder, which I clamped on to a workbench we had in the attic. I would sit on the workbench to stabilize it and grind away for hours, every time producing a small tray full of meal. It took at least an hour of grinding to get enough meal for one loaf of bread. As the winter progressed, we moved to the dining room in the back of the house. This room was not visible from the street and it was smaller, therefore easier to heat. There was not much heating material anyway, but the lengthy cooking process certainly improved the temperature. I had plenty of time to read during that long cold winter. I could not go out and my friends could not leave their homes either so I had little else to do than read a lot. I plowed through a number of big tomes on architecture and history, books I borrowed from friends. I had read almost all the books my parents had and their library was not a small one.

In mid–December, we got the devastating news of the German offensive in the Belgian Ardennes region. The German attack was a complete surprise. The Germans had managed to amass a large force that remained undetected despite elaborate preparations, a noticeable increase in train movements, and the disappearance from the front of whole crack units that were pulled back and kept in reserve. On a day carefully chosen for bad weather so the Allied air superiority was useless, they attacked with overwhelming force. The American divisions that came under attack were mostly not seasoned troops while the Germans brought in hardened SS veterans from the eastern front. The Americans fought bravely and offered well coordinated defensive action, but they were outnumbered and in a lengthy battle that was fought in snow and ice under very cold weather, the American line was rolled back. This battle was later named "the Battle of the Bulge," referring to the bulge in the Allied front created by the German penetration.

The battle raged until December 24 when the weather broke and the Allied air forces could finally come into action and destroy the German forces which had not reached their objective, which was to penetrate unto Antwerp and cut off the forces now in northern Belgium and southern Holland. We suffered a tremendous emotional letdown when this offensive started. We thought the Allies were strong and invincible and now saw that the Germans were far from beaten. When Christmas arrived, there was not much to celebrate. The battle in the Ardennes was over, but there was no movement whatsoever in our region. On New Year's Eve, we saw an astonishing breach of discipline among the German forces. The antiaircraft guns located around The Hague that were used to fend off the Allied attacks against the V-2 launching sites, burst out in celebratory New Year's salvos. From my perch in the attic, I could see an expanse of the sky that was filled with exploding AA munitions and tracer bullets. I realized this was unusual since the Germans were not apt to fire in vain and were known to be short of ammunition. In January and February, we got a lot of snow followed by many clear, very cold days. There was a curfew from 8 p.m. until 6 a.m. so people who could not make it home would have to find a place to sleep in some farmer's hayloft. Many people did this. There also were more people coming to our door asking for food. We usually would not give them anything since we did not know if this was a provocation and would lead to more and more people coming back. We preferred to give food to people we knew.

The town opened a soup kitchen nearby and we would go there to sample the fare. It was not much more than water with a fatty taste so we left it alone. We did eat tulip bulbs and sugar beets. Many people had little else to eat. The bulbs could be roasted on a fire and tasted reasonably good. The sugar beets required a great deal of cooking and preparation, and smelled and tasted awful. We fed them together with potato peels to my boxer dog Moro who almost did not survive the winter. We went to bed very early and got up late to save our energy and we washed ourselves rarely. It was too cold to splash in front of a washstand without warm water. The Zeylstras left us in January, why and whereto I do not remember.

The war came closer on March 3, 1945. That morning we heard a squadron of tactical twin-engine bombers come over, I remember seeing them through the kitchen window where I was standing doing my chores. Immediately after I saw them coming over in a tight formation, the bombs they had just dropped detonated with a tremendous bang. A second and third set of explosions followed, and we knew somebody nearby had been hit badly. It turned out to be the Bezuidenhout quarter of The Hague, the area closest to the border of Voorburg. An hour or so later, a wave of people streamed down our street that was known as a thoroughfare to the countryside. Many people looked dazed and distressed, some were still in their nightclothes.

I went out to a spot nearby where I could look at the skyline of The Hague and saw to my amazement and distress that it had changed. Several higher buildings and particularly church towers that for decades had been familiar sights to me as I bicycled to school across a patch of open land between Voorburg and The Hague, were gone. There were lost of fires and a great deal of smoke. About 500 people died. This attack turned out to be a mistake. It hit the wrong part of town. That evening I could see the fires better as the Dutch firefighters had little equipment left to fight fires in such an extensive area. The Germans had the good taste that night to fire off a V-2 in the midst of the conflagration. The rocket misfired and fell back into the bombed-out area, killing several firefighters working there. Almost everybody in Voorburg who had extra beds offered shelter to people from the bombed-out area. We got Mr. and Mrs. Houwingh and their daughter Annetje. Their son Frits was hiding elsewhere. These people were very pleasant guests and they did not stay very long since they found better quarters elsewhere. Later I got to know their son Frits quite well. He was a fellow student in Leiden in my year and a friend of Tilly, Netty's sister.

The snow had thawed and the winter was over, but the hunger continued. The German presence in our area was now reduced to some secondary or tertiary force – older men, Ukrainians who had been pressed into German army service etc. This made it better for me since I felt I could risk going out once in a while. However, it also meant that there was a mood of desperation among the Germans that could erupt anytime into some atrocity, and many atrocities were committed in those final days, including the shooting of Oom Bernard. People began to behave more and more lawless. They were now cutting down trees in the streets, right in front of our house. I remember waking up one morning hearing sawing, and looking out of the window, I saw two men who quickly cut down the tree in front of our house. They sawed off the main part of the trunk which was about 15 inches across, and carted it off, leaving all the branches and the leaves that had begun to sprout on the street.

By mid-March, the news from the eastern as well as the western front indicated that the end was near. We got information about the progress of the war through underground newsletters. The Dutch press, which was of course still adhering to the German party line, could not hide the continuing decline of the "third Reich." Our connection with the radio "through the telephone" proved helpful because it continued working although we had not had electrical power for several months. We could hear the German news broadcasts and being able to read between the lines knew that the Russians were in Germany, approaching Berlin, and that the Allies were also across the Rhine and rapidly moving towards a meeting with the Russians. It was very clear that it would not be long before we were free.

The Dutch government-in-exile had made a deal with Sweden and later Switzerland through which these countries would send ships with food to Holland. These ships had arrived in the small port of Delfzijl, in the province of Groningen, and negotiations started to allow this food to be shipped further on to the densely populated and starving provinces of western Holland. Finally, it arrived; just before we were free we all received a loaf of white bread and a package of real margarine. This food was such a delicacy for all of us that it tasted better than the best cake. Every family established its own rules for consuming it. Most people had each individual keep their own hoard and everyone nibbled from time to time on the bread.

Being hungry is a strange thing. You loose weight, of course, but it very much depends on your own metabolism and your age to determine how you will behave and how you will look. I remember going to bed cold and quite hungry and dreaming vividly about food. I dreamt about going camping and cooking my own food. I also remember how the long periods I spent in bed made my hipbone feel tender. Lying on my side without too much flesh to cushion my weight became noticeably uncomfortable. Everybody was thin and I have never believed the excuses overweight people nowadays have that they get fat even while they do not eat. I have seen a whole population get thin, without any exception. When you don't eat you loose weight. Men, my father included, were still wearing three-piece suits with ties. Their shirt collars were often hanging almost down on their chests. I had in the meantime gotten involved as a "gofer" with the local Resistance people who had some extra Swedish bread, and it was my job to deliver it to a few very needy people. It was a real experiences to knock on people's doors and find them open it very cautiously after quite a while, probably because they had to hide people inside. I then told them I was sent to give them a loaf of bread. They often wanted to pay me or make some gesture of gratitude. I told them not to make a scene because of the neighbors and left.

In the final days, the Allies made another deal with the Germans. The RAF and the U.S. Air Force were allowed to drop food in designated areas near the starving Dutch cities. The small airport of Ypenburg where the paratroopers had made a failed landing in 1940 was one of the areas where food was dropped. I could move around quite freely by then and went to see what was happening. It was a wonderful sight to see these huge bombers come in at almost tree top level and drop their loads. The British bombers dropped burlap bags with packs of margarine, flour and other foodstuffs. The Americans dropped large cardboard cartons with military emergency meals. Each box had to be opened and the contents, pieces of soap, ready made food, etc., had to be sorted. So the U.S. system was much less handy to use on a large population.

One American box somehow fell too early out of a B-17. It came down in the small front yard of a house directly behind us and I rushed over to see it. A group of neighbors gathered in front of the house. The family inside had grabbed the box and opened it and showed the contents through the front window. We all cheered. At that moment a Dutch cop arrived on his bike, waded into the small crowd and gave me a very hard slap on my head. I had said something like, "You misunderstand, we are just looking." He must have thought there was a riot going on, although the group of people was really small. But these semi–nazi cops who were well fed and armed had the idea that they were the only ones saving the country from anarchy. He fired his pistol into the air and pushed me into the house. He asked me a few questions, and I tried to explain we had just been a group of friendly neighbors cheering the receipt of the air mail package. I guess he accepted that and left, jeered by the crowd. Still he fired his gun and a further small misunderstanding could have lead to bloodshed. I still seethe when I think back to this incident, and I can well understand the feelings of people who have experienced some form of undeserved police brutality.

Towards the end of April, the Germans began to make it clear that the game was up. Seiss-Inquart gave a strange speech for the radio, which we could hear because of our telephone system. In it he rambled on about the fight against Bolshevism, which had become the excuse the Germans had found for waging war throughout Europe. He wondered what would become of the Netherlands in the future and asked at the end, *"Was nun?"* (What now?) Well we knew what now, and we could not wait until it happened.

The first few days of May were very strange. The Allies entered our region from the east, not from the south as we always had expected. They were already deep into Germany and political pressure was exerted on General Montgomery to make him swing part of his forces into the Netherlands to liberate us. He was in a rush to capture as much of Germany as he could before the Russians got there. He felt the liberation of many millions of hungry Dutchmen who had to be fed and who had to sort out their pent-up rage against their own traitors, was just a nuisance that could wait. The Germans occupying Holland would fall into Allied hands out of their own weight, it was thought. After feverish pressure from the Dutch government-in-exile, which had by now established itself in the southern – liberated – part of the country, a move was made to send the First Canadian Division in to clean out the German occupation of Holland. As was the case five years earlier when everything started, it was beautiful spring weather. Everyday I went on my mother's bike (without tires, but with rubber strips on the rims) to a bridge over the Vliet canal where the big highway towards the east entered Voorburg. A huge crowd was waiting there and it took several days before we saw Allied troops.

There was still a German soldier standing guard on the bridge and unbeknownst to him people crowding around him had put a small orange flower in the barrel of his gun. A nervous SS man came by driving towards Germany in a small car. When he saw the crowd he panicked, pulled out his pistol and fired. His aim was poor. He shot through his left front fender right into his tire. So he ended up trying to change his tire in the crowd and it was a wonder that he was not lynched then and there.

Strange skinny-looking men came by on foot, dressed in rags. They were escapees from a concentration camp and too cautious to say much or reveal where they came from or were heading to. Finally towards the evening of May 4th, a group of scout cars raced by. In it were a group of British officers, who looked to us incredibly well fed, well dressed in their battle dress and black berets and well equipped with brand-new-looking scout cars. These were the first Allied troop to enter The Hague. They moved in and looked around and raced out again. The next day the real force came. They were Canadian soldiers with Sherman tanks and many individual soldiers on motorbikes. Thousands of motorized troops followed and pandemonium broke loose. We heard the Germans had capitulated officially on May 5. Shortly afterwards the main forces in Germany itself surrendered unconditionally as the Allies had demanded. Hitler had committed suicide and Admiral Raeder, the former submarine commander, had taken over as substitute Führer only to throw in the towel after a day or two.

The next day I awoke and realized it was all over. I cannot describe the feelings that rushed through me. The future could be very uncertain. But now I could control my own destiny. I could go wherever I wanted and do whatever I liked. I was free! For those who never have lived under a repressive regime it is impossible to grasp how the release of pent-up frustration over the controls, threats and terror that have shackled your life for years changes you. Your entire outlook on life is suddenly different. There is hope, there is a future and there is freedom from fear. To be free is precious and worth any sacrifice!

14 : *The War Is Over.*
Now What?

I was a teenager when the war started. When it ended, I was for all practical purposes a twenty-year-old adult. But since I had not really been able to spread my wings during the last few years of the war, I was far from a "real" adult. I had spent years with my parents at home, saw mostly old friends living nearby, and was in a state of suspension in my development. All my friends were in the same position, so my lack of sophistication and "savoir faire" did not show and did not bother me. I knew all about war, bombing, assassinations and executions, torture and concentration camps, but I knew little about "life." I was a late bloomer. Compared with today's twenty-year-olds, and using today's vernacular, you could say I was out to lunch most of the time. But I did have a strong desire to catch up with what I had missed and to find out what the world was all about. Not surprisingly, I wanted to leave the nest almost immediately, hardly astonishing in view of all we had been through.

But leaving the place where I had been cooped up so very long was easier said than done. The country was devastated and there was absolutely no transportation. In the summer of 1945, Holland began the long and difficult road to recovery and like everybody else I had to use my own ingenuity to find ways to, at least temporarily, leave the nest. There were no hotels, summer resorts, camps or anything else in operation, so the only thing you could do was visit relatives or old family friends. And that is what I did that summer. I went to visit people I had known for years but had not seen for quite a while. They re-entered my life in a different fashion. They were adults, of course, and now they generally began to treat me as an adult too. Given the layers of respect and distance separating Dutch generations in those days, I felt I had stepped over a huge barrier and quickly gained a very different perspective of my relatives and old family friends. With the war behind us, we all turned over a new leaf. We rebuilt old relationships and exchanged stories about what had happened to us in the last year of the war when communications had become extremely difficult and it was dangerous to be too explicit in letters. The telephones had not worked for more than six months so letters were the only way to stay in touch. After the liberation we all stepped out of our wartime cocoon and we all began to inter-relate much more intensely with a broader circle of people. We could begin to live a more normal life. Having been deprived of direct contact with many people who did not live in the same area, my contacts with the outside world quickly multiplied.

The story of the first few months after we were liberated seem to offer a good point to interrupt the narrative and offer a few short vignettes. I will discuss life immediately after the war and give my impressions of my renewed contact with direct relatives and also my impressions of Netty's direct relatives (whom I learned to know much later, of course.) I hope that by putting them in perspective now will make them more recognizable when I mention them again later on.

In the first few weeks following the liberation I often went to The Hague. That was the first place where I could go and feel a little independent. I went there to nose around and buy cigarettes on the black market that sprung up immediately after the arrival of the Allies. Canadian and British soldiers would drive up to these black markets usually located on street corners, and swap their ample cigarette rations for all kinds of goods offered. Money was not accepted. Our Dutch money of the Nazi era had no value. We quickly got to know Canadian cigarette brands such as Sweet Caporal and MacDonald's. In addition there were the English brands such as Gold Flake, Players and Wild Woodbine. I guess most of these brands now have only historical value. I usually went into town with a group of friends. I guess we all wanted to see if there was any action. We found a place where we could dance. It was a perfectly respectable place, probably a dance school somewhere on the Noordeinde, the street where the Royal Palace is located. There was not much there beyond a dance floor and a record player playing music of the prewar swing era.

Hanging around outside, gathering up the courage to go in and pretending I was doing this every day, I observed a British soldier also hanging around and smoking a cigarette. We all craved their cigarettes, but I did not want to ask for one like many people did. Cigarettes were better than money in those days. They bought anything the soldiers liked to have, particularly love. The soldiers had an ample supply of cigarettes and that meant they could have almost any woman they liked. The soldier I saw standing there was smoking and when he was through, he tossed the cigarette butt down on the street. Immediately a man came out of nowhere and swooped in to pick the butt up. This was my first introduction to *"buk shag."* We called the tobacco we used for hand rolling cigarettes *shag* and to stoop in Dutch is *bukken*. So *"buk shag"* was the name given to tobacco that was to be reused and was gathered by picking up butts. Despite its questionable origin, this tobacco was probably better than the homegrown product we had used in the final year. After I had found the courage to pay the entry fee to enter the dancing place, I found myself confronted with another postwar phenomenon. The dancing and social scene was now domi-nated on the male side by the liberators. Soldiers from various Allied units, including the Dutch "Prinses Irene Brigade," a small unit that had been given the privilege of liberating The Hague. They were all healthy, well-fed guys with tans, nice uniforms and, most important, cigarettes and chocolate in their pockets. They also danced the "jitterbug" a new style of dancing unfamiliar to us poor ill-clothed and underfed wretches. We only knew how to dance the fox trot. Not much opportunity for us to pick up a nice girl. The Dutch girls (of the kind that would go alone to a dance hall) knew immediately where to find the right men and learned how to jitterbug through osmosis.

As could be expected, we had an explosion of sexual activity between Allied soldiers and many willing Dutch women. Despite the fact that the soldiers were routinely provided with free condoms, a wave of out-of-wedlock births started nine months after Liberation–Day and continued for quite a while. Virginal local boys like me had more success in meeting girls in the many house parties that were orga-nized after the liberation. At these parties we danced and necked a little. We made very little progress with the girls because most of us were still shy and not adventure-some and our girlfriends were equally inexperienced. There was little if anything to drink or eat at these gatherings, but we had fun nevertheless.

❧

Another new thing was the block or street party. Right after the German capit-ulation, people started to gather on the streets to chat, exchange news and meet friends. It was just so nice to be able to be outside in the evening with no blackout and no fear of being picked up by the Germans. One such gathering place in my neighborhood was the Prins Albert Laan, a side street to the Parkweg where I lived and a stone's throw away from our house. Frits Greup lived there and I had walked that street for many years going to the Montessori School. Immediately after the liberation, a large group of older and younger people started to gather there in the evenings. We exchanged war stories and many people revealed what they had done for the Resistance in the last year of the war. Frits had kept his family's radio hidden in their attic and had supplied notes on news broadcasts to the local underground press. Some people who had lived quiet inconspicuous lives came suddenly to the fore, emerging as active Resistance workers. For instance, next door to Frits lived a Mr. Fromeine who appeared to have been a leader in the local Resistance. He worked his way quite quickly into the interim military authority that was organized by the Dutch government to take power after the German occupation ended. Within a few short weeks, he walked around in a nice uniform with the rank of captain and having become important, stopped attending our impromptu street meetings.

To avoid chaos and anarchy, there was a need to reestablish law and order and for that reason, a plan had been worked out by the government-in-exile in London to create a military authority and initially give all powers to it. This authority, called *Militair Gezag* (Military Authority), would oversee all civilian authorities and start the postwar cleansing of all Nazi elements. There had been fears of riots and of people taking the law in their own hands by going after the remaining Nazis. There were also some subliminal fears of communist takeovers, strikes, civil unrest and other politically inspired activities. Remarkably, there was little of this and after some months the civilian authorities could take over again and the *Militair Gezag* people faded away. Electricity was quickly restored so we could play music on the street with a record player and we started dancing in the streets. Later when we could move farther afield the street parties died down, but it was fun and relaxing as long as it lasted that late spring and early summer.

Transportation was nonexistent and hitchhiking became *"de rigueur."* There was an unwritten rule that anybody who had wheels was more or less obligated to take on people who were asking for a ride. So we would walk along the road going to The Hague and hail a guy with a horse-drawn cart and ride along with him into town. Going farther outside town required knowledge of places where one could get a ride on a truck or similar vehicle. The Allies had made a fleet of trucks available to transport food and other necessities into the densely populated part of western

Holland. You heard along the grapevine where truck convoys were departing and went there to ask for a ride. Using that method I went to Arnhem to see Tante Jet, Oom Otto and Tineke. They had just returned from their forced stay outside the beleaguered city and reoccupied their house. The Germans had done very little damage to it and had not carted away any furniture. In general the Germans did not destroy much in the houses they occupied. However, in Arnhem they had started to take away furniture on a wholesale basis, robbing houses that were forcibly abandoned and bringing the furniture in large truckloads to the bombed-out cities in Germany. The house of Oom Otto and Tante Jet was spared from this for some reason. When I arrived at their house at Paulus Potter Straat No. 7, things were generally as before. They had worked hard, to clean up and get their house back in shape, of course, but most of their furniture and other things were intact. Several houses in the neighborhood had been less fortunate. There I saw damage from bombs and artillery shells and many broken windows. There was also some evidence of looting with people's possessions strewn all over. Very few inhabitants had returned to the severely damaged houses.

Harrietta Allegonda Hesselink, or for me Tante Jet, was my mother's elder sister. She was born on May 9, 1896. She was two years older than my mother. Throughout their life, the sisters were very close and they stayed close until they got too old and could not travel to see each other any more and were also too confused and deaf to enjoy each other's company. They grew up without a mother, although their stepmother whom I called "Oma Dik" probably did her best to act as a surrogate mother. Opa Dik remarried in 1901, when Tante Jet was five. Tante Jet and my mother were very different. In many respects they were almost opposites. When I look at pictures of the two sisters as very young girls, I can see the difference between them. Aaltje, my mother, looks confident and self-assured but more introverted. Jet looks more pugnacious and extrovert and that's the way they were. My mother was very strongly attached to her father. Tante Jet was probably equally attached to her father and sister but more closemouthed about it. She had a more detached, less emotional and more "matter of fact" attitude towards her siblings, her father, her own family and life in general. She married young and was less interested in intellectual pursuits. My mother was always reading books, sometimes quite "heavy" literature, including, for instance, the life of Don Quixote in old Spanish. Jet was not interested in literature. Compared to my mother, Jet was only an average student in school. She was less articulate but much better at sports. In fact, she must have been quite athletic when she was young. She could also be much more assertive in her relationships with others than my mother. I always had a very warm and good relationship with her and have the best memories of her.

Tante Jet was more practical in her decision-making and better coordinated and better at working with her hands. She was not as tall as my mother was and both were of sturdy Frisian build. Tante Jet was more interested in clothes and in her general appearance and dressed better than my mother. She had been engaged to Oom Otto since she was quite young. During World War I Otto was an officer in the Dutch army and served in a heavy-infantry guards regiment called the *"Grenadiers."* Tall men were chosen for this regiment. Oom Otto was tall. Another guards regiment, the *"Jagers,"* favored short men. The name *Grenadiers* is self-explanatory. *Jagers* is probably derived from the French *Chasseurs* and goes back to the Napoleonic period when French customs prevailed in the Dutch army. They were what we now call light infantry. Many words and general terms currently used in the Dutch army still are rooted in French and reflect Napoleon's domination of all things military in the beginning of the eighteen hundreds.

While Otto served in the army, my mother would tell me how she and her father would tease her sister Jet because she felt duty bound to write her fiancé every day and had to wash and mend his often well-worn underwear. In the evenings when she was writing Otto, they would ask her what she was writing about. Did she write what she had to eat and when she went to the bathroom, etc? Oom Otto must have been a very persistent suitor. When they married on April 26, 1920, a year and a half after the war ended, they must have been engaged for several years. Jet had only a high school education and had seen little of the world beyond the very provincial environment of Leeuwarden where both bride and groom grew up.

After school Tante Jet worked briefly as an x-ray assistant at the local hospital in Leeuwarden. I don't think she became a nurse—she wouldn't have had time to complete the course before she got married. Oom Otto's father was *directeur,* (manager) of the local post office. Unfortunately I know little else about Oom Otto's parents. I don't even know the name of his mother. I remember seeing a photograph of Otto's father, a lean man with a mustache and a full head of gray hair. His son, Otto Jan Jonas was born on February 3, 1894. A few years later, he had a second son, Jaap, whom I met several times. The father and both brothers seemed to prefer working for the government. That meant relatively low income but total job security.

Otto spent his entire career with the Dutch governmental land survey system, the *Kadaster* or cadastre, the official register of land ownership. Oom Otto was deeply involved in a system called *"Ruilverkaveling"* – reallocation through exchange – that over the years played an important role in bringing parcels of farmland together to a workable size. Most farms in Holland are small and farm families were traditionally large, when generations follow each other, the land is often split up into progressively smaller lots. The Dutch legal system, based on the *Code Napoleon,* gives each child and the surviving spouse an equal share of the estate of a deceased parent. When a farmer died, his land was divided among his usually numerous offspring. Consequently, a farmer can end up owning a collection of smaller randomly scattered pieces of land. Using a complicated system of swaps the government tries to mediate between farmers to give them more economically viable farms. When he was at the peak of his career, Oom Otto was in charge of a large area of the country and his official title was *"Ingenieur Verificateur."* On the Internet I found a review of a Dutch book that discussed the *Ruilverkaveling.* It is a doctoral dissertation by a lady called Gerrie Andela who grew up on a farm and describes the impact the reallocation of land in the 1950's had on Dutch farmers. It was an effort to make Dutch farms more productive in order to reduce subsidies. In addition, the government began to offer assistance and education to farm families to change their habits of cooking among the animals and eating meals in among the farming equipment. People were taught how to install hot water heaters and showers and were urged to use electric power instead of generators and kerosene. The result was a vast modernization of the rural population, but also a more boring landscape as roads were improved, canals straightened, and hedges removed. An interesting statistic is that in 1955 there were still 220,000 working horses in the Netherlands. Ten years later this number was halved. Oom Otto must have participated in the early stages of this effort, which was probably something he did not totally agree with.

Oom Otto's brother Jaap had a law degree and worked as official recorder (or registrar) of mortgages (*hypotheekbewaarder)* in the city of Zutphen. Oom Otto once told me he had hoped to become a notary, but did not pass the highly competitive exam required to be admitted to the government sponsored course that leads to an appointment for a profession that can be very lucrative. Notaries in Holland are really highly specialized lawyers who handle all wills, real estate transactions, corporate mergers and many other functions normally performed by attorneys in the U.S.

Otto and Jet Jonas started married life in Leeuwarden, renting a house on the Harlingerstraatweg next door to Anne and Mieke Deibel. Anne was a first cousin of Jet. So they did not stray far from the reservation. While Oom Otto's job was mostly administrative, he would travel frequently to settle disputes between farmers who not surprisingly always thought that the piece of land they were giving up was more valuable than the one they got in exchange. Their house was in a post–WW I development, built to alleviate a housing shortage. I have described the houses in my sketch of Anne and Mieke Deibel. Very simple small houses with virtually no luxury at all. After WW II civil servants were paid much better than before the war., but during his life Oom Otto was certainly not overpaid. He did have job security, but almost all his life he had to resign himself to counting every *"dubbeltje"* (dime). My parents were considerably better off. I do not think my father ever got any financial support from his wealthy parents, but he was simply much better compensated as an executive at Royal Dutch Shell.

This difference in income was a constant source of jealousy for Tante Jet. As Tante Jet grew older she commented more often about her disadvantaged position. This embarrassed my parents who could not do much about it anyway. Surprisingly it became less of an issue after Oom Otto's death. By that time the postwar socialist "cradle-to-grave" regime had taken hold and among many other things improved the compensation levels of civil servants and also the pension rights of their widows. For Tante Jet this was a godsend because in the old days widows' pensions in the Dutch civil service were scandalously low. I remember in the early days my mother – who could never keep any confidential information – saying that Oom Otto's salary was only 4,000 guilders a year. That is about $2,500 at the going exchange rate at the time. Not a big salary, of course, but it was more than it seems today as the purchasing power of money has decreased so much. It was probably closer to a salary of about $ 50,000 today. Most important, these compensation levels reflected the severe economic depression we went through in the thirties. Imagine what the income for a widow of a man earning that salary would have been! I do not want to leave the impression that Tante Jet was constantly referring to her lower level of spending money. She was usually cheerful and full of optimism, but she spoke often enough about money and her lack of it for me to remember it clearly. Despite their modest income, Tante Jet and Oom Otto still had a live-in maid. That was Jikke Boonstra, a typical big-boned Frisian girl who was always in high spirits and had the habit of listening in on our conversations and laughing loudly when somebody told a joke. I remember her lingering at the dining room door after serving something and with her head just around the door, bursting out laughing when she had heard a good story. In Holland such behavior would have been very much out of the question. In Friesland where relationships between different layers of society were and are much more democratic this was natural and common behavior and this was a Frisian family, after all.

My cousin Tineke, her full names were Jantina Aleida Jonas, was born on December 16, 1923. As a very young girl she was a reasonably chubby child. When she was a little older, she became quite skinny and as a young kid she was an active happy child with a funny falsetto voice which prompted our uncle Henk (my mother's stepbrother) to call her *Kraai,* (Crow). Tante Jet was always worried about Tineke's health, which in hindsight was totally unnecessary. Tineke had a habit of keeping her head a little sideways over her left shoulder. It was discovered that this was caused by a slight tightness in a tendon in her neck and she was operated on it to stretch the tendon. At the time, Tante Jet made quite a scene about this operation. Tineke herself did not. She always was a very levelheaded, matter of fact person.

My earliest memories go back to the time that the Jonas family still lived in Leeuwarden. In Dutch the name Jonas would mean Jonah, the biblical figure that explored the whale's interior. Oom Otto and Tante Jet would joke about that. They had an antique tile hanging on the wall showing Jonah stepping unharmed out of the whale's mouth. The name Jonas is not very common in Holland, but there are several prominent people of that name. In 1950 I would find my first job with a small investment firm in Amsterdam called Jonas & Kruseman. I suspect the name is of Scandinavian origin and refers to the first name Jonas (John) and not the man in the whale. In Leeuwarden, I would play in their backyard with Tineke and her friends. Both Tineke and I remembered how Jikke would come out of the kitchen to warn us that dinner was ready,

MA WITH TANTE JET AND OOM OTTO, CA. 1937.

rhythmically crying *"Piefje Peter handenwassen eten"* – she used Tineke's nickname *"Piefje"* and announced "wash your hands–dinner."

The move to Arnhem, probably meant a promotion for Oom Otto. It certainly meant a much more interesting life in a new environment in one of Holland's most attractive cities. They were thrilled with the move and very happy with the house they rented in the Paulus Potter Straat. In those days people often rented their house. The house of Tante Jet and Oom Otto was in a street where all the houses were new and more or less similar. Renting was, of course, a good solution for people without the necessary capital, to buy a house, but the system also made it impossible for them to build up equity in their property as is common in the U.S. Buying a house U.S. style with a small down payment and a big mortgage was impossible. The Dutch financial markets did not offer that kind of lending facility. Coming from flat provincial Friesland, the hilly and varied landscape of Arnhem with many forests and much attractive scenery within easy bicycling distance from their new home was a major attraction for them. They must have moved in 1933 because I remember visiting there for the first time after I returned quite sick from a cub scout camp in Doetinchem. That was also the time that Dr. Zwolle was asked to come and see me. Later on he became a friend of the Jonas family. During the battle of Arnhem in 1944, the Germans shot him.

Oom Otto worked in the city of Arnhem. He supervised a larger territory than he had in Leeuwarden and became prominent in the ranks of his profession. A high point for him was a big meeting for the countrywide profes- sional organization of which he was chairman, which was held in The Hague. He was decorated by the Queen and made a *Ridder in de Orde van Oranje Nassau,* a decoration frequently given to leading civil servants. I believe Oom Otto got his decoration outside the traditional channels, which was more of a distinction. Every year on the Queen's birthday, a long list of people who received decorations was published, organized in the newspapers by department and called *de Lintjes Regen* (the downpour of decorations). It was customary for everybody to scan this list and write congratulatory notes to those friends and acquaintances that were among the honorees. At that time Oom Otto and Tante Jet were staying with us as houseguests as they frequently did, and I remember being impressed by the elaborate floral pieces delivered to our house, festooned with ribbons in the colors of his decoration.

Over the years Oom Otto and Tante Jet became well established in Arnhem with a wide circle of friends. They made many bicycle trips through the countryside, played high-level bridge at the local bridge club, played tennis and enjoyed life in general. In 1933 the Depression was still in full swing of course, and Oom Otto cannot have made much financial progress. Their furniture was still the same as in Leeuwarden and over the years it became well worn. Still Oom Otto enjoyed a good time and liked to go out frequently for dinner with his family to the restaurant Royal, at that time the best eatery in town.

Oom Otto was tall with strong hands and a sharply chiseled face. He had a good head of silvery gray hair. I do not think I ever saw him other than with gray hair. He had a well-developed sense of humor and always treated me like a favorite son. I sometimes thought he treated me better than his own daughter. He was friendly and warm and never made the comments on the subject of wealth comparisons that Tante Jet was apt to make. Tante Jet and he seemed to me to be quite happy together, at least in the earlier years of their marriage. Later on, particularly during the war and in the years thereafter, they were less compatible and had some large differences. I guess the stress of the war got to them. They were both Frisian people and therefore more inclined to bottle up feelings and not discuss problems or show affection. After the war there were periods during which Oom Otto seemed to be uncommunicative, silent and sour. What was really the case I think was that he was deeply depressed. Small wonder after all he went through during the war. He and Tante Jet were out-spoken in their anti–German attitudes. Before I went to the Far East I was garrisoned in and old barracks complex in Arnhem and frequently visited Tante Jet and Oom Otto. At that time, Oom Otto seemed not to be so depressed anymore, clearly on the mend and more at ease with himself. Oom Otto died on March 10 1951, on a business trip, returning home in a train traveling from Amsterdam to Arnhem. He had a massive heart attack and was gone in a very short time. He was still in his fifties. This happened shortly after I returned from Indonesia.

Tante Jet was in many respects a "fun" aunt for me. She had a much better feel for what was of interest to me as a teenager and young adult than my mother who was more inclined to feel anything I did had to be tempered and moderated and who worried that I was less of an intellectual than she had hoped. During the war my mother was constantly afraid I would get in trouble with the Germans for showing my anti–German inclinations in word or deed. After the war she was constantly afraid I would get into trouble for drinking, mixing up with the wrong friends, etc. She was a person for whom the glass was always half empty. Tante Jet was inclined to think the glass was half full.

In the summer of 1945, right after the liberation my father had a talk with me about my future. I had unsuccessfully looked for a job and was still hoping I could find one in the shipping business. This was an interesting field for me and in those days there were still a number of major Dutch shipping companies active in the country. Most of them had survived the war reasonably well since they were able to move their ships out of harm's way. Many ships were lost through German and Japanese actions, but overall the bulk of the Dutch merchant fleet was intact. My idea was therefore not foolish, but I had zero experience and no skills to offer. So Pa sat me down and suggested I try studying geology in Leiden. This was, of course, a field he was very familiar with and he was hoping I would step into his footsteps and go in the same direction. I had never thought about geology as a profession, but since I had no idea what else to do I agreed that this might be an interesting career. Once this decision was made, the next step was how to get registered in Leiden and what to do about joining the student *Corps*. Being a student without joining the Corps and going through the obligatory hazing period was, of course, out of the question. I was rather late making these decisions which meant that all the rooms in popular places were taken and I had to search at the outskirts of town for a place to stay. As in many other instances in my life, I entered this project of becoming a student in Leiden totally unprepared. I had not made any plans in the months before the academic year started. I had not looked for any friends who were going in the same direction, and I was certainly not "briefed" or mentally prepared for this important step. I had no clue what being a geologist meant. I just wandered into it.

This is where Tante Jet came in. At the time she was visiting with us and realized I had no idea how to go about becoming a student. So she offered to go with me in the *"Blauwe Tram"* the tramway that connected Voorburg with Leiden and The Hague, and find out. She was a decisive lady and not easily put off. So we found out where the offices of the university were located, marched up to them, and I filled in the necessary forms then and there. Subsequently we went to the *Societeit*, the club building which was and is the center of *"Studenten Corps"* activity. There we found a side door open that I later learned was the kitchen entrance and inside the door, I found a student dressed in white tie and tails and a top hat who had been to an all-night party and was clearly quite well lubricated. This was Udo Suermondt, a man much senior to me and later on one of the terrors for us first-year victims of the hazing period. In those days I was still a clueless and easily intimidated guy and Suermondt was quite an intimidating apparition to me. However, he was not unfriendly and reasonably forthcoming and told me that all I had to do was show up on the day the *Groentijd* started, dress in old clothes, and they would take care of the rest. I don't know where Tante Jet was at that moment, but I am quite sure she was not inside the building. I am still grateful to her for pushing me in the right direction and helping me overcome my shyness and hesitation. She could be quite decisive. I do not remember if she helped me also with finding a place to stay, but I did find one that was really third rate but would do for a beginning.

After Oom Otto's death, Tante Jet stayed for a few years in her house and began to enjoy life. Tineke was already married and living in Indonesia when her father died. Tante Jet had never traveled anywhere with her husband except for a brief trip to the Harz Mountains in Germany before the war. She joined groups that went abroad in buses and met new friends. She rented out rooms in her house to a young insurance man. Postwar Holland had to cope with an enormous housing shortage so people like Tante Jet who lived alone in her house were obliged to take in people who could not find a place to live. To forestall having to take in people she did not like, she decided to find a "lodger." I have forgotten the name of the man she took in, but he was a nice, jolly life insurance salesman who enjoyed her cooking and was often away staying with his girlfriend anyway. Later Tante Jet decided to leave her house and rent an apartment in the center of Arnhem, which made it easier for her to get around. Her place was in easy walking distance of the shopping area and the station so she could go where she liked. She often visited my parents who by then lived in Wassenaar. At one point she had a boyfriend who was never shown to us. In those days it was not yet quite acceptable for older widowed people to have a relationship and my mother was very defensive about this very normal situation. My mother told me there was "nothing wrong with her sister having some 'love' in her life" since she had really never had a loving relationship with her husband. To me this seemed a bit exaggerated but possibly basically true. Towards the end of her life, Tante Jet became seriously deranged. She was found wandering around the square in front of her apartment with very little clothes on and she began to utter all kinds of often-unpleasant statements. So Tineke put her in a nursing home in Oosterbeek where she stayed for a while until her death in March 1986, almost ninety years old.

❦

Tineke was born in Leeuwarden on December 16, 1923. She was therefore about 14 months older than I was. I do not know what the origin of her first names was, but suspect she was named after Oom Otto's mother. She attended grade school in Leeuwarden and later in Arnhem, where she subsequently completed the *Hogere*

TINEKE IN 1944.

Burger School, the math and science oriented branch of our high school system at the time. Like her parents, Tineke was good at sports and several times beat me at tennis. She also was a good swimmer. She was about nine years old when the family moved to Arnhem. She experienced no negative effect at all from that move; in fact, she very quickly acquired a large group of friends there and continued to have a happy childhood. When Tineke became a teenager and went to high school, she had a boyfriend. She met him through common friends in the neighborhood and I met him when we went sledding on a winter day. Arnhem is one of the few hilly Dutch cities. The streets are therefore not just flat and horizontal like everywhere else. When there was snow this encouraged youngsters to go sledding and one of the most enjoyable ways of doing it was to tie a number of sleds together in a long train and so go down hill. No cars to worry about really because it was war and only the Germans had cars, and they had very little gas so they were not moving about that much. Tineke was a happy-go-lucky, gregarious girl with lots of friends. For me that was great because I was at that time socially somewhat more reticent and tagging along with my older cousin was wonderful. I had in those years a very close relationship with Tineke, I guess we both missed having no siblings so we naturally gravitated to each other in a brother and sister fashion. When the boyfriend came on the scene, I was naturally very interested in him and looked at him with a great deal of awe, particularly since he went to a merchant marine academy and wore a uniform. His name was Joop de Jong and he was a little older than Tineke, which added to his prestige in my eyes. In those days, Holland had a significant merchant fleet on the high seas. There were about eight Dutch shipping companies involved in world trade, all of them listed on the stock exchange. Today none of these companies exist any more except perhaps for the Holland America Line, a company that is in the cruise business and is only

Dutch in name. There were several schools training people to serve as officers on merchant ships. These schools were all boarding schools with a tough curriculum and strict military-type discipline. During the war they also offered a convenient escape from being drafted for work in Germany.

Shortly after he got to know Tineke, Joop went through a major crisis in his life when he discovered that he was adopted. The people he had always thought were his "parents" had never told him that. He found out by accident when he came to get his wartime identification card and was told by the officials who checked him in that he had a different family name than the one he always thought he had. In Holland it is very difficult to change a family name, usually you always keep the name of your birth mother or parents, and adoption of a child does not result in a name change. His "parents" were orthodox Protestants who were well meaning but obviously afraid to reveal the truth after so many years. So they exposed him to this incredibly rude shock. Later the romance cooled off because as Tineke told me in her usual dry fashion, "he needed a woman," and she was not willing to comply. It was typical for Tineke that she kept her cool and did not accede to Joop's demands and went on with her life.

As the war progressed, Tineke ended up in the hotel "Zilven" with her parents, exiled from Arnhem. It was there, immediately after the war, that she met Jaap Kort, her future husband. Jaap was an *onderduiker* – literally a "deep diver" or a person hiding out from the Germans. He grew up in Bilthoven in a fairly large family. He had one brother and two sisters. His father was like my father a mining engineer, working for the Billiton Tin Company in Indonesia. This made Jaap immediately acceptable to Pa. Unfortunately Jaap's father committed suicide at a fairly early age, probably while they were still living in Indonesia. Jaap's father was, therefore, a

TINEKE AND JAAP'S WEDDING. BEPJE IS BEHIND THEM.

subject that was rarely discussed. Jaap's mother was a tall lady who seemed somewhat colorless, taciturn and stern to me. Jaap was also a very tall man, which suited Tineke fine because she was tall too. After the war Jaap had to finish school and when that was behind him he started to show up more and more at Tineke's house in Arnhem. Pretty soon they were engaged.

I got along quite well with Jaap although he was not exactly my cup of tea. I always thought he did not have too much of a sense of humor. Jaap had to find a job, of course, which was not very easy immediately after the war. After some searching he ended up with the Royal Dutch Petroleum Company where Pa was in the top management. It is unclear if Pa helped him with a nudge in the right direction or not, but he was accepted and soon in a training program. My mother always claimed that Jaap owed his entire career to Pa's help, which was probably an exaggeration.

Tineke and Jaap were married in the spring of 1947. It was not a very grandiose affair since we were still recovering from the war and Arnhem was a shattered city. The evening before the wedding, we had a party at Tineke's house where I met Jaap's brother Kees and his wife and his older sister and her husband and also his much younger sister Bepje. I got along best with Jaap's brother and his wife. The older sister was named Tima and abbreviation of *Tin Maatschappij* – Tin Company, the company Jaap's father had worked for. Really odd to call your firstborn after your employer. Her husband was a social worker type who was director of a home for wayward boys and treated everybody else as if they were wayward boys too and in need of direction and instruction by him. We played some silly games and that was that. The wedding itself was only in the town hall since Jaap was more or less an agnostic. Oom Otto had arranged a nice dinner at the restaurant Royal, where we all gathered. During the dinner Jaap's youngest sister Bepje created a terrific emotional scene–crying and carrying on, clinging to Jaap as if he was going to be lost forever. Our side was just stunned by this outburst. We wondered about this young woman's emotional stability and pitied the young man she was planning to marry. Ultimately she turned out O.K. I understand, living happily in a somewhat isolated rural area in Canada.

Jaap was soon posted in Indonesia, but Tineke stayed home with her parents in Arnhem until her first child Jetty was born in December 1948. At that time I was also in Arnhem with the army unit I would go to Indonesia with. So I saw a lot of the Jonas family, visiting them in the evenings. I was among the first to admire Tineke's new baby, Jetty. Over the years Tineke and Jaap had three more daughters, Dorien, Suzanne and Karin. After Indonesia they moved to Venezuela and then to Nigeria and from there back to the Netherlands. When they were living abroad I did not see much of them, of course, but I did catch up with them in 1950 in Batavia (now Djakarta), when I was in an army camp waiting to be shipped back home and they were temporarily there, en route to some other place in Indonesia. Jaap was laid up in a hospital with some sort of minor ailment, and it was there that I noticed that not everything was going smoothly in their marriage. Tineke was enjoying the company of a doctor who belonged to my unit and who I knew was not a very trustworthy fellow. So I warned them about this doctor. I was absolutely certain that there was nothing serious going on between Tineke and the doctor, just a casual flirtation. But Jaap's reaction was totally over the top and I regretted having mentioned the doctor at all. In hindsight, it might have been a better solution if Tineke had run off with the doctor rather than stay with Jaap. Dorien was born a year later, in July 1951. Suzanne followed in 1954 and Karin in 1958.

When Oom Otto died in March 1951, Tineke lived in New Guinea, a God-forsaken outpost from where it was impossible to come home in time for the funeral of her father or even make a phone call. She wrote a long and very emotional letter to Tante Jet. I remember that letter since it was so long and rambling and so unlike all other letters Tineke used to write. She usually wrote in a very matter of fact style, but this letter showed she was under considerable emotional stress and bothered that she was so far away and unable to do anything.

Today people jet all over the world and communicate easily by phone, cell phone or the internet with places like Indonesia. It seems almost incomprehensible that only fifty years ago this was all still impossible. If you went overseas, you were stuck there until you went back. We only saw Tineke and her family when they returned to Holland on leave. Once they came to see us here in Riverside when they were en route from Venezuela to Holland. Netty and I had just settled down here and lived in a small rented house on Peters Road. We could not possibly put the entire family up so we found a spot for them in the Old Greenwich Inn near Tod's Point, which was not very luxurious but a good spot for the children. It turned out to be a success. We took them on several trips to the countryside and had generally a good time. I still have a movie of this visit.

In the late sixties Royal Dutch went through a lean period and began to down-size. Jaap was let go, probably with a decent golden handshake. He soon found another job with the Dutch government, looking after the oil exploration activities that had started in the North Sea. It was Holland's incredibly good luck that a large gas field was found in the north, in the province of Groningen. This gas field is still operational and has provided the Netherlands as well as parts of Germany and Belgium with abundant natural gas. In addition, oil was discovered offshore in the North Sea. The government obviously needed to supervise the offshore drilling and exploration activity. Jaap was involved in this. The family settled down in Gouda where they bought a house and Jaap commuted to The Hague. Tineke was quite happy there and her daughters all found good schools and developed a circle of friends. Netty and I visited them periodically when we were on vacation and I also came when I was on a business trip. When we visited everything seemed to be on an even keel. Tineke worked hard to make her house nice. She was good at sewing and cooking. Jaap seemed content. Little did we know that there were serious problems. I even heard later that Jaap occasionally worked off his pent-up frustrations by beating Tineke or the girls. I have no proof of that, but if it were not true, why would people talk about it? We got a signal several years earlier when Jaap showed home movies of their European leaves. Netty and I noticed that there were shots of a woman we did not know in those movies. This appeared to be Jaap's lady friend with whom he had had a relationship for some time. Strangely enough, he seemed to have no problem showing her within the context of a series of family vacation pictures.

One day we got word that Jaap had simply left without leaving any notice or explanation, just taking a few belongings, including his toolbox, a cowardly and very despicable act. Years later Netty asked Tineke why she had married Jaap in the first place. Her response was typical for Tineke. She said simply and in a very matter of fact way: "Because he was the first one who asked me."

After the divorce, Tineke was in a difficult situation and as these things go, the lawyers took a long time settling a reasonable alimony arrangement. Over the years Tineke often had trouble getting timely payments from Jaap and making ends meet. My father rose to the occasion and provided support and counsel to Tineke, and at his funeral Tineke spoke movingly to thank him for what he had done for her. Tineke had to move out of her house and got a small apartment in Gouda. For a while Karin, her youngest daughter, lived there with her. Jetty went to medical school at the University of Leiden and earned a M.D. degree there. She married Kees Kraayeveld, also a medical doctor. He is now a neurologist. They have three children and are now grandparents. Dorien married Han Lameris an anesthesiologist, a Ph.D. and a professor at the University of Amsterdam. They also have three children and Dorien is now also a grandmother. Unfortunately Han decided that he needed another wife and left Dorien. This divorce was luckily reasonably amicable. Suzanne married Harry Nahuysen, a physiotherapist. They have three boys. The marriage between Suzanne and Harry also broke up leaving Suzanne with serious problems since Harry developed an incurable disease, which made it gradually impossible for him to work and also negatively affected his behavior, which was less than desirable in the first place. Harry died in 2011. He had a difficult death that affected his sons very much.

Netty and I had the pleasure of inviting Tineke for a visit to the U.S. This must have been around 1972 or 1973. She stayed with us for a couple of weeks and we made trips in the surrounding countryside and went to the city.

In the evening of January 12, 1989, I came home from New York City and met Netty at the kitchen door. She said, "I have horrible news for you." Tineke had died that day of a massive heart attack. She was found in a chair at home, all dressed up and ready to go out with a lady friend to play bridge. I flew over for her funeral. It was January and the Dutch weather was at its worst. The days were dark and short, the skies were leaden and it rained incessantly. Han Lameris took me over to see her in the smallish funeral home they had chosen to use. It was a quiet Sunday afternoon. Beyond us there was nobody in the room where Tineke lay in her coffin. The only thing we heard was the son of the funeral director upstairs, noisily practicing on his drum set. The funeral was the next day. It poured. To my utter astonishment, Jaap showed up with his second wife, his former girlfriend. The cemetery had luckily a very proper auditorium where we could gather to say good-bye to Tineke. There were quite a few people, mostly friends of Tineke herself and of her daughters. Jetty spoke very well and I had an opportunity to say a few words too, so that there was a link with the older generation. Then we all went to the gravesite and after a few words there in the driving rain, we all went home.

My father's only sister Henriette Luise was born in Batavia (now Djakarta) on October 31, 1891. Her parents moved back to Europe when she was still quite young and she lived in Bloemendaal with her parents until she was married in 1931. Jet, or Jetje as we called her, went to school in Bloemendaal and to the gymnasium in Haarlem. She had a strong interest in literature and languages and had a quite extensive library at home. During the war when I often stayed at her house in Leersum, I browsed with great delight through her collection of books. All her books and everything else in her house were burned when the Germans set fire to it in the fall of 1944. I know little about Jetje's younger years. I have a suspicion that my grandmother had a strong influence on her and that her youth was not very free and independent. Oma had a strong personality and very fixed ideas about what was proper for a young lady and what was not. I know that Jetje studied to become a nurse, but I am not sure she finished the course, which was even in the old days a difficult one. She must have finished the gymnasium at age eighteen or nineteen that was about 1910. I do know that at the end of World War I she joined a Dutch medical team that went to Russia to help alleviate the horrific conditions at the eastern front where the German army had badly beaten the Russian army and the Great Russian Revolution was in the offing. The Dutch team established a hospital in St Petersburg, the city later called Leningrad and now St Petersburg again. When the Bolsheviks took over, the Dutch hospital team was told to leave. They left but took along two Russian young women, Elisabeth and Gertrud von Heuking. They were daughters of a Russian/Finish/German noble family who were endangered by the new Bolshevik terror regime. They were smuggled out as Dutch nurses in the proper uniforms. Elisabeth. or Betje as she was later called, became Tante Jetje's very best friend. She married a surgeon who was also part of the Dutch team, Dr. Joosten Hattink. They had two children, Coen who went to Leiden in my year and became a gymnasium teacher in classical languages (Latin and ancient Greek), and Thea, his younger sister who worked for many years at the Dutch Ministry of Foreign Affairs. We are still in touch with Coen and Thea. After her Russian adventure, Jetje returned home and probably stayed there waiting for a proper suitor to turn up. She was not exactly a beauty but certainly not unattractive. My father was physically very strong and healthy; I don't think he ever saw the inside of a hospital until he was in his nineties. His sister was not that strong, and certainly not at all athletic. My father was a good tennis player, an excellent Alpinist and a good horseman. Jetje also hiked in Switzerland, but her endurance was not great and her general attitude was more sedentary. Jetje worked for some time as a baby nurse, helping friends and others take care of their new born children immediately after birth. So when I was born she took care of my mother and me. When my mother went to Venezuela to join my father when I was a few months old, Jetje went with us. I guess she went back home after a while.

Later on my mother and she became quite close and traveled together. In 1930 they went on a tour to Spain to see all the sights and museums. This was quite an elaborate expedition. The group had prepared itself during the winter before by attending courses on Spanish art. Travel arrangements were in the hands of a professional, Bernard van der Hoop. He became my Uncle Bernard. Although I was very young then, I do remember distinctly how happy Tante Jet seemed and how radiant she suddenly became in those days. She had finally found the man of her heart. I remember her sitting in her living room upstairs in my grandparents' house, together with my mother, learning Spanish to prepare herself for her married life in the Spanish speaking Canary Islands. They had a lot of fun together and I do not think Jetje learned much although my mother spoke Spanish quite well.

Bernard Christiaan Marie van der Hoop was born on November 19, 1893 in Rijswijk. His father was a diplomat who was posted among other places in South Africa where Bernard spent part of his youth. His mother was a woman from an aristocratic family. Bernard also had a brother who ended up in Indonesia during the war I believe, and I think I heard he perished in a Japanese prison camp. But not much was ever heard from him, probably also, if my recollection is correct, because he was married to an Indonesian woman which in those days was still not quite acceptable. Bernard and his brother spent a lot of time in boarding schools, first in South Africa, later in England.

Oom Bernard had a well-developed sense of humor and would entertain us with stories about the Dickensian conditions under which he and his classmates lived in these schools. Food was always scarce, and in South Africa the boys would spend time in the weekends trying to catch roaming chickens that they could kill, pluck and cook in the woods. They would do that by selecting a large bush with sturdy twigs. They would make a noose out of a piece of rope and tie it to one of the twigs. Then they would bend the twig down to the ground and secure its end with other sticks so it would spring back up at the slightest movement. The noose would rest lightly on the ground and they would scatter some chicken feed in it. As the chicken would come to pick at the food, it would disturb the sticks holding the twig and with a rush would be hanged by its neck, caught in the noose. This device was called a "wippie," I remember. The name is self-explanatory. Sandwiches for the schoolboys were "buttered" by

TANTE JETJE AND OOM BERNARD IN LAS PALMAS, 1933.

lying them in a row and swiping a brush with molten butter over them. Older boys would torture younger ones by lashing them in the showers with wet towels, etc. Still Oom Bernard had fond memories of his English boarding school and proudly wore its blazer, a jacket in school colors, vertically striped. The family eventually returned to Holland and for some time lived in a small castle in Gelderland called *De Gelderse Toren* – the Gelderland Tower. It was indeed a tower, an almost totally round building that still exists. Bernard liked to hunt and fish, was a good shot and owned several firearms, including a shotgun and a revolver. He liked to fish for *snoek,* an aggressive fish that is found in the Dutch canals and is caught by using small live fish as bait. I still have a nice English metal fishing rod he gave me. He liked dogs and preferred the outdoors to city life. He looked like an Englishman, with sandy hair neatly combed back and a small mustache. He was for me an ideal uncle and great fun to be with. He was not an intellectual and I do not think he had much schooling in the formal sense of the word. But he had lived in many different countries, particularly in Argentina, and was not very well suited for life in the narrow world of the Netherlands during the depression.

When Tante Jetje and Oom Bernard got engaged, they started to look for Opporunities to live elsewhere. Bernard found a firm In Las Palmas, the capital of the island of Gran Canaria on the Canary Islands in which he could buy an interest. It was an "import export" business of the kind one would find often in outlying places where only a few things were produced and everything the population needed had to be imported. The wedding was quite an affair. It took place in the small church behind the house of my   grandparents.

Oom Bernard and Tante Jetje soon moved to the Canary Islands and my grandparents would visit them a few times, going there by ship, of course. My mother and I went there in 1936. I have described that trip. Gran Canaria was a wonderful place to visit. There were hardly any tourists at that time. Now it is packed with European tourists every winter and many retirees have chosen to live there because the subtropical climate is very nice.

A few years later it became clear that the sanctions the European powers had put in place to counter the Fascist regime of General Franco made doing business in a Spanish possession impossible. After a short

period in which Oom Bernard and Tante Jetje lived in a small apartment in Amsterdam while Bernard was trying to find suitable work, they decided to try to find a place in the country. They found the house of their dreams in the "Meezenhof" in the village of Leersum. It was a very simple but lovely and well-situated house. Oom

Bernard became an avid gardener and grew a prodigious amount of vegetables, which were canned. I believe that my grandfather financed the house and that he gave the couple an allowance. They lived very frugally and simply but were very happy in their new location and made many friends among the local people. We visited them often and during the war the Meezenhof became a refuge for my grandparents, my dog Moro and myself. Later the Germans burned the place down in a reprisal action against Oom Bernard and his Resistance unit.

My grandparents went back to Bloemendaal immediately after the war and found their house in reasonably good shape. I went to visit them there and heard from my grandmother some of the details of Oom Bernard's death. She also told me how hard it was on Tante Jetje who was at that time still in the eastern part of the country where she had close Resistance friends. Jetje wanted to live in Leersum again. My father handled her affairs and spent a lot of time negotiating with the authorities for a building permit. The reconstruction effort came only slowly off the ground. Building materials were scarce and priorities had to be set. Bombing victims and people like Tante Jetje who had been victims of the Nazi terror had priority, but Tante Jetje was not allowed to rebuild her house entirely as it was. She was only allowed to rebuild the ground floor, which contained the kitchen, dining and sitting room, veranda and the master bedroom with bathroom. She had to put a flat roof on top and had a stairway that led up to the roof. In this way, the house could be easily expanded with a second floor when this would again be possible.

Tante Jetje lived in her rebuilt house for about twenty-four years. She never got over the loss of Bernard, I believe, although she was level headed enough not to assume a victim attitude. She lived alone in the woods with her dog, a nasty little corgi whose herding instincts made her nip at your ankles when you walked with her in the woods. Jetje aged rapidly. She was by far not as sturdy as my father. She tired quickly and had a problem with swollen ankles as a result of poor blood circulation. She was a sweet woman I was very fond of. Netty also got along very well with her and we both visited her many times when we were just married in Holland, and she visited us once when we lived in Old Greenwich. She wanted to see with her own eyes how we lived and whether we had really succeeded in the U.S. This trip became a bit of a disaster since she caught pneumonia, which manifested itself during her flight back, and she became quite ill in the plane. Luckily she overcame this hurdle, but it soon became clear that she could no longer live alone. So Pa found a place for her in a small apartment that was part of a hotel in the nearby town of Zeist. She lived there for about a year or two in rapidly deteriorating health. She was very pleased that we named our daughter Janet after her. She died on April 13, 1972. Knowing that she would not last very long, I made a point of going over to visit her before she died to say good-bye and I returned later for the funeral. At the funeral ceremony were several people who had known Jetje during the war, and one lady I had not met before, spoke very movingly about that time. Pa was unable to speak and asked me to do it. I was very glad to oblige and have an opportunity to eulogize my favorite aunt.

Returning to the summer of 1945, life picked up its rhythm and the reconstruction effort started. Some people were able to make trips outside the country, but most of us had to stay put and try to make the best of it. Oom Frans de Clercq was among those who were able to find business reasons to visit Belgium and later Switzerland where he had old friends. He had managed to find a prewar car with which he could go to Belgium, and since the Dutch guilder was worth very little, he had to find ways to barter. He found out that the Belgians, who had been liberated a year earlier, were much better off and had little need for Dutch products. One thing they seemed to like was *Haarlemer Olie,* an old-fashioned laxative that was still available in certain pharmacies. So when I was staying with the de Clercqs that summer, Oom Frans would send us (Lucas, Thys and myself) out on bicycles all over Haarlem to see how many tubes of Haarlemer Olie we could buy. We got quite a few and that allowed Oom Frans to get some nylon stockings for Tante Ans, a new postwar wonder product we had only recently heard about. I stayed for a few days with the de Clercq family and got acquainted with the cow they had secretly kept in their garage. Oom Frans had a false wall built in the back of his garage, which created a small stable for the cow. When entering the garage through the door, it looked as though you were looking at the back of the structure, but in reality you looked at the false wall. There must have been a door in the back to get to the cow. The cow was not overly well fed since they had little grass left in their backyard. They did have a tennis court and the cow, now being liberated from his small stall, was out in the open and constantly walking back and forth in front of their back porch, obviously looking for food. The solution was to "walk" the cow in the park across the street. Oom Frans made me do this once, to my enormous embarrassment. There I was, crossing the street into the park, which looked somewhat like Binney Park in Old Greenwich. I held the cow on a sort of leash, but as soon as she saw the grass, she took the initiative and rushed over, pulling me along. The cow attacked the bushes and grass in the park ferociously, and I was forced to stand by, looking furtively around and hoping nobody would see me. After a short while, I managed to get the cow back into the backyard of the de Clercqs, pretending she had grazed for hours and was totally satisfied.

When the end of summer came I had to think about going to Leiden, and a new chapter in my life opened up when I moved to this wonderful old town.

15 : *Life Begins at Twenty*

In the early fall of 1945 I went to the small room I had rented in Leiden and prepared myself for the ordeal of the *Groentijd* – the novitiate or hazing period of the Leiden Student Corps. The next day I reported to the *Societeit,* the clubhouse where we were all registered. This was a chaotic situation where large numbers of older students were milling around, yelling at us and ready to pounce on us greenhorns. The men in charge were sitting in easy chairs on top of tables trying to control the multitude. Many were spiffily dressed in three-piece suits and wore fedoras or snap-brim hats and if they had the proper seniority, carrying a walking stick or a tightly rolled black umbrella. We, the *groenen* – the freshmen were a singularly poor-looking group. Imagine a group of young men who were told to wear old clothes because of the expected rigor of the *groentijd,* just a few months after a five-year war in which most of us had not had a chance to buy decent clothes for a long time! We looked terribly disheveled. We were all given a *groenenboekje* – a booklet in which our tasks for every day were printed and in which senior students could write comments and sign off when tasks were properly executed.

In contrast with prewar custom, we did not have to shave our hair off. There was a reason for that. In September 1945 there were many Dutch and German Nazis incarcerated in town and they were marched through town with shaved heads. So we were spared this extra indignity. We soon understood what the drill was. We had to address all older students with *Meneer,* sir, and use the honorific or *U* form when speaking to them while they would use the familiar *je en jij* form when talking to us. Sitting on chairs was prohibited. So when an older student wanted to "talk" to us while sitting in a chair, we would have to sit on the floor next to him. The day would start early and end late. We would have to go to older students' houses to wake them up in the morning. That meant we had to be there around 9 and talk to them or do chores like shop for bread, etc. After that we would have to go to the *Societeit Minerva,* the old club building where we would engage in various activities.

Membership of the *Corps* and *Societeit* were separate, but an integral part of each other. We were selected out to determine if we had talents for singing and or acting, etc. or if we could play a musical instrument. If we were talented in the eyes of our leaders, we had to practice for a cabaret performance that would take place at the end of the *Groentijd.* I had heard that being in the theater group was preferable because you could hang around the whole morning, learning a small role and not be bothered. The others had to do gymnastics and other strenuous stuff. In the afternoon we had lunch in the big dining rooms upstairs followed by a session at *Njord,* the student-rowing club down at the river. We had to march there in some sort of column, and once there we had to row large steel barges that took about twelve rowers, six on each side, plus a bunch of older students to steer and give us "directions." We had races in these barges, and while on land we had to do all sorts of silly stuff and be constantly harassed with questions and verbal insults by older guys. A standard trick was to load too many *groenen* in the boat and then "discover" midstream that the boat was too crowded and leave the excess guys on mooring pilings etc. only to be retrieved much later. After this water-sports interlude, we were marched back to the *Societeit* where we had to sit on the floor and be constantly interrogated by our elders while they were enjoying their *borreltje,* cocktail, drink of a shot of *Jenever.* Then it was dinnertime for us, always in the big upstairs dining room. The food was pretty awful. Food and also *jenever* and beer were still scarce. After dinner, down to the main room again with constant harassment, and finally at midnight we would have to sit on our haunches, form a sort of conga line and frog-jump around – *kikkeren.* Very tiring.

After a week of this, we were dead tired and when I went home for the first weekend, I fell asleep in the tram and passed my stop. This all sounds pretty gruesome and stupid and most of it was, but there were many humorous moments. The verbal harassment was not just yelling insults, it was much more in the vein of attempting to debate and corner the *groen* into making stupid statements or intimidating him verbally through intelligent debate. This was called *feuten* – a term derived from the word "fetus" indicating our lowly position of unborn human beings. A favorite question was "have you ever kissed a girl?" If you answered "no," you could be accused of being weird, a homosexual or worse, socially inept. If you said "yes," they would ask what her name was. If you told the inquisitor the name, he would explode and ask you if you thought the girl would like her name being mentioned here?

Being in this cauldron of activity, mostly in the old *Societeit* building, made us know many of the people in our year and most of the older students. The system was called *Kennismaking op voet van ongelijkheid* – introduction on a basis of inequality. Proponents insist it has great value in preparing new students for *Corps* life, and for society in general as they learn how to handle themselves in difficult social situations. When it was over, we had the cabaret in which we sang songs in stupid costumes and did silly dances. My role was that of a Utrecht student, the rival university, which we strongly believed did not really exist. The lyrics of the songs were usually highly scabrous, but since in those days it was not correct to print the actual lyrics as sung, the booklets given out before the cabaret had different, more sedate lyrics and everyone was eager to get the real lyrics and write them down. I had reasonable success with my part although it was not really racy. After the performance we were invited to have dinner with a group of older guys and all of a sudden we were on the same plane with them and would remain there forever. We sat on chairs that evening, of course.

After the *groentijd* we were officially first-year members of the *Corps*. We were more or less obliged to come often to the *Societeit* and sit there on the one sofa assigned to us. If you did not show up often enough you risked being declared *obscuur* – hiding in the dark, invisible. The *Societeit* was a large building in the *Breestraat,* the main street of Leiden. You entered a vestibule with an area where coats could be hung and where there was a big men's room complete with a kind of basin with strong handrails on both sides for those who had too much to drink and needed to throw up. The big main room was beyond a large formal staircase that led upstairs. At the other side of the building was a service staircase, which was the only one we were allowed to use as freshmen. In the big room were windows looking out over the street and a large bar on one side and a large fireplace on the other. The furniture was very beat-up and consisted of sturdy tables and chairs and a few easy chairs around the fireplace. As you gained seniority, you were first allowed to sit at the window and finally, when you were really old, you could sit in the "easy" chairs near the fireplace. There was a large reading table in the middle. Large brass chandeliers hung from the ceiling. A row of pillars ran through the middle, and on the backside of the room were a number of billiard tables. Upstairs were various ceremonial rooms and a library as well as the large dining room. The *Societeit* was a dark and gloomy place. There was little light. Power was still very scarce. It was somewhat dusty with dark wood paneled walls and beat up wooden floors and a penetrating odor of stale beer everywhere. Unfortunately the building burned down in 1959. It was rebuilt in a more modern style with basically the same interior, but the new building is in my view even more run down now than the old one ever was and misses the character of the old place.

At the beginning of our first year we had to form *jaar clubs* – year clubs, groups of about twenty friends, usually people who knew each other from high school. The idea was that these groups would become your nucleus of close friends within the much larger first year crowd. We had a postwar problem. Normally a "year" would consist of about one hundred and fifty new members. But we had a much larger inflow caused by the closing of the university for five years, which forced those who graduated from high school to wait until the liberation. So the *Corps* had to telescope about four years into one, causing a crunch.

To reduce the number of *Clubs* that could be formed, we were obliged to take in more people than we wanted, which made the group large and unwieldy and not really a group of close friends anymore. There was a hectic period in which the clubs were formed with several of us who had not been asked to join any group, wandering around aimlessly. It became in a way an unpleasant beauty contest. I had very few if any close friends among our year. So I had trouble finding people I could and or wanted to join up with. I knew several men in the year before us that was formed about six weeks before ours. This was really my age group, but since I had done my exam in 1944 and not the year before, I could not join them. That was a shame because they were automatically promoted to second year members with all the advantages attached to that. I was lucky to find Rob Laane also looking among the people in my year. Rob and I knew each other from the Haags Lyceum and we went out jointly to select a club. Rob is now my closest friend and the beginning of our friendship goes really back to that period in Leiden. We found a group that consisted mostly of kindred souls from The Hague and this group became the nucleus of our *Club.* They were: Jan van der Drift and Jan Frederiks, who were roommates and are now both deceased. Manus van Rijckevorsel, also now gone. Jan Willem Royer, who lived in Wassenaar and died there recently. Bart Schuur, who until recently lived in Belgium near Rob. Werner Hermann, the only one in our group who earned a Ph.D., who is a very successful dermatologist living in The Hague. Werner is Jewish and survived the war. His parents did not, but he never spoke about that to us. Gerard van Leeuwen, served in Indonesia in the army and subsequently went to live in Canada but came back to Holland and died there. Nico van Hasselt was briefly among us. We totally lost sight of him. In addition to the people from The Hague we found Rob van der Toorren who came from Haarlem and in later years lived in Heemstede near Netty and me with his wife and child. He emigrated to the US and disappeared. We also found four nice guys from the southern part of Holland. Klaas Bakker and Hans van Vloten, roommates who both became physicians and are now living in the south of Holland. And Peter and Pim Kreek, two brothers from Eindhoven. Peter died still quite young and suddenly. Pim lived in Wassenaar and died in 2005. Finally there was Klaus Angel, who was also Jewish and had survived the occupation with his mother and stepfather. His parents were very interesting people. They were both originally from Germany and psychiatrists, disciples of Sigmund Freud. Klaus did not stay long. His family emigrated to the U.S. and we lost all contact with him. I guess they had every reason to turn their backs on Europe. They lived briefly in a house in The Hague without a stick of furniture.

So we had about sixteen or fifteen members of the nucleus who were close. Most of them remained friends for the rest of their lives. There were quite a few additional members we had to take on because they could not find a home and whose names I have forgotten. They disappeared (became *obscuur*) fairly quickly after the first year. Later on there were people from Indonesia to be absorbed in the *Corps*. The ships with people who had suffered for three miserable years as prisoners in Japanese concentration camps arrived in late fall and early winter. When their sons arrived in Leiden and wanted to join the *Corps*, we were asked to take two of them into our club. In our case we got two friendly smiling Chinese fellows who went through the motions and afterwards kept to themselves. We did not see much of them either.

We then proceeded to the traditional *Club Inauguratie*, an event that could be called the pledging of the clubs. Liquor was still very scarce, but for this event each club got a ration of *jenever*, the corn-based Dutch gin which is very much an acquired taste. I still like it and drink it when in Holland. Somehow it goes down better in the damp Dutch climate. It is consumed "neat" in small glasses and for us greenhorns who had no training in drinking at all, the results were as could be expected, disastrous.

Soon I found a better boarding house. I rented two small rooms from a young family who had extra space in their attic. It was still fairly far away from the center of Leiden. The accommodations were far from ideal. I had to wash myself in a washbasin outside my rooms in the open corridor where the stairs came up from the floor below. There was no heat except for a small coal stove that I had to light myself. I had my own furniture there and spent the first winter of my life away from my parents in this cold hovel. In the spring of 1946, I had an opportunity to improve my lodgings when I could move to an establishment called *Chateau de Bisquit* located on No. 1. *Beschuitsteeg*. But more about that later.

Classes started soon after the *Groentijd*. I went to the building of the geological faculty and introduced myself to the two professors who were the principal docents there. My father, who had become a prominent member of the Dutch Royal Society for Geology and Mining knew them and told me that was the way it was done. This gesture appeared to be a thing of a more genteel and relaxed past. The professors were surprised to see me. Apparently most other students never made an effort to introduce themselves and just showed up to attend various courses. Geologists could take two different courses in the same discipline. One was heavily oriented towards metallurgy, chemistry and physics the other more towards biology and zoology. I chose the latter because I had always abhorred the chemistry and physics classes in high school. So we started to attend lectures in biology, one of the most boring subjects I was ever exposed to. An elderly professor rambled on and on about plant families and as was customary in those days, did not really teach a course. He just started somewhere in the middle and went on in excruciating detail about a small section of his subject, the history of plants. You were supposed to pick up the rest of the course from your textbooks. I also learned to dissect frogs and started to peer at fossils through microscopes. It all made little sense to me and I felt like a fish out of water in this environment. Perhaps I did not know how to study well and I certainly had no strong urge to learn all I could about geology.

That winter during the Christmas season, we had a visit at home from Oom Anne, Tante Mieke and Bas from Leeuwarden. Oom Anne, who had not driven a car for decades, had managed to wheedle a permit to buy one of the few new cars now being imported from the U.S. He got a Ford sedan that looked marvelous to us, gleaming and new. Oom Anne was a nervous driver and did not quite manage to enter our driveway correctly. He got a scrape on his brand new fender and from there on, Pa drove the car until they left again. Sometime later Pa also acquired a car, but not a new one. He could get a permit to drive a car, but not to buy a new one. He got a Hudson Terraplane, an American brand that like so many others does not exist anymore. This car was a two-seater with a rumble seat in back, a seat that you could climb in from the rear fender and that was hidden under a hatch when not in use. This vehicle had literally gone through the wars. It was a prewar model, of course, and had been "found" by someone who sold it to Pa. The front wheels were not the original ones anymore. They came off a military Jeep and the tires were military style too. But despite its strange looks, this car was a wonderful possession for us for several years. I particularly liked to drive it with the top down on sunny days. But before I could drive around in it I had to get a license. Pa tried to teach me at first, but that did not work out too well. Turning on to a small bridge in Voorburg with too much speed, I made the classic beginners mistake—forgetting I could brake and reassess the situation. I managed to scrape the front fender along the brick side of the bridge, which did not please Pa very much. So I decided to take lessons in Leiden from a professional driving school and got my license without a hitch. Once I got better at driving, Pa was very generous in letting me use his car. This opened fantastic new horizons for me.

In the early spring of 1946 the geological faculty arranged a study excursion to the Isle of Wight in England. This was a wonderful opportunity to finally get out of the country for a brief visit to a country we all admired very much and what is more, where food, cigarettes and drinks were plentiful. It is hard to explain how excited we were to be able to go to a place that had not been occupied and where our liberators came from. You needed special permits to leave the country and, more important, to get the foreign exchange you needed to pay for your stay. Our allowance was very small anyway. We got all that and we shipped out on the night boat from Hook of Holland to Harwich, England. We went in third-class accommodations of course. That meant you slept in real steerage accommodations, in bunks in a large open men's dorm in the lower part of the ship. The next day we arrived at the Harwich harbor where the train for London was waiting. Our first taste of an English breakfast as served on the train with ham and eggs, kippers and all the trimmings was for us the epitome of luxury. We could wander around London a bit before catching the train to Portsmouth, from where we took a ferry to Wight, and once on the island we took a small steam train that looked like a throwback to Victorian days to our destination, the small town of Ventnor. Despite the war and all the attendant work that had been done to fortify England against a German invasion, Ventnor was completely unspoiled. Like the surrounding towns and villages, it was picture book "merry old England."

We spent our days walking around and doing geological research on the very interesting rock formations, mainly on the cliffs on the beaches. We did not know the climate on the southern shores of England and found the weather surprisingly mild. In the evening we went to a local dance hall to meet the English lasses. We had only one female student in our group of about twenty so we had to branch out. I latched on to a girl called Joyce Hall who to me seemed the pinnacle of sophistication. She lived with her working-class parents in a small house in town and seemed to have no job. She was a tall, strawberry blonde who was quite good looking, a good talker and fun to be with. During the war she had served in the British Army's Woman's Auxiliary in an armored reconnaissance unit. I thought that was incredibly interesting. So we took long walks in the balmy evening and after I was back home I corresponded regularly with her. This helped my ability to write English considerably.

Our group stayed in a small but nice hotel for summer vacationers. Hiking around the pretty countryside was a real treat. We noticed that many small farms still used German and Italian prisoners of war as farmhands. These fellows walked quite freely around, wearing British army fatigues with a big yellow colored circle stitched on their backs. The population there accepted them as equals. That seemed strange to us. We were still full of hate, mainly towards the Germans and could not understand that these guys were so much at home there.

On our way back home a friend (Jaap van Rijn van Alkemade) and I stayed for a couple of extra days in London. I could finance that because Pa had given me some extra English money and had also referred me to the wartime office of Royal Dutch Shell that had been set up outside London in Richmond to replace the office in The Hague. I went there to pick up some additional cash from one of Pa's colleagues. You had to jump through all sorts of hoops in those days.

In the spring of 1946 London was still very much the same as it had been during the war. It was full of uniformed service men and women from all over the world. The pubs were jammed every night with military people. The Americans were very much in evidence, strolling around Piccadilly Circus, looking much more prosperous even as soldiers. Their uniforms were of better material; they had more money and swaggered around (as only Americans can) as if they owned the place. The U.S. Army Military Police had a truck stationed on Piccadilly Circus, which blared swing music through big loudspeakers and served as a container for drunken American service men. MPs picked them up and tossed them into the truck. When it was full it left to be replaced by a fresh one. Clothing was rationed so we went to the Jewish quarter where you could buy second-hand clothes. I bought a U.S. Army issue raincoat, which I proudly wore for years. I also bought a new hat in London. Hats were apparently not rationed. I had it carefully measured to fit my large head. It was a brown fedora, which became one of my proudest possessions. We all wore hats in those days.

Our stay in London was a great thrill for me. I had always been strongly Anglophile, becoming more and more so during the war, steeping myself in the romantic notions about upper-class life that prevailed in English literature of the time. I read almost all my mother's English books, such as *the Forsyte Saga* and several others by Galsworthy, also *the Rains Came*, a popular book in the thirties, *Rebecca* and several books by H.G. Wells and Charles Dickens of course. I also read

American books, *Babbitt* and *Main Street* by Sinclair Lewis, *Gone with the Wind* and others, but I found America still far removed from my world and the English lifestyle very attractive. Now that America has been my country for more than fifty years, I feel more at home in the U.S.A, but still like to visit England and find it a country where one can feel totally comfortable and at home. I also realize now that the genteel Britain described in the books I read during the war was quite far removed from the reality.

While in London, I ran into one of our fellow aspiring geologists who had also found a temporary girlfriend in Ventnor. He told me that his girlfriend had told him that Joyce Hall was married to a soldier serving abroad somewhere. This was a really strange baffling piece of news for me. I felt really funny that she had not told me. When I was back home I wrote her and asked her why she had not told me. I was like all my contemporaries then still very much a puritan who felt you should not associate yourself with the wife of somebody else. She responded that she had not wanted to spoil our friendship by telling me she was married. Strange. She was probably bored stiff in that little town and looking for a little diversion. I was glad we had not gotten too much involved, which was very unlikely anyway given my very prudish and "shy with women" attitude in those days. Just before leaving, Jaap and I both bought new bicycles in a store in Oxford Street. I bought one for Ma, because Pa had already bought one for himself on one of his trips to London. Jaap and I rode these bikes through London's heavy traffic to Liverpool Street Station where we shipped them to Holland to go on the same ship with us.

After this trip to England I decided that geology was not for me. I had found out that I could, after all, study law in Leiden, despite the fact that I did not have the required gymnasium high school diploma. You could study *Indisch Recht* – Indonesian law, which was essentially the same as Dutch law since the Dutch legal system was used in the Indies at that time. You had to learn some Indonesian local law based on local religious and ethnic traditions, but in general you could use the title you earned for a career in Holland that was no different from that of a person with a Dutch law degree. It was not necessary to go to Indonesia to get the advantages this background gave you. In those days and today still, many Dutch students study law without any intention of ever practicing law. It is seen more as a general background for business or any other career that requires an academic degree without any specific specialization. I decided to make the switch to law and told my parents, who appeared not to be very upset by my decision. Now I had basically lost another year and it was necessary to try to catch up. I decided to engage the services of a *repetitor*, a person who made a living by coaching students as a personal tutor. Nobody seemed to care if you attended a professor's classes or not. In fact, the professor would not notice anyway because there were so many students. So you could go to a tutor, who told you what to study to be properly prepared for the oral exam and who knew exactly what each professor liked to hear. There was no time limit and you could request an exam anytime, provided it suited the professor, of course. I decided to take no summer vacation except for a brief trip to Friesland to see Oom Anne and Tante Mieke. I was still an aviation nut and when I discovered KLM had opened a connection between Schiphol Airport, Amsterdam, and Leeuwarden, I booked myself on a flight. The plane was a former military DC 3. The flight was very short, of course, but for me it was a sensational experience. It was the first time I flew in an airplane! Leeuwarden airport was the old German air base. Flying there was not as idiotic as it would seem today when one can cover the distance by car in about 2½ hours. The train service was still very primitive and it took the better part of a day to get to Leeuwarden by train.

In the fall I passed my first exam, which we called *tentamen,* in Old Dutch law (the legal system that prevailed in Holland before the *Code Napoléon*, Napoleonic Law was introduced). Then I had to start working for the more demanding *Candidaats Examen* – the half-way mark of the Dutch law studies in those days. I again used a tutor to speed things up. In the late spring of 1946 I had found a room in the center of Leiden. The people who rented out this room and several others were relatives of the couple where I had stayed at first. I had told them I wanted to be closer in and they passed me along. The old house was located on the corner of the *Beschuit Steeg*, the "Biscuit Alley," loosely translated. It was on a canal called *Oude Rijn*, Old Rhine, less than five minutes walking from the *Societeit* in contrast to my old digs that took about a half hour. The room was on the third floor. As you entered the front door of the house you had to climb a steep stairway to get to the main floor, which was above a store. The family occupied a living/dining room there and two students had a large room overlooking the *gracht*. Up one more flight of stairs was the floor where I lived. My room was above the family's room, and two other students shared the larger front room also overlooking the *gracht*. My room was separated from theirs by two sliding pocket doors that were kept closed but were not exactly sound proof. This proved to be a major inconvenience because the fellow who was bedded down on the other side of that door was a particularly loud chap.

This was Menny Fruitema who would become a good friend and, amazingly, my brother-in-law when he married Netty's sister Tilly many years later. Since it was summer and most students were away I was at first not so much aware of my neighbors, but soon I got to know them well. It was a very nice group of people many of whom I have known for many years afterwards. Menny was an original whom we unfortunately lost in 1998. His father was a businessman with German connections who long before the war had married a German lady and Menny was their only son. Menny grew up in Bentveld/Aerdenhout, a suburb of Haarlem, very close to Bloemendaal. Menny would often refer to his parents as *Kale Hendrik en Blonde Ilse,* bald Hendrik and blond Ilse. Much later I heard that the marriage of Menny's parents was not ideal. His mother often left his father who was quite a bit older than she, to pursue affairs of her own. We did not know anything about that of course. Menny's home life was complicated. His parents lived most of the year in Berlin where his father had become Dutch consul. Having a German mother was also not easy, of course, during and immediately after the war. I met his mother only twice and found her a nice, attractive woman who spoke very poor Dutch despite many years in Holland. Menny would go to his parent's apartment in Zandvoort overlooking the sea to study. There Detta, a German woman who had been with the family since his birth, was spoiling him. Detta was more or less Menny's second mother and much later, after Netty and I were married and lived in Heemstede and Menny was still a bachelor, he would give wonderful dinner parties in his parent's place with Detta taking care of everything except the drinks. That segment was Menny's forte. When he was not studying, Menny had a habit of getting up late and going to bed late, often after lengthy evenings at the *Societeit.* He would then come home and start loud conversations or make speeches to himself or to an imaginary public outside the open window that woke me up. During the day he was also not exactly noiseless. His roommate, Jos de Jongh, was in contrast a very quiet fellow. After a while I found that Menny had a small heart so whenever he really started to irritate me I would barge into his room and threaten physical violence that calmed him down in a hurry. Still, he was a very interesting and special fellow to share a house with and with some major bumps in the road we stayed good friends until his death. Other housemates were Fokke Jonkers, who was downstairs with John Boumeester, and upstairs a chap by the name of Vismans who I would see again in New York City where he worked for the Peabody Coal Company.

About six months after my entry into the *Chateau de Biscuit,* as the house was called, Willem Witteveen arrived. Willem was older than I, but had first completed the MTS engineering school where many people found a refuge during the war. He decided to study law in addition to his engineering degree and ended up arriving

about a year behind the big influx in Leiden. When Jonkers and Boumeester decided to leave to go elsewhere, Willem and I teamed up and took their large double room. This resolved most of my noise problem. Willem also became a lifelong friend. I have a photograph of Willem and myself and Vismans standing on the street near the "*Chateau de Bisquit.*" There I am in my English hat and a nice American three-piece suit. This was a suit we had received as a gift from a lady in Omaha, Nebraska. She was a friend of my parents. They had met sometime before the war on one of their long ocean-liner passages, and she had been over to visit with my grandparents before the war. Mrs. Ruth Lionberger was a widow who had stayed in touch with us for many years. Immediately after the war she contacted us to see how she could help us and started sending large parcels with things she thought we could use and urged us to let her know what we really needed. This was mostly clothing. So she went around to her friends who had about my size and that of Pa and started shipping shoes, suits, etc. that these men gave her straight out of their closets. I think she even sent a ladies' coat for Ma, but sending women's clothing was much trickier, of course.

This was a true example of the limitless generosity many Europeans experienced after the war from America, mostly now forgotten. So towards the summer of 1945 I had a nice wardrobe of three American suits. This was extremely welcome because we still had to cope with a severe rationing system, which touched almost all aspects of our lives. Clothing, shoes, cigarettes (Mrs. Lionberger sent me Lucky Strikes by the carton), coal, fuel, gasoline, housing etc. etc. My parents and I corresponded regularly with Mrs. Lionberger to express our gratitude and appreciation for her generosity. In the summer of 1947 Pa went on a business trip to the U.S. to reacquaint himself with the newer oil drilling technologies that had been developed during the war. At that time he made a special side trip by train from Texas to Omaha to visit Mrs. Lionberger and thank her for what she had done for us.

As we emerged from the wartime scarcities, we often had the feeling that we were over-regulated and over-rationed. The bureaucracy that was put in place to organize the distribution of consumer goods and regulate the construction activity had become enormous. It became self-perpetuating and it took years until we had gotten rid of all encumbrances. We often felt that the bureaucracy kept itself alive by inventing scarcities where none would exist anymore or would have disappeared if we had opened up the market. We had a strongly socialist-leaning government in those days, and its stated policy was to use taxes not only to cover the government's expenses but also as a means to achieve political objectives. This became very clear in later years, but in the period immediately after the war the country was practically broke and needed considerable cash infusions. So we not only were subjected to extra high tax rates but also to a heavy "one time" charge levied on all taxpayers to cover war damages, which was based on one's reported wealth. This charge was called *Heffing Ineens,* Levy At Once. I remember my grandfather grumbling about this charge that was sharply progressive and must have hit him hard where it hurt most.

Student life got going in the spring and summer of 1946. Traditionally the *Corps* had two Balls each year. The most important one was the *Sempre Bal.* One of the *Corps'* most prominent suborganizations was the music ensemble called *Sempre Crescendo.* It had an orchestra that produced an annual classical concert of some merit. Their performance was held in the concert hall in Leiden and the Ball followed this performance. The other one was the *Toneel Bal,* the Theatre Ball organized by the people who liked to produce plays. You attended a play during the earlier part of the evening and afterwards there was a great Ball. Ours was in the *"Kurhaus",* an old hotel in Scheveningen. We went to these Balls with a group from our club, all dressed in white tie and tails, the customary dress for student Balls in those days.

I don't remember anymore where I got my costume. I think I owned a tuxedo and used its pants and rented or borrowed the coat with the tails. At first I had tried a jacket that belonged to my grandfather. He had once been officially introduced to the Queen and had to wear white tie and tails for the occasion. This event took place many years ago and the coat had been hanging in his closet since then. My grandmother, who never threw anything away offered it proudly to me, but when I put my arm into the sleeve, the lining proved to be totally decayed and came out in shreds with my arm. So I let that one go. You had a white vest and a shirt with a stiff front, with a wing collar attached with collar studs and a white tie. We had a few parties during the winter at people's houses where I got to know more girls. Rob Laane was a most valuable connection in that area. Somehow he knew an awful lot of attractive girls in The Hague and Wassenaar and introduced me to them. I went to my first *Sempre* Ball with Joke Nuchteren, a really sweet girl I knew from Voorburg. I also went dancing with her in Scheveningen one spring day, borrowing my father's brand new English Raleigh bicycle that he had brought back with him from a business trip to London. I put the bike in an official guarded place for bikes and got a receipt for it. When I came back the attendant told me the bike was gone! I am still mortified thinking about that event and remembering how powerless I felt. So I pedaled back home on Joke's bike with her sitting on the back.

In the fall of 1946 I went with Rob Laane to the Leiden Town Theater to hear Ruth Draper, an American artist well known for her monologues. I thought she was very good. During the intermission, we saw two girls Rob knew and he introduced me to them. One was Tilly van Kleffens. Shortly after that evening Rob got a note from Tilly inviting him to a party she was giving at her house in Wassenaar for her birthday. She added a P.S. saying, "by the way, maybe the fellow who was with you at the theater (I forgot his name) would also like to come." And that was how I met Netty. Rob and I went to the party, met with Tilly's mother as was customary and spoke with her for a few minutes. We also met Tilly's younger brother Pul who was then still very young and dressed in a "battle dress," the uniform the British and Canadian soldiers who had liberated us used to wear. The uniform had been scaled down for him ,of course. The other guests were young people from a neighborhood group Tilly and Netty called *de Soos* roughly translated the society or club. Rob and I thought these kids were somewhat below our level of sophistication. We were after all "university students" and rather full of ourselves. Netty was part of the group but kept herself a little in the background. We danced a little to a record player, did a few silly kissing games and had over all a nice time. Netty and I later confessed we both hated the kissing games.

I was immensely attracted to Netty, who was at sixteen still very young. Rob and I decided we would invite Netty and Tilly to lunch in my room. We wanted to see them again and decide among ourselves which one we would invite for the next Sempre Ball. At that time both Netty and Tilly attended the *Meisjes HBS* in Leiden, the HBS for girls. They walked from that school to the tram to Wassenaar, often passing the Oude Rijn where the *Chateau de Biscuit* was conveniently located. At this luncheon I decided to invite Netty, but Rob decided not to invite Tilly. We did not tell them then because we wanted to invite them separately. This must nevertheless have been a blow for Tilly. For girls, especially the ones who were Leiden students, an invitation to a student Ball was a big thing, and for the student girls almost a make or break proposition. On the day of the Ball I picked Netty up and escorted her to the house of Professor and Mrs. Cleveringa, who were friends of her father and uncle and considered a super safe address. Netty carried her dress in a box and we went by tram to our destination. Later on I picked her up again, now dressed in white tie and tails and we went to the restaurant where we had dinner with my club group. The photo of this dinner shows in the background two members of our club, Werner Hermann and Bart Schuur, who had both decided not to go to the Ball and just wanted to have dinner and spy on us. As far as I was concerned, the ball was a great success, and I believe Netty liked it too.

From then on I started dating Netty fairly regularly. We went to the theater, dancing in Scheveningen, etc. I got to know Netty's family better and she met mine. I remember one sunny day in Scheveningen where I was with Netty and for some reason we were to meet my parents and Tante Jetje van der Hoop. What startled Netty was that both Ma and Tante Jetje were dressed in the same summer dresses. Yellow affairs with green dots if I remember correctly. This was not as odd as it seems because in those days you bought whatever you could, and those dresses may have been the only shot they had for a new summer dress. We were joined by Pa and probably went to eat *Rijsttafel,* the Indonesian dinner we all liked very much.

Meanwhile a dark cloud arrived on my horizon. The Netherlands was involved in a long-term struggle to regain control over its former colonies in the Dutch East Indies, now Indonesia. Troops were sent over to reestablish order. The first Dutch military presence in Indonesia consisted of volunteers who were recruited immediately after the war, initially to fight the Japanese, later to go to Indonesia to suppress the local rebellion of the then-fledgling Republic Indonesia. Later it became necessary to reestablish the draft and send more troops. Special legislation was passed to make the movement of draftees overseas possible. Before too long I was called up to come to The Hague for a medical test. There I found myself among a bunch of Leiden "townies," tough guys who enjoyed the day and made fun of the students among them by calling them "George," which in Dutch sounds somewhat like "Sjors." It was common practice among those fellows to yell at students on the street, who were easy to spot because they were dressed much more formal. They would yell, imitating our slightly affected style of speech something like *"Zeg Sjors, waar ga je naar toe man?"* (Say George where are you going?) George was considered to be strictly an upper-class first name. So imagine their glee when our names were called and we got to me and they heard "Schieferdecker – George Peter." A great whoop went up. Still, I had a good time with this group. We were all walking around practically nude and made fun of each other's appearance. We particularly enjoyed a crude joke the medics played on a very nervous, jumpy guy who was clearly not playing with a complete set of irons. They were trying to take a look in his ears and found them clogged with wax so they brought a huge pump-like device to flush them out. A normal thing, but the guy was frightened and whimpered loudly. So they prepared to flush out his left ear and told him to hold the vessel that would receive the water coming out under his right ear. Which he did. A few moments later a doctor came to tell him the country would not need his services.

I was tested "fit for service." As was usual I got a student exemption until after my first exam, the *Candidaats* exam. I would have to report after I passed that exam and would then most likely be called up,— a prospect I was not looking forward to. I had nothing against serving in the military, in fact immediately after the liberation I had volunteered to fight the Japanese and wanted to become a pilot. I passed that medical too. But after the Japanese capitulated, I saw no reason to rally around the flag anymore.

In the spring of 1947 Willem Witteveen and I had an opportunity to improve our lodgings further when we learned there was a big room available on a house on the Rapenburg, the most prestigious address one can have as a student in Leiden. The Rapenburg is an old canal running through the heart of the old town. Our house was very near the old Academy building where the university was founded in 1572. The *Pieterskerk,* the old church from where the Pilgrim Fathers departed on their journey to America, was across the canal from the Academy. Our house at number 8 was a stately historic building with marble hallways, sumptuous rooms with high ceilings and ornate marble mantels in the rooms. The staircase was an antique gem with marvelous woodwork. The occupants of this house were an interesting group of mostly older students (senior in corps years to us). Several of them have remained good friends of mine over the years. In later years I had the pleasure of offering one of them, Ernest van Panhuys, a job at the firm where I worked in Amsterdam and we spent several pleasant years together. When I left for the U.S. we said a tearful good bye to each other and that was the last I heard from Ernest until he came to New

York for a brief visit. After that there was again complete silence despite all my efforts to stay in touch. Ernest died a few years later. Such is life.

During my stay at Rapenburg 8 Willem got heavily involved in volunteering for the NBBS (*Nederlands Bureau voor Buitenlandse Studentenbetrekkingen* – Netherlands Bureau for Foreign Student Relations), an organization that promoted contact with students in other countries and also travel for Dutch students to places abroad. This was in the postwar period an important effort because we could not travel just anywhere without elaborate arrangements for lodging and spending money (we were only allowed to take very little foreign exchange out of the country). Usually the arrangement was for Dutch students to go somewhere where they could work and earn a little money to spend afterwards for travel or vacation. Rob Laane and I subscribed to such a project in the summer of 1947 when we went to Sweden.

I don't think I ever studied harder in my life than in that spring of 1947 period or after it. I went up for my *Candidaat's* exam in the late spring and to my immense relief passed with the notation *"Met genoegen"* (With pleasure). This was better than just a passing grade. At least that was what I thought the professor said at the end of my exam. True to tradition I appeared in the ancient Academy building where the exam would be held in white tie and tails. Before the exam one had to wait in a little room called *het zweet kamertje,* (the little sweating room). In this room generations upon generations of students had sat nervously awaiting their exams and written their names (and sometimes drawn pictures,) on the whitewashed walls. I added my name. I hope it is still there. After the exam we had a party at the *Societeit Minerva* with an ample supply of *jenever.*

This step forward opened up the possibility for me to undertake a trip abroad. Rob and I enlisted as farm laborers and took a train to Sweden. The train ran from Holland through Germany to Denmark and from there we took a ferry over the *Øresund* to Malmö, Sweden. This was the first exposure we had to postwar Germany. Our train left the Netherlands during the day and ran past Hamburg and Bremen in the evening. These two cities were still completely bombed out, two years after the war. You could see the harbors where badly damaged cranes were hanging lopsided over the water. Along the tracks dozens of children were lined up begging for food. The Germans were not being well fed. When we came to a station we would walk around on the platform and look at the poorly dressed and poorly fed people wandering about. We would smoke a cigarette and make sure our cigarette butts would not be useful to them by grinding them out on the platform with our feet. We did not give a damn about the plight of the Germans. The war was still too fresh in our memory. On one of the stations I heard an older man say *Das sind die Sieger,* (those are the victors). I thought "you are damn right and you better not forget it." Still, the incredible devastation we saw in the cities made an impression.

In the middle of the night we passed the Danish border. As the sun went up again we saw an entirely different landscape, the totally pristine Danish countryside, untouched by war. Neat farmhouses with clear white walls and red roofs in the early morning haze an almost surreal sight after the devastation in Germany and the shabby and often also badly war damaged Dutch countryside. But then the Danes had hardly fought in the war. They were overrun in April 1940 and capitulated after five hours. After a ferry ride, we arrived in Malmö, Sweden. There we fell into the arms of the Swedish bureaucracy. We had to go to a hospital to be examined, go to an office to get working papers, etc. You could immediately see in the attitude of the Swedes that they had been neutral in the war, that little had changed there and that they were determined to stick to their rules and regulations. Even then Sweden was a country with strong socialist overtones and a state that kept a heavy hand in everything that went on.

In the afternoon we were guests of a group of Swedish students who wore white caps, similar to old-fashioned sailing hats. The girls wore the same caps. They did not make much of an effort to get to know us and spoke generally poor English or German. By and large they probably felt awkward towards us having been so neutral and prosperous all these years. They also seemed to us a little less mature than we were after all we had lived through.

From Malmö we went by train to our final destination, a farm that belonged to the Swedish noble family of the *Greve Bunde,* Count Bunde. The count lived in a castle nearby and a man called "the inspector" managed his extensive farmlands. The castle was called *Bosjökloster*. The countryside was lovely, rolling hills with many forests in between extensive fields with grain, potatoes and many other crops. We were housed in several houses that normally must have served as homes for farm workers. We had to wash in the kitchen sink and go to an outhouse if we wanted to go to the bathroom. In one of the houses we had a sort of dining room where an elderly Swedish woman cooked for us. She had a strong resemblance to the way Mrs. Claus, the wife of Santa Claus, is usually portrayed by Hollywood. She was quite heavy, always wore an apron and a scarf around her hair and had small steel-rimmed glasses on the tip of her round bulbous nose. She was officially addressed as *hüsmoor,* house-mother. She was a jolly type who cooked fabulous, very rich meals. At the farm we met our campmates. There were a few other Dutchmen, including a somewhat older guy who was a schoolteacher and spoke reasonably good Swedish, two Norwegians, two Slovaks from Bratislava and "Mr." Gunnar Zachrisson, a Swedish student who was our leader. Gunnar was a strange, somewhat effeminate fellow with long hair (unusual in those days) hanging in his face. While we worked in the fields he never did a stroke of work. He was supposed to organize our stay at the farm and arrange some entertainment. That he did. On Sundays a young man, a student of agriculture who also worked at the farm, would take us around on a flatcar pulled by a tractor. Sometimes we would go out dancing to villages where Swedish families had summer cottages. There would be big tents with a fenced off dance floor and a small band. Stern looking Swedes with uniform hats would guard the entrance to the dance floor. You could only dance if you had previously bought a ticket. There were a large number of attractive blond Swedish girls hanging around these dance places. They were spending their summer vacation there with their families and were bored. It was all very small-town innocent and nice.

Very near the farm was a lake where we would go to swim. Our work varied. We would be sent to weed a potato field or pick pickles. The fields were huge, the sun was very warm and we were far from fit for farm work. It was depressing to see how local farm women would come to a field and outpace us within seconds in weeding or picking. Still, we had a very good, very healthy time. I worked for a while alone cutting wood in a forest with Sverre, a huge Norwegian who was incredibly fit and strong. I guess our wartime experience and lack of exercise was very noticeable, but

the Scandinavians never commented on it. The countess, who was an attractive youngish woman, also invited us for coffee and cakes. Near the lake was a colony of small summer homes and we met some of the people living there, but nobody invited us to visit. However, the girls who lived there came over to see us. One of them was a particularly pretty girl named Britta Angverd. She went out with one of the Slovaks. When we left she gave a photo of herself to Rob and me, and when Netty and I got married a so called "Bridal Newspaper" was printed in which Britta's photo appeared prominently.

After about a month of hard work we were in much better shape than when we came. We were paid a nice amount of money and Rob and I immediately started spending it. First we went to Helsingborg where we bought clothes for ourselves. Among other things I bought a pair of shoes there that I kept all through Indonesia. When I came back they were worn out so I disposed of them by throwing them in the harbor just before debarking. Being able to buy good quality clothes was an unheard off luxury for us. In fact it was an amazing experience to be in a country that was untouched by war where all the houses were in excellent repair and everybody looked prosperous and well dressed and where all the girls seemed to be incredibly pretty. Rob and I had done some research and decided to spend a week in the small seaside resort town of Bostad. After a week there with marvelous weather and nice beaches we went home where I found my whole family including Tante Jetje eagerly awaiting me to hear the news about the outside world.

In the fall of 1947 I had the luck of being able to take another trip to England. I went there with a Leiden student field hockey team under the leadership of Jack de Meyere, a friend who was active in that sport. Fokke Jonkers, my former housemate, was also in the team as a goalie. For obvious reasons we called him Bill Jonkers in England. Jack said they needed a reserve player in case there was a problem with the regulars so this was a fine opportunity for me to enjoy a week or so in Oxford, Cambridge and later Loughborough, just hanging around and watching the others play. I had not played in years but thought chances that I would be called upon would be slim. Unfortunately somebody got slightly injured right at the beginning so I was forced to play. I have seldom felt so embarrassed in sports as at that time, playing with a reasonably good team and being the clear weak spot.

Still, it was fun to stay at the colleges of Oxford and Cambridge and be a guest of English students there. They were extremely hospitable. Most of them were quite a bit older as they almost all had served in the war for many years. Life in the colleges was a curious combination of pre–Victorian discomfort, and some very English and very nice conveniences. One or two students usually had several rooms together, a sitting room and several bedrooms. The rooms were quite cozy and nicely furnished, much nicer than ours in Leiden, in fact, but the toilets were very smelly antique affairs located at a great distance. Male servants would come in the morning to serve breakfast, clean up the rooms, take care of laundry, etc. Dinners were sumptuous affairs in beautiful Gothic halls served to a large number of students seated at long tables with the professors on a dais facing the multitude. After the games we would go back to the locker room where attendants had filled a row of deep bathtubs with steaming hot water. Showers were, of course, out of the question for English gentlemen. I remember that one evening I was the guest of a student in his room where we had a long discussion about politics. It turned out he was strongly in favor of the Labor Party, which had won the elections right after the war when Winston Churchill was basically told by the population that he was a good war leader, but that they wanted something else for peacetime. In the Netherlands we also had a socialist government and I was not at all in favor of it. I thought then, and still feel the same way today, that their level of interference and masterminding of every aspect of society and the economy down to the smallest detail went much too far and stifled freedom and free enterprise. He was, of course, of a different opinion and mentioned several facts about life in England before and during the war that did not apply to the Dutch situation at all. This made me realize that socialism and class had deep roots in British life. He said, for instance, that the distinction between the classes of British society was profound. The working class had lived for centuries under often wretched conditions, deprived of decent nutrition, and that whole generation of working-class children had "grown up without knowing what milk tasted like." In Holland there were differences between the classes, of course, and I had seen people in farming areas living under very poor and primitive conditions, but the overall gap between social layers was not at all as steep as in Britain.

Several years later I would visit London again and on a Sunday walk through Hyde Park saw a reunion and parade of a British army regiment. All the officers were in sharp, dark-blue business suits with bowler hats and umbrellas and marched with the umbrellas under their arms like drill sticks. They were followed by the so-called "other ranks" a group of jolly men in rumpled suits and floppy felt hats. The startling difference, however, was not as much in the outward appearance of the two groups, but in their length. The officers were all at least a foot taller! This was obviously a reflection of the better nutrition they had enjoyed when they were growing up. I made a movie of this parade and still have it.

At some point in the summer of 1947 I passed my driving test. As I mentioned, once I had my license, Pa was very generous in letting me have the old Terraplane, which gave an entirely new dimension to my recreational activities. I went frequently over to Wassenaar to see Netty and take her out to parties and on rides in the countryside. Sometimes Rob hitched a ride with us and we then put him in the "rumble seat" and when it was cold or rainy he would crouch low so he could let the lid down. We then purposely drove over curbs and other obstacles to shake him up a bit. I remember one glorious sunny day (rare in Holland) when Rob and I drove out towards Utrecht with the top of the Terraplane down. We enjoyed confusing drivers of passing cars by moving along with me hanging casually out with both arms over the driver's side while Rob was surreptitiously steering from the passenger side. There was not all that much traffic in those days; people drove slower and road rage and aggressive driving was still to come.

In the fall of 1947 I started to focus on the second half of my studies. I now had more or less caught up with my year and could take a more serious and deliberate attitude towards getting my law degree, i.e. attend more classes and spend less on tutors. As the year moved on I began to really enjoy student life since I now had reached my third year and could benefit from the privileges my more elevated status in the *Corps* offered. After New Year's 1948 I talked with Rob van der Tooren about taking riding lessons. Rob was a great equestrian and I thought that would be a sport I might enjoy. So I arranged for a few introductory lessons at the student manège where there was a riding school. Pa had a lot of riding equipment from his days in Mexico and from his prewar riding period. He had elegant riding boots and a nice pair of light riding pants from his Mexico days. So I took these over to Leiden and climbed on my horse. As I swung my right leg over the horse's back for the first time, my pants split at the seam. They were too old. So I took my first riding lesson worried about how I would be able to walk the short distance home with pants that were split through the middle.

When I got back to Rapenburg 8 there was a message that the army wanted to see me promptly. It appeared they had called me up and sent a message to that effect to my old address at *Chateau de Bisquit,* the messy Vos family there had never bothered to send this message on to me. They knew very well where I had moved to. Mr. "Pa" Vos had even helped me move my furniture over. He pushed a handcart with my stuff on top, moving at a trot and keeping in front of the tram. I trotted alongside. They were just sloppy people and had forgotten my mail. I made a few phone calls and found out that I was late to report and would have to hustle over to Arnhem immediately, where I would have to report for primary training, in order to avoid being punished for being late. I was totally shattered by this turn of events. I had to fold my tents in Leiden in a great hurry, say good bye to my friends and face an uncertain future without riding lessons. That evening I drove over to Wassenaar to tell Netty the bad news. When I said good-bye she kissed me, a gesture that raised my spirits a little and that I will never forget. I opened a new chapter in my life, which would bring many hardships and many difficult times, but also memorable experiences. My easy going student days were over forever.

16 : *Wearing The Queen's Uniform*

On a gloomy January day I traveled to Arnhem and went to the Menno van Coehoorn Kazerne, an ancient 19th century barracks complex. There I met with a grumpy sergeant major of the administrative branch who seemed annoyed by the prospect of having to check me into the army just when he was prepared to have a nice lazy afternoon. This was my first contact with the kind of professional army "lifer" who spends his time figuring out how he can do as little as possible while earning as much as possible and by all means retire as early as possible. There would be many more encounters with this kind of army man. He told me I was just in time in reporting for duty. If I had waited one more week, the MP, the Military Police, would have picked me up. Afterwards I was given a ride to another barracks complex, more modern and located on the outskirts of town. This was the Saksen Weimar Kazerne. At that place I received a mountain of uniforms, underwear, boots, belts and backpacks, etc., etc. The Dutch army of those days was completely equipped with British army gear, including weapons and tin hats. We wore the British "battle dress" as uniform, made out of heavy wool with a short jacket and pants with extra pockets on the thighs. We received a new uniform that was later tailored a bit to fit better, and an old used uniform to be worn in the field, and a heavy coverall- type uniform to be used in the field in summer and for greasy or dirty work. The barracks complex was alive with recruits being put through their paces for what was called "primary training," a six-week period in which recruits were toughened up to increase their endurance and teach them the rudiments of drill, weapons handling, etc.

I ended up in a large room with about 20 beds, two rows with doubles, one on top of the other. They gave me a bed, luckily it was the lower one, and a locker, and a corporal told me how to fold my clothes in the locker. He escorted me to a pile of straw where I filled my straw mattress. I dragged the mattress inside and dressed for the first time in the uniform the sergeant told me to use. It would be more than two and a half years before I got rid of it. Being new in the army is really a very odd experience. You are exposed to a new world with its own rules of behavior, its own terminology and slang and its own timetable, very different from the one I had been used to as a student. Here it was get up very early, rush to get ready for early morning report and inspections, fairly hasty meals consisting of generally lousy food and very early bedtime and lights out. My roommates were outside, being trained for something. When they got back and we got acquainted with each other, I discovered that my platoon of twenty or so men was the "clean up" group; it consisted of guys who were late in joining for one reason or another. There was another student type, who disappeared fairly quickly to the officer's school; there was Piet Plooy, a guy who had been late because he was in jail when called up. He was a man who stood out because he had already fathered a child. I forgot whether he was married or not. I think he worked as a stevedore on the docks in Rotterdam. There was a strange guy who moved very slowly and was a rural type from way deep in the provinces. He wore curious underwear that seemed a throwback to the previous century and refused to change to Government Issue underwear. There were several fellows with strange medical problems, who in my view should never have been called up. Next to me was a nice guy who had a very peculiar habit. He slept with his eyes open! I checked it several times and it was true. He had his eyes open and did not blink. We were called very early in the morning, 6 a.m. or thereabouts, "the sergeant of the week" would come around, switch on the lights, and blow his whistle. We had to dash out of bed to get halfway dressed, go to the toilet and "wash." Washing was a cursory affair because the water was very cold and the main challenge was to shave as quickly as possible since we had to be clean-shaven when inspection time came. The barracks building dated back to 1938 when the Dutch government made a belated effort to modernize its military, so it was not very old. However, the Germans had done a lot of damage to it and the heating system still did not work that winter, which was a cold one. A sergeant took me aside a couple of times to teach me the rudiments of drill I had missed. Soon I was up-to-date and could march around with the others.

The battalion I was in belonged to a guards regiment, "Prinses Irene." One of the few positive parts of being in the service was the physical training you got. The rule was that you had to be able to run two kilometers. About a mile-and-a-third. In the beginning I was totally unable to cover that distance running, although the sergeants would yell at us incessantly and threaten us they would take our weekend leave away if we didn't make it. We realized, however, that there were simply so many stragglers that it was impossible to keep that many people over the weekend. Since we would all be going to Indonesia, a program of inoculations and injections was started. Many men had never been inoculated against small pox, so they all got the scratches and before too long walked around with two big ugly sores on their upper arms. I got the same treatment, but it did not take, probably because I had been inoculated when I was a small child. We also got a combination of shots to prepare us for typhoid, tetanus and all sorts of tropical diseases. Those shots were really big, several men fell down in a heap after receiving them. I think we got three in succession, one every week. After the third one, I got a high fever so I had to stay in the room while the platoon went on a night training exercise.

We learned the infantry weapons – all English. The Lee Enfield rifle (a reliable but old WW I vintage rifle), the Sten gun (a lousy, light sub-machine gun), the Bren gun (a very good light machine gun), the PIAT (an antitank weapon) and the hand grenade. I still remember how baffled we were when a corporal gave us our first lesson on the rifle. He asked, "What is the purpose of the weapon?" We were stumped. He then proudly answered his own question. The purpose was "to destroy the enemy." We got some elementary training with our rifles on the local firing range. After six weeks we completed our "primary training." It was early spring and we were ready for more advanced training. While we had been confined in the barracks for our primary training, we were now allowed to go home on our first leave. We had a big parade through the streets of Arnhem with a large military band providing the right rhythm to march on. It was the first time in my life that I had participated in a military parade and I grasped the psychological value of drill and of marching with a band. The band made you march better and its rhythmic staccato pounding made you feel good and very soldier like. Napoleon and Hitler and all the German generals who served under him also understood this. They promoted band music as much as they could. When I returned home for the weekend, I quickly changed into my civilian clothes and went to Wassenaar to see Netty. In the weeks to follow we went to many weekend parties and went out as much as we could because I had the feeling I might be sent out to Indonesia before too long.

Our battalion was slowly being prepared for Indonesia, but for me another plan was hatched. The people with high school diplomas and students were being culled out to become officers and NCOs. For some reason I was not immediately selected for a test for officers school. It was probably because at that time of the year there was no new class starting. Later on, I was ordered to take the test and to my relief failed. If I had passed I would have had to serve longer. As it turned out I was sent to a NCO school and that meant six months more service anyway. Adding the officers training to that would have meant a year more. I was not prepared to do that.

In the early spring of 1948 I had to go to Harderwijk, a small garrison town in northern part of the province of Gelderland. In a complex called the Willem Frederik Kazerne was the so-called Kaderschool – school for noncommissioned officers. Among the ordinary soldiers these schools had a reputation of being particularly tough with very strict discipline. As I quickly found out, the stories were correct. I was less than happy to find myself there, but there was little I could do about it. It was still an infantry school, but we were organized in the English system where an infantry battalion had three rifle companies and one "support" company. This company was meant to support the rifle companies with heavier weapons. These support companies were all motorized. We used small tracked vehicles called "carriers." I ended up in the heavy mortar platoon. Beyond mortars the company had a heavy machine gun and an antitank platoon.

Our platoon consisted of guys culled from many different regiments. We were immediately thrown into a regime of constant bullying by sergeants who were more skilled, more "spit and polish" and senior to the ones we were used to. Most officers and sergeants had seen action during the war and all were good at maintaining a very strict discipline. We were ordered not to walk, but always run. There was a lot of attention paid to grooming and keeping our gear neat and an immensely high level of pressure to keep us moving all the time and give us very little time to accomplish our tasks.

During the day we would often have to change from track suits into uniforms or into working uniforms and back again and were given only a few minutes to do that. The rooms and barracks had to be kept spotlessly clean, and in the first week or so we were awakened several times and ordered to dress into full battle-gear and rush outside to stand at parade rest because a cigarette butt had been found in our building. This kind of stuff made me very angry because I realized that this was just a way of "breaking us down" to instill a high level of discipline in us. They had, of course, not found a cigarette butt.

We spent a lot of time training with our heavy 3-inch mortars. The mortar is an interesting weapon and very handy for infantry work. It was heavy to carry around, consisting basically of three parts, the ground plate, the barrel and the two legs that held the barrel up once its end rested on the ground plate. It could bomb an area of several acres at a distance of two to three miles with shrapnel bombs or smoke bombs or a combination of the two. Mortars always operated from behind hills, buildings or other cover and rarely saw the results of their fire. Forward observers were supposed to tell us what to do. The idea was to have the platoon of four mortars race up to its position in carriers, unload the mortars, which were in three pieces on the back in racks, put them together in a few seconds and start aiming them. Using a quickly strung-out telephone line, the forward observer would give us compass bearings to aim the mortars and the elevation he assumed we needed to reach the target. We would fire a few shots to get the proper bearing, and once we had zeroed in to the target fire a barrage of bombs. After that, we were supposed to pack up quickly and disappear. We trained endlessly with the carriers. We would sit in the open vehicles and on command dive out by swinging ourselves over the edge and racing to put the mortars together. Very tiring stuff, and as it turned out, all for naught. When we came to Indonesia, there were no carriers for us anymore and we had to move our mortars on trucks, leaving them in one place for weeks. Since we would all become corporals or sergeants, we were especially trained in directing the fire. There was a classroom with a sandbox showing a model of terrain with little houses, trees, etc. in it and we trained directing fire there. A sergeant- instructor sat under the sandbox to create puffs of smoke in the target area from below, to give us an idea of where our bombs were landing. This was quite interesting and fun to do. Beyond mortar training, we got ordinary infantry training, with many forced marches, night exercises etc. On Saturday mornings we had to run several kilometers just before getting dressed in our best uniforms for inspection and weekend leave. As we were constantly trained, the running did not present a problem anymore. We were very fit. We had to jump backwards out of trucks moving at about 25 mph, loaded down with rifles and packs. We forded small lakes and rivers with water up to our armpits. The water and mud work was particularly annoying since we would have to clean up our clothes, gear and shoes afterwards to be ready again for spit and polish inspections. We had belts and anklets made out of heavy canvas and brass buckles. We had to shine the buckles to a fare thee well and work the canvas with a sort of clay like compound that we would smear on with water so it would produce a nice even olive drab color.

The Saturday morning inspections could sometimes have a nasty effect. I remember one of my roommates being a little late for inspection because he went to the latrine. When he ran back to where we were standing, he got a little dust on the tip of one of his shiny boots. He was told to stay back because his boots were dirty. He could not go home that weekend. The poor guy was crushed. In Holland where all distances are short, all soldiers are used to go home every weekend. When I came home, I would quickly change into civilian clothes. This was actually strictly forbidden and punishable. What you had to watch out for was not to act like a robot and salute an officer when passing him in the street in civilian clothes. I would try to get the Terraplane to go see Netty. We then could have an evening and a day together. On Sunday afternoon, Netty often came back with me to Voorburg. After dinner I would have to get back in uniform and Netty would go with me to the Voorburg train station where I would start the trek back to Harderwijk. The trains used for military transport were often made up of old German cars with wooden benches in third class. The Dutch railways were certainly still not yet up to prewar standards. Traveling in the poorly lit old rattletraps to a small provincial town made me feel as if it were still wartime. I felt trapped in a world where all my movements were controlled by an outside force and where I had little opportunity to do anything I really wanted to do. Once we arrived in Hardewijk, large numbers of soldiers would pour out of the train and start walking back to the barracks. We would try to sleep as soon as we got back because a screaming sergeant would blast us out of bed again at six in the morning. The irritating thing was that a few guys would arrive much later in our room than most of us. They would stomp in, switch on the light, talk loudly and make all sorts of other noises, much to our irritation.

In Harderwijk I got to know Octave van Crugten, a fellow student also trapped in the army. He was being trained as a sniper, which was also a specialty. Oc used to hunt a great deal with his father in Limburg where he lived and the army probably found him a good shot. Oc and I very often had dinner in a small restaurant just outside the barracks gate. The food in the army was very poor in those days, especially on Friday when we had to eat fish because of the Catholics. They would serve very small frozen flounders that were not warmed up so they were very brittle, and when you tried to cut into them they would just splinter into small solid frozen particles. Oc and I became close friends and we saw a lot of each other in Indonesia.

That summer the discipline slacked off a bit and we did not have to run everywhere we went. We spent time at the army shooting range where we could use live ammunition and drive our carriers through the terrain. This was more interesting than the eternal drills with standing carriers we had been through. A less attractive part was the need to sleep in pup tents. We each had a waterproof sheet in our pack that could be buttoned together with the sheet of another fellow and so form a small pup tent for two. We had oilcloth raincoats that were intended to serve also as protection against gas attack, and we used them to sleep on so the moisture of the ground would not penetrate. My tentmate was my "slapie," the Dutch army term for the guy who sleeps nearest you, in my case above me. This was Stephen Lebküchner. Leb, as we called him, had an interesting background. He was the adopted son of a family from Culemborg, a nice, small historic town "between the big rivers" as they say in Holland. I believe his father owned a furniture factory there and he had grown up using his adoptive parent's name, which was, if my memory is correct, Grimberg. His birth mother lived in Germany and had the name the army insisted he should use because somehow that was considered to be his real legal name. Leb had a fairly big behind and was about as tall as me so we barely fit into our pup tent. We had a couple of cold, miserable nights and it was at that time that I swore I would never go camping anymore after I got out of the army.

It was during our time in Harderwijk in the summer of 1948 that the relationship between the Soviet Union and its East European block and the U.S. and the rest of Europe really began to sour. The Berlin crisis erupted. The U.S. Airforce in Germany and the RAF had to establish an air bridge between Western Europe and the city of Berlin, which was located inside the territory of what was then Communist East Germany, to fly in food and fuel since the Soviets had blocked off all access roads and railways to the city. As we stood in front of our buildings every morning for inspection and the flag was being raised, we could see the planes fly by. NATO, the North Atlantic Treaty Organization was still in its formative years, but we knew that we would be involved if there would be trouble. Not a pleasant thought. A more humorous interlude was provided several times by a stray dog that lived on the grounds and was nourished by scraps of food the guys working in the kitchen would throw him. Once this dog wandered over and when the trumpeter blew his bugle to call for the flag raising, he sat down, threw his head up and start howling. After that he wandered up to the flagpole, lifted his leg and peed. We thought that was just wonderful, particularly since the major, who was in command and stood alone in front of us, exploded in a fit of anger and ordered some sergeants to chase the dog, in vain, of course. Somewhere in the middle of our training there in Harderwijk we were promoted to private first class.

CORPORAL SCHIEFERDECKER.

When we came to the end of our training period, we were all promoted to corporal, a rank in which I would stay stuck for the next two years. We had to pass a written test for this promotion and I had passed for sergeant, but there were too many ahead of me who had made sergeant so they took the ones with the best grades first. As was usual in the Dutch army of those days, corporals had to act as sergeants, sergeants as lieutenants etc. This saved money and we were conscripts anyway so who cared? I think my bad marks were for one course in particular. This was a course on Indonesia, its population and its religions. It was taught by an elderly professional NCO of the colonial army who was waiting for his retirement and gave us some very poor information about the country where he had spent his whole career. So I proceeded to answer his questions with my newly acquired academic knowledge about Islam, etc. I should not have bothered. My teacher probably never understood what I wrote and gave me a fail. As I mentioned before, I also failed the test for an officers' course. I had to go to the town of Amersfoort with a couple of others. There we got a written exam and a physical test. In my case a doctor let me run over an obstacle course at the end of the day because he had forgotten to include me earlier in this test. He measured my time and commented that I was slow. I was because I was tired and also because he did not set his stopwatch right. He started his watch first and then gave me a start about twenty seconds later. After that he had a conversation with me in which he said, "I don't think you would be a very inspiring leader for a platoon of soldiers." I saw my chance and answered, "No." This spared me from another six-month training period. I guess I did not make a very gung-ho impression and that was how I felt, although I think in reflection that I turned out to be a reasonably good leader of men in the military and later in business of men and women. It's just that I always abhorred showing off as a zealot or advertising myself as a great leader.

We were all assigned to battalions that were going through primary training. After they finished this training we would join them and go to Indonesia with them. I ended up in the same barracks where I had started, the Menno van Coehoorn Kazerne in Arnhem. But before we went there we had a few weeks leave. Netty and I had by that time really fallen deeply in love and decided to get engaged. So I asked her father if I could have a talk with him and asked him formally for his permission to ___ry Netty. This was all, of course, not a great surprise for Netty's parents because I ___ regular guest at their house. I had gotten to know Netty's family well and ___ ___ I hoped they also liked me. When I passed the test for son-___ ___ration among ourselves, and then we went through the ___ engagement. This involved sending announcements ___ mostly friends and relatives of our parents and our own ___ organize an engagement reception at the bride's house. ___. Netty and I went to Bloemendaal in the Terraplane to ___ my grandparents. It was September and as often hap-___ humid air and the cooling soil caused a thick ground fog. ___ ___ening, we went through Heemstede and I drove down a ___ track running through the middle. In the fog I followed ___ ___aring on the location of the road. As we came to what later ___ circle, the tram tracks ran straight across the circle, but the ___ did not notice that, and in the center of the traffic circle ___ pole of the tram. We were not going very fast, but the car ___ ___etty who was and is not a heavyweight, was thrown with her ___ ___ield that broke. I was totally crushed by this event and had ___ ___could leave the car for repairs and get us back to the station ___ ___n home. We were both really depressed about this whole ___ ___he situation proved to be even worse as Netty appeared to ___ ___ to stay motionless in bed for a week or two. This accident ___ ___r engagement reception and ruined the plans we had for a ___ ___ade a great effort to let everybody know that our party was off, but to my mortification there were still a few people who showed up. I guess this accident would not have happened if I had been a more experienced driver, and Netty would certainly not have suffered through the headaches and other problems associated with a good-size concussion if we had used seat belts, a device that was totally unknown in those days. All I was left with was a deep sense of remorse. The official date of our engagement is September 19, 1948. This date is engraved in our wedding rings because in Holland wedding rings are bought when an engagement is official. To simplify matters you wear your wedding ring on your left hand when you are a Protestant and engaged to be married and shift it to your right hand when you marry. Catholics do exactly the reverse. How and outsider is supposed to know whether he is dealing with a married Catholic or an engaged Protestant is a mystery I have never been able to resolve unless you assume that the two population groups did not mix much in those days. When I arrived in America people interested in these matters such as secretaries in the offices where I worked, often asked me why I was wearing my wedding ring on my right hand. I got tired of explaining the situation and moved my ring to my left hand where it happily stayed ever after.

In Arnhem I met the platoon I would join and the fellow corporals that served in the company and shared a room with me. The van Coehoorn barracks were old and therefore closer to downtown. So it was easy for me to take the bus in the evening and go see Tante Jet, Oom Otto and Tineke, who had returned to her parent's house to await the birth of her first child while her husband Jaap was overseas. It was an opportunity to get a square meal, sit in a decent chair and meet my relatives. We proceeded to train the troops using all the knowledge we had acquired. In the beginning the guys regarded us with some dread because the school where we came from was in their eyes a place of incredible discipline and toughness and they feared we would treat them the same way as we had been treated. I guess that did not quite work out that way, but we were still incredibly fit compared to them and got some satisfaction out of testing their endurance.

As winter approached it became clearer when we would leave. To prepare ourselves for Indonesia, we got more shots but also a course in jungle warfare taught by two old and tired sergeants of the Indonesian colonial army. They gave us a course in the kind of patrolling they had been taught about fifty years ago, or perhaps even longer, to fight the rebels in Aceh, a province in northern Sumatra where the Dutch had encountered problems with Islamic fundamentalist fanatics for centuries. I doubt that these old geezers ever fought themselves in Aceh because their methods were ancient, to say the least. We were told to walk slowly in single file, very close together, looking right and left with our rifles and machine guns evenly divided between both sides. We would stop frequently to listen and walk as silently and unobtrusively as possible. If there was trouble we would close up and stand pat. I have no idea where these tactics came from. As soon as we were in Indonesia we started going on patrol, walking briskly and keeping a good 15- feet distance between each other so that an opponent with a machine gun could not easily mow us all down. In case of trouble we would follow normal infantry procedures and hit the dirt and look for cover. In my mind's eye I still see us walk slowly and solemnly through the snow-covered bushes near Arnhem, pretending we were in tropical Indonesia. We all understood that in the army one never asks why things are done a certain way. It is much more convenient not to argue and go about one's business.

I do not remember what we did for Christmas and New Year's Eve. But I am certain we all went home on leave. A highlight of the preparations for the tropics was the distribution of tropical uniforms. We received a floppy green piece of head-gear that was a poor approximation of the beret we wore in Europe but looked more like a collapsed cook's hat. We also received two green field uniforms plus a light khaki outfit for "dress" occasions. As it turned out, the folks who were in charge of supplies had scraped the bottom of the barrel and come up with the craziest sizes imaginable. The Dutch army had been sending troops overseas for almost four years and the country was strapped for cash. It was known that the conflict in Indonesia could not be financed much longer so we were probably one of the last of the bunch. Accordingly, we got leftovers. I remember that I got a green jacket that was more than extra, extra large and pants to go with it that were of a different material and would fit a small boy better than me. Our captain hit the ceiling and asked two officers from the supply unit to come watch us on parade. We were told to put on the worst fitting outfits we could find. It was a ridiculous thing to see us stand there, shivering in the winter cold looking like an army out of a third-rate funny movie.

On December 23, 1948, Henriette Albertha Kort was born. Jetty, as she is called now, was Tineke's first daughter and the first child of the generation that came after us. When I came back from Christmas leave I went over to admire the baby, a new development I was not quite comfortable with since I did not feel I knew how to react to babies. Tineke even came once with her baby carriage to the barracks and saw me drill a platoon on the parade ground behind the building and started waving at me. I guess I pretended not to see them. As we got closer to embarkation day, I suddenly got word that I had to move to an infantry company where they needed a corporal. The mortar platoons normally had more sergeants and corporals than ordinary infantry units because we had a more complex task to fulfill that required more leadership. The sergeant's stripes had been handed out and evidently I did not make the grade. Moreover, the sergeant's ranks had been swelled by a few men who had washed out of officers' school and were returned to us as sergeants. So I had to go to the Saksen Weimar Kazerne, where I had received my primary training. There I was put with the 3rd company under Captain Wolzak. The odd name of the captain literally translated means "Woolsack." He was not a bad egg, however. He was part of a group of officers who had been professional NCOs before the war and had joined as volunteers immediately after the war to go to Indonesia. They were, therefore going on a second tour of duty and were rewarded with a promotion to captain. Captains with the same background commanded several other companies of our battalion. They were allowed to have their wives and children join them in Indonesia and were therefore more interested in keeping the military routine going by the book and not get in trouble with too much military action. Since they had never gone to officers' school, they tended to be more focused on the smaller details of army life. They certainly were not out to prove themselves as fighting men and for us that was perhaps just as well. I was unhappy to be separated from the men I had served with for almost a year now and immediately began protesting that I was a heavy mortar man and had no infantry knowledge and that my expensive training as a mortar man was wasted. The captain did not pay too much attention to my pleas.

In February 1949 we were given our embarkation leave. I felt awful, of course, to have to leave Netty and to be sent away on a very uncertain expedition to the other side of the world as part of an army that I knew was at best poorly trained and even more poorly equipped. There was none of the "gung-ho" spirit among us that had characterized the volunteer army that preceded us. We were aware of the halfhearted attempts the Dutch government was making to negotiate a mutually satisfactory arrangement with the rebellious "Republik Indonesia" forces that would keep sovereignty in Dutch hands but would give the Indonesians more freedom and a form of self-government. As negotiations failed, there had been two attempts to force a solution with a large-scale military attack. The first one was called the *De Eerste Politionele Actie* – the first police action in 1947. At that time the Dutch government took the position that the self-proclaimed Indonesian Republic was not a recognized political entity because the Dutch East Indies were a Dutch colony and therefore under jurisdiction of the government of the Kingdom of the Netherlands and part of it. The proclamation of the founding of the new Republic was therefore not valid and viewed as a rebellion and the Netherlands' government had to take action against it.

This first action succeeded only partially because the United Nations intervened and ordered a cease-fire. A line of demarcation between the two sides was established more or less under the control of UN observers. Lengthy conferences followed again without too much result, and eventually the Dutch saw no other way open than a second police action that involved a massive attack on the area the Republic Indonesia occupied on the island of Java. Paratroopers were dropped on Djokjakarta, the capital of the Republic, and most of the Republic's territory was occupied. Republican leaders were interned on an island outside Java. This action was at first a success, at least militarily, but it soon became clear that we had to cope with a large population of millions of half-starved and poorly clad people who had been deprived of almost all medical care for several years. Moreover, as the Dutch troops advanced, the Indonesian forces, which consisted mostly of irregular guerilla bands anyway, melted into the mountainous areas and began to harass the Dutch from there. In addition, the UN stepped into the picture again and forced us to declare another cease-fire. It was in this situation that we ended up once we got to Indonesia. The second action was begun in late December and was over by mid–January. More manpower was desperately needed because the Dutch army was stretched to its limits after having had to occupy an enormous area. So when we arrived in February we entered an arena where a lot of action had recently taken place and where the two sides were still fighting a guerilla war.

Around February 11th I had to report back from embarkation leave. I had spent my leave at home with my parents and, of course, at Netty's house with her and her family. Netty and I had also gone over to Bloemendaal so I could say good-bye to my grandparents. A little earlier we had the rather comical scene at the dinner my grandmother gave for my parent's 25th wedding anniversary. (My parents were married on February 8, 1924, in Mexico City.) I have described this dinner in an earlier chapter. This time we were not in a festive mood, and it bothered me very much to see my grandfather cry when the time came to say good-bye. Here I was leaving to help put an end to a period in Dutch colonial history in which he had played an important role in earlier years. And it would not be a pleasant excursion either. When the day of departure came, I had asked Pa if he would drive me to Arnhem in the Terraplane so I would not have to take the dreary train ride with all my gear. We had been issued an olive drab American duffel bag, considerably bigger than the British ones we had used before but still not a very large piece of luggage for a trip to the Far East with a lot of military gear. There was not much room left for personal belongings. Netty gave me a large leather portfolio with two portraits of her in it, which I carefully packed. The fact that it was a flexible leather portfolio helped a great deal. It could bend and would not break in my bag. In Arnhem I also picked up an Italian-made Beretta submachine gun that I bought from a sergeant major who had "found" it somewhere between Normandy and Holland. He had served in the Prinses Irene Brigade, the Dutch unit that participated in the invasion of France and the subsequent march to the Dutch border. I had bought this weapon because I knew we would be in a free-for-all in Indonesia and that I would be equipped with a British Sten gun, a small submachine gun that had a poor reputation for accuracy and effectiveness. The Beretta used the same ammunition as the Sten but was considerably more elegant and a much better weapon. I stuck the Beretta in the center of my bag so it would not show too easily. We were not allowed to bring our own weapons but many of us did anyway. Oc brought a really beautiful German Luger pistol that the head of police in the village where he grew up gave him. I said farewell to Netty and Ma at our house and Pa and I drove off. It was a drive of about two and a half hours and we did not talk much. My father was never a great talker, and I did not have too much to say either. I was going to enter a very uncertain period in my life. In the dark February night we drove up to the gate, I kissed my father good-bye and lugged my big bag inside. The buildings were almost totally deserted because it was still quite early in the evening and there were not many people back yet. We had left early so Pa could get back at a decent hour. I found one fellow corporal in one of the rooms and chatted with him for quite some time as the others slowly filtered back. I believe the man I was talking with was J. Niemeyer. I do not think I knew his first name. I did not see him often in Indonesia because he served with another company, but I do believe he was killed late in 1949 in a village called Uteran. He was there with a small detachment guarding the road between Ponorogo, where our battalion was headquartered, and Madiun, the principal town in that area. He went to the local market place, the passar riding a bike and while there, probably looking to buy some food or eggs, ran into a group of the enemy who were hanging out there too. They killed him on the spot. Things like that would happen often in the fluid situation we were in, but it was a shame we lost him, just a few weeks before we would enter a ceasefire and withdraw.

I do not recall how many days we were in Arnhem, waiting for our orders to ship out. It cannot have been very long, but I think we would have needed at least a few days to establish who was present and who was not. It was not uncommon for guys to desert during their embarkation leave. Several did and the tragic result of that was that men who were not supposed to go were often told to ship out at the last moment to fill the gap. We had a cook in one of our outposts who was a victim of circumstances like this. He was the only child of elderly parents and their sole provider so he got an exemption from overseas duty. But some other cook deserted and he was grabbed to fill this fellow's place.

On the morning of our departure, February 11, 1950, we had to get up very early, at 3.45 a.m. in fact, pack our bags, label them, and get into formation outside. It was still a pitch-black night and quite cold. We were in our winter coats and had labels with numbers attached to our lapels. We marched off to a railway yard somewhere outside Arnhem where the train was waiting. As we marched downhill towards the train I noticed military police hiding in the bushes, and during our trip civilian police surrounded the train whenever it stopped. They were there probably because there was some fear that we would riot or create a ruckus or stage a mass escape. In those days there was still a communist party in Holland, and this party as well as other groups opposed our actions in Indonesia and tried to get a foothold among the soldiers. I do not think there was anybody in our unit who wanted to organize any resistance to our departure. We were a fairly meek group although one guy jumped out of the train once it was in motion. I don't know what happened to him. When daylight came, we were trundling through the Dutch countryside in our old steam train with wooden benches. From time to time we would see groups of people, relatives and friends of soldiers, waving along the railway track. Overall it was not a scene that made us swell with patriotic pride as troops going away to fight a war should have. It was more like a transport of prisoners, and I guess most of us felt trapped in a situation we had no control over. We felt fate had dealt us a bad hand. In the afternoon we chugged into Rotterdam and onto a track that was on a dock. We could just get out, find our bags and walk onto our ship, the Kota Inten this name means City of Diamonds. That name was a bit of an exaggeration. The Kota Inten belonged to the Rotterdamse Lloyd, one of the two companies that maintained regular passenger service between Holland and Indonesia. It was an old freighter. It had served as a troop ship on the North Atlantic during the war so it was equipped to carry a large complement of troops, but it was not really good for longer hauls like ours. The holds were insulated against cold weather and equipped with berths, and the air-conditioning was ineffective so the holds got very hot once we were in the tropics. I found my berth, I think I remember I was in the second berth from the bottom in a stack of four. It was just a pipe berth with canvas to sleep on. A set of wide metal stairs led to the deck. The accommodations were not ideal for a four-week cruise. As it turned out there was a thick fog and the ship did not leave the dock until early the next morning. We had time to get familiar with the ship, wander around and look over the railing where I saw our commanding officer, a lieutenant colonel named van Urk, leave in a cab to go into town probably for a nice dinner. The next morning we were awakened by a speaker system blaring Anchors Away and announcing it was 6 o'clock and time to get up. We would be bothered by that tune for the duration of the trip and hated it thoroughly after a few days. When we went to wash and shave we discovered the water we had to use was salt water, which was the reason we had been issued a small bar of salt-water soap. The crush of people around the few available faucets was enormous, as was the demand for the toilet stalls. To our consternation we found that the stalls had no doors and were open to view. The North Sea was not calm in February and the ship began to move which affected a number of guys. To my relief I was not seasick and would remain free from it for the whole trip although I had been quite severely affected when I made the trip to the Canary Islands with my mother in 1936. There we were on a gray day at sea in an old ship with a large complement of poorly trained and poorly equipped men. We wondered how long it would be until we felt cold weather again and would see fog around us. We were sent to enforce policies in the Dutch East Indies that were outdated, out of tune with the postwar trends in international relations that were poorly executed and not very well thought through. Old men in stuffy ministry buildings were sending a bunch of mostly nineteen-year-olds overseas to defend their ill-conceived objectives and some of these boys were going to die for them.

17 : *From Dutch East Indies to Indonesia*

As the troop ship Kota Inten with the 422nd battalion (a.k.a. 6-8 RI or the 6th battalion of the 8th regiment infantry) on board left the shores of Holland, on its way towards the Far East, I thought it might be appropriate to interrupt my narrative with a brief history of the country we were heading for. This country played an important role in the lives of my father, my grandparents and two of my great grandparents and in the life of Netty's mother and grandparents. It also played an enormously important role in the history of the Netherlands, its economy and its politics. As will soon become clear, it was originally never really a nation, but it became one. Indonesia, now the most important nation in Southeast Asia, was once a Dutch colony. An archipelago of enormous proportions consisting of thousands of islands, big, very big (Borneo, now called Kalimantan, is as large as Germany and France together) and small. Most estimates put the number at over 17,000 islands, ranging from small coral atolls to vast mountainous landmasses. From west to east the country stretches for 3,200 miles; it fills an area with boundaries reaching roughly from 6 degrees N to 11 degrees S in latitude and from 95 to 141 degrees E in longitude. That is a distance of 46 degrees in longitude. To compare, Miami is at approximately 80 degrees W and Seattle at approximately 125 degrees W – a distance of 45 degrees in longitude. So the map of the East Indies can be laid over that of the United States and more than cover it "from sea to shining sea." As the Dutch started traveling there, they gradually established the borders of their colony in treaties, mostly with the British, who often had overlapping interests in the region. At the outset, the Europeans did not pay much attention to the different characteristics of the peoples that lived on the many islands, to their tribal or racial backgrounds, their level of development, or their very different languages and religions. They came to do business and were initially not interested in territorial conquest. It is an enormously large country inhabited by a multitude of peoples with different traditions and racial backgrounds.

For decades the Dutch insisted on the premise that historic and traditional bonds inalterably linked the Indies to them. They steadfastly maintained that the Indonesian population desired nothing more than to be governed by wise Dutchmen who knew better than the natives themselves what was best for them. After World War II, when that policy became untenable, the Dutch proposed a federal structure for the newly independent republic. Realizing that there was great diversity among the people in their colony, they proposed a federal republic tied in various ways to the "Motherland." After many years of political turmoil, a disastrous military dictatorship, and presently a weak, not very effective, central government, the federal plan that emphasized local control seems to have been a better idea. The Dutch plan was inspired by the best intentions; however, it still stemmed from the patronizing ideas about Indonesia that prevailed in Holland. It was also somewhat self-serving since the Dutch could more easily stay engaged in a new country consisting of a number of semiautonomous republics, each based on ethnic or geographic characteristics and each with a different agenda. But the new nation became very quickly a single republic, which was much more difficult to influence.

In the old days, the Dutch called their colony Indië, a name that is usually translated into English as "The Indies." For generations they took a paternalistic, somewhat-detached interest in the country, viewing it as "theirs" to exploit and govern. They saw it as a wonderful country, waxed poetic about its natural beauty and called it the Gordel van Smaragd, the Belt of Emeralds. The people who went to the Indies viewed themselves (correctly) as pioneers who were building a great country with vigor, ingenuity and great skill. The inhabitants were seen as people who benefited greatly from the Dutch initiatives and magnanimity without contributing much more than manual labor. They were believed to be content under the benevolent Dutch authority and not to have any strong desire to be independent. They were seen as generally gentle peaceful people who liked to live the simple life, had little ambition, and were largely incapable of functioning like westerners. Against this background, the strength of the movement to achieve independence that rapidly gained momentum after World War II came as a rude shock. The startled Dutch thought the Indonesians, as they then started to call themselves, were without competent leadership and did not really know what they wanted and what they were doing. There was still a generally condescending attitude towards the leaders of the newly proclaimed Republic Indonesia and the belief was that most areas outside central

Java where the Republic was founded were not interested in joining the movement. It all came out differently. The Republic Indonesia is now a large important country with the world's largest Muslim population. The U.S. worries about its political stability and its influence in the Muslim world. It is rich in natural resources and at a population of 237 million is among the world's most populous countries. During the Indonesian struggle for independence, the republic's leaders turned out to be quite competent and able to deal with the Dutch government in a very skillful way, and they often outmaneuvered the Dutch in negotiations on the international scene. In contrast, the present Indonesian government often seems rudderless. It appears to lack direction and seems unable to take care of its most important problem – widespread corruption. Still, Indonesia is now a free country and no longer a colony. I had the dubious honor to be present at its birth.

I will never forget speaking to a soldier of the TNI, the Tentara Nasional Indonesia or the Indonesian National Army, a slim, very boyish-looking guy in a more or less self-designed uniform. We were in Ponorogo, a small city near the center of Java where our battalion was headquartered. He was the first opponent or Peloppor (as we called them) I met face to face. He was sitting in the back seat of a small automobile they had driven into town. This car in itself was a strange apparition for us. The Indonesian guerillas were not supposed to have cars. They must have kept it hidden somewhere and triumphantly hauled it out of storage to show us they were better equipped than we thought. A few days previously a cease-fire had been declared and it was clear to us that we would withdraw and gradually ship out to go home. The TNI people had come out of the hills from where they had been bothering us for months and were starting to negotiate with us over the terms of our withdrawal. I talked with the young soldier and arrogantly asked him how his small rag-tag band of people would manage to govern this vast country. Where would they be getting the people who had the skills to do it? He answered they might not have enough people with the necessary skills and they would no doubt make mistakes, but they would be making their own mistakes. In other words, what made me think the Dutch had a God-given authority to rule them? He was right, I was wrong, and they were now going to be free. It was a defining moment for me. Here I was a corporal in the Dutch army, standing in the hot and dusty center square of Ponorogo, called the *Aloon Aloon*, a large grass- covered area found in the center of most Indonesian towns, talking for the first time on a sensible one-on-one basis with an Indonesian opponent. He told me in a few words the quintessence of the Indonesian struggle for freedom. My great grandfather had been the highest judicial authority in his country, my grandfather had been a very prominent businessman here, my father and Netty's mother were born here and Netty's great-great uncle had been a governor general and now it was made clear to me that it was all over for us. We were finished and colonialism was too. I was told in no uncertain terms that we had no business being there.

In reading up for this chapter, I was struck again by the realization how much the world had changed since I grew up. I had always been taught that the Indies were well governed by well-meaning Dutch government employees who had only the best interest of the population in mind. That these authorities had studied the traditions, languages and history of the people they ruled over and had gained their gratitude and admiration because their subjects realized they could not handle the job themselves. I learned that the Dutch commercial, mining, oil and agricultural entrepreneurs working in the Indies were skillful, tough but just people who dealt in a fair and humane way with the native population. And if they happened to treat the native population unfairly, a government that protected its native subjects against exploitation would swiftly correct them. I understood that life in the Indies was not easy for Europeans because of the climate and the many tropical diseases, but that for many people it was a wonderful country to live in and that for their children it was a wonderful country to grow up in. It was a big country where people could spread their wings and rapidly build careers. It was a place where enterprising people could find opportunities that did not exist in the much more confining and small-minded society that existed in the Netherlands in those days.

I still have a book that came out during the war and that is entitled *Zo leven wij in Indië* – This is how we live in the Indies. The book came out in 1942 just after the war with Japan had come to Indonesia and had brought a quick and ignominious defeat of the Dutch forces there. Tante Jet and Oom Otto gave the book to me in 1943 on the occasion of my admission as a member to the Doopsgezinde Kerk. This church to which my mother and I belonged baptizes people when they reach age eighteen. The sensible thought behind this practice is that at that age people can be assumed to be able to think for themselves and make their own choice as to what to believe and what church they want to belong to. To be admitted aspiring members are required to declare their beliefs in a written essay and appear before a board of trustees to discuss their writings. Joining the church was seen as an important milestone in one's life and that is why I was given the book. It became immensely popular in Holland during the war because it dealt with Dutch achievements overseas. A nationalistic subject therefore, but apparently nonthreatening to the Germans because they were also of the opinion that the Europeans had a right and a mission to lord it over other less developed peoples overseas. The Germans probably had plans to take over in the Indies after they had won the war. The book discusses the life of Dutch people in the Indies in many different professions and businesses. Since I had vague plans to go to the Indies after the war and seek a career there, it was of great interest to me. The book is a compilation of essays written by people who each wrote a chapter about a segment of life in the Indies they were familiar with. Its language and the writing now seem almost childish and superficial, but at the time it was a generally admired book. The most astonishing part is that there is so little written about the native population. Hardly more than two or three pages deal with this subject. It is all about the Dutch, how they live and thrive there and what they have achieved. How they live in roomy houses, enjoy their cool evenings on the terrace, swim in their pools or play tennis. It describes the mountain resorts where the Dutch vacation and enjoy the cooler temperatures and the excellent boarding schools where they send their children when they live too far away from day schools.

A special chapter is devoted to the trip to Indonesia by air. Flying such long distances was then still very rare. The KLM plane is a DC-3, now considered a very small obsolete aircraft. The story follows the plane as it leaves Amsterdam and flies to the Far East making overnight stops at several exotic places where passengers are lodged in first-class hotels. The book becomes even more apocryphal if one realizes that in 1942, at the time it was written, the Japanese had interned the entire Dutch population, men women, and children, without any exception, in large squalid concentration camps where they lived under dreadful circumstances. We did not know this, and even our government-in-exile had no clear idea of the living conditions of the Dutch population in the Indies. So we blissfully read about life in the tropics as it was and hoped it would all end up right after the war was over so that we would be able to go back there and continue where we left off. Most people did not share the notion that things had changed forever. I found it fascinating to reread parts of the book. It is a return to what was almost a dream world in which we lived during the war, unable to visualize the postwar world and just clinging to the world we had lived in before all the trouble started. Dutch literature and textbooks about the Indies that came out in the period before World War II, and even directly after it, still reflect the old colonial attitude. It was only later, after the Indonesian independence that things changed.

More recently written Dutch books about Indonesia often lack balance, in my opinion. They tend to over-emphasize all the things that were wrong. But I have two excellent books that give a fairly balanced picture. One is called *Het Rijk van Insulinde* – the Realm of Insulinde (the more poetic name the Dutch sometimes used for the Indies) and a more recent second book *Afscheid van Indië* – Good Bye to the Indies – both written by H. W. van den Doel. The writer is a well informed historian and writes well. He paints a truthful and objective picture of the Dutch history in the Indies and in the second volume a riveting review of the difficult and often disastrous road followed by the Netherlands in its negotiations with the young Republic of Indonesia. However, the writer is too young to have been present in Indonesia before things started to change and unravel. Van den Doel still seems to put a great deal of emphasis on the ugly side of Dutch history in the Far East. He extensively quotes personal accounts of the brutality of the Dutch military in rebellious provinces in the eighteen hundreds and of the stupidity and insensitivity of the Dutch authorities towards the native population and to its desires for more independence and freedom. He cites stories about the rude and despicable behavior of certain planters in the outlying areas, and last but not least, the many atrocities committed by the Dutch army in the years immediately following World War II, some of which I witnessed. The writer gives a reliable record of all these actions that have cast a dark shadow over the history of the Dutch involvement in Indonesia. I believe he is correct in shining a bright light on all this because the truth must be revealed and omissions in the historic record must be set right. We have indeed spent too many years sugarcoating the Dutch colonial history. However, to be fair, an equally prominent place should be given to the good side of the history of the Dutch in the Far East and he does not give much room to that side of the equation. The Dutch presence in Indonesia was not characterized mainly or only by cruelty and stupidity. Most Dutch people who grew up in the Indies had a true and deep love for the country and its population. Many Dutch scholars studied the rich history and anthropology of the country and made major contributions to the historic record of it. Dutch writers wrote poetry and volumes of fiction as well as nonfiction about a country they truly loved. Dutch artists created paintings, sculptures, photographs and other artistic expressions that leave lasting impressions of a country with incredibly scenic beauty and a population that is singularly interesting and attractive. Much work was done by Dutch scientists in the field of agriculture to improve the country's crops and not only those that benefited the Dutch plantations, but also those that benefited the local population that made them grow better rice and other crops for local consumption. Not all the Dutch in the Indies were rough military men, uncouth planters and greedy businessmen out to make a quick buck and go back to Europe. Around the beginning of World War II, a large part of the Dutch population in the Indies consisted of teachers, scientists, doctors, missionaries and other religious persons who were all striving to improve the well being and education of the population. When I was in high school in The Hague, I had several teachers who had taught in the Indies. They would tell us about the wonderful life they had over there, about the forests, the mountains and volcanoes, the rivers and the many islands that made up the archipelago. They would teach us with great respect and insight about the people, the various tribes, their habits, languages and traditions. And above all they would tell us how gentle civilized and polite most Indonesians were. How important and advanced their culture was. These teachers genuinely believed that the Dutch had a historic mission in Indonesia and felt they should tell us about the country and encourage us to seek a career there. Most of these lessons were given during the war and the German occupation, of course, and nobody had a clue about the fate of the Dutch in the Indies under the Japanese occupation. It was probably just assumed that the Europeans there would be allowed to continue their normal life under certain restrictions in the same way as we ourselves lived under the Germans. That is probably the reason why a book about life in the Indies could be published and sold in great quantities despite the fact that it was unfortunately telling a story that was no longer true. Postwar historians have changed much in the way in which the history of the Dutch colonial empire is viewed in Holland. In my opinion, they now seem to have a tendency to go too far in the direction of criticizing the Dutch experience there. Perhaps this reflects a desire to restore the balance in the story or perhaps it is an expression of the much more liberal leanings of Dutch public opinion in the years after Indonesia achieved its independence. To use an expression that is nowadays popular, it is politically correct to be severely critical of the colonial policies of the Dutch and of the people who implemented it. The colonial period is now history all over the world and the younger generations have trouble understanding it. It is not too long ago that having colonies and controlling the native population, to serve what was perceived as their best interest, was for many countries a completely acceptable situation to be in.

❧

The history of Indonesia goes back to ancient times. It is rich, complicated and very interesting. It shows that this country had reached a high level of civilization long before the Europeans arrived. I will try to highlight some of the more salient points of Indonesia's history, very roughly and briefly. Since my family and Netty's have links with the Dutch period in Indonesia's history, I will naturally spend more time discussing that period although it was – in hindsight – quite short.

In the first few years after the birth of Christ, between the years A.D.1–700, people from what is now India moved to Indonesia and brought Hinduism with them. For centuries the Hindu religion prevailed in most of the more developed parts of Indonesia, particularly Java and Sumatra. In the same period, the first contacts with China emerged and Chinese merchants established contacts between Indonesia and the Han dynasty. Buddhism flourished in China in those days and Buddhist pilgrims traveled all over Malaysia and India. These pilgrims brought the first stories about an Indonesian kingdom on Sumatra called Çriwaijaya. Its rule extended over a large part of what is now Malaysia, it had connections with India, and its fame reached into Arabia. The island of Java also counted several kingdoms with those on East Java playing the most important role. The religion was initially also Hindu there and the language Javanese. Poetry and literature blossomed in that language. Around A.D. 770–800, the Hindu – Indian influence diminished and Buddhism began to mix in. The world famous Buddhist temple Borobudur was built in one of the more powerful Javanese kingdoms in that period. Later, the kingdom of Mataram (900 – 1220 about) located in central Java became an important factor in trade with the Moluccas, Malaysia and China and became a Buddhist stronghold. As the influence of Buddhism waned, the Borobudur became a ruin covered with volcanic ash and overgrown by jungle vegetation. Dutch scientists started its restoration in the early 1900s and in the 1970s an international effort was launched for a complete restoration which was completed in 1983. UNESCO declared the temple a "World Historic Monument" and funded its restoration. It was an enormous effort that involved shoring up the base of the temple with underground concrete supports. Unfortunately, it now appears these efforts were not completely successful because the temple's foundation seems to have become unstable again in recent years.

In the twelfth century, the first Muslim traders arrived in Java. They came from the empire of Gudjarat in India. This empire reached from Cambai in India into Canton China. It is often included in the Arabian sphere, which is erroneous for the Muslims arriving in Indonesia were not necessarily Arabs, even if they spoke Arabic. Arabic was a universal language, a "lingua franca" used by all Muslims in the same manner as Latin was later used by all Christians as a universal language. These merchants from Gudjarat and from Persia brought Islam to Indonesia. Spices shipped from Indonesia found their way to Europe from Gudjarat by way of Egypt and Venice. For centuries pepper was the most important Indonesian export product. It was grown on Sumatra and created a great deal of wealth for the merchants in Venice and later for the Dutch East India Company. Marco Polo even visited Sumatra in 1292. A year later, in 1293 the Chinese sent an expedition to East Java. It is interesting to see how even in those days the influence of China grew and how China became a world power. In the second half of the thirteenth century, the Mogul King Kublai Khan had conquered China, and Marco Polo's visit to Sumatra was made on his behalf. Until then China had ruled only in a token fashion over Burma, Indo-China and Indonesia. But Kublai Khan wanted more than just a few annual gifts. He conquered Korea, threatened Japan and made his power felt in Indonesia. King Kertanegara who ruled over East Java resisted and sent the Chinese ambassadors back with scarred faces. When the Chinese returned with a large expeditionary force, they discovered that Kertanegara had died and that East Java was in chaos. The Chinese were driven out in 1294 by Prince Wijaya, Kertanegara's son, who established the kingdom of Madjapahit, which ruled over Eastern Java, Madura and Bali. King Gajah Mada, a well-known figure in Indonesian history, succeeded him and ruled from 1331-1364. He established control of Madjapahit over all the coastal territories of the Malayan peninsula and the Moluccas. Gajah Mada conquered Bali and Sumatra and organized a fleet that restricted Malaysian pirates. He was therefore the first monarch to bring almost the entire archipelago under one authority. This contradicts the Dutch post–World War II position that Indonesia was never a real country and that historically the Dutch colonial authority provided the only glue that held it together.

In about 1368, China was liberated from the Moguls and under the Ming dynasty started a renewed expansionist policy towards its neighbors. Local potentates were offered an armistice if they submitted themselves to Chinese rule. To many this was a welcome offset against pirates and the taxes levied by Madjapahit. Malaysia prospered under Chinese protection while ruled by a Muslim prince. Around 1414 Islam spread along the shores of Sumatra and must have moved over to Java too since the first grave with Arabic inscriptions was dated 1419 and found in Gresik, a small coastal town north of Surabaya where I spent a few weeks in 1950. This was the grave of a rich Persian merchant. While Islam spread along the shore, the interior of Java remained untouched by it. The Ming dynasty in China disappeared in about 1450, which left Indonesia open to intrusions by European adventurers and Islamic proselytizers.

The Islamic/Portuguese period started in the beginning of the sixtteenth century after the first Portuguese ship arrived in Malaya in 1511. The Portuguese conquered

Malaya and visited the Moluccas. History tells us that the Portuguese colonizing activities seem to have been inspired by a crusader or conquistador mentality. The "Moors" had dominated the Iberian Peninsula for centuries and when the Catholic kings of Spain and Portugal regained control over their countries, they committed themselves to fighting the Islamic influence worldwide. At home in Portugal, the Portuguese tried to find a way to attack their former Arab and Berber conquerors – the "Moors" – from the rear or the south. When they reached the Cape of Good Hope, they were obviously much farther south than they intended and when they ended up in Malaya they found Moors there too because in their eyes any Muslim was a Moor. The Portuguese objectives seem to have been more romantic than the British and Dutch "just business" orientation but the results were the same. The greatest conquistador was Alphonso de Alberquerque, who succeeded Vasco de Gama as governor of Malaya (1509 – 1515). He triggered a holy war with the Sultans of Aceh, Demak and Ternate who were successful in defeating Alphonso. Despite his defeat, he continued to attack all ships carrying "Moors" thereby alienating local traders who had been doing business in these waters for centuries. Eventually he managed to conquer Malaya and make himself hated by the local population. This hatred must have been a reflection of the "Conquistador" mentality, which also cast a shadow over the relationship of most South American countries with Spain.

The Portuguese had also discovered the Spice Islands (Moluccas). Spices were a very desirable commodity in those days, particularly pepper and clove. Prices for clove moved sky high in Europe. The clove plant grows very slowly and cannot be easily transplanted and the transport costs were high too. Nutmeg was another specialty of the Moluccas. The profit margin on nutmeg when sold in Europe was 2,500% in those days, reason enough to get into the spice business.

The Spaniards came in 1521 when the ship Victoria visited the Moluccas on Magellan's first circumnavigation of the world between 1519 and 1522. The Victoria was part of what was left of the fleet of Ferdinand Magellan who had died in the Philippines in 1521, while on his way home after rounding Cape Horn. Magellan was born Fernão de Magalhães, a Portuguese nobleman. He offered his services to Spain and commanded a fleet of five ships that went westward around the globe. Magellan's objective was to avoid the Portuguese-controlled Cape of Good Hope and to prove that the Spice Islands were lying westward of the line of demarcation drawn by the Pope in the treaty of Tordesillas and therefore inside the Spanish sphere of influence. The treaty concluded between the kings of Spain and Portugal with the help of the Pope divided the world into two spheres of influence. The Pope drew a line across the globe, declaring that everything to the east of the line lay in the Portuguese sphere and everything to the west in the Spanish realm. Nobody seemed to realize that the world was round. But the division worked in South America where to this day the Brazilians, finding themselves east of the line, speak Portuguese. The fleet going westward discovered the Strait of Magellan. It experienced incredible difficulties and challenges on its voyage, particularly crossing the Pacific, which was thought to be only a small body of water. The fleet was now reduced to one ship and continued on to Spain, but its appearance was still considered a breach of the Treaty of Tordesillas. After the Spanish visit, the Portuguese realized they were spread too thin and moved to strengthen their position. They asked the local rulers of the Spice Islands for a nutmeg monopoly and established a foothold on West Java, near where Jakarta is now located. They closed a contract with the local sultan that allowed them to build a fortress that would ostensibly serve to protect him from inroads of Islam. Ultimately, they could not complete their contract, and soon afterwards they were denied access. By 1535 the entire north coast of Java had become Islamic and by the mid-fifteen hundreds, Islam was on its way to spread throughout Indonesia. The Portuguese tried unsuccessfully to bring Christianity with the help of a few priests. They had arrived as an invincible force, but later their invincibility proved to be questionable and they gradually lost power all over the Indies.

In June 1596, the first Dutch ship arrived in Bantam, near where Jakarta is now located. The crew was well received by the Portuguese and by the sultan who invited the Dutch to trade freely. The Dutch had been under way for 14 months and of their fleet's original strength of 249 men, 145 had died. The long duration of the trip and losses of manpower were a reflection of poor leadership and equally poor seamanship. There were many conflicts between the sailors and the merchants aboard the Dutch ships and when they set foot on land in Java their rude, ill-mannered behavior soon created problems with the Javanese. The main culprit for the expedition's misfortunes was its leader Cornelis de Houtman. De Houtman had overestimated his knowledge of the Far East and of the route he would have to follow to get there. The story we all learned in school in Holland was different. We learned that during the 80 year war with Spain, its King Phillip II – who had united the kingdoms of Spain and Portugal – closed all Spanish and Portuguese ports to Dutch shipping. So the Dutch had to go it alone. De Houtman was a very enterprising and clever man who went to Lisbon and visited the local watering holes to learn on the sly how to navigate to the Far East from listening to Portuguese sailors. This is only partly true. The Dutch were already sailing all over the world. The main reason why they hesitated to go beyond the Cape of Good Hope (they gave the cape its name) was lack of technical knowledge. After de Houtman's voyage, they quickly improved the design of their ships and their navigation methods. When de Houtman returned to Amsterdam, the businessmen who sponsored him decided to send eight more ships, followed by five more expeditions for a total of twenty-two ships. A few tried to go west, but of these all but one, Olivier van Noort, failed. Van Noort returned by way of the Cape of Good Hope so he may have been the first Dutchman to circumnavigate the world. The expeditions that went east lost only one ship, but most of the early ones were not profitable. However, subsequent expeditions turned out to be very profitable and the business orientation of the Dutch presence in the Indies was solidified through the formation in 1602 of the VOC, the Verenigde Oost Indische Compagnie, the United East India Company. This organization would become the sovereign authority over the archipelago for almost two centuries. This "multinational" was the first publicly traded company in the world and was listed on the Amsterdam Stock Exchange where until then only Dutch government bonds were traded. The Dutch settled in the Moluccas and traded peacefully in the area, but they were in general not well received there or for that matter anywhere else in Indonesia except, remarkably in Aceh and Madura, where they were seen as offering a useful counterbalance to the Portuguese. Throughout Indonesia, the Dutch competed successfully with the Portuguese. Ultimately, they got the upper hand because they were better sailors and had (by then) better ships. In 1607, the Portuguese left the Moluccas and since then the Dutch were in control there.

The early part of the seventeenth century is generally regarded as the period in which Islam became the dominant religion in the Indies. In that same period, the VOC strove hard to get a monopoly in the spice trade and to drive prices up by reducing output. Despite these efforts, the company was losing money for the first ten years of its existence and did not pay a dividend. The man who is credited with reorganizing the VOC and establishing a real colony in what is now Jakarta was Jan Pieterszoon Coen, the father of the Dutch East Indies. Coen went to Italy as a lad of thirteen and stayed there seven years. In Italy he learned the Italian advanced double-entry bookkeeping technique and became an expert administrator. He went to Indonesia and spent some time on Celebes (now Sulawesi). In 1610 he returned to the Netherlands, but in 1612 he was back again. He founded Batavia. In the past the same name was used for Holland. In 1620 Coen wrote a reorganization proposal for the VOC that was based on the premise that: 1) Trade with the Far East is necessary for the continued prosperity of The Netherlands and 2) The Dutch had the legal right to trade in the Far East and to monopolize it. He wanted to bring Dutch families over and drive Spain and Portugal out of the Philippines and China with a VOC fleet and the help of the Japanese emperor. These plans proved to be much too ambitious, but he did manage to reorganize the VOC's money-losing operation in Java. He is nowadays described as a narrow-minded, cruel man who was ambitious and promised huge profits to the VOC directors if they would just listen to him. In contrast, Dutch schoolbooks in my days portrayed Coen as a noble statesman who had done a great job in establishing our colony. It depends on one's point of view how history is perceived. Trade with Indonesia blossomed and attracted the enmity of the British. They laid siege to Batavia in 1619 but Coen beat them off, taking advantage of a dispute between the British and the local native potentates as well as a dispersion of their fleet, which gave Coen the opportunity to capture several ships. The British came to an accord with Coen and left. Coen died of a tropical disease in 1629.

Coen's old Batavia was built like a Dutch city with canals lined by houses that were standing close together. A few hundred Dutchmen lived there, believing that ventilation was bad, particularly at night. So they slept in the overwhelming tropical heat with all windows closed. The larger much more comfortable colonial houses with open verandahs and lots of cross ventilation came much later. The canals were used as sewers and were connected with the sea, which allowed some fresh water to flow in from time to time. The Dutch dressed as if they were in Amsterdam and went around in their heavy velvet clothes with "mill stone" collars and all. Bathing was considered unhealthy. The day started with a glass of jenever, Dutch gin. Men smoked their pipes all day to ward off the bugs. No wonder the mortality rate was high in Batavia in those days. For almost two centuries, thousands of Dutchmen worked like slaves to establish an empire in the Indies, and thousands died. Life was particularly hard for a few hundred Compagnie clerks, young men that were poorly paid, poorly fed and plagued by fevers. They got up at 5:30 a.m., started working at 6 a.m., and continued until 6:00 p.m. with a 30 minute break for breakfast and two hours for a midday meal. A citadel was built near the shore and a garrison of about 1,200 men was kept there to defend the town. The fortress was the center of government. Life was dull for the free burghers. The women had many slaves working for them, but the men worked very hard. The Batavians did not care about science, but there were a few writers, poets and painters among them and several important books were written. Non–Dutch clergymen were not admitted and the Calvinist Dutch Reformed Church was the only church allowed. All kinds of Indonesians were allowed to live outside the walls of the town, but Javanese were not permitted to live there. They were considered to be "treacherous." People belonging to many different ethnic backgrounds had to serve in the army and the police consisted mainly of Amboinese and Balinese who were believed to be most reliable. The VOC had strict control over people's lives and over trade in Batavia, but despite this there was quite a bit of corruption and smuggling with products being channeled abroad outside the VOC monopoly.

A large contingent of Chinese lived outside the city walls. They played an important role as traders and craftsmen. In 1740 rumors circulated that the Chinese plotted to overthrow the government and wanted to occupy the town. Among the Chinese there were contrary rumors saying that the Dutch were extraditing Chinese and throwing them overboard once they were on the high seas. The Chinese revolted and the Dutch reacted, killing many. The pattern of blaming the Chinese minority for all kinds of evil persisted through the centuries. Today there is still a large Chinese community in Indonesia, and throughout the country's history there has been friction between them and the Indonesians that stems mainly from the fact that many Chinese are wealthier than the local population. Their prosperity is resented and seen as a result of exploitation of the locals and not of intelligence and hard work. In the 1960s, a group of Indonesian generals organized a military coup to take over control of the country from the Sukarno administration. And when a little later a Communist regime took hold in China, a large-scale persecution of the Chinese was organized under the guise of hunting down communists. Thousands were killed and since then the Chinese in Indonesia have made a great effort to keep a low profile and assimilate. Many have now assumed Indonesian names and rejected their Chinese background.

In old Batavia the Dutch did not discriminate against other races, Chinese or Javanese. Intermarriage was common, but no other religion than Christianity was tolerated. Batavia was initially just a trading post. Men of the local Dutch citizenry, the free citizens, were obliged to serve in the schutterij, a kind of National Guard or militia. When my grandfather lived in Batavia, this militia still existed and he served in it as I described earlier. The sultan of Mataram ruled outside Batavia. He was an extremely cruel despot who killed hundreds in mass executions and ensured that Islamic laws prevailed. Around 1743 the VOC slowly began to transition from a pure trading company into a territorial power, dependent for its income on forced agriculture and over time, it began to spread its wings gradually over Java. The Dutch were not the only ones who oppressed the natives. There was also a good deal of exploitation of the local population by their own regents. When the governor general imported coffee trees, many native regents got rich by exporting coffee which they forced their subjects to grow. By 1750 Batavia was no longer the same as a hundred years ago. Houses were no longer built very close together. They now were roomier and located outside the old city. The Dutch started plantation estates on which they kept native slaves as labor. These slaves were generally treated more humanely than those working for the local potentates. The VOC made deals with the local regents and "rented" part of the north shore of Java to plant coffee.

At the end of the eighteenth century, the VOC controlled Batavia and environs, also the north coast of Java, Ambon, parts of West Sumatra and the Lampong district on Sumatra, the Banda Islands in the Moluccas, Makassar and Menado on Celebes (now Sulawesi). Still, this territory was only a small part of what later would be the colony of the Dutch East Indies. The Dutch traveled to the Netherlands East Indies for a long time, ostensibly to establish a colonial empire, but in the period before 1800, the commercial activity of the VOC was the principal purpose of their presence in the archipelago. Interest in the territories beyond Java and Madura and the Spice Islands developed only towards the end of the 19th century. This was the period when my great grandfather and grandfather lived and worked in the Indies, but a great deal of history had still to be written before they arrived.

Late in the eighteenth century, the VOC ceased to operate as a commercial enterprise. British competition proved to be too strong in many markets. Heavy losses were incurred, particularly during the fourth English war from 1780 to 1784. Not long after this war, the French Revolution took hold in France with the storming of the Bastille in 1789. The French Revolution shook up the entire western world and influenced the citizenry of several European countries, sparking revolutionary movements in many. In Holland the party called the *Revolutionaire Patriotten* seized power in 1795 and nationalized the VOC only to terminate its operations in 1799. The new regime in the Netherlands initially sought to bring the ideals of the French Revolution, *Liberté, Egalité, Fraternité*, also to the Netherlands East Indies. Forced labor was abolished and so was the forced planting of certain export crops called dwang cultuur. This idealistic interval was soon followed by a much tougher regime in the Napoleonic period. Napoleon had made his brother Louis king of Holland, and Louis sent a Dutch member of the pro–French Patriot Party to the Indies as governor general. Herman Willem Daendels arrived in Batavia in January 1808. He set about reorganizing the government and built up its defenses against the English who were the enemies of France and therefore of the French occupied Netherlands. His major achievement was the building of the *Grote Postweg*, the Great Post Road ran from Batavia in the west across Java to Surabaya in the east. This work was accomplished in one year at the cost of the lives of thousands of Javanese forced laborers. The road had obvious value for the defense of Java but also afforded much better control over the mainly unexplored and undeveloped inland regions. Daendels also went to work on the old Dutch town of Batavia. He founded Weltevreden, a new residential area with larger much more open houses with big verandahs and large gardens. He demolished a good part of the old town and filled in the grachten, canals the Dutch had dug to make Batavia look as much like Amsterdam as possible. Daendels acted more or less independently because he had little contact with the homeland, probably because the English dominated the seas. His regime came to and end in 1811 when the English landed in Java under the command of Thomas Stamford Raffles and beat the Dutch Napoleonic colonial army. Raffles abolished the forced labor system and stormed the powerful sultanate of Jogjakarta. This was the first European interference with the power of the sultanate. Raffles left in 1815. Napoleon had been beaten and the Dutch stadtholder, who had fled to England when the French Revolution overran his country, returned as King William the First, an ally of Britain. The British decided they would like to establish a strong Kingdom of the Netherlands with colonies, as one of several counterweights against France. So they returned the Indies to Dutch control and a new period began for the colony.

The departure of Raffles and the reinstatement of the Dutch government in Java did not result in an immediate Dutch takeover of control of the colony's territory. Many years of fighting small local revolts and larger uprisings had to be coped with before some semblance of Dutch authority was established. There were still not many Dutchmen in Indonesia. Newcomers were very much afflicted by the tropical heat, by depression and by many tropical diseases. There were many more men than women so there was much intermarriage between Dutch men and Indonesian women. Or more often, Dutch men had an Indonesian "housekeeper" or *Njai*. For the large majority the Indies was a temporary place to live. Yet, newer ideas began to break through in Holland. These ideas were based on the concept that the Netherlands had "something to offer" to the Indies. This philosophy would later be called the "Ethical Stream." However, there was not enough political power or manpower, for that matter, in the region to implement ambitious ideas. The borders of the colony were not secure either. The Dutch military strength in the Indies was frighteningly low. An agreement with the British government signed in London in 1824 improved that situation. England promised not to make any deals with the sultans in Sumatra. Singapore would remain a British possession and the British offices in Aceh were closed. The Dutch kept the sultan of Aceh independent at that time. Later on he would become a real thorn in the flesh of the Dutch government. In return, the Dutch gave up all possessions in India and Malaya. Unfortunately, the economic situation in the post–Napoleonic era did not improve. Prices for coffee and sugar dropped on the world markets because of South American and Caribbean competition. The local population was still paying taxes called landrente. Slavery was still not totally abolished. Slavery had existed for centuries and when the Dutch came, they tolerated it among the Javanese. The Dutch did put out an order, however, that forbade Javanese to be enslaved. Raffles forcefully put an end to slavery wherever he could. But it took until Jan 1, 1860, before the Dutch government officially abolished slavery in the territories of the East Indies in which it could exercise its authority. Earlier, in the years 1825– 30, a serious revolt in Java shook up the colonial regime. It turned into a full-fledged war. The war cost the lives of about 15,000 Dutch soldiers and 200,000 Javanese. It was led on the Javanese side by Diponegara, a charismatic leader who was seen as a "just king" and Islamic king. He promoted a terror campaign against those who cooperated with the Dutch and directed the people's anger also at the Chinese. Religious fanaticism was clearly on the rise and by 1826 the situation was so turbulent that the Dutch colonial future was in serious jeopardy. A system of *Bantengs*, or small fortresses was adopted. In these Bantengs the population could find refuge and the war was fought with small anti-guerilla units. This strategy proved successful in the end. In a last-ditch effort to regain power Diponegara proclaimed himself Sultan of Java, but he had to capitulate in February 1830. He died in Makassar in 1855. It was the final attempt of the old Javanese power elite to restore its culture and destroy the Dutch colonial power. They lost, and the real colonial period began.

In the newly emerging colonial system, the power of the Javanese elite was significantly reduced and the Dutch colonial government in Batavia became the supreme power. There was a great need for more centralized power because the colony was under severe financial stress. The Dutch tried unsuccessfully to exploit the colony on a profitable basis, but its government was heavily in debt. The difficult economic situation led to the implementation of the *Cultuur Stelsel,* a system of forced production of export crops. The system required each village to use one-fifth of its arable land for the production of export crops. No more than 66 workdays were supposed to be spent on this task. The system was meant to replace the old landrente, a land tax system that was an unsuccessful attempt to squeeze tax payments out of the impoverished farming population. The system is often cited as an example of the oppressive methods of the Dutch colonial regime. That assessment is mostly correct and around 1835 it began to meet with political opposition in Holland. However, as onerous as it seemed to be, it did make the colony profitable again. The rules imposed on the population by the system were really only enforced on the islands of Java and Madura. By 1860 Java had become a very profitable colony thanks to this *Cultuur Stelsel.* The other possessions, called *Buitengewesten,* or "Outlying Territories", were still mostly left alone. No income was received from them and there was a continuing effort to bring them under control. For instance, it took until 1849 before all rebellious local regents in Bali recognized Dutch sovereignty and in Borneo the Dutch fought Chinese strong-arm Kongsis, commercial cartels, until 1850. Foreign adventurers were also encountered. An Englishman by the name of Brooks settled in Serawak, North Borneo, where he had helped the local regent to quell a rebellion with his ship. He received land in payment for his efforts and established himself as a "white raja" there. The reign of his self-invented dynasty lasted for more than a century. An American adventurer from South Carolina by the name of Gibson smuggled weapons from Singapore to Borneo for the Chinese Kongsis. He was taken prisoner in 1852 but escaped, became a Mormon and settled in Hawaii where he became prime minister of the Hawaiian Kingdom. In Europe, growing press commentary on situations like these invited incursions by other nations and necessitated a more vigorous effort to gain control over the entire territory of the Netherlands East Indies.

Forced to broaden their efforts in Indonesia, the Dutch began to realize that their knowledge of the country and its peoples was still very limited. In 1842 a beginning was made with the establishment of academic training in the Netherlands of civilians for government functions in the Indies. Now the governing philosophy was that "the Netherlands could keep its colonies in the Indies only if the native population was treated with fairness and justice and above all with respect for its traditions, habits and prejudices." Scientists moved to the Indies to study nature, volcanoes, forests, etc. Mining engineers and geologists discovered all kinds of resources including coal and bitumen in Borneo. Missionaries entered the country in droves and the government tried to diminish the influence of Christian missionaries. It was feared they would create disturbances among the local population. The government took the position that it wanted to educate the population first, and as it had done before, it would not take a position on religion. A pastor who handed out a translated version of the New Testament among strongly Islamic people was even arrested.

Around the 1850s the Indies, or rather Java, contributed on average 19% of the income of the government of the Netherlands. The money served to pay off debt incurred by the Indies and the West Indies and African colonies and to finance the abolition of slavery. As the Dutch gained more authority over their colony and it became a profitable operation, they kept close controls over the Europeans who sought entry. People shipping out to the Indies were checked out in Holland before leaving and they were required to carry passports inside Indonesia. The surprisingly submissive local population was mainly controlled through local rulers who enforced the *Cultuur Stelsel* and received a percentage of its revenue. Sugar was the most important export crop in Java and the government controlled weight and quality of the sugar produced. Producers had to handle cutting and transportation of cane themselves. Because of the increased economic activity, the population of Java grew rapidly. From 3.6 million people in 1802, it rose to 9.3 million in 1850, 16.2 million in 1870 and 28.4 million in 1900. The growing demand for export products spawned an increase in the demand for labor and for food that had to be grown by the local population. The system did not create much opportunity for capital formation among the local population. Rather it created a universal level of poverty. There was a high degree of social and economic homogeneity that prevailed until the Second World War. The Indonesian people had a high level of freedom; there were no property owners oppressing a group of serfs – it was a system of "shared poverty." Better roads and railways opened Java to world markets and the natives benefited from the generally evenhanded and benign government established by the Dutch. On balance, the *Cultuur Stelsel* is believed to have been beneficial for the population, but it was a system that put a feudal imprint on them and it gave them little opportunity for a higher education. European-trained people filled all the top positions. There was a clear need for a better education system.

In 1856 Eduard Douwes Dekker, a member of the new academically educated civil service, started accusing the colonial authorities of supporting corrupt practices by local rulers. He used western norms of behavior as the model against which government should be measured, and after just one month in the field as a junior government representative, became an "activist" and a supporter of the local population, which in his opinion was oppressed. He soon left his position with the government and returned to Europe where, using the pseudonym Multatuli (I have suffered much), wrote a book called Max Havelaar. This book became a classic in the Netherlands and was translated into many languages. It is the story of a civil servant like him who became the advocate of what we now would call the civil rights of his subjects who were severely oppressed by the local native ruler. The writer was not anti colonial – independence was just a concept that was too far-fetched in those days – he advocated a just colonial regime. He saw the European born government person as the messenger of a just society. In 1863 Douwes Dekker's voice was heard, or perhaps the tide had already turned and the general trend was more towards reform of the colonial philosophy. A new minister of colonies came into office, a Mr. Fransen van der Putte, who proclaimed, "Java has paid its debts, now we have a debt to Java." Reforms came. The first high schools were established, a HBS and a gymnasium, all in the Dutch style. These schools facilitated the career opportunities for Indo-Europeans. Drastic reforms came in 1866 when the *Cultuur Stelsel* was abolished. The number of European government employees was increased and the colony was no longer put on a feudal but on a more liberal, modern footing. An Assistant Resident was placed next to each native Regent. Thus, the Indies became a colonial state in lieu of a large plantation. The Sugar law (Suikerwet) of 1870 allowed private enterprises to lease raw land for 95 years from the local population. Javanese could buy farmland. Europeans could not. The law protected the population against western capitalism but also allowed development of larger scale agricultural enterprises. The old idea to leave the natives to their own devices and support the local elite was abandoned for a much more hands-on system. Around 1870 the tobacco culture in Sumatra was started. The sultan of Deli, an area that became famous for its high-quality tobacco leaves used for cigars, made land available to Europeans and tried to get them interested in tobacco growing. Coolies to do the work were hard to find, and there were instances of unreasonable punishment, beatings, etc., by plantation managers of those that tried to escape. The managers governed the plantations without any government controls. These conditions leaked out and raised concerns in the Netherlands. The Deli Maatschappij, the largest and best-known Dutch tobacco company, was founded in 1869. My grandmother Dorothea Estella Stibbe was born in 1871 in Palembang, the largest city on Sumatra, a great distance from Deli. I guess my great grandfather's placement as a judge in Palembang reflected the extension of the Dutch government to the outlying areas. There probably was not much in the way of a government presence in Sumatra before the Dutch civil service increased its work force and its reach there. No doubt, the family benefited from the improved economic situation in the colony, and as a judge my great grandfather must have also benefited from the more enlightened approach the government took towards the population.

The Dutch efforts to establish control in several outlying areas with military force proved to be very difficult, however. Most prominent in the minds of most Dutchmen is the struggle to control the rebellious strongly Islamic people of Aceh, or Atjeh as the Dutch spell it. Aceh is an important state or province located on the tip of Sumatra, the part of this huge island that points at India and is separated from Malaya by the relatively narrow Strait of Malaya. The Achenese are a people who throughout history have fought fiercely for their independence and who are stricter in their adherence to the rules of Islam than most other Indonesians. Recall that the Dutch concluded a treaty with the British government in 1870–71 that gave them total sovereignty over Sumatra. A first effort to control Aceh in 1873 ended in defeat. There had been rumors that Italy and the U.S. were interested in doing a deal with the sultan of Aceh. These circumstances prompted more action by the Dutch army, but local resistance grew.

There were some Dutch efforts to study Islam and Aceh seriously. Professor Christiaan Snouck Hurgonje, a notable Islam expert who taught Islamic history in Leiden, had traveled to Mecca which in those days was still part of the Turkish Ottoman Empire. He spoke fluent Arabic and managed to spend several months in Mecca where he studied local customs and met Indonesian pilgrims. He found the Indonesians generally inclined to tolerate the Dutch authority over their country because they felt that being ruled by the British or even worse, the Chinese would be a much less desirable situation. The Acehnese, however, were fanatically opposed to any rule by any infidels. They were the most doctrinaire Muslims of all and absolutely not inclined to submit themselves to the authority of the Dutch. Snouck had to cut his sojourn in Mecca short because the French vice consul in Mecca committed an indiscretion by letting it be known that Snouck was not the Moroccan dignitary he pretended to be, but a Dutchman. Snouck wrote a book about his experiences and his thoughts on how the archipelago and particularly Aceh could be pacified and colonized. For several years the Dutch army in Aceh assumed a defensive but inactive posture. A new governor general, van der Wijck, assumed office in 1893, the year my father was born in Batavia. Van der Wijck decided to take action in Aceh and on the recommendation of Snouck appointed a Major van Heutsz to lead the campaign. Johannes Benedictus van Heutsz is Netty's great-granduncle. Van Heutsz had written an article on "How to conquer Aceh." He wrote "Only he who shows that he has real power and can have his will obeyed everywhere and under all circumstances, also if necessary by using his strong arm efficiently, will be the man who can bring Aceh to total submission and can place his foot on the neck of the brave and liberty loving Aceh people." Van Heutsz started an aggressive and very harsh military campaign, smoking out resistance wherever he could find it and going after individual tribal heads one by one until he had pacified the region. He gained a level of respect among the local population because he followed Snouck's advice and gave conquered regents most of their powers back as long as they stayed peaceful. He used loyal tribesmen to serve on the Dutch side. Using small aggressive units led by Europeans, he abandoned the system whereby the Dutch mostly stayed behind a line of defense. He moved into the interior. In 1898 van Heutsz was a colonel and named governor of Aceh. He is described as energetic, a go-getter, and free of all pre conceived notions. He is said to have given the army its self-confidence back after years of enforced passivity against an aggressively attacking enemy. After gaining the submission of most of the leaders of the revolt, he managed to capture Teuku Omar, the leader of the revolt in, 1899. The administration of Aceh was left to military men including a colonel van Daalen, a relative of our friend Albert van Daalen, and Henricus Colijn, later a top executive in Royal Dutch Shell and subsequently also prime minister of the Netherlands for many years during the period of economic depression in the 1930s. Van Daalen made several forays into the interior during which his troops acted particularly harshly, killing large numbers of men, women and children. His defenders say that the number of casualties could have been a great deal more over time if less aggressive action had been taken. Van Heutsz, now a general, became a national hero after the Aceh rebellion was quelled. In 1904 he became governor general of the Netherlands East Indies, a position he held until 1909. He was very much aware of the need to gain control over all the parts of the archipelago claimed by Holland. Especially in New Guinea there was a need to establish a Dutch presence after Britain and Germany made moves that seemed to indicate an interest in this huge island. Ultimately, the Dutch claimed and kept the eastern half of New Guinea. The "Aceh method" was applied in moves to pacify the outlying parts of the archipelago. Ceram, Borneo and Celebes were occupied, followed by Sumba, Sumbawa and Timor. Bali continued to present big problems. The Dutch tried to stop the local custom of "widow burning." The Balinese, who are Hindus, followed the custom of burning their dead on large ceremonial funeral pyres, and when a man died, it was customary to force his wife to join him on the funeral pyre. After the Balinese plundered a stranded Dutch ship, van Heutsz had a motive to move in. His action resulted in a collective suicide of the Balinese rulers who rushed the Dutch troops with hundreds of fighters, armed with primitive weapons. In the following mêlée, the entire retinue of the raja was killed. Van Heutsz termed the behavior of the Balinese as "not so nice." When accusations about his actions in Bali came from Dutch parliamentarians, he called it "just gossip from nattering members of parliament." The military government gradually improved the situation in

Bali, and about 1908 the war was over.

While France, Germany, Italy and Britain were occupying huge areas of Africa in the years after 1880, the Dutch limited themselves to the Indonesian archipelago in a sort of "ethnically rationalized imperialism." Gradually the archipelago became one political unit, and later on Indonesian nationalists saw the Netherlands East Indies as one country. Accordingly, van Heutsz is now regarded as the founder of modern Indonesia. I have tried to find out what record van Heutsz achieved in his career as governor general. There is very little information about him beyond long and emotional stories about the atrocities committed by the Dutch troops in Aceh under his command and later particularly those under command of Colonel later General van Daalen. When van Heutsz became governor general, he traveled to Aceh and fired van Daalen who was then governor of Aceh. This move was inspired by political pressure from Holland after disturbing news reports were received about the way in which Dutch authorities carried on in the region.

What I do know about van Heutsz is that he was an energetic man who undertook a difficult task, the pacification of Aceh, and succeeded. For many years, he was celebrated as a national hero in Holland and monuments honoring him were erected.

After World War II when opinions about colonialism, war and the way in which people in Indonesia had been treated changed, protesters damaged the monuments. In the sixties, left wing activists believed it was their duty to deface these monuments in order to express their indignation with things that happened almost a century ago. They tried to rewrite history retroactively and wrote about their brave acts of vandalism in detail. Where patriotism was once considered an honorable aim, it was old hat in the sixties and rejected. Words such as fatherland were politically incorrect since they were too gender specific, but motherland was equally unacceptable. So monuments that bear inscriptions like den Vaderland Getrouwe – faithful to the fatherland – are now hopelessly old fashioned. The Internet bears witness to these rants and very little else can be found that gives an objective picture of the man van Heutsz was. From speaking to Netty's mother about him, I know that van Heutsz was born a Catholic in Coevorden in 1851. He died in Switzerland in Montreux in 1924 as an agnostic. Mammie said that he was embittered about the political situation in The Netherlands and refused to move back to his homeland despite strong urgings from Queen Wilhelmina who wrote him several letters telling him that he should end his days in the Netherlands. After his death, in the nineteen twenties, van Heutsz' body was exhumed in Montreux and brought over to Amsterdam where an elaborate mausoleum was built to receive his remains. This mausoleum still exists in a cemetery called the Nieuwe Ooster Begraafplaats. Van Heutsz was perhaps the most controversial man in Dutch colonial history.

In May 2003 the Indonesian army started a large-scale military operation in Aceh against a small band of separatists who were successfully holding out against the government and were perceived to have broken a cease-fire agreement. A massive sea-land attack was launched. The fact that rich natural gas fields were discovered in the province was an important issue in the background. The Acehnese have remained rebellious through the centuries and their separatist movement is seen as a serious threat to the country's unity. As the French say, "plus que ça change, plus que ça reste la même chose." On Christmas day 2004, a major earthquake erupted in the Indian Ocean, very close to the southwestern shore of Aceh. The quake did major damage to Aceh's capital Banda Aceh, but what was much worse was the Tsunami wave it triggered. The Tsunami rolled over Aceh's shoreline, killing tens of thousands of people and leaving the area devastated. It also destroyed a good part of the coastline of Sri Lanka, Thailand and India. It is considered the worst disaster to hit the world in this century. Efforts to bring relief to Aceh, by far the worst hit area, were slow to start. The Indonesian government at first did not react fast enough, and its officials showed signs of being confused and overwhelmed by the magnitude of the disaster. What is more, the area was still in a state of rebellion and under military control. Accordingly, journalists were not allowed to enter the area and the Indonesian military was initially reluctant to let foreign aid organizations come in. After about a week of indecision, aid workers were allowed in and a U.S. navy flotilla, including an aircraft carrier with forty helicopters, was helping the devastated population.

Soon after van Heutsz left office, the so-called "Ethical Period" I referred to before began in the Indies. Representatives of the Dutch government began to see themselves as big brothers of the indigent population, brothers who had to protect their charges against the oppression and corruption of their own regents and lower authorities, *Pathihs, Wedanas* and *Assistent Wedanas*. A policy that was based on "Moral Obligation" replacing one that was profit oriented and that leaned towards exploitation of the Netherlands East Indies. There was a notion that Holland had to pay back the many millions it had extracted from the Indies in previous years. A theory of "guardianship" over the population took hold. At the turn of the nineteenth century, there was great poverty among the population of Java. Taxes levied

458

on the Javanese were used to finance expansion outside Java and as the *Cultuur Stelsel* was removed, the government paid gradually less back to the population for growing certain crops. Also, population growth added to the problem.

In the mid–1880s the sugar industry experienced a serious crisis as European governments began more and more to protect growers of sugar beets and a disease hit the sugar cane growers in Java. Consequently, sugar producers paid less rent to the locals on whose land they were growing their product. What impact these events had on my grandfather's business is unclear, but it is perhaps the reason why he left Indonesia in the late 1890s. The more benevolent policies of the Dutch resulted in the building of irrigation projects with dams etc. for the benefit of the population, extensive promotion of farmer education, and cheap credit. Medical care was improved, but in 1930 there were still only 1,030 doctors for 60 million people! A school system was developed and locals were trained to serve as teachers in it. The goal was to develop the population towards self-government with emphasis on training the Javanese elite. By 1940 40% of the children between the ages 6 –9 years had received some form of simple elementary education as a result of these efforts in the education sector. There were a few vocational schools, but there was not enough native small industry to employ those who graduated from these schools. Very few native students received a higher education. The first high school for the native population was opened in 1919. The Technical University of Bandung was founded in 1920. Sukarno, the leader of the Indonesian independence movement and the first president of Indonesia, graduated from this university in 1926. In 1924 a law school was opened and in 1927 a medical school. However, the ranks of the Binnenlands Bestuur or BB, the Department of the Interior, the government authority that ruled over most of the territory of the colony, remained closed to native sons. The school for future government executives, which was formerly located in Delft, was closed in 1900 and moved to a more academic level in Leiden. I assume my great uncle George Stibbe, my grandmother's elder brother, went to this school in Delft because he started working in Indonesia in 1888.

When my great grandparents arrived in the Dutch East Indies around 1868 the new era in the colonial society was about to begin. They came with a ship that still went around the Cape of Good Hope. The Suez canal opened in November 1869 and the first Dutch ship passed through it in 1871. This event greatly facilitated the movement of people and goods between the Netherlands and its colony. It also facilitated communications. Recall that in those days communication by cable was still in its early stages so that almost all communications were by letter.

In 1870 the Dutch parliament passed a Sugar and Agriculture bill that opened the cultivation of export crops in the East Indies to private enterprise. My grandfather Max Schieferdecker, who arrived in Java in June 1882, was in a business that benefited from this change in the legislation, which was a move away from the old colonial society dominated by government-controlled economic activity to a more open market. Opa Schieferdecker arrived on a ship that still had to anchor in the roadstead outside Tandjong Priok. The harbor of Tandjong Priok, where I arrived with the Kota Inten, was built between 1877 and 1883. In 1880 there lived 59,903 Europeans in the Indies, mostly on Java. The native population then exceeded 19.5 million! Opa arrived just in time to witness the greatest explosion the world had ever seen, the eruption of the volcano of Krakatoa. The eruption and the tsunami it caused killed 36,000 people on Java and Sumatra. I cannot recall my grandfather ever talking about it. However, my grandmother mentioned it several times. She lived then in Batavia and recalled the skies getting pitch dark in daytime and the earth rumbling, while volcanic ash rained down. Beyond Java, Sumatra became an important center for European settlement because of the tobacco plantations that were developed there, beginning in 1863. The most important city in Sumatra is its capital Palembang, which is located in the southeastern part of the island near Java. My grandmother Dora Stibbe was born there in 1871. It must have been quite a pioneering existence there in those days. In Deli, the tobacco area, that is more to the north on the side of Malaya, Medan is the most important city. Medan was founded about 1890. The tobacco planters lived a lonely existence. They were allowed to marry a European woman only after residing in the area for six years. Consequently, many had an Indonesian "housekeeper" called a Njai. In 1900 there lived only 501 European women in Deli! Since 1848 it was legal for Christians to marry non–Christians, so many could marry their concubines and they did, which resulted in a large population of Indo–Europeans in the country.

The eighteen seventies brought great change to Dutch society in the Indies. In the old days (using a Malay term) often called Tempo Doeloe (or nowadays spelled Dulu), society was predominantly male and somewhat static. As the economy boomed and new arrivals from Holland came in greater numbers, other aspects of society changed too. There were more "nouveau riche" types around, living in large houses. A half-million Chinese moved in, mainly to work in mining for Chinese cartels, or "Congsis," outside Java. On Java itself Chinese began to participate in business and banking. Indo-Europeans became a larger group who through lack of opportunity and education were often poor. Many Europeans suffered from tropical diseases. Critics saw Dutch society in the Dutch East Indies as a cultural desert. The only entertainment available came from amateur musicians and theater groups. A French observer called life in the Indies with the typical cultural snobbism only the French can muster: Une societé sans art, sans réligion, sans idéal. Still, several notable books about life in Indonesia were written in those years. In 1880 there were only 60,000 Europeans living in the Dutch East Indies with 481 women per 1,000 men. In 1930 the Dutch population had grown to 240,000, of which about 70% lived in Java. There were 840 women per 1000 men in 1930. Life became more "European" in the thirties. Most Europeans lived in the cities and they were still a small part of the total population. The number of academics was also still low. In 1934 there were 768 engineers with a degree from the Technical University in Delft in Indonesia while there were 2,684 in Holland.

Nationalism and the independence movement among the local population started only in the 1920s. This late start may be due to lack of national sentiment among the different very diverse components of the population, the realization that they belonged to one country and also perhaps the generally gentle and compliant attitude of the Indonesian people, a national characteristic. However, a few Dutch observers had felt for some time that an independence movement was coming. The well-known Dutch writer Louis Couperus said in 1901 already that autonomy was only a question of time. For many Asians the Japanese victory over the Russians in 1905 was an important milestone in their quest for autonomy. It showed that the white man was not omnipotent and that Asians could beat him. The Indian National Congress party in India dates back to 1885, and during World War I the British government already made some concessions to the Indians. The U.S. also had a presence nearby when they occupied the Philippines in 1898 and gave that territory partial independence in 1916, promising to withdraw in due course. Feeling the heat, the Dutch reacted with characteristic pomposity by calling this U.S. promise a "mixture of western ignorance and eastern impatience." Still, an attempt was made to decentralize government functions to diminish the powers of the bureaucracy and transfer more power to local authorities. A new western-trained locale elite began to become noticeable, and a few voices of enlightened government officials who wanted to give the local population a stronger voice in government were heard. On the other hand, fears arose among the Europeans that the population was being radicalized.

The ethical movement of the "enlightened" government officials was thinking in term of linking the Indies permanently to the Netherlands and building a beautiful future for both by improving education and democratic institutions. The cry was, "A people who have been sleeping for centuries have awakened." By the end of World War I, Indonesians heard about Wilson's fourteen points, which included a broad sweeping statement about colonialism that had a beautiful ring but was difficult to implement as were his other points. It said in characteristically fuzzy language that there would have to be a "free, open-minded and absolutely impartial adjustment of all colonial claims." A feeble attempt was made in Indonesia by the installation in May 1918 of the Volksraad, a people's council somewhat representative of the population that had powers to consult and advise, but not legislate. Initially this council had 38 members, among which only 15 were Indonesians. Later it was enlarged to 60 with 30 Indonesians, partly appointed and partly elected. Naturally, the Dutch continued to be firmly in control. As the socialists became a vocal party in Holland after the first war, they argued for making the Indies an independent part of the Kingdom, but this movement found a great deal of resistance and as a result more conservative policies began to take over in the twenties. The ethical movement protested but lost its influence. Communism also infiltrated Indonesia and the PKI, the Partai Kommunis Indonesia, was formed. Later I would meet fanatical remnants of this party fighting us around Madiun. The PKI even plotted a revolt in 1926, but the police got wind of their plans and rolled the plot up.

Gradually the ideas of the ethicists that felt the population could be educated to become cooperative with Dutch long-term plans was shattered and more forceful policies were followed to keep order. One of the offshoots of the harsher policies was the construction of an internment camp for Indonesian revolutionaries in New Guinea in Boven Digul. In the thirties, a big chasm emerged between the Indonesian nationalists and the Dutch government. The Dutch had no more desire to grant more independence, and the Indonesians became more and more radicalized. The Great Depression and its impact on world markets and certainly markets for Indonesian products played a big role in the hardening of these positions. Exports of three major commodities suffered. Rubber had become Indonesia's most important export product – Indonesia produced 37% of world output in 1928. Oil and sugar were second and third in importance. Oil production started in 1892 and eventually Royal Dutch Shell had become the largest company in the Indies. Exports to the U.S. and Japan increased while those to the Netherlands diminished. The market crash of 1929 was a tremendous blow to the economy of the Indies and the insistence of the Dutch government to hang on to the gold standard for its currency – the Dutch and colonial guilder were linked – further worsened the situation in Europe and overseas.

Sukarno, who had graduated in 1926 from the new Dutch engineering university in Bandung as one of the first native sons, was the most prominent among the student nationalists. He coined the name Indonesia. His main position was non-cooperation with the colonial powers. Indonesians studying in the Netherlands also became politically active. In 1927 they formed a party called Perseritakan National Indonesia the PNI that later became the Partai Nasional Indonesia. This party still exists as the leading political organization in Indonesia. They composed the national anthem, Indonesia Raya, and designed the red and white flag. Several governor generals tried to respond to the nationalist pressures, at first by following the ethical policies of "association," later by yielding to conservative pressure from the European community by arresting Sukarno and putting him away in Boven Digul. There were tremendous battles between more ethically oriented government officials and conservatives. When Sukarno was freed again in 1931–his four-year sentence was reduced to two years–he had gained enormously in stature. A critical event was the 1933 mutiny on the Dutch battle cruiser Zeven Provincien, an old WW I vintage craft. Indonesian crewmembers mutinied, locked up their officers, and started drifting around. The rebellion was quelled by bombing the ship with a navy seaplane. One bomb was dropped which killed nine crew members, three of whom were Dutch. It was later revealed that the mutiny was prompted more by social motives than political ones since the navy had implemented a salary reduction for all hands. The conservative Governor General de Jonge, who retired in 1936, restored order. His motto was, "we have been here for 300 years and may need another 300 years before some form of independence can be achieved." The Dutch simply did not see the rising tide of the independence movement and there continued to be a deep schism between Dutch and Indonesian societies. The contact Dutch people had with Indonesians was mostly only with their house servants who were regarded as loyal and willing to sacrifice. They saw the nationalist trend as "oriental" and irrelevant. There were virtually no reforms and old-style government prevailed.

❧

Meanwhile the external threat grew. Japan needed oil, bauxite, rubber and many other products. The Dutch realized that their military power was insufficient to fight Japan. The colony had a "small-country size" army, mainly used to keep order in the interior, not trained to fight an exterior enemy. The Dutch navy in the Indies was active and well trained but numerically at a grave disadvantage to the Japanese.

The airforce was in the same position. After World War II began, the Dutch tried hard to buy fighters and bombers from U.S. manufacturers wherever they could but the U.S. was rearming itself and could not spare too many first- line modern planes. Moreover, the need for reinforcements from the U.S. for the British RAF in Europe was also strong. The systematic efforts to reduce defense budgets in the depression years had brought military readiness to a very low level. On December 8, 1941, one day after the Japanese attack on Pearl Harbor the Governor General Tjarda van Starkenborch Stachouwer declared war on Japan. A brave gesture that had to be made to support our Allies. Tjarda counted on the protection of the British Navy. But the horrible calamity that befell the Allies in Asia soon began to take shape when on December 10 Japanese planes sank two British battleships in the Indian Ocean, the brand new Prince of Wales and the older Repulse. These battleships came over from England to help defend Singapore. They sailed without air cover and were an easy prey for Japanese dive-bombers. Also, Guam fell on December 10, followed by Wake on the 11th and Hong Kong on the 25th. The Japanese reached Rabaul in Australian New Guinea on January 24, 1942. The Japanese attack on the Netherlands East Indies logically focused on first capturing the oil fields in Borneo and then getting a foothold on Celebes. The British General Wavell was put in command of all land forces between Burma and Darwin, Australia. The Dutch Vice Admiral Doorman was given command of a joint naval strike force. Tarakan, the island on the shore of Borneo where one of the largest Dutch oil fields was located, fell after a 24-hour fight. The Japanese had threatened anybody who destroyed the oil fields with a death sentence. Despite this the fields were dynamited and two civilian Dutch government officials were beheaded and 76 other civilians were forced to walk into the sea and were shot.

On January 25, the Japanese landed in Menado, the main city of Celebes, and Singapore fell on February 15. The fortifications of Singapore were all directed towards the sea, but the Japanese came over land, marching rapidly down the Malaya Peninsula. The defenders, although numerically stronger than the Japanese, did not put up much of a fight. Their excuse was that they were responsible for a large number of women and children trapped on the island city. A look at the map will show that Singapore held the key to all of Indonesia and after it was lost, the Allied supreme commander decided to leave Java, leaving the Dutch alone to face the over-whelming force of the Japanese army, navy and airforce. A number of Dutch fighter aircraft had been sent to defend Singapore and were lost there, further depleting the air power available for the defense of Indonesia. Admiral Doorman and his fleet had cruised up and down the Java Sea for several days, trying to find Japanese units that could be attacked. He lost several ships in these forays, some to air attacks and a few that ran aground due to faulty navigation, which gave the Allies reason to doubt the local knowledge of the Dutch. When a large Japanese invasion fleet approached Java, the Allied strike force decided to engage them. They elected to do this during the night because they had little or no air cover. Admiral Karel Doorman knew he was doomed and said so when speaking to his staff in Surabaya before the battle. Chances that they could damage the Japanese invasion forces enough to make them turn away were slim. So he went to sea and gave the order, *"Ik val aan volg mij"* – "I am attacking, follow me." These heroic words have become part of Dutch history and folklore. We have learned later that his actual signal was different. It said, "All ships follow me." Still, this attack reflects the bravery of the naval strike force, which was operating against enormous odds. The Allied squadron had been hastily pulled together from several navies. Their signal systems were poorly coordinated, radio frequencies did not match and armaments and ship speeds we very different. In the ensuing battle with several Japanese heavy cruisers, which outgunned them, the entire force was wiped out. The Japanese had only light losses. The Allied crews were exhausted after many days of uninterrupted action and heavy losses and when the battle started Doorman had already lost almost all his destroyers. Two Dutch cruisers, the de Ruyter and the Java, and the British heavy cruiser Exeter went down. The American heavy cruiser Houston and the Australian cruiser Perth also sank. This battle was without doubt the most dramatic engagement of the Dutch navy since the wars against England in the eighteenth century. Admiral Doorman, who perished, became a national hero in Holland. He is linked through marriage with Netty's family. Netty's aunt Nini, her father's sister who died young in childbirth, was married to a naval officer, Dick Hetterschij. Doorman's first wife Justine (they were divorced), married Dick Hetterschij after Nini's death.

After the battle in the Java Sea, the Japanese could land wherever they wanted on Java. They did so promptly and met with relatively little resistance. The Dutch army fought the invasion in several spots but could not muster a vigorous coordinated resistance. While the Dutch airforce and navy fought heroically in the brief war with Japan, the army did not perform well. It was an army that had spent most of its time in policing the colony and fighting local insurgencies. Many native soldiers were less than eager to fight and Dutch reservists showed an equally low level of fighting spirit. Leadership was weak and modern equipment not always available. It was decided not to fight the Japanese when they landed but rather to attack them after they were moving inland and were presumably more vulnerable. The Germans made the same mistake when they wanted to fight the Allies after they landed in Normandy. The German General Rommel wanted to throw the Allies back into the sea as soon as he knew where they would land. His successor decided to draw back and attack the presumed still weak forces once they had landed.

The Dutch forces capitulated on March 8, 1942, after just one week of fighting. Surprisingly, almost all army units followed orders to surrender. Only a few small units of the colonial army, the KNIL, tried to start a guerilla-type resistance. The Japanese soon rolled up most of them, sometimes because the local population turned them in or because they were unable to find sufficient food. In the very rugged terrain of New Guinea, one group managed to stay undetected for more than a year. When the Japanese found them, they beheaded their commander, a heroic Indo-European lieutenant, and shot the other members of his unit. The harsh treatment of prisoners of war was most likely also a reason why little further resistance was organized. The enthusiastic reception the local population gave the Japanese in the beginning of the occupation came as a rude shock for the Dutch. When the Japanese forces landed and marched into towns and villages, the natives greeted them as liberators with the "rising sun" flag. They must have prepared these flags in advance. The loss of prestige by the Dutch who thought the Indonesians regarded them as omnipotent was enormous and lasting. It was a sea change in the relationship between the Indonesians and the Dutch that critically and permanently influenced the behavior of the native population towards their home-grown independence movement.

Soon after the Japanese occupation was completed, steps were taken to incarcerate all Dutch citizens. In the beginning of May 1942, all Dutch men over seventeen years old were arrested and put in camps that were hastily built in city neighborhoods. Soon women and children followed. In total 29,000 men, 25,000 women and 29,000 children were interned in Java. Indo-Europeans were exempt, but surprisingly, not in Sumatra. The level of discomfort suffered by the internees was not uniform. It depended on the Japanese camp commanders. Many of these commanders behaved extremely cruelly, for instance forcing women and children to stand for hours in the burning sun while their tormentors stood in the shade. Women and men had to bow daily to the Japanese flag in honor of the emperor and suffer many other indignities. It was often thought that for a Japanese officer it was in a way a "loss of face" to supervise a camp with women and children rather than be in the field fighting the enemy. Particularly heartbreaking are the stories of children left in the camps without parents or of boys who were forced to leave their mothers to go to a men's camp after reaching the age of fourteen or sometimes even younger. In the beginning, prisoners in most camps could trade with the native population outside, but later in 1944 when rules were tightened, this was prohibited. Food rations were brought down to starvation levels. At that time, the Japanese began to realize they were losing the war and took revenge on their prisoners. Overcrowding and disease made the camps a living hell, especially in the last few months.

The men had a particularly hard time, especially the prisoners of war. Many men, military personnel as well as civilians were transported to Burma to work on the notorious Burma railroad. Of the 18,000 Dutch POW's sent there 3,100 or 17% died. On Sumatra 5,000 Dutch POW's died building the Pakanbaru Railroad. The official history of the Netherlands during World War II contains much information about life in the camps during the Japanese occupation of the Indies. In many camps the treatment of prisoners, especially the men was dreadful. Beatings, torture, and hunger were the order of the day. Many prisoners were summarily executed – they were shot, beheaded, hanged, or beaten to death. Despite this there were still many cases of heroism. There were prisoners who had hidden radios they had built clandestinely and allowed them to listen to news from Australia. There was a female doctor who forcefully opposed her tormentors, went to the commandant, pounded on his desk, demanded better treatment of her fellow women prisoners, and got it. There were several escapes, some successful but most not. As time progressed, the food situation got worse and towards the end men, women and children in many camps were close to starvation. Hunger edema, a condition we also frequently saw in Holland in the final year of the war, was a common occurrence, as was diarrhea and many tropical diseases. Since the camps contained people from every layer of Dutch society, there were of course heroes and cowards, generous people who shared everything they had and those who hoarded money and food, people who stole from fellow prisoners and every other form of human vices. Overall however, most prisoners behaved admirably under very difficult circumstances and many Dutch families were reunited after the war.

What happemed in Indonesia after the Japanese capitulation was dramatically different from the generally joyous liberation Holland experienced. At first the Japanese ignored the nationalistic movement of the native population, but when the tide began to turn Sukarno was supported in many ways. In January 1943, he traveled to Tokyo, and was permitted to establish a militia in Indonesia called Barisan Pelopor. This name caught on and we called our opponents always *Pelopors* (pronounced with a silent e - the word means pioneer/trailblazer). The Javanese liked to serve in this army because they were given uniforms and better food. After the capitulation of Japan, the Japanese gave arms to this army and to military auxiliaries called HeiHo's. The Japanese-inspired anti western "Greater Asia Movement" became Sukarno's principal political aim. Sukarno was convinced that Germany, Italy and Japan would win the war. The Indonesian population had greeted the Japanese invaders as liberators but learned soon that they were treated almost as badly as the Europeans who were put in camps. The occupier disrupted the food supply because of ill-informed policies. The rice distribution was particularly chaotic. Hunger and poverty were soon a common occurrence. Only the black marketers, often Chinese, and the outright collaborators prospered. The Japanese garrison was thinly spread over the archipelago and many disruptions in the local infrastructure were left unattended. So by the time the war was over, the country's economy was in shambles and lawlessness was widespread.

On August 17, 1945, shortly after the Japanese capitulated, Sukarno declared the independence of Indonesia and formed a government consisting mostly of well-known nationalists who had either collaborated with the Japanese or opposed them in a fashion. This government was shocked when the Japanese made no effort whatsoever to transfer power to them. They wanted to act independently, however, and went ahead on their own. As soon as the authority of the Japanese military could be challenged, a horrible period of looting, murder and plunder erupted with bands of self-appointed nationalists, who had often been armed by the Japanese, roaming the cities and the countryside. They attacked the camps of the helpless Dutch civilian prisoners. This period is known as the Bersiap period. It took a long time before Allied troops arrived to liberate the people in the camps. About 3,500 Dutch prisoners who must have thought they had survived the war were killed in the Bersiap period.

Allied war plans initially included an attack on Indonesia by American forces that were preparing for an invasion from Australia. This plan was abandoned when the "Island Hopping" strategy was adopted, and the Americans moved rapidly in a thrust towards the Japanese home islands and the Philippines, bypassing Indonesia. When it became clear that there was no need to occupy Indonesia and many other territories in between to beat Japan, the British forces that were moving into Burma and Malaya from India were given responsibility for Indonesia. Lord Louis Mountbatten, a cousin of the king and supreme commander of the British forces, had no great desire to commit too many troops to Indonesia after the war was over.

He had not prepared for this task anyway and did not have sufficient manpower. He concentrated his forces in the main cities and avoided large-scale actions. The internment camps were now again protected by the Japanese POWs under British orders, and evacuation was terribly slow. The world had changed.

The American Secretary of State Sumner Welles (a less than prominent member of the Roosevelt administration who was later replaced), referring to the Asian colonial regimes declared that he could not imagine a postwar world "that was half slave and half free." Mountbatten was convinced that long term resistance against the nationalists was futile. In the fifties Mountbatten would serve as the last viceroy in India and turn that country over to its own nationalists a move that resulted in an enormous bloodbath between Hindus and Muslims who ultimately split the country into India and Pakistan. When the British commander General Malaby was killed in Surabaya during the Bersiap period, vigorous action was finally taken. In the battle of Surabaya 14 British soldiers died and thousands of Indonesians were killed. Then the evacuation of the internees was finally speeded up. I have searched in vain for statistics about the number of Dutch people who were interned by the Japanese and the number of victims. It is probably not possible to get accurate statistics on these matters as the mortality in the camps varied greatly from area to area, depending on the treatment people got from local Japanese commanders. For instance, of the people interned in North Sumatra 4½ % did not survive while of those imprisoned in Mid Sumatra 10% perished and in Southern Sumatra it was much worse – 37% died. Of the people interned on Java, 16% died. Recall that the total number of Dutch people living in Indonesia was surprisingly low relative to the size of the country. One book I read gave an example, comparing the size of the entire Dutch community in Indonesia with the population of the city of Utrecht in 1940.

It took until July 1946 before the Dutch authorities could take over in what little territory they could reclaim as their colony. Lieutenant Governor General van Mook, a man who was second in command under Tjarda van Starkenborgh and who had managed to escape at the last moment to Colombo, was put in charge. He would play a very significant role in the ensuing battle for the freedom of Indonesia. Van Mook was a man of the ethical school who was also a realist, and he tried to negotiate establishment of the Federal Republic of Indonesia, the Republik Indonesia Serikat. He met with opposition from both sides. The Indonesians were opposed, and at home right-wing people, including me and many friends of my parents and grandparents, regarded him as a traitor who was ready to sell out our precious heirloom. The rejection of the federal plan by Sukarno's Republic was a bitter disappointment for van Mook because he had an agreement with them that they would accept the plan and play a role in it. As carnage continued in many parts, the Dutch sent more and more troops. The first two divisions that went were volunteers from Holland who ended up spending up to three years in Indonesia after being told they would have to serve at most two years there. An infamous colonial army captain named Westerling purged Celebes of pro-republic elements. Thousands died and journalists at home made him into the incarnation of the atrocities the Dutch military were accused of committing. He would resurface after the Dutch were ready to leave forever and make another foray. Today the Dutch still wrestle with the question of the behavior of the Dutch military in Indonesia. More about that later. The Dutch supreme commander General Spoor thought in 1947 that a quick limited action could stop the Republic. He reached the oil fields and mines near Palembang on Sumatra and captured Surabaya and part of East Java and Madura. This so-called "police action" (the name was chosen to indicate a purely internal affair) stirred up considerable foreign interest and the UN sent in a "Commission of Good Services" that was supposed to mediate. The commission consisted of two Australians who were pro–Republic, a Belgian who was pro–Dutch and an American who was neutral. Negotiations were started with the Republic. In the event, Sukarno who was a skilled propagandist, gained wide international recognition. When his communist faction rebelled inside Republic–controlled territory in Madiun, a place where I would spend much time later on, he repressed the rebellion brutally. This caught the attention of the U.S. since the cold war was heating up and suddenly anybody who was anticommunist was a friend of the U.S.

The situation between the two belligerents, confined to "demarcation zones," became untenable. A second police action started on December 19, 1948, just before my battalion was shipping out. Its objective was to eliminate the Republic. Initially it was successful. All of the Republic's territory was occupied as the Sukarno forces faded into the countryside and started a guerilla war. While a futile effort was made to establish the Federal Republic, the UN Security Council demanded an immediate cease-fire, which was supposedly in force when I arrived. As I discovered, this was hardly a peaceful arrangement. The unit I belonged to ended up in this quagmire, and it took a year and a half to extract us from it.

This chapter may be extremely boring to many readers and I trust those for whom this piece of history is of no interest will skip it. It is important to me, however. Reading up on the history of Indonesia has given me a new and fresher perspective on the Dutch colonial period. It has become clear to me that the Dutch have really only been masters of the Indies in its entirety for about fifty years, not four centuries as I had always assumed from the history books I read in Holland. When I was in Indonesia I quickly understood that the Dutch army did not have "a snowball's chance in hell" to overcome the independence movement and that this movement was entirely justified. The ineptness of the Dutch negotiators who were trying to protect Dutch interests and the interest of many separate ethnic groups of the Indonesian population was monumental and after many agreements and understandings with Sukarno's republic failed, the Federal Republic of Indonesia was organized anyway. I was there at that time and saw it collapse into the arms of Sukarno's Republik Indonesia within weeks of its formation. After that, the Dutch did not even try anymore. They just let the situation deteriorate into chaos. The more I think about it the more I feel we as soldiers were given an impossible task to perform with inferior equipment and extremely poor leadership. The public in Holland was not interested anymore and was kept totally in the dark about our activities. Only notices with black borders and the names of men that were killed appeared in the papers. It makes me angry to think of the men we lost needlessly, of the money that was wasted on us and of the good years of our lives we gave for a cause that was ill defined and impossible to fulfill. In my opinion it would have been much more appropriate for the Dutch press to direct its criticisms, decades after the military actions took place, at the weak political and military leadership at home and in Indonesia that permitted these events to develop rather than the few overwhelmed men who tried to maintain order in a chaotic country. We left 2,500 good men behind and in 2010 the Dutch government officially confirmed that the date of inception of the Indonesian Republic was August 17, 1945 and not December 17, 1949, the date on which sovereignty was officially turned over by the Dutch and which until then the Dutch had insisted was the actual date. So it had all been in vain

18 : *Indonesia*

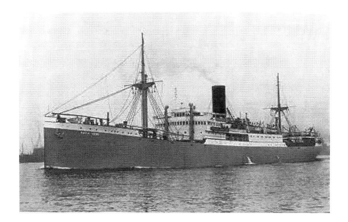

The Kota Inten (built in 1927) was packed with soldiers. She carried not only our battalion but also a detachment of marines and several other men belonging to other units. Some 1,300 men in all. We slept on bunks made of canvas stretched in steel frames with ropes. Four high. These bunks were vertically so close together that lying in your bunk, you would poke the one on top of you with your shoulder when you turned over. While the guy below you would do the same to you. I was unlucky and got a middle bunk. Our large U.S. Army issue duffel bags were stacked in an open section in the middle of the hold where there were hatches covering the opening to the hold below us where trucks and other equipment were stored. Whenever you needed something out of your bag, you had to dig for it among a pile of duffel bags in competition with several others. The passageways between the rows of bunks were about three feet so there was not much room to stand

and get dressed or undressed. The North Sea, the Channel and the Bay of Biscay are not very welcoming bodies of water under most circumstances and certainly not in February. The ship began to move and people started getting seasick. This was not a pleasant experience what with the crowded conditions we were in and the very poor ventilation of the holds. On board we did not have to stay together with our units, so we could wander all over the ship, certainly in the first few days when a high percentage of the men were seasick. We could also sit in the larger "recreation" room to write letters etc., provided we could find a seat

There we would also have to go to be checked in or out or get paid or get on lists or off lists etc. The officers were quartered in the middle section of the ship where they had a few cramped cabins that were used for paying passengers in the old days. The Kota Inten moved at a speed of about 13 knots (that's about 4 knots slower than the cruising speed of my lobster boat Strider) so she was not exactly a speedboat. In the North Sea and the Channel, we had a few very rough gray days, and I remember being in the dining area for breakfast where they had nice hard-boiled eggs with bread and nobody there to eat them. Everybody was sick and I could pick up three eggs of fellows who had tried to eat and had to rush away. Several men were so sick that they lay for dead in corners of the deck. One had found a pipe on which he could sit while keeping his head outside a nearby porthole. He was deadly afraid of getting violently sick again if he would leave his perch and come inside. To avoid the worst seas the Captain decided to move further west towards the Isle of Wight and make a loop back to Portugal. It was a strange feeling to be so near the island where I had such a good time three years earlier in my first postwar trip abroad and to see its lights glittering in the evening gloom.

When we approached the coast of Portugal, the sun broke through, the sea became calmer, and I could see the shoreline with small white houses on it. On an early grayish morning, we passed the Rock of Gibraltar fairly close. I was standing on the bow and could see dolphins scooting along with us and playing around our bow. I had never seen dolphins before. The Rock of Gibraltar looked gray and grim like the fortress it was. You could clearly see the military installations there that had had been so crucial in the war. You could also see the large concrete slab the British had built on the side of the rock to collect rainwater.

Crossing the length of the Mediterranean took several days. We had flat calm seas and our troops came back to life. This meant that I was forced to endure the close proximity of many men who were loud, profane and generally uninteresting and uncivilized. I hated the environment and withdrew as much as possible with friends like Oc and others. I wrote many letters. I wrote more than 160 letters to Netty during my period in Indonesia and underway to and from there. Since every letter consisted of three sheets and each sheet was covered on both sides, I covered more than 960 letter size (8 ½ x 11in.) sheets with my small scribbling. Netty wrote me more often. She sent me 190 letters! In addition, I wrote my parents and friends regularly. There was no other way to communicate effectively except maybe when possible with telegrams, but that was out of the question in most places where I would end up. We have saved all our letters and before writing this chapter I read all my own letters and many Netty wrote. They gave me a perfect flavor of the time, a real time capsule, with lots of detail I had forgotten. It was a strange sensation for me to read my own observations again, and it was heartwarming to see my expressions of love for Netty repeated more than 190 times and her even more frequent responses in the same vein. It was a miserable time for me, but it was certainly not uninteresting. I have no record of any other time in my life that is as precise and completely documented and I will therefore spend more time on detail in this segment than on any other period of my life. I can only hope it will be of some interest to my readers.

On board I spent a good deal, of time trying to be transferred back to my old mortar platoon and in addition, trying to get an assignment to the military judicial service. I wanted to see if I could serve with that branch of the military since it would, hopefully, afford me an environment in which I could continue my studies. My friend Frits Greup served as a lieutenant with the military court in Batavia, but he had already earned his law degree and was, therefore, of more value to this branch. I thought I had a good connection at the judiciary through a Major Schaap, the brother of one of my mother's oldest friends, Leida Schaap. Mr. Schaap was serving in Batavia as a military judge and had said by letter that he was willing to help me. Many people who had like me "candidate of law" degrees served as clerks with the military tribunals so it was not a far-fetched idea. As it turned out much later, this major was exactly the wrong connection for me. He was not highly regarded by his colleagues, who considered him an eccentric. He was viewed as a bit of a light-weight in the military judicial system and certainly not an officer with the clout I needed. I did not know this and spent a lot of time and effort trying to contact him by telegram via my parents. He was slow in answering and eventually proved very ineffective. Perhaps nobody could have done anything for me anyway, the way the military works. The army seems to have a knack for not using people for the jobs they are best qualified for but rather for things they are totally unqualified for. Because of these efforts and also because I celebrated my birthday during my first week on board, I received more telegrams than anybody else on the ship. I gained great notoriety because the names of people who had received telegrams were broadcast over the ship's loudspeaker system so the recipient could come to the office of the radioman to collect them.

When we reached Port Said we got our first batch of mail and could send off our first letters home. In Port Said the ship was tied up to a mooring, very close to the shore. You could clearly see the commotion on shore and in the streets. Egypt was still under occupation by the British army and their men and vehicles were visible in the streets. Policemen wearing fezzes and carrying shotguns, pistols and large long bullwhips were keeping order among the riffraff on the docks. Next to our ship was a crowded emigrant ship heading for Australia, loaded with eastern Europeans – people we called Displaced Persons (DPs) in those days. They were folks who had been displaced by the Germans during their march into the Soviet Union and did not want to return home or people who had subsequently been driven out by the Russians and could not find a place to live in Europe. Australia opened its doors to these DPs since they wanted more people but were still restricting their immigration to Caucasians only. Asians and blacks were not yet admitted there.

In Port Said we were given an opportunity to change some money and buy things from a designated group of traders who came aboard with their trinkets. In addition, a swarm of people in small rowboats surrounded our ship yelling at us in all kinds of languages, trying to sell us stuff. We were told to be careful in dealing with them because they were the worst rabble one could find anywhere in the world, and after looking at them, I agreed. They could curse in Dutch and used the foulest Dutch words imaginable. Clear proof of the good educational work done by thousands of Dutch sailors and soldiers who had preceded us. A light rope with a weight was tossed up at us and a basket was used to move goods up to the ship. Many of us, including me, bought soft leather zippered travel bags, which enabled us to separate some of our more valued possessions out of our duffel bags and make them more accessible. For some reason we were not allowed any more luggage than this one duffel bag, but once on board we could have more pieces of luggage. Like all the others, the Port Said bag I bought was poorly made, and the cheap zipper was soon busted, but for the time being it was wonderful to have a better way of keeping my more valuable things separately.

After waiting for about a day in the harbor with engine trouble, we were included in a southbound convoy and around midnight went on our way into the canal. A large searchlight encased in a heavy wooden crate was attached to the bow to help us navigate, and two very grubby-looking Egyptians in dirty nightgowns were on the foredeck with their small rowboat. It was their job to row out a dock line if we had to stop in the canal and could not go forward anymore. The next morning found us well into the canal. The desert sun was very bright and the air was remarkably clear. Despite the fact that we were now well into Egypt, it was still quite cool and we were still wearing our woolen winter uniforms without feeling uncomfortable. We passed antique looking signal stations along the way, which served as marking posts for passing convoys. In the distance in the desert, we could see British tanks maneuvering, using their guns with live ammunition on practice targets. Along the Egyptian side of the canal was a roadway, and you could see people moving along it in cars or trucks or riding camels and donkeys. Many men were hanging around the water's edge and several demonstrated their disdain for us by lifting their grubby skirts and waving with their penises at us. Eelco Apol, who had gone through the canal much earlier had written me about this interesting way of waving at passing European soldiers so I was on the lookout for this phenomenon and enjoyed seeing it.

I had received 11 letters in Port Said so I had plenty to read. I also got word that I would be able to return to my old mortar platoon once in Java. This was excellent news that was confirmed by Captain Wolzak. Beyond my natural desire to be with my old buddies, my preference for the mortars stemmed mainly from the fact that the men in that platoon had been chosen because they were more intelligent, a major factor in making life among them more bearable. The normal infantry, the 3rd company I was in at that time, were the bottom of the barrel in intelligence and that showed in their day-to-day behavior. Loud, stupid, profane and generally difficult to deal with. I was amused to read in a letter from my mother that she hoped I would be able to play a lot of ping pong since there would probably be little room for deck tennis (a game she knew from her days on ocean liners). I read this while sitting on deck on my proud possession, a fruit crate, jammed in among hundreds of men.

On February 25 we entered the Red Sea and it began to get warmer. We broke out our tropical uniforms. Among the infantry officers I found an ensign named Bronsgeest who was nineteen years old, and the son of the owner of a small grocery store in Voorburg where my mother sometimes bought her groceries. As a young boy, he would come to our house on his bike to deliver my mother's purchases. He had only three years of high school. I was praying that I would be able to stay away from this character. As it turned out, my prayers were not heard. All the platoon commanders were still ensigns and would only become second lieutenants in Indonesia. Another economy move by the Dutch government. As we entered the Indian Ocean, it became more and more intolerably hot down below. One of the farm boys near my bunk had brought a huge Dutch cheese from home, one of those wheel-like things about a foot in diameter and more than four inches thick. Every night, sitting on his bunk, he would cut a piece from it and eat it. In the heat the cheese began to soften up dangerously and smell noticeably. The floors of the shower rooms were made of steel plate and since we showered with salt water, the plates were covered with a thick slimy layer of red rust. This situation got worse in the heat and made it very tough to towel off and emerge with clean feet.

The first officer of the ship told me he had served on cattle ships and observed that they took better care of the cattle on those vessels than the people he was transporting on this ship. Every morning we had to form up for morning parade. Wolzak was keen on keeping the discipline in his company. So we stood there while guys from other units could just hang out and watch us, making sarcastic comments. We were ordered to sunbathe a fixed amount of time every day. This was supposed to toughen our skin for the tropical sun. When the ships' crew rigged canvas awnings over all the decks, giving shade nearly everywhere, we were still told to sunbathe in the shade. Oc and I tried to stay sane by talking about parties we had attended in recent times. I told him about the party Netty and I had given for our engagement in Kasteel Oud Wassenaar, a castle near her home. Hard to believe, but this was less than a month ago. Oc told me about a royal ball he had attended with friends at the Belgian Court in Brussels. Here we were in the Indian Ocean, dangling our legs over the side in our gym shorts discussing court protocol. In the Indian Ocean we were allowed to sleep on deck. Lying on the steel deck, not bothered by too many people around and looking at the tropical starlit sky was a wonderful experience. The stars are clearer and much more visible in the tropical sky. There was no ambient light and there were many falling stars. It gave me some privacy and a chance to think about Netty and my uncertain future.

We played a lot of bridge. My steady partner was a fellow corporal Joop Groenendijk who studied agriculture at the Wageningen University. Joop and I played the "one two clubs convention" and had it down pat. We entered a duplicate bridge drive against the officers in their nicely airconditioned saloon. We ended up in fifth place and would have won if we hadn't made one fatal mistake. We were not invited back. We met several ships on our trip. We passed the

Willem Ruys, a luxury liner of the same company as our tired old tub. The Ruys was homeward bound from Indonesia. It was afternoon and its decks were empty. Everybody was probably enjoying a siesta. As the ship went by at a high rate of speed, I saw one lonely gentleman standing on the promenade deck, looking with some surprise at our ship packed with cheering soldiers and festooned with drying laundry. We had to wash our own clothes as well as we could with salt water and used to dry them in the sun. On March 7 we were passed by another troop ship, the Waterman. This was a former American troop ship that was believed to have much better accommodations than ours. This ship left Holland five days after us and passed us at full speed. The Kota Inten's speed was further impeded by frequent engine problems. For at least two full days we drifted around the Indian Ocean without making any headway while serious repairs were made. For entertainment we received King Neptune on board. He and his retinue proceeded to baptize hundreds of people clad in bathing trunks and roughly smeared them with oil and grease to create a dreadful mess on deck. We also had some games like a tug of war between platoons. The hero of this event was an outsize gorilla-like guy who was in one of Captain Wolzak's platoons. He was extremely powerfully built, like a professional wrestler, and could only talk in monosyllables and grunts. I had already had disciplinary problems with this guy as he tried to intimidate his buddies with his physical strength. His name was Schonewille and his nickname was Bul. Later on, he would cause a tragedy in our company.

In the night of March 9, almost four weeks after departure, we approached the harbor of a small island called Sabang. It is near the western tip of Sumatra and therefore the westernmost outpost of Indonesia. In the old days this island had been a coaling harbor for Dutch ships and was now used as a place where troopships would stop to allow the men to get on shore and stretch their legs. As we entered the harbor we saw that the Waterman was still there. Being near land was an incredible sensation. We were tied up to a wharf that was very close to a village or kampong as Indonesian villages are called. The warm air brought a smell of land, of vegetation and charcoal fires, a different and very tropical experience after four weeks of salt air and sea. The next morning we had reveille at 5 a.m. and were on land at seven. The dense tropical vegetation and the tremendous heat struck us like a ton of bricks. We walked around a bit with Captain Wolzak explaining the various aspects of life in the tropics. That evening we left for Batavia.

The Straits of Malaya is a relatively narrow body of water and it was filled with smaller and larger ships traversing it to and from Singapore and other Asian destinations. After Sabang, the harbor of Batavia called Tandjong Priok was a different thing. Since Indonesia is a huge archipelago, transportation by ship is important and so are its harbors. The Dutch had built the harbor in my grandfather's days and established a shipping company called KPM Koninklijke Paketvaart Maatschappij, (Royal Packet Company) that connected the many islands of the archipelago. What struck me immediately was the size of the harbor. It was immensely large in my eyes and had dozens of KPM and other ships berthed in it. It was my first impression of the size of the Dutch "empire" in the Far East. So much larger, and so much more economically powerful than its home country with its crowded cities filled with small houses and narrow streets. Here one sensed the presence of a truly large economy, and I was awestruck that the Dutch, a small nation, had built all this.

Sometime after the ship had tied up at a pier, I was again called on the PA system and found that two of my lifetime friends, Lieutenants Frits Greup and Eelco Apol were looking for me. This was a wonderful surprise. After some negotiation, I was allowed off the ship in the custody of Frits and Eelco. They took me sightseeing from 10 a.m. to 4 p.m. in Eelco's jeep. I had my first glimpse of colonial Batavia, its old downtown, the Benedenstad, and uptown the more modern quarters. We had lunch at the Royal Yacht Club, courtesy of Eelco. It was for me a wonderful break after a very rough trip.

On March 16, after almost four weeks and five days on the ship, we finally came to our destination, Surabaya. The ship was met by a swarm of dockworkers, little brown muscular men who took our duffel bags and ran down the gangway with them. Another surprise. These people were quite a bit stronger than me although they were two feet shorter. We were trucked through Surabaya to a camp outside town, on the way to the hinterlands. We were put in huge hangar-like sheds where we were issued stretchers! It appeared the normal regulation collapsible canvas-covered field cots were not available for us. They would come later we were told so for the time being we had to make do with stretchers, much narrower and more uncomfortable than cots. We received mosquito netting to hang over our beds and weapons and ammunition. We were not told where we would go, but we heard there was a lot of trouble in the interior. To my immense relief I was able to take my first good Indonesian style bath there, with fresh water that was stored in large drums. In Indonesia one bathes with a small bucket that is used to scoop water out of a large tank, usually a cement basin in a shady room which keeps the water cool. Using a shower with running water is not effective since the water pipes get hot and the water in them never cools off enough. To bathe this way is called to *mandi*. We all got quickly adapted to it and used it exclusively. It was still hard to get used to the heat, and we did not have a proper way of washing our sweaty uniforms.

After a few days spent hanging around the transit camp, we were loaded on trucks on March 20th and traveled inland in a convoy of 72 trucks escorted by armored cars and men on motorcycles. I noticed Bul Schonewille loudly roaring, standing up behind the cab of a truck with a machine gun pointing forward. A real warrior-like position. The cavalry who drove the armored cars had swept the road several times in an attempt to eliminate the well-known practice of shoving an explosive charge or old Japanese aircraft bomb in one of the many drainage conduits under the roads and exploding them under a passing convoy. These devices were called trekbommen – literally translated "pull bombs" because they were usually triggered with a rope pulled by a guy (or sometimes even a child) hiding in the bushes or rice paddies next to the road. Many of our men were killed or hurt by these devices. We drove past Modjokerto to a large town called Kediri, which turned out to be our destination. Along the road we could see the impact the war with the Republic of Indonesia had on the local population. Kediri and environs had only been under our control for about eight weeks. In contrast, the area that had been under Dutch supervision since the end of the war with Japan and consolidated by us in the first police action was relatively prosperous. The area we now entered was exceedingly poor. It had been under Republic control for several years. Javanese people normally look clean and well groomed. While they often have little money, they dress in clothes that are in good repair and clean. The people we saw here came out to beg for food when we were stopped. They looked unusually disheveled with dirty and unkempt hair and dressed in rags. They had suffered from the blessings of the independence movement. My first conversation with an Indonesian was with a very dignified-looking woman who came to talk with us. She spoke perfect Dutch without a heavy Indonesian accent or any grammatical mistakes. Later I always wondered where she came from and what her background could have been.

In Kediri our company – I was still with the 3rd company of Captain Wolzak – was billeted in a school building. We were put in the classrooms, very simple rooms with a lot of cross-ventilation and doors and windows on both sides. The sergeants and corporals were in a room together and each platoon also had its own room. Wolzak and his staff and the kitchen were across the road in a fairly large building. We set up our stretchers, hung our mosquito netting over them and cleaned and prepared our weapons. We had found machine-gun positions with sandbags and corrugated iron roofs around the perimeter, which had obviously been built by our predecessors. We were told to improvise one-man positions by digging them in between the larger machine-gun positions so we could run out and take cover there when there was an alarm. Around 10 p.m. we were sitting around preparing to go to bed when there were several sudden bursts of machine-gun fire. We quickly extinguished all lights and ran outside to our designated spots because Captain Wolzak came out of his room and yelled "Alarm." A great deal of confusion ensued and there was much more firing. When we had established some order and the firing stopped, there was an eerie silence. We were told to return to our rooms and as the men came back very quietly from their positions, I stood on the grass in front of the building, trying to find out what had happened across the street. I wanted to speak to the men and make an effort to calm them down. Several came over to me and whispered that two men had been killed and that there were several wounded. Of the men in my room, one sergeant and a corporal were completely shell-shocked. They started vomiting and crawled in their stretcher beds, oblivious to whatever happened further. Wolzak had telephoned for help, and within a reasonable time we had an ambulance on site, and later a few armored cars of the KNIL, the Royal Netherlands Indies Army, our colonial army, arrived. The men with these armored cars were dyed-in-the-wool professionals who were calm, wearing flip flops on their feet and sporting clean, nicely laundered uniforms. They presented a stark contrast with us, sweaty, nervous and upset newcomers. They proceeded to fire a couple of rounds with their cannon into the surrounding kampongs and a few bursts of machine-gun fire on top, aiming at nothing but darkness. I think they did this just to reassure us. The young ensigns tried to restore order and get people who did not have to stand guard to go to bed. As it turned out, we had many cases of shock and nervous breakdowns and only a few who had the nerve to stand guard. Since I had remained calm, I was told to go behind the school building and take charge of a position we had built there that afternoon on top of an old car. There was a junkyard full of old cars behind the school and we had taken the seats out of old cars and hauled them behind our sandbags, to sit on. I sat there with a guy who was so shaken up that he trembled for about an hour vibrating the car seat in a most unpleasant way. After several hours there, looking at the strange unfamiliar scenery of the tropical night, I began to see people everywhere among the strange contours of the car wrecks. Later I found out that banana trees have leaves that move in the breeze with a motion that looks like walking people. I did not shoot, however, and told the guys with me that the lights they saw were fireflies. I finally told the ensign who came by from time to time that I needed some sleep and went to bed, only to be awakened again after a few hours to go back on guard duty because they could not find anybody else.

The next morning I pieced the story of the night together and came to the conclusion that Schonewille had been in one of the machine-gun positions, and he and his buddy had gotten nervous from the unfamiliar things they saw. They had no idea what fireflies were and were spooked by their little lights. They thought they saw people moving toward them and started firing. When the alarm was sounded and several people ran toward them from the rear, they turned around and opened fire on them too. A clear case of "friendly fire." Nothing was said the next morning and in the days afterwards. A third man died the next day in hospital. Schonewille was taken away in an ambulance that night, still roaring but with a serious nervous breakdown and we never saw him back. The official version was that we had received enemy fire and had responded. I went to the funeral of one of the killed men at the local Catholic church. The Catholic priest, an officer in our battalion, wailed the usual prayer "requiescat in pace" and the commander of our battalion spoke. This was a martinet, a lieutenant colonel called J. J. van Urk who had been a noncommissioned officer in peacetime and had all of two years of vocational school education to his credit. He mispronounced the name of the dead man and made a hash of his speech. We called him "*Jan Jurk*" (jurk meaning dress in Dutch), for no particular reason except maybe the lack of leadership ability he showed, a weakness the enlisted men can intuitively recognize very quickly. The troubles of our company were not over yet. One guy shot himself three times through the hand in order to get a medical dismissal. Instead of going home, he was going to be court-martialed.

After a day or two I went on my first patrol. We had a KNIL veteran as guide-monitor. The drill was to let two men walk a fair distance ahead to serve as point men so they could draw fire and alert the others. I had to pick the point men. I decided to nominate myself and one other guy for that role and took a brisk walk through Kediri in the early morning. I learned to bottle up my fears and not show them to the men in my group. Later I overheard the guys talking about me in an admiring tone; they spoke about my courage in a language that cannot be translated. They called me de sjokkie, the jockey, which referred to the baseball style US marine cap I wore. I had bought it in a war surplus store at home because I very much disliked the strange beret we had to wear. The hat reminded the guys of a jockey cap. Later- on I would wear only my woolen dress beret I had brought from home. The whole episode in Kediri left me feeling very angry about the lack of proper leadership we had in our battalion. I was outraged about the stupidity of sending nineteen year-olds who had arrived four days ago in Indonesia into a town the Dutch army had occupied only very recently and put them out on guard duty without anybody with them who could coach them. The fact that we got KNIL escorts after the fact proves that someone realized that a big mistake had been made that had cost three poor country boys their lives. And farm boys they were. Some had spent the whole war period in their rural district and had hardly ever seen a German. Some did not know how to handle a telephone. I wrote Netty that I wanted to go to the safest spot on earth with her when this all was over and for the first time started to talk about going to the U.S.

As we came to the end of March, I was still in the same infantry company and walking patrols. We were told to patrol only the broader streets and stay out of the Kampongs. We were to look for members of the TNI (Tentara Nasional Indonesia), National Army of Indonesia, who wanted to surrender, and we handed out pamphlets describing the Dutch plans for the future of Indonesia in rosy terms. The Dutch planned to establish a Federal Republic the Republik Indonesia Serikat. This format would stress local control in the hands of the many different ethnic groups living in the archipelago. Our equipment on these patrols was O.K., but we had only four Brens, light machine guns, in the company. According to the book, we needed nine. Later on we got more, but initially our company was sent into harm's way with insufficient firepower. The Lee Enfield rifles our guys were issued were of 1918 vintage but still good. The men were soon put on 24-hour town garrison's duty with an additional night thrown in for good measure. Really heavy duty and the food was none too good. I like Indonesian food, and as soon as I could I would go to the local Chinese restaurants. Our cooks were just getting used to cooking rice, another stupid mistake. Why not have the cooking done by men who had been there for a while, at least during the first few weeks. Whenever we got rice to eat, the guys threw lemonade over it, treating it like a Dutch dessert called "rijst met bessensap," rice with berry juice, while making chickenlike clucking noises, indicating they thought rice was chicken feed. They were meat and potatoes people. I wrote to Netty that I hoped all these sacrifices were justifiable in light of the future of the country, but I doubted it. There was a guy in my squad who had already lost a brother in Indonesia, whose father was handicapped and whose mother was a nervous wreck. From time to time, he himself suffered from attacks of hysteria.

Finally, on April 4, I was transferred back to the mortar platoon. What a relief! No more daily parade and forced gymnastics. The mortar men were in a nice villa, with a good babu (an Indonesian woman servant, mainly to do the laundry). The babu was Mina, a quiet, nice-looking woman who stayed with us for a very long time. She had a small daughter who also stayed with her. My friend Leo de Zoete, the senior sergeant in the platoon, also a university student, made sure nobody bothered Mina. The mortar platoon had a radio and it played at night. During the day the power was off. It was the first time I heard decent music in eight weeks! I wrote Netty that I still had not fired a single shot and went on night patrol with regulation hobnailed boots so everybody could hear us coming.

Here I had a nice place to sleep and was able to display Netty's portrait for the first time and – surprise – there were no comments from the others. Also, I was allowed to have a fairly large wooden chest made by a local carpenter to put all my belongings in. Captain Wolzak's company did not allow chests. We finally could exchange our stretchers for regular fold-up cots. We bought mats made out of rattan, a thin bamboo-like material, the kind Indonesians used to sleep on. These mats put over our stretched canvas beds were cool to sleep on and made our beds roomier. Also we could tuck our mosquito nets under these mats and so keep them away from us. This prevented the mosquitoes from biting us through the nets.

I wrote Netty that several thousand men had been killed in Indonesia and that most of them rested in a large military cemetery in Surabaya. Yet when our convoy drove through Surabaya, not one of the many European men and women on the streets waved or greeted us or showed some appreciation in any way. On watch during the night I sat in a little bunker looking at the beautiful mountains in the distance where one could see many lights in the villages. This was Republic country. Life went on as usual there. I had time to philosophize and reflected my pessimism about Europe's future in my letters. It was cold war time in Europe and we in Holland were vulnerable. Militarily we were dangerously overextended and our economy was still very fragile and recovering from war damage. Like most everybody in the Western world, we overrated the powers and influence of the Soviet Union.

WITH DUTCH TRAINED POLICE.

On April 17, I wrote that I was being sent with a squad to a company of the Grenadiers, a unit that had been in Indonesia for three years and was burned out. The mortar platoon meanwhile was moved to a village just outside Kediri where life was considerably less comfortable. It was Easter and I went to church, mainly to have an outing and be able to meditate on my own for a while. I caught up with Oc, who had the splendid job of being in charge of the battalion library and canteen, including the liquor supplies! Talk about putting the fox in the hen house. Oc and I went to Toko Oen, the best Chinese restaurant in town, and had a nice Easter meal. I kept corresponding with Major Schaap and Frits about joining the judiciary, but nobody gave me much hope. With a sergeant whose name was Pasop, which translated means "watch out," and a mortar squad we moved to the Grenadiers. They were billeted in an old sugar factory called Mridjan. As it turned out the Grenadiers were under strength, having lost many men to death, illness and other problems. They told us one of their trucks had just run into a cleverly disguised trap, a big hole in the road where they were ambushed and lost four men. I went on my first night patrol where we went into an area where we set up an ambush hoping to catch some TNI. To no avail. I was quite scared in the beginning, but being uncomfortable, cold and wet soon changed my anxiety into a general feeling of disgust. We had a long march and ended up in a place where a TNI company had just left. As usual, they had faded into the countryside. We destroyed their phone lines and radios. As we left, we walked downhill along the edge of a field and came under well-aimed machine-gun fire. They had returned from their hiding places. I dove into a ditch after a bullet hit the heel of my right boot. The captain of the Grenadiers, a guy who knew his way around, told us to keep marching quickly downhill, making sure the peloppors could see us, but he left a small group with two or three Bren guns hidden behind some rocks. The TNI guys came after us across the field, cheering themselves on, thinking they had driven the *Blandas* (white men) away. Then the men we had left behind suddenly opened up and killed about twenty of them. The rest fled in disorder. This was real good action, I thought. A few days later, we again went on a big expedition into the interior. We went to a place a spy had mentioned to us. We gave him a uniform to

wear so he would not be too conspicuous and took him along, just to make sure he had not sold us a bill of goods. We went a distance in our carriers – the Grenadiers still had them, but we never got them – and after a while started climbing the mountains on foot. We waded through two rivers on the way up and one on the way down. We took the long way up because we could not trust our spy and had to be alert to ambushes. We were incredibly successful though. We found a huge ammunition dump containing Japanese, Dutch and English weapons, about eight tons of ammunition, field glasses, etc., etc. We blew the whole lot sky high and returned along the easier route as the spy had proven to be reliable. We had walked from 0930 until 1700 hours, without getting anything to drink. A very exhausting but rewarding outing.

With the Grenadiers we saw more action in a few weeks than I had seen before or would see in the future. On one trip we were trundling along a dike with our carriers when we came under fire again. We jumped out and ran up the dike where we saw two TNI guys fleeing into the rice paddies below. Both were shot. These were the first dead people I saw in my life. Despite all the things that happened to us during the war, I had never seen a dead person up close. The two very young guys had been sitting behind the dike and shot at us from there, probably aiming into the air. This was rather typical behavior for the "peloppors." They were not very determined opponents if push came to shove. If they had been more aggressive and gung ho, we would have had a much tougher time, I think.

We participated in another action where we brought our two mortars along and were told to fire at a distant village. The people living there were believed to have been a source of trouble for our folks. I did not want to do that because I figured our bombs would arrive literally out of a clear blue sky in a kampong where people might be moving around. They would hear the distant bangs of our mortars firing, but not being front soldiers would not know what it meant, and then all of a sudden the bombs would rain down on them. I was ordered to fire 40 bombs, 20 for each of the two mortars we had. I did not say anything to anybody, but just gave my people a little more elevation so the bombs would fall short of their target and land in the rice paddies. Before we went back to our own mortar platoon we participated in a ceremony where all the Grenadiers got a medal for the years they had served and one, not more than one, drink of jenever. They said they wanted to go home and did not care about the medals or the drink for that matter. They had been overseas for about three years. It was a very nice bunch of men. Very capable and unemotional soldiers who could hit a cigarette tin off a wall 20 yards away, with a Bren machine gun, firing from the hip.

We returned to our own platoon around May 5, full of stories about how the older guys we had been with handled the war we were in. Our platoon was now bil-leted in a facility of the electrical company ANIEM. For me it was a funny thought to be there since my grandfather had been one of the founders of this company and its chairman of the board for several decades. There was a western-style house with some other buildings and a small generating plant. It was very well protected with barbed wire and machine gun posts. Obviously, it was important for the town to have a secure source of electricity. We had gotten used to wandering around a bit and my old buddy Lebküchner and I walked into town and found a young Javanese artist who sold me the small water color I still have. He also made a charcoal portrait of me, complete with mustache, that I proudly sent to Netty. She was not very happy with the result because he had made me look like an Indonesian, she wrote.

We had for unknown reasons been equipped with a brand new Japanese heavy machine gun that we put in one of our small bunkers. A few nights later, we came under heavy fire. This happened often. The peloppors would sneak up during the night and open fire, sometimes with heavy machine guns and other weapons. They would fire for quite a while, and the guys receiving the fire were always afraid they would advance and attack us. But that never happened. The peloppors were happy firing away and screaming all kinds of insults after which they stopped and went away. Our mortar people had never been under fire except my squad, and there was a great deal of nervousness firing back and fearful running around. Leb was prostrate on the floor of our room and claimed later that he had been looking for his glasses. In the bunker with the Japanese gun sat a friendly guy who was trained as a driver for the carriers that never arrived. In civilian life he was a baker in a small village and let it be known to everybody within earshot that he was not a hero and that his sole aim was to get safely back home to his bakery. He told his buddy in the bunker, *"we moeten dit ding aan de praat krijgen"* (we have to get this thing to start talking) and then cried out *"zat ik maar in m'n bakkerijtje"* (I wish I was back in my little bakery). They got the gun to start talking and after a while it was all over. All had gone rela-tively well and our ensign had been nervous but had not lost his head.

The next day a captain from the staff came to observe and give us a post-mortem. We knew this individual from the ship and knew that he was still shell shocked from his previous tour in Indonesia. We were told he would hide under his desk whenever somebody started shooting. He always insisted on traveling in an armored car while we just wandered around. He now had the gall to criticize our ensign loudly, within earshot of the enlisted men, for wasting ammunition by firing back and for not having organized a counter-attack by trying to move out and behind our attackers. We were "punished" by this captain with an order to establish an ambush during the following night. For us it meant we had to lie in the mud near some rice paddies for a couple of hours without talking or smoking while being eaten alive by mosquitoes. A small group had to walk ahead in a circle and try to scare up whoever might be there and drive them into our arms. We all thought this was totally uncalled for. We heard what the possible reason was for this strange order. The United Nations Commission that supposedly controlled our cease-fire was in town and did not like excessive firing by us. We also heard that our commanding officer Lieutenant Colonel van Urk had been recalled to Surabaya under suspicion of having committed some malfeasance during his first tour of duty. Perhaps the captain who visited us had hopes of filling his position, which made him extra difficult. We never saw Jan Jurk again and I do not know what happened to him. It was May 10 and I was reminded of seeing the first bombs drop on my village Voorburg. And here I was nine years later still in a

ON PATROL. GETTING A DRINK OF COCONUT MILK.

489

warlike environment. The next day was Netty's birthday. I celebrated it by lying again in another night ambush for three hours without result.

'A few days later, we heard we would move to the area of Ponorogo, a town near the border between Central and East Java, in the mountains and close to a larger town called Madiun. As we left Kediri on May 13, we heard that our supreme commander General Spoor, who was a professional KNIL soldier and much beloved by the troops, had been ordered by the government to evacuate Yogyakarta, the capital of the Republik Indonesia. He had protested this order to no avail. Underway to Madiun we saw much war damage and passed many army outposts, some heavily fortified. Much land was uncultivated and the population looked poor and shabby. Near Madiun the situation seemed better. People worked the fields again and Madiun itself was a nice town, totally intact, cool because it was higher up in a mountainous area. People were well dressed and there was an army

café with a sign that said "Tonight Cabaret." When we got to Ponorogo, we found ourselves in a smaller, much more run-down town. It would be our battalion's headquarters. I was told that I had to go immediately to an outpost called Sampung. I had to take one mortar and three guys. My mortar was to be used as a defensive weapon in the outpost. When I got to Sampung, hungry, dirty (a couple of hours in an open truck on very dusty roads will do a real job on you) and tired, I found to my great distress that the officer in charge of this post was none other than Dijkhuizen, the nineteen year old grocer's son from Voorburg.

The mortar guys we replaced were part of the original volunteer division, which had been more than three years in Indonesia after having been promised they would stay at most two years. They were finally going home and left immediately in the trucks that had brought us. There was no mandi place so we had to bathe in a river nearby beneath a bridge that had been blown up. Corporal Kees Gruys, a former mortar man who had been sent to this infantry platoon, greeted us with great joy. Gruys was already settled in and in pajamas, the usual evening attire in the field. There was one volunteer left behind. He was our radioman. He was in regular contact with our battalion headquarters by short-wave radio using Morse signals. This was the only way we could summon help or report enemy action. The patrols we sent out had no radios and if anything happened we would only know when somebody made it back. The radioman also was regularly in wireless contact with TNI radiomen in the mountains. They would exchange friendly and not so friendly insults. We were billeted in a strangely built, large rambling house located at a T-crossing between two roads in this tiny village. The house stood next to a small stream and also near the larger river where we bathed in the gray chalky mountain water which was nice and cool. Next to our house, on the other side of the small stream, were the remnants of a small cement factory with large chimneys for the kilns. The village consisted of small bamboo houses and a few more substantial ones, mostly sitting along the road to Ponorogo. Our house was located at the end of the row of houses, at the point where the road sloped down to the river. It had one large open room in front and a few smaller rooms to the side. It had a tiled roof which was an advantage as it kept us dry during rainfall and did not have the rats and bugs that usually lived in the roofs made of palm tree leaves. The walls were made of plastered brick as is usual in Indonesia. From behind the house we had an unobstructed view of Mount Lawu, a beautiful 10,700-ft. volcano.

Ensign Dijkhuizen had a reputation of doing crazy childish things, and the guys in his platoon told me they just refused or ignored his orders when they thought he went too far. On one of our first days there he went on patrol in shorts and shirtless, with a pistol and a sword as a side arm. It was a klewang – a short cutlass-like sword used by the Dutch colonial army. Sort of like the great white hunter or a kid playing cowboys and Indians. Soon after my arrival, I spoke to him and told him that the mortar men would not go on patrol since they had to be at the post at all times to operate the mortar whenever this was required. He accepted this readily. I did this to make sure my men would not be put in dangerous situations by this nut. There were no babus available yet at the post, and we couldn't wash our clothes anywhere else but in the river and that was awkward. We had plenty of equipment problems. One of the worst was – socks. The army had equipped us in Holland with three pairs of thin tropical cotton socks. These wore out quickly with all the patrolling we did (sometimes more than 20 kilometers a day) and with the rough washing system the babus were used to. The babus would clean clothes by rubbing and beating them on rocks in the river, using plenty of soap of course. Almost everybody had written home for socks and I had done so too. Netty had sent me many pairs of woolen socks that were sturdy and good for patrols. Most other guys had socks from home too, but some were unable to get them and they walked around with their bare feet in their boots. Another problem was lighting at night. We had no electricity, and no generators. All we had was a few candles issued by the army. We made small kerosene lamps from cigarette cans and used those to write and read by at night. Later on we received a nice kerosene pressure lamp from an organization in Holland that busied itself by sending helpful packages to us. I got really mad, months later, when I went to visit the Brigade staff in Madiun and found they had not only electric light but also a plethora of good gas lamps in their offices and barracks just in case the power went out. It was a real poor man's army and as usual the pipeline to the front went past the bureaucrats, and they kept the best stuff while we had to do the dirty work. In talking with the volunteers we relieved, I was once again impressed by their fighting spirit. They were truly mature and professional soldiers, the best our army ever had. They were volunteers who had been kept much too long in Indonesia and were bitter about that. We were conscripts, just going through the motions, hoping to go home soon.

After about a week in Sampung we were suddenly attacked. During the late evening of May 21, we came under heavy fire from all sides around us. From the top of the hill behind the old cement factory, from across the road, between the houses abutting our kitchen, and from across the river where the bridge was blown out. From the bridge area came heavy machine-gun fire. We held our fire, but I decided to use my mortar. I had set the thing up in a small triangular courtyard surrounded on two sides by the house and on one side by a high wall. In the preceding days, I had figured out where the mortar had to stand so it could fire without the bomb striking the edge of the roof of the house. It would have been very unfortunate if the bombs had hit the roof and fallen back among us. The bombs would destroy everything with shrapnel in a radius of about three hundred yards. The problem was that the mortars were supposed to be used in the field at distances from the target of two miles or more. The bomb had to be dropped down, tail first, into the barrel. As it slid down the barrel it would hit a pin at the bottom, and this would ignite a cartridge that would propel the bomb on its way to the target. Around the ignition cartridge the tail had four metal fins and in between the fins you could clip extra charges that would increase the distance the bomb could travel. Theoretically, you could not fire without at least two extra charges. Using just the ignition charge was called "charge zero." The bomb would then sort of wobble out and, we hoped, not drop too close by. In the days before, I had measured the distances to potential targets and the elevations we could use. I ordered my guys to fire three bombs in close succession, all with the illegal and dangerous "charge zero," aiming the two first ones across the river to where the machine gun was firing. I peeked over the sandbags to see where they would land. By great good luck, they fell exactly where they were supposed to drop and the machine gun was silenced. I fired one more bomb 180 degrees away from the first target, up the hill behind the cement factory, and that was the end of the fusillade. We never had any more trouble at Sampung. I am not sure what effect my bombs had, but the next day I went across the river and saw where the first two bombs had hit. I am almost certain that they wiped out the machine-gun crew. While we were being shot at, the peloppors yelled insults at us and the radioman, who was good at the language, yelled foul insults back. I had an uncertain feeling in my stomach after this episode, probably mainly because I did not know the platoon I was with and had no confidence in them. They had not had much experience under fire and acted quite nervous. The ensign's youthful, cowboy-like behavior did not help either. The next day I had a smoke bomb fired at the hill behind the factory, so I could see where it landed and make sure I had the right range in that direction too.

I got gradually used to my new environment. The platoon sergeant was Nico Molenaar, one of the few better-educated people in the gang. He was a catholic from Den Haag and knew Rob Laane who regularly sat near him in their church. Small world, but for a small country not a very strange coincidence. Nico adhered strictly to his religion and every evening yelled loudly *"Ja... avondgebed Katholieken"* – "Yes... evening prayers Catholics." An invitation that was hardly conducive to quiet religious introspection. Nico was a good guy, a little hyperactive and brusque. He was high-strung and not very well liked by the men. Later on I would have a great deal of contact with him in Surabaya and we became good friends. The general quality of the infantry soldiers in this platoon was low. I complained in my letters to Netty of their loud and vulgar behavior. This was nothing new for me, of course, but being cooped up in one room with a bunch of louts like that and being unable to go anywhere after dark was a real trial of togetherness.

A few weeks later a superior TNI force with heavy machine guns ambushed a squad of our platoon. They had one man wounded almost immediately so they could not move and were finally relieved after six hours by another squad with whom they were supposed to rendezvous. When they did not show up, the others had come looking for them. This was a lucky break in a situation that could have been disastrous. Another guy from the liberating group also got wounded with a shot in his knee. They had been stuck there, insufficiently armed while the peloppors yelled at them in Dutch from a distance of about two hundred feet, *"Jullie zijn bang"* (you are scared)! If they had had a light mortar and a radio, the whole situation would have ended differently. As it was, they were stuck in a rice paddy while under fire from a palm grove. It seems they could not or did not want to use the usual infantry tactic of keeping the TNI under covering fire and sending a small group in a flanking move to get at them from another side or even behind. The wounded were luckily not seriously injured. One of the people with the platoon was the Protestant pastor of our battalion who had come along with the patrol out of curiosity. He had come to visit his flock and spend a night or two with us to find out what life in the trenches was like. He came back from this patrol a shattered man. He had a dent in a cigarette case he carried in his breast pocket. A ricochet bullet had hit him there. The guys who were with him in this outing said he had been a general nuisance and a fearful scared-stiff whiner. I believe he never went out on patrol again after this event. I observed that even the quality of our spiritual support was below par.

We heard that a round table conference had started between the Dutch government and the Republic Indonesia under UN auspices. This news and the constant Chinese water torture of further bulletins telling us about a coming agreement that would undoubtedly end with a withdrawal by us gave us very little reason to take big risks. Dijkhuizen was soon replaced and we got a new ensign who was also a university student and turned out to be a fellow I could get along with very well. He opined that he was not going to take any risks or fight hard for this rag-tag bunch of unreliable people (meaning the Indonesians). I agreed with him. Initially I liked to be part of an effort to bring back law and order to our former colony before turning it over in an organized manner to its rightful owners, but now I began to dislike the people of Java more and more and only wanted to get back home. We now had several babus on our outpost to do the laundry. Some of them came with us from Kediri and liked the idea of making good money. Their husbands protested initially, but when we gave each of them ten guilders, they thought it was O.K. for their spouses to leave. One young woman actually used us to escape from an elderly husband she had been forced to marry. She hid under a tarpaulin in one of our trucks when we left for Ponorogo. I wrote to Netty that I found the population dirty, miserable and unreliable.

The same martinet Captain de Boer, who berated us in Kediri for wasting ammunition, came back to tell us we should use our bayonets (really!) more and save ammunition. This idiot was a professional sergeant major before the war and now lived like several of his colleagues far above his normal social level. He tried to tell us how to fight the enemy closer up without using unnecessary ammunition, yet when he had to go to one of our outposts in Ngawi, one of the more dangerous ones, he ordered an armored car for his transportation. On June 2 I wrote Netty that we had a lot of dysentery among our men and were drinking only tea made with boiled water, and we had to wash our mess kits in boiling water before eating and try to stay as clean as possible. Nico Molenaar left the post with a nervous breakdown. He could not control his men and became paranoid about what he saw as their threats to his own safety.

Life in Sampung began to become routine. Our place was quite high in the mountains, so the nights were cool and we could sleep with blankets. We got twice-weekly visits from a convoy that brought mail, food and supplies and was used to ferry people back and forth to our headquarters in Ponorogo. I now was away from home for four months and for most of that time had not seen a white woman, viewed a movie or had a drink. The jenever pipeline was not yet functioning. Across the street from the house where we slept was our kitchen. This platoon was fortunate in having an exceptionally good cook. The poor guy had been given an exemption from going overseas because he was the sole breadwinner for his elderly parents, somewhere in the backwoods of Brabant. However, when one of the men who was supposed to go did not return from his embarkation leave, this poor chap had to take his place, drop everything and leave on very short notice. He produced good Indonesian-style food, now preferred by almost everybody. He had hired two men from the village to act as his coolies and do the washing and heavy lifting. He cooked so well that we were afraid our captain would notice it and take him back to Ponorogo. Accordingly, we instructed him to produce lousy food whenever anybody from the staff came to visit. This was a well-understood routine for everybody in the platoon. The cook was a roly-poly fellow, a hard-working, dedicated and friendly soul who was always ready to feed us, sometimes at strange hours when patrols had to go out. The food supplies were not always adequate, and we got food from the local population (chicken, eggs, vegetables, etc.) in exchange for some of our stuff. For instance, from time to time there was no bread, a deadly sin for Dutchmen who want their boterhammen for breakfast and lunch. Instead of bread we were then fed crackers of World War II vintage out of large tins, the same ones we received right after the liberation as our first rations. They taste and look like hardtack. While they tasted like fine cake in 1945, we now found them tough, dry and unsavory.

Another interesting character was our medic the hospik as we called him. He had a room next to the ensign's quarters in a small house across the small stream where he "practiced." The medic was a very willing but somewhat feeble-minded slob. In fact, he was such a slob that I wondered how a guy with such incredible messy and unhygienic habits could ever become a medic. He would diligently treat us for heat rash, a common ailment in the tropics that affected many of us, particularly in the crotch area. He used his shaving brush to liberally apply an ointment that was very effective, but quite painful when its cooling alcohol first hit your skin. Most evenings you saw men running out of his shack firmly holding on to their crotches with both hands. That meant the stuff was working. He also applied bandages, and when he had to replace a bandage and did not know where to put the old one, he would tuck it into his pocket. As he got hot and sweaty from his exertions and wanted to look for his handkerchief to wipe his face he would reach into his pocket and absentmindedly wipe his face, with the old bandage while concentrating on his job.

We had occasional contacts with the population of the village. At one point we attended a party held to celebrate the circumcision of a small boy. This was an event held in accordance with the Javanese Muslim religious traditions, the so-called adat, the religious laws. The partygoers, all men, were sitting on the floor around a rectangular table that was about two feet from the ground in the Indonesian tradition, eating food served by the women who were bustling around. The small boy who was the direct reason for the party wandered around with a dazed and pained expression. Under his sarong he carried a little bamboo cage strapped around his middle that protected an at that time very vulnerable part of his anatomy from being touched by his clothes. In the countryside, most women wore sarongs falling down from their middle with a bodice or blouse on top. The top of the sarong was held up by a broad belt like contraption that was really a sash made out of narrow, woolenlike cloth that they wound around their bodies. This sash functioned as a support for their tummies and kept them warm in an area where people often catch cold in the tropics. Men usually wore shorts and sometimes a shirt or nothing on top. On formal occasions men also wore sarongs with a nice shirt. If we saw somebody with a suit or more citylike attire, we would stop him for questioning because he did not fit in.

In my letters to Netty and hers to me, we started discussing our future. We fantasized about our life as a married couple, sometimes quite naïvely, but usually realistically with a great deal of moaning and groaning by me about the time I was wasting and the many years I had lost already as a result of war and military service. I was unhappy with the responses I got from my parents on my questions and comments about my plans for the future. My parents either did not respond, or restated their opinions about the need for me to get back home first and study from there, so there is no real correspondence. I rejected that and said that I wanted to be on my own, get back to Leiden and work there. I hoped they would understand. Ma responded by telling me about their outings and trips abroad and detailed descriptions of the food they had consumed at various dinner parties. Sometimes I sounded a hopeless note about my future. I realized I was halfway with a study of Indonesian law and was witnessing daily the demise of the Dutch government system that applied this law. I heard various rumors from letters friends sent me about the possibility of my study direction being channeled back into a Dutch law curriculum, or worse, being totally shut down in a few months. The latter alternative would make all my work worthless – not a good prospect. I also worried about the postwar economy in Holland, which was moving along on a far from inspiring rate of growth with still a lot of unemployment.

Many of the soldiers around me were thinking of taking advantage of government offers to emigrate to Australia or New Zealand after being demobilized. A nice guy I had befriended had asked me to give him English lessons. His name was Hommes; he was a real character and a terrific slob, very unmilitary. Once when the captain came to inspect our post Hommes was posted on guard duty. We did this regularly, whenever a "higher up" was expected. Everybody knew it was a totally phony move, but when higher-ups were coming we had to put out a man on guard in full uniform with steel helmet. Some of us had British field uniforms with removable buttons so they could be washed easier. Hommes had lost all the buttons of his uniform so he had put little pieces of string through his jacket, his helmet missed its chinstrap and his shoes were like blocks of dirt and mud. He got a very bad rap for his appearance. We all preferred American style uniforms that were made of stronger material and had fixed buttons.

Another character was a fellow we called "de zwarte roek" (the black crow). He had a dark complexion, black hair and fiery dark eyes. He told me he had Spanish ancestors. I cannot remember his real name. This fellow was a good example of the work ethic many people from the small Dutch towns still had. The roek [rhymes with "book"] worked in a roof tile factory near Leiden and was, therefore, an expert on the subject of roofing. Looking up at our roof, from the inside out, we realized that we saw a lot of daylight and that the rainy season when it came, would bring a deluge inside the house. So we started talking about the poor shape the roof was in and the roek added his expertise. We then deliberately started telling him he did not know what he was talking about. This upset him so much that he climbed on top of the roof and in the course of two or three days re-laid all the tiles. He did a superb job. When we were building a sandbag machine gun position we purposely did it in a clumsy way until he came, looking at us and telling us we did it all wrong. We then told him he was all wet and within five minutes, he was hard at work and we could relax.

On the political front, we heard in the beginning of June that Yogyakarta, the capital of the Republic that we then called Djokjakarta, was returned to the Republic. Oc came to see me with a convoy and told me the TNI was infiltrating Ponorogo with six companies of infantry, well armed and sometimes even uniformed. This created a dangerous situation for us. We were moving towards a cease-fire but were not yet there

497

and we were outmanned and outgunned in town. Their intelligence about our movements was perfect. We found mines every morning on the road to Madiun and every night there was trouble in town. To keep their heads down, we now used artillery to fire systematically at all the kampongs around Ponorogo. Not exactly a good way of winning the hearts and minds of the local population. Our battalion lost another man, bringing the total up to six. The infantry company I am now with had to cover about 300 square kilometers with its 100 men! A hopeless task. We got a separate room for us four corporals, which was a Godsend. This way we had more privacy, could talk quietly among ourselves and were not constantly exposed to the conversation level prevalent among the men. We got a radio given to us by a private organization in Holland that cares for the well-being of the troops in Indonesia. The radio was very nice, it operated on batteries, but typically Dutch, there was only one set for the entire company so we had to share it with the other four platoons and pass it on to them after a few weeks.

Among the thoughts I conveyed to Netty are that I longed for having a nice conversation with somebody, preferably Netty, dressed in a nice suit, in a nice room. All these weeks in the outpost, dressed in just athletic shorts and slippers and never being able to sit in a nice chair were beginning to take their toll. I also discussed my belief in God. I wrote that I prayed in bed before going to sleep but was not sure whether I really believed in God. How should I envisage Him? I was not sure, and as I write this, more than fifty years later, I still have not worked out this enormously important question. My sage comment is, "You have to decide what your attitude is on all kinds of questions and situations in life, and if you cannot decide what your answer is, you have to search." Well, I am still searching.

Eelco wrote me to say he was living the good life in Batavia, as liaison officer with the UN people there he resides in the world-renowned hotel "Des Indes" and had a borrel every day with them. I thought Eelco's good fortune was well deserved. They kept him away from his wife and young daughter much too long. We heard that we now had evacuated Yogyakarta and donated 150 trucks to the Republik. It would be nice if our battalion could have ten of them. Our equipment is far from ideal. I would get very angry when our guys stole from the dirt-poor Indonesians; many other NCOs tolerated it. But how can you prevent a coarsening of moral attitudes if you let people do heavy duty with poor equipment and no entertainment whatsoever on these outposts. It was now July and I was six months in Indonesia, and I was writing letters at night with a self-made oil lamp.

I had hoped to be able to go to Surabaya to visit a doctor or a dentist, excuses to get away for a few days. I could only seem to get as far as Madiun. On July 7, I wrote that I finally made it to Madiun and slept in the Brigade staff headquarters. They had electric light there, something I had not seen in a long time. They also had 86, count them, eighty-six, beautiful kerosene gas lamps hanging there, just in case their power fails! On our post we didn't even have one gas lamp. The doctor in Madiun agreed that my feet were bad and I hoped it might help me get into the judiciary. Sitting around in Sampung was beginning to get to me. We made no progress, we could not find the enemy, we could not get the population on our side, we made many mistakes, and we were drowned in paperwork and incompetence. My petition for transfer to the army justice branch is finally typed up for me with the required seven copies, the cease-fire was coming, and the Republik was trying to gain "turf." I bought a better small kerosene lamp for myself in Madiun and headed back to the boondocks. Meanwhile we had two Red Cross nurses coming regularly to Sampung. They treated the local population. It is remarkable, but minutes after they arrive, people stand in line. That is what old Indonesia hands call the "*kabar angin*" (the letter or news that travels with the wind). News travels very fast among the population by word of mouth. I vividly recall the case of one man who was covered with ugly frambesia lesions, the size of walnuts. He got a shot of penicillin and when he returned for a follow-up visit, he was completely cured. This man was obviously extremely happy and grateful. This is just an example of how much positive help we could give with simple means if we only had a chance. The Republik recognized the propaganda value of these medical teams and forbade them immediately after they gained control. They could not care less about the well-being of the population. I went back to Madiun for another medical check- up to get a lower rating that would declare me unfit for infantry duty. I hoped this would help me get a job where I could do work that was more intelligent. Pointing at my feet, the doctor said, "Schieferdecker has such strange feet that he doesn't have to come back." I spent the night in the field hospital, which was located in a nice building. I slept like a rose in a nice bed, the first time in seven months that I slept on a soft mattress in a nice bed with sheets. The next morning there was a bit of a dispute between me and a new medic who had just come on duty. Unbeknownst to me I had ended up in the ward for venereal diseases, and when he saw me leaving in the morning he thought I was a patient who was escaping his clutches.

Around this time, mid-July 1949, a large offensive action was planned involving several infantry companies plus support. Our brass evidently thought this was their last chance to flex their muscles—it may also have been a strategic move to make our opponents understand that we were not just caving in but were willing to defend our territory forcefully. Whatever it was, it turned into a monumental flop, a prime example of poor planning and organization. It showed the disastrous lack of military know-how and organizational ability of our officers. We started out with what was planned as a large encircling movement to capture a large force of peloppors. To make sure the peloppors were there, a small reconnaissance aircraft flew over the area involved. Since this had never been done before, the peloppors understood quickly what we were planning to do and melted into the countryside as they had done many times before. One of the companies of our battalion ended up marching for three days without food and without being able to change their clothes or sleep under mosquito netting. When it was all over, about 50% of the men came down with malaria. They still did not have a good pair of socks and their radios did not work either. When they arrived at the prearranged spot where they had been told trucks would pick them up to return to their base, there were no trucks. There had been a misunderstanding and the trucks and staff officers had gone home thinking everybody was accounted for. Nobody missed them and they had to march another 60 kilometers to get back. Later my colleague Frans van Tongeren, one of the corporals I roomed with in Sampung, was sent away with a squad to be part of another large action in the mountains, again to go hunt peloppors. One of our mortars had to go too, loaded on horses! I wondered what sense this all made. The big shots of the Republik were set free and our ambassadors were talking with Sukarno while we had to take big risks and go after the small fry. Frans's patrol came back after two days in the mountains. It was too risky to go further. They found beautifully kept villages with nice working schools for the children. No wonder our guys are beginning to wonder why we are here. They have no idea of the broader economic interests the Dutch have in the region and think we are only there to defend the financial interests of the big shots. Life in Sampung, meanwhile, was nice and easy with no discipline at all. The men were sleeping when they wanted and dressed the way they wanted.

The chief medical officer in our brigade complained to his wife in Holland about our need for decent socks, and she started an action to have them produced by volunteer women's knitting groups. Unfortunately, it appeared the government was unable to supply the women with the proper wool yarn!

We achieved zero progress since the "police actions" The Dutch press believed the TNI had been reduced to just a few bands of irregular brigands and had been beaten. We know this is total nonsense. A cook out of our headquarters in Ponorogo was shot through the head while climbing off a truck after attending a soccer match and other units lost 35 men in Kediri in one week. We heard that in Holland the country publicly mourned the victims of a plane crash but ignored the daily losses in Indonesia. Since the beginning of our actions in 1945, we lost more than 2,000 men in Indonesia. Nothing happened day in day out in Sampung and Ramadan was starting, the most dangerous period of the year. It is in the 9th month of the Islamic year, a sacred period in which people fast from sunrise to sunset. It is known to be a period of increased religious fervor.

On the first of August we heard that a cease-fire would take effect and on the third it is official. We now would reduce our patrol activity to a radius of about five kilometers around our post. Just to keep us from getting too cozy with the TNI. At the same time, I learned that my request to join the military judiciary service was declined. Frits Greup had already written that my chances were very slim since there was an oversupply of men with my qualifications and a diminished need for them. I got a letter written by a lieutenant who was, as I noted from his army number, a year younger than I. Sitting at his desk in Batavia he wrote I had to take this disappointment like a "man" and should realize "we all had to sacrifice, some more than others etc." This ridiculous document did not surprise me much and did not affect me much either. Life went on. I went to Ponorogo to see the dentist. He worked with an old-fashioned drill, which he activated with a foot pedal. I remembered that in the old days, Ma's friend Wally van Ramshorst practiced dentistry in The Hague with a similar primitive installation. Of course, she had to do my cavities because she was a friend! The army dentist was friendly and had a parrot sitting on the top of the drill who delivered commentary on the proceedings.

৵৩

It was beginning to get confusing, chaotic and dangerous in Ponorogo as the TNI infiltrated and did not stick to the cease-fire rules. We had a tank rumbling around town to intimidate the TNI folks and keep them at a distance. There were red white Indonesian Republik flags everywhere. Where did they come from? Whenever we searched a house, we certainly did not find any! One of our patrols in Ponorogo met a TNI patrol that was so well dressed that they thought it was a KNIL (our colonial army) patrol. The TNI stole cars from the local authorities and police force that worked under our supervision and then drove into town in them. Theft of weapons from several units was also a growing problem. Our ability to control the situation was rapidly waning. I had been about four months in Sampung – useless time spent just loafing around. In this atmosphere, the behavior of our protestant pastor stood out as particularly idiotic. He was said to have recommended the public execution of a prisoner by us just before the start of a soccer game against the locals. This was his suggestion for a strategy to keep the population from revolting.

Suddenly after six month of isolation and boredom, the army decided to provide entertainment. For the first time we were visited by a movie unit, a jeep with a generator and a projector. Just when they were all set up to show us our first movie in four months, it started to rain. The wet monsoon had come! The Lord must have sent us a message saying that we did not belong in this country. We also finally got a volleyball net and ball and can play. In addition, we got a cabaret performance. A Belgian troupe we thought was very good, especially since they had two white actresses, fading beauties who had clearly been through the mill but who sang reasonably well. In reality it was of course a more than third-rate performance. Which sane Belgian cabaret actor would agree to come to Indonesia, be with the Dutch army in a war zone and drive five hours along bumpy dusty roads in an open truck to perform in a shack for a bunch of soldiers? You must be seriously broke to go to such extremes.

Word from Netty's Oma and mine came that the skimpy attire of our babus, as shown on a photograph I sent, shocked them. The dear old souls had a mental picture of an Indonesia that is no longer valid. Moreover, the babus simply do not have the material to make the clothing required for the traditional sarong and kabaya (a thin, usually white, long sleeved jacket worn over their bodices) as was usual in the old days when the Omas lived in Indonesia.

Finally our battalion got a new commander, a lieutenant colonel by the name of Both. He used to serve with the cavalry in armored cars in East Java and the gossip among the men was that he was a good officer. In private life he was a lawyer in Arnhem. So we finally got somebody who is not a recycled prewar sergeant. We needed leadership. On East Java our battalion was known as the unit with the worst discipline, but also the best results. We all feared that we were now heading for a period in garrison, hanging around under increasingly tight discipline. We had an amusing incident in a village called Balong, a place similar to Sampung. A corporal there had written to Prince Bernhard in his capacity of Inspector General of the armed forces, complaining that he was stationed in this outpost and that they did not even have a Dutch flag to display proudly above their outpost. Apparently, the Prince got quick action. General Baay, the man in charge of all of East Java, who was despised by his entire command, arrived at Balong with the flag and a fifty man military band. Each outpost had to send ten men, properly dressed of course to attend the flag raising ceremony. The general traveled in a convoy of four heavy armored cars. He must have been scared out of his wits because he seldom ventured outside Surabaja. He also must have been mad as hell to have to leave his comfortable house and go through this exercise. Noticing the commotion, the local population fled, fearing a military action. The general told us that sovereignty would be turned over on December 31 and that in anticipation of this event, systematic withdrawal would start soon. Using the occasion, Baay brings a "surprise visit" to our post and finds only ten men there on watch duty with a corporal in charge. He was told that the others were out on patrol. This was all a total fake. We never had a formal watch system with corporals in charge, and the men on patrol are lurking about a half a mile away, waiting until they see the general leave again. The general was pleased with his inspection and upon seeing an empty waste paper basket exclaimed: "See here they have *gezelligheid*."

The new company commander of the second company is known to be a heavy drinker. We now have a wind-up gramophone, "borrowed" from a Chinese family in Ponorogo, and when he showed up we played and old German drinking song that happens to be among our small collection of records: *"Trink Trink Brüderlein Trink"* (drink little brother, drink).

We finally received a nice big gas lamp that lights up the place at night as never before. This lamp is part of a "jungle crate" containing all sorts of gifts sent to us from Holland, financed by private donations, not the army. Our official ration is still one candle per 30 men, per day! In the tropics it gets dark quite early and the evenings are long. But, oh wonder, we get a supply of good socks! That is a small point of light. On September 22, I wrote to Netty that I was beginning to get thoroughly fed up with being idle all day. I wanted a job! I felt that I was living like an outcast, sidetracked by society. "Here I was, a disheveled corporal who spends his days in idleness, while in Holland a sweet beautiful girl is waiting for him." We were having more and more disciplinary problems. I heard that my old bridge buddy, corporal Joop Groenendijk, has been demoted to private in the third company. More problems with Wolzak and his eager beaver sergeant major Nieuwkerk, I guess. Several men in that company were being court-martialed for insubordination. It is not only the men that showed strain, our equipment was showing wear and tear too. Trucks frequently broke down. This was not surprising since many of them were acquired from the British Eighth Army and date back to the campaign against Rommel in North Africa and have been shipped from there over to Burma to help fight the Japanese. Five years of hard duty is enough to kill any truck.

One evening in Ponorogo at the mortar platoon, Lebküchner acted funny, started pointing at his mouth and could not talk anymore. They thought he had gone nuts. It appeared that he had been taking such a big bite out of a sandwich that his jaw became unhinged. Two sweating doctors had to spend several hours punching Leb around, trying to make his jaw snap back. It finally succeeded. Another mortar man was on patrol one night and a truck came to pick his group up. As he was about to climb into the truck, it started moving and he fell backward into a bed of cactuses. His back looked like a porcupine and he had to spend several hours in the hospital while they were removing all the needles one by one, by candlelight of course.

In my letters to Netty, I worried about unemployment in Holland, the threat of war with Russia, the atom bomb and more. I realized that it had been six years since I finished high school and I still have very little to show for it. I wanted to start a career, but did not have a clue in what direction I wanted to go. My calculations were that we would not go home until the spring of 1951. The TNI is now "allowed" to go anywhere they like, except within a three-kilometer perimeter of our post. There was some irony in these rules because the TNI wandered around wherever they liked anyway. Life moved slowly at our post. Dusk was the best time of day. It was cool then and we would walk around near the river in our pajamas.

When it got dark I hated to get back into the stuffy old dark house. We played cards at night to kill time. We did not play for money because cash had no value here. The population did not accept our money, they lived in a pure barter society. What had value for us was cigarettes and sometimes we wager our entire monthly ration on one game of Twenty One. The loser had a bad month with a strong nicotine craving. This happened to Kees Gruys who got carried away one evening and ended up sans cigarettes. Netty sent me many packages and I get excellent English cigarettes from her. "Craven A," my favorite brand. So I could help Gruys out with a small donation. I gave bridge lessons to several guys and still taught English to a bulb grower who worked really hard at it. He wanted to emigrate to Australia or New Zealand when we would be demobilized.

Then all of a sudden, on October 7, I got orders to leave Sampung and rejoin the mortar platoon. It was strange, but I felt a little sad leaving. It was after all a good post. Cool (mostly) because we were up in the mountains, quiet, and I had a nice little room with two friends. When in Ponorogo I got a letter from Ma who told me that they had to put my dog Moro to sleep. He was very old, of course, but I had hoped to see him again on my return home. I had a real hard time that night thinking about my old friend who was the nicest dog I have ever had. The mortar platoon left Ponorogo and moved to Madiun where we ended up in a house with electric light! What a luxury. Suddenly I could take an evening walk on a nice street with nice houses and nice shops. For me it was a double pleasure not only to be in Madiun but also to be back among the men of my old platoon. I was also lucky because I got a letter from Netty that was only four days old, an amazing event if compared with today's postal service. The position of the Dutch army in the field was becoming more and more difficult. When the infantry platoon I was with left Sampung in a large truck convoy, the whole village was festooned with red and white flags, the colors of the republic, and the population stood at attention along the road. We did not have such a bad relationship with them, after all, and I think that they wanted to express their appreciation for what was after all a quiet and orderly period in their lives. The "peloppors" who moved in were commanded by a subaltern who could not read or write. They asked for cooking equipment because they had none and they had no beds. They were going to get them "in the village" they said, so the folks in Sampung would soon know what freedom and independence meant for them. As we arrived in Madiun, the last remnants of our battalion came in from Ponorogo. They were bitter. The TNI who came in were poorly clad but had heavier machine guns, etc., than we. We took the flag down, presented arms and the Indonesians stood by laughing. So it goes. Now the TNI in Ponorogo were fighting splinter groups consisting of communist and Islamic fundamentalists. They are training hundreds of recruits, and they still had Japanese instructors, we hear. On October 18, we were told that our battalion will go to Pasuruan, a town on the shore, roughly southeast of Surabaya. Our lieutenant colonel will go ahead to find out what the situation is there. He decided to go with another officer and three men for protection. I was the one chosen to go with two men for this superb job. So I pick Burger and another fellow to come with me with two bren guns, and we piled into the back of two jeeps and roar off along the bumpy and very dusty roads leading back to civilization. A quick and wonderful end to a very strange period in my life.

We went directly to Surabaya where I plunged into western civilization for a couple of hours, looked at the good looking women, the nice, well paved streets, the stores, cafés where you can sit and have a drink. Wonderful! We hung around the staff headquarters of our division where our commander had business with the bureaucrats that were crawling around there in large numbers. On to Pasuruan with a side trip to Trètes, a mountain resort where I found the most beautiful mountain scenery I had ever seen in Indonesia. Later on, I would learn that Netty's grandparents had a vacation home there when they were living in Surabaya. We stayed for one or two nights with a cavalry company, which used to be Colonel Both's unit in Pasuruan, then we went to Bangil, the town where the recently arrived mortar platoon will be billeted on the train station with the task of guarding trains. This was a routine we got used to very quickly after we were acclimated to the civilized world in which trains roll on time to their destinations. We had to sit on the trains in groups of three or four men and somehow make sure the TNI does not stop or attack them. It is more a matter of being present than anything else because we would not know what to do if we were seriously challenged. Luckily, nothing happened.

I particularly liked the run to Malang, a nice mountain town where it was cool and quite western. Sometimes we would sit in fourth class, the class used by the local population on their way to and from market, with lots of luggage and food carried in baskets or in a piece of cloth. The train to Malang has more luxurious passenger accommodations. First class was even air conditioned with a system where a fan blows over blocks of ice. We were, of course, always riding in first class although we were not supposed to, not being officers. We were never given a hard time though, and whenever I rode the train, I regularly walked the length of it to make our presence visible. The houses where we lived were small and practically on the tracks. The advantage of being on the station is that we could shower under the large hoses used to fill the steam locomotives with water. When you pulled a chain, a virtual waterfall would cascade down. Riding the trains was better duty, I think, than being in town and having to participate in the elaborate town guard system our battalion has designed.

On November 1, 1949, I had a particularly hard day on the trains. I had to get up at 4:30 a.m. to make my first train and did not get back before 6:30 p.m. This is tough because on the hot train we could not take our afternoon nap, a tropical tradition we all adhere to. You got up quite early, started work around 6 a.m., go on until about noon, had lunch and go to bed for about two hours. In the afternoon, you worked again, and in the evening when it is nice and cool, you stayed up quite late. Rumors were flying again that legislation will be passed to allow a longer stay for us in Indonesia. But then a General Buurman van Vreden spoke up and said we might be back home by September 1950! He said he would even try to make it before July. Naturally this is very important news. It was the first time somebody higher up actually mentioned specific dates. I realized I might be back after a year and a half, almost a shame for all the effort! I had trouble sleeping after hearing this news. I consoled myself with the thought that for me it has not all been for naught. I had matured and become more independent, I learned much about Indonesia, learned to hate the military, learned to cope and fend for myself under all circumstances. As I wrote these thoughts down in my letter to Netty, I added that I am more in love with her than ever. Hope for a reunion springs forever.

Meanwhile the situation with the new republic was far from orderly and settled. The TNI was now fighting the Darul Islam, a fundamentalist group in pitched battles. It was obviously a power struggle with several groups trying to fill the vacuum that would exist after we pulled back. From Netty I heard that armchair strategists in Wassenaar were saying the Indonesians need the Dutch after all and we should launch a third police action to teach them who is boss. This is a virtual impossibility. We did not have the equipment nor the manpower and definitely not the will to fight anymore. We knew the UN would do nothing and the US would not help us. In Batavia our troops had to parade before General Buurman van Vreden and Sukarno, the self appointed President of the Republik Indonesia. The TNI even asked us to give artillery support for some of their actions on East Java. The world had changed since last year when we were forbidden to use artillery by the UN or even by our own civilian authorities, who always wanted to protect the population.

On November 9, I heard I would be transferred to the IVG, the intelligence unit of our battalion. Oc had been in this group for some time but had an opportunity to go to the judiciary branch. He was after all a candidate in Dutch law and I was not. In my letters home to Netty I began to focus more and more on home and less on my life in Indonesia. I learned that Rob Laane and Jan van der Drift would soon complete their law studies. They would have jobs next year when I would return, not an encouraging thought. Initially I was not happy with the move to the intelligence group, although I realized they lived like princes and could not be touched by anyone. No officer could interfere with the IVG. I was moved to a small house on the main street in Bangil where I found two soldiers and an Indo–European spy-translator. I was now in charge of this place and commander of the IVG detachment Bangil. A Lieutenant van Zuuren was my new commander. He told me that I had to work with my brain and could not use the practices the IVG was known for anymore, arrests and serious interrogations with quite a bit of torture.

I had to gather information on the local situation by interviewing the local people of importance, Dutch as well as Indonesian, and especially try to find out as much as I could about the battles between the TNI and the Muslim faction. Very interesting! We had a radio for information and bicycles to ride around in the town. We even had a typewriter. I had to write situation reports and keep a daily log. I was very happy with this assignment and planned to work hard. Finally a job, something to do, and on top of that a job that presents an intellectual challenge, albeit a minor one.

As I write this, the war in Iraq is over on paper, but the postwar trauma is far from concluded. The chaos that plagues the US forces there has many similarities with the situation in Indonesia when we were trying to pull out. The history of the Indonesian Republic in the decades after our departure shows a picture of corruption, military dictatorships and economic disasters in what is essentially a rich country and many terrible political upheavals. It all does not bode well for what may transpire in Iraq and in many other countries in the region and in Asia that must get to self-government and some form of democracy. In November 1949, I got reports of mass killings in West Java by the Darul Islam, a fanatical branch of the Islamic community. In one village, 200 people were killed by these people dressed in KNIL uniforms. The TNI had trouble with setting up a supply system to support their men. Up until now, they had established what amounted to a legalized extortion system that forced the population to feed their troops.

From the Netherlands came news that Netty was preparing to go to France as an au pair. She had planned this with her parents for quite a while. Tilly was already there and I believe the family where Netty would be staying were acquaintances of Tilly's host family. Netty told me that Willem Witteveen had also completed his studies and that Paul Beversen, my best boyhood friend whose parents were pro–German during the war, does not have to serve in the army because of his parents' political background and can complete his studies also. Go figure! I got a big Sinterklaas package from Netty. Very welcome.

My work in Bangil was purely intelligence. I was not allowed to put anything on paper beyond the reports I wrote and destroyed after sending them out. I used to keep a diary with brief notes on my doings since I left Holland. I was not allowed to continue doing that so the diary abruptly stopped in Bangil. Our plan was to withdraw in a wide circle around Surabaya. Our battalion would be the one but last to leave. First 421 battalion would go, then us, 422, then finally 423 battalion, which came last to Indonesia. My job was to interview locals and ferret out information, mainly to protect our forces. There was always a fear that we would be suddenly attacked by some new Indonesian group that might want to achieve cheap glory by scoring a few hits on us. I had to use my own initiative to see how I got my information. I visited representatives of the leading Indonesian politicians that were cooperating with our plan for a federal republic. Among them was a member of the New East Java Parliament. This legislative body was formed to start the Republic

East Java. This man was deeply concerned about the inroads the Djocja Republic was making on his territory. Another source was the station master, a nice guy who is Indo–European like most of the lower level civil service people. I also visited the leaders, self-appointed or not of the main minority groups, the Chinese and the Arabs. These visits were interesting. The Chinese was a sneaky fellow who worked both sides of the road. When I visited his house, he played the Dutch armed forces radio station so loudly that conversation is almost impossible. At the same time he displayed a big red and white republican flag in his home, but he told me the best thing to do was for us to start a third police action. I asked him why he displays the flag if that is his opinion. He grinned sheepishly. Just trying to survive and do business, I guessed. This man treated his Indonesian servant girl who brings us something to drink like dirt. She had to sit on her haunches and shuffle forward in a sitting position, the way the Indonesian servants were supposed to approach their masters in the old days. I thought it was a disgusting display. A more interesting fellow was the head Arab. Arabs have always lived in Indonesia, mainly as traders in gold and jewelry. He received me in his house and served very strong coffee in tiny cups. You heard the noises of his household in the background, but the women were invisible. We would soon abandon all these more or less well-meaning people. The thought bothered me and, I felt ashamed about the situation but did not know what to do about it. An Amboinese retired sergeant who lived in town told me that he was told he could stay behind at his own risk. He had twenty years of service in the Dutch colonial army and no place to go! I attended several meetings with our battalion commander and his TNI opposite, Captain Ichdar who served as a corporal in the Dutch KNIL in the past. The TNI fellows were generally poorly educated and their behavior reflects a desire to be seen as tough and knowledgeable by their peers. So every time we came up with a simple practical suggestion concerning our withdrawal and its timing, they respond with "we do not agree." We went to make a tour of several outposts of the local police force who have been trained and armed by us. These men were deserting in droves because they were afraid the TNI would see them as traitors. The TNI captain Ichdar and one of our officers spoke to them to reassure them and to try to keep them functioning. I didn't think it would help much. These fellows were all spooked and would most likely return to their villages and probably take their weapons with them to give to the TNI as proof of their real allegiance. There was a textile factory in town run by a Dutchman. He did not want us to show up in his factory because he was preparing for independence and wanted to be inconspicuous and not known as a friend of the Dutch army. Still he offered to take me to Surabaya in his new American sedan. What a treat! Closed windows, no wind, real springs, soft seats. I had been looking around for a gift to send home to Netty and my parents. The only thing we could think of that is available here in large quantities and good quality is pepper. So in Surabaya I bought eight cans of pepper and shipped them to Netty. I guess I bought a lifetime supply for about twenty people.

On December 5, it was Sinterklaas, the holy man came by our little IVG house in Bangil in a jeep. He was sweating profusely and not in a good mood anymore. He had been on the road in his costume and drinking beer since 9 a.m. and got to us by 4 p.m. It turned out to be a buddy of mine, a huge guy by the name of van Tricht who had managed to stay out of trouble taking care of provisions, clothes, etc., while being a terrific specimen who could have been an excellent infantry man. I do not recall any further Sinterklaas celebrations in my house. I had two soldiers with me, Lodder, a nice guy from a good family, his father was a lawyer in Amsterdam and Büscher, also a nice, quiet, intelligent chap. Then there was the Indo– European man, actually more a teenager who had been a protégé of our lieutenant van Zuuren. His name was Richard van der Heiden. Despite his purely Dutch name, he is Indonesian in his behavior and lifestyle. He often hung out in town and I did not know what he is doing there. He was supposed to be our spy and translator, but at this time there was not much to spy or to translate, and my own "Bahasa Indonesia," the language used and in my days called Maleis (Malay), was sufficient to deal with day-to-day situations and simple conversations with our sources. Richard had also become quite cozy with the woman next door, another Indo–European who lived with two daughters in a tiny house, similar to ours. She was happy with our presence for security reasons, but worried about her future, of course. I visited her once or twice and felt sorry for her; I gave her a strong hint to keep her daughters away from Richard who was not very trustworthy, I thought. We also had a live-in babu who does our laundry. The house we live in was small. It had a small veranda on the street where we would sit in the evening. A living room with an adjacent room where our babu slept and two bedrooms in back. Behind the house was a small garden with an outbuilding where we had our bathing facility and a toilet with the traditional hole in the ground set up. In back was a wall with a gate to the outside world. We slept happily in this house, which was completely open to the world outside, and we did not have anybody standing guard at night.

Meanwhile the chaos around us worsened. Captain Ichdar was taken prisoner by another TNI faction and after his release was extremely upset at his own Pasuruan

TNI group. Many local government people who had been appointed by the Dutch wanted to quit, and another five policemen disappeared with their weapons. I wanted to turn the town over to the TNI so they could cooperate with the police force before it had completely melted away. Captain Wolzak – can I ever get rid of this man – was opposed to this idea, so I tried to work around him. There was total chaos in town. TNI press gangs went around to the Chinese and "asked" for large amounts of money. They set up roadblocks to shake passersby down. In Pasuruan there were 120 policemen gone.

In our house, we got a raw taste of the situation when one evening we discovered that Richard van der Heiden had disappeared, taking two rifles and my personal Beretta submachinegun. While we were sitting on the front porch, he had slipped out through the gate in the back of the small garden. For me this was a very serious situation. Losing a weapon means invariably a court martial for the responsible man, and that was me. I immediately called van Zuuren, who arrived with Wolzak. After a conversation with me they decided that I should put a lock on the clothes chest in my bedroom in which we kept our weapons and then break it so they could claim I had everything under lock and key as the rules require. Van der Heiden then became the thief who broke into the closet in my room. I sensed that van Zuuren worked this out with Wolzak because as it turned out, van der Heiden was not on our payroll and therefore not really an official native member of the IVG, just a pro-tégé of van Zuuren. Ergo, in court I could have claimed that I employed Richard believing he was a legitimate member of our staff, which would have been bad for van Zuuren because he was responsible for Richard's presence in our house. Luckily, unbeknownst to Richard, I had hidden the three magazines of the Beretta in another place. So he was probably never able to use this gun. The whole thing was nicely covered up and I felt extremely relieved. I was grateful for Captain Wolzak's attitude in this matter and told him so in a respectful manner.

Then a new man joined us. He was a jeep driver who had been in prison for about a year for causing the death of one of his fellow soldiers. When we were just in the country and still in Kediri, a group of drivers were horsing around in a room, playing "chicken" by tossing a loaded rifle around. The rifle discharged accidentally, killing a boy by the name of Vis. Vis came from Warmond, near Leiden where his family ran a marina and boatyard, well known to me and close to the house where Netty and her family spent the last winter of the war. Our man was convicted of manslaughter and put in jail. Once he was discharged from prison, nobody knew what to do with him so he was sent over to the IVG.

On December 17, we departed from Bangil, leaving it to the TNI, and I was moved to a sugar factory named Tulangan, closer to Surabaya. The Dutch people running the factory were not really all that happy with our presence there because they were hopeful they could stay in business after our departure and therefore did not want to be seen as closely aligned with us, the occupying Dutch army. In a letter to Netty I described the first Dutch management people I met at Tulangan as "stuck-up snobs." They wanted at first to put all of us up in a windowless little room with a wooden door, a place where the babus slept on their little rattan mats. I told them this was not acceptable. They changed their minds and offered a small pavilion, a sort of guesthouse in the backyard of the assistant manager. This was very nice; I stayed there with Lodder and Bücher. Kloosterman, the driver, was reassigned elsewhere, thank goodness. In Bangil he used to preach all evening about how much he had read and how much he admired Einstein because according to him Einstein had the right philosophy about life, which came down to the statement that "everything is relative." Finally, I put him in his place and explained that as far as I knew, the relativity theory of Einstein was a mathematical formula that referred to the relationship between space and time. I said I had no knowledge of higher mathematics and no idea how Einstein reasoned this all out, but I was certain that his, Kloosterman's, interpretation was nonsense. That shut him up for several days to the amusement of all three of us. As my father used to say, people with just a little knowledge are more dangerous than those who are just not very well educated and are without pretensions.

To my utter astonishment, Eelco suddenly showed up in Tulangan just after we had settled down in our pavilion. He was on business in East Java and had found out where I was and drove over. A very nice surprise, and wonderful to see an old friend. Eelco told me that to his annoyance he was held back from repatriating with his division because he was supposed to have a key function. He acted as a liaison between the military and the civilian authorities, I believe. His division was the first unit of conscripts who went over to reinforce the volunteers who were already there. It was called the *Zeven December Divisie* – the Seventh of December Division, after the Japanese attack on Pearl Harbor, the event that changed the world in Asia forever.

My assignment at Tulangan was a secret one; it was to clean up the old IVG posts in the region. The name IVG was removed from our vocabulary because it had a very bad reputation among the population. It was our secret police and spy organization rolled into one, and it was known for treating its prisoners very rough. Indonesians who worked for us had to be removed and given other places to live and new identities.

Our predecessors in this area did nothing for these people. Now, at the very last moment we had to step in. The whole issue of our actions in Indonesia bothered me very much at the time I was there. I remembered, how later on in Surabaya, I saw a German movie called *Die Mörder sind unter uns* (the Murderers are among us). It was a story of the adjustments Germans had to make after the war, to living with people who had committed atrocities. After seeing the movie, Oc and I agreed that the murderers were also among us, and that we had learned nothing from the war period when we were the oppressed. Now that we were the oppressor in Indonesia, many of us behaved almost as badly as the Germans. As a generalization, this was true, but I would not want to say that we all behaved badly and that our regime was a Nazi–like terror regime that resulted in thousands of victims. Far from it. We were in general a benign group of people who often felt betrayed by the Indonesians and their, to our western minds, sneaky and devious behavior. Most Asian cultures, including the Indonesian, regard straight answers to questions as impolite. It is not "yes" or "no," but always "maybe" or "perhaps." To questions posed in Malay we often got responses in Javanese, a different language we did not know while we had good reasons to suspect the person we questioned knew how to speak Malay perfectly well. These communication problems often lead to violent reactions from Dutch soldiers who were mostly uneducated about Indonesia and the people there.

The worst incident I witnessed myself took place just before the cease-fire when I was on a small convoy moving from Sampung to Ponorogo. When our trucks came around a bend in the road, we suddenly saw a man on a bicycle who was much better dressed than the farmers we were used to see along the road. The man made the mistake of jumping off his bike and running into the fields. A natural reaction of course, but in this case a stupid thing to do. We stopped our trucks, and a sergeant whom I knew quite well jumped off and ran after the man, firing his sten gun. When he caught up with him in the distance, I could see him beat the poor man with the steel butt of his gun. He returned to the trucks and we drove on. That evening the sergeant was bragging to all who wanted to hear how he had killed the man and how his beating had badly bent the butt of his gun. I did my best to spread my version of the incident, which was that the victim was totally unknown to us and had only been running away. There was absolutely no reason to kill him. He was unarmed but suspect because of his bike and the way he was dressed. To top it off, the sergeant took the bike with him to Ponorogo.

Tulangan was a sugar factory, run by a Dutch company. Like all other sugar factories, it grew its sugarcane on land owned by the local population. Locals were encouraged to lease their land every two years or so to the sugar factory for the planting of sugarcane. The Dutch have always tried to protect the indigent population from large colonial enterprises who would try to buy their land from them, which could ultimately impoverish them. The factory would harvest the cane, mill it and refine the sugar. The plant was managed by a small team of Dutch people, mostly technicians who lived with their families around it. Being in there among these Dutch people was a new and different chapter for me. Our pavilion had a real ceramic washbasin, the first one I had seen since leaving home. The houses were nice and grouped around a wide road. They were uniform in design. Two larger houses, for the boss, the administrateur, and his second in command, were located in the center. The factory was also on the road and narrow gauge railway tracks ran everywhere to move the cane at harvest time. It was December and Christmas was near. Most of the Dutch families had gone to Surabaya for the holidays. Captain Wolzak had arrived with part of his company. It seemed impossible for me to shake this unit. I had spoken with the top man, a Mr. de Groot, a real throwback to prewar Holland. In contrast to older Dutch/Indonesia hands who were usually rugged individualists, often tough, self-made men who drank a lot of jenever and could cuss a blue streak, this man and his wife were devout orthodox Protestants. They called each other *vadertje en moedertje* – daddy and mommy and were very straight-laced. Later on, I learned that in their personal and business dealings they were as inflexible as their religious background would suggest. I had a little talk with *Vadertje* as we now all called him behind his back, and told him my family had strong connections with his industry and that my father was on the board of Krian, a sugar factory nearby. That changed his attitude to me quite a bit. I also learned that his oldest son was going to Leiden and would be a groen, i.e., an aspiring member of the corps. So I could be of some help to him if as and when I got back home. Because of this meeting, I was invited for the family Christmas dinner on Christmas day. But before we had this event, we had a small Christmas Eve dinner with our group. I bought eight chickens, not very fat ones, and the babu cooked them for us. We had beer and jenever.

The third company also had a Christmas dinner. Gifts from home, cheese, roggebrood (special black Dutch bread) and cigarettes were distributed. These gifts all came from private donations. The army provided nothing. The dinner at the home of the Administrateur, a.k.a., *Vadertje*, was very nice. Captain Wolzak was there too. Our host and hostess scurried about, sang psalms and read from the bible. They exclaimed "God bless you meneer Schieferdecker." It was all very well intended, of course, and for me a wonderful experience to sit at a nicely set table with a white tablecloth in a real home with a family. At this dinner party I met Wim and Ieneke Opstelten. This young couple was about my age. Wim had graduated from the school in Deventer, Holland, where people trained for executive level jobs in tropical agriculture. They had a very small son Arnoud and lived across the street from *Vadertje en Moedertje*. We soon discovered that we had a great deal in common and that they were the only people there I felt at home with. They also liked to talk to me since I seemed to bring a breath of fresh air into their very isolated life among a group of people with whom they were not always comfortable.

The next day I went to Malang to see Oc, who was in the hospital with a bad case of malaria. The Opsteltens invited me to spend New Year's Eve with them, and also to come over for Ieneke's birthday. I could sit with them in their living room and talk about home and Netty, subjects I could never discuss with my comrades in arms except Oc. In the years to come the Opsteltens would emigrate to Australia where Wim initially had a very tough time getting his feet on the ground. He worked in a factory and Ieneke cleaned offices. After a while, Wim found a new and much better career path as an executive at CSR, the large Australian sugar company where he worked for many years. We stayed in touch through the years, mainly Christmas correspondence between Ieneke and Netty. We saw them a few times in Holland when we both happened to be there on vacation. When Netty and I went to Australia in 1994, we visited them in their retirement home in Peregian Beach, near Brisbane. We had a wonderful week with them, exploring the very scenic area they lived in. In 1997, Wim and Ieneke came to the U.S. to go with us on a trip to Alaska. Sadly, Ieneke was stricken with cancer shortly after that vacation and died after a prolonged and difficult illness. We are still in touch with Wim, of course, and he came to see us here in the U.S. in 2002. My brief visit to Tulangan yielded a lifelong friendship. A few years ago, Jim Anathan, the father of Julie, Richard's former wife, gave me a series of books written by a famous Indonesian novelist, Pramoedya Ananta Toer, about a young man who grows up in Surabaya. Tulangan plays a prominent role in these stories. Curious. Pramoedya is called the "preeminent prose writer of post independence Indonesia" by the Encyclopedia Britannica.

At the end of the year 1949, which had been a strange and difficult year for me, sovereignty over Indonesia was turned over to the new Federal Republic which would prove to be extremely short lived. My stay at Tulangan, which had been a very pleasant one, also proved to be short. I spent a great deal of time driving around, often with van Zuuren, the lieutenant who was our commander. We visited old IVG posts and tried to take care of loose ends there, mainly people who had been loyal to us and were now left behind. I do not think we achieved much, but we did our best. We moved to Sidoardjo, a town nearer Surabaya. One evening in a heavy monsoon downpour, van Zuuren stopped by to say he had orders to go to Batavia, where he had "business." A few days later, we heard he had been called back because he had problems with the military police about some affair. I never got to the bottom of it.

On January 3, 1950, there was a large manifestation in Sidoardjo attended by an enormous crowd. Half of them seemed to be in favor of the new republic of East Java, the other half was pro-Republic–the Yogya, Sukarno, faction. Some people in the crowd yelled at us and said we were dogs and should be their servants, using the word *djongos*, the word we used for male servants. We were now a small remaining IVG group and we had to be very careful moving around. Many of us were under threat to be reassigned to the infantry, a terrible fate of course after so many months of comfortable living as "spooks." Luckily, I managed to stay with the right crowd and continued to be among the untouchables, the ones that stayed out of the clutches of the infantry officers who were gunning for us and wished to see us join their dreary units. I visited Tulangan again to attend Ieneke's birthday. The entire sugar factory crowd was at the party and my comment to Netty is that they were a *"burgerlijke banale groep"* – a petit bourgeois banal bunch. Wim and Ieneke agreed with this but had to live with them so they coped. Netty was now in France and I wrote her more than ever to help her get over homesickness. I also got the bad news that Opa van Someren Gréve, the father of Netty's mother, died on January 6, 1950. It was tough to get news like that and to know that the only thing you can do is write a letter. We were then moved to Modjokerto, a market town located at a point where several roads cross near Surabaya.

In Modjokerto we had a rude awakening. We were included in the staff company of our battalion we got an office with native employees and official office furniture. We had to be well dressed, punctual, have a real military morning formation and, a real insult, we had to fetch our own food at the kitchen. In Modjokerto I was thrown in with the whole ex–IVG group. There were several people I had known for some time, but not known well. A standout is the Sergeant Major Nicolaas Louis Tenty. He was a member of the KNIL who was detached to us in Ponorogo. As a KNIL man, he was beyond the reach of our brass, a position he used frequently with great skill. I had of course seen him several times and spoken with him and Oc told me a good deal about him, but now I had a chance to get to know him better. Tenty came originally from Limburg, the same southern province where Oc came from and lived. People there speak a very strong dialect that is somewhere between German,

Flemish Dutch and northern Dutch. It is very hard to understand. Tenty was well educated and attended the gymnasium, I believe. He could speak very good Dutch and prided himself for being of a good family. Somewhere along the line, he got in trouble with his parents and decided to leave for Indonesia to join the colonial army there. He had been a sergeant major with the intelligence branch there for a long time and spoke fluent Malay. He was a pudgy man with a nasal way of speaking and great fun to be with. He was a very heavy drinker – a certified alcoholic. He often started his day with a couple of slugs of jenever and once he had the taste, he kept going. Like many heavy drinkers, he could camouflage his level of inebriation very well and could function in a manner that was close to normal even after having drunk the better part of a full bottle of jenever. Tenty's function with us was totally unclear. He was just there and lived his own life among us. He had a surrogate family of his own, two Arabian girls he took care of. The Indonesians had killed the parents of these girls after it became known that the father was spying for us. The older of the two girls was Tenty's mistress and the younger one was sort of kept in tow. They were dressed like Indonesian women, but in looks quite different. Taller, slimmer and finer boned than the average babu. The oldest was called Aisha; I do not recall the name of the younger one. Aisha was a lively cheerful girl and very pleasant to have around. They kept themselves at a fair distance of us though, in the Arab tradition. They would cater to all the major's whims and took his drinking in stride without comment. In the evenings when the major wanted some entertainment, he would call out *"Aisha menjaji"* or something to that effect which meant "sing." The girls then would protest and fuss, but eventually they would sing with nice clear voices. Their repertoire consisted of some of the Indonesian songs we liked. There were not all that many and some were not acceptable to the soldiers around us. When they sang the Indonesian national anthem for instance, we would get immediate angry reactions from men quartered around us who did not understand we were doing this just for fun. A favorite of ours was Bengawan Solo, a song about the river Solo:

This is a lovely song. I found it back on the Internet and discovered it has become a standard Indonesian song. When Netty and I were in Jakarta in 1988, we were in a restaurant where they had a small orchestra. I asked them to play it for us and they did. It was a very special sentimental and moving moment for me.

While in Modjokerto we heard that a Dutch colonial army commando unit had started a revolt. A captain Westerling of Indo–European background decided that the "real" Indonesians did not want the Republic so he went on a rampage around Bandung, a government center near Jakarta in the mountains. He occupied the TNI headquarters in Bandung. His troops were generally well-trained hardened fighters who had fought the peloppors for many years and were unwilling to accept the new political situation. They had little trouble getting the upper hand over the local TNI although they were numerically very small. They caused a real crisis in Western Java, and their action resulted in much bloodshed mainly on the side of the TNI. Our credibility as a party to an agreement was also in jeopardy, of course, and there was some anxiety among our brass that the movement would catch on in East Java and become a real countrywide problem. Major Tenty and I went on a trip inland to see if we could spot any Westerling sympathizers. Luckily we found none and the whole thing became a fiasco for Westerling who was hauled before a court martial and put in prison. Later on he surfaced in Holland and became a kind of right-wing idol.

A few days later, some of us went to Surabaya to say good-bye to Lieutenant van Zuuren who was shipping out to the Netherlands, facing an uncertain future there. I was jealous to see him leave on a nice ship. That afternoon in the city, I saw a parade with Sukarno as the main character. It was already becoming clear that the Republic East Java was a nonstarter and that the Yogyakarta republic was taking over. It was a strange sensation for me to stand in the enormous crowd with a revolver in my pocket and see the man who until very recently was our enemy number one drive by in an open jeep a few feet away. They had trucks with heavy machine guns mounted on top in front and behind him. It would certainly have been a real blood bath had anybody tried to take a pot shot at Bung Karno – brother Karno as his followers called him. He was clearly establishing his presence in East Java as the national hero and the leader of the revolution against the Dutch.

To my joy and surprise a new lieutenant arrived who turned out to be an old friend of mine. Theo Kraayevanger, whom I had known since the Haags Lyceum and who went to many parties with Netty and me. He was assigned to us for a short period. Theo had been longer in Indonesia than I, but spent all his time on Celebes, the island that is now called Sulawesi, a much quieter place. He decided not to go permanently back to the Netherlands, but to emigrate to New Zealand, a favorite destination in those days among Dutch people who wanted to leave the country's difficult economic climate and find a better future elsewhere. In fact, emigration was encouraged by the government. The authorities promoted emigration for soldiers who were going to be demobilized and many people, particularly those who knew a trade or were farmers went permanently overseas. Theo wanted to try to become a professional soldier in the military police which in Holland is called the marechaussee. If he could not secure a spot there, he wanted to emigrate. He had an interest in farming, but to my knowledge did not know much about it. His sister Wanda was also a friend of ours, and we met her and her husband Willem van der Vlugt again in Curaçao in 1995 on Menny's seventieth birthday party. She told me Theo had died a few years before but had a good and prosperous life in New Zealand. In Modjokerto Theo and I talked nonstop for two nights about old times. He was a nice, open and straightforward man. Unfortunately, he did not stay long with our unit. It would have been a real boon for me to have a good friend in command.

In this age of cell phones, tape recorders, email, the Internet, fax machines and worldwide telephone service it is hard to understand that all of this did not exist in 1950. As a very special service, we could make a recording of our voices on a small metal gramophone record, the size of the old 78-rpm records. You had to speak your message into a mike and the record was prepared after that. I sent it to Netty, together with the wooden needles required to play it on a record player, but I was not very happy with the result. My voice was sometimes barely audible and you could hear the trucks roaring by in the background. Expressing my love and longing for her in this way on a hot afternoon with many people hanging around and listening in was a total fiasco. I wrote Netty that I had many bad moments, calling the Dutch army the most mind-numbing and mean institution known to man. Netty wrote that her mother is busy trying to decide what she – Netty – should do when I come back. In those days parents still thought they could guide their children through life even after they were legally adults. I did a lot of daydreaming about life when I got back, about my future and even designed a house for us in my mind.

The internal conflicts in the TNI continued. The UN now got into the act and the U.S. State Department too. They were, of course, looking towards their future relationships with what is after all a huge South East Asian country with a large Muslim population. A U.S. representative by the name of Jessup visited Yogyakarta and walked around, according to my letter "as if it was all his (or the U.S.'s) doing." I felt betrayed by what I thought was our big friend, the U.S.A. The sultan of Yogya seemed to sympathize with Westerling, the sultan of Solo was pro–Dutch, there were TNI units that were pro–Dutch too and others that were pro–Japanese (still an influence, although beaten.)

I heard we were going to a town called Gresik on the shore north of Surabaya. On a visit to Surabaya I had to adhere to the new rule: we could only walk around in town UNARMED. For me there was a solution. I had a nice revolver as part of my IVG equipment. I put my six-shooter in my pocket and cut a small hole in the bottom where the barrel could fit in. During my visit to Surabaya I seemed to continue to be in a blue mood. Having absolutely nothing to do was probably the main reason for my frame of mind. I told Netty that I did not like the city. It looked to me like a place full of greedy people. Perhaps a natural reaction of a man who came from the boonies where there had been a lot of fighting and very little comfort and found the people he was defending enjoying life and paying little attention to the soldiers who protected them. Life went on. I noted that the young Indo-European women were overly voluptuous, the Dutch women heavy and matronly, the Javanese sneaky, the Dutch men vulgar and pompous and the Dutch children whiny. On top of all that, I declared that the buildings in town were ugly. TNI soldiers clomped around town in shoes given to them by us that were often too big. For an Indonesian who has spent all his life going barefoot, owning a pair of shoes was heaven. It meant he has arrived. A few weeks later, I returned to Surabaya and found the place quite nice because I had friends there and had something to do. As Kloosterman would say, "Einstein said it right; it is all relative."

Gresik turns out to be a fishing village surrounded by fish ponds and salt flats, used to make salt and breed fish and of course, also breeding millions of mosquitoes in the process. It was still quite interesting. Its architecture was very different from what we were used to seeing. It had a center square surrounded by buildings, mostly with two stories and with walls made out of yellow sandstone clay. Interesting turrets and small towers, etc. Oc visited me there and told me he has nothing to do at all either, he said whole offices are told "Sorry, there is nothing to do, so enjoy yourself." Our lodgings there were primitive and we were unhappy to be attached to a regiment we did not know, with a lieutenant colonel who in private life was a music teacher. Still, he may have beeen better than the man we had in Modjokerto who had all of two years of vocational school. Herman, another character of our group who drove around in an old one-ton truck he dearly loved and called *Oude Schicht* after the truck of a Dutch Cartoon character *Tom Poes*, built a corrugated steel roof over a small terrace on the second floor of our building where we could sit in the cool evening breeze. It took Herman more than a day to build the roof, but he was very pleased with the result, sweating profusely, he offered it to the Major. It was ready, just in time for my 25th birthday celebration. I bought saucijze broodjes and loempias in Surabaya that were consumed by our group with plenty of jenever and beer. The major was in excellent shape and Aisha served and we asked her to sing afterwards. There was a drunken exchange after the singing with some of the guys downstairs who happened to also be from Limburg and objected to the songs Aisha sang as being too pro-Indonesian. The major staggered downstairs and gave them a piece of his mind speaking in pure Limburg dialect and that was that. The party went on and was a great success. The major showed me a picture of a Dutch girl he was engaged to when on leave in Holland. Unfortunately, she would not come to Indonesia. This poor man had a lot of mental baggage and memories he drowned in jenever.

A few days later Theo invited me to come to Surabaya for a nice Chinese farewell dinner. He was going home after all, before traveling to New Zealand. I found a place to sleep with Nico Molenaar who was now in charge of the division's sports equipment. A wonderful job for him and he handled it well. Nico introduced me to two of his Dutch nurse friends, Carla Roes and Hanneke Kjaer (a Danish name), who work at the navy hospital in town. These two ladies – and they are ladies, an unusual sobriquet in the world we live in – would later-on become very good friends of Oc and mine and be of great help to bring us back to civilized life.

On March 2, 1950, I celebrated two years in the army and one year in Indonesia. A year spent among men-only, with much misery, but also much humor. It was never a real war though. I hoped to be home in four months. Then I would have to be reentered into polite society. I realized I had forgotten almost all I learned in my law studies and looked at the future through rose-colored glasses. I told Netty that I wondered sometimes how I managed to stay true to her while all around me men are breaking their vows and promises to wives and fiancées in Holland. My conclusion was that my love for her is just too strong. It was now just a matter of a few months.

In mid–March 1950, I suddenly got a one week leave to go to Trètes, the mountain resort where Opa and Oma van Someren Gréve had a vacation house. It was a very nice resort with a pool and a canteen. We were lodged in small bungalows. It was cool and wonderful in the mountains. We were not allowed to stray very far away from the resort, but I still went to a waterfall where we had a splendid view of the plain with Modjokerto and Surabaya over the horizon. I imagined how nice it must have been to be there in the old days, when Oma and Opa lived in Surabaya. A prim Dutch lady who runs the local library in Trètes refuses to lend soldiers certain books. She declared, "These books are not suitable for you!"

Back in Gresik the oppressive heat hit me hard. It is the period when the monsoon is almost over and the weather is changing, always a bad time in the tropics. In my letters, I continued to express pessimistic feelings about the economic and political outlook for the Netherlands. I saw the country as broke, overpopulated and economically and militarily powerless. Thousands of people were returning home from Indonesia, military as well as civilian, without any hope or money. My views on the Dutch economy and outlook were perhaps correct on the shorter term, but longerterm, history proved me to be totally wrong. Holland became a rich and prosperous country in the sixties and seventies and the loss of Indonesia had no long-term impact on the Dutch economy. I wrote my parents regularly with my thoughts about these matters but never got much of a response and began to realize that I was becoming more and more detached from them.

In late March, Oc told me that he got a job at the Krijgsraad, the Military Judiciary or Court Martial. A nice change for him. He moved from total idleness to a busy job. We learned that we would have to leave Gresik in a week, and our prospect is being billeted in steel sheds with 400 of our battalion comrades in Perak, the harbor of Surabaya. We met with our lieutenant and made clear to him that we expected him to defend our position as an independent group of people who have to operate away from the troops. He may succeed, but it is strange that we, the "other ranks," have to prompt him to protect his men. Sergeant Major Tenty went over to look for better quarters and our lieutenant agreed with everything. Luckily, Tenty found a place. It was a nice house in a good neighborhood in Surabaya. I got a new assignment. I now had to wear civilian clothes and wander around the neighborhood, keeping an eye on our American neighbors. Our new location was splendid. It was in the center of town and within walking distance of all the nice places, nightclubs included. In the evenings, it was a pleasure to walk around the well-lit streets and watch my American neighbors enjoying themselves in their air-conditioned homes. It is the first time in my life that I saw air conditioning in use in a house. The windows of the house were closed and seen from the hot sidewalk everybody inside seems supremely comfortable.

In mid–May, East Java had to be completely empty of Dutch troops. Our friends, the nurses have to stay because they signed a contract with a fixed duration. They are upset at being left alone without any protection.

The Indonesian Central Bank suddenly devalued the currency. We had to cut our bank notes in half and use one-half as currency exchangeable into new money at a sharply reduced rate. The other half we could convert into 3½ %, 40-year government bonds for half their value. Transferring money to Holland also became suddenly very complicated. We get a Dutch guilder for every three Indonesian ones. It used to be one for one. This was a real blow for men who were sending money home to their families and for people who wanted to leave the country. Their savings in guilders were now cut in half and then reduced by one third because it was now "foreign exchange." Therefore, they can transfer now only one sixth of what they thought they had out of the country. A raw deal for the people here. I heard that Dean Acheson, the U.S. secretary of state met with Oom Eelco. The U.S. had offered Indonesia financial help to recover from the "Dutch oppression." The Lingadjati Agreement that established the Federal Republic of Indonesia was now worthless with the influence of the Sukarno Republic rising rapidly. Meanwhile Australia, a country that had given us a hard time throughout the struggle here, now insists that we stay in western New Guinea. Since World War I they have had sovereignty over the formerly German eastern side, so their interest has changed dramatically.

In April my grandfather Opa Schieferdecker celebrated his ninetieth birthday. I sent him a letter, of course, to celebrate this momentous event, and I received a neatly typed letter in response. Not bad for the old pater familias. It was beginning to be fun in Surabaya for me, at least socially. Nico Molenaar was there and offered us generous transportation in his jeep at all times. There also was Mike van Rossum, a soldier we have known since the Kota Inten. He was a scion of a wealthy expatriate Dutch family who grew up in Italy and Switzerland, quiet intelligent but totally undisciplined and without much formal schooling, at least the kind that yields diplomas that are useful to get a job in The Netherlands. Mike was hopeless as a soldier, he lost all or most of his equipment, looked extremely sloppy and was generally a headache for his sergeants. But he was excellent company for us and he and Oc became good friends. Much later Mike married, and for a while he and his wife became more or less permanent house guests at Oc's house. They stayed so long that Oc had to let them know that his usually boundless hospitality had reached its limits. Mike drank a lot in Indonesia and continued on this path afterwards. In later life he developed a serious problem with alcoholism. He died in the 1990's.

At Easter Oc and Nico went to an elaborate Catholic Church service, and Mike and I had to wait for hours for this event to end. Our friends, the nurses, invited us for a rijsttafel Easter lunch at their mess. This was a wonderful event. I do not recall who was there with Carla and Hanneke beyond Oc and me, probably Nico. I don't think Mike was in the inner circle there. The nurses had their own compound with a large central mess building surrounded by a square of low small houses each lodging two women. In front of their rooms, shaded by large trees, they had a *platje*, the Dutch/Indonesian word for a small terrace where we would sit when we visited them. They had excellent accommodations compared to ours, but they were in rank equal to officers and, of course, women. They also had a tennis court there so we went to play tennis many times in the early evening when it was still light and a little cooler.

With Mike I explored the seamier side of life in Surabaya. We frequented Tabarin, a bar where Mike was a well-known guest. It had an orchestra, "band" would be an exaggeration and behind the counter was a fading beauty whom we called Mrs. (with her name, which I have forgotten.) She had long discussions with us and we consumed too much jenever. The nurses disapprove of our "bar" stories, and I noted in my letter to Netty that I was drinking too much, which was particularly uncomfortable in the mornings as the dehydration alcohol causes, combined with the heat made the hangover extra bad. I decided to cut down on my liquor intake. I had enough money to lead a good life in Surabaya because I had an arrangement with a family who were distant relatives of Mammy in which Pa would deposit money for them in Holland, and they would give me money in Indonesia at a – for me – very favorable exchange rate. For them this was still a very good and cheap way to transfer savings to a financially more stable country.

On the streets in Surabaya, life was getting tougher day by day. We always traveled in groups of three or four, just to be on the safe side. We also took guns along again. For me the group approach was not always possible. I once even went way inside a kampong – an Indonesian settlement usually consisting of thousands of small bamboo houses. It was evening, the place was dark, only lit by small kerosene lamps in the houses, and there were smells of food and charcoal fires everywhere. I went there with a sergeant buddy to gather intelligence by interviewing two Indo–European women who lived with their family. We went there by betjak, a pedicab. This was a three-wheeled vehicle with a two-person seat between the two front wheels for passengers and a driver who pedaled from behind, pushing the thing along. They were omnipresent means of transportation in Indonesian towns and cities and we often used them but seldom to go deep into the kampongs. It was a great relief for me to finish this trip without incident and return to the busier center of the city. During the ride I had my hand on my revolver and was on the lookout for a chance encounter with some band of TNI fellows who were roaming around everywhere. Such encounters were highly dangerous in those days. The TNI had little discipline and its members were inclined to use their weapons frequently. There was a general increase in crime in town because the judicial system was crumbling. In April four Europeans were killed, including two Dutch marines.

As all my bosses in the intelligence service went home, nobody seemed to know what my job was. Finally, I got a wonderful assignment. I had to go to the Dutch army harbor command in Perak, the harbor of Surabaya. There I would join the office staff, but my assignment was to find out what the Indonesian army was doing and not office work. I was billeted on Perak Boulevard, in a sergeant's mess, a pleasant small house. The boss-man there was a sergeant major who was in the Dutch Irene Brigade, the small Dutch contingent that was formed in Britain and participated in the D-Day landings in Normandy and marched all the way to the Netherlands. He had now been in Indonesia for five years. You would think a grateful nation would send a man like him home with honors. To the contrary, they kept him extra long because he had expert knowledge of the shipping and transport situation. I could roam around the harbor on a bicycle or later even on a motorbike. The three sergeants in my house accepted me very kindly as a new housemate and even taught me how to ride one of their big old English BSA-army motorbikes. This was fun; I even once or twice rode the bike into Surabaya, but the negative was that I did not have a valid army driver's license so if the MP would have stopped me it would be very troublesome. I therefore confined myself to put-putting calmly around the harbor, watching for theft of army equipment and interviewing TNI men who traveled by ship with their units to and from the outer islands. They were easy to talk to and eager to give any information you wanted, still naively believing in the superiority of the white man.

What was of interest to us was information of troop movements to Ambon. The Amboinese, faithful servants of the Dutch military, had been abandoned by us and had now declared independence. This situation would over time present the Dutch government with many headaches, but when I was in Surabaya these troubles were far over the horizon. Our battalion was still in the harbor, billeted in terribly hot and noisy steel sheds. They said that they were slowly going mad. Sometimes they had no water and barrels with water had to be trucked in. Then they had to bathe outside in full view of the population. The food was bad. Naturally I was happy to have a nice house to live in and visited my comrades on my motorcycle. Nevertheless, I had to be careful, not to excite a jealous officer or NCO who would be angry at my obviously luxury existence. The situation with the battalion was so bad that word had even reached the Dutch Parliament where questions were asked. The response of the minister was that the boys were happy there because it would be only for three weeks. At that time, they had been there already for five weeks! The good Dutch people who had elected him believed him because he was a minister. In those days, people were questioning authority much less than today.

I hated Surabaya, but was still fascinated by its melting-pot society, its perversity, its tensions and its multiracial environment. One evening we witnessed a good illustration of the situation in town when Nico drove me home and we passed an automobile junk yard in which homeless people and other undesirables were living among the car wrecks. We saw a line of TNI men trying to clean the place out. In the half-dark night, they advanced towards a mob of screaming men who danced in front of their weapons. Then we heard a scream, a couple of bursts of fire and saw several men drop. We drove on and wished each other a good night. We hardly talked about what we had seen. We agreed that we had a pleasant evening. Life was cheap in Indonesia.

On May 1, there was a May Day parade in which portraits of Marx, Engels, Stalin and Mao Tse-tung were carried around. An indication of things to come in the country. It was still unusually and uncomfortably hot. On May 5, we celebrated the anniversary of the liberation of Holland and we had a day off. Nico drove us to Trètes for a wonderfully cool day. In the harbor the next day, I saw the old Kota Inten again. This time she was used to bring Amboinese army families home to their island. In the hold I saw a terrible mess with baskets, kids, women nursing babies etc. The Amboinese independence movement became more and more aggressive.

In the evenings I was still nosing around town in civilian clothes. Very pleasant but of little use to the Dutch army. Ma wrote a long dissertation about the party they held for Opa's ninetieth birthday. She described the food in detail but did not react to my long diatribes about the political situation here. That was very frustrating. Oc came to say that Frits Greup was in Surabaya. I went to see him and found him little changed from the old days. He had a sheltered life working at the court martial. I also went to a wedding party in town. One of the sergeants who had temporarily been with us in Gresik married an Indo– European girl whose family he claimed was part of the Dutch nobility. He said her name was Jonkvrouwe Goldman (Dame Goldman). I doubted his assertions but kept my mouth closed. The party was at the bride's house where everyone was sitting in a large circle talking and eating. Typically Dutch. The father of the bride, a small mousy-looking man, was there but his wife was in the kitchen sitting on her haunches Indonesian style, in front of a charcoal fire cooking. The bride could be glad she had found a husband who would take her to Holland, out of the Indonesian mess.

The Kota Inten returned to our harbor loaded with all the Dutch people who were stationed in the Moluccas. They told me that it was a tragic situation there that was getting worse by the day. The Ambonese wanted to fight until death and had ammunition for three years but no food. They had reinstated Dutch as their language and played the Dutch National Anthem, *het Wilhelmus* upon the departure of the ship. It was a very moving but also deeply embarrassing moment for the departing Dutchmen.

In late May, I heard I could petition for early repatriation as a student so I could be home in early fall by the time the university year starts. I sent my petition in as fast as I could, of course. On a weekend, I visited the Opsteltens at Tulangan. They were very worried about their future there and had decided to emigrate to Australia. Wim thought he would have to start out working as a truck driver. Tough. Word from home was that my father and Netty's Dad had talked together about my future. The Pa's were talking about my future without me being present, did they realize I was twenty-five years old? One of their conclusions was that the law degree was losing its weight. So they may have concluded that I should stop my studies. Who knows? I hoped that they would tell me some day what their thoughts are. I was now going every day to the office of the harbor command. Nosed around in the harbor and had a generally pleasant time, but I was hoping there would be news on my petition for early departure. One very rainy day with a heavy sea running, I was outside the office looking over the Straits of Madura. I saw a large Indonesian prau, sailing down towards the harbor, a beautiful sight. The ship was square rigged in the old-fashioned style and looked like an old East India man coming down for spices. A wonderful picture that is still in my mind's eye.

In early June, we were invited by our nurse friends for a big dance to celebrate the anniversary of their mess. It was a marvelous party but very hot. I brought two shirts and used them both. Nico was in love with a nurse, not one of our two friends, and bored Oc and me with his amorous problems. Oc told him to keep his affairs to himself. We made fun of poor Nico

SURABAYA, TALKING WITH OCTAVE AND HANNEKE

at the party. He sweated as much as we did, but he sweated particularly in the seat of his pants so it looked as if he had wetted them, and this made him more uncomfortable than he already was. We were the only non officers at the party but also the only ones who had bought corsages for our hostesses, a small victory for the people who knew how one behaves.

In the harbor, I saw the Sibajak off, an old, large passenger liner loaded with women and children. I spent a whole day on board, enjoying the air-conditioning, drinking their good Dutch beer and stealing toilet paper. It was a sad sight though. Wives of generals and colonels put in one big pen with two hundred other women, Indo–European families who were leaving the country where they grew up and belonged, leaving everything behind. When the ship left, the national anthem was played.

Netty asked me what Hanneke looked like, and I told her she is quite good looking with a nice figure and a round face. A serious and conservative girl. Hanneke's father died in the period we were there. He had been sick for a long time, but it still must have been a heavy blow for her. When Netty and I lived in Heemstede, we caught up with Hanneke again who worked then as a nurse in a navy hospital nearby. We became good friends.

On June 20, the heaviest earthquake in fifty years hit Surabaya. This was an unusual sensation for me. I was in our little house, writing letters, as always, when the lights went out and the ground started to heave under me in a rolling fashion, the dining room lamp swung back and forth and the trees outside were swaying. The water in the large gutters along the street sprang up in plumes. After a few minutes of movement it stopped. For about twenty seconds it was deadly quiet outside when it was over. Then all of a sudden, the kampongs exploded in noise. Dogs barked and people banged on pots and pans to ward off the evil spirits.

Reading Time Magazine regularly, courtesy of Pa, I got more and more worried about what was later called the cold war in Europe. I feared more military conflicts with the Russians and their satellites. When the war in Korea broke out that summer, the misgivings of our troops were reaching a fever pitch. Our men feared we would be sent to the U.S. for training and then to Korea. After getting a series of injections, I am declared "medically and socially" ready for Holland. I had to sign a paper in which I declared that I was not aspiring to receive any government-subsidized schooling. Heaven forbid I would have cost the government more than I did already! In my letters to Netty I got really serious about the Russian threat and told her she should try to escape to the U.S. while I fought it out. No sense sticking around when the Russian steamroller comes your way. In my next letter I apologized for my war psychosis. Still, my letters were a reflection of the times we lived in, in the fifties. A conflict with the Soviet Union was considered a distinct possibility.

We took Carla and Hanneke out for dinner and to dance afterwards in Tabaris. They did not belong there, but we danced until we dropped and they loved it! It turned out this was our farewell party. On July 6, I got orders to leave as soon as possible for Batavia (Jakarta) by ship. I had to assemble all my papers myself since I was now almost a unit on

my own. I did this on my motorbike. Very convenient. Oc went by plane with people from his office. Saying good-bye to Carla and Hanneke was tough. They lost friends who came by regularly and gave a good deal of *gezelligheid*, now they are stuck with Nico who will also go back soon with the 422 battalion. On July 12, I shipped out on the Merak, a small steamer plying between Batavia and Surabaya. I felt elated to be leaving and guilty to abandon so many good friends. In accordance with my rank, I traveled third class or really steerage. About twelve people brought me to the ship. A doctor even came to the ship to sign my smallpox certificate, which at the last moment proved to be not in order. Once the ship left the harbor of Surabaya, I had a real feeling of departure and impending homecoming. A wonderful sensation. I had a bottle of jenever, which I drank with three others, one of whom indulged a little too much. He threw up overboard, losing his glasses in the process. The next day we arrived in Batavia and were transferred to a transit camp in the suburb called Meester Cornelis where I found hundreds of student friends all gathered there returning to Holland "for study reasons."

We were told we would be leaving on July 21 on a Norwegian ship called Skaugum, that was used to bring immigrants to Australia. The Dutch government chartered it to take troops back on the return voyage. We hung around the transit camp, bored and waiting for news. The food was bad, but the people who are processing us were well organized and efficient. After a long search, I found Tineke and Jaap. They were in Batavia on their way to another assignment, New Guinea I believe. Jaap was in the hospital and Tineke was hanging around waiting for him to be released. She struck up a friendship with a doctor who was known to me as a ladies' man and very bad news. I also visited with Mr. Kramer, a friend of my parents who had a job with the Dutch government at that time. He came to fetch me in his nice car and we had dinner in town. Oc and I also escaped the camp to investigate a nightclub called Le Chat Noir. This establishment had become notorious since Captain Westerling was a regular there and was sitting at the bar while everybody was futilely searching for him all over town. Unfortunately I did not see much of

Batavia. Later in 1988 when it had become Jakarta, Netty and I briefly visited the city, but then it had been changed radically by the Republik Indonesia with many high-rise buildings and other prestige projects that ruined the old city that was known for its shady streets lined with large trees and beautiful, roomy, old houses. Much of the old colonial atmosphere was gone in 1988. Many houses looked run down and over-crowded and large broad avenues had been built with huge office buildings and no trees which made them very hot and barren looking.

We boarded the Skaugum on July 22 and the ship left Tandjung Priok, the next day at 5 p.m. Rumors were flying about Korea where the American army suffered horrible losses and was asking for help from its allies. We also heard we were going to have nice cabins aboard with beds with decent mattresses and sheets. Minutes later the story changed and we would be relegated to a hold again. As it turned out, we did get nice cabins, sleeping six people, in bunks with mattresses and sheets. I tried to get a cabin just for people from Leiden, but that did not succeed. The ship was reasonably well air-conditioned and quite comfortable in many other respects. Oc was appointed to the ships police and quickly got me a job with the same unit. This was one of the better jobs one could get. Every day we had to be on duty for a couple of hours, just wandering around with a red armband with a "P" on it and keeping order. Beyond a large group of military men who scalled up, the ship transported mainly members of the KNIL and their families. Most of the KNIL people were Indo–Europeans, many of whom had never been in the Netherlands. Our job was mainly to direct young women with small children to various doctors' offices and other places where the military continued to do whatever an army does in the paper-shuffling department. Some of the passengers were only used to life in Indonesian army camps and were, for instance, unfamiliar with western style toilets. They would squat on top of the toilet seat. In one amusing incident, a fellow decided to sit on the ship's railing to relieve himself. Below him was the ship's hospital where air scoops were used. These scoops would stick out of the portholes and draw in a nice stream of cool ocean air. In this case, something else blew in. A doctor saw what was happening and stormed topside to find the culprit calmly sitting on the railing with his pants down.

I do not recall much of our trip back, and I do not have a record of the trip since we had no opportunity anymore to write letters home. Just before I left I received Netty's one hundred and ninetieth and last letter. She really supported me tremendously with her letters throughout my ordeal. My last letter to her was almost a farewell from something that had become a very dear part of my life, Indonesia.

The ship was nice, clean, fast, and not overly crowded. Compared to the Kota Inten it was a luxury liner. The passage through the Suez Canal was smooth and uneventful and as we approached our destination, Amsterdam, we were issued woolen European style uniforms that were true to form, old, used, and ill fitting. In Batavia, I had made clear that I did not want to be brought home by bus. I had asked my father to pick me up in a hotel in Amsterdam.

The morning of our arrival we were all up early. In the distance, we could see the coast of Holland. As the ship came closer, it struck me immediately how densely populated our little country was. Compared to Indonesia with its green jungle shoreline and the wild shores of Egypt and Saudi Arabia along the Red Sea where you saw rugged mountains and no sign of life for several days, Holland appeared very crowded. Beyond the low lying dunes you could see roofs of houses, chimneys of factories, church steeples and many other signs of habitation. To get into the harbor of Amsterdam, the ship had to enter the locks at IJmuiden. When we entered the locks, we were suddenly home among the Dutch people. Hundreds of family members were packed around the locks, calling out for their "loved ones" (as we say nowadays). Houses and bicycles were everywhere and an ice cream vendor was doing business in the middle of this festive crowd. I suddenly saw Tante Jetje wandering around in the crowd. She had taken a cab from Bloemendaal to greet me. That was very touching.

Once we docked in Amsterdam, we had to listen to a speech by General Baay, the man we regarded as an incompetent leader who had caused many needless casualties in East Java. Nobody paid attention to what he said. Shortly afterwards we were on home ground and loaded into buses. I took the Amsterdam bus which after dropping a few people off at their homes came to the Hotel Americain where I would meet Pa. He soon came and he loaded me in his new Ford car, stating, "It does not have a scratch yet." This was clearly in reference to what he feared I would soon do to his new automobile. In Voorburg I was greeted by Ma in the hallway of our house and as I entered the living room I found Netty. We embraced for a long time while Pa and Ma discreetly stayed away. A new life would begin for me, and I would have to find many answers to many questions, so many that I was often totally overwhelmed by them. Still, I was home safely and the military was suddenly far away.

❧

This time in Indonesia had made a different man of me. I was considerably more mature, but in the months to come, I had to go through a long period of adjustment. The Dutch army just dumped us back into society, straight from the boat. No handholding, no financial help or assistance with employment or with health care. The Dutch army left 2,526 dead behind in Indonesia. Of these 1,162 were killed in the first seven months after the second "police action." This was the period when I was there. So we lost on average 166 men per month. It was a high risk period and I was lucky to come out in one piece. In recent years, Holland sent small detachments of troops to various trouble spots as "peacemakers" under UN auspices. These men are transported by plane, stay away for two or three months or even get permission to have their wives or girl friends flown over to places like Cambodia for leave. When one or two were killed, the national uproar was enormous with big headlines in the papers. Hundreds of government employed handholders and social workers swarmed all over the troops. With us, nobody cared. Sometimes there were small lists in the papers with the names of those who had been killed. There was little or no press coverage of our actions. We were a defeated army and part of a bad part of Dutch history. God only knows how many of our men were suffering from what is now called "post traumatic stress syndrome." I think this experience and its aftermath, the feeling of having been treated shabbily, been poorly equipped and poorly led, made me feel much less connected with the Dutch nation and its people, who mostly had not given a damn about us. It made my departure in 1958 to America much easier.

As a footnote, in the 1990s – fifty years later – the Dutch government decided to do something for its veterans and gave each a gift of one thousand guilders, about 500 dollars at that time. After a few years, I decided to accept this overwhelmingly generous offer and following a lot of formalities centered around proving that I was still alive I got the money. About two hundred euros. Thanks.

19 : *First Job and Marriage*

In my first days home I spent a good deal of time with Netty, of course. I also bought a lot of clothes. The post-war rationing system of textiles was gone and you could buy good quality clothes again. After so many years in uniform and often in skimpy rags in Indonesia, I had a great urge to dress well again and look good. I had two suits made by expensive tailors and bought several other outfits off the rack. It was still summer and Netty and I went to stay with Tante Jetje in Leersum. Her house had been rebuilt, at least partly. There was still a housing shortage and building materials were scarce, but as a war and resistance victim, Tante Jetje had priority in getting her house rebuilt. The new

Meezenhof was built on the same footprint of the old burnt-down one with almost the same layout inside. However, there were still restrictions on the size of the house that could be constructed. So she was only permitted to build the ground floor, with a staircase to the flat roof, which eventually could be finished off into a second floor.

In Leersum a picture was made of us, which is one of our favorites. It was summer and we were in the country, but I still showed up in jacket and tie. We dressed that way in those days. To be honest about it, I have tended to dress more formally all my life. That was perhaps due to my father's influence (he was always properly dressed) and the style of dress of Leiden students in those days. Casual dress for everybody came only much later.

Netty had come back from France before my return. I cannot say much about her adventures there, because I was not present. Also, this is mainly my story, at least until Netty and I were married, and I don't want to describe her early years and also cannot do justice to writing about what Netty did during the time I was in Indonesia. She stayed in the wonderful old town of Montpellier in southern France. She worked as an au pair with the Lafont family. Mr. Jacques Lafont was a lawyer. Netty took care of their two young sons. Madame Lafont's mother, Madame de Fleurieux, a very distinguished lady, was particularly nice to Netty. She owned a castle called Boisseron near Montpellier where the family often went on summer weekends. In 1956 Netty and I made a vacation trip to Spain by car and stopped in Montpellier to visit the Lafonts. This was a nice visit. However, it was somewhat of an anticlimax for Netty who had warm feelings for this family with whom she had become very good friends. When we arrived, they had obviously completely forgotten that we were coming and had to improvise a dinner and a room for us. We left the next day realizing that some people do not put all that much value on friendships that seem tight at the time when convenient to both parties and later are not valued as much. She had very much hoped to see the boys when we visited but never saw them again.

In September I went back to the Societeit in Leiden to be present at the first day of the groentijd – the initiation of new members. As is customary on the first day, the door was barricaded by older students who wanted to keep those students out who were considered unworthy of dealing with the novices. They are known as obscuur i.e. fellows who are not known as active participants in the day-to-day Corps life and now come to lord it over the poor novices as if they are big shots. As I could have expected, the fellows at the door did not know me because I had been

away for almost three years. They were perhaps now in their third year and considered themselves now very senior members, but they were certainly junior to me and
I thought they were just young jerks and told them so. I angrily explained that I had
been in Indonesia and was not going to be prevented from entering by them. After
a short scuffle, which I won, I was inside together with Toon de Mol van Otterloo,
a friend who was in the same position. Still, this small incident made me feel I was
not welcome anymore and did not feel at home in a group that had what seemed to
me juvenile and silly traditions and practices. The Societeit was dominated by fellows who had not been in the army and were in my view slackers who had been dealt
a much better hand than I. I was wrong in my anger, of course, but I think it was
understandable. I did not come back to the Societeit for many years.

At that time in September, I had still not made arrangements to move back
to Leiden and to find rooms, etc. I was still drifting around rudderless. One evening Netty's father asked me to come in his study for a talk. He was very good at
that sort of one-on-one discussion. He was as always friendly, understanding, wise
and interested in helping me. We discussed the rather uncertain outlook for my
Indonesian law studies. The faculty was actually in the process of being closed down
and "arrangements" were made for those who were like me, hung up halfway. Since
Netty and I did not want to wait too long before getting married, Pa van Kleffens felt
I should not attach too much value to the Meester in de Rechten – the law degree I
was seeking and move on with finding a job. With some reluctance, I agreed. It was
time to earn a living, but how? I had no clue how the world worked and no skills to
offer. Pa van Kleffens offered to see if his good friend Kees Schimmelpenninck (C.
J. Baron Schimmelpenninck van der Oye), who was sole principal in an investment
brokerage firm in Amsterdam called Jonas & Kruseman, could do something for me.
A few days later when I was visiting Netty, her parents returned from having dinner in
Amsterdam with the Schimmelpennincks and announced happily that I could come
and join the firm as a trainee. And that is how I got into the investment business.
No lengthy studies of job opportunities, no soul searching about the correctness of
my choice. I grasped this opportunity with both hands and the idea that I could have
reflected on it some more or even rejected it was just not an option for me. It just did
not occur to me that I had any choice. I just had a strong urge to get on with making
a living, and I was willing to take any decent job that came my way regardless of what
it was and where it was. I had, of course, absolutely no knowledge of the world of
finance. As the saying goes, I did not know the difference between a stock and a bond.
I will always gratefully remember the efforts Netty's parents made to get me started in

life. They did not hesitate to use their influence with a friend to help me and set up visits and dinner parties with the Schimmelpennincks to cement the deal.

Ever since those days I have never hesitated to use my own private network of friends, relatives and acquaintances to further my career and that of others. This is not to say I favor nepotism or "sweetheart" deals or using cronies to get a job one is not really qualified for or to bypass others. I think that if somebody recognizes you as a good fit for a certain position, it is perfectly normal to accept his or her recommendation for it. That is what makes the world go round. I got all the many different jobs I have had in my life through connections with friends and acquaintances. I never went around knocking on doors or mailing out my résumé blindly. In fact, I often had to write my résumé after being interviewed because my interlocutor needed one for his files. Later on I learned from outplacement people that they recommend their charges to do the same. To use relationships and do as much networking as possible. Visit all the people you know and ask them "what do you think I should do" and "with whom else do you think I should speak." If they want to hire you they will do so, if not they will pass you on to other people who may be interested, provided you ask to be passed on.

Before getting married and going to work, I wanted to have a dermoid cyst removed which had started to bother me in Indonesia. It was a small, bean-sized bag under my skin on my coccyx or what I would call tail bone that was aggravated by riding around for years in military vehicles without springs and with hard metal seats or no seats at all. The surgeon called it *"de jeep ziekte"* – the jeep disease – and said it was a very common thing and just a small operation. It was, but after a few days in the hospital when I was back home, the wound got infected and I had to go back to the surgeon's office. He proceeded to cut the wound open again and scraping it out. He did this while I rested on my knees on his examination table, like a praying Muslim and without any anesthesia. I do not think I have ever experienced as much pain as that evening. When I climbed down from the table, my legs almost buckled under me, and I was glad Pa had come to pick me up and bring me home by car. For several weeks, I had to have my rear end bandaged by a visiting nurse and I carried a bright red blow-up rubber ring around to sit on. It was with this ring in hand that I met Mr. and Mrs. Schimmelpenninck for the first time at the van Kleffens' house. Luckily they did not seem to mind at all and I was told I was welcome to start at the office as soon as I could. On a day when it rained as it can only rain in Holland – coming down in buckets for hours on end – I took the train to Amsterdam and started a search for a place to live. I found a place in the Jan Luyken Straat, a nice street near the Rijks Museum, where an elderly landlady had a reasonable room for me. It was a gloomy place, however, and I kept trying to move in with Oc, who had found a nice room in a boardinghouse in the Vondelstraat near the Societeit of his (Catholic) Student Corps. Before too long a room became available there and I quickly changed. Beyond Oc there was another man there, Bob van der Kun, who was a friend of Oc's. Bob worked at a bank and the three of us enjoyed each other's company at dinner served by our landlady and going out in the evenings from time to time.

The day I entered the offices of Jonas & Kruseman, or Jokru as we always called it – using its telegram address – I stepped into a very conservatively organized business in an old historic building at the Herengracht in Amsterdam, staffed by friendly and helpful people who mostly had been there for decades. Jokru's business was that of a Commisionnair in Effecten – a stockbrokerage. In the Dutch tradition that meant doing business with individuals and small institutions, handling their investments in securities, safekeeping their securities, keeping cash accounts for them and performing all kinds of other services, such as paying bills, estate planning and fiduciary work. Quite a bit more, therefore, than what a classic sales volume oriented American brokerage firm used to do for its customers. Most Jokru clients kept us busy with small remittances, bill payments and other trivial transactions and not with investment services. We charged a small fee for each service we performed. We functioned more like a small private bank than an investment firm and the volume of our stock exchange business was very low most days. Although the war was five years behind us, the Dutch economy and its financial systems were far from back to their pre-war shape. The enormous economic damage done by the war and the German occupation was still noticeable everywhere, certainly in Amsterdam, the nation's financial center. The city had not suffered much material damage in the war, but the viability of its businesses had been severely impacted. The only place where physical damage was noticeable was in the section where the ghetto had been. This was the area where the Dutch Jews had been concentrated before being transported to the camp in Westerbork, the place from where they were loaded into trains with cattle cars and moved to the death camps in Poland. Towards the final winter of the war when everybody was hungry and looking for firewood and all the Jews were gone, there were many empty houses in the ghetto and the people of Amsterdam had broken into them, looking for wood. They took entire staircases, floor boards, wooden beams and many other parts of mostly old buildings. Several houses caved in or were torn down afterwards to avoid risk for the surrounding houses. On my way to the stock exchange, I would occasionally walk through this part of town and see the gaps in the rows of houses as a visible reminder of one of the worst atrocities the world has ever seen.

The Amsterdam business world also had to struggle out from under a mountain of necessary but still irksome postwar measures. The stock exchange, the oldest one in the world, was burdened with many regulations. Since most Dutch securities in those days were in bearer form, which means that physical possession usually signifies ownership, the true owners of securities stolen in wartime were often hard to find. The Germans and their Dutch helpers had simply taken possession of all Jewish-owned investment portfolios and sold them off. The authorities had devised an elaborate system to retrieve these stolen securities and to prevent black marketers, who owned securities they had received in payment for wartime deals, from enjoying ownership of their ill-gotten gains. We had an *Effecten Zuivering* – a securities cleansing operation. All bearer securities had to be registered and transactions could only be settled if the securities were delivered with a certificate proving the security had been registered and had a "clean" provenance.

In addition, we had a very strict foreign exchange control regime. The country was poor and it was necessary to prevent capital flight abroad, particularly into the U.S. dollar. Transferring money abroad was not possible and travelers who had to go to the U.S. and other hard currency countries were severely restricted in the amount of money they could take with them. We could not buy foreign securities from abroad, only pre-owned ones from Dutch citizens. Therefore, transactions in foreign securities, historically an important area of the Amsterdam stock market, were almost nonexistent.

The war and its aftermath still overshadowed the business world and people were trying to survive rather than make it big. The structure of investment portfolios was risk averse and heavily slanted towards the safety and security offered by fixed-income securities. Stocks were bought for yield – for the dividends they paid, not the earnings growth they promised – and price stability was preferred over volatility. Companies issued skimpy annual reports that told the shareholders little about their business and promised more of the same rather than optimistic forecasts. It was perhaps not only the war that impacted investment thinking in those days, but also the Depression that preceded it. The 1930shad been tough for the investment business. Most employees had weathered the Depression with the firm, working for the two brothers Jonas, the founding fathers of the business. It was never quite clear to me where the name Kruseman came from, but the Jonas brothers, although dead for several years, were still spoken off with great affection and reverence by my colleagues. *Meneer Piet* was the dominant one of the two. He called himself Jonas van 's Heer Arendskerke. He had bought a country farm/estate in Zeeland that allowed him to legally extend his name with this lengthy appendage. His brother, *Meneer Eduard*, was mild mannered and clearly less pushy than his sibling and always was just Mr. Jonas.

The brothers had built a business that had a very high reputation as a sound first-class firm with a distinguished clientele. Much of that was still intact when I came and it stayed that way, although the pressures of the postwar economic environment brought inevitable changes that worked out less well. The brothers had no sons so they invited Mr. Schimmelpenninck to join the firm at a young age. This must have been around the mid–1930s. When I came Mr. Schimmelpenninck was sole partner. Over the years we would become quite close, and I have to thank him for much of what I learned in the seven years that I worked at Jokru. Schimmelpenninck belonged to a very distinguished old family. He had lost his father early in life, and as he told me, his mother was too strapped for cash in the thirties to enable him to attend a university. He had to go to work right after high school. He did exceedingly well at the firm, right from the start. He was a very energetic, charming and gregarious man who had a knack for getting along with people. He was very smart with a good mind for financial problems, an excellent public speaker and a very good writer who could dictate letters in Dutch, English and French without having to get a draft first. He was very tight with money when it concerned relatively small expenditures, but amazingly easygoing when it came to using the firm's cash to make loans to people that turned out to be poor credit risks. This "penny wise and pound foolish" mentality affected his business negatively over the years. In my opinion, it would have been better if we had used our energies to become a first class investment firm rather than making feeble efforts to make loans to various businesses with shaky financials.

As a partnership we did not have much capital beyond the net worth of the sole partner, and I thought we used our clients' credit balances the wrong way. Mr. Schimmelpenninck set himself on a course of trying to stay small and surviving by working along the edges, running a combination of businesses rather than look for growth as an investment firm. He certainly had the prominence and the brains to do the latter, but he preferred the former. His investment philosophy reflected the attitudes of the people he had grown up with. The old guard made little or no effort to research the financial record of a company and relied heavily on what they heard from friends and acquaintances and on "hunch."

Mr. Schimmelpenninck was a long-time member of the board of the Amsterdam Stock Exchange, served on the board of several large listed companies and had a major interest in a lucrative business of issuing bearer certificates against U.S. shares owned by a trustee company, similar to today's ADRs (American Depositary Receipts that are traded in the U.S. and are issued here against foreign securities held in trust). His strategy of staying small and his motto "it will last our time," as he often expressed to me, ultimately prompted me to leave and seek my fortune in America. I just did not want to spend the rest of my life in a business environment that offered little or no opportunities for growth. Still, making this break was a very tough decision because I was very fond of my boss.

The offices of Jokru were on the second, main or parlor, floor of an old historic house on *the Herengracht* and Charles Dickens would have felt completely at home there. The ground floor was as usual used for kitchen and service purposes. Our vault, was built into the ground floor but was accessible only from the second floor. Up a short flight of stairs one came on to a landing with an opaque glass wall with a door and a small window with a buzzer. Employees entered the office through the door next to the window. All securities were delivered through this window. Clients who came to see Mr. Schimmelpenninck were ushered in through another door. On the front side, where the gracht (canal) was, were two rooms, one the principal (parlor) room for Mr. Schimmelpenninck and his secretary and the other for the two *procuratiehouders*, managers who could sign for the firm. Each room had one phone.

In the back and open to the *procuratiehouders* room was a large office area with three rows of desks. The desks, made of solid oak, were positioned side by side and faced each other. Each row had three or four people on each side. There was one telephone in the middle of the first row, placed on a platform that could swing around so many people could use it. In the middle row was a primitive switchboard staffed by Juffrouw Drijver, Miss Drijver, to handle calls for the three or four phones. All the employees, many of whom had worked together for twenty years or more, addressed each other as Miss. or *Juffrouw* or Mr. or *Meneer*. No first name familiarity here. However, they did use the familiar *"Je, Jij and Jouw"* amongst themselves but not when addressing me. As is customary in the Netherlands, Mr. Schimmelpenninck was addressed as "Mister" with the honorific "U" of course. In contrast, when he spoke to his employees he always used the familiar form, for the men, using only their last name, and for the women *"Juffrouw"* followed by the last name.

There were no electronic or electromechanical devices in use. The typewriters were all manual. I think there were four in the office. Adding machines were mistrusted, and not needed because the bookkeepers could add up numbers faster than anybody operating a machine could. All books were kept by hand, and purchase and sale confirmations as well as monthly statements were handwritten in beautiful curly handwriting. Including the two managers, there were about fourteen employees. Over the seven years I would work at Jokru, I got to know them all very well. Many of them lived quiet lives without much excitement as one could expect of office clerks who had not seen a raise in many years and were just emerging from ten years of economic depression with a five-year-war period added on. Yet, several of them were interesting people with surprisingly varied backgrounds.

In the front room resided the two managers, Mr. Lette van Oostvoorne (another self-acquired, add on name) and Mr. Swijters. Lette was the son-in-law of "Dr." Heineken the largest and most valued Jokru client and the CEO and chairman of the board of the beer empire that bore his name. Mr. Heineken had received an honorary doctorate from some university and henceforth was called Dr. Heineken by everybody. Just before I came, the Heineken accounts had been pulled out which was a tremendous blow to the firm. It was not quite clear to me why this happened, but it certainly did not strengthen the position of Lette who was in my opinion not the brightest light on the Christmas tree. He spent most of his time babbling on the phone with society friends and handled the account of our most successful credit client, a firm managed by a Mr. Holtzhaus. Later the Heineken daughter divorced him and his hold on his position at Jokru weakened further. Right after his divorce, Lette no longer came to the office in a large Kaiser Fraser car but with a tiny two-person Fiat 500 which prompted Mr. Verbrugge to ask him, "gut meneer, is ie gekrompen?" (gee sir, did he shrink?). Mr. Swijters had come up through the ranks. He had been prominent in the Resistance movement during the war and earned his promotion partly to that but mostly to his ability to be a good office manager.

In the back room were all the others. I was given a desk on one side of the first bank of desks, between Mr. de Bree and Mr. Moonen. Mr. de Bree was a very modest man who lived a life of "quiet desperation," as novelists would say. He had lost both his parents at a very young age and had been raised in the old city-owned orphanage, which is now a museum for the City of Amsterdam. Children who were under the care of this institution used to wear uniforms which were on one side red and the other black, the colors of the city of Amsterdam. De Bree had still been subjected to this indignity, which could be seen as giving the orphans a stamp of being "different" for the rest of their lives. Apologists claimed it was viewed as a batch of honor by the orphans. De Bree had married a mousy German woman who was a maidservant in town and came from East Germany, the part that was overrun by the Soviet army. She had not heard from her parents or any other relatives since the war. The de Bree's had several children. He never told us much about his family or what he did in his spare time. The only thing he said from time to time was, *"Het leven is duf"* (life is dull).

Mr. Moonen was much livelier and would become my great friend. He was a true Amsterdammer, or *Mokumer* as the local dialect calls it, and came from a working-class family. His father had worked in a factory and when he retired from his lifelong job, he received a nice watch and a medal (a low-level decoration of the Order of Orange Nassau) and a hearty "thank you" from his bosses but no pension, of course. That is the way it was in the good old days. To make a living after retirement, his father operated a small cigar store where he worked almost until his death, and Mr. Moonen went there each week for an evening to keep the books. Mr. Moonen's wife was also a former German maid servant but much livelier and more attractive than Mrs. de Bree. The Moonen's had two sons and lived in a small apartment until Mr. Schimmelpenninck offered Moonen a side job as manager of a complex of houses for low-income, deserving people. He was on the board of the charitable foundation that owned the property. It was at a canal, the Ruysdaelkade, east of the Rijks Museum. Moonen lived there for practically nothing and in turn collected rent from the people living in the complex and kept an eye on things. He loved living there because his place was more centrally located and had a view over the canal, and it related in many ways the history of Amsterdam. He enjoyed telling me about the conversations he had with the tenants, mostly simple, old retirees, as he made his weekly rounds to collect rent. Moonen had a great interest in the city's rich history and traditions and over the years as we walked back and forth from the office to the stock exchange he would take me on different routes and tell me about the buildings, the neighborhoods and the people we saw.

De Bree was working on the cashing of interest and dividend coupons. All securities we kept for clients had sheets of coupons attached and when a dividend was declared, an ad appeared in the papers telling us which number coupon to clip and what would be paid for it. The same happened with interest coupons attached to bonds. De Bree later became cashier. Moonen's job was to handle deliveries of all securities and making sure securities that had been purchased ended up in the right deposits and were entered properly in our books. To that end he kept enormously thick books called *Nummer Boeken* – number books. If one of our clients had bought a security, it was physically delivered to our office and entered by hand in Moonen's numbers book, with the date of trade, from whom it was bought and the name of the client. Often clients kept their securities in custody with special separate custodian banks, either the entire security or only the front leaf or mantel, while the coupon sheet stayed with us. So after receiving the security our client had bought, Moonen often had to deliver all or part of it out again to a custodian. This whole cumbersome system was reversed in case of a sale. I believe it no longer exists, but there were good reasons for people to have separate custodians, because Jokru was a partnership and if it would have gotten into financial difficulties; creditors could attach the securities belonging to its clients. Shortly after the war there had been a famous bankruptcy of a brokerage firm which left many of its clients with large losses.

Runners made all deliveries by hand, riding around town on a bike. Our runner Schooneberg, when not on his rounds, was sitting at a small table at the end of our row. His one passion in life was *Blauw Wit*, a football (soccer) club that belonged to the top competition league in Amsterdam but was a perpetual underdog to the much more powerful Ajax club, which was supported by Moonen and others. So every Monday morning when *Blauw Wit* had lost again, Schooneberg's week started badly. Somehow he seemed to relish his position as the underdog. In front of me sat Juffrouw van Vuuren, a good-looking, cheerful, sturdy woman who lived in Halfweg, a village half-way between Amsterdam and Haarlem. She commuted by tram. When I had acquired a car and came to work in it on Saturday mornings, I often gave her a ride home and joked she helped keep my small car on the road under windy conditions. Miss van Vuuren was in charge of the vault and had to take care of the securities of our clients. Most people had their own portfolios, bundles of securities tied together with string, but stocks everybody owned, such as Royal Dutch, were kept together with the names of the owners written on a scrap of paper and attached to them with a pin. She had to haul all the coupon sheets out whenever a dividend or interest coupon had to be collected and clip the coupons by hand. Next to her was a young girl, who was her assistant and general roustabout, and on the other side Mr. May. May was a jolly man who was better educated than the others. His job was to credit all client accounts for dividends and interest received and handle stock dividends, rights offerings etc.

Behind me was the second row. On my side was Miss Drijver, the telephone operator, and Mr. Haape, the cashier. Haape was a small old fashioned looking man with a goatee, pince-nez glasses and fairly long, curly grey hair. He would soon retire, but when I came he was still very much in evidence. He had a hot temper that flared up when too many deliveries came at the same time in the morning. He kept a thermometer on his desk and complained constantly about the temperature, which he thought was often too high. This was not altogether nonsense. There was no air conditioning and there were no fans. The ladies kept the windows tightly shut except on hot summer days, and many people smoked. With so many people in one room, the air got quite thick from time to time. Mr. Haape's plaintive voice exclaiming, *"vijfenzeventig graden"* (seventy-five degrees), was often heard. Mr. Haape also had been fiercely anti–German during the war, and when the Germans proclaimed Holland would henceforth be on Central European or Berlin time as opposed to its own time, he refused to accept it. He still kept his watch religiously on what he called "Amsterdamse tijd" (Amsterdam time) and was angry that the Dutch government had kept the Central European Time after the Germans left. Whenever we spoke about the time of day, he would give us his version, which sometimes led to confusion. In his vacations he liked to take long walks, probably without Mrs. Haape whom nobody had ever seen. He would go to the Hook of Holland and walk along the beach all the way to the top of North Holland in several days.

Facing Mr. Haape was Mr. Verbrugge, the head bookkeeper, one of the smartest employees. He kept the accounts for the firm and all clients in long hand in big books that were carried every evening, together with Mr. Moonen's numbers books, down to the vault, for safekeeping. Mr. Verbrugge was married but childless. He and his wife had a boxer and since that was my favorite dog, I had many discussions about boxers with him. Over time his face was beginning to look more and more like that of his boxer since he would constantly talk about his dog, while pulling faces and making noises like the animal.

Next to him was Miss de Voogd, a lady of a better social background than most. She was well spoken and articulate but very plain and not in good health, a typical example of the often difficult life unmarried women had. There were not many opportunities open to them. She assisted Mr. Verbrugge and hand-wrote many of the account statements for our clients.

Finally there were Mr. Fruitier and Miss Rientjes in the corner. They handled correspondence and Fruitier was also a runner from time to time. Fruitier did the filing and Moonen would prod me to watch him look puzzled when he could not quite remember the alphabet anymore and would mumble it from the beginning to find the letter he wanted. Miss Rientjes was also a source for many chuckles. She was a bit of a hypochondriac and had a tendency to claim she had also experienced every ailment, no matter how strange, that other people were talking about. Once Swijters had an accident that happens to many Dutch men when they are a bit careless climbing on their bikes and slip off the saddle, hurting their crotch on the bar. When he was telling us about that in guarded terms, of course, Miss Rientjes piped up and said she had had that too. Everybody yelled *"Dat kan niet"* (that is impossible).

Everybody knew that our former client, the very rich Dr. Heineken, was a lecherous old man who frequented the bars behind our office on the Rembrandtplein, often with young ladies of questionable reputation. On her way home Miss Rientjes had seen him reel around a few establishments on the Plein. The next day she mentioned to her colleagues what a hard-working man the old Dr. Heineken still was, making the rounds in the evening, inspecting all the cafés for his beer business. Everybody snickered.

My first assignment was to go with Fruitier on his errands. The objective was to introduce me to the business center of Amsterdam and the location of the offices of the firms and banks we did business with. My entire training was geared towards learning the details of the business from the ground up and only from an administrative point of view. Little or no attention was paid to investment research or trading techniques. I had to acquire all I knew in that area myself through trial and error. Moonen thought I should first of all learn all about his world of settling transactions and delivering securities which was all important to him. I soon understood that the business was run along old-fashioned lines and that I should pay attention to all these administrative details if I wanted to be useful.

I enjoyed going to Jokru every day and my social life in the evenings at my lodgings improved significantly after I managed to move in with Oc in the Vondelstraat. In the weekends I went home of course and Netty and I met as often as we could. We planned to marry the next summer and that put us under great pressure to find a place to live. This was no easy task since housing was still extremely scarce. We looked in Heemstede, a place we knew because it was near Bloemendaal where Opa and Oma Schieferdecker lived. Initially we developed plans to buy the top floor of a house near the station and renovate it so we could live there independently from the people downstairs. We would have to build a new staircase outside in the back of the house and do some extensive renovation inside. We liked the location, but upon further reflection the whole idea was too cumbersome. Looking around we found a street where a developer was building several rows of houses. Under the rules of the housing allocation regime, you could not move into a town and buy or rent an existing house. These were reserved for the locals. You could only move in if you had a "residence permit" and it was virtually impossible to get such a permit if you came from elsewhere and had not worked locally for a number of years and wanted to rent a place in town. To live in Amsterdam, for instance you had to put your name on a waiting list and when a place became available, the housing authority would notify you and tell you where you were supposed to live. You had little or no choice to select a place to your liking. However, you could buy a newly built place and move in. This was a rule intended to support the floundering construction industry. These conditions made it extremely difficult for newlyweds to settle anywhere unless they had the money to buy a newly built house, a strange circumstance in a country that was moving more and more towards a socialist welfare state that tried to level the playing field for everybody. Luckily Pa was more than willing to support us financially in this venture. He helped us in selecting the house and in the negotiations with the builder. Thus we had a place to settle in after we got married. My salary at Jokru was still minuscule, but I thought we could swing the deal using the proceeds of a small portfolio I had inherited from Oom George and my father's support. We signed up with a developer for a house in the Alberdingk Thymlaan no. 35 for the then, for us, enormous sum of 35,000 Guilders, which at the going rate was equivalent to about $9,200. We loved the site, which was in a quiet street close to the station. Most important, our side of the street backed up to a small *slootje* (little canal), beyond which were the wooded grounds of a large estate that would most likely remain undeveloped. Our living room would look out at the greenery of this estate. In crowded Holland, it is and was terribly difficult to find a place that does not look out at other rows of houses. This was a tremendously exciting development for us, and we started planning feverishly for the wedding and the house. Our wedding date would be June 30th 1951. Mammie van Kleffens quickly stepped in and took control of virtually the entire wedding organization leaving little room for Netty to put in her two-cents worth. But that was the way most weddings were organized in the days that parents still had a lot more control over their children, even when they were well in their twenties.

Things were looking up for us in many ways. In early 1951 Mr. Schimmelpenninck called me into his office and said he wanted to send me to New York City for a brief visit on a special assignment. I accepted with great glee, of course. As it turned out a Jokru-related company that issued Dutch bearer certificates against American stock certificates it held in trust, owned a large block of shares of General Motors. G.M. had decided to split its stock two for one, I believe, and instead of simply issuing a new certificate for each one held, they wanted stockholders to turn in the old ones and issue new paper against them. This transaction presented a huge problem for our company, which carried the simple name of *Amsterdamsch Adminstratiekantoor voor Amerikaanse Waarden.* Later I often got a chuckle out of my American friends when reciting this name for them, and I would add for extra effect the name of the holding company that issued shares for Philips Electronics – *N.V. Gemeenschappelijkbezit van Aandelen Philips Gloeilampenfabrieken.*

The problem our office faced was how to transport the certificates to New York City without incurring horrendous insurance premiums. Dutch insurers were not eager to take on a high dollar risk since dollars were as scarce as hen's teeth in Holland. G.M. would supply duplicates of any securities lost, but that would take a long time and our office was legally obligated to supply U.S. certificates for any Dutch ones turned in for redemption at any time. If all or part of our shipment to the U.S. was lost, we would still be obligated to supply original stock certificates to anybody redeeming our shares. As it turned out the lowest premiums would be charged if the securities were put on a ship in the purser's safe with a reliable passenger going along on the trip. The reliable passenger, in this case me, would hold one key to the safe and the purser the other one. On fairly short notice I got a visa for a brief business trip to America and boarded the Westerdam of the Holland America Line. This ship was a combination freighter/passenger vessel. Space was still scarce, so all passengers had to double up, except me because of my key.

The crossing was very comfortable and seas were calm despite the season – it was February. The passengers were mostly business people, a few emigrants and people who went to visit relatives who would pay for their stay in America. Among businessmen, bulb growers were a big group. They traveled every year to the U.S., rented a car and drove all over the country to visit stores and dealers who sold their bulbs. The barman told me they were a rowdy bunch on the way out, but on the return voyage they were all subdued because, as he put it, when they come back "mother is standing on the dock to greet them." As I mentioned in an earlier chapter, the woman who was my father's first wife was also on board, at least I suspect it was she. When we arrived, I entered New York Harbor the proper way, seeing the Statue of Liberty from a ship arriving from abroad. We docked in Hoboken, N.J., the traditional destination for the Dutch ships. Mr. Schimmelpenninck was there. He had taken a plane over and brought two friends from Brown Brothers Harriman along whom he had persuaded to help bring the securities to the transfer agent downtown. I met Frank Hoch, a Swiss–American and Maarten van Hengel, a former Dutchman there. Nine years later those two would be my bosses at Brown Brothers. Frank had brought his car and we packed my suitcase with the certificates in its trunk. Earlier, when I passed customs, I was asked by a surly customs officer, "What's in that suitcase?" I responded, "One hundred thousand and fifty shares of General Motors." (I am not sure anymore if that was the right number, but I knew the total number and it was huge.) He was baffled and said, "No kidding," opened the suitcase, lifted the corner of one package a little and let me go. At the General Motor's transfer agent's office we met with a friendly low-level executive. When Mr. Schimmelpenninck asked him if we were the biggest shareholder of G.M., he said he did not know, leaving us comfortably basking in the belief that we were tremendously important. G.M. has many more much larger shareholders, of course, such as pension funds and large mutual funds.

Brown Brothers had reserved rooms for us at the St. Regis Hotel, a pricey place for dollar-poor people. As Mr. Schimmelpenninck had some other business to do, I had a few free days to spend in New York City before returning. It was cold and it rained a lot which negatively colored my first impressions of the world's greatest city. The view from the deck of our ship had been overwhelming, of course. It is difficult to describe what you think and feel when you see the massive cluster of buildings in downtown Manhattan looming through the morning haze, and you have never seen anything like it before. But once I was on the streets of Manhattan, I thought the city was kind of unwelcoming with impersonal streets lined by ugly brownstone buildings with fire escapes protruding from their facades. The building boom that changed New York City in the past thirty years had not yet started so I saw many more impersonal brick buildings than there are now. People were in a hurry and taxi drivers snarled in unintelligible English. On the other hand, when I asked a man in Macy's if he could tell me how to get to Gimbel's, he brought me over there himself and when he heard I was from Holland, asked all kinds of interested questions.

I even managed to get lost trying to reach the hotel where the Dobsons stayed. They were a young Shell family from Houston I had met aboard ship and who had been at our house as guests of my parents. You would think it would not be hard to find a place with all the streets and avenues numbered and at right angles, but if you turn the wrong way at the outset it can get confusing. After some back and forth, I found the Dobsons. The restaurant in their hotel was old style New York, noisy with a guy playing an organ in the corner, dimly lit with candles in little reddish glass bowls on the tables and a menu of large steaks with baked potatoes. Drinks were very potent, too. I still had to learn how to sip an American cocktail.

During my stay I even had to report to the U.S. Immigration Department. You entered a large room with row upon row of wooden benches like a station waiting room; you would sit down on the bench farthest away from the authorities and slide along, gradually working your way forward to the almighty Immigration Agents who barked out your name as your turn approached. The officers were impersonal and snarled at us, and I got a taste of what it must have been like to be an immigrant arriving at Ellis Island. Our hotel was first class and the dry overheated atmosphere inside it had a kind of antiseptic feel. After a few days of rain, when the sun started to shine on a Sunday, New York City all of sudden looked friendlier, and when we left I was much more intrigued by it and wanted to come back. Before leaving I went to a ladies store to buy a blouse for Netty. It was the latest thing in American fashion, a sort of wash and wear nylon contraption that did not need ironing, unknown in Holland. I picked out a saleslady who was about Netty's size, and she tried on various things for me. She was very helpful and friendly and tried to sell me much more than I could afford. I think Netty liked the blouse, but I believe the nylon material was uncomfortably warm to wear.

When we went to board our plane home, we experienced air travel as it used to be. We took a cab to the KLM agency on Fifth Avenue where all passengers were booked in right in the office. A bus picked us up and drove us to Idlewild Airport (later JFK), which was still under construction. There we boarded our plane directly from the bus. No fuss, no waiting and no security check. As is still the case, the American authorities were not interested in people leaving the country. For me that was surprising and compared favorably to all the rigmarole one had to go through when traveling from country to country in Europe. Coming into America was and is another story, of course. This was my first transatlantic flight. Our plane was a Lockheed Constellation, a sleek-looking four engine prop plane. We stopped in Gander, Newfoundland, where we walked around for a while and I was struck by the pale pasty-white complexion of the girls behind the coffee counter. They were half way of living through a long dark winter with little sun. The plane was very comfortable with large, wide seats similar to what you find now in first class. But compared to today's jets, it vibrated a lot. We had to make another landing in the middle of the night in Prestwick, Scotland. There we had to wait for a few hours as they fixed one of our engines. Today's jet engines are much more reliable and seldom fail, but in those days almost every other flight was subject to some mechanical delay. Sitting in the lobby with Mr. Schimmelpenninck for several hours, we had a long talk. He gave me a detailed description of his firm and its employees and I had the comfortable feeling that he saw me as a comer and somebody he could confide in. Throughout the seven years I worked there our relationship remained excellent and I became more and more his right hand man and a true "insider."

When I returned back home, I felt like a hero. I had been to a country where everybody wanted to go but few people really could travel. America was then also a superpower but in many respects perhaps more admired than now. It had a rich, dollar-based economy with unlimited resources and opportunities where everything was possible, and people lived a life of luxury surrounded by all sorts of wonderful new gadgets unknown in Europe. I told my friends who were listening enviously and with open mouths how I had seen trucks loaded with wrecked cars that were not all that old and that despite their lack of old age had been flattened like pancakes and were trucked out to be melted down. This while in Holland every car was carefully repaired and kept running for decades. We could not imagine that you would just press a car into a pancake and bring it to a smelter. I also awed them by telling how I had seen a man walking in a New York street in a rainstorm. His umbrella blew out in the wind, and he promptly stuck it in a garbage can without breaking his stride for a second. My father had one umbrella that he owned for years. This prized possession was carefully repaired by an umbrella repair shop when it showed a defect. I had gotten my first taste of the postwar consumer economy.

When spring came, preparations for our wedding got more and more serious. Netty was often very frustrated by her inability to control her mother and have a say in the organization of her own wedding, but on the other hand she received a large quantity of household goods, towels, sheets, pillowcases, blankets, dust cloth, etc., etc., everything that belonged to what was called an uitzet (trousseau). We still have some of the sturdy Dutch things Netty received at that time in our household, and now sixty-plus years later I sometimes run across a kitchen towel that I recognize as being an original from the trousseau. Steamrollering right along Mammy also decided who would be invited to the wedding party, which turned out to be mostly relatives and a few friends. Our own, younger, contingent was small and restricted to Eelco and his wife Louky (since Eelco was married he could not serve as usher), Frits Greup, Rob Laane and Octave van Crugten, my good friends and Bruidsjonkers, or ushers, and Tilly, Netty's sister; Lucia LeFèvre Netty's favorite cousin and Jetty Terwogt, Netty's (then) best friend.

But I am ahead of my story. In Amsterdam I started going to the Stock Exchange, which was a major and most welcome step ahead for me. The Amsterdam Stock Exchange is considered to be the oldest in the world. It is located kitty-corner to the famous exchange building designed by the renowned Dutch early modern architect Berlage. In tourist brochures The *Beurs van Berlage* is often called the stock exchange, which is incorrect. In my days it was a commodity/insurance/shipping exchange which we called the *Koopmansbeurs* (the Commerce Exchange). The stock exchange is located in a less famous, more old-fashioned nineteenth century building next door. It had a large, open trading floor with a kiosk in the middle, a small building that had a projected tickertape running around its roofline. On the floor were a large number of people who all had their prescribed positions. These were the *hoekmannen*, or specialists, who each were authorized to make markets in a certain number of securities. Along the walls were a large number of wooden booths with usually a table, a few chairs or benches and a phone. Most banks and investment firms had a booth where they could sit and do their business.

Several years before I came, the Amsterdam Stock Exchange had admitted the commercial banks as members, a decision that many brokerage firms saw as a fatal mistake. It severely curtailed the business and growth prospects for the much smaller pure brokerage firms as the banks developed their own trading and investment departments and used their power over their clientele to capture a larger and larger share of the trading volume.

Most inactive securities were traded on the basis of one daily price. The specialist would match all buys and sells together and arrive at a price that was established on the basis of his "book" and the buy and sell limits he had. Active stocks were traded in a so-called *"open-hoek"* wherein the specialists (there were usually two competing firms dealing in each security) were trading with each other and whoever else joined their "crowd." This was done in a so called open "outcry" system. It was in the *open-hoek* that the real fun was. Whenever there was an announcement or an event, positive or negative that focused a lot of investor attention on one stock, say Royal Dutch Petroleum or Philips, the crowd surrounding the *hoekmannen* could be huge and the pressure of the bodies of the traders, pushing and shoving to get to the center of activity, could be enormous. In an open hoek you could trade with whoever heard your bid or offer and by making a quick note in your beursboekje, a special small book we all carried, the deal was done. After the close you would go around and find your counterpart and confirm the trade. It was all done on the principle of "my word is my bond." Normally you would just enter your order with a hoekman either with a limit or for execution at the market or "middle price" between high and low which was the customary way to settle all transactions.

It took me a while before I was authorized to trade on the floor, but when I became a *gemachtigde bediende* – an authorized clerk, I did trade often and found the atmosphere at the exchange fun, interesting and invigorating. Today the trading floor of the Amsterdam market has changed drastically. It is full of desks, computer screens and electronic devices using trading systems that are very different from the ones we were used to. Once I was authorized to trade, I took the place of Swijters at the exchange which allowed him to stay at the office and run the place there. Everyday I walked with Moonen to the Beurs and sat there for about two and a half hours, handling our business and calling clients to tell them what was going on.

Over time I made several good friends at the exchange, mostly young men who worked for other firms. We organized a group of young Beurs people that got together from time to time and invited speakers. One time, when I was already more than six years at the exchange, we organized a big charity drive for the Princess Beatrix Cancer Fund which was a great success. We threw a big party on the floor for a lot of people who had never been at the exchange and sold shares to the public that had been donated by the companies involved. My big coup was to get a certificate of Royal Dutch for the auction which was worth about four thousand guilders, a huge amount in those days. I managed to get it from Mr. Piet Feith, Pa van Kleffens' best friend who was the chief in-house lawyer for the company.

My first steps on the exchange were much less auspicious, however. I had my share of mistakes and costly errors, the worst one, and it still hurts when I think about it, was a sale that should have been a purchase of a stock that was not all that liquid so that the transaction could not easily be reversed and the firm had to swallow the trade for a few days before we could get out of it.

The stock exchange was famous for the antics of its membership. Many men on the floor were independent operators, small one-or two-man firms, day traders or specialists in areas like options (in those days a very small, esoteric part of the business.) These independents came every day to the exchange determined to have fun. All sorts of sophomoric stunts were executed and newcomers were targeted for special attention. I was targeted too, but as usual, I do not seem to be a very attractive target for people who look for a vulnerable soul to tease or give a hard time in some hazing procedure or other. One of the favorite tricks was to stand next to you, say on your right and tap you on your left shoulder. You would of course look left in the direction of the tap and find nothing. A man reading the paper or quotation sheet could find it suddenly aflame. We all smoked everywhere, certainly on the floor of the exchange, and a newspaper was a tempting target for a guy with a lighter. A fellow who had been married decades ago on December 21st, the longest night, was always serenaded on his wedding anniversary with a chorus of men singing the bridal march. A man who had a hot temper and was often very agitated when things did not go his way was called hete Dirk – hot Dirk. As he agitatedly paced the floor of the exchange with somebody he had buttonholed, waving his arms and arguing, a group would start following him around (unbeknownst to him). The group would suddenly burst out singing *heeete Diiirek, heeete Diiirek,* to the tune of the Volga Boatmen opera number.

The bosses and partners of the larger firms would come to the exchange after lunch and walk around discussing issues with each other and ignoring the horseplay of the little guys. On the floor of the exchange I rediscovered a friend from boy scout days, Adolf Sirtema van Grovestins. Adolf had joined a stock exchange firm called Beels & co, de Clercq and Boon Hartsink. Ever since we were frequently in touch with each other, and Adolf often stayed with us in the U.S. when he was here on business. He had a brilliant career in the investment world, moving from one bank to the next as they merged, and ended up as a managing director of ABN Amro, the largest Dutch bank. We sailed in the Virgin Islands with Adolf and his wife Louise and always made a point of visiting them when in Holland. Adolf's death on February 27, 2011 came as a tremendous shock for us. We remember him fondly.

A serious matter I had to pay a great deal of attention to was our honeymoon. This was a complicated assignment because we did not want to stay just in the Netherlands, we wanted to travel abroad. But I did not have all that much money and needed to select a country where the exchange rate with the guilder was favorable. Switzerland was very pricey and out of the question, so was France. Austria was the best bargain. That country was just emerging from being part of the Third Reich of Adolf Hitler and eager to attract tourists. We needed passports and visa and Austrian schillings, which you had to get in cash from a bank. We could not buy travelers checks and credit cards had not yet been invented. I wanted to travel in style with my bride and bought tickets to fly to Innsbrück with KLM. I selected a hotel Igler Hof in a little village outside Innsbrück called Igls. This proved to be a good selection. It was a nice resort near town so when the weather was not good we could take the tramway into town and enjoy ourselves there. Otherwise we could go swimming in a lake and hike all over the mountains.

As the big day approached, I rented a car from a local Amsterdam garage. Car rental companies did not yet exist. We would use this car to escape from Wassenaar to Amsterdam and go to the hotel where we would stay before departing the next day by plane. The car was a little Skoda, a Czech-made car that was not very glamorous but served the purpose. In addition to these preparations I had to buy a morning coat and top hat for the wedding. I should have rented this outfit because I rarely used it afterwards, but I felt I had to have my own to be a really well-equipped groom.

In Wassenaar preparations were reaching a fever pitch. Long before our wedding date Netty and I had jumped through all the hoops to become members of the Doopsgezinde Kerk, our church. We had found our most favored pastor willing to marry us in the main church in The Hague. We had registered ourselves in the town hall in Wassenaar and arranged for a civil marriage ceremony as required by Dutch law. The plan was to go to the town hall first in a procession of limousines and get married in front of the civil authorities there. This ceremony required us to bring two witnesses, which gave us an opportunity to honor people that were dear to us. I chose my grandfather, who was then ninety-one years old, and Eelco Apol. Netty chose her grandmother Omi van Someren Gréve and Oom Eelco, her uncle. We would then go to the church in The Hague where the "real" marriage ceremony would take place. After the service we would have a brief reception in the church to greet all the people who had come to the service. After that event we would return to Netty's house where we would have a dinner for the entire wedding party. The party consisted of our bridesmaids and ushers, Eelco and Louky Apol, Mr. and Mrs. Schimmelpenninck, the pastor and his wife, Mr. Jaspar (see below), Tante Jet and Tante Jetje, Oom Eelco and Tante Margaret, Oom Wim and Tante Soph, Oom Errie and Tante Pia, Lous and Jean Paschoud (Mammie's youngest sister and her husband), Pul and Til and our four parents, of course.

A few days before the wedding date we had a serious problem. Or rather, Til had a problem. Til worked in Geneva at that time. She would be one of Netty's bridesmaids and planned to come a few days in advance. She had organized a ride home with another Dutch girl who owned a car and had to go to Holland. Somewhere in northern France they had an accident. The car left the road and turned over in a ditch and Til broke her leg. She was transported to a rural hospital where the local doctor did an excellent job setting her leg and the Catholic nuns who ran the hospital treated her very well. The dilemma was how to get her home after she was allowed to travel and how to find a replacement for her in the bridal procession. A friend of Pa and Mammie van Kleffens, Mr. Jaspar who was a high official with the then just organized Benelux, the trade organization for Holland, Belgium and Luxembourg, offered to have his chauffeur pick Til up. Netty's cousin Lucy Lefèbre was happy to jump in and be a substitute bridesmaid. Mr. Jaspar was hastily added to the wedding party. He arrived with Tilly in his big Buick with chauffeur. Like all higher Dutch multinational bureaucrats of the postwar era Mr. Jaspar had immediately availed

OUR WEDDING. JUNE 30 1951.

himself of a big car with driver, and this time this extravagance proved to be very helpful. Til could stretch out on the back seat and be reasonably comfortable. When she came home, Til was in good shape and cheerful, but her leg was still a mess. She could definitely not walk behind her sister entering the church.

I rented the Skoda a few days early, which allowed me to go back and forth between Amsterdam and Voorburg. The protocol required that during the dinner there would be speeches by the two fathers, a few uncles and whoever else felt the urge to speak. At the end of the dinner, the groom had to make a speech in which he would thank his parents for raising him, his in laws for entrusting him with the bride, and respond to all the other speeches. Then he had to say a few words to his bride and all in all he had to stitch this all together into a reasonable presentation. I spent my time driving back and forth in the Skoda rehearsing what I wanted to say. I still do this when I want to rehearse for a speech I have to give. I find driving a car gives just the right isolation and background noise to enable me to focus on what I want to say, and I can speak out loud without feeling embarrassed.

I remember little of our wedding day. It was a stressful experience for both of us. I had the speech to worry about and also the names of all the people that might show up in the church. Netty had no speech obligation, but she was expected to remember all the presents we had received and thank the givers for the right present if they showed up in the reception line. We had a list of the presents handy and our ushers helped with this problem. One of them would announce the guests by name as they came down the .line and another would quickly look in the list to see who gave what and whisper into Netty's ear "Mrs. Jansen one soup spoon" or words to that effect. The photo album we have of our wedding shows our bridal party leaving Netty's house, all the men in striped pants and tails and top hats and the ladies in festive dresses and hats. Nobody looks very cheerful, although there are some smiles. A wedding is a solemn and serious event in Holland. We all clambered into one of the limousines that were ready for us and drove off to the town hall. In view of the importance of the guests, (not the bridal couple), the mayor had provided a police motorcycle escort so we were whisked over in no time. The town hall of Wassenaar is an attractive building; it used to be an old country estate that sits in the center of a beautiful park. The ceremony was dignified and brief and we were soon on our way to the church. There our favorite pastor, Dominee Tuininga married us. Wedding ceremonies in Dutch churches are not as brief and crisp as American ones. It is more or less an entire service with a sermon of some duration and several psalms being sung before a couple ties the knot. For me this all went by in a daze and only after we were at the reception did I begin to get my bearings again. Many people came, including almost all the Jokru employees in a bus hired for the occasion. This was very touching. They had been somewhat taken aback by my response to their question as to what I wanted to have as a present. I said I would like to have a nice tool kit. They thought this was much too prosaic, but I got a nice tool kit anyway and I kept it and used it for more than fifty years, which cannot be said about many other things we got.

Once we were back in Netty's house, we found an immense L shaped table laid out in the living room and caterers and waiters swarming around. Netty's father spoke first. He spoke from the heart and very well. He was good at speaking on his feet. After my father and many others spoke, I made my speech. It was at the end of the dinner, and I believe I succeeded reasonably well, despite the constant tugging at my sleeve by my mother who was seated next to me and thought I was making too many risqué comments. I was only trying to make it fun. It was a beautiful sunny day, and after the dinner we went into the garden where Tante Margaret took pictures of us with the new Kodachrome color film she had acquired in America. Color pictures were still a new phenomenon then. It was late afternoon when Netty and I had a chance to change into street clothes and drive off in our little car, which had of course a number of empty cans tied to it and a sign "just married." I had foreseen this and taken a knife along to cut off the cans. They were triumphantly brought back to Netty's house by a neighborhood dog. But there was little I could do about the rice they had thrown into the car. When I brought it back to the garage in Amsterdam I was worn out and no longer apprehensive about my newly married status. I just told them, "I just got married, and they threw a lot of rice into the car." The first night together of our married life was spent in the Doelen Hotel in Amsterdam.

The next morning we took a taxi to Schiphol. Everything was still very genteel and calm there at this airport, which is now huge and very busy. Passengers could sit on an outdoor terrace, sip the inevitable Dutch *kopje koffie*, look at the planes and wait until their departure was announced. Netty was taken aback by the small size of our plane, an old wartime DC-3 (Dakota), but there was little she could do about it. To our pleasant surprise Tante Maragret was also waiting for a plane on the terrace. When we entered our plane we discovered that Netty was seated way up front and my seat was in the back. We managed to convince the stewardess (flight attendants came later) that we were newlyweds who wanted to sit together, and we took off on what was Netty's first flight. The plane bounced along to Bavaria and from there to Innsbrück, for quite a while following a seemingly very narrow valley to the airport. You had the impression that you could look straight into the living rooms of the houses on the hills on each side. We arrived on a pleasant sunny day in the capital of the Austrian Tyrol. Our hotel Iglerhof was nice and we had a wonderful time there. I had been given a three-week vacation, which was an exception. Jokru employees normally had only two-week vacations, but when I asked Mr. Schimmelpenninck for three, he caved in.

After a while I discovered that I might not have brought enough money along for three weeks and was quite alarmed about it. I wrote my father (telephones were seldom or never used internationally) asking for help. I knew he had clout in Austria because he was overseeing the Austrian Shell oil fields near Vienna run by the local company called *Rohölgewinnungsaktiengesellschaft*. He managed to get the head man there to send me some cash through a local lawyer. Soon a solemn looking Innsbrück lawyer showed up with a briefcase full of banknotes. I signed a receipt, and we could continue our honeymoon in good style. We took many hikes in the mountains around Igls. One day I decided to suggest to Netty that we could climb the mountain ridge on the other side of the valley in which Innsbrück was located. You could also get there by cable car, but that would cost a lot so we climbed up. Halfway Netty stretched out in the grass and announced she could not go any further. Luckily I convinced her that we just had to go on because there was no cable car stop nearby. I was hugely relieved when she got back on her feet and marched on, avoiding our first marital crisis. We also made a trip by rented car and driver to Bolzano in Italy across the Brenner Pass, the pass where Hitler and Mussolini had met several times, in a different era, not too long ago. On another excursion we went to Salzburg. In the evenings we would dance in the hotel bar. A local orchestra played what the Austrians thought sounded like swing music but resembled more the Tyrolean music they were used to. Several times we went to the local lake for a swim. It was all quite simple and rustic, but we had a wonderful time.

Since our contractor had not finished our house on time, we had asked Opa and Oma Schieferdecker if we could live with them in Bloemendaal for a while. We had some of our furniture brought over there and settled in nicely. Every day I rode my bicycle to the Bloemendaal station and commuted from there to Amsterdam. Netty had a few brisk battles with Oma in the kitchen as both got up early determined to make my breakfast. Ultimately she decided that Oma had the upper hand in her own house and let it be. In the evenings we would sit in our own living room, the one Tante Jetje had used many years ago, and had a cup of tea. Opa would come to visit and enjoy our tea. He would say, "At last, a real cup of tea." Oma was a very health conscious lady and always made excessively weak tea for him. We thought that at his age, he was ninety-one, consuming strong tea really did not matter anymore.

We were given a nice young male boxer dog which we called Janus. He was a wonderful cheerful puppy, but unfortunately Janus" life ended early and cruelly. He broke away from his leash while walking with Netty and got run over by a car. We buried him in Opa's backyard next to Duco's grave. The death of Janus was a real tragedy for us and Netty was very upset about it for quite a while. In late fall, our house was finally ready, and we started our move to begin our life together in our own house – at last.

For today's standards our house was quite simple, for us it was a palace, a treasured home. We lived there for seven years, until we left for America and we were very happy there.

Our address was Alberdingk Thymlaan 35. The Dutch don't go for easy street names if they can help it. Our street was named after a well-known Dutch writer. As is customary in Holland, a whole neighborhood will have names that have some generic link. In our case it was writers. All the streets in our neighborhood had writer's names. Sometimes it is painters or birds or flowers, you name it, they have it. Some of the names, like ours, are hard to use abroad and hard to spell out for non–Dutch speakers, but that does not seem to faze the bureaucrats who think them up.

We had a backyard that looked out over the grounds of an estate, not very well manicured but therefore freer than most other Dutch houses. The small canal behind us meant that we were responsible for the upkeep of its banks, in line with the Dutch system that controls all the intricacies of the vast system of waterways in Holland. As soon as we were expecting our first child we built a sturdy fence along the water, of course. Our front door was on the side of the house, facing the door of our neighbors. At first we had no car and no garage. We built one later. Downstairs were basically only two rooms, the kitchen and the living/dining room which had a big window looking out over the backyard. The kitchen fronted the street. Next to the kitchen was the coal shed with a side door where we kept the coal we burned in our central heating. The furnace was in the kitchen. There also was a toilet downstairs. Upstairs were two larger bedrooms and a small one and a bathroom which had a toilet, a shower and a washbasin. One of the bedrooms also had a washbasin. On the third floor we had an attic in which we later built a bedroom for our live-in girl. This room also had a washbasin. That was all. There are many photos and movies now on DVD showing this house. We were very proud of it and took extremely good care of it.

Moving in was a snap. We did not have much furniture and what we had came from different directions. Our dining room table and chairs came from an antique dealer in The Hague where we had bought it. Our bedroom furniture came from Amsterdam. We still have the dining room chairs and we only said good bye to the bedroom furniture more than fifty years later when we left our house in Riverside for our apartment in Greenwich. We soon settled in and developed a routine. I commuted from the Heemstede station to Amsterdam and Netty ran the household and built relationships with our neighbors. The street consisted entirely of new houses so everybody was new to the area, which facilitated contact. The Dutch are not that easy in building neighborhood relationships. Your neighbors have to be of the right age, class and background, etc., before you make a move. It was not long before Netty announced she thought she was pregnant and that signaled another big change in our lives.

20 : *Heemstede*

Years before I was married and still an unattached, uncouth young male, unburdened by too many life experiences and devoid of wisdom, I never shirked from expressing opinions on almost everything. One of my favorite targets was marriage and married bliss, and I used to make jokes about getting hitched and building a little nest with twelve of everything and getting trapped in a stifling quagmire of household implements. But soon after Netty and I were married and settled down in Heemstede, I changed my tune, not because I felt I had to, or out of shame or regret, but simply because it was just so much fun, so wonderful to be together every day in our own place and to share all our experiences – important ones as well as unimportant ones. We enjoyed furnishing our house, acquiring various and sundry pieces of furniture, and the many other sometimes mundane things one needs to run a household. I never would have thought when I was in my early twenties that I would be so enthusiastic over what nowadays would be a very small and primitive washing machine or a small refrigerator, but I was. We hung pictures, installed lights and radios, set up a ping- pong table in the attic and worked in the small garden. In our first winter I learned how to keep the coal-burning, central-heating furnace going when we would be gone over a weekend and get the big pieces of slag out after we returned. As soon as we occupied our house, tradesmen and a gardener came to offer their services. Those were the days! People were actually competing to get our business. Our gardener came with a bakfiets – a tricycle pedaled from the rear and a large wooden container between the two front wheels, to carry his equipment. This very hard-working man, called de Winter, soon progressed to a motorized bakfiets and from there to a small truck. He reflected the rapid economic growth Holland was enjoying at the time. We established a policy that gave the business, if we needed it, to whoever came first and made a good impression. Netty investigated all stores nearby. It was still a time without super-markets so you had to go to the baker, the butcher, the dry goods store, etc. They also delivered their merchandise to your house if you wanted. Later on the Dutch would also fall victim to supermarkets where you had to get your own merchandise and carry it out yourself after receiving impersonal service at the checkout counter, but at that time, we were still unaware of this new trend.

In early 1952, after Netty discovered she was pregnant she became a patient of Dr. van Luin, a general practitioner nearby, who would deliver our first two children. He was a very nice man, the epitome of the family doctor, who had his practice at his house. He was always ready to make house calls and radiated confidence. We trusted him implicitly and were certain he knew his way around medicine. We had a cold winter and I got worried that Netty was walking around pregnant and almost barefoot, so I invested in a pair of English sheepskin boots for her, and we went out to the stores in Amsterdam to look for a winter coat. This coat, a grey, fuzzy, fake-fur job was our pride and joy and our first major investment in clothes. Over the years there was much more to follow, of course. As Netty got bigger, we also wanted to buy some clothes for her to wear while expecting her child. This proved to be an odd experience. In most stores we found women who looked at us with a measure of disdain and who responded to our inquiries, sniffing that they did not have any special clothes for expectant mothers. This prompted me to say at one establishment, "Well, you know Miss, it does happen sometimes."

That first summer, with Netty very pregnant, Pa van Kleffens decided to organize a vacation for his entire family in the Vosges area in France. He had a taste for the unusual and for out-of-the-way places, and came up with a small hotel called *L'Auberge du Frère Joseph.* This was a small family hotel in Ventron, a hamlet in the Vosges, the hilly area near Strasbourg. Pa and Mammie drove there with Pul in their small British made Austin car that was called Eva. It was a white car. Its predecessor was also an Austin. It was black and called Adam. Netty and I took the train to Strasbourg where we were met by Pa. We arrived fairly late and it was dark. Pa was a somewhat eccentric driver who tended to drive along the center of a road, assuming the stripe painted there was intended to help drivers keep their cars centered on the road. When he met oncoming traffic, he would move to the right with a graceful swerve and after the other car had passed, swing back to the middle. As we drove along the dark countryside, we began to suspect that Pa did not really know how to find his way back to the Auberge. But nothing was said. There was a hair-raising moment when we almost sideswiped a farmer who was walking in the dark along the edge of the road, pushing his wheelbarrow. The real moment of truth came when Pa zoomed up a steep hill and on the top plunged into what seemed to us a dark pit because Eva's headlights were still aimed into space. Netty squeezed my hand as hard as she could and held tight until Eva landed back on the road, going steeply down-hill. Shortly after that, Pa got lucky and saw a sign he recognized and we were there.

To say the hotel was primitive did not do it justice. It was beyond that. The rooms were dingy with wooden floors and wooden creaky beds. In our room we had two very strange beds with Netty sleeping in what seemed to be a wooden feeding trough for cows, while I had to stretch out on a double bed with a convex mattress that forever made me roll off the side. There was only a small washbasin in the room and the toilet was at the end of the hallway. We soon discovered that the place was a destination for day-trippers who came by bus to eat and visit the shrine of Frère Joseph – Brother Joseph, a long dead recluse who had lived in the woods nearby. The shrine was a little old block-hut with a small window behind which they had propped a picture of the recluse. The problem was that the day-trippers would all use "our" one and only toilet, promptly stop it up, and make it flow over so that if we had to go to the bathroom after the pilgrims had gone, we were often compelled to wander outside into the woods. The food was excellent, however, and the family that ran the place charming. Father, mother and about ten children were all busy running the hotel and restaurant.

The area was beautiful and we took a couple of short walks, went swimming in lakes and toured around in Eva. I do not recall how we did the car trips because Eva was a truly small car that seated four at most, and we were with six. After a day or two, Til had joined us, coming from Geneva. We got a little worried about possible medical assistance there in the wilds because Netty was, after all, well into her seventh month. The proprietress of the Auberge told us not to worry, the nuns down in the village knew all about midwifery, and she had successfully brought her ten children into this world with the help of the nuns. At the Auberge the proprietor proudly showed us his new car, a new invention. It was a Citroën 2CV or Deux Chevaux a strange ugly duckling of a car, very light, with very low gas consumption and very practical. It would become a kind of cult car for European young people adhering to an "alternative lifestyle." In the fifties, most inhabitants of the French countryside drove old pre-war jalopies hanging together with baling wire and tape. The 2CV was aimed at that market and it was a tremendous success for decades.

In the final week of August we knew that the big event could happen any minute. We had Dr. van Luin on standby, and had made arrangements with the Flora Kliniek, a maternity clinic just over the border in Haarlem. In the early morning of August 29, 1952 Netty said that she felt the baby was getting ready to enter the world. I called a taxi and called Oma Schieferdecker in Bloemendaal who had been planning to visit with us that morning. Oma accepted my message that she could not visit us because she was about to become a great grandmother, with equanimity and did not say much more. A few minutes later she called back to say, "Freddy says it is impossible." Freddy was Freddy Klein, the retired nurse and family friend who lived with Opa and Oma and took very good care of them. Oma considered her the expert on all things medical. I said that maybe Freddy was right, but I was not going to take any chances. I called the office to say I was not coming in and got back to the taxi people to tell them not to wait any longer because it was a childbirth situation. That lit a fire under them. The cab came immediately and the driver looked worried and apprehensive, but we zoomed off to the Flora Clinic and arrived without any problem. We were ushered into a little room. I was told this room was usually not used for birthing, but business was booming that day and somebody else was ahead of us in the delivery room.

Dr. van Luin came and a nurse told me to stand at the head of the bed, out of the way of the proceedings. In the Netherlands fathers are allowed to attend the birth of their children. In the U.S. they are often not permitted to be present. There are some recent exceptions. This prohibition stems probably from fear for lawsuits that could be brought by less than fully informed plaintiffs. Thus our litigious society prevents many American men from experiencing one of the most moving, amazing and wonderful experience they can have in their lives. The nurse said she hoped I would be able to attend the procedure without causing her trouble by fainting; adding that recently a father had become weak-kneed and fainted. As he slithered to the floor his head got jammed between two vertical bars of the bed, and they had more work with him, having to saw him free, than with the young mother. Netty believes

L TO R - OMI, GEORGE, NETTY, MAMMIE

in natural childbirth, and most Dutch doctors do too. I was completely awestruck by the stoic and tough way in which Netty behaved in this for her totally new and very painful event.

Dr. van Luin had kept a running commentary going, so I knew what was going on from minute to minute. He pointed out to me how the baby's head became first visible, just before it emerged. After what seemed an eternity the baby emerged, covered in a substance that seemed to me to resemble white lard. The doctor lifted the baby up with both hands, held it upside down, by its feet, and said, "It's a boy." Soon after that everything including our new baby was cleaned up, and we had a wonderful peaceful moment together as a family. The helpless, "useless bystander" feeling I had experienced all morning was aggravated further when they told me to go home so mother and child could have some rest.

I clearly remember how I walked home from the bus stop. It was a beautiful, warm, end-of-summer day. It was late in the morning and our street was very quiet. It suddenly dawned on me how my world had totally changed that day. I now was the father of a child. I had a strong feeling of being connected with the past and the future through the birth of our son, and I was completely at peace with the great change this event had brought. I realized that few things really matter in life, and that among the most important experiences one can have, parenthood ranks very high if not highest.

I had to tend to quite a few details: reporting the birth at town hall, and sending out announcements and, of course, calling our parents and grandparents. Ultrasound scans were still unknown, so throughout Netty's pregnancy we had no idea if we would get a daughter or a son. We had selected names for both genders and as was customary, given those names to the printers who would prepare the announcements. For a boy we chose George Bernard Max, naming him after three people who were close to us. My father, my uncle who was executed by the Germans in the last weeks of the war and my grandfather. I had spoken with Tante Jetje to ask her permission for using Oom Bernard's name. She said that would be wonderful and asked me not to forget Opa who would be delighted if we used his name too. Accordingly, we added Max, which was perhaps also helpful in creating some distance between our son and George Bernard Shaw. We had delivered the envelopes beforehand with all addresses written by hand by Netty. We used traditional Dutch formal birth announcements, a small envelope that contained a calling card with our name and address (Mr. and Mrs. Schieferdecker – van Kleffens) and attached to it in the left-hand top corner with a tiny, light-blue ribbon, a small card with George

Bernard Max on it. If it had been a girl the ribbon would have been pink. These announcements went out promptly and over the coming days would result in an avalanche of flowers, presents, telegrams, cards and letters.

Our parents and grandparents were delighted to hear the great news. When I called Netty's family in Wassenaar, I got Pul on the phone. Mammie had already left for the station since we had called her earlier to say we were going to the clinic. Pul called his father in his office and as a true-to-form monosyllabic teenager, said with a somber voice, *"Het kind is er"* (the child is there). I believe Pa jumped in his car and caught Mammie before she got in the train. Anyway, they both arrived and visited Netty as soon as this was possible. Netty was radiant and in very good shape and well taken care of.

We had asked the daughter of friends of my parents, Anneke van der Bel, to come and help us for a few weeks when Netty came back home. Pa came from Wassenaar to transport his first grandchild home. Anneke arrived a day or so ahead and took charge. I quickly understood how lucky I was having Netty running our household. Anneke was a registered nurse and quite handy on the nursing side, but as a cook

L TO R: PA, OUR DOG MAX, OPA WITH GEORGE, ME.

and housekeeper she was not up to par. She asked me what I would really like to eat and for some stupid reason I made a mistake, confusing bovine organs, and said "kidneys" instead of "liver," which I like very much. Anneke looked puzzled but proceeded with her chores. The next day when I came home, the house smelled like the wrong end of a horse barn. Anneke had bought a huge kidney and was stewing it in a pot, releasing a heavy urine smell. I cannot recall how we ate it, but I did give it a try. It was horrible. When I saw Anneke bathe George in a washbasin, taking him out of the water with a quick swing so that his head passed a hair's breadth away from the faucet, I realized we would be lucky to escape unscathed from Anneke's regime. We did, and all three of us survived.s

When George became a healthy big baby, we took him around to show him off. We had a "pram," not a stroller like they have nowadays, but a four-wheeled contraption that had a detachable upper body in which George could sleep and sit. The frame with the wheels could also be folded up. So we could transport our son to relatives and friends either by public transportation, rented cars or walking. We also decided to complicate our life further by acquiring a dog. Max was a boxer, of course. We bought him from a farm family. He was a grown dog, completely house broken and very friendly. He quickly became a valued member of the family and soon developed a deep attachment to George. George could poke his finger in his eye or tug his ear, it did not matter, Max would just move his head out of the way and continue his snooze. One evening we went with our whole family to Bloemendaal and took a picture of four generations of Schieferdecker males, Opa, Pa, George and myself with Max. This picture is one of our prized possessions.

What cast a shadow over the first years of our marriage was the political situation in Europe. The postwar relationship with the Soviet Union had soured over the years and the Communist threat from the east was very real. America no longer possessed a monopoly in nuclear weapons. The Russians had developed their own and had made a great deal of progress in building intercontinental ballistic missiles that posed a threat to the entire free world, which now included West Germany. On our side of the iron curtain, Communist parties in Italy and France were on the rise and were potent forces in local politics. The Soviet Union controlled virtually all of Eastern Europe and had established satellite states, "Peoples Republics," in all of the countries in its sphere of influence.

In 1949 NATO, the North Atlantic Treaty Organization, a defense pact between the U.S. and all free Western European nations, was established. This treaty required all participating countries to supply troops for the defense of the West. The Dutch government decided that its Indonesia veterans were a good source to muster an active reserve to train for a fight with the Russians. Consequently, I was called up again to report for training. This turned out to be a complete farce. A few years earlier, we had been required to turn in all our equipment and uniforms on a chaotic day in the small town of Deventer. They had lists for everybody and knew exactly what was issued to you in Indonesia or later on the troop ship home. We had to bring it all back and were fined for whatever was missing, which was quite a lot.

Now almost two years later, we had to come back and receive new equipment. In the summer of 1951, just after we were married, I went for the first call up to Eindhoven where we were in a barracks camp near Oirschot. All my buddies from Indonesia were there plus a few strangers we did not know. Netty came to Eindhoven for a few days and stayed in a hotel near the station there, and I would sneak out at night to join her, leaving a rolled-up blanket in my bed to suggest I was fast asleep. Our training was ridiculously poor, and morale was as low as it could be. We really did not want to be in the military anymore. The Dutch had thought up a new system, which was to let everybody go home with his uniforms, all his equipment and his weapon so we could all be called up in a jiffy and join our units fully armed. I came home with a Sten gun, which rested in one of my closets and was only of great interest to Pul who wanted to see it whenever he came to visit. The well-trained, well-armed and much younger Russian army would have had little trouble with us. They were not more than about three hundred miles away. As usual, we never saw the mortars we were trained for. We had one big exercise at about battalion strength whereby we were supposed to storm past a group of higher officers in a mock infantry attack. We were all so disgusted with the whole theatre that we did not run but sauntered past. The rear was brought up by Corporal Voorhoeve, a man I knew well from Indonesia, but whose first name escapes me. Voorhoeve was a very intelligent, intellectual type who hated the military and demonstrated this by slouching past the officers, holding his rifle by the end of the barrel, dragging the butt through the mud. He almost got arrested by the MP and court-martialled for that.

The second call to arms took place in midwinter. I believe it was in the winter of 1952, just after George's birth. This time I had to go to an area near Roosendaal, near the Belgian border, very close to the town where Rob and Liesbeth Laane now live. Here we had to stay in tents. It was snowy outside and it was freezing hard. When I got to my tent, I found that only one of my tent-mates had arrived before me. This was a guy from Volendam, the village near Amsterdam where all the tourists go to look at the people in their traditional costumes. He was not in his costume but in multiple uniform layers. He wore all the clothes he had and was still cold. He told me he had been unable to get the gasoline stove going and had been so cold the night before that he went to bed with everything on, including his boots and his overcoat. I do not recall what we did there all day, but I do remember that it was bitter cold. Trying to wash and shave in an open tent with only cold water was a real treat. I decided that this was enough for me and went to the doctor to say I had a strange right leg with a knob on it that was bound to get irritated again by my boots as it had been many times before and that I had bad feet and could not walk very far. The doctor was a reservist, too, and seemed to understand that I had better things to do than hang around a bunch of tents in the middle of winter. So he sent me to The Hague for a medical checkup, and lo and behold, I was declared unfit for further military service! I was finally free from the army and could go home and go on with my life, unmolested by the government. Thus ended my military career – one of the more difficult chapters of my life.

At Jonas & Kruseman I began to make a little progress, enough to start thinking about a car. In the 1950s wage scales in the investment business were still extremely modest, and this was certainly the case at Jokru. The explosion in compensation for investment bankers, traders, analysts and money managers would come thirty years later. Next door to Jokru was the office of another brokerage firm called Alsberg Goldberg. As the name suggests, this firm was owned by Jewish people. During the war, Mr. Schimmelpenninck had been able to roll it into his own and make it "disappear." It was, of course, resurrected after the war, but there was not much left of it except for the two administratiekantoren it ran. As I explained these businesses were independent trust-like organizations that issued bearer certificates against underlying original securities. The one for American securities was by far the biggest. It had an interesting selection of holdings of what were then blue chips. G.M. and G.E. still exist and G.E. is still a blue chip, but Woolworth, Curtiss-Wright, American Hide and Leather and Republic Steel are all gone. The second trust office that issued certificates for European securities, in reality just less actively traded Dutch ones, was much smaller and proved to have less potential. Mr. Alsberg, who had started both businesses, had selected the stocks we used for our certificates, and he picked good ones. He was a very nice, erudite, soft-spoken man who was in poor health, probably due to his experiences during the war when he had to go underground for three or four years. It was almost immediately clear to me that he was not in good shape and not up to the rough and tumble of regenerating his business. The firm had a staff of a few old hands who kept it going. Mr. Alsberg died fairly soon after

I joined Jokru and Mr. Schimmelpenninck took over. He gave me a function with these two administratiekantoren, which gave me a power of attorney, and that meant every time one of our certificates was cancelled I had to go to a bank vault with Mr. Slagt, the manager of the firm to retrieve the original stock certificates. There was a fair amount of activity in this area as arbitrageurs were buying in Amsterdam and selling in New York and vice versa.

Whenever there was a split-up, we had to issue additional certificates and these had to be printed and signed by hand. Each certificate for ten shares got a signature. This effort gave me plenty of writing cramps and reduced my signature to an illegible scrawl. Dear reader, just try to sign your name five hundred times. After a while you may even write something totally different as your attention wanders. The trust had a small three-man board that would meet once or twice a year. This little business was a gold mine. A small fee was charged on each cancellation or issue of certificates, and when dividends were paid and had to be distributed, a little bit was skimmed off the top on the exchange rate of the dollars sold against guilders. The directors received what for me seemed huge bonuses, and I also got a piece of the action. Thus I was in the strange position that I made more on this sideline than on my actual day-to-day job.

My improved financial situation allowed me to go to a Renault dealer in Haarlem who had used Quatre Chevaux cars for sale. This was a French version of the Volkswagen but by far not as sturdy and well put together. Still it was transportation, and it was cheap. Our first car was a beige, four-door job with a tiny stick shift. We could put George in his bucket on the back seat, and Max on the floor lying across the center beam, and off we went. Netty also took driving lessons and quickly passed the elaborate and difficult Dutch driver's test without a hitch. Netty had trained and had taken the exam in the driving school's car so she had to switch over to the Renault. We went to a big parking lot and started driving around. I soon learned that my efforts to teach and my comments were not welcome. I was told: *"Hou je mond ik kan het nou hoor!"* (Listen, shut up, I now know how to drive!) And that is the way my driving commentary was and is kept at bay for the rest of our lives.

Much of what happened around us in Europe was interwoven with our family life. In 1952 the European Coal and Steel Community (ECSC) was established. This supranational organ marked a new beginning in European relationships between countries. It was based on the so-called "Plan Schuman". Robert Schuman was a well-known French foreign minister who came up with the idea that future Franco–German conflicts could be avoided if these countries (and a few others) ceded their control over their coal mining and steel manufacturing industries by turning it over to an international authority. This would practically eliminate the ability to rearm and wage war for any of the participating countries. This plan was launched in 1950 and ratified in 1952 by all the countries involved. Pa van Kleffens, who had spent most of his career at the Dutch ministry of economic affairs, was intimately involved in the earlier negotiations establishing a customs union between Belgium, the Netherlands and Luxemburg called Benelux. The Benelux and the ECSC were the forerunners of the European Economic Community or EEC, founded in 1957 by the Treaty of Rome. At that time, the Benelux was already a working organism, which greatly facilitated trade and movement of people between the countries involved and gave its three small European member states more of a voice in international affairs. From the beginning, Pa also worked as a leading negotiator on the team preparing Dutch membership of the ECSC, and as the organization took shape, he decided that he wanted to serve as a judge in the court of justice that was set up to decide all disputes that would inevitably arise among member states of the ECSC. This was a very important assignment because the court was to be the first functioning supra national judiciary institution in the world, with real authority over a number of sovereign governments. After much to and fro, Pa was appointed as the Dutch judge in the court. He was very happy to get this new assignment that would give him an opportunity to spend the final years of his career in a very interesting and challenging function and gave him an opportunity to use his legal talents in helping to break new ground in international law.

In early 1953 Pa moved to Luxemburg, where he initially stayed in rooms rented from a local widow who lived in a large old house in town. From there he went back and forth to Wassenaar. Mammie stayed home for a while. Netty and I visited Pa in the summer of 1953 when we went with our Renault on vacation to Switzerland and France. It was a memorable visit. The widow's house was a complete throwback to the nineteenth century. The rooms were dark with dark wood paneling and chock-a-block full of overstuffed furniture. Heavy drapes were held up by thick cords with big tassels and were hung behind the windows of all the rooms, letting very little light in. In the hallway and on the stairs were bronze statues on marble pedestals, interspersed by potted palms. We slept in a bedroom that resembled a mausoleum. Its curtains were stifling. We commented to each other that this place was exactly what Pa liked since he preferred the way people lived in the nineteenth century. As the court began to get organized, the judges immediately started to assume the lifestyle of what later would be called Eurocrats. They received very generous tax-exempt salaries and could select large automobiles and hire chauffeurs to drive them around. Pa told us with considerable irony in his voice how the judges had argued over the design of the uniforms of the chauffeurs. The hat was a particularly sensitive subject since ostentatious uniforms and large hats were not desirable in postwar Europe. As time went on, Pa and Mammie found a nice large apartment in the outskirts of the city of Luxembourg and lived there for a number of years. Mammie enjoyed the social life among the Eurocrats in Luxembourg and most of all the receptions at the court of the grand duchess of this little operettalike Grand Duchy. Just before we left for America, we spent a few days in Luxembourg with Pa and Mammie. Their apartment was beautiful and large, and we thought they were very happy there.

Meanwhile Rob Laane had moved up in the hierarchy of the Rotterdamsche Bank and was appointed co-director of the Haarlem office, a very nice job for him. Haarlem is the capital of the province of Noord Holland and has a fair amount of industry and other businesses, which gave Rob's bank a nice share of loan activity. In addition, the bank had an active brokerage and portfolio management business. We found out that Mevrouw Meyer, the lady who lived next door to us, was interested in renting out a room in her house. Rob took the room and became our next door neighbor, which was great fun. Rob was also keenly interested in getting motorized transportation. He started out with a bromfiets, a motorized bicycle. These bikes with little engines that made a terrible racket were extremely popular in Holland in the fifties and sixties. It gave people greater mobility without requiring a drivers' license or a registration. These bikes were the harbingers of what would become the Dutch infatuation with automobiles that has now filled the towns and villages with parked cars and clogged all highways to the saturation point. I remember Rob zooming around the Alberdingk Thymlaan with his youngest sister Edith sitting on the back seat, screaming in anguish about his less than perfect maneuvering. Rob's bromfiets period was short lived. He soon got a driver's license and invested in a Renault, similar to ours but newer. Soon we would jointly vacation in Austria, forming a mini- convoy with our two Renaults. More about that later.

Our life in Heemstede revolved around our small family and our friends. My parents had moved to Wassenaar in 1952 after Pa's retirement from Royal Dutch Shell. A developer had built the house Pa bought at Groot Haesebroekse Weg 17-B, and it proved to be a good choice. It was an ideal retirement home for them and my parents lived there happily for more than forty years. Ultimately, it proved no longer quite as ideal as it was in the beginning – it had too many steep staircases. I have described the initial lack of enthusiasm Ma felt for moving to Wassenaar. However, she lived there quite happily and made many new friends while her old friends from Voorburg and The Hague kept coming to see her for a game of bridge, often chauffeured by Pa. My parents had more time on their hands after Pa retired and visited us often.

On one of those visits, on Sunday morning, February 1, 1953, they told us they had heard over the radio (nobody had television then, but Pa religiously listened to all the early morning news broadcasts) that a bad flood had hit a good part of the provinces of Zeeland and Brabant. The night before, a very heavy storm had started to blow, but we just thought it was a winter storm and gave no further thought to it. I had taken Max out for his evening walk and noticed that it was blowing very hard. So hard in fact, that Max would lie down on the street whenever a particularly forceful burst of wind hit us, keeping his head low while his ears were flying out horizontally. I also noticed that a few roof tiles had blown off a neighboring house, but all these things were in my mind just part of a very bad storm. What had happened that night was a rare coincidence of several forces of nature. We had a full moon and the attendant unusually high tide that night. The storm was of hurricane force and blew out of the northwest. The prevailing wind in Holland blows from the southwest, and a storm from any other direction is extremely rare. The force of the wind blew large bodies of North Sea water into the English Channel, which became a large funnel with an outlet that was not wide enough. Consequently, the water was pushed with great force against and over the dikes of the Low Countries, breaching them in many places. As the water cascaded into the low-lying polders, whole villages were swallowed up, and many larger towns flooded too. Large land areas were inundated, and it soon became clear that the Netherlands faced a catastrophe of biblical proportions. About 1,600 people died and the property damage was enormous. This event, which became to be called *"De Ramp"* (The Calamity) dominated life in Holland for a long time. Our friend Rob van der Toorren, who worked for a large public works contracting firm, was one of the first people we knew who had visited the affected area. He came back completely shattered about what he had seen. This was unusual since he was normally a self-assured, somewhat boastful person who tended to inflate his own role in situations he told us about. Not this time. He was deeply impressed and very subdued. He told us about the loss of life he had seen and the enormity of the damage the area had suffered.

Much help came from many countries and from the American forces in Germany. Large collections were held for the victims, and the members of the stock exchange were extremely generous, putting large amounts of cash into collection baskets. The Dutch government started almost immediately to plan for the construction of a large system of new dikes, floodgates and other works to prevent a reoccurrence of these floods. This project, which was called the Deltawerken (Delta Works) became an undertaking of world renown and is an example of the ingenuity the Dutch have in matters of water management and flood control. It was of course a matter of concern that so many dikes proved to be unstable and unable to hold water pressure from the inside, but the war years had taken a toll on maintenance and it was clear to everybody that the storm was an extremely unusual one. Still, all existing dikes were raised and reinforced and the whole recovery effort presented the Dutch economy with another severe burden after the war and the conflict in Indonesia.

Beyond having our old friend Rob Laane next door, we made several new friends and strengthened old relationships with people living near us. Rob van der Tooren was a member of my year club in Leiden who had like me been called up and forced to interrupt his studies. In his case, it was medical school. Rob played his cards better than I and ended up as an officer in a special intelligence service branch of the Dutch navy, stationed in Singapore. Like me he had not gone back to his studies. In Singapore Rob met and married Josette, who had grown up there and was the daughter of the Belgian consul and an American mother. Rob and Josette settled in the Haarlem/Heemstede area and we saw a great deal of them. In the beginning Josette only spoke English and we got the impression that she was lonely. Rob worked at Blankevoort, a large construction firm. He seemed to enjoy the work, which often brought him to London. They had a little son who became one of George's playmates. I do not recall when they announced their departure, but one day Rob told us they were emigrating to America. If my recollection is correct, this was possible because Josette had an American passport. This enabled them to go to the front of the line of people waiting to emigrate.

In the 1950s, the Dutch government, believing there would not be enough jobs at home for Holland's growing population, encouraged emigration on a large scale. Information bureaus were opened, subsidies granted and regular radio broadcasts detailing the ins and outs of emigration were produced. Many families, especially from rural areas, went to Canada, Australia and New Zealand. However, going to America was another proposition, and people who wanted to go there were facing a long wait. Rob and Josette left and we never heard from them again.

Another lady from Singapore, or more precisely from Malaysia was Jill van Huystee. Jill married Dick van Huystee in Malaysia when Dick was working there on a tobacco plantation, learning the trade. Dick's father owned a tobacco brokerage firm in Amsterdam and Dick worked there after he returned home. Although Jill's parents were Dutch, her father was a Dutch diplomat, she spoke English better than Dutch and was a friend of Josette. The van Husytees became very good friends of us and of Rob, and later on when Rob married, Liesbeth Laane. They also had a son, Marc, who was George's age and therefore also a playmate. The van Huystees lived in a house nearby that was formerly a servants quarters on an estate in Heemstede. They had a nice tennis court on the grounds and we played there regularly with them and other friends. During our time there, the van Huystees gave several fabulous parties. One of them was a costume party, and Rob and I appeared as Hillary and Tensing (the New Zealander Sir Edmund Hillary and his Nepalese guide Tensing, the first people to climb Mount Everest), who were big news in those days. Dick and I were both enthusiastic movie makers and Dick's films of a party we gave on our departure for America and of a farewell dinner Rob and Liesbeth gave are still cherished scenes in our family archive of old movies.

In the midfifties Dick's father died suddenly of a massive heart attack. This left Dick with the job of rescuing the firm and dealing with all the estate problems that crop up when a partnership suddenly terminates. One day he called me at the office to ask my advice after his bankers, one of the larger major banks, gave him a hard time about his credit line, questioned his solvency and unexpectedly demanded much more security than his father ever had to give. I checked with a friend who was with another, smaller, bank who said they would be more than happy to have his firm as a client, giving him the same credit line as before. So Dick switched his account and left his old bank holding the bag. This episode made me feel good about my ability to help a friend by using common sense and knowledge of the politics of the financial scene in Amsterdam.

Dick had an eye for the ladies, he was a real charmer and a fun guy to be with. Jill was a very attractive woman who was a little awkward in her relationships with people, especially men. Their differences eventually led to a divorce, when Dick took off with the wife of a neighbor and friend of the Laanes (much to their embarrassment.) I saw Dick several times when I was on business in Amsterdam. He eventually sold his firm to the Deli Maatschappij, the largest Dutch/Indonesian tobacco firm, where he became a member of the top management. He visited me once in New York City with his second wife and her daughter. That was the last time I saw him. He died sometime later, I believe in the late eighties, of a heart attack. He was a good friend.

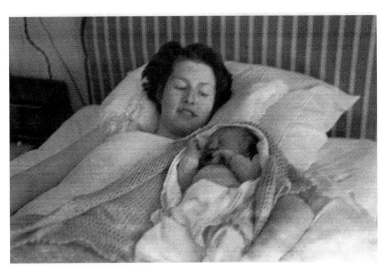

ADRIAAN EELKE MATTHIJS ONE DAY OLD.

In the summer of 1953 Netty became pregnant again and our second son Adriaan arrived on March 21, 1954. Long before this event we had decided that this baby would be born at home. That was much *gezelliger* (cozier) in our opinion, and we had everything planned well ahead of time. We went to the local *Groene Kruis* (Green Cross) organization (an outfit in Holland where you can rent wheel chairs, crutches and other medical implements for temporary home use) and rented extension legs to put under Netty's bed so it could be made considerably higher. To make things work well we also needed to have a good nurse in place some time before the event. We found a nurse who came highly recommended and whose name was Tilly. She arrived at our house, delivered by her family in the family car. Her father had brought the family dog, too, and demonstrated how he could make the dog jump over our garden gate. After this impressive performance, Tilly's parents left with the dog, and Tilly settled in. She soon proved to be a good nurse and a wonderful person to have around. Calm, handy, a good cook, very good with George and above all a very good sense of humor. She was great fun to have with us for a few weeks.

Anybody who knows Adriaan as an adult will not be surprised to learn that he arrived at a decent time, midmorning, and on a Sunday. Everything went very smoothly after Adriaan announced his imminent arrival very early in the morning. Nurse Tilly was asleep in our guest room, and I awakened her as soon as Netty noticed the first symptoms and organized everything efficiently. Doctor van Luin arrived in time. For a second time I had the privilege of witnessing the birth of one of our children, this time in our own house which made the whole event so much more special and wonderful. It was another boy and we knew immediately what his names would be. Adriaan, Eelke, Matthys – named after Netty's family, her father,

her little brother who drowned in 1945 and her sister Tilly (Mathilde.) During Adriaan's birth, which went very smoothly, Dr. van Luin again gave a running commentary, clearly showing his knowledge of, and interest in the phenomenon of birth. When the placenta came, he showed it to me with what he called the "tree of life," a beautiful pattern of vessels and veins inside a maroon colored mass of tissue, which was much larger than I had expected. Checking it on the Internet, I noted that doctors are required to inspect the placenta immediately and that some experts even require examination by a pathologist. We did not go that far. Everything seemed to be O.K. and Dr. van Luin asked for a pan to put the placenta in and told me to get rid of it. Not knowing what better to do, I went downstairs, got a shovel and buried it in our small garden on the side of the house. When all the necessary work was done, I invited Dr. van Luin for a glass of sherry and a cigar downstairs in our living room, and we had a very pleasant long visit there, chatting about all kinds of subjects. Later I got in trouble with my mother and mother-in-law because I had called them before Adriaan's birth to say it was imminent and had forgotten to call again when our new baby was there, so these good people spent much more time on tenterhooks than was necessary.

After a few weeks, when Tilly had gone home and everything seemed to be going well, we had a bad scare with our new little baby. Whenever he was fed, and Netty believed strongly in breast-feeding, Adriaan started to vomit with great strength, ejecting all the precious mother milk he had just ingested. We summoned Dr van Luin, and he quickly saw what it was. Adriaan had Pyloric Stenosis, a condition some three-or four-week-old babies have. The muscle controlling the outlet of the stomach is too strong, and as the baby grows, it is rapidly getting stronger, thus almost blocking the stomach's outlet. As more food enters the stomach during a feeding, it has no outlet and is forcefully expelled. The doctor showed me what happened. He put the small baby on his back after a feeding and bent him a little backward by holding his hand under his back. I saw the stomach clearly delineated under Adriaan's rib cage and you could see how it was contracting to expel the food. Adriaan had to be operated on. A pyloromyotomy had to be performed, a cutting away of part of the muscle, to weaken it. We were assured that it was a quite common, routine operation and that there was nothing to fear. Still, it was very tough for us to bring Adriaan to the hospital and leave him there; visibly weaker and smaller than he was a few days earlier.

As often happens when you have to deal with something medical that you have not heard of before, you suddenly discover that many people say that they know all about it and that they or their children have had the same problem. At Jokru, Klaas Lette told me that one of his two children, also a boy, had the same operation and had come out of it without any problems. These inputs are always welcome and reassuring. It seems mainly boys are affected with Pyloric Stenosis. Overall, it did not take more than a few days before Adriaan was home again and totally cured. During Adriaan's stay in the hospital I went there regularly to deliver his mother's milk we had carefully gathered with the help of a pump. Netty went too, of course, and she told me that one morning she came into the ward where Adriaan was and saw the nurses coddling him and carrying him around. He was a favorite patient there, all of four weeks old. This episode gave us a small impression of the fragility of life, particularly at a very young age. We were inclined to take good health for granted, and continued to do so, but this little warning taught us that a lot can happen in a very short time and that your life can change profoundly without any warning.

In the summer of 1954 Netty and I went for a summer vacation visit to Austria with Rob Laane. We went in two cars, two tiny Renaults, and Rob took a girlfriend along, Lon van der Graaff, a young woman we became very fond of. We had a grand old time in a village called Ötz in the Ötztal. The weather was not very good, but as Europeans we were used to that. We felt like kings, driving our little cars along the German Autobahn to Bavaria and from there to Austria. Our first stop was in a part of Germany, just over the Dutch border, which at that time had been annexed by the Dutch. Luckily this bad idea was later abandoned and the area was returned to Germany. Lon would join us later and for this section of our trip, Rob had offered a ride to another young lady he vaguely knew. When we came to the small hotel where we would have our first overnight stop, it appeared there were only two rooms and to our immense enjoyment Rob had to share his room with this young woman, who turned out to be a great talker but not somebody Rob really enjoyed having in his bedroom. Our next stop was Ulm in Bavaria. I believe Rob had a better sleeping arrangement there and could rest peacefully without having to listen to the chatter of his friend. We had a very good time in our hotel in Ötz which was simple, but nice. Rob and Lon were chastely lodged in separate rooms. I took movies of the trip and they are in our archive. On the way back we stopped in Frankfurt. There we saw the impressive work done by the Germans to rebuild the extensive war damage Frankfurt and many other cities had suffered. Construction work went on day and night around our hotel, transforming the city into what is now a major financial center with several high-rise office towers.

In late 1953, Netty's sister Tilly had become engaged to Frans Terwisscha van Scheltinga, a young member of the staff of the Dutch Ministry of Foreign Affairs. Frans worked at the ministry in The Hague, concentrating on the area of Dutch involvement with supranational organizations that were proliferating after the war. He told me his job was different from that of the people who worked in the Dutch diplomatic service in various countries, called the *Buitenlandse Dienst* (the Foreign Service). This meant that he would mostly stay at the ministry throughout his career as opposed to having to move from country to country every four of five years. He would not travel very frequently, but he did go to Geneva and there he met Til. They hit it off very well. Frans was the only son of the mayor of Wijchen, a town near Nijmegen. He had a degree from the Catholic University of Leuven, Belgium. He probably went there when his part of the country was liberated and the rest was still occupied and because it was a Catholic school. The Terwisscha family was strictly Catholic. In the Holland of the 1950s this was still a big deal and presented a problem. Not so much for Netty and me, but certainly in the eyes of Pa van Kleffens, who never set foot in a Protestant church but still regarded anybody who was a Catholic with suspicion. The fact that Frans had not gone to Leiden but to a university in Belgium added another hurdle. Frans took all these problems in stride and did his best to be as forthcoming as possible. Soon Tilly and Frans were engaged and the plans for their wedding were being made. It was impossible for Frans not to have a church wedding, and Til decided to become a Catholic. Today the attitude towards religion in the Netherlands is very different. All religions are suffering under lack of church attendance and membership. Churches are no longer used. They serve as discos and entertainment or community centers. Convents are closed and there is a painful lack of Catholic priests and Protestant pastors. So in retrospect all the fuss about Tilly's wedding seems a throwback to ancient history, but at the time it was very real for all of us. Tilly went to see a local priest in Wassenaar and had a crash course in Catholicism. In the spring of 1954, on May 22, they were married in the Catholic Church in Wassenaar and a nice reception and bridal lunch followed in the Kasteel Oud Wassenaar, an establishment that was very near by. I do not know where Adriaan was at the time of Tilly's wedding, but I do remember that Netty was still breastfeeding him and from time to time had to dash away from the party to do her motherly duties. A high point of the wedding was the arrival of a telegram from the Holy See giving the couple the papal blessing. This caused some consternation with Frans's relatives who wondered who could have arranged such a high honor? As it turned out, Oom Eelco was the culprit. He had visited the Vatican on a diplomatic mission and asked the secretary of the pope, the Cardinal Montini, for the favor of the blessing on Tilly's wedding day. Pa van Kleffens walked around proudly announcing we arranged that. Later on Cardinal Montini became pope himself. Til and Frans bought a newly built house in the Marialaan, a section of The Hague that had been bombed out in 1945 and was being rebuilt. Their oldest child Elise was born on March 13, 1955.

In the spring of 1955 we bought a new Volkswagen "beetle" car. This was a big event – now we had a new car. It would be our pride and joy for several years. We built a garage next to our house so the VW could be properly garaged. The original Volkswagen factory is in Wolfsburg, which was in the British occupation zone. The British got the factory going as soon as they could, to provide jobs for the masses of unemployed that were causing an economic problem in Germany. Ironically, the Volkswagen became such a success that it completely captured the market for small cars in Western Europe, much to the disadvantage of the British manufacturers who were also trying to switch their production from war to peace. One of the strange disadvantages of the original design was that it had no gas gauge. When the tank ran empty, you could turn a lever with your foot, which opened a small reserve tank with presumably enough supply to get you to the nearest gas station. I invested in a gas gauge and some other instruments, including a radio that made the car more civilized in my opinion. The Dutch taxed everything, including radios at home as well as in cars. You had to carry a card that showed you had paid your taxes and bureaucrats with binoculars were lurking along the highways. Every car they saw approaching with an antenna was stopped to check the radio license. Our Volkswagen was silver blue and carried the license RP-25-50. Royal Peter was what the RP stood for, I claimed.

That same spring I drove the VW to Geneva. Mr. Schimmelpenninck had a very close relationship with the partners of the Bordier banking house in Geneva, particularly Mr. Raymond Bordier. It was customary for young people like me to be sent out to foreign correspondent firms for brief periods as interns. I had asked for this assignment because I thought it would widen my horizons and it did. Bordier was a typically Swiss and very conservative old-fashioned firm. I got a small table in the room where Mr. Eduard Bordier sat with his "procuriste" a nice man called Orsini, I believe. Every day Eduard went to the stock exchange with Orsini, and I tagged along. The exchange was a small affair where trading was done in the Corbeille – basket system. This was analogous to the old Paris Bourse where people would stand around a round barrier, the basket. Trading was done by going down a list of the securities listed on the exchange. Officials sitting inside the basket announced the names of the securities to be traded and kept track of the transactions. When the list was completed, there was a period of open trading in the more active securities. All trading was done in the "open cry" manner. I had great trouble following what was going on but eventually understood the basics. I went to several departments at Bordier to see how they operated and also took the train to Zurich to visit a Bordier connection there and see the market. The Zurich market was much more active and important than Geneva and has remained so. I had found a room with Mr. and Mrs. Tremblay, acquaintances of Eduard Bordier. This friendly elderly couple lived in an old house near the center of town. All my conversations at Bordier and with my hosts were in French, a real tough assignment but very helpful to improve my limited knowledge of that language. After a few weeks, I began to wonder why Eduard Bordier had not invited me for lunch or any other small social get together outside the office. I knew they were very formal and stiff at Bordier's, but thought it was perhaps up to me to invite him. So I did. This invitation flustered him quite a bit and he started with a stream of excuses, his wife had been sick, they had been renovating their apartment etc. He asked me to have lunch with him in a restaurant with his wife, which was very nice. Raymond also asked me to come to his house in the country, which was a lovely place. In Geneva people went to the office at eight in the morning and took two hours for lunch at home between noon and two, and then returned to the office until about six. During the weekends I drove to Lutry near Lausanne, where Omi van Someren Gréve, Netty's grandmother, had a nice apartment with a view of Lake Geneva. I also saw a good deal of Lous and Jean Paschoud, Mammie's younger sister and her husband, a lawyer in Lausanne. I think that Omi liked my visits. She cooked Indonesian food for me and I took her on long rides into the countryside which she loved to do. In my memory she was an elderly lady, but checking her age, I note with some surprise she was "only" seventy three at that time, a lot younger than I am at the time of this writing. On my way back from Geneva I drove to Paris where I met Netty. This was an idea of Mr. Schimmelpenninck who had offered Netty a trip to Paris to link up with me. We had a few nice days there together and then drove home.

In the fall of that year we made a vacation trip to Spain and Portugal. We drove down by way of Bordeaux, San Sebastian, Burgos and a small town on the border of Portugal, Ciudad Rodrigo. In Spain we stayed in paradores, hotels run by the Spanish government's tourist office, whenever we could. These hotels were excellent and often located in tastefully renovated old country houses or castles.

In those days Spain was still a backward country, a dictatorship with General Francisco Franco in charge. The roads were empty, the hotels were cheap and the food very Spanish. Oom Eelco and Tante Margaret had invited us to come see them in Lisbon and recommended that we come in fall to avoid the summer heat. Near San Sebastian, we stayed in a parador, which was next door to the grottos of Altamira, where the famous prehistoric rock drawings were on view. I believe these caves are now closed to the public because the constant stream of visitors polluted the air in the cave and threatened to deteriorate the paintings. We thought the drawings were very interesting and special, but the pictures we had seen of them were considerably clearer because the photographer probably used much brighter lights than the few small light bulbs we had to cope with. We also saw the cathedral of Burgos. The parador in Ciudad Rodrigo was particularly interesting and stands out in my memory as a highlight of the trip. The town was still completely surrounded by its medieval walls and the parador was in a castle built into the wall. At sunset we walked around the town on the top of the wall and had dinner in an old vaulted room. The next morning we took a walk outside and saw the farm people coming to market, all on foot or on donkeys, some driving a pig along with a stick or carrying a bunch of chickens. A step back in time, almost to the life Spanish masters have depicted in their paintings. When we entered Lisbon we discovered that nobody spoke or understood English, French or German. In Spain we had managed with French combined with vigorous arm and hand signals. The Portuguese were different. We had to find the street where Oom Eelco and Tante Margaret lived. We were at the outskirts of town and one of the bystanders in the crowd we had attracted finally came with an excellent solution. He pointed at a city bus that was waiting to start its route and spoke to the driver. We followed the bus, making all the stops and when we were there the driver signaled that we had reached our destination.

Oom Eelco and Tante Margaret lived in a very large apartment. We were ushered into our room while their driver Antonio took our VW to a garage where he had it completely serviced. We did not see our car again until we left. Tante Margaret had two or three maids, waiting on us hand and foot. At first we thought they had stolen most of our stuff because they had grabbed our bags and unpacked them, taking all our dirty clothes. A few days later everything was back neatly washed and ironed. Oom Eelco, who liked to be always precisely on time, told us that he would offer us a drink at six thirty. When I went down for our drink, I saw the library empty and dark so I told Netty that there had to be some mistake. Not so. I had been two minutes early. At exactly six thirty, he was sitting in his den, as if he had been there for hours. At dinner we sat in the formal dining room with a uniformed maid standing in the corner to cater to our wishes. There also was a dinner party in our honor. For this event I had brought my tuxedo. After dinner we had cigars with the men while the ladies went to the drawing room with Tante Margaret. Oom Eelco, who could not stand cigar or cigarette smoke, positioned himself under a fan which he had had built in the ceiling just for this purpose. We had a wonderful time there; Tante Margaret took us around on many sightseeing trips, including a Portuguese bullfight where the bull is not killed but subdued at the end of the fight by a swarm of little men in special costumes with red woolen, gnome like hats. At the end of our stay we visited the country house Oom Eelco and Tante Margaret had built in a village called Almoçageme, north of Sintra. The house was built by combining three hovels that had been owned by local fishermen. It was situated on top of a rock cliff and had a tremendous view of the Atlantic Ocean. I learned from Oom Eelco that the nearby lighthouse at Cabo de Roca is only a little bit more east than the most western point of Ireland which is at 10 degrees west.

This visit to Oom Eelco and Tante Margaret cemented our relationship with them. We found that some of the criticisms we had heard within the family of their regal lifestyle and cold attitude towards members of the family were exaggerated. They lived a very disciplined life and liked to live in style which was only reasonable as Oom Eelco had been minister of foreign affairs, ambassador to the U.S., Chairman of a plenary United Nations Session and many other functions. Moreover, Netty and I are not adverse to decorum. We find it often more to our liking than the casual, "let it all hang out" style of many people nowadays.

On the way back from Portugal, we spent a few days in Madrid to see the Prado, Segovia and Toledo. We drove back through France, mostly in a soft autumn mist. A memorable trip. When we came home and stopped in Wassenaar where Pa and Ma were helping to take care of our sons, we were greeted by Pa in tears, telling us that Opa Schieferdecker had died on October thirteenth. Just a few days before our return. The funeral and cremation had already taken place. We were completely taken aback by this. We did not understand why Pa had not tried to reach us. Although we had not let him know exactly where we would stay overnight, he was somewhat familiar with our route. We certainly would have been able to speed up our trip to get home before the funeral. Today a cell phone call would have resolved the problem. The death of my beloved grandfather saddened me tremendously. He was the only grandfather I had known well as an adult.

Before Opa's death we had had ample opportunity to visit him and Oma with our children and we did so frequently. In his final months, advanced old age weakened him considerably. He could no longer move up and down the stairs, so his bed was put in Oma's salon downstairs. There we had seen him for the last time before we went on our trip. Freddy Klein was a tremendous help for Opa and Oma. She stayed and lived with Oma until her death.

My efforts to learn more about the way business was done abroad continued, and to my delight I got permission to go to London for a few weeks to spend time with a brokerage firm Mr. Schimmelpenninck was close to, Vivian Gray and Company. A partner there, Guy Thompson once got a huge order from us when one of our clients received an estate with a large portfolio of South African mining stocks – mostly gold. We did not know much about the mining industry in South Africa and believed it to be a risky area to invest in, so we decided to sell the entire portfolio. This was a nice piece of business for Guy Thompson, one of the Vivian Gray partners. During my visit, Guy took very good care of me, invited me to his house for a week -end visit and introduced me to one of his partners who would take me under his wing on the floor of the stock exchange. But first I had to be approved by the Board of the London Exchange. I received a blue button to wear so I could enter the building, but I could not trade of course. The London Exchange was a very peculiar and interesting institution. It was located in Throgmorton Street. An article I saw described its architecture as "Early Victorian Lavatorial." It had indeed that aspect with many long walls with white tiles and a very large trading room with marble pillars and high glass ceilings with smudgy glass through which a glimmer of sunlight could enter. At the entrance stood a porter in a magnificent uniform, a blue coat and a black top hat. He kept an eye on the people entering and leaving the building. Immediately inside was a large washroom where you went to wash up.

London in those days was still a very sooty town and you had to clean yourself up frequently. Everybody had open coal fires at home and the soot was everywhere. The famous London fog was caused mainly by soot particles, which thickened the fog and made it smell sulfuric. There was soot on windowsills, on office walls and especially on the clothes of Londoners. When entering London by train you would ride through endless grim-looking neighborhoods with row upon row of identical low, two-story working-class homes, each with at least two chimneys on its roof, often belching smoke. A remnant of the Industrial Revolution, which had brought Britain to its powerful position in the world because it had plenty of coal to fuel its factories and heat its houses. On the floor of the exchange, the "jobbers" were the specialists who made markets on a continuing basis in a large number of securities, stocks, as well as bonds. The brokers would execute their transactions on the floor, and all trades were posted by hand on large sheets hanging on the walls. No ticker tape or any electronic device. Sometimes there was a sudden interest in a security and a swarm of people would form around the jobbers, but mostly the trading flowed orderly and calmly during the day. Settlement was once a month, I believe, which caused a great deal of activity in the brokers' offices.

If you wanted to reach a broker on the floor, you went to one of the porters with a top hat who would climb into a kind of pulpit attached to a pillar and start bellowing the name of the person you wanted in a very deep and sonorous tone. Vivian Gray's exchange headquarters was in a so-called "box," a very small, grubby and dingy office across the street where a nice jolly woman kept order, collected information on trades, handled phone calls and made tea on a small gas stove that sat on the floor. There were a couple of desks and some rickety chairs and that was all. I learned that the English did not care at all about having nice offices. They did have nice homes, though.

The main office of Vivian Gray was a few blocks away from the exchange, somewhere in the maze of narrow streets and alleyways that make the City such a charming place. The office was a rabbit warren of hallways, up and down stairways and various rooms. I sat in a room with a nice man whose name I have forgotten. He was an administrative type who suffered from an ulcer he got during the war, serving at sea on convoy duty. His assistant was a sweet French woman who had married an English service man. They called her Fifi, although her name was different. Then there was Gordon, a gregarious broker who spent every Wednesday night in town with his girl friend and the rest of the week at home in the suburbs with his wife and family. Gordon took me along for lunch and many coffee breaks.

They would start the day around 9:30 – 10:00 a.m. and break for coffee at 11. Then at 1 p.m. it was lunch time for an hour or so and by 4 p.m. everybody went home. On Monday morning nobody arrived before 11 a.m. They had recently switched to a Burroughs mechanical bookkeeping machine that rattled away in the room next to us. A woman operated the machine that kept track of all their accounts. She was busy from early morning until late at night. Guy explained to me that she worked like hell and with a smile, said, "she's German." The old machine, the one that had recently been replaced, sat in the hallway, and nobody had yet bothered to remove it. Our office had a grimy window that looked out on an interior airshaft. Its walls were painted and you could see how tall the cleaning lady was because she had swept the soot off the walls as high as she could reach and what was too high stayed black. While the offices were grubby and quite primitive, almost Dickensian in appearance, the men working there were all very well dressed. Everybody wore dark blue or grey three-piece suits. Some brokers were even dressed in morning coats with striped pants. The gentlemen working for the so called "Government Broker," the firm that was authorized to trade bonds for the treasury, were always in morning coats and top hats. Most others wore bowler hats. Nobody wore the snap-brim grey or brown hats I used to wear in Holland. One day, in the middle of the week, I wore a suit I was very proud of; it was a grey "Prince of Wales pattern" suit, made to measure in Holland. When he saw me that morning, Gordon asked me if I was "going on a weekend." I realized I was seriously "out of uniform," a country yokel in a weekend suit.

I roomed in a place called International House, an institution that offered cheap rooms to young people from all over the world who were working in London. My room was lousy, but it was cheap, and they organized dances and gatherings from time to time. Overall, it was a very nice stay, and I loved the atmosphere in the City, its camaraderie and easy-going life style. Most of the City scene as I knew it is now gone. High-rise buildings have gone up and the stock exchange was torn down and replaced by a new building, which in its turn has become obsolete in a very short time as the old trading system was replaced by an electronic system that does not require a large trading floor. Also, the soot and the fog are gone as London forbade use of fireplaces and coal-fired heating systems.

I liked to wander around London in the weekends. I made a movie of soldiers rehearsing for some kind of flag ceremony, carrying what was supposed to be the flag as a floor cleaning rag on a broomstick. The sergeant major in charge of the drill was a sight to behold and the volume of his voice was true to form. I also saw and filmed a reunion of veterans of what must have been a guards regiment. All the officers were in dark-blue suits and wore bowler hats. They all carried tightly rolled black umbrellas. There was a military band, and when it started to play, the officers started marching uniformly holding their umbrellas under their right arm, with the handle around their elbows, like a drill stick. Behind them marched, what the British call "the other ranks," dressed in rumpled suits and wearing all kinds of hats. What was really remarkable about this parade was that the officers were all a foot taller than the "other ranks," a reflection of the British class system that for many generations knew a different, less healthy diet for the lower classes. Postwar Labor governments and other vast economic changes have drastically altered the social structure of British society. I guess the lower classes are now better fed, but they still dress differently than the "upper upper" people.

The year nineteen-fifty-six was a turning point for us. The political situation between Soviet Russia and Western Europe heated up and so the always difficult and complex political balance in the Middle East was disturbed. In June the Egyptian government under General Nasser nationalized the Suez Canal, which had been owned and operated by a semiprivate French company. A task force of French and British army, navy and air force units attacked the canal and took possession of Port Said. At the same time, the Israelis attacked Egypt through the Sinai desert and took positions at the eastern bank of the canal. The US vigorously protested this action. It forced the attackers to withdraw and supported a UN force to take their place. This was a major political and diplomatic defeat for the British and the French. It introduced the Soviet Union into the Middle Eastern political scene for the first time and created a popular anti-Western movement in the region that continues to this day. Despite the U.S. intervention it also strengthened the not completely groundless suspicion among Arabs that the Israelis, Europeans and Americans play hand in glove. In the fall of that same year, the political situation in the Soviet-dominated part of Europe also began to shift. In June there was an uprising in Poznan, Poland, that was suppressed by Russian troops. This revolt signaled the beginning of the Polish resistance against their Russian oppressors, which culminated, years later, in the strikes in the Gdansk (Danzig) shipyards under the union leader Lech Walesa, who would ultimately become president of Poland. In October the Hungarian people staged an uprising against their Russian-appointed government. The people demanded free elections and the withdrawal of Soviet troops. Initially the Russians withdrew, but later they put a new puppet president in office and invaded the country in force. The Hungarians had hoped for support from the U.S. and European forces, which did not come. The risk of nuclear war was too great, and the Eisenhower administration did not feel it was militarily strong enough to make a fist, which could have deterred the Russians. After heavy street-fighting Budapest, was retaken by Russian tanks and more than 200,000 Hungarians fled to the West. At home we heard dramatic broadcasts from the remaining free stations in Budapest pleading for help and telling us about the carnage in the streets. Netty and I decided that we would not want to live through another occupation, this time by the Russians, with knocks on the door in the middle of the night. We began to think seriously about moving to the United States or Canada.

Our life, meanwhile, was not negatively affected by the threat of war. Over the years we learned to live with the prospect of another conflict. We just pushed it to the back of our conscience. We had many parties and gatherings with our friends in Heemstede. Netty and I organized a large party at our house that was preceded by an automobile rally. Dick van Huystee and I had carefully prepared an itinerary that participants had to follow full of trick questions and strange events, such as a ferry operator we had bribed to get angry when asked by drivers if he had a pretty wife. I believe it was a success. There is a movie of this event somewhere. Since Netty needed help with our two children, we started with a young girl who came during the daytime. Annie was helpful and not bad looking, which may have been the reason she got in trouble and became pregnant. Soon after she left to have her baby, Netty discovered that many items of her inventory of baby clothes were missing. Obviously Annie had been stocking up for her baby. I hit on the idea of getting the priest of her Catholic church involved. He had everything back in no time. After this event we decided to start looking for a more stable live-in girl.

We advertised in the newsletter of our church in hopes of getting a girl from a rural area that would be more used to steady housework and more stable. This is how we got Aukje. Aukje Okkema came from Friesland, from the little town of Grouw. She was a big boned tall girl, not exactly slim, but proved to be very nice to have in our house. We built an extra room in our attic for Aukje, and I got the impression that she was happy to be with us. Aukje was pining for the love of a young man in America. She had visited relatives in Iowa one summer with her parents and there she met what seemed to us, from a photo, a loutish yokel out of the hinterlands. He sent Aukje his picture, standing in front of an automobile with his electric guitar. In other words, he signaled that he had all the equipment a young man in the Elvis Presley era needed. Aukje thought he was serious, which he obviously was not, but it kept her hoping. Aukje worked out very well as a mother's helper, and we could trust her completely with the children, which gave us much more freedom to go out evenings, etc. An interesting footnote; during Aukje's tenure with us the Dutch government's socialized medicine system came into being, giving practically everybody free medical care. Aukje, who was not very well informed about daily events, nevertheless caught on to this right away and started complaining about all kinds of ailments almost the very day the system started working. Before that time she had hardly ever seen a doctor.

As I look back on this period, I feel more than ever that this was the best time in our lives. True, the world around us was in turmoil and the Europeans had not quite given up their penchant to fight each other or to fight with the inhabitants of their colonies. But despite that, we were happy, we had a nice house, we loved each other, had two healthy little boys and not many cares in the world. Aukje would take care of the boys when we wanted to spend an evening with friends. We had a small car to drive around in. We were good friends with several of our neighbors. For me especially, I lived without the gut-wrenching stresses and personality clashes my later career in New York City would bring. Life at Jonas en Kruseman went forward without too many ripples. I was not in daily competition with others, and I was making a reasonable, albeit low, income.

Why even think about giving this all up and venture out into the unknown in America? I think I gradually concluded that my job had not much prospect beyond where I was. Even in the unlikely event that I would have become a partner in a few years, I do not think the firm generated enough revenue to support two well-paid partners. I saw how other firms in the business abroad grew the volume of their stock exchange business, witnessed their emerging research efforts to improve their stock selection and their ability to gauge the economic outlook and market prospects, and came to the conclusion that Jokru was not only a small firm, but an anemic one, a bit of a backwater with only very limited prospects. Whenever I broached the subject of trying to attract new clients with a market letter or better in-house research or other methods, Mr. Schimmelpenninck discouraged my initiatives. He did not do that in a nasty or adversarial way, he just did not have much use for my plans. His motto was that if we would stay small, it might last for our time. The national banks and the three or four larger private banks were actively expanding their research and investment information activity and it was clear to me that our clients would eventually demand similar services from us or leave, and we already lost quite a few people who felt we were not a good fit for their investment needs. The firm was shrinking. Gradually the notion that I would have to go elsewhere was growing in my mind. The problem was that I could not look for a job with another Dutch firm without causing a nasty disruption. This was simply "not done." There was a cozy collegial atmosphere among Dutch securities firms. Everybody knew everybody else, and Mr. Schimmelpenninck was an important man in that world as a member of the board of the Stock Exchange and of several larger listed companies. If I would have put out feelers among other firms, I could only do so with his permission. Otherwise it would backfire immediately. So the idea of trying to make a change in Holland to a firm that offered more aggressive growth prospects was an impossibility. The thought that the investment industry in America was light-years ahead of the state of affairs in Amsterdam was no news for me or any of my Amsterdam contemporaries. The logic for me was that if I wanted to learn more, I would have to go to America.

If I could tough it out there I could stay, and if I were unsuccessful after two or three years, I could always return. In case I would have to return, I could start with a clean, unencumbered slate and would be free to join another Dutch firm and apply my newly acquired knowledge there.

I started thinking about making a move to either America or Canada and began to educate myself on the subject. An important consideration for us was the future of our children. People we talked to about the subject told us that the American education system was excellent and offered possibly better opportunities to our children than what Holland had to offer. They were at that time young enough to make a complete change without ending up with the problems that might arise later if they would switch from one country with its own system and language to another.

George and Adriaan were, of course, the center of our life. They both started to walk and talk at the time they were expected to do so and soon they were indoctrinated with the Dutch *Sinterklaas* tradition. Saint Nicholas, or *Sinterklaas* in Dutch was a saint who lived in Turkey in the third century. He was known as a friend of children. The Romans exiled him to a far-away prison where he died. He was elevated to sainthood and many miracles are believed to have been performed by him over the centuries. Most of them were to help children. The Dutch tradition is to celebrate the arrival from Spain of the saint every year and he usually arrives by steamer. He lands with his white horse and his servant, Black Peter, or *Zwarte Piet*. This servant is probably a throwback to ancient history when the "Moors" dominated Spain. Despite his advanced age, the saint goes on his white horse over the roofs of the houses followed by Black Peter who climbs down the chimneys to see if there are any good children in the house who have left their shoes in front of the fireplace with something in it for the horse to eat. Usually a carrot. The next day the children will race down to the fireplace and to their astonishment will find the carrot gone and in its place a small present, usually special Sinterklaas treats or a small toy. This goes on for several days until the actual day, December 5, when the good saint visits schools and houses. He brings presents for the children who believe in him and in the evening grownups gather around the dining room table to exchange gifts, which are usually wrapped in a surprise package and often come with a poem that makes fun of the recipient. A lot nicer and better paced than the frenzied unwrapping of gifts on Christmas morning we now have to endure. There is an element of fear, however. *Zwarte Piet* carries a big sack in which he puts naughty children to bring them to Spain, and they are never seen again. I can vividly remember how apprehensive I was when the saint visited our school. I was aware of my many misdeeds committed during the year and not at all certain they would be overlooked. Also, children who had been naughty might find the *roe*, a bunch of twigs used to punish children with in the old days, or a few lumps of coal, in their shoe in the morning. Modern child psychologists shudder at these primitive methods of frightening children and nowadays every child is good. Nobody is naughty. Still Tilly, Netty's sister, once found the *roe* in her shoe, while Netty, the goody good shoes of the family, got a nice present.

In the days before December 5, the fireplace ceremony is conducted in the evening, before bedtime, and children will have to sing traditional Sinterklaas songs in front of the chimney so the saint can hear them. I made a movie of this event in Heemstede showing George and Adriaan singing. Adriaan is still too little to know the right words and irritates George, who tries to make it a good performance. I also filmed a Sinterklaas evening at our house where Frans appears in the bishop's costume and hands out presents. Adriaan is overcome with fear for the visitor, but George holds his own and so does his friend and neighbor Jopje Swens and Jopje's sister Elaine. Elies is there, unaware she is facing her own father, and the grandparents participate in the festivities. A wonderful scene to remember.

We sent George to kindergarten, the *Kraaijenester Kleuterschool*. This school still exists at the Kraayenester Singel. He liked it there. Netty or Aukje would walk to the school with Max and Adriaan in a stroller to bring George and pick him up later. We had several cold snowy winters, and snow was an invitation to go to the only sizeable hill in the area, the high dune in Bloemendaal called Het Kopje where there was a smooth road running down from the top and hundreds of people would come to ride their sleds down. We used my old "Flyer" sled, very sturdily built in the U.S. out of steel runners and hickory wood. Our grandson Alexander has it now. In my mind's eye, I still clearly see how we once went to the park Groenendaal in Heemstede with the sled and on a small hill put George on it. Down he went, with much more speed than I had anticipated, but he steered the sled nicely between the trees. When I saw him streak downhill, I thought "Oh my God, what have I done, he is going to crash!" I made a movie of the sledding in Bloemendaal and of George pedaling his new tricycle in our street. At school George was exposed to all the germs a child could possibly accumulate. He got several good ones, including scarlet fever which required a penicillin shot a day. The visiting nurse would come to our house on her bicycle to administer the shots. George, sitting in his bed, could look out over the street and when he saw the nurse coming he would start to yell in a voice laden with anxiety: *"Daar komt de zuster!"* There comes the nurse!

That summer we went for a second time to Spain, this time to the Costa Brava, the Mediterranean shore then just beginning to become popular. We had a wonderful time in Tarragona and later in San Feliu de Guixols, a beach resort where we had the great pleasure of seeing Oc's sister Yvonne with her husband, Louis Hustinx. On the way down to Spain, we had stopped in Montpellier to see the Lafont family where Netty had been as an au pair. I have described this somewhat disappointing encounter in a previous chapter.

Meanwhile Jokru had moved to another building, across the Herengracht, at no 522. Here we had the Alsberg Goldberg people, the two administratiekantoren and Jonas & Kruseman under one roof. I now had a desk, or rather a large antique table in an anteroom next to Mr. Schimmelpenninck's room, which was the principal room overlooking the canal. We worked much closer together now, and I was in many respects his right-hand man, doing a lot of trading and letter writing for the firm on his behalf. Letter writing, Jonas style, was done very much in the old Dutch tradition. You could never start a letter with "we" or "I." There always had to be a neutral beginning or one that referred to the addressee. Mr. Schimmelpenninck had a special, very gracious and old-fashioned style of writing, and I often imitated that, sometimes a little tongue in cheek. The letters always ended with a salutation in line with the addressee's rank or the rank we perceived him or her to have. *Pour épater le bourgeois* as the French say. The Dutch have now largely abandoned the system that we still used with gusto; it was a formidable collection of encomiums. A little man, tradesman, etc., would be a *WelEdele Heer* – a really noble gentleman. A student at a university (or as the student almanac stated, "students and other important people") was a *WeEdelGeboren Heer* – a truly nobly born gentleman. Someone who had graduated from a university and had, for example, a law degree of *Meester in de Rechten*, master of law, was a *WelEdelGestrenge Heer*, Mr… truly noble and austere gentleman, Mr…(the title). My father was an engineer with the academic title of Ir. So he was *De WelEdelGestrenge Heer* Ir. A. A. G. Schieferdecker. Had he been a professor he would have been *HoogEdel Gestrenge Heer* – a highly noble and austere gentleman. With noble titles it went in another direction. A baron was a *HoogWelGeboren Heer* – a highly wellborn gentleman, and so on. A churchman who was also a Ph.D. would be *WelEerwaardeZeer Geleerde Heer* – a most honorable very learned gentleman. So we started our letters with this type of honorific, without the name. At the end we would say: "We remain your obedient servant.' *Uw HoogWelGeboren dw.d.* All this gave the firm a certain *"cachet,"* of course, but you had to make sure you had the right handle for everybody. I had an office diary with all the honorifics with explanations on one page that was about a foot long.

I worked together with Mr. Schimmelpenninck's secretary, Mevrouw Vredenberg, a nice lady who sat in my room and was a good linguist and very good with the honorifics of all our clients. She had married and divorced a German, so she was fluent in German; she also was good in French and could seamlessly follow Mr. Schimmelpenninck's dictation in that language and in English. I made a movie of the office, taking as many shots as I could outside. The movie is in my collection of old movies and gives an impression of the people I worked with.

During my stay at Bordier I had seen the Burroughs mechanical bookkeeping machine they used, and I convinced Mr. Schimmelpenninck that we should modernize part of our system as a first step into the twentieth century. Electronics were still to come, but I had an army buddy who represented a German office machine company that made machines that had a memory and addition and subtraction capability that allowed us to prepare neatly printed client statements with special slips with details for each dividend and coupon payment. This was a revolutionary development, but it worked well.

When I was in Leiden at Rapenburg 8, one of my house friends was Ernest van Panhuys. When I moved in, Ernest was still in the army, having been called up after the war and unable to get out until several years later. He eventually got his law degree and found it hard to get a job in the financial sector where he wanted to work. During the war Ernest had been a big man in the Resistance movement, one of the true heroic Resistance people I have known. He received het Verzetskruis – the Resistance Cross, a high decoration, for his services. He was a most amusing and cordial man to have around, but as I later discovered a little strange in his work habits. I suggested to Mr. Schimmelpenninck that we might try him out, thinking that he could replace me in case I went overseas. Ernest went to the stock exchange with me and I indoctrinated him in the Jokru bookkeeping system. Ernest insisted on continuing to live in Leiden so he commuted every day to Amsterdam and often drove home with me to Heemstede to take the train home to Leiden from there. He became a good family friend and Netty served him many meals, which he ate with gusto. When we left for the U.S. Ernest said good-bye to me with tears in his eyes and presented me with a pair of golden cuff links. To my surprise, he never answered my letters after that. When he came for a visit of Amsterdam Stock Exchange people to the New York Stock Exchange, I asked him why he had never written. He gave me a strange excuse. However, I remembered from working with him that he appeared to have great difficulty writing something down, particularly on the floor of the exchange when we were under some pressure and had to cope with a large number of transactions. Maybe he had dyslexia or some other form of writer's block. Despite this lack of correspondence, I have the best memories of Ernest who died in the late nineties after having married a French lady he met somewhere on a trip. I think he even had children with her. In his final years, he lived in a mansion in Warmond, near Leiden. I believe he left Jokru two or three years after my departure.

As time went by, I had told Mr. Schimmelpenninck of my desire to spread my wings and try my luck overseas. He reacted very nicely and said he thought I should make a trip to the U.S. and Canada to evaluate my prospects there. Perhaps he hoped I would come back chastised by the difficulty of getting a reasonable job in what would be a very different environment for me. We had several contacts in the U.S. and Canada and over the years I had nurtured them. An important relationship for us grew out of our holding of stock in American Hide and Leather, one of the U.S. companies for which we issued Dutch stock certificates. The company had fallen on hard times, probably because its business was in an industry that was not any longer showing great prospects for earnings growth. In Fort Worth, Texas, there was a small leather goods company owned by the Tandy family. This company merged into American Hide and Leather and Tandy's founder, Charles Tandy, effectively took control. The company changed its name into General American Industries. Tandy had served in World War II and had noticed how leather crafts were used in military hospitals for rehabilitation of wounded servicemen. He wanted to set up a chain of leather goods stores offering various hobby products. Later on, he bought a small chain of New England stores that catered to radio hobbyists called Radio Shack. This became the now well-known consumer electronics company of the same name and General American Industries disappeared. The reason why American Hide and Leather was attractive to Tandy was probably its listing on the New York Stock Exchange, in those days a valuable asset. For a new and young company that wanted to grow rapidly, there were numerous hurdles to get a listing. A better way was to take over a company that was already listed, and then change its direction. To effect a takeover, holders of large blocks of stock were sought, and so we came in contact with a New York lawyer, Coleman Burke, who represented Tandy. Coleman started to call us by phone, in those days still a unique experience. We studied the material Coleman sent us, and decided that it was in the interest of our certificate holders to vote for the transaction and thereby gained the gratitude of Coleman.

Another contact we had was Frank Hoch, then a rising star at the foreign investment department of Brown Brothers Harriman. The name would suggest they invested abroad. In reality, the department handled the U.S. investment interests of the numerous foreign clients the firm had. Frank regularly visited Amsterdam and became friendly with me. I had also met him earlier in New York City when we came there for the exchange of General Motors shares.

Since it was difficult to get a U.S. emigration visa, I also wanted to look at Canada where we knew several people through Mr. Schimmelpenninck's involvement with an ailing mortgage bank that operated mainly in Alberta. This bank, called the *Vereenigde Transatlantische Hypotheek Banken,* had made numerous mortgage loans to farmers in Canada and issued bonds in Amsterdam to finance these mortgages. When the Great Depression hit, most of the poor Canadian farmers defaulted on their mortgages and the bonds became almost worthless. In the postwar economic upturn, these bonds gradually regained some value because they represented a claim on farmland. Mr. Schimmelpenninck was chairman of a committee that tried to recover some of the lost value on behalf of the bondholders. He made several trips to Canada to work on this project and many Jokru clients invested in the bonds since we knew about the prospects for a modest payout.

In the Dutch investment environment of those days this was entirely proper. I guess nowadays it might be regarded as insider trading, even though all the relevant information was made public in advertisements in the financial press. It was a typical example of the investment style of Mr. Schimmelpenninck and many others in Amsterdam. Instead of buying shares in a company with interesting long-term prospects, they preferred to go for a modest but almost certain return on investment. There was still so much pessimism around that only very few people saw a more distant, but better, investment horizon.

I embarked on a trip to the US, Canada, and Curaçao in the early spring of 1957. Mr. Schimmelpenninck had added the West Indian stop because he wanted me to see the two notaries in Willemstad who specialized in setting up tax-sheltered offshore investment pools. The government of Curaçao had passed a number of laws that facilitated setting up tax shelters. They wanted to become the Switzerland of the Caribbean in anticipation of a future shutdown of the Royal Dutch Shell refinery on the island that was, by far, the major employer. The notaries were the only people on the island who could prepare the required legal documents. They were politically well connected and had a heavy hand in the drafting of the laws.

I flew to Canada in a KLM DC-9 prop plane. My first stop was Montreal. The city had not yet had the facelift that made it much more attractive in later years. I found it a gloomy and unattractive place with a huge pit in its middle in which you could see all the railroad tracks coming into the main station. My hotel was near the

St Lawrence River, and I was surprised to see that the riverfront, which could have been quite attractive, was just a clutter of factories, wharves and railroad tracks. In the new world, business and industry came first. Nice parks on the banks of the river with promenades and lots of greenery would come later. Montreal would host the summer Olympics in 1976 and transform an island in the river to a major Olympic site and spruced up the city in a major way. This effort cost an enormous amount of money, and the city is still working off its debt load.

I visited a Canadian bank that was owned by the Nationale Handelsbank in Amsterdam. The men I met there were friendly but not very encouraging about my chances to make a go of it in Canada. Despite the country's easy immigration policies, the local investment and banking community was kind of a closed shop where people from abroad were not welcomed. Canada's banking laws were still very restrictive and tightly regulated the types of business banks could engage in. The banking people introduced me to a few brokerage firms. I was very nicely received by several brokers and one family even invited me to come to their country home outside Montreal for a Sunday. Whenever I raised the question of my coming over, I did not get too much of an enthusiastic response from my hosts. I decided that I would only come across the pond if somebody offered me a job because he thought he could really use me in his business and did so with considerable enthusiasm. I realized that I could not uproot my family just for some vague plan with questionable prospects. It had to be more solid. I took a tourist tour of the city and found out that the French speaking community lived in its own world and did not have much contact with the so-called "Anglophone" group. The business community, certainly the investment and banking people, were mostly English speakers, and they almost all lived in nice villas on Mont Tremblant, overlooking the city. Much later the whole scene in Montreal would change and the French speakers, who represented a voting majority, took charge and caused considerable disruption in Canada's economy by making life so difficult for the Anglophones that many moved to Toronto.

After Montreal I went to Toronto, taking the night train, a special experience. You got a berth in a Pullman-style car where you slept behind a curtain in a long corridor. The next morning all the men gathered in a communal washroom for a shave and wash-up. My business contacts in Toronto were not very good, and the whole visit was not more than a day in which I did not learn much. If I only had learned beforehand about large Toronto-based international investment banking and brokerage firms like Wood Gundy, and had been able to get an introduction there, my life and career might have worked out differently. It all depends on who you know and whether you are "on the right street corner at the right time."

After going back to Montreal I took the Greyhound bus to New York City. I did that in order to get a look at the American countryside. It was a nice ride that took the entire day. The bus went into what probably was Vermont and upstate New York, which immediately looked more prosperous than Canada. It was perhaps the drab streets of Montreal where winter was almost but not entirely gone, with the strange tasteless-looking houses with high stoops, that lead to front doors on the second floor, that turned me off, but I decided that Canada was not for me.

I had made a deal with Mr. Schimmelpenninck that I would pay half of the expense of the trip. This made me more comfortable with the project, which was, after all, designed by me as a reconnaissance operation for my personal benefit. So I had reserved a room in a cheap place, the Times Square Hotel. This was definitely not a good choice. It was a run-down, seedy hotel in the Times Square area, which in those days was a lot seedier than it is now. I had a very bad room, and in the hallway, I noticed a bullet hole in the elevator door. I still had to learn that in America a cheap hotel is not just cheap, it also attracts people you do not want to mix with. I called Hans Schuyten, who asked where I was staying, and was horrified by my choice of abode. He quickly got his friend John Hartwell to sponsor me for a room at the Harvard Club.

Frank Hoch, who lived with his wife Lisora and young son in a nice house in Irvington on Hudson also invited me for a weekend visit. I had a long talk there with Frank about emigration, and what it was like to move to the United States to live. He made a comment that stuck in my mind. "When you want to live in America, you have to take America as it is." So true. Most Europeans keep comparing Europe with America when they are here and tend to forget that they are in a different world that does not have necessarily to be the same as theirs.

The most productive contact for me resulted from a weekend with Coleman Burke and his family. He introduced me to a group of his friends in Short Hills, New Jersey. There I met Jim Morrison, who was a vice president with First Boston Corporation (FBC). I also met another friend of Coleman's who was a partner in a well-known Wall Street firm, of which I cannot remember the name. As it turned out, Morrison was involved in developing the foreign business of FBC and was interested in talking to me. Ultimately, FBC would hire me and arrange an emigration visa for my family and me. Two contacts had worked out well and proved to be key determinants of our future: Hans and Nancy Schuyten convinced me to bring my family to Connecticut, and Coleman Burke was instrumental in getting me my first American job. Further confirmation of my lifelong belief – one should make use of all the contacts and all the help friends and acquaintances offer. Provided you do not make a pest of yourself, of course. Coleman also touted the advantages and pleasures offered by the area of Short Hills, New Jersey, where he lived. If I had followed through on his recommendations, I would no doubt have ended up as a golfer with all the frustrations associated with that pastime. In the event, I ended up as a Connecticut sailor, heavily involved in a sport I love but that also has its frustrations.

During my two-or three-week stay in New York City, I benefited from the hospitality of Brown Brothers, Harriman. This firm has a long-standing tradition of opening its doors to young people working for the numerous foreign firms they do business with. Frank Hoch ran the foreign intern/trainee program and I was offered a desk for a few days and was given the opportunity to visit with several departments of the firm to see how they did business. Oom Eelco also gave me the names of a couple of people he thought I should see. So I went to see David Rockefeller at the Chase Manhattan Bank, who received me in a very friendly and noncommittal way. I had some trouble finding him because I picked the wrong entrance to enter Chase. It was the Wall Street entrance for securities deliveries. As I approached the counter and asked for Mr. Rockefeller, the clerk there said he did not know who that was and, in a typical New York manner, sent me away as a nuisance inquiry interfering with his job. Luckily, a man in the background overheard our conversation and proved to be a little sharper. He recognized the name of the president and major stockholder of the bank and directed me to an elevator that brought me to the right floor. Unfortunately, the problems I had to get access to the office of the bank's president caused me to be a little late for my appointment. I saw Mr. Rockefeller again when Netty and I were standing in line for a buffet on Parents Day when George was a freshman at Middlebury.

Another Oom Eelco contact was an equally high-level one. Robert Lovett was a partner at Brown Brothers. He had been secretary of defense in the Truman administration and later, during the Kennedy administration, he was one of the people the President Kennedy used as private advisors "a back-channel." He had a special phone in his office with a sign on it saying that when this phone was ringing and Mr. Lovett was not in his office, "it should not be picked up under any circumstances." It was a direct line to the Oval Office in the White House, and they did not want just anybody to speak with the president. Mr. Lovett was a very nice man who showed a genuine interest in me and years later, when I came to work at Brown Brothers, invited me several times to come down to his office for a chat. It was, of course, interesting for me to meet with these people who operated on a level I would and could never attain, and it was not clear to me what networking with these extremely important people could really do for me. After all, I was just seeking an entry-level position in Wall Street. I never told Oom Eelco and thanked him warmly for his efforts.

U.S. regulations did not allow boarding a KLM plane for Curaçao in New York. I had to go back to Montreal to continue my trip. I took the train back and had a nice dinner with an officer of the bank I had previously interviewed with at his apartment in the city. He plied me with scotch and wine, and when I had to get up at four in the morning to catch my plane, I was seriously hung over. After we had been flying for a couple of hours, I told the stewardess of my predicament. She said she had a surefire cure and offered me a Bloody Mary, a drink then completely unknown to me. It worked. The plane landed in Havana, this was before the Castro period, so I got a little exposure to Cuba and its Spanish-speaking officials who were brusque and uninterested. Curaçao was friendlier and immediately showed a "Dutch touch." One of the first things I saw was a Dutch ANWB (the Dutch automobile and travel association) road sign outside the airport. I went to my modest hotel and settled in for my first visit to the Caribbean. There would be many more to follow. In the following days, I visited the two notaries (Dutch government appointed legal officials who handle all corporate and real estate ownership and domicile changes as well as wills, etc.). These gentlemen had a nice operation going for themselves. They were busy setting up offshore corporations domiciled in Curaçao, which enjoyed very favorable tax treatment. I also visited with the local banks and paid a visit to the governor general, Mr. Speekenbrink, an old colleague and friend of Pa van Kleffens. What was particularly nice was the presence on the island of Cor Roodenburg – a man I had known since we both started out as geology students. When he was called up in the military, Cor had chosen to become a career naval officer. He now was the governor's naval attaché. Cor's brother was also a navy officer and served on a destroyer that was based on the island. The destroyer, quite a big presence for the Dutch navy, was there because there was a latent threat from Venezuela. Most of the oil Royal Dutch Shell recovered in Venezuela was shipped to the Curaçao refinery for processing. Venezuela was a military dictatorship that cast eyes on the Dutch island. I spent several evenings at Cor's home with his nice young wife and little son. I was also invited for a navy style, very good *Rijsttafel* – Indonesian meal on Sunday morning aboard the destroyer. A wonderful experience. On my way back my plane flew by way of Caracas, Venezuela, where I briefly met with Frits Greup and his then wife Deetje at the airport. Frits was posted there on his first assignment in the Dutch foreign service. The next stop was Paramaribo, Dutch Guyana. From there we crossed over to the Azores, then a dirt-poor island where somebody knocked on the door of my stall in the men's room after I had gone in, to hand me the two sheets of toilet paper I was allocated to use. When I landed at Schiphol, Amsterdam, I knew that if I wanted to leave Holland, I wanted to go to America and not to Canada, Curaçao or any other place. I felt I had a good possibility for a job with First Boston Corporation and decided to work on that.

Making plans is always easier than implementing them. Netty and I spoke with our parents and I kept Mr. Schimmelpenninck informed of our doings. Our parents were generally supportive; my father even said to me in private that if he were my age he would do the same thing, a statement that really warmed my heart and did make me feel less guilty about removing the only grandchildren my parents had from their immediate environment. Fax machines, e-mail, and cheap transatlantic phone calls did not yet exist, so it would be mainly by letter that we would be able to stay in touch. Once we had moved over, I wrote my parents weekly and Netty did the same with her parents. Many of these letters were saved and give a good impression of our first years in America. But a great deal had still to be done before we could leave. I wrote many long letters to Jim Morrison and he eventually came across with a genuine job offer and an offer to arrange emigration papers for us. He offered me a job in the sales and trading department for the princely sum of $7,500. a year. This posed an immediate dilemma for me. What did this salary mean? Could we live on it? I corresponded with Hans Schuyten about this subject, and he asked his secretary to work up a family budget based on that level of income. I spoke with many people who had visited the U.S. or lived there and got mixed reviews. I wrote Oom Eelco, who encouraged me to go ahead. As the days went by and our visa application was processed, the reality of what we were planning to do set in, and I had many a moment when I felt as if two big hands around my neck slowly closed my throat.

We went on vacation in the summer of 1957 to England. We drove our Volkswagen in the very early morning to Ostend, Belgium, and boarded a ferry to Dover there. We drove from the ferry to Lyme Regis, a small seaside resort in Devon. We discovered that England was not yet blessed with an express highway system so we meandered from one city or town to the other, and it took us forever to cover a distance that on the map did not seem very far. I was even more impressed with the achievement of the Allied armies who had prepared for D Day and invaded France, starting from an area where all the equipment had to be funneled down to various small harbors along a very old road system. Lyme Regis proved to be a charming old, somewhat run-down place, where elderly Britons bundled up in raincoats sat in beach chairs on a windy beach, with no sand, just pebbles, watching the turbulent sea. We toured around and saw Stonehenge and returned by way of the New Forest, Salisbury, and London where we still could park our car in front of our hotel near Piccadilly Circus! Once off the ferry in Belgium we dove immediately into an inviting looking restaurant and enjoyed the first really good meal after almost two weeks of steady exposure to the English kitchen, which at that time was not yet up to the level where it is now.

When our visa came through – I was given preference status – it was "fish or cut bait" time. We had to go to the American Consulate in Amsterdam and submit ourselves to all kinds of inspections and medical tests. They took x-rays of our lungs and fingerprinted us, asked if we were or had ever been a member of the Communist party, etc., etc. After that we had to wait and confront the reality that we would most likely be leaving Heemstede before too long. We started selling all kinds of things we could not use in America such as appliances, our radios and record player. Pa and Ma took Max and they found a family who lived on a farm who were willing to take Max for the final years of his life. We found a buyer for our house, a young family that lived down the street in a smaller house. We gave a big farewell party in Oma Schieferdecker's house in Bloemendaal (we asked Oma to go away for a few days). Mr. Schimmelpenninck gave a very nice farewell party for us with the employees of Jokru, and Rob and Liesbeth Laane and many others did the same. It was tough to say good-bye to our life in Holland, our home and our relatives and friends, and I still find it remarkable that Netty and I went through with our plans to start a new life in America. It must have been the risk-taking entrepreneurial genes of our ancestors that helped us to persist. We packed all our belongings in a big crate that the movers said would be delivered to our door in the U.S. I decided to go ahead by plane and spend a few weeks alone, trying to find a place to live for our family. Netty would follow with George and Adriaan by ship, which we thought was less stressful and allowed her to take more luggage. Then came the day when Netty drove me to Schiphol, where I boarded a plane for New York to start what would be the biggest adventure of our lives. Unwittingly the KLM people gave me a send-off that made it easier for me to say good-bye to my homeland. For some reason the ticket counter wanted me to come back, and thinking I was a German, started to bellow over the PA system: *"Herr Schieferdecker wird gebeten sofort zum schalter zu kommen..."*

21 : *America*

On April 27, 1958, I arrived at Idlewild Airport in New York City aboard a KLM DC-7 propeller plane and took a cab to the city. The driver was a real old-fashioned New York cabbie similar to the ones you nowadays only see in commercials – white, middle aged, English speaking with a strong New York accent and knowledgeable about the city and its geography. Today you usually deal with people from all kinds of third- world countries who barely speak English and often do not know their way around the city. I had a very friendly conversation with my cabbie. I told him I was a new immigrant to the United States, which gave him an opportunity to give me a lecture on life in New York City. When we passed the large cemeteries in Queens that occupy prime real estate with splendid views of the city, he declared, "These are the only New Yorkers who are not in a hurry." I went to the Hotel St. George in Brooklyn, just across the Brooklyn Bridge, a place the First Boston people had recommended because it was only one stop by subway from Wall Street and very moderately priced. My cabbie wished me all the best in my new life in America and I went up to my room. The hotel does not exist anymore, but it used to be a Brooklyn landmark and was once famous for its swimming pool and large ballrooms. I noticed that it had known better times – much better times. It was a run-down place with elevators that still required operators to run them and a lobby in which strange people were hanging around. My room was on one of the upper floors, and my window looked out on an inner court with only a small bit of sky showing if you craned your neck up at the top of the window. It was a tiny room with a small bathroom and a single bed. Suddenly, after the bellman had put my luggage down and left and I was alone, the enormity of the step I had taken hit me hard. I chocked up badly, and tears welled in my eyes, not so much because I felt sorry for myself but because I realized I was responsible for making a living for our little family here in this suddenly very strange looking city and had no clue how to go about it. After about half an hour in which I felt more miserable than I had ever felt in my life, I went to bed not feeling all that great about the adventure I had started. But first I had to settle down and get used to the time difference.

The next morning I had recovered and went to First Boston (FBC) where Jim Morrison and his staff received me. I was introduced to many people on the trading floor and importantly to a group of young college graduates who were in a training course. I would join this group to get used to the firm's business and its people. I soon became friends with several of them and they helped me greatly in getting used to Wall Street, FBC and bachelor life in New York City. Two men in this group were especially kind and helpful to me, Mike Strang and Sam Yonce. Mike was a Princetonian who had traveled in Europe, spoke some French, and was interested in my background. Mike grew up in Colorado and regaled me with many stories of his life out on the ranch of his grandfather and father. To show his western roots, he wore a belt with a fairly large western buckle with his business suit. After a few years, I lost sight of Mike, which I regretted because he was an exceptionally nice guy. He went back to Colorado and worked as an investment banker there. Later he became a politician and was elected to the House of Representatives. Now he is a rancher. Sam was a Yalie with whom I remained friends for many years. He married and lives in Greenwich and did business with me when I was at Eberstadt.

In the following weeks I was quickly propelled up on a steep learning curve, which was a wonderful experience and helpful in forcing me to adjust quickly to American business practices and lingo. I was put in an accelerated training program where I spent time in the research department, the investment banking department and several sections of the sales and trading department. The place where I would spend most of my time was the FBC trading room, then one of Wall Street's best and biggest. The company had recently moved into new space on Broad Street, almost directly across from the imposing facade of the New York Stock Exchange. I discovered to my astonishments that FBC was not a member of the exchange and that this was an advantage because it allowed them to trade securities listed on the exchange at net prices in the over-the-counter market, i.e. without having to charge the fixed commissions the rules of the exchange then required its member firms to charge. Shades of things to come. FBC could make its own markets, set its own price levels and act independently of the specialists who controlled price formation on the floor of the exchange. In contrast to Amsterdam, bonds were traded mainly over-the-counter in New York, and bond trading was by far the biggest business at FBC. Compared to today's trading rooms with hundreds of traders staring at computer screens, the FBC operation in 1958 was small beer, but at that time, it was up to date, big, and considered state of the art. Remember, electronic devices did not yet exist. Even the word "electronics" was not yet part of our vocabulary. Each trader was sitting in front of his own switchboard with a number of direct lines to the firms they were dealing with. The government bond trading desk was the most important one with half a dozen traders sitting in a semi-circle facing a large blackboard on which office boys wrote bid and asked prices. Each trader specialized in a separate segment of the market: Treasury bills, short-term bonds, long-term Treasurys, federal agency bonds, and even bankers acceptances. For me the volume was astonishingly large, with "round lots" of $100,000 and trades of one million or more routine. Traders had direct lines to their most important contacts in other firms and shouted out their trades and other information relevant to their business. In round lots of treasurys the "spread" between bid and asked was usually paper thin at not more than 1/16th of a percent, or a "steenth" as they would cry out, or sometimes even 1/32nd of a percent. Prices were chalked up on the big black board so the entire room could see how the government bond market was evolving. Municipal bonds, issued by state and local authorities, were traded at another desk. This was a very different business with hundreds of issues outstanding and much smaller numbers of bonds changing hands in each trade. However, the spread was much wider in this market so that each trade could yield quite a decent profit.

I ended up at the corporate bond desk where the bonds issued by U.S. corporations (many) and foreign entities denominated in dollars (a few, mostly Canadian) were traded. The stock desk was relatively small. This group specialized in utility stocks and bank and insurance company stocks. The latter two categories were not listed on the exchange in those days.

They also made markets in a number of stocks that had been offered in past underwritings managed by FBC. One of the over-the-counter issues traded there was Haloid Xerox, a brand-new, small company that had developed a process that made it possible to copy documents without having to photograph them. This was the beginning of a major breakthrough in document handling. We were used to typewriters that produced originals with copies that were made with the help of carbon paper. If you wanted to make a copy of an existing document, it had to be photocopied. Haloid Xerox's first small public offering of stock had been handled by FBC. In the FBC mailroom, they showed me the Xerox machine, a large cumbersome affair but still a fascinating new technology. Later Xerox would become one of the hottest growth stocks, and the company would record astonishing growth worldwide. Then when its patents ran out and its turf was invaded by the Japanese, the company was caught flat-footed without a good plan for the future and its stock declined precipitously, only to recover again much later to become a respectable, somewhat-dull player in a mature document-handling industry.

Other desks were for salesmen who covered institutional investors and for the syndicate department that handled the marketing of new issues brought out by FBC or by syndicates in which it participated. All communications were by phone or by telex, a system that nowadays has declined significantly in importance but still exists. A number of male typists sat at large clunky machines that rattled out incoming messages and received outgoing communications that were being banged out on keyboards. Internally we communicated with small sheets on which we would write a message. Boys were constantly running around to pick up messages and deliver them. What I was witnessing was essentially a large distribution machine where securities resulting from FBC deals, and syndicates organized by it or others, were distributed rapidly among institutional investors and traders and where markets were maintained to facilitate distribution of outstanding issues in the so-called after market.

In addition, FBC was a major factor in government bond trading, thus helping the U.S. Treasury in its efforts to create liquid markets for its bonds. FBC's relationship with the U.S. Treasury Department was of extreme importance to it and whenever there was a new government bond issue being offered, FBC went all out to sell it. Invariably the issue was earmarked as "attractive."

The top management of the firm was in the hands of two men who were very different but in a way complementary. Through Mike Strang, who was good at gossip, networking and digging up important background information about our bosses, I learned what kind of people they were. George Woods was Chairman, he was a somewhat enigmatic figure who was believed to be ultra-smart and was generally admired. He was a man who had come up through the ranks, starting out as an office boy from Brooklyn and rose to his position at the top through sheer grit and determination. He was completely self-educated and a good example of what America offers people who want to get ahead in the world. George was responsible for several key relationships he had built up with organizations like the World Bank where FBC became one of the major underwriters of this important postwar institution. He traveled often and did not bother very much to get to know us underlings. I was told he was a great admirer of the theater and invested some of his private money in the financing of plays, a very risky business that could lead to a quick loss of the entire investment or, in rare cases, a real home run. Jim Coggeshall, the president, was a real Bostonian, scion of a wealthy family and a total opposite to George Woods. I gained the impression that Woods was more "Mr. Outside," the man who brought in the important investment banking contacts while Coggeshall minded the store. My first and only visit to the latter's office came at the appointed time. Mike Strang had alerted me to the fact that Coggeshall would sit behind a clean desk in a nice office and would have the name of his visitor written on a card, hidden in a small half open drawer of his desk. He would surreptitiously glance at the card while greeting you as an old friend and leave the drawer open a bit so he could re-check your name and background. Sure enough, when I came in Jim, or rather Mr. Coggeshall for me, peeked in his drawer and started a general conversation. He welcomed me warmly, commented that I had "an interesting background," and after a few pleasantries I was on my way again.

FBC had several floors in the building it occupied. The investment banking or so-called "buying department" was upstairs. The trading and sales department was on a floor below it. The research department was on the same floor as the buying department and worked almost exclusively for it. While the research department looked incredibly sophisticated to me as a newcomer, it was, if compared with the work done by many firms in later years, a very simple operation doing mostly basic statistical comparisons. As part of my training program I spent a few weeks in the research department. There I learned how American investment firms conducted their research, quite a difference from the very haphazard way in which we used to inform ourselves of investment opportunities in Holland. A senior analyst specialized on each of the three industries in which FBC did most of its investment banking work – banking and insurance and public utilities. There also was a senior man who kept track of the basic industries. He was a nice, somewhat pompous individual, who used to spout predictions on car manufacturing and steel production and sat in a small office with big pictures on the wall of large steel plants belching black smoke. Environmental concerns had not yet reached us. Young associates prepared statistical comparisons for investment banking purposes. This was difficult grinding work that required intense study of many annual reports. It was amazing for me to see how much more information American companies made available to their shareholders and how much additional information could easily be gathered on all kinds of general subjects, business and finance as well as other areas. Clearly the Americans had a big advantage over the rest of the world in their ability to quickly gather data on any subject of interest and use it. I found my new young colleagues generally bright and well informed but not burdened by a great deal of knowledge of facts. They were always busy to gather more information and use it for the business at hand. My traditional European educational background was much more geared to learning many facts that often had no use in practical life, but knowing all those often-random facts created a misplaced sense of moral and intellectual superiority among Europeans over the "superficial" Americans. With the coming of the Internet, the entire world is now able to research any subject of interest and tap into databanks all over the world. This American invention has leveled the playing field for all of us and over time will hopefully remove many barriers in the relationships between people.

I also learned there was a mysterious government apparatus called the SEC – the Securities and Exchange Commission. Everybody at FBC had a healthy respect for the SEC and its long arm. FBC had created a solid "firewall" between its investment banking operations and the sales and trading departments by putting them on separate floors. The separation of both departments was rigorously enforced and as a trainee I was allowed to sit in on a few of the daily investment banking meetings but was told in no uncertain terms that everything that was discussed there was strictly confidential and could in no way be relayed to the sales and trading people on the floor below.

There was also a clear difference in culture between the two groups. The sales and trading people in general were a rowdy, easy-going bunch with lots of joking and horse play while the investment bankers were more cerebral. They felt they were the financial intellectuals, people of a higher caliber. Through the years to come, I would see these differences come and go and the point of gravity in firms shift from one group to the other, depending on how much money was made on each side of the fence. The information submitted to the SEC in special filings was, of course, available to us and was used for the spreadsheets we prepared for the "buying department." Most of the work done in this area was rather routine number crunching for utility companies that wanted to offer bonds or issue new equity. FBC had very strong connections with a host of utility companies. Bonds were traded on a "yield to maturity basis." If you knew the coupon and the maturity, you could figure out the yield with the help of yield tables we had. Again, electronic hand-held calculators did not yet exist. When you knew the rating of a bond, i.e. how Standard and Poor's evaluated the quality of the borrower, you could compare a bond on a yield basis with similar issues of the same quality and maturity and determine an equitable price. In Holland I was not used to that system. There, bonds were redeemed gradually by drawing numbers by lot, so you never knew the exact maturity of an issue. If you owned a hundred bonds, you could on a given date see seventeen or so being called by lot which left you with a holding of odd size. You could only compute a yield based on an average maturity, a much less accurate system that did not allow precise pricing of a portfolio.

Later when I had returned to the bond-trading desk, I could see how a new issue was launched and priced. A senior man from the buying department would descend into the trading area and check recent trades in comparable issues; he then would go around the salesmen and test the waters on the sell side. He would price the offering in line with the market, get a previously formed syndicate in gear, and launch it. The syndicate department handled the allocation of the securities offered among a large number of buyers. On those occasions, trainees like me were used to lend a hand with the heavy phone traffic. For me this was a moment for clammy hands and a nervous stomach. I still had trouble understanding phone calls with people who spoke rapidly using special investment lingo and rapidly spouting numbers with staccato voices, often with a distinct New York accent, a strange dialect for me. Underwriting syndicates or the names of the firms bidding on bonds offered in the competitive bidding market, mostly utility bonds and municipals, were listed on a big board. The FBC people felt far superior to almost all other investment banking firms in the street except for Morgan Stanley. The latter was the "white shoe firm" par excellence. They did not even have salesmen in those days, their syndicate department would just parcel all their juicy deals out to the hoi polloi, the other firms that had stooped as low as to have a sales department. Merrill Lynch was seen as an upstart firm, just a big broker for small investors now trying to elbow into the upper ranks of the investment banking business. Then there was the long, long list of firms that do not exist anymore. How the world has changed!

Another major social change I witnessed in the years I spent working in New York City was the breakdown of the color bar. In 1958 there were very few if any African Americans at work in Wall Street. It was as if the color bar came down at the Fulton Street subway stop. Even the shoeshine man who came around every day to shine our shoes at our desks was an Italian immigrant who could barely speak a word of English, but he was white. At the stock trading desk, then a modest operation compared with the huge bond business, I sat next to Howard Cox, a very precise little man who had his hair carefully plastered on top of his head, parted in the middle, with not a single strand out of place. Howard had a dry sense of humor and was constantly jabbering on the phone with buddies at other firms who also liked to joke around. Obviously Howard was not a major profit center. He traded convertible preferred stocks, a fairly rarely used security. When people wondering how the market was doing called out "how are stocks," he liked to yell "yes" pretending he heard somebody call his name. Howard was an old-fashioned, All American bigot who told me there had been big rifts in the firm in the days of the McCarthy hearings when Senator Joe McCarthy had the entire country in an uproar as he started a witch hunt, pretending to discover Communists everywhere in the government. McCarthy was eventually brought down, but it was clear that he had many supporters among populist right-wing elements in American society and in Wall Street. An interesting episode involved Howard's only daughter who was recently married. A picture of the bride appeared in the local paper of the New Jersey town where he lived. He wanted copies made of the newspaper article with the newfangled Haloid Xerox machine they were operating in the mailroom. He was horrified when he saw the result. His snow-white princess appeared with a black face. The new technology was O.K. for text but not yet totally up to snuff for pictures.

The glass ceiling, which prevented women from attaining leadership positions in Wall Street, was also firmly in place. There were a few well-educated women in the research department, but the majority of women working at FBC were secretaries and clerks. Most of the secretaries were nice Irish girls from Brooklyn. When I saw Jim Morrison's secretary with a black spot on her forehead, I warned her she should look in the mirror because she had gotten some soot from a building on her face. She explained to me it was Ash Wednesday and everybody went to church that morning to get blessed and get a dab of ashes from the priest, a custom I had not heard of in Holland.

In those first weeks, I had to get used to a new job, work in a different language in a totally new working environment and at the same time find a place to live for my family. A stressful situation to be in under any circumstances, but for me there was also the time pressure. I knew when Netty and the boys were going to arrive, and I realized I would not be able to pay for a hotel for the four of us for a long time. I simply had to find a place to live on very short notice. I was confronted with a bewildering choice of options. It became rapidly clear that living in Manhattan with two little boys who would have had to go to an expensive private school was out of the question. We would not be able to afford the rent on an apartment big enough for our family, and it was made clear to me that the public schools were simply not good enough. Also, the tuition bills of a private school would be out of the question for us. I had to find a place in the suburbs where the schools were better and free. There were so many different places I needed to investigate, and I had no idea how one region compared to another. Used to the social strata of Dutch society, I knew that these did not apply to life in America, but I gradually became aware of subtle differences in the backgrounds of my colleagues at FBC and how their choice of residence was influenced by these differences. Many FBC people lived in New Jersey. That was an obvious choice since the commute by train and Hudson River ferry was easy and quick for a downtown office location. When the World Trade center was built and the Hudson River tube station was placed right under it, it became even more convenient. Several younger FBC people who were married but had not yet had children lived in what were called "garden apartments" in New Jersey. These complexes of low buildings, each contained several apartments with their own front doors and placed in a more or less park-like setting, were ideal for them because they could be rented. I also had my mind set on renting because, if I could help it; I did not want to use up all my reserves by buying a house with the risk that we might not like the neighborhood or the school system. I wanted to keep my powder dry until Netty was there and could help me decide where we wanted to live. One of my new colleagues at FBC lived in the Montclair, New Jersey, area and he volunteered to let me see his house and go around with a realtor friend. I liked the houses there, but having seen the area where Coleman Burke lived in Short Hills, I could see the difference.

Also I did not know much about the school district. It all looked very foreign and disjointed to me and the recently developed neighborhoods of very similar looking houses seemed very alien. They were often placed somewhere in the middle of nothing on a horseshoe shaped cul-de-sac with no clear connection to a town or village, just a plot of land some developer had been able to buy. The woman I met in a house that was in my price range was nice but did not seem to be a person I could envision as a neighbor who could become a friend of Netty's. I also went to Connecticut, where I met with the wife of Dave Baker, Jim Morrison's right-hand man. She was a realtor and showed me several houses in Darien, where she lived. Here I had a more settled impression of the neighborhoods, but the prices were out of reach for me.

I kept going to the Schuytens on weekends. I had met Hans when he visited Holland as a boy with his brother Herbert and his mother and aunt, the Mullemeister twins. Hans' grandparents, Mr. and Mrs. Mullemeister, were close friends of my grandparents, from their days in Indonesia. They had twin daughters, Liz and Mans. Liz married a Mr. Schuyten who emigrated to the U.S. before or during World War I. I seem to remember that he was a conscientious objector to the draft and preferred to emigrate with his wife Liz. Mans, who wanted to be near her twin sister, emigrated too and stayed to live with her sister's family all her life. She became a college professor. The family settled in Seattle, where Mr. Schuyten prospered and raised a family of five. There were four boys and a girl. Hans married Nancy Ehrlichman and they had four children, a son Peter; twin daughters Candy and Cathy; and Vicky, a third daughter. Nancy belonged to a prominent Seattle family. Her family name got in the news in the early seventies when the Nixon administration's Watergate scandal broke and John Ehrlichman, Nixon's presidential advisor for domestic affairs, was convicted for involvement in the Watergate affair. John was Nancy's brother. He made several bad decisions, but he remained loyal to the president he served and paid the price for it. Hans and Nancy were very helpful to us when we settled down in Riverside, and when I was alone in New York waiting for Netty's arrival, they invited me several times for weekend visits to their nice waterfront house in Stamford. When Thys de Clercq came to visit us from Montreal where he was then working, we introduced him to Hans who helped him find a job with American Express Banking Corp where he was a vice president. I got along very well with both Nancy and Hans, but particularly with Nancy. She was an attractive woman who had long talks with me about life in the U.S., which was helpful in giving me an idea of what would lay ahead. Nancy also introduced us to several of their friends who lived in or around Riverside, mostly members of the Christian Science Church to which Hans and Nancy belonged. One couple, David and Dotty Osler, became good friends. Nancy introduced us to the Thomfordes, and through them we found our first home in Riverside. So we have every reason to be grateful to Liz and Mans for putting us into contact with their family in Connecticut, and we were more than willing to take their devotion to family photography in stride. Liz and Mans always traveled with a camera and took an innumerable number of pictures of the people they encountered on their travels. The first time I learned about this hobby was in the period when I was in the army and home for the weekend. Liz and Mans had come from the U.S. by ship with their car. This was not unusual. After the war many Americans toured Europe in their own cars. They came to Voorburg and immediately insisted on positioning us all in our front yard. Mans set up a tripod with her camera and Liz bustled around our group waving a handkerchief so Mans could be sure to get everybody in the viewfinder. This was a comical scene with these two twin ladies – both with short cropped hair and identical flowery Mother Hubbard dresses and sensible shoes – going through their routine. It soon became clear why they were so experienced. They traveled with huge albums full of pictures of their offspring with lots of children, all people we had never seen. They would insist on showing us all these pictures, pointing out who everybody was on each snapshot. Later in Stamford, I met them again at Hans and Nancy's house, and Nancy strictly forbade them from showing me their pictures, fearing it would bore me to tears. Then one afternoon they offered to show me Old Greenwich and Riverside. We drove to the Shorelands neighborhood where Hans and Nancy had lived earlier. In a quiet side street, they stopped and hauled out their albums, which they had hidden in their car, to show me their entire collection, all the time begging me not to tell Nancy. It took about half an hour to see all the pictures and we were on our way again. I had been ambushed!

It was upsetting for us to learn during our first year in Riverside that Hans and Nancy were getting divorced. Hans had fallen in love with a Chinese woman he had met on a business trip to Hong Kong. Nancy remarried, had a happy second marriage and died in November 2005. Hans died in Shanghai on December 31, 2010.

Nancy helped me in my efforts to find a place to live. At the Schuytens I met a family who were Christian Scientists like the Schuytens and friends of them. These were the Thomforde's, a nice young couple from Texas. He worked for Shell in Houston but was now in New York for a stint at the U.S. head office there. He had just learned that he was going to be sent to the Netherlands to spend time at the Royal Dutch Shell headquarters in The Hague. For them this was a big adventure and would be their first trip to Europe. They were eager to speak to somebody from the Netherlands who could enlighten them on the pitfalls of life there. In the fifties America was still far ahead of Europe in the many material things that make modern life agreeable. I assured them they would not have to bring a supply of Kleenex tissues and toilet paper, but impressed them of the need to bring umbrellas, raincoats and sweaters. During our conversation I found out they lived in Riverside near Stamford and were renting a house there. I immediately asked them if I could see the house and if I could perhaps take over their lease. They responded positively on both counts, and after I saw the house and made a number of phone calls to the realtor who was their rental agent, I managed to get the lease turned over to me. The Thomforde's were leaving shortly after Netty would arrive so that was a good fit too. That is how we ended up at 16 Peter's Road in Riverside. Netty and I have always felt that it was a stroke of extraordinary good luck that we found Riverside, a community where we have lived very happily for more than forty-five years.

I had now taken the first step on the road to making us true American suburbanites. The next question was transportation. I did not want to spend money on a new car either, and when I heard that another family in the Christian Science community, the Stiefels, were planning to trade their station wagon in for a new one, I offered to buy their old one. This was a large Pontiac, a true Detroit iron, its distinguished color scheme, pink with grey, was a little extreme, but as a totally inexperienced European I preferred to buy a car from people I knew over plunging into the world of second-hand car salesmen. This monster car served us well for a few years and gas was still cheap. If I remember correctly, gas was about 35 cents a gallon. The big car proved particularly useful when we had to move to another house and when we had to pick up Tineke and Jaap Kort and their four daughters, plus a mountain of luggage. from the airport. After I bought the car, I parked it near the St. George Hotel in Brooklyn and drove it around the city in the weekends. I drove down the Henry Hudson Parkway, along the Hudson River and passed over the George Washington Bridge, which then had only one level, and got familiar with paying tolls everywhere I went. I cruised around New Jersey and headed back to Brooklyn via the Holland tunnel. There I got a little confused about the signals a cop was giving while directing traffic and received my umpteenth culture shock when the cop stopped me and started to yell at me as if I were a criminal. Looking into his angry, red, Irish face framed in red hair, I realized I was far away from Holland where cops used to address you as Meneer (Sir) and would generally correct your minor traffic infractions by addressing you in a polite, but half mocking style rather than yell at you using foul language. There were many more culture shocks to come.

Life in the United States in the fifties was very different from life in Europe. Nowadays the global markets have taken over and when going from one continent to the other it becomes more and more difficult to find significant differences in the amenities that make modern life convenient. Try to buy a present for friends or relatives abroad, and you will find how hard it is to select something that is not already well known and readily available over there. The all encompassing leveling of the playing field caused by television, the Internet and the opening of virtually the whole world to trade had not yet taken place in the fifties. America was an island of prosperity, way ahead in many respects. People felt secure in their homes and in their jobs. Everyone was moving ahead to better positions, better homes bigger cars with more chrome and larger tailfins, and the moms of almost all kids were home when they returned from school. In the schools, kids had teachers who dressed up for their job. Male teachers all wore neckties. Female teachers had their hair done in a beauty salon and wore high heels. At the FBC office we all wore hats when we went out of the office. Several salesmen wore bowler hats in winter. In summer everybody wore a straw hat. So I bought one too. It was a brown snap-brim number made out of light straw. Many men wore boaters in summer. The summer hats were worn from Memorial Day until Labor Day weekend when they disappeared simultaneously as if somebody upstairs had pulled a switch. We also wore thin summer suits and I bought two right away when it started getting hotter. They were wash-and-wear Haspel suits that you could throw in the washing machine to clean. Very practical but not always very crisp looking. The women working at FBC all wore dresses and shoes with high heels. Many wore hats when they went out on the street. TVs were a fairly recent phenomenon and all broadcasts were in black and white. The sets took about five minutes to warm up after they were turned on and remote controls did not yet exist. People would decide beforehand which program they wanted to watch and would settle down in front of their sets for the evening. There were seven channels in our area and every house had an ugly-looking TV antenna on its roof. Cable TV did not come until the seventies. Almost everybody had a TV set. In Holland very few people had TV and Dutch broadcasts were limited to the evening hour on one channel. The government regulated TV and had ordered that nobody should waste time watching TV during the day. For us, American homes were marvels of convenience and full of interesting gadgets. The big refrigerator-freezers were new to us and so were the dishwashers and large washer and dryer machines everybody had. Using a coal burning furnace to heat the house as we did in Heemstede was a curious ancient practice in the eyes of our new American friends. Then there was the new fad of barbequing. I was told that if you landed in Houston on a late Saturday afternoon in summer, the entire city was enveloped in a blue smoky haze caused by thousands of people burning steaks in their backyards.

When the time came for Netty to arrive, I drove the big Pontiac to the Hudson River piers where the Statendam would arrive with my entire family on board. It was a nice sunny day and it was beginning to get much warmer. When the ship came in and the passengers came down the gangway, I did not have to wait too long before I saw Adriaan, striding down the gangway in a blue Dutch boy's suit and his rosy cheeks extra bright on account of the warm weather he was not used to. As a child, Adriaan had rosy cheeks for many years. This frequently elicited friendly comments from people in stores, elevators, etc. I am sure Adriaan is happy that he does not have this distinguishing touch anymore, but for me at that moment, seeing Adriaan appear was a priceless picture that I still have in my mind. Netty followed, and I still remember the blue dress she was wearing that day. George was there too, of course, and a few seconds later we were together again, hugging each other. The luggage was carried off the ship and had to be inspected by customs and then we could drive off to the hotel I had reserved for a few days until the Thomforde's would have moved out. I had chosen this hotel because it was used by Shell for its employees with families, and Jaap and Tineke Kort had stayed there when they came through New York on leave from Venezuela. I had met them there during my earlier visit to New York and thought it would be a good place for us too. Unfortunately, we got a room without any view, just a window looking at an inner court. This created a problem for Netty, who had to spend the whole day in the hotel. So she often went to Central Park, getting the boys used to the New York scene. We had a little kitchenette that allowed Netty to cook up a small meal for us in our first days as a family in America.

Our first venture into Connecticut was a trip to the Schuytens for dinner. We met Hans in Grand Central Station and took the New Haven Railroad to Stamford. Hans told me later that he had enjoyed meeting the boys in their "Sunday best" Dutch outfits. Clearly we had to learn to dress down to meet American suburban standards, but this had to wait until we reached Riverside. I had already made an effort to dress down when I stayed at the St George Hotel in Brooklyn Heights. I often went on walks there along the promenade, a wonderful place built over the Brooklyn Queens Expressway, where you could see the skyline of lower Manhattan in the background with the busy East River in front. Walking there on Saturday mornings, I noticed young couples strolling with their baby carriages (no strollers yet) all dressed in casual clothes. In Holland we were still much more dressed up, even in our leisure time. I went to a store in Brooklyn and bought a leisure outfit, which later on proved to be too much Brooklyn and not enough Greenwich. It was totally wrong for the Greenwich suburban crowd, but at that time I thought I fitted right in on the promenade.

After a few days we could move into "our" house on 16 Peters Road in Riverside. Our furniture had not yet arrived, but Nancy Schuyten lent us beds and we had a few other odds and

16 PETERS ROAD.

ends in the house such as a kitchen table. For Netty this initial period in America was very rough. Setting up housekeeping in a totally new environment without furniture and only a few pots and pans we had hastily bought was no picnic. The first day I went to the office I decided to walk to the station and when I returned I promptly got lost. I remember walking through the tunnel under the railway tracks near Ole Amundsen's boatyard and not knowing how to get home from there. We were extremely fortunate in one aspect. Next door to us lived the McCready family, Jane and Jack and their sons Jimmy and Robby, both the exact same age as George and Adriaan. The McCready's were of immense help to us in getting us established in our new environment. Soon many other families would pitch in too, mostly people we met through our children's schools. All these people gave us a lesson in American style neighborliness, friendliness and openness to strangers that was totally new to us as people who had grown up in a much more structured society where helping neighbors did not come naturally. Jane introduced Netty to the neighborhood stores in Old Greenwich and to the school system. Jane would baffle me by being able to quote all the prices for various groceries she bought at the supermarket. A sharp intellect wasted on the grocery shelves? Hardly. We learned that in contrast to the Dutch fixed-price economy we were now in a world where the market economy reigned and prices could vary sharply depending on which store or region you were in.

Adriaan went to the kindergarten school at St. Paul's Episcopal Church where he quickly became a celebrity, being "from faraway Holland." George went to the Riverside school. Both boys adjusted very quickly to their new environment and the unfamiliar language. As true Dutchmen, Netty and I had preconceived notions about the bad influence TV would have on our children so we held out on buying a TV set. What happened naturally was that George and Adriaan went over to the McCready's whenever they could to watch TV so we had absolutely no control over the programs they were watching. It did help their English vocabulary though, and one of the first sentences Adriaan could say was, "We are sorry, but we are experiencing technical difficulties," a statement often heard in those early TV days.

Soon our furniture arrived. Contrary to what we had been told by the movers in Holland, the big crate containing all our belongings was not delivered to our door. It had to be unpacked in a warehouse in Manhattan before a customs inspector. It was an annoying experience for me to see all our possessions spread over the floor of that warehouse, roughly handled by inattentive movers who cracked jokes about some of our, for them, strange-looking household implements. When our things finally arrived at Peters Road, it came in a truck with one driver/mover who had to carry everything up our fairly steep driveway. I saw him carrying one of our prized paintings, the large one depicting a Dutch village under a sunny sky, wrapped in heavy paper. Pieces of its frame were breaking off and falling on the grass in front of our house as the mover stumbled up to our front door. Still it was nice to have our own things and to be able to make our house "gezellig."

As the American summer began to become noticeable, we realized that we were not well prepared for the heat. The house all of a sudden seemed very small and the heat became oppressive, certainly for our Dutch metabolisms. Netty was particularly afflicted by the heat. She would flee into the basement where it was cooler and just sit there for a while. I don't know if she cried there, she never told me, but I would not be surprised if she had. This was a very trying and unhappy period for her. I bought an air conditioner, stuck it into the back window of our living room so that we had at least one cool room. At night we had all the windows open and a few fans working upstairs. Then came the moment when the Connecticut Turnpike – now I-95 – was opened. It was a brand new link in the interstate highway system that President Eisenhower had advocated. He had seen the Autobahn network in Germany and realized it had been built mainly to move troops quickly and efficiently, and not just to give Nazi party members nice roads to travel on in their Volkswagens. Our road had many toll stations where you tossed a quarter in a basket to be allowed to drive on. A quarter for us was a lot of money. It was almost a Dutch guilder at that time, and my parents when they came to see us were shocked by the cost of this toll system. The bridge over the Mianus River was not ready when the turnpike opened, so all the traffic exited and entered at exit 5, the one that circled behind our house, so close that at night it felt as if the trucks were shifting gears practically inside our bedroom.

The Schuytens had also introduced us to Dave and Dotty Osler who lived nearby and would over the years become dear friends. The Oslers introduced us to the beautiful park Greenwich has on Tod's Point. Dave owned a Mercury, a small 15-ft. wooden sloop that he kept on a mooring near the town dock. This beautiful park was a revelation to us and we quickly decided that sailing was the thing to do as a family. Healthy, not very expensive and nearby. I went to Ole Amundsen's boatyard and negotiated the purchase of a fiberglass Mercury. Low maintenance boats made of fiberglass with aluminum spars and Dacron sails were just beginning to come on the market, and for us this type of boat offered an ideal way of spending summer weekends and vacation time. We got a mooring at Tod's Point and started sailing. I had waited impatiently for our boat to arrive and as soon as it was there, I made the classic mistake of going out as soon as I could, instead of waiting for a nice calm day. Without paying attention to the blustery wind that was blowing that day, I went out with George and Adriaan, both wearing life preservers, of course, and strapped in the sails in order to tack out of the cove. The boat sailed fine, but we also got a great deal of water over the bow and we got very wet. George was a little frightened, but Adriaan braved the water coming in over the bow and sat on the cockpit floor against the mast, getting soaking wet but showing a brave smile. Another picture that is still engraved in my mind. It did not take long for me to understand that we had to get back and wait for a calmer day to get used to the boat. We also went to the beach at Tod's Point and from time to time we took the car to drive around the Connecticut countryside. Coming from a crowded flat country where the weather was often bad, the American summer with many hot sunny days offered us wonderful new opportunities to explore the area we lived in. We enjoyed the dense woods and the hills with interesting rock formations and the parks such as Bear Mountain Park.

When driving around we got a sense of the vastness of the country, with houses widely spaced and no fences around their yards, and lots of woodsy areas where trees grew helter-skelter and just fell over wherever they died with nobody bothering to clean up the detritus. This was different from Holland where the houses stand close together in rows and trees are also mostly planted in rows, and when a tree falls over it is always quickly removed to maintain the general sense of orderliness. The McCready's and the Oslers introduced us to barbequing, and using a pit we found in our backyard, we started to experiment with this national pastime. We also bought a portable barbeque which we loaded in our pink monster station wagon and used for picnics outdoors on our exploratory trips.

At FBC I concluded my training program and was put to work in the foreign bond department, which was supposed to trade with non–U.S. customers. I soon discovered that FBC was doing a great deal of business with several British firms, particularly a London brokerage firm called Kitcat and Aitken. This firm was acquired by the Royal Bank of Canada in 1986 and closed in 1990. Jim Morrison was the principal contact for this business, and he gave all the orders to a man called Vinny on the sales desk who had worked there for years. Vinny was not the sharpest knife in the drawer, but he did know how to protect his turf, and it became soon clear that he had no intention whatsoever of letting me in on it. The business we did with firms on the continent was minimal, mainly because most European countries still had strict controls on the transactions residents could do in foreign exchange, particularly dollars. We did some business with Swiss and Swedish banks, institutions in the two countries that had stayed neutral during the war and had become quite prosperous, doing business on both sides of the fence. But on the whole, FBC did little business with Europe outside the UK, because we did not have a regular brokerage type business and did not make stock recommendations. We were strictly wholesale. I was included in most luncheons with visitors from abroad, mainly, perhaps, to show the visitors that FBC was making an effort to become more internationally oriented. We had two public offerings of note, the first postwar bond offering in dollars by Japan, a country that still was in need of money in those days and the introduction on the New York Stock Exchange of the shares of KLM Royal Dutch Airlines. My involvement in these deals was minimal, which was logical in the case of the Japan offering. I knew absolutely nothing about Japan, its economy or its securities markets. However, it would have made sense in my view if I had been given a small role in the KLM offering, if only because I was Dutch. The KLM offering was a tough one because it had all kinds of restrictions, mainly tying initial buyers down for quite some time, making them investors rather than free riders who could "flip" their holdings as soon as they saw the stock go to a sizeable premium over the offering price. Several European firms got caught in this rule and were forced to keep their stock for a while. I could have done a better job there explaining the characteristics of the offering to them before they got caught, but I was not in the loop and had no ongoing dialogue with these customers. I began to get the feeling that Morrison did not quite know what to do with me. He made little effort to get me involved and was a poor mentor, not having the gift of explaining himself clearly and keeping most of his affairs very close to the vest. On the other hand, I worked in a group of people, mostly bond traders, where I had a great deal of support and gained an enormous amount of experience. While I realized I was not going forward in my career, I was not going backwards either, which was easy because I was practically at the bottom of the FBC totem pole. It was quite a comedown from the status I had at Jonas & Kruseman. I had to lay low for some time and see how things were developing. But I did worry very much about the wisdom of my move to the U.S. in those days.

When autumn came we experienced our first New England Indian Summer and saw the brilliant fall colors we had heard about. We organized a trip to Vermont to see the colors. Many more trips to that wonderful state would follow over the years. In fall the United Nations General Assembly is held in New York City and Frans Terwisscha, then Tilly's husband, was part of the Dutch delegation. He joined us on our trip and Edith Laane, Rob's younger sister who was also in New York on

UN business, came too. We loaded up the Pontiac and cruised up to Bennington, Vermont where we found a motel. For George and Adriaan a highlight of this journey was the availability of TV in the motel rooms because they were still TV deprived at home. I took a memorable shot with my 8 mm film camera of George being dragged out of the darkened room to see the beautiful surroundings. He was very upset because the cavalry was just coming over the hill to fight the Indians on the black and white screen, and who cared about fall colors in such a situation!

Over several visits to the U.S. we got to know Edith much better, and she became a great friend, particularly of Netty. Later on she married Sir John Boynton, an English government official she met during another diplomatic gathering in Rhodesia (now Zimbabwe). John also became a good friend. He had special ties to the Netherlands since he was a major in the British Army and his unit had helped liberate the southern part of our country in late 1944. Every year John faithfully attended his regiment's reunions in Holland. The 2005 reunion was to be the last one. The veterans were getting too old and their number had declined drastically, and with Prince Bernhard no longer there it was hard to find a proper official to take the salute on their parade. I believe it was the mayor of the town of Wageningen who saluted the British warriors in 2005. He was a young man who was probably not yet born when the war ended. John died in January 2007, much to our regret. We had seen him last on a big luncheon party Rob and Liesbeth Laane gave to commemorate their fiftieth wedding anniversary and their eightieth birthdays. It was a beautiful midsummer day in 2006, exceptionally warm but John was in good shape. Sadly his health deteriorated fast in the following months.

We lured Edith to come to a party a group of FBC bachelors were giving in their apartment. The rooms were chockablock full of people and spirits were high. The hosts knew what they were doing when they introduced Netty and Edith to the American martini. The ladies had no clue about the impact of that fabulous libation and soon got the giggles. After that party we had plans to go see a Broadway play called Two for the Seesaw and would meet Frans there. When we arrived at the theater we were very happy and Frans was stark sober and irritated also because we were late. As we entered the balcony of the dark theater and were stumbling down the stairs to our seats, the high heel of one of Edith's shoes got caught in one of Netty's shoes and we caused a major disturbance. We enjoyed the play but did not remember much of it. This party and many other gatherings we had with FBC friends were a highlight of our first years in the U.S. The camaraderie we enjoyed there was unusual. It was a singularly nice group of people FBC had recruited. The idea was good, but over time the company was not able to retain these people. Hardly anybody stayed and most of them found good careers elsewhere in Wall Street.

As we settled in on 16 Peters Road, I started working in the yard. In front of the house was a large crab apple tree that to our disgust produced millions of tiny rotten apples. I cleared the hill behind the house, that was overgrown with weeds to create a better play area for the boys. When the leaves came off the trees, we raked them together and according to custom, burned them on the curb of the street. A wonderful autumn ritual that is now history because of environmental concerns. Each fall the smoke of burning leaves is now replaced by the soot produced by the large diesel engines of whole armies of large trucks and backhoes the Town of Greenwich sends out to clear the streets of piles of leaves, probably adding more pollutants to the air than the fires had done before.

Winter came and it got colder. Netty and I decided that we could not let December 5th go by without a Sinterklaas event for the boys. They were still believers, we thought. So we made a big manikin out of my purple bathrobe with a head made out of a basketball and a red and gold cardboard miter. When I came back from the office in the dark, I placed the Sinterklaas on the front door porch, rang the bell loudly and ran around the house to the back. I was just in time to see George run back from answering the door with a panicky face exclaiming "Sinterklaas!" We had some presents for the boys and created a little Sinterklaas celebration. That was the last time we stuck to this typically Dutch tradition. Later when Richard and Janet were small, we would be invited to gatherings of the Dutch community where Sinterklaas appeared in full regalia, but for our children the impact was just not there. Our good friend John Hafkemeyer often suited up for the Sinterklaas role among the Dutch community in New York. He did a marvelous job.

During our first months in Riverside we had also linked up with Erry and Pia van Someren Gréve, Mammie's younger brother and his wife. They had lived for some time in America. Errie worked with various engineering firms, mostly in sales. They had two sons, Peter Hans and Robert. We had met them in Holland after they had returned from the Far East and they had attended our wedding. Erry and Pia had spent the war partly in Australia and partly in the U.S. Their sons were both American born and therefore citizens and as time went on we developed a close relationship with Errie and Pia and their boys. They lived in an apartment in New Rochelle. Later when Erry landed a better job, they moved to Greenwich. It was nice to have relatives nearby in a new country, especially for Netty. Erry was a man who had many good qualities, he was very good with his hands and a born engineer.

However, he frequently seemed to have problems with interpersonal relationships and had trouble holding on to a job. He always tended to blame his bosses, his colleagues and others for his problems. Over time we began to realize that Erry himself was the problem. He had a way of setting up people's backs when thwarted or contradicted and totally lacked flexibility in dealing with people. Pia was a nice warm woman, a little high strung and a very fast talker, but full of vim and vigor. Peter Hans was in high school, almost college age, when we came to America. Robert was still in junior high. Peter Hans was a nice slender gentle boy with dark hair and large dark eyes. Robert was stockier, blond and more athletic and also more pugnacious. As a small boy he was quite a hell raiser. When Erry and Pia returned from Indonesia, where Erry had a government job, they spent some time with Netty's parents. Mammie loved little Robert, but he was a handful and on one memorable day he managed to set fire to the bushes of a nearby neighbor's garden and ran away in panic after he saw what he had done. The firemen had to come to put it out. Sadly, almost the entire family was stricken with cancer. Over the coming years Peter Hans died first, then Robert and finally Erry. Pia lived the longest. She died in a nursing home in Holland. But these events were still far in the future in 1958.

When the year-end holiday season came around, we enjoyed our first exposure to the overwhelming American Christmas celebration with all its gimmickry, schmaltz and commercialism but also its genuine good cheer and warmth and spiritual involvement. We had shopped around for a church that would approximate our Dutch church experiences as closely as possible. We found the Congregational Church best suited for us. Its services struck us as simple and much more "protestant" than the Episcopal Church. We had attended a service at St. Paul's Episcopal Church in Riverside and felt as if we were in a Catholic environment. Nothing wrong with that but not something we were accustomed to. The First Congregational Church in Old Greenwich made us feel much more at home, and we particularly liked its senior pastor, Dr. Daniels, a man who turned out to be a most beloved man in the community. We sent the boys to Sunday school at this church and began to attend services there from time to time. Like everybody else we dressed up for church, I wore a business suit and Netty bought a small hat especially for this purpose. With a Christmas tree in the house and presents under it, we began to resemble a Norman Rockwell type American family. The Christmas services at our church struck us as very beautiful and impressive and full of warmth.

Three weeks before Christmas I had received a Christmas bonus check for $100. from Jim Morrison. My friend and colleague Dick Dunham told me that it was an insult, and I realized it was not the biggest bonus in the world, but I did not know what to do about it. Another and very different aspect of the Christmas ritual was the office party which in those days involved a lot of heavy drinking with the attendant loosening of tongues in conversations with the bosses and other bawdy behavior between male and female participants. FBC was no exception. The company threw a big party in the Broad Street Club, a lunch club in our building. As we trickled in we found a dance floor with a band, a buffet and a large number of big round tables on which were glasses, ice buckets and bottles of scotch, bourbon, gin, etc. You just poured yourself a glass and started drinking. Luckily I was now more familiar with American drinking habits and the potency of the libations people used to consume. I danced with a pretty young Irish secretary who exclaimed, "Throw me, Mr. Schieferdecker!" I did not know what she meant until I saw that my European style of dancing the fox trot was totally out of synch with the way Americans danced. I just did not know how to do the lindy and confessed my ignorance. She must have found me a terribly boring dullard. The party soon became a little messy and after we had spent some time there we (the group of younger people I was now part of) went uptown to Greenwich Village where we visited the apartment of one of the girls in the research department. I ended up sitting next to a German fellow who worked in the accounting department and used the occasion to tell me in German about the problems he had with his Jewish/American mother-in-law and the reason why it made no sense to own a car when living in Manhattan. His mother-in-law kept

dominating his wife's life and his car had broken down on a street and when he was trying to push it uphill into a garage, the cops gave him a ticket for parking illegally. He then told me *"Ich bin besoffen"* (I am drunk), and went home. I took a late train home, glad to be out of it.

At home we had prepared Christmas gifts for the boys. Netty had bought second-hand skates for George and a new pair of beginners' skates (with double runners for stability) for Adriaan. We also found some plastic toys in the supermarket. George got a space station with rockets and astronauts and Adriaan a fire station with hook and ladder trucks etc. These really cheap toys proved to be roaring success. George and Ade are still talking about them. You do not always have to buy expensive things to make a child happy. When there was ice on the pond in nearby Binney Park we went over to skate. I put on my Dutch Frisian skates, the ones you tie on with leather straps and made quite a splash on the ice where nobody had ever seen skates like that. Immediate references were made to Hans Brinker and the Silver Skates, a book I used to own in Holland. My parent's friend, Mrs. Lionberger from Omaha, had sent it to me when I was young. Sadly I had to tell them that Hans Brinker was an invention of the American writer of the book and totally unknown in Holland.

As we rolled into our first American spring as a family, Netty got more and more used to her new environment in Riverside, meeting with other women who got her to join a couple of social organizations. The boys flourished in school and my job at FBC dawdled along. Visitors began to arrive. I believe the first ones were Pieter Boot and his wife Cissy. Pieter was an officer in the Dutch merchant marine and would end up as captain of one of Holland's largest passenger liners. From time to time he could bring his wife along on a trip and so they came to New York harbor. They slept in our basement for a few nights and seemed to have a good time. Cissy was an attractive young woman whose presence was a godsend since Netty got very sick for a few days with the flu and terrible migraine headaches. A few years later Pieter and Cissy divorced. Pieter never got over it and became deeply depressed and much later died tragically.

That second summer Pa and Ma arrived. They were anxious to see their only son and his family again and were determined to make the best of their stay here. This time Netty and I moved to the basement. Then sixty five and sixty years old, Pa and Ma donned bathing suits and went to Tod's Point with us. Pa went sailing with me and we made trips in the countryside with them. The high point was a trip to Vermont for a two week vacation in Dorset. It was very hot in Riverside that summer and I was anxious to find a place where we could escape the heat. One of my colleagues at FBC told me about Vermont and recommended the Dorset Inn there. We made reservations, with Pa footing the bill, of course, and climbed into the Pontiac. It turned out to be a very good choice. Ever since then Dorset has been one of our favorite places to go in Vermont and it is still almost unchanged from the way it looked on our first visit there in 1959. The Inn was run by a very friendly couple, Fred Whittemore and his wife. Fred was a kind and talkative man who paid much attention to the boys and quickly became Adriaan's hero. They had a small swimming pool behind a house across the highway where the boys spent hours jumping in and out of the water, learning to swim in the process. There were barbeques in the backyard of the inn, and when Ma's birthday rolled along on August 24th, the waitresses came to our table at dinner to sing "Happy Birthday" – for us a completely new experience. To our consternation their singing made Ma cry. In the evenings we sat in the rocking chairs on the front porch watching the nonexistent traffic go by. A very nice vacation that gave us a good and long-lasting memory of a memorable time spent with my parents in a beautiful part of America. Pa and Ma came and went by ship. They had nice pictures of their captain's dinner in black tie with the captain. They were not used to flying yet, but that would come later. After Pa and Ma got back home, Omatje, my sweet little grandmother, died on September 19, 1959. It was sad for Netty and me to have a death in the family without being able to grieve with our parents and participate in the funeral. It simply did not occur to us to go over for a quick visit. That was not done in those days.

During their stay here I spoke with my parents and explained that I was planning to stay in America for at least several more years and that we needed to think about buying a house. I had discussions with Frank Hoch of Brown Brothers, Harriman, who had told me I might be able to join his firm as an analyst of foreign securities. So my prospects for a better salary improved which could justify buying a house. My reserves were just enough to buy a modest house with a mortgage, but with some support from Pa it would be easier and I would not be entirely without reserves. As always Pa promised to help and Netty started scouting around for a house.

We had some very firm ideas about the type of house we wanted to buy. It could not be what was called a colonial because they all had windows with muntins and the attendant many small panes and we were used to the Dutch type house that had big windows to let as much sunshine in as possible, a scarce commodity in America. We wanted to be near the school in Riverside and near the station and not surprisingly there were no houses with big sunny windows in the area we had chosen. We did not realize of course, that the colonial style houses were built that way for a reason. They had small windows and low ceilings so they could be kept warm in winter and keep the sun out in summer. The postwar building boom had picked up on that style of house and built millions of them and they are still being built. We thought the Dutch approach to homebuilding in a rainy sun-deprived environment was superior.

As Netty went from house to house she got more and more frustrated and finally the realtor showed her a house he said he was sure she would not like. She liked it. It was a colonial, but it had large window panes without muntins in the lower part of its double hung windows and that small detail did the trick for us. We liked the house and started looking into a mortgage and tried to find another renter for the Peters Road house. All this worked out quite well, and in the fall of 1959 we made the move to what was then 82 Summit Road, Riverside. The house was on the corner of Spruce Street, a short walk from school and station. Really ideal. While we lived in Peters Road we had learned to paint and to hang wall paper. We tried to liven up that place, which was painted dark beige inside as was fashionable in the postwar period. We made all the walls off-white and wallpapered the stairwell, which was a major achievement for people who did not come from a "do-it-yourself" culture. We quickly got the hang of it and marveled at the, for us, unknown world of American home decorating technology, water based paint, paint rollers and roller trays, wall paper that had glue on one side and only needed to be made wet to stick to the wall, etc., etc. We now had to do it all over again in our new house. I would go there in the evenings and paint for a few hours, doing the broad stroke easy work while Netty came during daytime when the boys were in school and did the more precise work of painting the woodwork of the windows. A realtor found a nice young couple who had no children to take over our lease and soon we could move in. Dave Osler helped me move. We did it with our own cars and only had to make a few trips. We had not yet acquired the overwhelming amount of "stuff" young families in America normally have. The house on Summit Road, the yellow house as we later called it because it was painted light yellow, became a very pleasant and happy house for us where we would live for more than seven years and would probably have stayed longer if we had not outgrown it.

In the spring of 1960 I had a number of meetings with Frank Hoch and Maarten van Hengel, a Dutchman by birth who would become my boss. Frank's idea was that investment by American investors in foreign, then mainly European, securities was bound to come and since Brown Brothers, Harriman did a considerable amount of business in American securities for foreign clients, it behooved them to reciprocate by using foreign portfolio ideas for their own U.S. clients. Brown Brothers, Harriman was then and is still now an unusual hybrid type of firm. BBH, as we all called it, was a bank, but it was not a bank with a federal charter, it had a New York State charter. It was a partnership and as such almost unique in the banking world. At the time there was only one other bank left in Wall Street that was a partnership – Laidlaw, a much smaller one. As a partnership BBH could also do business as a stockbroker and be a member of the New York Stock Exchange. The firm did a significant portfolio management business for American domestic clients and its large Investment Advisory Department was supported by a very well staffed investment research department. Frank worked with Maarten van Hengel and Bill Horn, an older very nice and gentlemanly man who like Frank had the title of manager. Maarten was assistant manager.

The bank had a very horizontal structure. It was basically run by its partners who operated in loose groups. Beyond partners BBH only knew managers and assistant managers. Frank and Bill had built up a significant brokerage business with foreign, mainly Swiss and British, banks and investment firms. This business benefited from the idea that BBH as a bank could act as a secure custodian for the holdings in U.S. securities of these banks and instead of paying a custody fee they could compensate BBH by sending it brokerage business. As could be expected, the Swiss would then turn around and charge their clients full custody charges and brokerage anyway. So this was for them Gefundenes Fressen (found grub) as the Germans (and the Swiss probably also) say.

Over the years I would learn a great deal about the methods of the Swiss banks. They did business in a typically frugal and unexciting way but had invented a major gimmick. They accepted clients with so-called numbered accounts, totally anonymously; only one person in the bank would know the real identity of the client. With this method they attracted a large number of clients from all over the world who wanted to avoid taxation at home or had darker, more sinister reasons for hiding their wealth. South American strongmen and assorted scoundrels are as welcome as prosperous French petit bourgeois who were all supposed to have a Swiss numbered account together with a liver ailment and embonpoint. This Swiss system was supported by Swiss federal laws that conveniently made it a crime for bankers to reveal the identity of their clients. While in most Western countries the authorities can demand opening of bank accounts for inspection by fiscal or judicial authorities, the Swiss were forbidden to do so and could therefore guarantee complete secrecy to their clients. Individual cantons in Switzerland would go a step further and allow domicile for corporations in a tax-sheltered environment. Cantons like Zug became famous for attracting businesses that way. A famous case was Mark Rich, accused by the US judiciary of serious crimes and securities fraud. Rich escaped to Switzerland by jumping bail here. He established a thriving commodities trading business in Zug. He was later pardoned by President Clinton just before the end of his term. Marc Rich's ex-wife had made heavy contributions to the Clinton campaigns and became a friend of the first couple.

The department where I would end up at BBH was called the Foreign Investment Department which was a bit of a misnomer since they did not invest abroad – they served clients from abroad who invested in U.S. securities. As I soon would learn, there was a considerable amount of genteel politicking going on at BBH. This was not peculiar to this firm, it happens everywhere were people get together to do business. It has lead me to conclude that in my business career the only serious problems I encountered were always people problems. In Wall Street where most firms operate without much structure and organization and prima donnas are present in every conceivable area of financial activity, office politics abound. Frank soon became partner of BBH and Maarten was made manager. Bill Horn was already a manager. Maarten was the office manager for all intents and purposes while Frank occupied himself with loftier problems of doing business with continental investors, mainly in Switzerland, France and Italy. The business with London and with the very powerful Scottish investment trusts had been captured by another partner, John West. This business was at least as important as the transactions we did with the clients on the continent, but if you would listen to the noises made by Maarten you would never think so. Yes, Maarten was a noisy fellow, big brash and domineering. He was determined to also become a partner and worked very hard to achieve that goal. Still, we became good friends and I was very saddened to learn that Maarten died of emphysema on December 29, 2006. Beyond managing the department, Maarten was responsible for the business BBH did with the Netherlands and Belgium. In business volume those countries were small pickings. He would have a long hard road ahead to partnership. Curiously Frank died almost four months later on April 13, 2007.

At BBH I began another training period that proved to be very helpful. I spent time with most if not all analysts who taught me the key ingredients of their work. This was necessary since I would have to go out to Europe and find attractive investments in many different industries. I had to cover the waterfront, become a generalist, and could not specialize by focusing on just one industry. The plan was to try to latch on to new research efforts emerging among European firms that were producing industry research on a Europe-wide basis. My first stop was Pierson Heldring

& Pierson in Amsterdam. It was a historic moment for me to step into the hallowed halls of this first class Dutch firm, no longer as a minor competitor but as a friend who would be allowed to see some of its inner workings. Pierson was part of a consortium of European firms who had joined together to produce investment research on a level that was more up to US standards, a major job because the information available on European companies was still much scarcer than what American companies revealed about their operations. So the research produced by this group while covering all of what was then the beginnings of the Common Market economy was heavy on basic industry information but light on specific company data. It was still virtually impossible to make comparisons on a company-by-company basis, selecting, for instance, the best steel company among French, German, Dutch or Italian companies. The Common Market was not a single economy but a collection of sovereign national economies that were each subjected to different trends that often moved in opposite directions and with separate incompatible legal and political systems. This situation still obtains, almost fifty years later.

I had not been in Holland for almost three years and it immediately struck me how little progress towards a more open financial market had been made, how people still lived in the rather confining small town atmosphere I had left behind in 1958, and how much it rained! I had become accustomed to New York City rain which came down only sporadically, albeit sometimes in buckets but not all day long. In a New York office panic would break out among the women if they discovered it was raining at the time they would have to venture out to go home. They would produce umbrellas, plastic overshoes to protect their spike- heeled footwear and plastic rain caps to save their bouffant hairdos. In Amsterdam people just stoically suited up in their rain gear, climbed on their bikes and pedaled home along the "Herengarcht" in the pouring rain. Nothing special, just a day-to-day occurrence. I had never before realized how wet Holland was, but now I sensed how the climate must have a lasting impact on the Dutch. It makes them gloomy, the glass is always half empty kind of people. I was staying with my parents and had rented a car in which I drove back and forth to Amsterdam and later to Brussels to visit the Banque Lambert, the Belgian banking firm that was part of the new research group.

The flight that brought me back to Holland was special for me. KLM had just received its first DC-8 jet planes and I was on one of the early flights in this superb new aircraft. It was a wonderful experience. No vibration, a calm, very-high-altitude flight that took considerably less time than before. BBH did not pay much in salaries and over the years my financial progress proved to be dreadfully slow, but they traveled first class. We always sat "up front" in planes and stayed in first class hotels. I had no trouble getting into the habit of traveling that way. But my first jet flight from New York to Amsterdam did not go as smoothly as planned. As we approached Holland there was ground fog in Amsterdam so the pilot decided to divert to Düsseldorf Germany, a smallish airport. Instrument landings were probably not yet advisable with this brand new plane. After a long delay, we climbed back on board to find that KLM had loaded up the first class with Germans who had a ticket for Amsterdam and kept racing back and forth to take in the scenery below. We flew low over foggy Holland, and it was interesting to see how church towers and factory chimneys stuck out above the layer of what looked like cotton wool. After I landed Pa picked me up, and at home in Wassenaar I had to sit down with Ma and Tante Jetje, who had come especially to see me, and tell them about our life in America. I had brought an 8 mm movie and some slides to show them and other friends to give an impression of our life on the other side of the pond. Over the coming years I would make movies and slides that I would send over to my parents.

After Amsterdam I visited Brussels, Frankfurt, Paris and Milan. As could be expected, the differences between the people and their way of doing business in these financial centers were great and sometimes amusing. In Brussels I was brought over to the headquarters of the research organization I mentioned before. There analysts worked on huge reports on the basic industries of the Common Market. The steel report, for instance, carried dozens of pages on the steel-making process, how it was done and where, but little if anything in the way of crisp, well-reasoned recommendations. It dawned on me that I would have a tough job coming up with specific investment ideas and well-funded reports on stocks that represented a participation in companies that were very attractively priced relative to similar American ones and that showed superior prospects for earnings growth, because there was very little information available. Only extraordinarily attractive opportunities would induce BBH investors to take the currency and geographical risks attendant to foreign investing. That in a nutshell would be the problem I would encounter in the coming years and would not be successful in overcoming. It would take several decades before Americans would invest significant amounts of money overseas. We were too early.

In Frankfurt I reported to Herr Direktor Langhoff, a big bully who barked immediately, *"Sind Sie Händler?,"* (are you a trader?) When I responded that I was an analyst, he lost interest in me and referred me to a bunch of young traders who were working the phones on a trading desk. I was astonished to notice that these men were not only actively trading for their clients, but were also buying and selling for their own account, free-riding on almost any order they handled. Obviously they were doing very well for themselves. They took me to a sumptuous dinner and the next day introduced me to a Herr Doktor so and so who turned out to be the research director who was working on producing a systematic data base on all publicly traded German companies. He ultimately completed a very useful guide book that was ignored by the traders who were not interested in investigating what they were dealing in. I had returned to the investment Stone Age.

In Paris I visited the director of a bank who said he could resolve all my problems. All I had to do was recommend a mutual fund run by his bank that invested in European securities. He happened to sit on the board of the fund and could personally guarantee that it was a marvelous investment. He did not listen to my questions proffered in hesitant French and just pontificated.

In Milan I met with two nice guys who took me to lunch in a fine restaurant in the famous glass-covered shopping gallery near the Duomo. They said I should try risotto Milanese since I was in Milan. I agreed and started on a huge plate piled high with rice. When asked what else I wanted I said "just coffee." Oh no! That was not the idea. The risotto was just an appetizer and I had to eat another huge portion of duck followed by a sumptuous desert. Obviously I provided these men with a nice opportunity to have a good meal before they went home for their traditional afternoon siesta.

Back in New York I started working on my first research reports on European companies. I decided that I would select only one or two very high quality companies in each country and would focus on them with the help of overseas sources and BBH analysts. I was trying to find companies that were benefiting from the postwar economic recovery of Europe and that had something unique in their business that might make them attractive to American investors. Starting to write these reports and finding an acceptable format for presenting basic information proved to be very tough. I found out that my ability to write understandable English needed improvement. I was greatly helped in this by the partner in charge of research, Bud Newquist, who sat down with me for several hours and questioned every statement I made, challenging my facts and my way of expressing my thoughts, and correcting my writing in general as we went along. A tremendously important learning experience for me.

I soldiered on and after a few months was able to write acceptable reports. BBH people were real sticklers on language. It seemed as if the content and the writing style of their research reports was more important than the investment value. It was a tough but very useful period for me. Once again I came to the realization that

I was about a decade behind my contemporaries in America. My education for what it was worth did not equip me to work profitably and effectively in finance, and the years wasted during the war and in the Dutch military did not help either. I had to accumulate knowledge on

OOM EELCO AND TANTE MARGARET IN 1978.

my own and as quickly as possible. I could see in my colleagues that American institutions of higher learning with all their shortcomings somehow prepared people much better for the challenges of real life than the European schooling I had been exposed to. Brown Brothers provided a nice fuzzy cocoon for me in which I could work on my education without having to worry too much about the longevity of my job. There was not much pressure to perform or much job-related stress at BBH. Most of the younger people I was friendly with hoped to become partner, virtually the only way to make money there, but only a few were chosen and many left the firm to go elsewhere.

My next trip abroad was to London. There I was the guest of Oom Eelco and Tante Margaret. Oom Eelco had decided that the reason for his self-imposed retreat to Portugal as ambassador in Lisbon was not valid. Tante Margaret's health was better than expected so he looked for another assignment and was appointed as ambassador of the European Coal and Steel Community at the Court of St. James. Not a bad job. The ECSC was a work in progress but diplomatic posts had to be established and Oom Eelco lived in a very sumptuous two-story apartment in Kensington Palace Gardens, across the street from Kensington Palace where part of the dysfunctional family that rules Britannia lived. Princess Margaret, sister of the queen resided there with her then husband the photographer Tony Armstrong Jones. So in a way our aunt and uncle were keeping up with the Joneses. The street was in a gated community, but not in the sense of today's heavily fortified neighborhoods in the U.S. You entered through a stone arch guarded by two elderly men in top hats who were, of course, unarmed.

I had my base at Kleinworth Benson, a firm BBH was close to. At Kleinworth I found a genuine research department where I got much helpful information on research sources for UK and European securities. The atmosphere at the department was a bit Dickensian. Analysts sat all together at small tables in a large room. The man in charge told me he insisted on total silence so there wasn't much conversation. Later on I moved to the Dorchester Hotel, not a bad place to stay either. Oom Eelco and Tante Margaret honored me by giving a dinner for John West and me. John had come to London on his biannual business trip and helped me by introducing me around. I guess this dinner party made a serious impression on John. It was a nice dinner prepared by their cook and served by their butler who would also serve breakfast for Oom Eelco and me. I was of course familiar with the City, but the BBH connections were something special. Most memorable for me was a visit to Rothschild's were I was introduced to Evelyn de Rothschild who chatted nicely with me and offered assistance. All this was many levels above where I could operate, but the intention was good. The contact man at Rothschild's, I think his name was Roger Blake, invited me to his home for drinks followed by a performance of the Sadler Wells Ballet and supper afterwards. We saw Swan Lake with Margot Fonteyn, the world-famous ballerina. It was an unforgettable experience and seeing the ballet from the Rothschild's private box was special. Ever since I have enjoyed ballet and Netty and I still like to go to the Metropolitan Opera when there is a good ballet. The music is beautiful and the performances are for me more attractive than a concert because of the combination of good music with the visual enjoyment of the ballet.

The winter of 1960–61 brought much snow. George and Adriaan built snow forts in the yard and we celebrated Christmas the American way, with a tree with plenty of electric lights and an avalanche of presents for the boys. Netty and I became more settled in Riverside, the boys were doing well in school and were now fluent in English. We encouraged them to speak English and neglected keeping up their Dutch. We thought that a language overload would not be good for them and might cause them to stutter. Nonsense of course, but that is what we thought. Life was good.

22 : *Old Greenwich and Riverside in the Sixties*

While we were busy settling down in America, the world around us was changing rapidly. We discovered we were now living in a country that was a world power. That was a big change from being part of a little country where news of happenings in international affairs could only be seen from the point of view of powerless observers rather than direct participants. In America you were in the middle of whatever happened in the world and certainly in the center of the perpetually adversarial position the U.S. had to take in its relations with the Soviet Union. Every morning when I picked up the paper at the Riverside train station I was reminded of that. Reading in my retirement about the postwar years in Europe and in America, I often wonder how we could just live our life almost oblivious of the dangerous situation surrounding us. We knew what was going on, of course, but we just went on with our lives while there was a real threat of being blown out of our existence as a result of some slight misunderstanding between what were then the two world powers, the United States and the Soviet Union. Like everybody else around us we were just busy with our own life and that of our children and did not pay much heed to Soviet threat or to the millions of people all over the world who suffered under terrible regimes. We hardly understood how lucky we were to find ourselves living in a country that people from all over the world want to move to even if they claim to dislike it. A country that is loved by those who live there and often criticized if not hated by those not living there. A rich country that has shown extraordinary generosity towards less fortunate nations for which it is often not even thanked and sometimes even blamed for not giving enough. A strong country that projects its power around the globe, protecting countries in Europe, South America and Asia from antidemocratic influences while those being protected often seem to resent being shielded by a nation that is so powerful militarily. A nation that has an impact on the lives of many people in many places, sometimes helping them and sometimes harming them. A great nation that in our lifetime gained a very powerful place in the world, militarily, economically and culturally. When we still lived in Europe, the French were talking about la Coca Colonization, an apt way of expressing European distress with the onrushing influence of American culture and political and commercial power. Now, in the twenty-first century, the tide has turned. Americans are worried about foreigners buying up their companies just as the Europeans were worried about American interests becoming too large in their economies. We see China, India and a resurgent Russia as new competitors and bemoan our inadequacies in manufacturing, education and economic growth.

The Korean War was part of the cold war with the communist block. It started while I was still in Indonesia. It lasted until 1953 and towards its end involved Chinese intervention, which resulted in an undeclared war between China and the U.S. It cost many American lives and ended in a stalemate that brought the American forces back to the 38th parallel, precisely the area where they were attacked by the North Koreans when it all began. The Communist dictatorship of North Korea continues to this day. It is an absurd regime that flaunts all rules of democracy and normal human behavior between nations and people. China, meanwhile, has now changed completely and has embraced capitalism to a certain degree, but for the Chinese people democracy is still to come. China's economy is booming and growing at an enormously fast rate. But in the fifties and sixties, China was still a dictatorship subjected to the whims of its leader Mao Tse-tung, whose bizarre projects to build the Peoples Republic of China into a workers paradise brought death, starvation and misery to untold millions of people. It is estimated that 30 million people died as a result of the starvation, the mass murder and disruption orchestrated by him in his "Great Leap Forward," his numerous purges and his "Cultural Revolution." When it came to killing, Stalin and his Soviet regime were no slouches either. Reading Aleksandr Solzhenitsyn, we learned that he estimated the regime claimed 60 million victims in its concentration camp system that he called the Gulag Archipelago. Many of these people were dying in the fifties and sixties, a period in which the West experienced extraordinary economic growth and rapidly increasing wealth. I guess we did not care much about all this carnage since the victims were Communists and part of the "enemy."

When I was still at First Boston we read on the Dow Jones news ticker, now a relic of the past, that in Cuba a revolutionary called Fidel Castro had emerged out of the Sierra Maestra and managed to dislodge the corrupt regime of Fulgencio Batista, a military dictator. Everybody thought this was a positive development that would bring a more democratic regime to the island nation. Little did we know that Castro would start a pro–Soviet communist dictatorship that would give Uncle Sam a tremendous headache for a very long time. At this writing, more than fifty years later the problem remains unresolved. Fidel's health is going downhill, but his regime is firmly in charge. Thousands of Cubans have escaped to the U.S. and have found a warm welcome here. Thousands of Haitians, who are also escaping a bad regime and extreme poverty on an island near Cuba, are not welcome here. That's politics. The Cubans have established a firm and politically powerful base in the Miami area and our politicians listen to them very carefully. The Haitians do not have any political clout and suffer the consequences of that.

Soon after I moved over to BBH, the presidential campaign of 1960 moved into full swing. On January 1 John F. Kennedy, then a not-very-well known, young senator from Massachusetts announced his candidacy and quickly became a strong Democratic candidate. He said he wanted to get "America moving again," suggesting the Eisenhower administration had been sitting on its hands. Statements like that are hard to contradict. You have a nation where the vast majority of people are doing reasonably well, there are no scandals in the administration and the world is at peace. Now we wax nostalgic about the peaceful and stable Eisenhower years, but at the time many people thought it was a good idea to shake things up a bit and move to a younger team in the White House. Kennedy exploited this by promoting "vigor" which sounded like "vigah" in his Boston accent. He threw in a cold-war scare

82 SUMMIT ROAD IN FEBRUARY 1960.

by announcing he wanted to eliminate the "missile gap," which he falsely claimed existed between America and the Soviet Union. Kennedy's father Joseph was a very wealthy man who made his money in the liquor business during the Prohibition era and later on in the stock market as a speculator. He was a generous contributor to the Democratic Party and as such was rewarded with an appointment as ambassador to the Court of St. James in the late1930s. During the early war years, he expressed doubt about the viability of the British nation in light of the German conquests in Western Europe and recommended that the U.S. broker an attempt at peace with the Hitler regime. This did not sit well with Churchill and Roosevelt, of course, and Kennedy Sr. was replaced. Two sons of the large Kennedy clan served bravely during the war. The oldest, called Joe, was killed in Europe in an experimental plane that was loaded with explosives and supposed to go on a pilotless mission to Germany after the crew bailed out. Unfortunately the plane exploded too early with its crew still on board. Jack Kennedy served in the Pacific in the navy as skipper of a PT boat, a small, very fast torpedo boat. During a night engagement Jack's boat was "T-boned" by a Japanese destroyer, and he and his crew spent several days on a small deserted island close to other Japanese occupied islands before being rescued. To get help Kennedy managed to swim to an island that was in American hands.

Kennedy was a very intelligent good-looking man who looked fit, but wasn't, and who projected a sense of being actively engaged in his campaign and in his interesting plans to improve the economy, education, general well-being and many other projects. He quickly became very popular, not the least because of his glamorous wife, the former Jacqueline Bouvier, a beautiful lady with a background in Newport and New York society. This couple with their two young children took the nation by storm and made it very tough for Kennedy's opponent Richard Nixon, who was Eisenhower's vice president, to mount a successful campaign. A major turning point in favor of Kennedy was the TV debate the two candidates conducted. It was the first TV debate ever held. Nixon had refused makeup and looked strangely pale and sweaty. Kennedy was telegenic, looked cool and composed and acted well organized. The public opinion was that Kennedy won the debate hands down. Curiously, people who had listened to it over the radio gave the nod to Nixon and Netty and I did not think Nixon did all that poorly either. Our reaction was that Nixon as Eisenhower's vice president had more experience and could be trusted to carry on where Eisenhower had left off. It was the beginning of the era of campaigns where a new and fresh face could win over experience, simply by saying he or she would bring "change." As the senior partner of BBH,

Tom McCance exclaimed during a luncheon where we discussed Kennedy with some clients, "what has he done?"

Nixon had a reputation as a "red baiter," a strong anti-communist and a man who could handle the Russians as he had proven in the then famous "kitchen debate" where he was seen on television speaking with Khrushchev during an exhibition of American products in Moscow. The two were looking at a modern American kitchen that obviously was something the average Russian had never seen. Khrushchev blustered that the Russians could outperform the Americans in technology, saying they would "bury us," and Nixon effectively countered him. The elections came and Kennedy won by the narrowest margin in history. He got 49.7% of the popular vote against 49.5% for Nixon. It is still unclear if Kennedy was helped by the Democratic machine in Chicago run by the corrupt Mayor Daly. But Nixon did not ask for a recount. Kennedy was the first Catholic to become president. He overcame this serious religious hurdle with ease. Once elected he assembled an outstanding cabinet and recruited advisors who were a cut above the quality of people Washington had seen before. Most of them were academics from Ivy League universities with solid reputations in their fields, a team that came to be known as "the best and the brightest" after a book that was written about them. So many books have been written about the Kennedy years that one would think they lasted for decades. Unfortunately they lasted only two years. In that Ivy League environment, Lyndon Baines Johnson, a senator from Texas with a great deal of experience in Congress, looked like an oafish country bumpkin. Johnson was chosen as vice president to get the southern Democrats into the Kennedy camp and provide a balance between the Northeast and the South. Kennedy started with great momentum. He delivered a memorable speech at his inauguration with many sentences that are still being used. One in particular: "Ask not what your country can do for you, but ask what you can do for your country." Clearly he had very good speech writers. He and his attractive wife and young family became immensely popular all over the world. People identified with him, women swooned over Jacqueline and men, imitating Jack's hatless style, stopped wearing hats, a calamity for the hat-making industry. The media fawned over them and now more than forty years later they still do. The young president projected a feeling of a new beginning and a bright future. You still see images on TV of the Kennedy years. In those years the press was much more discreet than it is now and protected the Kennedy image. Nothing was heard or written about the president's peccadilloes with many other women, including a girlfriend of a known mobster or about his severe back problems which made him much less fit than he tried to look.

In those first years at BBH I traveled frequently to Europe and established interesting relationships with people in the investment business. In years past Frank Hoch had built a system of offering internships to young people from European banks and investment firms who all got a desk with us in the Foreign Investment department. Some of them stayed for several months and built lasting friendships with BBH employees. I enjoyed this aspect of work at BBH very much and invited several of these trainees to our house and sometimes out for a sail. Many reciprocated whenever I or both Netty and I were in Europe. Unfortunately we are not any more in touch with any of these people. Frank's approach to the trainee program was systematic and well organized. He made sure that they were not wasting their time and returned with warm feelings about BBH, which hopefully would last throughout their career and boost business between us. It was a smart idea that worked well. In contrast to other firms where foreign visitors were often ignored, the people at BBH had plenty of time to spend on foreign interns. Everybody was on a fixed salary that was usually on the low side. Some would say, "I don't know how much longer I can afford to work for BBH." The lack of profit incentives created a calm and relaxed atmosphere in the office that was not conducive to pursuing new business aggressively. I would experience that lack of aggressiveness as almost nobody paid any attention to my efforts to recommend foreign investments. Most of the infighting was not about competing with others in the market place but about positions within the firm, and many young colleagues were hoping to become partner some day. The odds for this were extremely low if you counted the number of candidates versus the number of available slots, mostly occupied by elderly gentlemen who were hanging on for dear life. I often thought that if all the people hoping to become partner made it, they would be hanging from the rafters in the oak paneled partner's room, looking down on the old roll top desks. The prevailing culture at BBH caused many ambitious people to leave while the more bureaucratically inclined stayed.

For me this period at BBH offered time for adjustment to life and work in America and it was beneficial to me that I was not under great pressure to produce results. I am grateful to BBH for providing me with a perch from which I could gradually adjust to my new environment while earning a modest living, for having taught me to write research reports in reasonably good English, for giving me an understanding of how the upper layers of American society worked and also for the friends I made there.

As I traveled around Europe I decided I had to develop a short list of European stocks I could recommend on the basis of their relative attractiveness. I also had to build a case for the prospects of the economies in which these companies were operating. In addition, I had to select stocks by comparing their attractiveness within their industry relative to other European companies in the same industry. For instance if I thought the German market and economy were attractive and I wanted to recommend an investment in the chemical industry, I had to make a choice among several big companies, such as Bayer, BASF and Hoechst, all three descendants of the old IG Farben concern that was split up by the Allies after the war. To make a judgment on price you had to know the company's earnings. This was, at best, a guessing game in the Europe of those days. Most European companies went to great length to hide their true earnings. Annual reports were often laughably obscure in their discussions of earning power and longer-term corporate strategies. It soon became clear that it was very difficult for me to generate interest among BBH portfolio mangers for investment opportunities that seemed more like a shot in the dark than a sound investment decision. The BBH approach to investing in the U.S. was methodical if not plodding with every portfolio selection based on a "top down" economy to industry to company selection process. There was an Investment Policy Committee of partners who worked on a portfolio diversification plan based on their opinion of the relative attractiveness of individual companies and industries. The research department developed a stock selection list, and portfolio managers had to base their portfolio selections on this list and on the industry diversification the firm had chosen. Moreover, they had to send a memorandum to the committee asking for approval of every transaction and offer a rationale for it. This cumbersome system was not conducive to active portfolio management and resulted in mediocre investment results. Smart portfolio managers would know which stocks were favored by the partners and put those stocks in their portfolios to curry favor with their bosses, regardless of their relative attractiveness in the market. Moreover, nobody could react quickly to unforeseen developments, positive or negative because a mem-orandum had to be written before action could be taken. The same committee also approved recommendations made by the research department; this worked counter-productive for analysts who wanted to make imaginative choices. On the other hand, the firm could boast that all portfolios were managed "by the partners" as if these gentlemen had some otherworldly ability to look into the future and oversee hundreds of portfolios and get results that kept clients happy. The system produced limited choices in stock selection, but the portfolios built by managers were not identical and investment performance was therefore not uniform throughout the firm. Most of the money BBH managed was "old money" belonging to people who were more interested in preserving principal and getting good income. The partners themselves mostly belonged to that group. They were risk adverse and found the banking business of making loans something that could only be approached with the utmost care. They preferred to gather deposits from their banking clients and invest them in municipal bonds that yielded tax-exempt income to them rather than going out and taking risks by making loans to creditors thus producing taxable income for the partnership.

As I made the rounds among European banks and investment firms, I built relationships with the people who produced the best research one could expect given the scarcity of information. I also asked them to introduce me to companies they thought were attractive investments and tried to interview people on the staff of these companies so I could cultivate relationships with them. The results of these interviews were meager at first, but I was hopeful I could build more confidence in the companies I was visiting as time went by. It was sometimes amusing to sit in an office with a man who was obviously not very knowledgeable about his company's true earning power and try to milk him for information. After listening to sometimes very lengthy descriptions of a company's wonderful business results and extraordinary favorable future outlook, I always asked: "Since everything seems to be going so well in your very big company, I find it hard to believe that nothing ever goes wrong, that no mistakes were made and that there are no problems whatsoever." This sometimes brought us back down to earth and occasionally elicited useful comments.

As my analytical skills improved and my reports were approved for publication, I anxiously awaited the first transactions. Nothing happened. It was quite clear that there was no incentive for BBH clients and portfolio managers to invest abroad. The dollar was strong and the U.S. market was promising and reasonably priced and offered plenty attractive investment opportunities. Why take the extra risk of going abroad when local markets offered sufficient opportunities? Why risk "the partners" ire?

I became friendly with many BBH analysts and found it very beneficial to sit down with them and find out how they went about their business. Several other New York firms made an effort to move into the foreign investment field and a so-called "splinter group" was formed within the New York Society of Securities Analysts, a venerable institution that organized luncheons every day where poor food was served and you could listen to presentations by corporate executives. I applied for membership of the NYSSA and was admitted after being vetted by their membership committee. This was a major step in the right direction for me and I am still grateful for the enthusiastic support my application was given by my friend Walter Goode, one of the two heads of the BBH research department. The foreign investment splinter group organized weekly luncheon meetings which I attended regularly. The group was small and everyone knew everybody else. One member who frequently attended and usually kept to himself was George Soros, who later became a world-renowned authority on currency speculation. George worked then for a firm with German roots, Arnhold and S. Bleichroeder. He started a fund for that firm and later went out on his own to start a private equity fund called Quantum Fund. He was immensely successful with this fund and became a multimillionaire if not a billionaire. In later years he performed a major coup when he shorted the British pound in anticipation of its devaluation. His position was heavily leveraged and so big that he was a major factor in forcing a devaluation. He became known as the man who broke the Bank of England. In later years George was a well-known sponsor of many left wing and liberal causes, sometimes making comments that were a little off the wall. In 2004 he spent millions trying to prevent the election of George W. Bush, claiming he was a Nazi. On the other hand, he also spent millions on efforts to improve healthcare and education in underdeveloped countries and on promoting democracy in countries that used to be part of the Soviet block. I became friendly with several other members of the foreign investment group that, over the years, helped me find my way through Wall Street.

In the spring of 1960 the FDA approved the birth control pill which soon became known as "the pill." The drug companies who developed this contraceptive offered a huge investment opportunity. We did not know it then, but this event and the subsequent legalization of abortion by the Supreme Court would have a major impact on our society. We were entering the turbulent sixties, characterized by major societal changes, by the women's liberation movement, student uprisings all over the world and a general change of attitudes towards authority, government, the military and more. The pill drastically changed the mores of younger people and today continues to impact behavior. The children of the generation that went to war and came back determined to create a better life for their families broke loose from the bonds these families had lovingly built for them. Boys started to live together with their girlfriends and having a "companion" rather than a spouse became more and more acceptable. Family planning was now de rigueur and conservative organization such as the Catholic Church were and are fighting an uphill battle against the forces that are undermining the moral standards they have promoted for centuries.

Strangely, now that we had all kinds of ways to prevent unwanted pregnancies, births out of wedlock began to increase all over the world. For many years Netty volunteered for Planned Parenthood and came home with stories about the girls who came there to obtain contraceptives. They were mostly so unattractive, uneducated and so obviously unsuited for parenthood that we became convinced that the prevention of unwanted pregnancies was a good thing in our society, but the hedonism that became a symbol of the late sixties was obviously an undesirable offshoot. After the Supreme Court ruled in 1973 in Roe v. Wade that abortion was legal, the mostly religious opponents of abortion became an enormously important force that politicians had to take into account. So called "right-to-life" fanatics have even gone to the extreme of justifying the murder of doctors who perform abortions. How you can approve a murder under the banner of "right-to-life" remains a mystery to me. I have always thought that the abortion question should be primarily resolved by women because they are, after all, bearing the children. Oddly enough, the most fanatical right-to-lifers are almost always men, none of whom has given birth to a child as far as I know. An interesting side effect of legalized abortions is the reduced crime rate we experienced beginning about two decades after abortions became legal. It has been pointed out by economists, that the reason why the crime rate went down can be found in the lower number of young males being born in milieus that would normally produce criminals.

In our little family the Cub Scouts made an entry. George and Adriaan were friends with the Elliot boys, George with Peter and Adriaan with Chris. The Elliots lived on our street and were a popular family. Jane, the mother, helped Netty get used to some of the more intricate parts of American motherhood, which included serving as a "den mother." George was the first one to appear in uniform and at age six or seven participated in the "Pinewood Derby," an event of major importance for boys of his age. They had to build small wooden racing cars, of a carefully prescribed size and weight, using kits handed out by the scouts. They had to race them down a wooden track that looked like a miniature ski jumping ramp. Two cars raced against each other and the winner was selected by elimination. George was then already good in working with wood. He produced a good-looking little car that he painted orange. To give it the right weight I drilled a hole in the bottom of the car and took some lead to reach the exact weight. I then melted the lead and poured it in the hole, and to our surprise and satisfaction the car had the exact required weight. When race day came we went to St. Paul's Church where the ramp was set up and started racing. George's car ran nice and straight thanks to George's precise work on the wheels and kept winning. Some boys he beat got angry and claimed he had too much weight. Eventually George triumphed over the entire field. After his victory his picture appeared in the Greenwich Time. I believe Jane Elliot was den mother at that time. Sometime later when Adriaan got into uniform, Netty was in charge. We had a competition between dens that could make the best presentation on a theme of their choice. Adriaan was in those days always intensely busy with machinery he made out of cardboard boxes and all kinds of odds and ends. Using all kinds of mysterious pieces of equipment, he produced handles, throttles and wheels that drove imaginary machines that he made growl and hum. Netty and I decided to put this hobby to use in building a space station with astronauts. Our basement turned into Cape Canaveral with a cardboard rocket and boys walking around with their heads stuck into ladies' cardboard hat boxes with a small cellophane window cut out. This turned out to be a huge success that got the boys really involved and I think it won a prize when it was demonstrated before the scouting authorities. This event may have been the zenith of the scout involvement of our boys. They soon lost interest and resigned from the organization.

Through the Oslers we had become friendly with Roland and Jacqueline Bryan who lived across the street from the boatyard of Ole Amundsen where I had bought my Mercury sailboat. The Bryans were great cruising sailors and owned an old wooden boat called the Old Lea. For us cruising was a new world. We often visited together and one evening we decided that our boys were old enough to be left alone for a few hours while we went down to the Bryans for a drink and a chat. Until then we had always hired babysitters to watch over our children and had worked our way through a long list of women and girls with varying success. We had barely settled down when we got a panicky phone call from George telling us that Adriaan was in great distress because somebody had touched his toe while he was trying to sleep. We hurried back and found both boys wide awake and Adriaan in tears. We made a big display of inspecting all the nooks and crannies of the house and to our relief came up empty. There was nobody around who could have touched Adriaan's leg. Another evening spent on parenthood.

My memories of our days on Summit Road are closely intertwined with our life as a family. Our boys were soon used to going to Riverside School and after school they were normally picked up by Netty, but from time to time they walked home on their own. On nice days I walked to the station. Sometimes George would get up early and walk over with me. On warm days I would have breakfast in the screened breezeway between the garage and our kitchen and George would appear, ready to give me a hand and walk down to the station. I do not think anybody would do that anymore. Children are now constantly supervised by their parents and bused over to play dates rather than left to their own devices. On one occasion Adriaan left school and decided to change his walking home routine to spend some time playing with his girlfriend, Mary Ann Noferi, who lived nearby. When Adriaan did not come home at the expected time, Netty was, of course, getting worried and as time went by got really panicky. She alerted the police and a search party was mobilized. Shortly afterwards Adriaan walked home, unaware of the turmoil he had caused. The next day his friend Chris Elliot tattled to their teacher Mrs. Fogg, and she made Adriaan stand in front of the class as an example of what not to do when walking home. Mrs. Fogg also decided that Adriaan was left-handed because he picked up a pencil with his left hand when asked to start writing. Despite Netty's protestations, that settled it. Adriaan became a left-handed writer. Mrs. Fogg goes down in our family history as a not very popular or competent educator.

In early 1961 Netty discovered that our third child was coming. This joyful event necessitated a whole range of urgent preparations. In the U.S. pregnancies are handled differently, less *gezellig* (cozy) than in Holland, but also in many respects more efficiently and with more care for potential mishaps. There were more doctors' visits and more tests. Netty went to see Bob Wyatt, who with his wife Mary later became friends. That summer we went to Holland with our entire family. Netty went first and I followed a few weeks later, combining my visit with a business trip. Taking advantage of the grandparents' eagerness to take care of our boys, Netty and I went on a vacation to Vienna, Austria which was a wonderful change for us. We decided to do this trip because with Netty pregnant we could not travel all that much or go hiking in the mountains. Vienna offered many interesting opportunities for sightseeing and small trips and we had a very good time. We learned that the Viennese take life easy and that waiters are used to people who sit on café terraces for hours with one cup of coffee and not in need of further service. Netty was constantly thirsty and would frequently ask me to secure a glass of water. When I asked the waiters for this the answer was always sofort (right away) and nothing would happen for what seemed an interminable time. We also discovered that it was equally tough to get the check and pay. Even standing up and walking away for a few steps did not have the desired effect. During this vacation we heard that the East German communist regime, prompted by Khrushchev, had decided to build a fence around their territory. All summer thousands of East Germans had left the "Peoples Republic" and crossed into West Germany, obviously preferring the horrors of capitalist society over the communist paradise they were now being confined in. While in Vienna we rented a car and drove to the Czechoslovakian border. We found a small river marking the end of the free world with watch towers in the distance. A grim reminder that many people were living cooped up under a dictatorial regime while we were enjoying our vacation near by.

The American relationship with the Soviet Union was not going very well in those days. In 1960 the Soviets shot down a U.S. U-2 plane that was making a photo reconnaissance flight over their territory. The U.S. initially denied the flight was theirs, but when the pilot appeared to have successfully bailed out, ending up in Soviet custody, little could be denied. President Eisenhower was hugely embarrassed for having told a lie when he said there had been no U.S. flights over Soviet airspace. After that episode, Khrushchev immediately started to behave intransigently in all international forums he participated in. A Big Four meeting in Paris collapsed and in October Khrushchev came to New York City for a UN meeting and made a spectacle of it by pounding on his desk with one of his shoes and yelling in Russian during a speech by British Prime Minister Harold McMillan who supported the UN intervention in the Belgian Congo. The cold war was close to becoming a hot one. Not a good climate to encourage Americans to invest overseas.

As soon as Kennedy was elected, Khrushchev tried to intimidate and test the young president. Fortunately he did not succeed. On April 12, 1961, the Russian Yuri Gagarin became the first man in space, an event that did not help American morale as the threat of Soviet superiority in space became a real one. On May 5, Alan Sheppard was the first American in space, but his flight was a very short one and more a hastily arranged propaganda gesture. While it seemed that the threat of an all out nuclear war between Russia and the U.S. was remote, the competition for world dominance continued. Meanwhile, the situation with Cuba worsened. Kennedy approved a landing by CIA-trained Cuban exiles. On a Sunday morning I was surprised to read in the New York Times that this landing had taken place. For me it was astonishing that a covert operation of this size could be organized without anybody noticing it. Actually the press, or what later would be called "the media," knew all about it, but there was a tacit understanding between the White House and the media that they would not mention it. This became the famous Bay of Pigs landing where a group of brave, ill-prepared Cuban men were sacrificed without air cover. Kennedy had called off the air support the day before thus dooming the expedition. Two hundred died and 1,797 were taken prisoner. It took years before the imprisoned men could return to the U.S. This was a big blunder on Kennedy's part.

The landing was planned during the Eisenhower administration, but he gave the go ahead and then caused it to fail. Like so many other negative things, this tragedy was soon erased from the American collective memory and certainly in the years to come from the heroic and glamorous image left by Kennedy.

On November 27, 1961, Richard Peter Schieferdecker was born in Greenwich hospital. Sonograms were still unknown, so we were in suspense until the last

moment about the gender of our third child. After dutifully honoring both grandfathers, we decided to name our third child, if it were a boy, after ourselves. When Netty was a very young girl she was apparently a roly-poly cherubic child, and her father used to call her Dik which means "fatty" in Dutch (in a nonoffensive way). He kept using this nickname for a long time, even after we were married and Netty was a very slim beautiful young woman. So we arrived at the name Richard and added Peter for good measure. When Richard Peter Schieferdecker announced his arrival, it was early evening and we rushed to the hospital where I was told to hang around for a couple of hours. I decided to go for dinner to a nearby steakhouse called Nino's, and when I returned to the hospital I was just in time to meet the doctor who had performed the delivery and to get the joyful message that we had another son. The doctor was Dr. Hofmann who was filling in for Dr. Wyatt. The first words Netty said (in Dutch) when I entered her room and kissed her was, "It is always so wonderful to hold such a sweet little thing in your arms for the first time."

In early 1962 I traded the old Pontiac in and bought a brand new Mercury Comet with a manual shift and no air conditioning. It was a so-called "compact car," smaller and lighter than the big Detroit Irons. They were then all the rage because gas prices were going up, reaching outrageous levels, even climbing beyond 35 cents a gallon. In late spring that year we hired a baby sitter and took off on a trip to the South. This was the first of many longer road trips we would make in our life, enjoying the American countryside and the many unexpected things you can find along the road. To gain some mileage we spent the first night in New York City where we saw the musical No Strings. That was a good introduction for our trip to the South because the theme was a love affair between a white man and a black woman. I thought the show was excellent and still remember the theme songs.

We traveled to the Outer Banks and to the Blue Ridge Mountains in North Carolina where we ended up in a very nice rustic hotel with bungalows and a trout pond that produced excellent trout for dinner. It was called Nantahalla Village near the Cherokee reservation. Many years later we would return there on a trip from Houston to Washington, D.C. with our Dutch friends the Witteveens and found the place run down and terribly unattractive. Along the way we noticed signs on restaurants and other public places with ambiguous texts that said something like "we reserve the right to refuse service to anybody, etc." The Equal Rights Amendment and the emancipation of the South were still to come. In 1958, the year we arrived, the police arrested a biracial couple in Virginia who were happily married. Their crime was living together while not of the same race. It took several decades before this outrage was rectified and the couple could return to Virginia.

We had beautiful weather on our trip and traveling by some of the Civil War battlefields we got a whiff of the tragedy that had taken place almost a century ago. The South has a certain lure, an atmosphere that you notice particularly in spring that makes it a romantic place with great charm despite some of the rough edges and the ugly aspects of racial prejudice that was until recently so prevalent there. The people were courteous and friendly, as they still are, and we greatly enjoyed our first vacation of travel in America.

Sailing became over time a more and more important part of my life and by necessity also that of my family. I joined the Old Greenwich Yacht Club and the Greenwich Cove Yacht Racing Association. In summer the latter group participated every week in races held in Greenwich Harbor and in the Sound just outside. One-design racing was still very much alive then. The Mercury class, in which I participated, had the smallest boats. Many other classes raced, such as Rhodes 18s, Bulls Eyes, Luders, Quincy Adams, etc., etc. In recent years all these classes and those that came after them such as Flying Scots and Ensigns have disappeared, and at this writing we have only one-design class left that is racing regularly – the Etchells. This is a sad reflection of the busy life younger people have nowadays that makes it hard for them to come out every week and race and also of the increased wealth of younger families that enables them to buy larger cruising boats that often sit unused at the dock. For about two seasons I raced with George as crew. We had very little success. I was not very skilled in getting the most out of my little boat, and I also found that my keel boat was much slower than the centerboard Mercurys we competed with so we constantly were in the lower end of the fleet. On one of those races I asked George to tell me the numbers on the sails of the boats ahead of us – the others were always ahead of us – and he said, "I can't see it, it's all a blur." We found out quickly that he needed glasses and from there on out all our kids got glasses despite the fact that neither Netty nor I ever wore glasses except for reading purposes later on.

Roland Bryan sold the Old Lea and bought a very nice wooden ketch the Daybreak. This was a good cruising boat and Roland started to work on me to also buy a bigger boat. After a while I did that and acquired a 22ft fiberglass boat with minimal cruising accommodation. This was a Pearson Electra. We called her Eclipse. It was my first step on the fatal escalator that leads to a compulsion to buy ever bigger boats, an affliction every sailor seems to suffer from. Urged on by the Bryans, we began our cruising career. Our first cruise was to Port Jefferson on Long Island. This was for us a long day sail, and when we arrived there we felt as if we had crossed an ocean and accomplished a major journey to a foreign country. After spending the night in the very cramped quarters of the Eclipse we sailed over to the Norwalk Islands where we spent another night, and the third day we headed for home. There was a nice breeze out of the north east so I decided to go downwind with the spinnaker up, which would enable us to beat the Bryans home. Unfortunately the spinnaker immediately hour-glassed around the forestay and would not come down. So we returned to the cove with a nice light blue spinnaker tied up in knots. Many more strange incidents and nautical pratfalls would follow. A well-remembered incident followed a few weeks later. Netty was away on a trip to Europe and I was in charge of George and Adriaan. I decided it would be wonderful to go for our first ever evening sail using the battery-operated navigation lights the Eclipse had. Everything went extraordinarily well. There was a nice soft evening breeze and the Eclipse slid through the water in the twilight. Sailing at that time of day has a particular fascination because it gives the impression of greater speed as the wind is still there but the seas are calm and glassy. We switched on the lights and headed for home. Unfortunately I had forgotten there was a big rock between Indian Harbor Yacht Club and the entrance of the Mianus River. We hit the rock with a hard thud, and Adriaan slid forward and hurt his head on the edge of the cabin. Luckily there was no serious damage to ship or crew, and I snuck back to our mooring urging the boys to keep quiet about this episode.

In the late summer of 1962, the U.S. Air Force flying reconnaissance over Cuba discovered activity on the island that seemed to indicate that missile sites were being built. The cold war was heating up again and Khrushchev had allowed this very hostile act to commence. In the fall this situation erupted into what later would be called the Cuban Missile Crisis. The Kennedy administration decided to take decisive action after it had irrefutable proof that the Soviets were building missile launching sites virtually on our doorstep. At that time I was on another business trip in Europe and remember well how ambivalent I felt about continuing my travels within easy driving distance of the Iron Curtain, an area Netty and I had left for precisely the threat we were now facing. I was sitting in a high speed train going from Brussels to Dusseldorf and had a conversation with a German gentleman about the nuclear threshold and the question whether the Soviets would dare step over it. It was spooky. In the event, the crisis was the one moment in the cold war where we were closest to coming to actual warlike action. The U.S. sent out warships to intercept Russian freighters on their way to Cuba, carrying missiles. In a tense standoff, these ships were forced to turn back. In the UN Security Council, the U.S. made its case, bolstered with aerial photographs showing the missile sites under construction. Soon afterwards an agreement was reached and the Soviets backed off, removing their missiles and showing them uncovered on freighters so that US planes could verify their departure. What was not known at that time was that the Soviets got something out of the bargain too. The U.S. pledged to remove its missile sites from Turkey, a U.S. ally, next door to the Soviet Union. For years the Kennedy administration basked in the glow of heroic decisive action, staring down the aggressive Russian moves in the face of a nuclear Armageddon. We did not know better than that the Soviets had blinked. Now we know that they really did not blink all that much because there was a deal. We do not know why both sides kept it quiet.

In early 1963 I decided to stop smoking. I had a bet with Dick Carpenter, my favorite colleague at BBH, that we both would try to stop. One day we went to lunch and we both forgot to take our cigarettes along. We worked in a large, open office without partitions so everybody heard what everybody else was saying. Judy Byrne, a very nice young woman who worked for Dick and me, overheard our conversation and hid our cigarettes. When we came back, Dick went immediately to the newsstand downstairs to buy a fresh pack of cigarettes. I decided to give it a try.

I managed to get through the evening and the next morning I felt like a hero for not having smoked for about eighteen hours and decided to continue. Since then I have never smoked again and now it really bothers me when somebody smokes near me. I cannot understand how Netty managed to survive living with me, puffing away for years, particularly in winter in a car with the windows closed.

In February of that year our little world was almost turned upside down. Across the street from us, on the other corner of Spruce Street and Summit Road was a house that was rented out to a French couple. Michel and Thais Bonnet were in America for a limited time. Michel worked for Mobil Oil and commuted with me to New York. Netty became good friends with Thaïs, a good-looking, lively and well-educated young woman who had been a teacher before she married. As extrovert as Thaïs was, as introvert was Michel. As the French say: "les extrèmes se touchent." He was quiet and conservative in his opinions, but he did have a dry sense of humor that came out from time to time. One morning Thaïs was babysitting Rich while Netty was playing badminton. When Netty returned Thaïs told her she smelled a strong sewage odor in her house. Naturally she was worried about the odor because she had a young daughter, Servane, who was almost exactly the same age as Richard and had been born in Greenwich. Netty decided to go and take a look in the basement where they had an oil tank for their furnace. She tried to look under the tank to see if the source of the odor came from there, but it was too dark there and she asked Thaïs if she had a flashlight. Thaïs went upstairs and came back not with a flashlight, but a burning candle. They opened the garage door, adjacent to the basement and at that moment there was a tremendous explosion. Netty caught the brunt of it since she was standing in front of Thaïs. There was no car in the garage. The garage door blew completely out and that allowed Netty to run outside and roll around in the snow because her clothes were on fire. Thaïs did the same, I believe, but she was not as seriously burned. There was of course a great commotion in the neighborhood and several ladies rushed out to help and take the children in. Rich and Servane were still in the house. Somebody called me in the office and Dick Carpenter who happened to have driven in, immediately offered to drive me home. When I arrived I found firemen working in the house and lots of people milling around. I heard that Netty and Thaïs had been taken to the hospital and that the children were with neighbors. I rushed over to the hospital and found Netty on a stretcher with a horribly burned face. She said in Dutch, stom hè (stupid right?) It was stupid of course to use a candle, but the idea of entering the garage was a natural move. The explosion burned the entire front of Netty's face and part of her hair to about the middle of her head and also the parts of her hands that were exposed. Thaïs also had burns on her hands. I spoke with the fire chief and learned that a contractor for the gas company had been working in the street and one of his machine operators had simultaneously hit a gas and a sewer line, so that the gas traveled uphill in the sewer line and entered the garage through a small catch basin in the middle.

I now had to move quickly to keep our household running. I found a babysitter lady who was willing to live with us for a while, told George and Adriaan what had happened when they came back from school, and parked Rich with the Bryans who had also just had a young son called Richard and were therefore equipped to handle small children. A good occasion for me to learn how much Netty was doing every day and how well organized she was. Mrs. Blackman arrived. She was nice lady who seemed to have decided it was her task to teach me, an ignorant immigrant, how to behave in America. I called Netty's parents and mine to tell them about the accident. In those days international calls were still a real project, involving operators and long waiting times. Once you got your connection, there was no chance for a relaxed conversation. Everybody knew it was very expensive especially in Dutch eyes because the dollar was still strong and expensive and worth a lot of guilders.

I started a cycle of daily hospital visits. Netty and Thaïs were together in a sterile room and visitors had to wear sterile gowns and masks. This was because the wounds were kept exposed to the air and not bandaged. A new system that worked out very well for Netty. She only lost her freckles and after a long healing process that took more than a year, there was little left of her injury, but we did not know that at the time of course and feared she would be permanently disfigured, a terrible prospect for my beautiful young wife. I kept George and Adriaan out of the hospital because I did not want them to see their mother in the condition she was in, and they were not allowed inside the room anyway. We had much attention from friends and neighbors, and I learned from a secretary at BBH that the accident was even mentioned on the radio. Since I did not know what financial troubles lay ahead for us, I asked our lawyer, Ellery Smith, who lived across the street, for advice. He told me the gas company was a client of his firm, but a trial lawyer in Stamford would be willing to take on the case for me. His name was Epstein and he handled it very well, had a photographer take pictures of Netty and started suing the gas company. As the weeks went by, we began to see that the outcome was more favorably for Netty than we had feared. Mrs. Blackman did an adequate job and was duly impressed when Oom Eelco came over to see us.

What Netty missed were Rich's first steps. I still see him suddenly get up on his legs and start staggering around the living room sticking his arms up in the air as small children do when they learn to walk and with the hair on the side of his head sticking up straight as it would do for a long time. When Netty was looking more presentable, I brought George and Adriaan over to visit. They reacted amazingly calmly to the situation. I had briefed them of course, but to see their pretty mother so changed with half her hair gone and a face full of crusts and bandaged hands must have been a shock for them. After a few weeks Netty was released, and we could start working as a family again.

That summer I decided we should go to an area where there was not too much sun and heat to allow Netty's face to heal. So we went to Maine, a state we had not yet visited. George and Adriaan went with us, Richard was left home with a sitter. We went to Boothbay Harbor to the Newagen Inn, a family hotel that still exists. We took a small cabin there where we had two rooms. Ever since we have loved Maine and have traveled there often, by car or boat. We also learned to appreciate the lobster bake. I have a picture somewhere where we are getting ready to eat lobsters cooked on seaweed bed on the rocks at the Newagen Inn. George and Adriaan are standing there with lobster bibs on. Their body language shows clearly that they are very worried about the prospect of having to eat a lobster. We had not told them that they would get hamburgers. We all had a wonderful time there.

During that summer a civil rights movement organized a very large demonstration in Washington, D.C., and Martin Luther King held his famous "I have a dream" speech in front of the Lincoln Monument. In those days America gradually awakened to the need for positive action to end racial discrimination. African Americans, as they are called now, were then called Negroes (with a capital N,) this replaced the word "colored," which was felt to be derogatory. Later on the term "Blacks" became generally used. I still think blacks is the right term just as whites is the correct term for Caucasians. Netty and I have always been in favor of equal rights for all races and in the sixties I even used to contribute to the NAACP (the National Association for the Advancement of Colored People).

Another major hurdle appeared in my path in 1963. The Kennedy administration proposed legislation to introduce an "Interest Equalization Tax." This tax was designed to restrict foreign borrowing in the U.S. and purchases of higher yielding foreign bonds by Americans. Our interest rates were lower than those in Europe and Japan. The tax would hit all dividends and interest income received from abroad by U.S. residents with a 15% charge. This legislation would of course affect ownership of foreign securities very negatively and was the death knell for my little foreign investment business. The ambushes foreign governments could set up unexpectedly through legislation or adverse political developments were often cited as the biggest risks of investing abroad. These risks were accepted as long as the rewards were commensurately greater. Here we had a problem caused by our own government. In hindsight it seems clear that in the sixties U.S. markets were not ready for large scale investments in foreign securities. The rewards were not yet obvious because the local market was very reasonably priced and much more transparent than the European markets that were not yet coming out of their postwar slumber. Also, the big boom in Japanese and other Asian stocks was still to come.

As we began to get to know more people in Riverside, we became good friends with Will and Inge Cates. Will also worked in Wall Street and had an equal interest in foreign securities. After the war Will had worked in Germany with Radio Free Europe, a CIA-funded broadcasting operation that beamed Western news and ideas to countries behind the Iron Curtain. Inge was a native Berliner and had survived the war and Russian occupation in that city. She was a slim and very friendly person who once told me she was gang- raped by a group of Russians immediately after the fall of Berlin. The way the Russians behaved in Germany has been a well-known fact that for many years was denied by the Soviets and brushed aside by the Allies. The Germans themselves also decided to repress it and move forward, mainly because they themselves felt responsible for incredible atrocities committed against people in the countries they occupied, against the Jews and against the inhabitants of Russia, Poland and the prisoners of war they captured on the eastern front. The Cates had a daughter Barbara, who is exceedingly smart and later went to Princeton, learned Russian and now works at the State Department. At the CIA Will had also learned Russian. He was a man of the world who loved women and bourbon and anything else alcoholic. Inge and he were people of broad interests who loved classical music and good food. They were fun to be with. Unfortunately Inge developed a heart problem that stayed with her and caused her death at a fairly young age. After a decent interval, Will married a lovely French lady, but also died fairly young of throat cancer, not surprising for a man who was a heavy cigarette smoker. Will wanted me to go with him to Congress in Washington to testify against the Interest Equalization Tax. I declined, partly because I mistakenly thought the tax was a good measurer to help the dollar, and partly because I did not feel I was up to it as I did not feel sufficiently skilled in public speaking in English. Over the years we would have many wonderful dinners, outings and sailing cruises with the Cates.

After their first visit to us in the summer of 1959, Pa and Ma realized it would be better to come by plane and avoid the summer. Now they got used to flying and during their second visit here we made another trip with them, this time to Washington, D.C., where we went by train and stayed in the old Willard Hotel, now completely renovated into a luxury caravanserai with prices reflecting the cost of rebuilding it. The boys were thrilled to be in a hotel and we went to see all the usual sights. A memorable event was Adriaan getting lost in the hotel's elevators. Adriaan, as usual not afraid to push any button he could reach, liked to go up and down in the elevators. Until he took one that did not stop in the dining room area. We were waiting there for him to have breakfast. When he did not show up, I started a search party and finally found him somewhere in the basement area with a beet-red face from the stress. Mammie also flew over several times, but Pa van Kleffens stayed put in Holland, saying he was claustrophobic and could not bear being in an airplane. Once we had Pa and Ma and also Mammie with us at the same time, and we went in force to Vermont where we stayed in the Woodstock Inn, a nice Rockefeller owned resort. I cannot remember anymore how we managed to put them all up, but suspect Pa and Ma went to stay across the street with the Bonnets. Many more visits would follow, which was a joy for us because it made us feel our parents liked to be in America and approved of our move there. Other visitors included Omi Gréve who stayed part of the time with Erry and Pia. They had moved to Greenwich, at first in a rented house on Parsonage Road and later in one they bought nearby in a cul-de-sac on a side road off Parsonage. Omi endeared herself to me by cooking many outstanding Indonesian dishes, some of which required a full day's preparation with all the attendant smells. Tante Ans de Clercq, the mother of Lucas, Thys and Jan, who was widowed after Oom Frans died in a car accident in South Africa, also stayed with us. She was a great help for Netty when Rich was still very small. It was fun for us to have visitors because we could not really move around all that much with three small children, and the visitors brought stories and life experiences we enjoyed. But I am way ahead of the history of those days.

On November 22, 1963, in the later part of the afternoon, I was working at my desk at BBH when I noticed a commotion in our department. Secretaries were standing together in the middle of our floor and people scurried around. I soon was told what had happened. John Kennedy, our president, had been shot in Dallas. We did not know much more. We all felt as if we had received a body blow. This was a horrible event in our country's history. We soon heard Kennedy had died of his wounds and the whole cycle of events that would later on become well known evolved. There was the swearing in of Lyndon Johnson as president in the plane that carried Kennedy's coffin home to Washington. We wondered: was this a plot against our nation by some foreign entity? Who did it, how many people were involved? As it turned out the Dallas police almost immediately caught the culprit, Harvey Oswald, a strange malcontent who had lived in the Soviet Union and tried to get into Cuba. He was caught in a movie house after also killing a police officer. Oswald had bought a cheap, high-powered rifle with a telescope sight by mail order. Another example of the terrible consequences America's free gun culture can have. He had brought it to the warehouse of the Texas School Book Depository where he worked. During his lunch hour he found a window that overlooked the road were Kennedy's motorcade would travel and from there fired three shots that killed the president and wounded John Connolly, the governor of Texas. Two days later in a chaotic scene Oswald was brought out into the basement of the Dallas Police Department to be brought to court. The basement was filled with press, TV camera men and uninvited onlookers. In the melee that followed a man by the name of Jack Ruby, operator of a strip joint who had no business being there, stepped forward with a gun and killed Oswald as he was held by two big Texas state troopers in ten gallon hats.

Immediately after the news of the assassination, we all went home, some of us feeling bewildered, others quite emotional and one of my colleagues who shall remain nameless said, "Well, he was an extremist and that's what happens with extremists." The spokesman had very strong right wing political convictions. The whole country went into mourning as it tried to cope with the loss of a young president whose élan and lifestyle, often referred to as "Camelot," had created an enormous worldwide reservoir of good will for the United States. Frank Hoch, who had always seemed to me a buttoned-up man, immediately drove to Washington with a friend to pay his respects to Kennedy, who was lying in state at the Capitol Rotunda. We all had the day off for the funeral, a very moving event that was covered on TV for hours. Most everybody still remembers the picture of Kennedy's young son John, about five years old saluting the coffin of his father as it went by. A little contrived, but it hit home with most people who sensed the tragedy behind this gesture of a well-trained small child. George was old enough to understand what was going on, and at one point we were standing in our living room when George said he was glad this was not a plot by the Russians but the work of a "malcontent." I am not sure anymore if he used that exact word, but do remember he used a sophisticated term which surprised me.

Shortly before Kennedy was killed another assassination took place in South Vietnam. There President Diem was assassinated in a coup that later turned out to be supported, if not ordered, by the Kennedy administration. It was an effort to promote a less corrupt and more democratic Western-oriented government in South Vietnam as the regime in North Vietnam became more and more under the influence of the Soviet Union. American advisors were sent to the country in fairly large numbers and the whole Vietnam problem gained prominence in the media and the expression "domino theory," dating back to the Eisenhower administration, was frequently used. It was shorthand for the fear that communist influence gaining ground in one country could gradually affect other neighboring countries and thus allow whole areas to become vulnerable to Soviet dominance. In the case of Vietnam, Laos, Cambodia, Malaysia and Indonesia were seen as being under threat. Against this background the growing U.S. involvement in the conflict between North and South Vietnam is understandable although it turned out to be a monumental mistake that cost more than fifty thousand American lives and many many more Vietnamese, Cambodians and others. Years later the American forces were forced to withdraw in the first war the country ever lost and in the event, the domino theory turned out to be a mirage. Was it all for nothing? Sadly I think the answer to this question is –Yes.

President Johnson escalated the war by using a totally harmless and perhaps even non-existent nightly encounter between U.S. navy destroyers and North Vietnamese gun boats in the Gulf of Tonkin as a means to whip up a mood of outrage in congress that led to a pro-war vote. In 1965 the first American combat units landed in Vietnam. From that point forward, this war became more and more a divisive issue in American society. It tore the Democratic Party apart because Lyndon Johnson was a strong supporter of staying the course and fighting on until victory while many traditionally liberal democrats wanted to end the war. Among Republicans there was also a split that stemmed in part from negative feelings about the war and in part from the ambitious social programs Johnson rammed through congress. He called these programs the Great Society. They were very ambitious and very expensive programs. This, in addition to heavy spending for the war, led to a "guns and butter" policy which triggered a wave of inflation that took decades to overcome.

Gradually the Vietnam War became an issue of great controversy. Huge peace demonstrations were held and we saw the emergence of the so called "counter-culture" movement of young people who were unhappy with the world they lived in and particularly with the Vietnam War. The Beatles, an English rock group that came on the scene in the early sixties, became over time symbolic of this culture. When the Beatles made their first trip to the U.S. in 1963, they were still dressed in modish, three-piece suits and wearing neckties, but they had longish hair, which led people to call them "mop tops." Much more was to come. And hair styles became wilder and longer as the years went by. Earlier Elvis Presley had come on the scene swiveling his hips thus earning the sobriquet Elvis the Pelvis. But he still produced a melodious repertoire rooted in the so totally American Country Western music style. We had seen the many "Do Wop" singing groups of men with long sideburns and strange-looking, tight-fitting polyester suits together with women with bee hive hairdos, gyrate over American TV screens. But now this all disappeared when Rock 'N 'Roll took over. Music began to mirror the mood of the times and the rebellious mindset of the young people. Music got louder and louder, lyrics got raunchier and raunchier musicians looked like wild cavemen in strange cloth. It was the beginning of the Hippy period, a time in which young people rebelled against society by living in communes with free sex and open drug use idling their time away and rejecting the education and lifestyle of their elders.

Luckily we as a family escaped the devastating impact the new youth culture had on many families all over the world whose children became drug addled zombies or useless members of a society that ultimately had no place for people who wanted to reject all conventions.

In 1961 or 1962 Netty and I took steps to try to become members of the Riverside Yacht Club. We had visited the club house on many occasions and believed this club would be a wonderful place for us and our family to enjoy the water. The Bryans also had applied. In those days there was still a waiting period of several years, and in the winter of 1963-64 we were pleasantly surprised when we were asked to meet with the Admissions Committee. It appeared we would be admitted before too long, so I realized I would soon be able to have a boat at the RYC mooring field with launch service and other amenities so I began to dream about getting a bigger boat that would enable us to cruise longer and farther. Roland Bryan convinced me that buying an older wooden cruising boat would be a good deal for me because they were so much cheaper than the fiberglass boats that were coming on the market in increasing lengths. So after considerable searching, I found a 30 ft. Malabar Jr. sloop, a cruising boat that had been very popular immediately after the war. The boat was located at the City Island Yacht Club, which was a club combined with a boatyard, a very convenient idea for me. I spent many winter weekends there crawling under the canvas cover, removing the cracked old seals between the mahogany deck boards and replacing them with new, nice-looking ones. The boat also needed some yard work such as new garboards and better sealing between hull planks. She had a gas engine and slept four with an enclosed head and an alcohol stove. All we needed. After considerable agonizing searches, we came up with a name we were sure nobody else had thought of. Volante, a music term meaning "moving with light rapidity." The name was somewhat overdone because she turned out to be a slow boat. I told the manager of the yard what the new name would be and could he please paint it on. I started to spell it. He said, "Don't bother; I know the name. There is another one with the same name out there on a mooring." The boat was really very completely equipped, with a nice wooden dinghy and good sails made by Valentine on City Island.

In the meantime Netty discovered that she was pregnant again. This most welcome news would, as we immediately understood, not be without problems. It

meant that we would have to think about a bigger house, but for the time being we could manage and wait for the big day. In early 1964 we learned that we had been admitted to the RYC and when the club opening came along we hastened over to show we were going to be good members. Netty was at that point over-due. We were unfamiliar with the elaborate ceremony the RYC organizes every year that includes the firing of a big cannon that is only used for this occasion.

When the gun was fired to announce the raising of the flags, Netty was startled out of her wits, and sure enough, our daughter Janet arrived that night in Greenwich Hospital. This time Bob Wyatt officiated and came out of the elevator to tell me we finally had a daughter. As a fellow RYC member he correctly guessed what had prompted the birth. We thought Jeannette would be too tough for the average linguistically challenged American so we made it Janet and we added Alise, a combination of my mother's name Ali and Netty's mother's name Elise. Her third name was Henriette after Tante Jetje, my father's sister and a favorite of ours. When Netty came home from the hospital we had hired a lady to help her out, a Mrs. Bauer. She was a nice, gregarious woman who had only about one or two teeth left in her mouth, and when I asked her what her husband's business was, she startled me by telling me he was a dentist. Little Richard ordered her around by yelling BAUER! Rich had developed quite a personality by then, with a great liking for TV. There was little left of our good intentions of shielding our children from the perceived bad influences of TV. Richard usually announced that he wanted to "wash keewee" and particularly "Jackie Bleesont," his version of the name of Jackie Gleason, a very popular comedian at that time. Adriaan and George preferred the Three Stooges, a group of comedians who excelled in pratfalls and scenes in which they regularly hit each other over the head. All very uplifting stuff that many years later may have planted the seed for Richard's first job after college with the ESPN Cable TV Network.

When summer came it was time to bring the Volante to the Riverside Yacht Club. Roland Bryan was willing to help, and we went to City Island to pick her up. The hull was painted a beautiful white, the planking was tight, the bilge dry, the mast and boom neatly varnished. She was ready. We motored out and raised the sail. Everything went well and when we reached the club, we lowered the sails and started the engine. It started fine, but when I pulled back on the throttle and shifted into "forward," nothing happened. It appeared the shaft was turning, but the propeller was not. We struggled into the harbor under sail and got onto our mooring and went home. A tremendous downer. It appeared the prop was supposed to be attached to the shaft with a key, a pieced of metal that fit into a groove on the shaft and a matching one on the prop. I got it fixed after a lot of trouble, hiring a police diver and finally hauling the boat out again to get a new key in.

Roland had planned a cruise to Nantucket for our two boats, and as I learned later was always determined to start his cruises on a certain day, ready or not. He had brought his Daybreak up the Sound to Stonington I believe and we would sail up there in the Volante with the two older boys and Roland and Jackie. Roland wanted to save time and start in the evening, right after we were back from our respective offices, and sail through the night so that we could pick up his boat in the morning. We left and found ourselves in a fairly lively sea with a lot of wind, luckily behind us. As night came we realized we had no clue where we were. We saw all kinds of lights on shore and on buoys, but we had no radio direction finder, and Loran or GPS had not been invented yet. The seas became more and more confusing and at night seemed more threatening. At one moment Netty and Jackie looked aback over the transom and were almost paralyzed when they noticed a huge wave coming at us. It passed under us of course, but they did not know that. Sometime in the middle of the night with waves cresting all around us, Roland announced, "we are in the Race." We were not, of course, the boat was much too slow and the distance much too great to have reached that turbulent body of water between Long Island and the open ocean. Morning found us all exhausted somewhere near the Thimble Islands, half way down the Sound. We finally reached our destination and discovered that the only ones who were fresh and ready to go on were George and Adriaan, who had slept through it all in the forward bunks.

As it turned out this cruise was far too ambitious for beginners with an unproven boat. The weather was stormy and rainy, and we did not make as much progress as we had hoped. One of the problems with the Volante turned out to be the engine which was located under a hatch in the cockpit. The hatch was not water tight and water always penetrated into the engine compartment. As the distributer cap got wet, the engine got no spark and failed. Sometimes it would suddenly work again. So when we entered the Point Judith, the Harbor of Refuge, half-way between Fisher's Island Sound and Newport, we were sailing and with a great deal of trouble got our sails down. I planned to motor in between the breakwater and anchor near Roland, who was there already, snugly at anchor. At the critical moment when we entered the breakwater, the engine refused to start so we raised the jib again and tried to sail in and anchor near Roland. The holding ground turned out not to be very good so we dragged anchor across Roland's anchor line. Once we had disentangled that we lurched back into the harbor and heard a heavy toot from the Block Island ferry that was leaving point Judith and had no plans to change course even while we were directly in front of it. At that moment Adriaan, who still had a tendency to push buttons and flip switches, tried our started button again, the engine started, we turned around and found an anchorage as if nothing had happened. Later we found an essay George had written for his English class in which he related this incident and commented, "I have never been more scared in my life."

We continued on to Newport, then still a fairly rough fishing town. We never got to Nantucket, but we reached Edgartown and took a few days of rest there. On the way back we had another engine problem near Block Island that slowed us down and made us reach the island only at dusk. This cruise was to be the beginning of many adventures on the water. As we got more experienced and had better boats, it all became much easier, but we had to learn the hard way that it is better to start slowly, be well prepared and cover short distances gradually getting to know the boat and its peculiarities. It now seems almost irresponsible that we went out in that old boat with two of our then young children, leaving the other two behind in the care of a babysitter. We never even had the boys wear life preservers during the trip because we had taught them how to swim and thought they could handle themselves well on board. In general we had very little safety equipment on board and no radio. But that was the way it was in the old days.

In November 1965 the north east U.S. experienced a power black out of immense proportions. I was caught in it when in Grand Central Station sitting in a train that did not move for hours. It was an old train pulled by a diesel engine that generated its own power. Sitting there in a nicely lit carriage while everything around us was dark made it difficult to leave. I was with our neighbor and friend Frank Clowney and we finally decided to leave the train and walk to the Princeton Club where Frank was a member. The great station hall was lit by enormous flood lights the firemen had installed, but the streets were dark yet amazingly calm. People were volunteering to act as traffic cops on intersections where the traffic lights were out. There were long lines in front of all pay phones. So we were unable to reach our wives and ask them to come down to pick us up by car, a risky expedition anyway which we felt was inadvisable in light of the possibility of riots and looting. So we stumbled down to the Princeton Club, rang the bell and when inside discovered that every chair, sofa, and table was occupied by people who had arrived before us. So we went to the library and stretched out on the carpet there. During the night it got gradually colder as the heat was off too of course. Finally in the morning, power came back and I went to a barbershop to get a shave and went back to BBH. In hindsight this seems a really gross overestimation of my own importance. I could have gone home and taken a shower and a nap and nobody would have blamed me, but I still had and have this odd Dutch idea that you HAVE to go to the office when you are supposed to, come hell or high water.

The mid sixties also marked a major change in the life of Netty's parents. After several successful years on the bench of the Supreme Court of the European Coal and Steel Community, ominous clouds appeared on the horizon for Pa van Kleffens. I believe his term was six years, after which we all assumed he would be reappointed, as were all his colleagues. Unfortunately there was some intrigue going on in the Netherlands which made Pa's post a desirable plum for another jurist with stronger political connections. A Mr. Donner was interested in the job and worked his political friends to get it. There appeared to be a political impasse for the dominant Socialist party which prompted a need for some help from the Protestant, more conservative party Donner belonged to and they made a deal. Pa van Kleffens was the sacrificial lamb. He had no political ties to any party, which proved to be a big mistake. He thought that as a judge he should be as neutral as possible and not be beholden to any political group or party. After an extended period of heavy intrigue and much pulling and tugging, he had to give in, leave and return home. For him this must have been a tremendous blow, but he bore it with great fortitude, and since the Coal and Steel Community afforded him a very generous pension, he could buy a nice, large country house in de Steeg, a village near Arnhem. He always wanted to live in the more rural eastern part of the country and this location was ideal for him. Mammie went along, but not without much protest. She had enjoyed the life in Luxembourg, perhaps even more than Pa, who was more inclined to enjoy a quiet evening at home rather than a reception at the palace of the Grand Duchess of this little operetta state. Mammie wrote long flaming letters to us wherein she poured venom over the people who were trying to unseat Pa and also bemoaned the fact that her husband was a gentle man, not a fighter.

In the end, Mammie liked life in de Steeg very much and they lived there for many years very content and happy. They found many old and new friends there and enjoyed the first house they owned outright. The house in Wassenaar was rented. Nobody understood why Pa had never bothered to buy it from his landlord or looked for another house nearby. Pa just liked things the way they were and resisted change. In de Steeg Pa and Mammie became friendly with many local people, particularly the Dikker family, who ran a small farm called the Carolina Hoeve in the middle of a state park near the van Kleffens house. The Dikkers lived in their farmhouse surrounded by a few fields and in summer baked pancakes and waffles for passing tourists. Mr. Dikker kept a horse and a small jitney owned by Pa. Whenever Pa wanted to take a ride with his grand children, he called the Dikkers, they would hitch the horse to the jitney, and off they went. Pa was a meticulous man with a heart of gold and a strong sense for justice. When Dikker was pressured by the province to give up his farmhouse and move to the village because his pancake operation did not fit in with some bureaucrat's idea of a nature park, Pa stepped into the breach and defended his friend. They won the case and old Dikker was forever devoted to Pa.

In the sixties I was not the only one who made frequent trips to Europe. Netty went several times with the children. She went over with Richard and Janet and had given the children sleeping pills so they would sleep through the night flight. The pills had the opposite effect, and the kids spent the night racing up and down the aisles, helping the flight attendants and turning Netty into a zombie.

In the years that the van Kleffens' still lived in Luxembourg George and Adriaan also went alone, to stay with my parents in Wassenaar. Pa and Ma made a great effort to show them the country where they were born. Later they did the same for Rich and Janet, but by then they were much older and sightseeing was more of a burden to them. I can only hope that these trips have helped our children to understand Holland and Europe better. On their first trip alone we went to pick George and Adriaan up at Kennedy Airport. The plane arrived on time, but our two boys were not there. Naturally Netty and I were frantic. The KLM man behind the arrival's counter could not help us much beyond saying they were not on the passengers' list. In those days KLM flew two daily flights into New York and as it turned out Pa and Ma had delivered the boys to the airport and waved them good bye as they went into the restricted customs area under the guidance of a KLM employee. The flight was overbooked and the two young children were of course an easy target for bumping so they were told they would have to wait a few hours until the next flight. They did arrive with the next flight, and I started a campaign to make clear to KLM that they had acted totally wrong and caused us extreme anxiety. I wrote several letters without much effect. I got a response from some low- level functionary who wrote a clumsy "explanation." I learned again that the Dutch are not good at apologizing or admitting errors. They always try to find some complicated explanation that is supposed to justify their behavior. Since then we have avoided KLM like the plague and flew dozens of times across to Holland with other airlines. When they were older George and Adriaan went solo. George was the first one to go and when he came back we took him for an afternoon sail to hear what he had to say. As is usual with young boys, the information he provided on what must have been a nice long vacation in Holland was meager but one incident he related was humorous. The Dutch had developed a system in which bakers, butchers, grocers, etc., who were still delivering daily to the homes of their customers, could go on vacation. In the Dutch mind, competition that would take advantage of a baker who was sunning himself in southern France was unfair. They all had assigned areas in which they could do business and if one went on vacation, the baker handling the adjoining area was instructed to take care of the customers of his competitor until he came back and vise versa. To make his work easier, perish the thought that he would get too tired delivering bread to all those extra houses, he was allowed to position his cart in a central spot, and customers had to go there to get their bread. No door-to-door delivery during vacation times. So Oma gave George the task of going to the baker and getting the bread. As happened often with Ma, she was not satisfied with the result. The wrong bread, too old, etc. So we asked George what Oma had said about the baker boy taking advantage of a young kid from America. *"Lelijke Beetle kop"*

(Ugly Beetle head), she had said. The Beetles had penetrated the vocabulary of the world, even with old folks in Wassenaar, and beyond that their "mop-top" hair style had engulfed the local bakery staff. Adriaan also spent time in Holland. He became a prominent helper in the kitchen of the Carolina Hoeve helping the Dikkers with the preparation of pancakes.

When George reached the age where he would have to go to what was then called the Junior High School, now Middle School, we investigated the possibilities of going to a private school. We found Brunswick, a private boy's school in Greenwich, to our liking. It was a school where there seemed to be good discipline, small classes and considerable emphasis on academics. We were under the perhaps mistaken belief that the junior high left much to be desired. We heard stories about kids smoking pot and large classes without much discipline. The Greenwich High School, on the other hand, had an excellent reputation and we knew that. Brunswick is now a much larger school with a waiting list for new students. Then it was easier to get in. George had very good report cards and admission was a matter of a visit to the assistant headmaster and he was in. Brunswick proved to offer a very good environment for George, Adriaan and later Richard. We never regretted sending them there. They found good, often lifelong friends, got a good education that lead to admission to excellent colleges and they learned how to study, how to write decent English and how to speak in public. Almost immediately George proceeded to get on the Honor Roll, and seeing his name in the paper, listed there among the very good students, made us feel we were making a good investment and that our move to America was yielding results.

In the later sixties it became clear that we had to look for more space for our family. We started looking around and found a house we really liked, made a bid on it and were outbid by another couple. We then heard that an old hotel on the shore called the Shorehame Club was going to be demolished and that the property would be split up into small lots of which several were waterfront. This hotel was a place where New Yorkers used to summer in the days that Old Greenwich was still called Sound Beach.

Waterfront properties were in those days as attractive as they are now, but not as pricey and building styles were still modest. The era of the McMansions in Greenwich was still to come. After much debate we decided to buy a lot provided we could build the house we wanted there. What I had in mind was a so called "modular" house. Not a prefab but a house built out of standard modules. The company making these houses was called Techbuilt and was the creation of a group of young architects in

Cambridge Massachussets. The idea was that each house was built in the "post and beam" construction with high cathedral ceilings and generally contemporary style. We liked the design and started to puzzle a house together within the limitations of Techbuilt. This meant that you started out with a simple house, four walls with a roof. There were modules of, I believe, four feet, so you could make the house four feet longer or shorter, but not wider. We designed a house with a L-plan with lots of large windows looking over the water. We also decided to make it two stories high with the main living quarters on the second floor. This way we could better protect ourselves against hurricanes and floods. I went to Cambridge to talk about the type house we wanted and an architect there drew up the plans on very short notice. I had a hassle with the investors who had bought the old hotel and were financing the development of the land. They did not like the design of our house. This resulted in a big improvement in the design of the house. I went back to the drawing boards and with the help of the architect added a big deck up front on the second floor, shaded by the roof that protruded out. This was approved and was more expensive of course, but in hind sight added a major feature to our house which we enjoyed tremendously. We found a builder willing to put the house up and proceeded to order the materials from Techbuilt. What happened then was that Techbuilt sold us almost all the wood, aluminum window frames, and insulation, roof materials, doors, etc., etc., trucked it

over to Old Greenwich and dumped it on the site. The cost of these materials was based on Massachusetts prices while building in Greenwich was then as it is now much more expensive on a per-square-foot basis. So by having it all trucked over and delivered on site, we acquired a Greenwich house at a Massachusetts price. The building trades union in Greenwich

8 SHOREHAME CLUB ROAD, OLD GREENWICH.

had gotten wind of our plan and were picketing the site, but our builders said the union guys were Greenwich men and therefore would not start picketing before about 8:30 AM so they ordered the truck driver to come at 6 a.m. which he did, asking all the time why he had to come so early.

We also decided to take additional precautions against storms, and had pilings driven into the very swampy ground of our tiny lot. We put the foundations of the house on these pilings and decided not to have a cellar but just a crawl space under the ground floor. We made the first floor into part garage, part bedrooms for George, Adriaan and Richard, plus a bathroom for them, a small furnace room and a TV room. Upstairs we had a big living room facing the water and next to it a dining room, behind that the kitchen, a den and a room for Janet plus two bathrooms and our own bedroom. All these rooms upstairs had cathedral ceilings and were quite large in size. We started building in the early spring of 1966. Not surprisingly, it took much longer than we had anticipated to finish the house. Summer came and with it a serious spell of hot weather. We had sold our house on Summit Road to John and Lennie de Csepel, who later on would become good friends. We had to leave our old house, but the new one was not finished yet. Leaving what he called the "Lellow House" was a major trauma for young Richard and he let us know his dissatisfaction with loud howls. Like all children, he preferred everything to remain the same.

A major hurdle to occupying the new house was the permit we needed from the electrical inspector. Our builder used only nonunion people and our electrician had a great deal of trouble

getting his work approved. The crowning blow came when the inspector decided to go on a two week vacation, leaving us waiting until his return. I always felt that the fact that we used nonunion people played a role in the delays we encountered. One of our new neighbors, the Pritchards, who had also built a Techbuilt house and with whom we had become friendly, offered to run a long electric wire to our house so we could at least operate a refrigerator and one lamp in our living room while we were camping out in our new abode. We had hired a mother's helper for the summer, a girl from Berea College in Kentucky, a school where people from the rural areas there could get a decent education. The college produced dozens of girls who were eager to come to our area and help families with children during the summer. Our girl was called Fran. She was a jolly, chubby young woman who took it all in stride and was probably used to more heat than we were. Fran would come back to stay with us for several years until she finished college.

It became gradually clear to me that I had no future at BBH. The Interest Equalization Tax had killed my little niche. The real business of the Foreign Investment Department was basically a brokerage serving the bank's foreign correspondents – banks, brokers and institutional investors. It was tightly controlled by Frank Hoch and Maarten van Hengel. We did not do much actual portfolio management work and spent most of our time dealing with administrative problems and answering investment questions from our many clients. There was a lot of letter writing. Overseas telephone calls were still in their infancy and too expensive to do on a regular basis. We had Telex, of course, but that was cumbersome. Every Friday a letter was sent out to a large number of clients. For this job we used a machine that could print out the letter with the proper address and salutation for each recipient. These letters were airmailed out so they would be over in Europe on Monday morning. The text was mainly a review of our research reports that came out that week and opinions on stocks on our Selection List. Leighton Waters, a wonderful man who sat across from me, would dictate these letters every Friday and their content was treated as if it contained information of the utmost importance. Leighton would work very hard all Friday on this product. Clients seemed to like this letter and rewarded us with brokerage. Leighton was an ardent sailor and all summer participated in races near Rumson, New Jersey where he lived, and on Monday he would relax and dictate long memos about the protests that had been filed in the previous weekend's races. Unfortunately he died very young.

Since Frank Hoch handled Switzerland, Italy and France while Maarten did Holland and Belgium and John West England and Scotland (the Scottish investors were very important clients in those days), there was little room for anybody else. The Swiss and UK relationships were by far and away the most lucrative. My friend, Alexander Ercklentz, handled what small business Germany produced in those days. Germany had still not fully recovered from the war. Its economy was booming, but after they were permitted to invest outside the country, German investors had little interest in putting their money in US securities. To a certain extent this was also true of French and Italian banks. Since I spoke some French, Frank decided that I should work with him on France. We traveled there together and visited many correspondent banks who received us very well but produced little business. On the flight back I glanced over to Frank, who was sitting next to me, and saw he was writing a report on the trip with a negative evaluation of my abilities as a French linguist. I realized there was not much perspective in this business for me and started to look around.

Through friends in the institutional brokerage business I had heard good things about two investment advisory firms, both with Boston origins. Historically Boston law firms had done much trust and estate work for the "old money" in that city and over time had gone into money management, leaving the law practice for what it was. Also non law firms that were established to render unbiased, pure investment advice for a fee originated in that city and of these two names stood out: Loomis Sayles and Scudder Stevens and Clark. I got introductions to both through broker friends and found Loomis mildly interested but Scudder much more receptive.

As often happens in life, I had arrived at the right moment. They were facing a vacancy because a woman who was one of their senior portfolio managers was leaving to become a broker. I spoke with two partners there, Buzz Coxe and Spike Thorne. They made me an offer that was much better than what I was making at BBH, and I decided to take another plunge into the unknown. Later on I learned that my entrance at Scudder was a bit awkward because Coxe and Thorne had circumvented the hiring system they had been laboriously developed and agreed upon exactly to avoid random hiring like they did with me. Another partner who was on vacation and who listened to the impressive name of Quincy Adams Shaw McKean, leaving little doubt about his ancestry as an American blue blood, was in charge of hiring managers and training them. I guess I was lucky, because I am not sure I would have passed the intensive screening of Shaw McKean. Shaw was a somewhat pompous man who did not fit the profile of the average Scudder investor who was more relaxed in relationships with colleagues and more focused on investment results and caring less about the form and style of letters and internal memoranda. However, what Shaw understood very well was what investment managers call "client handholding," that is, paying attention to your clients and making sure they were always aware that you were thinking of their interest. Later on I got along quite well with Shaw, but he insisted on me going through a training program before letting me loose on their clients. I quickly learned that being at Scudder was very different from BBH. Scudder was a very horizontal organization where investment expertise and thorough knowledge of all kinds of securities, stocks as well as bonds, was assumed. You had to be on your toes at all times and you had to move fast. This was different from the often somewhat sleepy BBH culture. Scudder had two senior partners, Hardwick Stires and George Johnson. Stires was older and retired soon after I came. George Johnson was a wonderful leader, kind and easygoing in his relationships with the people in the office. He was a skilled investor who enjoyed talking with us about investment problems. Below these two there was a layer of several partners. The portfolio managers were classified as either senior or assistant. There was a large research department, including a group that specialized in fixed income securities, a new arena for me. BBH's foreign clients were not very interested in bonds because they got higher yields in their home countries in those days. The culture at Scudder was totally different from the BBH style of mostly elderly partners who kept their distance and preferred to sit in their paneled partner's room behind roll-top desks. I managed to get on Shaw McKean's good side by writing a detailed report on Rank Xerox, which was the European arm of the U.S. Xerox Corporation, in those days a growth stock par excellence. Shaw needed the report for a client he deemed very important. I knew that company quite well, and Shaw was pleased with the result and I guess the report convinced him that I could be trusted to handle clients correctly despite the fact that I had not been hired by him.

After a few months I was made a senior portfolio manager and given accounts to handle. Being in a nice office of my own on Park Avenue with my own secretary, within a short walk of Grand Central, was a really important step up for me. My first very own secretary was not a great success. She was an Italian lady who was not able to handle the fairly complex portfolio accounting secretaries had to do at Scudder. Then Joan Crowl came into my life. Joan had just graduated from the renowned Gibbs secretarial college and turned out to be a wonderful person to work with a very quick study and a whiz at reconciling bank custody statements with Scudder appraisals. This sound simpler than it is; in normal times it is quite a job, but at Scudder it was more than that. The portfolio accounting at Scudder was done on a IBM punch card system, similar to BBH. Then came the beginnings of the digital revolution and Wick Stires, a computer buff, bought a brand new IBM 360 machine for a million dollars. This machine would be a tremendous step forward in record keeping. It was installed in a special big room in our building with a raised floor to accommodate all the wiring and a special dedicated air-conditioning system to handle the heat all the large machines were throwing off. I understand that this whole installation had about as much memory as a high end PC has now. A special team of experts was hired to make the transition, and they proceeded to build their data base from one of two punch card files that in hindsight proved to be the wrong one. When the result came out and we were getting ready to send appraisals to our clients we were horrified. We were looking at page after page of complete gobbledy-gook. It was a huge disaster and sorting this out for each client was no small task. Joan did a flawless job. Ever since then I made sure Joan would stay close to me and later on she moved with me to Eberstadt and eventually became manager of our entire portfolio administration there. Much later she re-emerged as a colleague of my friend and right hand man Richard Johnston who made her a partner in his investment management firm. In between all these moves Joan married Al Giannotti and raised a family with three sons. A really remarkable career and proof of the thesis that you can really get somewhere in this country if you are smart enough.

In the winter of 1966, just before joining Scudder, Netty and I went sailing in the Caribbean for the first time in our life. During a boozy evening at the Riverside Yacht Club, Roland Bryan had struck up a conversation with John Thomas, who had bought an old cruising ketch home ported in the Windward Islands. This was the Island Belle, formerly owned by J. Linton Rigg a well-known yacht designer, who sailed her all over this wonderful sailing paradise and wrote a book about it called The Alluring Antilles. I have a copy of the book, which seems almost primitive and idyllic in its approach now that the Caribbean has been flooded with charter boats and large cruising ships. This trip would convince us that the Caribbean was the place to be in winter and afforded us a peek at the islands before all the tourists came. Roland somehow managed to convince the owner of the Island Belle that we would be glad to sail in his boat for a week (for free of course) and that in exchange he could sail a week with Roland's Daybreak here in the U.S.

We flew to Castries in St. Lucia where we found the Island Belle with its captain Lionel Hodge, a man from the island of Anguilla. Lionel was a wonderful, mild-mannered man who was assisted by a young guy he had recruited from his village. Lionel proved to be a decent cook and a good sailor. As it turned out, the owner of the boat wanted to see how things worked out between Lionel and us before starting serious charters. Our flight over was on a prop plane from Antigua that made stops at almost all islands, leaving the starboard engine running while the door on the port side was opened. We sailed from Castries to Soufrière where Netty and I decide to take the dinghy ashore to look around. This caught the eye of a local policeman, who rode his bike over to the dock and asked if our ship was cleared in or out. We said we were cleared out in Castries and that left him with the big question, how we could be there on land while we were cleared out and no longer supposed to be on his island. This serious and puzzling problem made him take us to the police station where he started a very involved radio discussion with his commander, who judging from his voice, was an Englishman. Finally the voice asked the cop, "why are you keeping these people?" It was the first and hopefully last time Netty and I were arrested. We had a wonderful sail from there to all the well-known islands. We anchored overnight in the Tobago Keys where there were two other boats beyond ourselves. Nowadays it is packed with hundreds of boats during every night in the season. A man, who, surprisingly, was white came to us from one of the flat islands nearby and sold us some crayfish. He was a member of the small fishing community on Bequia Island that is of Scottish descent. Lionel proceeded to cook the crayfish in a pan that was a little too small. He did this by holding half of them in his hand and sticking the other half in the boiling water. We ended up in Grenada where we met an older Riverside couple, Ted and Dorothy Helprin, who would sail back to St. Lucia with Lionel. This couple became good friends in later years. This cruise was an eye-opener for us and a wonderful experience. I showed up at Scudder for my first day with a big tan. In the coming years we would make many more trips to the islands, usually on a so-called bareboat charter.

Anybody reading about the sixties will find much emphasis on stories about the youth revolution, the "hippie" movement, the demonstrations against the war in Vietnam and all the social unrest generated by the antiwar movement. Netty and I were not unaware of these developments, but our life like that of most other people just went along unaffected by the turmoil among the young people. Luckily our children were mostly also not touched by the drug culture and antiestablishment youth movement. We saw very bad examples of families basically loosing their children to the "Age of Aquarius." You could hardly miss what was going on in the world. TV and newspaper coverage of all the parades, riots and other disturbances was intense. President Lyndon Baines Johnson, a man who had wielded immense power in the Senate for many years before he became vice president under Kennedy and who succeeded him after the assassination, made a string of decisions on the Vietnam War that resulted in a huge increase in American troops over there and the subsequent escalation of the fighting. American casualties rose by the day and many people including Netty and I became thoroughly disenchanted with the war and the way in which Johnson conducted it. In addition to fighting the war, Johnson, always the big-spending politician pushed through a series of ambitious, very costly social reforms. LBJ as he was called was fated to go down in history as the man who lost the war in Vietnam at tremendous cost in human life and not as the president who brought very important social change that affected our country positively. In the public eye, his "War on Poverty" and the actions he took to promote racial equality were totally overshadowed by the war.

In the summer of 1967, Netty and I took a vacation in California. Since this was my first year at Scudder, we could not take any long vacations. Switching jobs brought me back to two weeks vacation a year, a scandalously short period in the eyes of our Dutch friends who were now moving into the new world of more than four weeks' vacation with many other holidays, sick days and personal days added. At BBH I had also only two weeks vacation and since I had been there seven years, I had accumulated modest pension rights. These were wiped out when I left because they had not yet vested in my name. What price glory?

In California we landed in LA, rented a car and started looking for a motel near the ocean. That proved tough. It was a Saturday night and the entire population of LA seemed to have moved towards the beach. Utterly exhausted, we found a place near a railway junction way inland where trains moved all night loudly blowing their horns. We visited Disneyland and wondered why people paid a hefty fee to enter the park only to pay again for a short ride after standing in line for a long time. We drove to Santa Barbara and from there inland to truly beautiful Yosemite Park and ended up in San Francisco.

The whole trip opened many new vistas for us. We experienced the heat near Sacramento followed by the wet coolness of San Francisco. We drove into this city, with our AC on at full blast when we suddenly noticed a woman crossing the street in a fur coat. It was really cool in San Francisco. We visited the Haight Ashbury district where the "hippies," a new phenomenon, were on view. Cars with proper couples (like us) with disapproving looks on their faces were cruising bumper to bumper along the streets looking with disbelief at the scene presented by the cavorting members of the youth revolution. They all had long, unwashed hair and strange clothes, many had bare feet, odd and unhealthy in the cool and foggy weather. They wore beads and sang songs with guitars, pounded on drums and rattled tambourines. None of their musical efforts were melodious or of any artistic value. Nobody did any work and sitting on the stoops of boarding houses seemed to be the generally accepted way to spend the day. We did not see it, but we assumed they were all smoking pot and often high on drugs. What we did see were couples who obviously had practiced free love, sitting on the sidewalk with their babies. This was a truly disturbing sight. What chance would these babies have for a normal life, an education and a decent place in society? We learned that in SF hotel rooms do not need to be air conditioned and after we opened the windows of our room in the St Francis Hotel, we heard the hippies pounding on their bongo drums in the park across the street throughout the night. There would be many more years to come of antiwar demonstrations by young people many of whom were well meaning, but the predominant attitude of the demonstrators was antiestablishment, not just anti war. "Make love not war," they yelled, and "Hey, hey, LBJ, how many kids did you kill today."

The quality of life in New York City began to deteriorate seriously in the mid sixties. John Lindsay a young fresh republican politician became mayor in 1966 following Robert Wagner who had run the city in the old style with cronyism and machine politics, hiding rapidly growing economic and fiscal problems. Wagner allowed the public sector employees to unionize which became one of Lindsay's biggest problems. As soon as he came into office he was confronted with a subway strike run by an Irish union boss called Mike Quill. Speaking on TV in his strange Irish accent Quill publicly ridiculed Lindsay calling him a "pipsqueak." This strike almost brought the city's transportation system to its knees. We had to walk to our offices and women began to put on sneakers carrying their high heeled shoes in a bag. It was the beginning of the end of "heels" in the office and it signaled the emergence of sneakers as acceptable wear in almost any social setting. The city's tax base began to erode as rents rose and many old manufacturing businesses left and middle class families followed suit by going to the suburbs. Crime increased, and when the garbage men also went on strike and garbage piled up in the streets we had a situation that prompted comments of "Bombay on the Hudson." But we continued to work as if nothing was amiss. Despite his problems Lindsay was elected to a second term after resigning as a Republican and becoming a member of the small Liberal party. Beyond his union problems he coped with a tremendous snow storm that upset people in the outer boroughs who claimed he neglected snow removal in their areas while favoring Manhattan. It would take decades before the city returned to a safe, prosperous and orderly place where people liked to live and work. The situation in New York City was not unique in our country, but since it was New York it was as always more pronounced and on the leading edge. It reflected the difficult transition from postwar prosperity to a period of economic uncertainty and social upheaval in which racial problems flared up and all kinds of groups began to assert their right to be heard.

One morning at Scudder I saw on the front page of The New York Times a photograph of an American tank rolling through the dense Asian foliage, the type of terrain I knew so well from my years in Indonesia. On top of the tank were several bodies of American marines. Most were probably already dead, others were severely wounded and covered with bloody bandages. This picture really turned me off on the war. I suddenly saw the utter uselessness of fighting an enemy hiding between civilians in a country that was fairly densely populated and covered with thick foliage.

The photograph was taken during the so-called "Tet" offensive, which occurred after the American troops thought they had beaten the Viet Cong and thrown most of them back into North Vietnam. Totally unexpectedly, during the Vietnamese Tet Holiday, the Viet Cong swarmed over our positions in many places, inflicting severe losses and even managed to penetrate into Saigon, the capital where the Americans were headquartered. It was a tipping point in the war and an enormous blow to the prestige of the U.S. and the South Vietnamese puppet government.

At Scudder I often worked with Hamilton Chase, a very nice gentlemanly partner who lived in Old Greenwich and was then married with Anya Seton, the well known author who wrote the Winthrop Woman, a history of Old Greenwich in the days of the early settlers. Ham invited us over for drinks at their place in Binney Lane where we met Anya. We had dinner afterwards at the Riverside Yacht Club. Anya showed us a room full of the books she had written and all the translations of these books in foreign languages, including Dutch. Ham ran a mutual fund that invested in foreign securities, a difficult thing to do under the IET. The only thing he could do was work with existing holdings. To avoid the tax, he could only buy new holdings by using the proceeds of a a sale in the same amount. Through him I met many foreign visitors who came to scout out Scudder's operation, and I convinced the firm that it was worth a try to go to Europe and show the flag. This was a difficult trip for me, because unlike BBH, I had nothing to offer in return and the concept of managing money for a fee like Scudder did, without getting brokerage commissions or custody fees, was a strange novelty for the Europeans. When I told people I visited that we were offering our portfolio management skills, most of them were not receptive. We were invading their turf. On a visit to Paris a Frenchman asked, "Do you want me to commit arakiri?" I had a week end in Paris and visited with the Bonnets who had returned there from a stay in Africa. They took me on a nice tour through the countryside and lunch in a small country restaurant of the kind only the French know where to find. We also visited an interesting family who lived in an old converted farm house. The host was an elderly man whose face was deformed as a result of wounds he had received when serving as a fighter pilot in WW I. We met his grand daughter there who was a student at the Sorbonne in Nantère, the out-of-town campus of that famous university. She told us about the student life there in a place that lacked the character of the old university in Paris proper. She gave us no indication of the serious student revolt that would erupt the next day in Nantère. She probably did not know what was coming.

Monday found me in the middle of an old-fashioned French revolution. Special riot police were everywhere. They were tough hombres with high lace up boots wielding long rubber truncheons and carrying submachine guns slung over their shoulders. I got some inkling of the problems these movements give parents when I visited a gentleman at Banque Louis Dreyfuss who was on the phone pleading with a young son who was only high school age, he said. The boy wanted to demonstrate in the streets, and the father was worried about his safety and opposed to this plan.

One evening I went for a lonely dinner to a small restaurant near the Place de L'Étoile. All of a sudden the waiters rushed outside and came back wheeling their mopeds into the restaurant. A few minutes later I heard what sounded like an ocean wave. The rushing noise came from the footsteps of a mass of thousands of students who were marching down the boulevard chanting, "Liberez nos camerades." It became clear to me why Baron Haussman had designed Paris with very wide boulevards. That made it much harder for the riot-prone Parisians to erect barricades. I was sitting next to the window and the students were banging on it as they walked by. I wondered what I would do if they would come inside. I decided to keep a table knife handy, but that was luckily not necessary. The riot police or, Garde Republicaine, were beating up the students without much regard to convention, but the remarkable thing was that there was not one fatality.

In the plane going home I read a book that had just been published in France and that had received enormous attention. *Le Défi Americain* was written by Servan Schreiber, a well-known French journalist, who argued that the American economy was stronger and more resilient than the European and particularly the French economies and that US technological prowess was a major driver behind the American economic growth. He believed that America was rapidly becoming an invincible world power. He pointed out that the U.S. let old basic industries die when they were no longer competitive while the European system was more inclined to let those industries survive, supported by government subsidies while all kinds of regulations prevented the development of new technologies in Europe. This all sounded like beautiful music to me because it seemed to justify the move I had made to America a decade ago and also argued strongly in favor of investing in American companies, the investment approach I was now promoting. When I got back to Scudder, I told McCullough, the firm's economist about the book. He immediately jumped on the idea the writer had developed and made it the theme for his next cycle of client presentations. When I asked him if he would not like to read the book first and offered to translate portions of it for him if he could not read French, he said that was not necessary. He could guess the drift of the argument and that was all he needed. A typical example of American blindness to the value of ideas from intelligent people living abroad.

In contrast to Paris there were many more deaths in the U.S. when the black people rioted after Dr. Martin Luther King was killed. Dr. King was shot in Memphis on April 4, 1968, where he was to support a civil rights cause. His assassination was a turning point in the civil rights movement. The assassin was a white man of the "red neck" variety who had a grudge against black people. I will always remember seeing King deliver his speech on TV in front of the Lincoln Memorial. It was the "I have a dream" speech. A statement of remarkable eloquence that set a tone for the legislation that followed that with a delay of some hundred years gave black people equal rights. The killing of MLK, as he is now often called, triggered serious rioting in the black neighborhoods of many major population centers. Bands of enraged people rampaged through their neighborhoods and torched stores owned by whites. Whole shopping centers went up in flames with the result that the people living there were deprived of neighborhood shopping opportunities. Curiously, the mobs never penetrated any of the wealthier white areas. We all feared this would happen, but it did not transpire. This murder of one peaceful man was not enough.

There was another heart-wrenching assassination in America in that year. Bobby Kennedy, Jack's brother, was shot in a hotel in Los Angeles on June 5. In the fifties Bobby had served in the Department of Justice and was part of the team of the notorious Senator Mac McCarthy's hunt for Communists. He ran his brother's presidential campaign in 1960 and became attorney general in his brother's Cabinet. His record at Justice was good. He was very strongly pro-civil rights and his persecution of the Mafia and corrupt Teamster Union leaders was aggressive and successful. After his brother's assassination, he stayed on with LBJ for nine months even though the two hated each other. He had been his brother's closest confidant and served more as White House counsel than as AG. That created a curious situation because as Attorney General he was part of the government and obligated to maintain the separation of powers. After he left the Johnson administration, he ran for the Senate for New York although he had barely ever lived in that state. When Senator McCarthy, who opposed Johnson for the democratic candidacy, began to falter, Bobby jumped in and started a run for the presidency. He was killed early in his campaign. I never had much sympathy for Bobby. I saw him once when he was paraded through New York City on his election campaign. He seemed much shorter than I had expected and had a fixed, toothy grin on his face. He impressed me as a ruthless opportunist, but he managed to gain the public sympathy and after his death he became part of the Kennedy "American royalty" myth the media continue to pursue to this day.

That winter we ordered a Seawind ketch from the Allied Boat Company in Poughkeepsie. This was our first true cruising boat. The Seawind was a solidly constructed ocean-going boat, very seaworthy, but a tad slow in the light winds in Long Island Sound. A sister ship had already completed a circumnavigation, the first fiberglass boat to do so and the skipper gave a presentation at the New York Yacht Club that I attended. I even had dreams of crossing the Atlantic someday with this boat. We named it Postiljon. Netty's great grandfather Willem van Someren Grève was a sea captain, and we have a picture of his Postiljon, a three-masted barkentine which he sailed on the Holland-to-Indonesia run carrying mail. Hence the name *Postiljon*, a French word which had been adopted by the Dutch. It means "mail rider," a mail carrier on horseback, and is spelled postilion in French. The man who brings a love letter to a girl is called a *"Postilion d'amour."* We thought this name would be known and easily pronounced by Americans, but that was not the case. From the first day the name was a problem for Americans, particularly on the radio. I learned by heart to spell "Papa Oscar Sierra Tango India Lima Juliet Oscar November." This boat became a real joy to own and carried us on many long cruises. In preparation for my imagined transatlantic crossing, I started a course in celestial navigation, and Netty made it quite clear to me that if I ever wanted to undertake such a trip, she was not going. I took delivery of this boat in Mamaroneck and sailed it over to the Riverside Yacht Club with George and Adriaan. I wanted to document this boat, thus avoiding an ugly number on the pristine new bow and preparing it for trips to foreign countries. But I discovered I could not document it unless the owner/captain was a U.S. citizen. This prompted us to overcome our inertia and take the steps required to become U.S. citizens. We had planned to do it for some time, because Rich and Janet were US born and traveled on U.S. passports while the rest of the family was classified as "resident aliens." Also, I thought we should prepare for the eventuality that George and Adriaan could be drafted into the U.S. military. I thought they would have a better chance of becoming officers and/or getting better assignments as citizens and avoid the ordeal I had to go through as a corporal in the infantry. So I prepared the papers and we went to a place in Stamford where a nice man asked us a few questions. He wondered who had prepared the papers and when I said I had done that myself he commented that I had done a better job than many of the lawyers who usually prepared the papers for new immigrants. We went to the court house in Bridgeport with Adriaan and George, and the four of us were duly sworn in amidst a motley group of people from all walks of life, some of whom were unable to sign the papers and many were unable to understand what they were supposed to do. We wondered what would become of a country that let in so many people that seemed unable to cope with the simplest instructions in English but it still seems to work.

We enjoyed living on the shore in Old Greenwich. The summers were especially pleasant. We had a small beach in front of our house and sailed a little Sunfish sailboat from there. The Bryans had also bought a piece of land in our compound and built a nice contemporary house there. So Netty and Jacky spent much time on the beach with the two Richards and Janet. In the evening we had dinner on our deck, overlooking the Sound, and at night we could see the full moon over the water with its soft light reflecting in it. In the distance was the lighthouse of Eaton's Neck, always blinking. In winter the weather was less benign. We had several severe storms and in our first winter we even had a north easter that flooded the entire area. We feared for our expensive top soil and newly seeded lawn, but it all survived without any severe damage, probably because the heavy rains drained the salt water away.

Netty was busy in those years. Very busy. School buses did not yet exist in Greenwich so she had to car pool with a number of other women in the neighborhood to bring George and Adriaan to Brunswick and Rich and Janet to the Old Greenwich School. I have no recollection of how she managed to do all this and stay sane. Still she managed to keep the house in perfect order and every day put a tasty meal on the table. It always irks Netty and me when people ask Netty, "Did you work?" Raising four children and running a household was lots of work in our opinion. We think it is more important to spend a lot of time on raising your children rather than having a career and leaving the child care up to hired hands.

We had many visitors from Holland. My parents came and one winter Netty's parents came. We belonged to an organization called the Riverside Dance Group. Every winter they held a number of black tie dances at the Riverside Yacht Club, some preceded by dinners at people's houses and some with dining at RYC. These were fun parties and being among smaller groups spread over several houses gave us an opportunity to get to know a large number of people. We danced to true swing music produced by a band conducted by a Yalie who always wore a red jacket and who had known better times. Still, he was greatly admired by the ladies, and after many urgent pleas he would always grudgingly agree to sing "On the Road to Mandalay." A song with the words from Kipling's poem. They were pleasant evenings with a decorum that is alas now mostly missing from our lives. At one of these dances we showed up with Netty's parents. That was a great success.

Later I offered Tineke a trip to America and a visit with us. She loved staying with us and I was glad to be able to give her a vacation she could use after her difficult divorce and all the troubles she had afterwards. We have saved a movie I made during this visit in which Richard plays the leading role as a magician. He had developed a great interest in performing magic tricks and over the years got quite far advanced with it. This hobby made it necessary for me to travel to the Times Square area with Richard to visit shops that sold magic tricks. These places were often located in less reputable streets, but that did not faze Rich. We would trudge down a street where ladies of the night were plying their trade, and arrive at a dingy, nondescript building, go up in a dark freight elevator, open a big grey steel door and find ourselves suddenly in a brightly lit wonderful place full of people interested in magic and salesmen performing tricks behind their counters. Unfortunately Rich does no longer practice magic.

In the sixties Netty and I became more active in the First Congregational Church of Old Greenwich. We regularly attended services and found some very nice friendships among the Church's members. I was invited to become an usher and on certain Sundays I would be present to help people to their seats. The senior Pastor was Duke Potter who invited me to become a trustee. Potter was a member of the yacht club and owned a Seawind ketch like ours. He went on long cruises every summer and generally took his ministry very easy. I soon discovered that many church members objected to Potter's way of handling the church's affairs and to his lackluster sermons that brought very little inspiration to his flock. Throughout the many years

NETTY WITH JANET IN THE FALL OF 1964.

of the Vietnam war he managed to completely avoid mentioning this conflict in his sermons and acted as if it was of no importance while it was tearing the country apart. I do believe I did some good as a trustee and later as Chairman of the Board of Trustees by reorganizing the Church's investment portfolio that was handled in a very casual way by a stockbroker who was a very friendly man who did his best, but was a "seat of the pants" investor who never produced a decent investment report for the trustees. So we had to remove him and replace him with a true custodian and an investment committee. My church problems escalated when we

had a revolt among the membership organized by some very dedicated choir members who wanted to remove Potter. I then discovered that it was very difficult to fire a pastor. We tried all kinds of avenues mainly through the United Church of Christ organization to which our church belonged. Ultimately Duke got the message and retired. He was replaced by a senior pastor from California who also turned out to be a poor choice. At long last we got Tom Stiers, a wonderful man who stayed for many years, and became a very popular pastor. In the mean time Netty and I drifted away from the church, not for any specific reason, just inertia and a very busy job on my part and lack of conviction on Netty's side. All the hassles I witnessed with church politics certainly reduced my enthusiasm for organized religion, but did not present a really good excuse. We are still members of the church, but rarely show up. I now call myself a deist, and Netty is more an agnostic, something she really always was.

When Janet learned how to walk she started to run. Whenever I think back to our time in Old Greenwich, I see Janet running around the house. I remember standing outside on the lawn talking with our neighbor Don Zuckert when I saw Janet speeding away from the house towards the Zuckerts. For some reason I did not want her to go there, so I called her over and she changed course immediately and came to me. Don Zuckert was stunned. His two little boys, who were usually out of control, would never have come over, he said. Janet turned out to be the only truly athletic Schieferdecker, and the only one who would play varsity sports (field hockey and lacrosse) in the Greenwich Academy and in college.

One day we heard from Netty's young aunt Lous Paschoud (Mammie's younger sister) who lived with her lawyer husband Jean near Lausanne, Switzerland. She had a daughter Carole who had graduated from high school

and wondered if Carole could stay with us for a year or so as an au pair, learning English and helping Netty. We thought that was an excellent idea. After she arrived I took Carole with me to New York City and showed her how to use the train and subways and introduced her to the New School where we entered her as a student for some courses in Basic English, etc. Janet called her "Cavolla" and we enlisted her in a driving school so she could help Netty with the transportation situation which steadily becoming more complex. Over time we realized that Carole had some quite serious mental problems. She could or would not understand that she was supposed to help with our household and our two small children. We later on discovered that she went every week to the New School but did not take any notes and just dreamed her time away in her room in our house and in school. She was immensely proud, however, when she got her drivers license. When I was in Geneva on a business trip I called Jean Paschoud to tell him we were concerned about Carole. He said, "Yes, we have a very strange daughter." I almost asked why they had unloaded her on us without any background information, but I didn't. Several years later Carole got engaged and was tragically killed in an accident when she was driving with her fiancée.

Lous and Jean had a summer house in Italy and Carole arrived equipped with a large number of photos of the interior of the house with Lous posing in almost each shot. We saw them occasionally when we were in Switzerland. They were more interested in socializing with the movie stars and other celebrities who inhabit Switzerland for tax reasons than in keeping up with us. Some of the celebrities were clients of Jean. A very famous one was Charlie Chaplin. In 1987, after Charlie had died, crooks dug up his body and disappeared with it. They called Jean's house to demand a big sum of ransom money in exchange for returning the body. Lous answered the phone and told them nobody was interested in the body and they could keep it. The body was later found abandoned near Lake Geneva and the crooks were caught. Over the years Mammie and Netty tried to keep in touch with Lous and Jean and their two sons Félix and Louis (Féfé and Lolo), but the contact dried up, mainly because the Swiss branch of the family did not seem much interested in their relatives. This bothered Mammie very much in the final years of her life. After Mammie's death we heard from Lous in the eighties that Jean had died after many years as a severe Alzheimer's patient. Lous died several years later, lonely and unhappy. In her prime she was a beautiful woman who yearned for a glamorous life and never seemed to realize that most of her friends were not real friends and that family ties are often more important than fly-by-night acquaintances. Nobody bothered to contact us to inform us of her death.

Life went on. Both George and Adriaan did well at Brunswick and were often placed on the Honor Roll which was published in the Greenwich Time to our not inconsiderable pride. Once during a class graduation ceremony George was complimented by Mr. Everett, the beloved Mr. Chips-like head master, for having successfully completed a math test that had been prepared for a higher grade and was mistakenly given to him. George got his driver's license in 1968 and started driving our Volvo. We had bought this car in Holland, and Netty had picked it up there one summer and drove it around afterwards we shipped it over to the U.S. in the fall. I picked it up on the Brooklyn docks, which was an experience in itself. This car became the boy's transportation and eventually went to college with George.

At Scudder I assisted Decatur Higgins, a more senior portfolio manager with a new account, the pension fund of J Ray McDermott, a New Orleans-based oil service company. Scudder had the good practice of always putting two people on larger, more important accounts. That way there would always be continuity even if one of the two left the firm. This was a lesson I remembered. It was also interesting to be involved with a really big pension fund of a fascinating company. The McDermott people were big no nonsense men, all engineers with slide rules sticking out of their shirt pockets. Their annual report showed how they had built an oil rig for Alaska in their Louisiana plant. The towering rig was put on its side and towed around the Horn to Alaska where it was put upright in its exact place. This was accomplished on the one day of the year that tides and currents allowed it.

Through a major London brokerage firm we also got an account that was intended to be a higher-risk portfolio that aimed for above-average, more speculative returns. I was given this account and enjoyed working on it tremendously. I dealt with David Brooke, a scion of a prominent English noble family. It was fun to become a gun slinger and take often speculative positions. Unfortunately the research department at Scudder did not produce the ideas I needed and the market kept slumping. My performance was better than the market, but not good enough in the eyes of the client and after a few years of hard effort, we lost the account. The Scudder research department went through a difficult period, which cost portfolio managers much grief with their clients. In 1968 and 1969 the market was basically unchanged, and in 1970 we started a decline reflecting an economic downturn. But the analyst's pot was stirring and one of our best men, a drug analyst, left to start an investment advisory firm of his own with a few friends. Other analysts tried to come up with ideas that were not based on sound research but just mirror imaged the flavor of the day in Wall Street. One of these ideas was "conglomerates." Firms sprouted up often led by investment banking or deal-making types who bought a number of unrelated businesses and then put them together in a conglomerate. The operative word was "synergy." If you bought a company that installed sprinkler systems in buildings, called Automatic Sprinkler, you could buy a company that made

fire trucks or one that made paint or anything else that with a great deal of imagination could be thought to have a business objective that was compatible to all the
other companies in the grab bag. The result was a conglomerate that as the sum of
the parts was often given a higher price-earnings ratio than the pieces it was made up
of individually. A premier and successful conglomerate was Litton Industries. When
our investment in Automatic Sprinkler and several others was mauled in the market,
we lost faith in the analyst who saddled us with the need to talk to clients and explain
why we went so wrong. I was stunned to learn a few months later that this very same
analyst was made a partner in the firm. This shattered my confidence in the firm and
made me susceptible to propositions I received from others.

When I was investigating brokerage firms I asked several friends for input, and
through Will Cates got in touch with Francis Williams, a friendly older man who
lived in Riverside and was a former commodore of the yacht club. Fran, as we called
him, was a partner at F. Eberstadt & Co., a small specialized investment banking
firm in Wall Street run by Ferdinand Eberstadt, a formidable personality in the business. Fran had survived and prospered under the crushingly domineering regime
of Eber, as he called him, by always agreeing with him. As a hobby Mr. Eberstadt
had established a mutual fund that was managed by his firm, called the Chemical
Fund. This somewhat peculiar name for a fund stemmed from recognition of the
chemical industry and its then fledgling younger sister the drug manufacturers as the
premier technological growth industries in the 1940s. It indicated that the fund had
an investment objective that was strongly oriented towards technological growth. In
later years when electronics and data-processing technologies became the dominant
growth industries, we often had trouble explaining the origin of the fund's name and
positioning it as a technology growth fund.

Mr. Eberstadt had introduced his son-in-law Peter Cannell, into the firm. Peter
was a smart and capable investment man who made desperate efforts to broaden the
firm's base by getting into the institutional brokerage business and establishing an
Investments Advisory Department. The investment record of the Chemical Fund
was very good and the idea was to build a portfolio management business on this
record. I was introduced by Fran to Peter Cannell and spoke with him, not in an
effort to join his firm, but to find out what he knew about some firms I had talked
to. One evening I was at home in Old Greenwich when I received a call from Fran
saying Peter Cannell had left the firm with Bill Breed, the man who was running the
Investment Advisory Department, to establish a money management firm of their
own. Would I be interested to speak with Mr. Eberstadt to see if I wanted to take

over the department? I was, of course. I had several lengthy conversations with Mr. Eberstadt in his office on Broadway, near Wall Street. The job seemed very attractive and appeared to have the full support of all the senior people in the firm. There was, however, not too much business on the books. I was assured that I could, if successful, count on a partnership. This all sounded very attractive and led to another wrenching decision. I decided to take the plunge and started to speak with the Scudder people to announce my departure so that we could make a smooth transition. This was not an easy step. The Eberstadt firm was dominated by its founder and the reason Peter Cannell left was quite obviously his inability to establish a solid platform for himself in an area away from the total control of his father-in-law. Ironically the world would have changed for him if he had only waited a few months longer. A little later I got another call from Fran Williams saying that Mr. Eberstadt had died suddenly and that the firm would carry on as before and that the offer made to me was still valid and unchanged.

Obviously this unexpected change introduced a new risk factor into the equation for me and later on I would discover that the death of its founder had a significant impact on the firm. The firm did not have much capital left after the estate was settled and there was an obvious power vacuum. But all this became only clear to me after I took the plunge, deciding that Scudder did not offer the same long term opportunity I would have at Eberstadt, where I could run more or less my own show. More or less because as my department became more successful many people tried to get a foothold in it and several severe turf battles would develop as we entered the seventies. The break with Scudder was difficult but went smooth. I was particularly touched by a visit of the senior partner George Johnston, who came to my office to ask if there was anything specific that had made me decide to leave. We talked about the poor research results and the strange decisions to make failing analysts partners. George discussed all this frankly with me, and I experienced once again that the only opportunity you have to speak openly and frankly about a business is when you are leaving it. George became a friend and I would later on meet him and his wife at several investment gatherings. Unfortunately he died suddenly in the eighties. The move to Eberstadt was perhaps the greatest jump into the unknown I would make in my life. It would work out well, but that was, of course, not known when I went back to work in downtown New York.

23 : *The Seventies*

The seventies were a period of political turmoil and of very difficult economic and stock market conditions. Against this background it was remarkable that my business continued to grow in leaps and bounds and that our family prospered.

The history of the period called "the seventies" did not start precisely on January 1, 1970. It started two years earlier, in 1968, the year Martin Luther King and Bobby Kennedy were killed and the Vietnam War went from bad to worse. President Johnson lost most of his political clout and announced he would not run again. In the previous four years he had escalated the war in Vietnam to such a level that public opinion turned massively against him. His Great Society programs did not bring him the political support he needed even while they brought us Medicare and increased other social entitlements to a thus-far unseen level hugely benefiting less-advantaged Americans. Johnson's resignation from the political scene he had dominated for many years left a vacuum and presented the Republicans with a unique opportunity to regain the White House. The Vietnam War had become an extremely polarizing issue in America. It was sometimes called "the Dinner War" because the daily TV news broadcasts aired around dinnertime and fed American households with a never-ending stream of pictures showing gruesome scenes of intense combat with soldiers getting hurt and villages being devastated. Young people demonstrated and college campuses became centers of antigovernment activity. Johnson's administration assumed a bunker mentality, but his secretary of defense Robert McNamara kept telling the nation that we were gaining ground on the enemy. He ran the war and the Defense Department with a Harvard Business School approach, making presentations with charts showing a growing "body count" of Vietcong dead and statistical progress in the fight that was bound to bring victory if we would just hang on for a little longer and brought just a few more troops to the front. "Winning the minds and hearts of the local population" became an often used term to indicate the thrust of the American strategy in Vietnam. The huge Vietcong and Vietnamese military and civilian casualties did of course not help in achieving that goal. The local population generally sided with the North Vietnamese.

The 1968 Democratic Convention in Chicago could not unify the badly split party and turned into a disaster. Large numbers of young people came to Chicago to protest the war and some of them even managed to get inside the convention hall creating further disruptions. Richard Daley, the mayor of Chicago, a prototype of the old line Democratic machine politician, ordered the Chicago police to beat up the demonstrators and clear out the parks where they had gathered and pitched their tents. The melee that followed was widely broadcast on TV and was called by some a police riot. Even TV reporters inside the convention hall were roughed up by security guards. It did not help the cause of the already weak democratic candidate Hubert Humphrey, known as the "happy warrior." He had served as vice president under Johnson, a role in which he had supported the war and was completely marginalized by his boss.

Richard Nixon, who had lost in 1960 to Kennedy by a very small percentage, prevailed this time and got elected, also by a narrow majority, 43.4% of the popular vote versus 42.7% for Humphrey. Nixon ran on the promise that he would put an end to the war, but soon after his election he faced reality and understood you could not just walk away from it. He broke his promise of immediate retreat and tried to achieve a military advantage, if not a victory, by training more South Vietnamese and bringing them into the fight. This approach was bound to fail because the South Vietnamese regime was corrupt and unpopular and the troops we trained had a very low morale. He escalated the bombing of North Vietnam that was started in 1966 by Johnson when the first huge six engine B-52's rained bombs on the flimsy houses of this tiny country. North Vietnam was fairly defenseless against these air attacks, but not entirely. The Soviet Union supplied it with more and more sophisticated antiaircraft missiles and American aircraft losses began to rise. The antiwar movement now began to agitate against Nixon and over time it succeeded in identifying him with the war more so than Johnson who had started the whole thing. Things got really bad when Nixon invaded Cambodia without asking permission from Congress, claiming this country provided a safe haven for the Vietcong. On May 4, 1970, a few days after Nixon announced the invasion of Cambodia, students at Kent State University in Kent Ohio organized a protest against the Cambodia incursion and for some reason the Ohio National Guard was called out to quell what they thought was a riot. They opened fire on a group of unarmed students, killing four and seriously wounding one. This outrage was extensively investigated and ultimately explained as an unnecessary and clumsy reaction by a group of poorly trained and badly commanded guardsmen. Nixon made the situation worse by using derogatory terms in describing the victims and praising the guardsmen. A group of young high school and college students decided to organize a protest against the Kent State massacre in the Wall Street area with a protest march that passed close to my office on Broadway where they were met by a group of big, beefy construction workers, wearing hard hats, who came from the World Trade Center construction site, yelling "U.S.A. all the way" and started beating up the students. Wall Street men and lawyers tried to stop them but couldn't. The construction workers were organized by their union leaders and felt they should support the troops in Vietnam. The army in "Nam," as it was called consisted mostly of conscripts out of working-class families while the protesting college kids got deferments because they had the money to study. The Vietnam war had become a class war.

In recent years TV reporting, which has traditionally always hewed more to the liberal point of view, continues to show the Vietnam War as a Republican-sponsored conflict rather than a Democratic one. Nixon's stiff and awkward persona did not help him either, and soon he became a favorite target of cartoonists, comedians and newspaper writers. This may have led to Nixon's paranoia about the press and the "enemies" he believed were trying to do him in. Still he was reelected in 1972 by a landslide, gaining 60.7% of the popular vote against his weak opponent, Eugene Mc Govern, who got only 37.5%. This victory was more due to McGovern's lack of appeal and perceived ultra left-wing leanings than Nixon's popularity. Nixon's paranoia increased despite his overwhelming and historically very significant election victory. Immediately after his victory, Nixon ordered his staff to draw up a list of his enemies and planned to go after them. But his opponents soon got the upper hand when the Watergate scandal broke. It appeared that during the campaign the Washington police had arrested a group of burglars who had gained entry into the Democratic election headquarters in the Watergate office complex in town. Then it was established that the burglars were no ordinary criminals but operatives working undercover for the Nixon campaign. The Nixon administration made the huge mistake of not immediately disavowing the burglars but began to call it a "second rate burglary" and got enmeshed in all kinds of lies and illegal acts in trying to cover the whole thing up. Congress called hearings that became a fascinating daily TV show. In these hearings a great deal more than just the break-in floated to the surface. We were shown political espionage and sabotage, improper tax audits to "get" opponents, illegal wire tapping and a secret slush fund that was used to silence the seven men who participated in the burglary. Later on it was also revealed that Nixon had a tape recording system in his office that had hundreds of hours of recordings proving that the president of the United States had engaged in obstruction of justice and several other criminal acts. These events led in 1974 to his resignation. He was the first president to do so. If he had not resigned, he would certainly have been impeached. His vice president, Gerald Ford, became president. Somewhat later Ford, an honest, down-to-earth politician, caused a major controversy by pardoning Nixon. This move probably cost him his reelection, but years later most responsible commentators and historians, Democrats as well as Republicans, agreed that he had acted wisely by terminating a long drawn out procedure and worldwide scandal that would damage the already badly tarnished image of the country even more.

In 1971, long before he had to step down in disgrace, Nixon made a historic move by making an overture to Communist China and going there in person, accompanied by Henry Kissinger, his national security advisor. Kissinger became a renowned star diplomat with excellent political skills who negotiated the peace accord with Vietnam and managed to survive the Nixon disaster almost completely unscathed. The opening to China signaled the beginning of the decline of the dictatorship created by Mao. Nixon had obviously some positive attributes and was very engaged in foreign policy. If he had only been able to repress his conspiratorial tendencies that made him totally ineffective, he would have been a pretty good president. The new China policy was a master stroke that sent shock waves through the world. It isolated Soviet Russia and marked a major turning point towards a better, more open world.

For us in Riverside and for most other Americans, the opening to China was of no great importance. We had no idea that in the near future China would become an enormous economic world power. Everything the Nixon administration did was completely overshadowed by the scandalous Watergate hearings. Over the early seventies, I became more and more critical of the Nixon administration. In my letters home – I still typed a weekly letter to my parents – I began to spout more and more anti–Nixon sentiments, which prompted Ma to ask me if I would please not be so critical of what was in her eyes a good president who kept the Russians in place and pursued sound conservative policies. Ma's comment reflected a general attitude then prevailing among many people in Europe with more conservative leanings. They did not think the shenanigans revealed in the Watergate hearings were all that serious and should be categorized under the title "boys will be boys," or perhaps better, "politicians will be politicians." They put much more stock in Nixon and Kissinger's firm handling of foreign policy.

Naturally Nixon's problems affected the markets and therefore my job at Eberstadt. The market does not like uncertainty and in the months preceding Nixon's resignation we had plenty of uncertainty. Moreover, the international scene was far from stable. In 1976 Israel launched the "six-day war." This war, in which Israel reacted with a preemptive attack to Egypt's expelling of UN peacekeepers from the Sinai and deploying a large force there, resulted in a tremendous victory for Israel. It attacked Egypt, Syria and Jordan at the same time and gained control of the Sinai Peninsula, the Golan Heights, East Jerusalem, the West Bank and the Gaza strip. Today the aftermath of this offensive is still with us and a source of unending problems between Israel and its neighbors that trigger continuing U.S. diplomatic peace efforts that always seem to fail. Every president since Ford has tried to get the Palestinians and Israelis to come to an agreement about sharing the land of what once was Palestine. My sense is that people in the Middle East have conflict in their genes. They have lived for centuries surrounded by enemies and are perfectly capable of continuing to live and thrive in that mode. They pay lip service to Americans and UN people but have no illusions about a future of peace and prosperity in the region. Their loyalties are family first, then their tribe or village and nationhood comes last, if at all.

Picking up the pieces of the departed asset management people at Eberstadt was no picnic. Joan Giannotti had not come over yet, and I had a secretary who had worked for the old group and whose loyalties were obviously with them. She would call them frequently and rejoice at their efforts to set up a new business. She did join them after a short stay with me. I had Russ Ferro, a clever young man, working with me who had done administrative work for my predecessors and could give me background information on the small number of clients they had. I called the clients and tried to establish some rapport with them, but that was not easy. We had a few small institutional accounts that were of course of prime interest to me, but there was no established, well-formulated written investment policy or stock selection list. All these very basic things had to be set up and communicated to the clients. I had to establish an Eberstadt investment philosophy that I believed in and could be used on the longer term and could share with the outside world.

Major factors in my new environment were the mutual funds Eberstadt was running. The Chemical Fund was well established and had a solid reputation. It was a so called "load" fund, which means that the broker/salesman who sells the fund receives a commission out of the amount invested so that the customer starts out with an investment that has a market value of slightly less than the amount he contributed. The fund employed a number of wholesalers who visited brokerage firms across the country to recommend the funds. The battle between load and no-load funds continues to this day. Knowledgeable people will buy "no load" funds managed by reputable large investors. Less knowledgeable customers will still buy the funds through stock brokers who act as professional intermediaries and introduce them to the funds they think are best for the client and thereby earn a commission. In 1970 the mutual fund world was still rather small compared with the plethora of funds the public is offered today. I am not absolutely sure, but I believe there were in the seventies not more than two or three hundred funds listed in the daily price list the Wall Street Journal used to publish. Now there are about 8,000 funds and the variety and choice of investment opportunities through participation in a professionally managed portfolio is virtually endless.

As I mentioned, Mr. Eberstadt had started the Chemical Fund in 1938 as a hobby and later added the smaller Eberstadt Fund that was managed by Jerry Jenks, a well-known analyst and professional investor with whom I would become quite friendly. The Chemical Fund was managed by a team of people including Francis Williams and John Vandeventer. John was a very nice man who lived in Greenwich. He was a knowledgeable investor and became a friend. After the death of Mr. Eberstadt, Bob Porter became president of the fund management company that acted as the manager and distributor of the funds.

The firm was incorporated after the death of its very dominant founder, aand the presidency went to Bob Zeller, a lawyer who had been a partner in the well known Cahill Gordon firm and had worked with Mr. Eberstadt on deals. Mr. Eberstadt had designated him as his successor. Over the years this would create a problem because Zeller was the head of the investment banking department that had under Mr. Eberstadt been the firm's prime moneymaker. In the glory days, many important deals were done by the small but well-respected firm. In the years I was there the investment banking side of the firm became an almost useless appendage as it seemed unable to get any meaningful business and was living on a reputation gained in bygone years. Like Charles Dickens' Mr. McCawber, it always seemed to expect that some really good business would be turning up just around the corner but whenever we peered around that corner we saw nothing. Nevertheless Bob Zeller remained in charge and Bob Porter had to play second fiddle, constantly trying to explain how important the funds were for the firm. The funds had impressive boards of directors who were given, in my opinion, far too much power in portfolio decisions and approval of investment ideas. New York State law requires each fund to have a separate board. In Massachusetts funds are treated as investment trusts and one single board of trustees can oversee a large number of funds. At Scudder the funds were domiciled in Massachusetts, and the board of trustees of the funds was treated well but was not involved in the details of portfolio management. Just before Mr. Eberstadt's death, the firm had started an institutional brokerage division. That group was led by Pike Sullivan, a blunt but very effective institutional broker, and Ed Giles, an extremely smart and friendly man who had been an analyst with the Chemical Fund and who would over time build a large, well-regarded institutional research department with a charming eclectic style. In the seventies this department became the most important moneymaker for the firm, far outdistancing the investment-banking side. I had to navigate between all these forces. In the beginning, my department was a loss leader for the firm, but that changed rather quickly. We broke even in about two years and after that became hugely profitable.

Larger pension funds had noticed the excellent, long-term performance of the Chemical Fund portfolio and wondered why they could not benefit from that, rather than suffer the often mediocre-to-poor performance of the bank trust departments that traditionally ran their portfolios. It was important for these pension funds to achieve good performance numbers because these results affected the annual contributions they had to make and in the long run the actuarial assumptions that governed their future contributions. The bank trust officers who ran the pension portfolios of their corporate clients were risk averse and used to dealing with all the legal ramifications of the trust business. They paid less attention to investment performance, often deliberately avoiding newer and more exciting areas, such as pharmaceuticals and technology stocks, as too risky. Their focus had historically been on earning a trustee fee and their investments were geared to earning dividend and interest income, not on investment performance. What I had learned at Scudder was that pension funds were interested in the total return concept, i.e. build up capital gains in a portfolio to make it grow and thus reduce actuarially required contributions and cover expenses out of income and capital gains. The simple idea behind this concept was that companies that used their earnings to grow and not to pay dividends were the ones that would give investors the best long-term returns. The record of the Chemical Fund showed many years of consistent growth in asset value. Consequently I had to build my business on its performance because no pension fund would hire a manager who had not been in business for a long time and achieved a creditable record.

My big break came when we received an unexpected visit from the manager of the pension fund of Allied Stores. His company ran a number of well known department stores all over the country and had a sizeable pension fund. We organized a meeting where he was seated in our board room with all the people we could muster. Porter and Williams gave presentations about the Chemical Fund, and it was left to me to make the real presentation he was looking for and ask the pertinent questions, such as how his pension fund was structured, what his investment objectives were, what he expected from his managers, how much investment discretion his managers had, etc. Ed Giles said later that I was the only one who seemed to know what he was talking about. This was, of course, not unusual, because I was the only one in the group who had ever dealt with a pension fund. However, it also gave a hint of the problems I would face in the future dealing with the Chemical Fund people who thought they were masterful investors and did not realize they really were just lucky people who had followed an investment approach based on buying high-quality growth stocks that had become highly popular. The market in those days loved the so called "nifty fifty," and Chemical Fund benefited from that, owning a portfolio that was almost totally focused on that group. It ended up with large holdings of IBM and Xerox, hardly hard to find stocks that outperformed the more stodgy cyclical stocks. The funds benefited over the years from the nifty fifty bonanza and could pay dividends to its shareholders at a steady level simply by selling a few shares of IBM or Xerox. My problem came when the trend favoring high quality growth stocks ended and we had to find other investments. This made my portfolios diverge from the Chemical Fund and ultimately out-perform it. As the investment advisory business grew, we were forced to drop the Chemical Fund formula and relied more and more on our own stock selection and portfolio performance, which luckily was good.

In 1970 George graduated from Brunswick School. Before going to college he spent a good part of the summer working on a cattle ranch in Nebraska. He went there with his Brunswick friend Burton Dickie. Our old friend Thys (Matthew) de Clercq worked in those years for a family investment company that owned large tracks of ranch land in the western U.S. Thys got George and Burton jobs there to help with the branding of young calves and other chores. When we called to ask if he had a good time out West, he said he was too bushed every evening to do much more than sleep. After he was finished branding calves, he was put on a tractor-mower to cut hay. The plot of grass land he had to mow was so large that it took him a whole day to complete one circumference.

George had applied to many colleges and we expected he would receive many acceptances. He had, after all, been on the honor roll throughout his years at Brunswick, had been editor of the school paper, had scored high in his SATs and done many other things. I took him to see many colleges and we thought he made a good impression. We let him write his own application. That was a mistake. He did not type his applications and we were unaware of the existence of the coaches people nowadays engage to lead their children from their freshman year at high school to a good college. We were naïve and George was probably way too modest in describing his own achievements or his parent's background. We never learned. We made the same mistake with our other children, never paying too much attention to their written applications. Saying you live in Greenwich and your father worked in Wall Street were two big negatives in the eyes of the mostly liberal-leaning admissions people. Not mentioning that your parents were immigrants and that your father had clawed his own way up to a decent living while working in the capitalist cesspool called Wall Street, was a mistake they all made. When the day came for George to receive responses from the colleges, he dejectedly looked at a stack of rejections and only a few positive replies, including the ones he had chosen as his "safeties." But luckily there was one standout. When we had visited Middlebury, George had a very good interview, and we were hopeful that school would invite him to come. They did and in the fall of 1970 George went happily to what turned out to be an excellent school for him. Netty drove him over to begin the next important step in his life. She met his new roommate, a nice young man from Texas, who said he would probably become a writer and live in poverty. The roommate also was surprised to learn that Netty was George's mother and not his older sister. Netty always looked very young and pretty and still does, and at that time she compared very favorably with the other ladies that were dropping of their kids.

In the fall we returned to Middlebury for "parents weekend." In line for the buffet lunch, we found ourselves standing in front of Mr. and Mrs. David Rockefeller. We spoke briefly with them and I reminded him of my visit to his office many years ago with an introduction from Oom Eelco. This found an immediate response and we were just becoming good friends when a man from the Middlebury Endowment Office swooped down on us and told Mr. Rockefeller that he did not have to stand in line because he was seated on the dais. The lesson was that money talks in the college world. I did find out that the Rockefellers had a daughter who was a freshman in George's class and told him we did not mind him loafing around a little as long as he would pay a great deal of attention to a wonderful girl whose name we just had learned. This wise counsel fell on deaf ears, naturally. What we quickly learned from George's going to Middlebury was that the departure of a child to college means the end of his or her childhood and life under parental control. They leave the nest and rapidly become individuals who make their own decisions. They are still very much part of the family, of course, but their role in it changes drastically. This is all to the good and a natural development in life as it should be, but for us as parents it also was an experience that was a little melancholy.

For the summer of 1971 I planned a cruise in the Postiljon to Nova Scotia. I still had ambitions to go further offshore with this wonderful little ketch and thought a trip across the Gulf of Maine would be a good start. I had already sailed to Nova Scotia with our friend Roy Megargel, who owned a large heavy wishbone rigged ketch called Stormsvalla. He wanted to cruise Nova Scotia with his family and to get there he had recruited a group of men to go nonstop to Halifax. It was a nice, uneventful cruise until we got to our destination. In a fresh breeze we came storming into Halifax harbor under full sail and saw the famous Nova Scotia schooner Blue Nose coming out, loaded with tourists. We turned left into a cove that was supposed to be the harbor of the Halifax Yacht Club but discovered that the place was empty except for a few dredging barges that had strung heavy steel cables across the harbor, directly in our path. We quickly came about and lowered our sails to stop the boat just in time. In this somewhat panicky maneuver our chart blew overboard so we were now "blind." A wonderful man came rowing out in a small dinghy to tell us the club had moved to a nearby river, and when we told him we had just lost our chart, he said "wait a minute," rowed back to the old club house, ripped a chart off the wall of the bar and brought it back to us. This was our first introduction to the nice people who live in that beautiful Canadian province.

My crew for my second cruise to Nova Scotia consisted of John Hafkemeyer, a dear Dutch friend who was Dutch consular general in New York City. John's assignment was to find American businesses interested in establishing themselves in the Netherlands. This was a tough nut to crack for him because Holland had already become quite prosperous, and the elaborate social safety net the Dutch were stringing up was costly for employers. So the advantage of lower-labor cost and a business environment that was friendlier than the one prevailing in the United States did not really exist there anymore. John was a bachelor and a cheerful soul who knew next to nothing about sailing but was very good company. George came along as my first mate, and he had his friend Burton Dickie for company. To save time George and Burton had brought the boat to Stonington, and John and I joined them there. We took off the next day and passed through the Cape Cod Canal by night. After we were at the level of Provincetown we ran into thick fog that enveloped us for the rest of the trip. The problem now was to find Nova Scotia. Easy enough if you could hold just a steady course. However, the Bay of Fundy is known for its strong tide currents that can set a small boat miles off course in a few hours. We had no GPS or Loran – neither of these navigational helpers had yet been introduced to recreational sailors. All we had was a Radio Direction Finder that we used to try to find the signal of a large buoy that marked the southern tip of Nova Scotia. That was to be the one and only point of reference for us. We never found the buoy and could not detect its radio signal either. We then used a method I had read about, which was to run along a course and take depth soundings at predetermined time intervals, mark them on a strip of paper to match the scale of the chart and see where they fit. As we approached the Nova Scotia shore, our depth sounder indicated we were gradually getting closer to land and that told us where we were, approximately. We knew there were fast-moving ferries going from Maine to Yarmouth, and when night fell again and we saw a very bright light and suddenly heard a very loud foghorn, our attention was quickly focused. George rushed to the bow with our little beeper horn to respond to what we thought was a very large ship. As we came closer, we saw it was a lighthouse and that confirmed we were close to land. We found a cove in which we dropped anchor and went to our bunks exhausted.

Early the next morning we were awakened by shouts from a fishing boat who asked if we wanted some fresh mackerel. We declined, but these fellows could tell us where we were – close to a small village called Pubnico, a French-speaking enclave in a mostly Anglophone province. We went there and tied up in the harbor, the only yacht among a large number of lobster boats. We were very well received by the locals and became friends with the local fishermen, who flocked aboard when they discovered we had plenty of beer. They helped us get ice from the fish factory and got a fuel truck to come and fill our tank with diesel.

We rented a car and drove around for a day and then started the 24 hour crossing over to Maine. In Southwest Harbor, Maine I called the office and heard from Joan that George's birthday date had drawn a very high number in the draft lottery which meant he would not be called up to serve in Vietnam. We celebrated that evening in a restaurant and made so much noise that other guests left in disgust.

After a few days in Maine we headed back, leaving Boothbay Harbor with our spinnaker up and a nice breeze behind us. We sailed all day on this tack, making good time. When we reached Newport, we left the boat there and went home. The trip took less than two weeks. A wonderful cruise I remember fondly. Adriaan stayed home because he wanted to be with his friends, which is, as I discovered always a very important element in any teenager's life. I believe he was sorry he did not go along, but he never told me. Netty was in Holland with the two little ones.

At Eberstadt I began to find out that Bob Porter was a restless man who liked to engineer drastic changes. He had little patience with the status quo and liked to throw his weight around where he could, playing the role of a big decision maker and captain of industry while he was in reality only just running one well-known, medium-sized mutual fund complex. Bob decided the firm had to move next door, probably because the lease at 59 Broadway had run out and 61 Broadway offered more space for less money. So he engineered a move that put the investment banking department on the top floor and the brokerage department on the floor below it, together with the funds and my small operation. Amazingly, a nice corner office was prepared on the top floor for "Mr. Eberstadt" despite the fact that he had died almost a year ago. This was done to mollify the estate, a group we would continue to wrestle with for years to come. The estate had to see physical evidence of their continuing ownership of the firm, and Ferdinand Eberstadt's furniture was put in place in that room to prove that. Another offshoot of the problems with the family was the need to find a job for Andrew Eberstadt, a cousin of Ferdinand who had worked as a broker but became a problem there because of his inability to focus on doing business and tendency to waste other people's time with long winded conversations. So why not make him head of Investment Advisory? The arrival of Andy was the beginning of a trend of sending me people who either did not fit in anymore at the brokerage or mutual fund departments or wanted to leave and were offered an opportunity to work with me as a counter to stepping out the door. Several of these transplants worked out very well but not all. Andy was a prime example of a complete misconnection. He was given a nice corner office next to mine and started making phone calls from behind a desk piled high with miscellaneous unread pieces of paper. Several months later he was still making phone calls without any visible result. Andy proved to be neither a help nor a hindrance to me, but I could have used a more powerful person who could market our advisory services effectively. I believe Andy was a case of attention deficit disorder that was never properly treated. He was a nice fellow and we could get along very well, but he produced nothing for my business and his outsized compensation was a drag on my P&L statement. After a while he left of his own accord "to spend more time with his family," as the trite phrase goes.

698

In the interim we had acquired another pension fund account, this was Canadian Industries, a Montréal-based subsidiary of the British ICI company. The pension fund manager of that company had independently come to the same conclusion as the Allied Stores manager and searched us out to run a piece of his pension fund. Now with two pension accounts with about twelve million dollars in assets, the Investment Advisory business became a much more important part of the firm and the struggle for control began. Bob Porter was a lawyer by background and was inclined to spend much time on the legal ramifications of running a mutual fund. He was a pompous man who was kind to me but held me back for many years, trying to keep control of my blossoming business that kept growing and became eventually much larger and much more profitable than his fund business. The board of the Chemical Fund consisted of a number of distinguished scientists, medical people and Roger F. Murray II, a professor of the Columbia Business School who was one of the well-known investment thinkers in the fifties and sixties. This heavyweight board would review all investment recommendations made by analysts and sit in judgment on all transactions made by the fund. In the early days, this was a great plus, but later it became a burden as portfolio manager after portfolio manager felt thwarted and second-guessed by a group of elderly men, which made quick action and flexible investing impossible. Porter catered heavily to this board and over time began to fancy himself a great investment genius, but he was enough of a politician to avoid being responsible for specific investment decisions. That was left to John Vandeventer.

I needed the Chemical Fund as a proof of Eberstadt's long-term investment performance and therefore had to pitch my tent on the fund side. In reality I felt the analysts of the fund were not doing very innovative work and leaned much more towards the firm's institutional brokerage side, where a growing number of first-class analysts were making a name for themselves and for the firm by developing good investment ideas. Ed Giles had an interesting leadership style. He sought out people with industry, engineering or scientific backgrounds and cared less whether they had MBAs in finance or a background in investment research. It was an eclectic group. Pike Sullivan handled sales. He was a successful salesman whose main claim to fame was a very strong relationship with the man who ran the investment portfolio of the Allstate Insurance Company and funneled a significant amount of business to Eberstadt. The salesmen he hired were several notches above the typical backslapping, three-martini-luncheon stockbroker types. They were intelligent people who could present complicated investment propositions well. Ed and Pike built a great institutional brokerage firm that put the Eberstadt name on the map again after it had almost eclipsed after the death of its founder. In his final years, Ferdinand Eberstadt had looked with great suspicion at the brokerage side and once had even told his people to stop trading on the exchange because he feared bankruptcies among brokerage firms when a paperwork bottleneck had put several firms in jeopardy. The old-fashioned, back-office, green-eyeshade procedures were overwhelmed by the volume of trades when the market took off in the sixties, forcing firms and the New York Stock Exchange to come into the twentieth century and adapt quickly to using more computers. Luckily our people remained able to trade. A few years later Eberstadt was a major institutional brokerage firm with lots of business and an income stream that put investment banking and mutual fund management in the shade.

Pike Sullivan felt I needed better marketing of our investment advisory business and I agreed. Rather than let me find a candidate, Pike said he had just the man for me, which turned out to be a friend of his called David Adams who had an advertising/marketing, but no investment background. Adams joined me and soon proved to be a problem, basically because he seemed to be constantly agitating to shift the leadership of portfolio management to Pike's group, away from me. He had no clue about the way in which the institutional asset management business worked and would barely listen to my efforts to guide him. He started out by ordering a very expensive brochure. That was a good idea, but as it turned out we hardly used it. Most firms in my business had developed brochures that promoted their skills and investment record. He hired a professional writer and a photographer and would not cooperate with me on the text or the layout, arguing that only professional writers knew what to say and how to say it. The result was a booklet with big photographs of Pike and Ed, Dave and me and none of the Chemical Fund people. When Bob Porter saw the proofs he got upset and insisted that a picture of him with Fran Williams should be included too. Adams also started to invent titles for him and me, trying to get around the fact that we were both just floating around in the very loose firm structure. He made me portfolio director, a rather absurd job description. He knew on which side his bread was buttered and spent a great deal of time in the brokerage department. We solicited and won several accounts that came to us through Johnson and Higgins, an insurance brokerage firm that had started a pension fund consulting business. They would invite several managers to make presentations before the pension fund board and would then help the board make a decision. This was the beginning of a new business of consulting that grew out to enormous proportions and often became a real problem for us. I can only remember one account Adams got independently, that was Campbell Soup. For the rest he wasted an awful lot of my time and ran up considerable travel expenses. After a while I noticed that in his presentations before what we called the "gate keepers" of pension funds Adams confused his listeners by talking up the skills of the institutional brokerage side much more than the fund side. This was realistic if you took short-term results as a measurement, but most pension people wanted to see a record of consistent long-term performance and an unchanging investment approach or "style." The Chemical Fund had those qualities, although its performance in recent years had not been more than average as it reflected the lackluster market of the early seventies. After about a year Adams went too far when he started marketing the "High Risk Fund." This fund was a portfolio in which the firm's shareholders could invest for their own account. It was run strictly in-house by Pike Sullivan and Ed Giles and had excellent results. But its risk profile was much greater than most pension funds could accept. For me it was intolerable that my marketing side would peddle something that had an image that was radically different from the one I had carefully built up in the pension fund world. I had to go to Porter and tell him this was an unacceptable situation. Luckily he backed me up, and Dave Adams was let go the same day.

My business continued to grow and I needed staff. Looking for a person with portfolio management skills was not easy because the culture at Eberstadt, particularly the fund side, was frugal if not downright cheap. The market for investment managers was beginning to boom and people were asking more compensation than Porter was willing to pay. Underneath this frugality was the fear that my department would become a place where people were paid more than at the funds. So I considered it a particularly lucky development that we were able to hire Richard Johnston in 1972. He had been managing money at the Franklin National Bank, an institution that was in financial trouble and had to let go of a large number of portfolio managers, causing a temporary glut in the market. He turned out to be a wonderful addition that helped me manage a growing and increasingly complicated business. In his early years at Eberstadt, Richard earned his MBA from New York University, studying hard in the evenings and weekends to achieve this goal, a very admirable tour de force. He never left and stayed with me until the end and became a good friend who now manages Netty's and my portfolios at his own sizeable asset management firm.

As accounts kept coming in, Gerry Goodwin, a smart young analyst at the fund side joined my department. Gerry had expressed his desire to broaden the scope of his work to Bob Porter and was sent over to me to become a portfolio manager. He was a good addition. Now I had two portfolio managers and could give each a number of portfolios to take care of. I had learned at Scudder that client "hand holding" is very important in the money management business. Portfolio managers should not have too many accounts and clients should feel that their account receives constant attention. I also learned that one should never leave the impression that the account is the sole bailiwick of one person. It is the firm's account and the firm's investment policies should govern the securities selected for its portfolio. Finally I always made sure I would participate in client meetings. There were two reasons for that policy. First it is better to go with more than one person, particularly if you are going to meet with a committee of several people. It is human nature to attack somebody who is alone much more forcefully than two people. We were, in the seventies, working in often very difficult market conditions and many pension fund committees were unhappy with the investment results of their account. Most clients were reasonable about it and understood that we could not "walk on water" as the saying goes, but the difficult markets required client companies to contribute more to pension funds than they liked. In rare instances we would have very tough meetings. The second reason for me to show up with the portfolio manager was the possibility of the manager leaving the firm. A situation you always had to reckon with in the highly fluid Wall Street environment. This could create a vacuum and I wanted to avoid that and show the firm had continuity. Also, I wanted to avoid the manager getting too close to the client and leaving for another firm with the account.

In 1973 we decided to have a family reunion in Switzerland. It basically grew out of a plan Netty and I had to go to Switzerland and rent a chalet for a month. We chose Les Diablerets as a good place to go to, close to Geneva and its airport and in the French-speaking section of the country, which would be useful for the language skills of our children, we thought. With some help from Lous Paschoud we found a nice house that would become a base of operations for us. George had found a girl-friend in Middlebury – Maggie Murray, and did not want to come along, but when we invited them both he jumped at the opportunity. Adriaan was traveling with his Brunswick friend Peter McGee. Adriaan was now a freshman at Lafayette College in Easton, Pennsylvania and Peter was at Lehigh University in nearby Bethlehem. We went over with Rich and Janet, then still youngsters. Near the chalet was a nice hotel where the grandparents Schieferdecker and van Kleffens took rooms. The result was a wonderful get-together with my father's old Swiss friend Tell Bersot and his wife also in attendance for a day or two. The Bersots lived near Lausanne so for them it was almost next door. We made numerous hikes up the mountains, and although the weather was not always all that good, we had a very good time. Our kids came drifting in and out at sometimes strange hours. George and Maggie, for instance, arrived near midnight. We were all sound asleep when they knocked at our door. They had taken the last train from Montreux and found a man on the train who walked them over to our chalet. They would never have found it on their own. A few days later Adriaan and Peter arrived and made a great impression on Opa van Kleffens by telling him their adventures traveling through France and Germany. In Chapter 7, I described the evening entertainment Adriaan and Peter provided with their travel stories and Richard with his magic tricks. Adriaan showed his proficiency in French by bellowing *"Bonjour"* every time he entered the chalet. That was the extent of Adriaan's French as far as he was concerned.

When Netty's parents were leaving we went with them to the airport in Geneva and in my mind's eye I still see her father walk away. He walked with some difficulty because he had problems with an arthritic hip. This was the last time we saw him alive. A few days after we returned to Old Greenwich we were having dinner when we got a phone call from Pul. I heard Netty cry out and rushed to the kitchen where the phone was. She had just heard that her father had died suddenly from what we later learned was probably an aneurism. We returned to the Netherlands for his funeral. George and Adriaan were both still in Europe and attended too. Netty loved her father very much and for me he was a wonderful older friend. I write this as I am eighty-seven years old and believe Pa's death at seventy three was early for today's standards. I think his unhealthy life style and total lack of exercise were major factors in his early death. Lots of smoking and a couple of glasses of Dutch gin before dinner and absolutely no exercise are a bad combination.

Another development would have a major impact on our future as a family. Before we left for Switzerland, Netty had looked at a house in Riverside she basically liked, but she felt it looked gloomy inside, mainly because of its interior color scheme and tired furniture. It also had a garden that promised to be very nice, but was neglected and needed a lot of work. When we were back she went to see it again and was told the asking price had been lowered. She saw that the house was now empty and the interior looked considerably more cheerful because it had been completely repainted in off white. She asked me to come take a look and we both liked the house instantly. We had always been more partial to Riverside than Old Greenwich because most of our friends lived there. Also, we had become somewhat disenchanted with our house near the Sound. We had spent several nights in our beds with the house shaking while a nor'easter was pounding the sea wall in front of it and the close proximity of neighbors we had little in common with and who caused constant problems in our homeowners association was beginning to annoy us. So we were ready to make a move. The fact that my financial position had improved considerably as my department grew and threw off more and more earnings for Eberstadt played a role too, of course.

I was now a shareholder in the firm and got good bonuses. While in our house in Old Greenwich we had received a lot of the antique furniture out of the house of my grandparents, including the 17th century grandfather clock I loved. This clock fit perfectly under the cathedral ceiling of our upstairs hallway, but could not fit in the Riverside house unless we raised the ceiling. We asked our friend Giff Reed, who then ran a local contracting firm with excellent craftsmen, if he could do something about that. He proposed a high tray ceiling in the living room which closed the deal for us. We made a bid and soon were owners of 15 Pilot Rock Lane in the Harbor Point Association. We did not have a totally unobstructed water view anymore, but we got a really interesting garden, full of remembrances of the elaborate formal gardens of an old estate that used to occupy the entire peninsula. Our house was part of a group of some thirty-three houses. We had a rose garden with a lovely little pond in the middle and another formal garden behind the house, also with a small pond. There was a swimming pool in a downright romantic setting, surrounded by old stone balustrades. The garden contained many different trees, some very old and large.

As we studied the history of Harbor Point, we learned that it was originally the summer home of Jacob Langeloth, a wealthy New York City businessman who was born in Germany and made his fortune in the metals business. He was one of the founders of American Metals, Climax Molybdenum. He married an American woman, who was much younger than he, and she started building the house that she called Walhall, after the German mythical place where the Gods lived. Stones were shipped in from quarries in the midwest and landed at a dock specially built for this purpose. The house had been located next door to our property, on a hill with spectacular views of New York City to the west. On the other eastern side of the house, one could descend into the formal gardens in the midst of which our house now stood. Our house had been built in a moderately contemporary style with big windows and simple lines which we liked. We have always felt that the style I call "phony colonial," with quasi old-fashioned shutters and coach lamps on both sides of the front door and many pillars, did not reflect a

15 PILOT ROCK LANE IN 1974.

durable sincere style. After the tray ceiling, we would make many more altera-
tions with the help of George's growing architectural skills. We became very
fond of this house and lived there thirty years, leaving it only after we began to
realize that we were getting too old to deal with the complications of owning a
house and an elaborate garden. The example of my parents, who stayed much
too long in their house until it became impossible for them to move, also played a
big role in our decision to leave. The house was not as big as our Old Greenwich
place. But we could cope with fewer bedrooms because our two older children
were beginning to leave to start lives of their own. The Walhall estate was put
on the market in the fifties and a syndicate of farsighted Riverside residents had
bought it to prevent developers from cutting it up into small lots with smallish,
ticky-tacky homes, which was done everywhere in those days. They then developed the place into a really nice park-like setting fit for more substantial houses.
Their venture was not immediately rewarded with success. In those days waterfront properties on the market for $15,000 were not snapped up very quickly.
Fifty years later, they went for several millions! When we moved in, many of
the original inhabitants were still living there. Now they have almost all been
replaced by younger, wealthier people who in many cases tore down the houses

they bought to replace them with gaudier and larger structures. Our house will probably be torn down also.

Immediately after we closed on our new house, the Organization of Arab Petroleum Exporting Countries, or OAPEC, plus Syria and Egypt declared an oil embargo. This group was part of the larger OPEC that in later years became a major player in Mid–Eastern politics. It wanted to support an Arab opposition against Israel. The war of 1967 had been a great success for Israel and changed its military posture in the region. Then came the Yom Kippur war in 1973, which was started by its neighbors expressly during the most important Jewish holiday. This conflict brought Israel initially almost to its knees but ended also in a significant defeat for the attackers. The Nixon administration had taken immediate action to assist Israel after it was attacked in the Yom Kippur war and started an air lift of weapons and supplies to its ally. The oil embargo was in retaliation against this support. The Netherlands was included in the embargo because it had also sent weapons and other support to Israel. The stock market collapsed in response to the war and the Dow Jones Average dropped from above 1,000 to around 600 by the final quarter of 1974. The price of gasoline shot up and the Greenwich real estate market swooned to the point where hardly any transactions took place. This put us in a tough spot, with two houses, two mortgages, a bridge loan and two kids in college. It took until the late spring of 1974 before we sold the Old Greenwich house. Amazingly, the buyers were a couple that had sold their house in Harbor Point! Netty always said she was impressed by my calmness during this stressful period of multiple home ownership, but I certainly had a feeling of immense relief when our realtor friend Jean Crocco called to say she had a serious buyer for our house and had a bid.

Still, the house dilemma did not prevent us from celebrating the fiftieth wedding anniversary of my parents. We decided to make our arrival in Holland a surprise. I asked Tineke to provide cover and invite Pa and Ma for a dinner at her house to celebrate their anniversary and called restaurant Royal, in The Hague, then one of the best in town, and made a reservation for a private room. We invited Mammie and Pa and Ma's old friends the Bersots who came from Switzerland and Tante Mieke and Bas as well as Grote Bas and his wife Sjoukje and Tineke with her four daughters, including two husbands. We flew over and went to a hotel in Amsterdam. We really enjoyed that little vacation, an incognito visit to Holland, without being obligated to visit numerous relatives and friends. We noticed that the gasoline shortage, with long lines at most gas stations that had seriously affected the American economy, was nonexistent in Holland. There was a gas station in front of the hotel and the attendants there seemed to have plenty gas and little to do. Ma was overjoyed when we called her to tell her what the plan was and the dinner was a great success.

Nixon resigned in August 1974. The Watergate affair and particularly the attempts to cover up all kinds of related misdeeds overwhelmed his administration. The Democrats in congress were after him and disclosures such as the discovery of tapes on which all conversations in the Oval office were recorded did not help. The tapes reflected a man who was obsessed with the idea that everybody was trying to plot against him. They also revealed how profane Nixon was in his private conversations. The term "expletive deleted" frequently used in the transcripts became part of the American language. I have always felt that people that use a lot of profanity were insecure, frustrated, or just using a veneer of civility in their day to day behavior with others while hiding a much cruder inner core.

George gave us an unexpected surprise when he called me in late spring and asked if we would have any objection to him not graduating with his class at Middlebury. It turned out he had been unable to complete his thesis. Since graduation was about a month away, what could we say? So we did not have the pleasure of going to Middlebury to see our eldest son march down in a cap and gown to get his diploma. Instead he came home and spent the summer and part of the fall writing his thesis in our basement. After he completed his magnum opus, he graduated cum laude in February 1975, which was a huge relief to us. His thesis was a good one. It is entitled "Matthew Arnold: The Energetic Man and the 'Unpoetical Age.'" It is very well written but tough to understand. It is possible that Maggie distracted him from writing although she was a hard worker herself and could understand George's predicament.

In the summer of 1975 George married Margaret Arnette Murray. We had met Maggie's parents several times before the wedding and found them to be a peculiar couple that came across to us as much older than we were. I was fifty at that time and Netty forty-five, and we both felt we were still young and full of pep. Maggie's father, Arthur, was a lawyer who worked for the Internal Revenue Service. They had always lived in apartments in Manhattan and when we got to know them they lived in a very nice building on Central Park West. It had always been Charlene's dream to have Maggie's wedding in the Plaza, but Maggie had a stubborn streak and was determined to avoid that watering hole at all cost. So the wedding party was at the St. Regis. Because the Murrays were Catholics, we had a very restrained marriage ceremony in a small chapel on the Upper East Side. The party at the St. Regis was very nice and I think Charlene was satisfied with it. In my mind's eye, I still see my three sons leaving in George's little car to go to New York for George's wedding. We had passed another milestone in our life. The couple soon went to Chapel Hill, North Carolina, where Maggie started working at Duke University for her masters in English and George became a waiter in a local country club. When people asked me what George was doing after his graduation and marriage, I would hide my disappointment at his lack of career building and told them he had a job in the food distribution business. George would soon find other more intellectually challenging work in the Duke University Hospital Pharmacy, where he became an inventory records clerk and later a purchaser. Adriaan was now a sophomore at Lafayette and decided to start living off campus, an arrangement that worked well for him after he had found the right place. Also in late 1974 Adriaan began his long and varied career as an automobile aficionado with a definite and permanent bias towards very large cars such as Lincoln Continentals. He found one that had been driven by an elderly lady who had passed away. I do not know if she only used the car to drive to church, but it was close. It was a large, beige monster that he really liked.

Gerald Ford became president after Nixon resigned. Nixon had made him vice president after the original VP, called Spiro Agnew, stepped down following a conviction for extortion, bribery, tax fraud and conspiracy. In those years our nation entered a period that lasts until today in which students of the national mood detected that confidence in government and the integrity of politicians decline drastically. Ford was succeeded by Jimmy Carter. He did not want to be called James, it had to be Jimmy, a man of the people – a peanut farmer from Georgia. Jimmy was an Annapolis graduate and had been a nuclear submarine commander. I saw him when he spoke to a group of investment people in the Waldorf Astoria and was favorably impressed. He looked trim and fit, had a nice grin and seemed to have good ideas. He ran on a promise that as an outsider he could heal the problems in Washington. Unfortunately, he turned out to be a mediocre president who made a number of questionable decisions, tried to micromanage everything and let his wife Roslynn sit in on Cabinet meetings, something that had never been seen before. He brought his young daughter, Amy, to state dinners where she sat at the table reading children's books. To top it all off, his beer swigging, hayseed brother Billy Carter became a real embarrassment. Carter had a naïve born-again Christian attitude to foreign policy and thought that people would agree with his proposals if he was just open and sincere and trusting. When Carter became president in 1977, the world economies suffered from a period of stagflation and went from bad to worse, the price of oil went through the roof and gold hit an all time high. The Fed had to raise interest rates to very high levels to counter the inflationary trends. Abroad, the Iranians revolted against the Shah, whose suppressive regime had been supported by the U.S. for decades, and got a cleric, the Ayatollah Khomeini, out of exile in Paris to become head of state of what was called an Islamic Republic. Khomenei had escaped to France loaded in a plane while rolled up in a carpet, an anecdote my father found incredibly funny. *"Ze hebben die vent opgerold in een kleedje"* (they rolled that bugger up in a little rug), he would say with a broad grin. It was the beginning of a new era of Muslim fundamentalism that is still troubling the world today. Carter could, of course, not be held responsible for most of these misfortunes, the economy follows its own path regardless of who is president, but the American public became thoroughly disgusted with his administration. The crowning blow was the takeover of the American embassy in Teheran by Iranian students calling themselves Revolutionary Guards. The embassy's personnel was taken hostage and stayed incarcerated in the building for 444 days. A major problem for Carter and a major blow to American prestige in the world. Things got worse when Carter launched a top-secret attempt by a Special Forces unit to free the hostages that failed and turned into a disaster. At the end of Carter's first and only term as president, the voters turned towards the Republican Party and elected Ronald Reagan, a former governor of California and movie actor. Netty and I did not know what to think of Reagan who seemed to be a quixotic figure, a tool of the far-right wing of the party who often left the impression he did not know what he was talking about. For Carter, the Iranians added insult to injury by waiting with the release of the hostages until the very day Reagan was inaugurated in January 1980. Over time we began to appreciate Reagan's style of governing better and found him a president who had an uncanny ability to sense the mood of the American people and who was a shrewd negotiator while acting with a certain level of detachment. Handwritten notes released after his death revealed that he was far from stupid and had a real knack for words.

Despite the very shaky political scene and very difficult markets, our business at Eberstadt was flourishing. The fund people had bought another fund, the Surveyor Fund and merged it with the Eberstadt Fund, retaining the name. With the Surveyor Fund came Bill Miller, who was a portfolio manager/analyst and who made it quite clear he did not want to work for the fund any longer. Bill became a very valuable addition to my team. He was a good investor with a somewhat volatile style who could get along well with important clients and who added a new level of nervous energy and curiosity to our group. Gerry Goodwin by then had left us, but we found a replacement for him in Ed Keeley, who had previously worked as an analyst in

Ed Giles' department. It took Ed Keeley a while to adjust to becoming a portfolio manager, but once he had the hang of it he also became a very good one and a solid support for our research oriented portfolio strategy.

In 1976 Adriaan graduated from Lafayette College. His major was international affairs. He wrote a 225-page thesis entitled, "U.S. Hegemony and Latin American Dependence." A very good piece of work. My parents came over for the occasion and spent some time with us. After his graduation, finding a suitable career was a big problem for Adriaan. The economy was in a slump, we had raging inflation and most companies were not hiring. Through Bill Hare, a good friend of ours he got an introduction to the Continental Insurance Company and was hired in the International Department. This was a great relief for Adriaan and put him on track for a distinguished career in insurance. He immediately moved to the city and rented a walk-up apartment on the Upper East Side. When we visited it, we burst out laughing. Ade had hung all his pictures at his eye level, which is a fair distance above everybody else's. In 1978 Adriaan was transferred to Brussels, where he began a new chapter of his life.

At the end of 1976 we organized a family trip to Holland. The Netherlands in the seventies had started to change drastically from the country we had left. A strong left-leaning political trend, locally called "progressive," had taken hold and Dutch society became more and more regulated and state controlled. Although as a country they had nothing to do with the Vietnam War, students protested in the streets against it, and a hippy-like culture took hold of young people, particularly in Amsterdam. The government regulated small business owners and nobody could open a store without first passing an exam and being approved so as to not cause too much competition for existing stores in a neighborhood. Everybody took time off between Christmas and New Year's and that custom still prevails. You would think that restaurants and bars would be wide open in such a prime holiday time, but they were not. The people who worked there also had "rights" and were too busy going to the winter sports rather than making an extra buck. We wanted to organize a dinner for our relatives and on another day a reception for our friends in a nice place. We discovered our thinking had become too American, we thought people would jump at the opportunity to cater a large party, but found to our despair that almost everything was closed. It was very difficult to find a suitable place that was willing to take our money to entertain our friends. Ultimately we found a restaurant where we could give a dinner for our family and a cocktail party the next day for a large number of our friends. It was not the best place, but it was O.K. Our dinner went well, and among the speeches given young Richard excelled. He had taken quite a few sips of the wine and delivered an inspired speech in which he roasted his oldest brother in a friendly way. The turnout at our cocktail party was surprisingly great. It was a typical Dutch winter day with rain coming down horizontally, in sheets. Despite that everybody showed up. We saw many people we had not seen in years and that was a delight.

In the later seventies the U.S. economy was in trouble. The price of crude oil soared and other commodities also saw historically sky-high price levels. Reflecting the rapidly rising inflation rate, gold rose to what was then an all time high of $850 an ounce and the value of the dollar declined accordingly. Interest rates rose and by the end of 1978 the prime rate reached 21.5% when the Federal Reserve decided to step on the brakes and put an end to this madness. This all made for a horrible economic environment for investors and it is still surprising to me that my money management business continued to grow. What helped us tremendously was that despite high interest rates people were not attracted to bonds because of the attendant high rate of inflation and looked for a safe haven in equities. By the end of the decade we had more than a Billion in assets under management. We had a number of prestigious accounts. Several of the Bell Telephone companies became our clients: first Pacific Telephone in San Francisco, then Pennsylvania Bell Tel and New York Tel and finally AT&T. Good relationships with clients begat other accounts. I became quite friendly with Adrian Cassidy, a true gentleman who ran the Pacific Telephone investment and financing operation. He obviously liked what we were doing and when he retired from Pac Tel and became trustee of the Getty Trust, which had ambitious plans to build the new Getty Museum in Los Angeles, we got that account also. In addition we had a Kodak account and also a Rochester Telephone one, Eaton manufacturing in Cleveland and Monsanto and Emerson Electric in St. Louis and Hughes Aircraft in LA. The good part of these larger pension funds was that management was obligated to fund the pension account on an annual basis and so every year the gate keepers had to find a home for more and more money. This gave us tremendous growth despite the difficult markets.

Like all good parents, we put music on the curriculum for our children. George had guitar lessons, Adriaan piano, Richard ditto and Janet had an episode of trumpet playing. None of these stuck except Richard's piano efforts. George gave up his guitar, Adriaan has a beautiful piano at home and still plays chords on it and Janet's trumpeting found its climax in the concert the Riverside School band produced for our local heroine, Dorothy Hamill. Dorothy won the gold medal in figure skating in the 1976 Winter Olympics in Innsbrück, Austria. We knew her parents, who were members of Netty's Riverside Dance Group. When Dorothy returned home, the band played in front of her house. It sounded like a slightly tired Mexican Mariachi band. Rich had piano lessons after Netty bought a small piano for the edification and enrichment of her brood. Mrs. Fink in Old Greenwich was his teacher and she organized annual recitals at her house. After we sat through the stumbling performances of several pupils, Richard would come on as the last player and he would invariably perform magnificently.

Later he got lessons from Stuart Hemmingway, a blind young man who lived in Riverside with his parents, another dance group couple. Stuart was a superb pianist despite his handicap. Now Richard still plays and still takes lessons in classical piano in Boston. His playing has been a joy for us for a long time, and when we lived in Riverside, it was also appreciated by our neighbors who would comment how much they liked to hear him play Scott Joplin in summer when we had the windows open.

During the Nixon administration, Will and Inge Cates moved to Washington, D.C. Will received a political appointment as deputy assistant secretary of the Treasury. He enjoyed that job very much and marveled at the level of expertise he found at the Treasury and the high-quality of the research available to it. After a while though, the Washington environment got to him and he experienced times of great frustrations. We visited the Cates on a nice spring weekend and Netty and I toured the city in a bus. It was the time of great antiwar demonstrations and the Mall area was crowded with college kids milling around looking for some action. When some kids crossed the road in front of us, a grumpy man in our bus told the driver to "run them over." Later we learned George had been in town with a group of fellow long-hairs from Middlebury. His group had left early, he told us, because it had been too much of drug scene. They drove back to college for at least an eight-hour trip, which may have cooled off their political zeal. Luckily that was about the extent of George's political activism, at least to our knowledge.

It was a time of great divisions in the American population with younger people turning more and more antiwar and antigovernment while older folks were inclined to support the Nixon administration and tolerate the war. Nixon's men called the older ones "the silent majority," a term that is still being used by politicos who are living under the illusion that there is real support for their views and that they would be victorious if only those in favor would come forward. The Watergate scandals that followed would change the attitude of the American public towards government and significantly reduced their trust in it. It was further evidence of the public skepticism towards all that represents government that will not go away. It started with Watergate and it continued. It would only get worse.

Moving the Investment Advisory department forward at Eberstadt was a wonderful task. To accommodate clients who wanted to offset common stock investments with fixed income, I wanted to establish a fixed-income department. Hunting around I found what seemed to be a good bond man with marketing abilities. Otto Holmberg had worked at Morgan Stanley and checked out well there. After a few years he unfortunately did not turn out to be a very good fit. David Dievler, the Eberstadt chief administrative officer, suggested that I get a promising young man from his staff to help Holmberg and beef up the bond group from an administrative point of view. This was William Huff, who was a good fit and who blossomed into a crackerjack bond portfolio manager. Bill quickly realized we had to offer something better than just a capability to buy Treasurys. He became an expert in so-called "junk bonds" or better "high- yield bonds." These were lower-rated bonds issued by mostly industrial companies. If you did your homework properly and selected issuers that were financially in good shape, these bonds could yield considerably more than Treasurys. In fact a portfolio consisting of say twenty different high-yield bonds would yield a return that was so much better that you had to lose two or three holdings to bankruptcy before the return would be equal to Treasurys. Over time Bill got a respectable list of clients and also ran the money market fund the mutual fund people wanted to establish to try to keep shareholders who would redeem their shares in Chemical Fund and wanted a safe haven that yielded a decent income. Bill is now a very wealthy man who runs his own investment firm.

The nation celebrated its two hundredth anniversary in 1976. The Riverside Yacht Club together with many other area clubs organized a trip to New York Harbor to view the parade of tall ships that was the largest event of its size in history. Enormous crowds were expected and special precautions were taken to give us safe passage. We went by train to Grand Central Station and were packed into a very crowded special subway to get to downtown. At the Battery we boarded a Staten Island ferry that would be our reviewing platform. We drifted around in the harbor to see the truly spectacular scene. President Ford reviewed the parade from an aircraft carrier anchored near the Statue of Liberty.

It was a beautiful sunny day with sparkling waters and low humidity and the ships were spectacular. There were square riggers from all kinds of countries, including Russia, Spain, Portugal and Brazil. In between, a flotilla of Dutch flat bottomed boats bobbed along looking very small amongst the tall ships. These Dutch boats had come over in a special transporter ship that functioned as a floating dock for them. They would return the same way but not before visiting Riverside. The whole event was an incredibly nice experience. Maybe it was the sense that we were finally at peace and on this beautiful day we felt a sense of unity and pride in our nation and its achievements. On the way back we walked through the downtown area where I worked. The streets were empty and peaceful, and we felt that we were part of a truly historic moment and were enjoying a really wonderful holiday.

The following Tuesday evening we went to RYC to go out for a short sail. In the parking lot I bumped into a man who was running around announcing in a heavy Dutch accent that a flotilla of Dutch boats was coming down the Sound from New York and wanted to find a berth. They had been rebuffed at another club and nobody had made any clear arrangements for anything. This came as a complete surprise. Although the club was closed as it always is on Tuesdays, I was able to mobilize the manager and the commodore and we received the mostly Frisian group as well as we could. We transported most of them to our house and offered our pool and whatever we could find in food and drink. The following Thursday they were still at RYC and participated in our traditional Thursday evening Vespers Race. It was fun to see the big sideboard Dutch *"skutjes"* sail on the relatively short course with sturdy Dutch girls winching in the heavy sheets when tacking. The group seemed to take our hospitality for granted and left without showing much appreciation to the club. The following year Netty went to Holland with Janet and visited some of the participants in Friesland, where the reception she got was a disappointment.

Meanwhile at Eberstadt things were in motion. With the Chemical Fund now approaching one billion dollars in assets and my advisory department moving well over the one billion dollar mark, Bob Porter began to worry about the future of the brokerage business. Events in later years would show that his worries were totally unfounded and that the stock market boom that was beginning to develop and would last until the end of the century would deliver spectacular results for the institutional brokerage business. But there were hiccups of course and every time the market declined Bob would get into a pessimistic mood. He wanted to safeguard his personal investment in the firm and detach it from the vagaries of the brokerage business. The solution was to split the firm and seek a merger with a company that would be willing to buy our money management business and not the brokerage side. Bob had good connections in Boston and knew the people at Putnam Fund Management. George Putnam was an old acquaintance and distant relative. Some years before, Putnam had been bought by the large insurance brokerage firm Marsh

& McLennan. Marsh was cash rich and constantly on the prowl to find profitable ways to deploy its cash reserves. It had a flourishing consulting subsidary called Mercer that operated in the actuarial and employee benefit consulting businesses. Although it could be seen as somewhat of a conflict of interest, because Mercer also consulted in the area of selecting asset managers for pension funds, Marsh believed that buying asset management and fund management firms was a good fit in its business plan.

With the help of smart lawyers, Porter arrived at a construction where Eberstadt stockholders would exchange their stock for Marsh shares with the asset management executives getting most of the Marsh shares and the others basically being bought out by them. The net effect for me was that I would get a holding of a listed stock in exchange for shares in a privately held company. This was a huge advantage for me and Porter was obviously in the same (much bigger) boat.

We would spin off from the Eberstadt firm into two wholly owned subsidiaries of Marsh & McLennan, Eberstadt Fund Management (EFM) and Eberstadt Asset Management (EAM). Initially EAM and EFM were kept together under one CEO. This was John Hill, a very intelligent Texan who had been a second-or third-level bureaucrat at the Energy Department. This newly formed department was created to cope with the energy crises the nation faced in the seventies after the oil embargo and other problems. To make clear we were no longer affiliated with a brokerage firm, both companies moved to new offices on a floor below where the advisory department had been moved some time before. This move away from the brokerage side was actually a good one for my business because I always had to cope with consultants insinuating that there was a conflict of interest and that we would somehow be beholden to the stocks recommendations of the brokerage firm or obligated to buy positions they had invested in or were underwriters of.

At Eberstadt we had a colleague named Bill Janeway who was one of the two sons of Eliot Janeway, a very prominent economist and financial writer. Janeway's approach to economics was a mix of fundamental economics, politics and worldwide macro trends, and he put much emphasis on what was going on in Washington. His son Bill was also an economist who had gone to the London School of Economics. He became a valued asset for the Eberstadt institutional brokerage department because he gave a coherent and consistent approach to economics that was in many respects the same as his father's and was closely linked to what was going on politically in Washington and the world at large. His ideas were very useful to me because they helped me crystallize my thinking about the markets and my never ending efforts to make sense of what was going on around us. Macro events such as the Nixon resignation and the energy crisis could not be ignored when thinking about the markets and the economy, and ever since those days we have lived in a turbulent world where markets were moved by random developments that impact stock prices.

To build an investment strategy only on fundamental research of individual stocks without paying attention to the forces that were driving stock prices in general was and is in my opinion a bad investment approach. Bill Janeway knew John Hill and recommended we talk to him from time to time to get a good background view on what Washington was doing to cope with the energy crisis. Soon John joined the firm and gradually moved over to the mutual fund management side where he probably saw better opportunities. He became what we called our energy guru. And that is how John Hill became my boss after the breakup of Eberstadt and the merger with Marsh & McLennan. In the late seventies it had become necessary for all investment people to focus hard on energy problems and the attendant investment opportunities, and John Hill found himself in the right spot at the right time. When the Saudi Sheik Yamani, one of the principal players in OPEC, spoke at the Plaza Hotel as a guest of Morgan Stanley, the meeting was packed. I had a good seat and observed in wonderment how times had changed and how powerful the oil producing countries had become. Here we were all basically groveling before this man who was a well-educated and clever diplomat, but he represented a desert kingdom that had basically only its enormous crude oil reserves as "raison d'être." He did not say much, but he seemed friendly enough. Over the years the Saudis would continue to be best friends with the U.S. even while there were strong indications that they were financing various terror groups run by Muslim extremists. It all went under the guise of "we need to make sure we keep our hand in."

The Marsh decision to buy us was not greeted with great enthusiasm at Putnam. Beyond being a major mutual fund manager and distributor, much larger than us, they also had a large investment advisory business, and the people in charge there immediately feared repercussions from clients who would think we were one and the same outfit. Luckily we had very little overlap among our clientele, and we orchestrated a carefully executed plan to make the news public at the same time in the same manner to all our clients. The overall Putnam operation was run by Robert Reilly, who initially became our boss. Bob was an intense and totally administratively oriented man who paid little attention to investment problems but focused heavily on the accounting and nitty-gritty of the fund business and especially on compliance with all the rules funds have to live with. David Dievler, the former CFO of

Eberstadt, had also moved over to the fund side, and he and John Hill were subjected to a constant stream of memoranda from Bob Reilly asking for immediate response. I had read an article about a machine that had just been put on the market that could duplicate a document and send it over a phone line. A forerunner of the fax machine that would later on briefly become a device used by everybody in lieu of using the U.S. mail. I mentioned it to Dave and he proposed it to Bob, who was ecstatic and started to use it immediately, sending one memo after another over to us.

After the free-form Eberstadt operation we had entered the land of big corporations and began to wonder what we were getting into. But things would change soon. After a few months, we were surprised to hear that Bob Reilly was leaving. I never learned what the background of that was. He seemed firmly ensconced in the Marsh world. It started a series of leadership changes that became difficult to live with. The Marsh people decided that John Hill would be the new head man of Putnam and ourselves. A remarkable promotion for a man who had never run a company and had zero investment expertise. He was a good talker, and he had gravitas and a certain "presence," which impressed many people. As an old Washington hand, he knew how to slide through the bureaucratic web.

For me it was a step up to be closer to the throne. John had started a new fund for us called the Eberstadt Energy Fund that was intended to take advantage of the great demand for investments in the energy sphere. This initiative created a great deal of good will for him, although the fund was very small and would remain so. John had a taste for the perks the Marsh people were enjoying, and soon we had a driver with a large black limo at our disposal that would bring several of us who commuted through Grand Central Station to the train every evening and would drop us off or pick us up at the airport. Not bad. When we moved to a floor below our old Eberstadt location, John built a large office for himself complete with a private bathroom with a shower. All unheard of luxuries for those of us who were used to the frugal Eberstadt approach. He also bought a set of very expensive prints of the Hudson School that lent prestige to our less-than-impressive quarters. One evening after we had made a client presentation, I don't remember where, we were sitting in a hotel bar for a nightcap with John. I also cannot remember who else was with me, but it must have been one of my portfolio manager colleagues. Suddenly John announced to us that he was leaving to join a small private investment company. He was keeping control over the Energy Fund, however. The Marsh people now decided to put another Putnam man in charge. He was Martin Hale, a very nice fellow I could get along with well. Martin was a Harvard Business School classmate of Bill

Miller. He lasted about six months and then left to join a portfolio management firm started by another Putnam alumnus.

Finally the Marsh people decided to remove the intermediaries and let Dave Dievler and me, together with Larry Lasser, Martin's successor at Putnam, report directly to Ian Smith, the second in command at Marsh who headed up Mercer. Ian Smith proved to be a wonderful man to work with. He was soft spoken and very smart, a Canadian of English extraction. His right-hand man, Tom Waylett was equally nice and approachable but kind of disorganized and apt to not respond to memos or phone calls. One day I discovered that Tom was interested in race horses. At Harbor Point several neighbor friends were also interested in the track and our friend John Phillips had organized a wonderful weekend for us in Kentucky with a visit to the Kentucky Derby. We traveled the right way, with seats in a private box where lunch and drinks were served. As a joke I had invested a tiny amount of money with them in a syndicate that owned a race horse called Scuff. So I was limited partner in this group and had the stationary to prove it. The stationary showed horses on a vastly over-designed masthead and on the left a list of the partners. I used that stationary to send a memo to Tom and got an immediate answer. He wanted to know everything about my horse. After that I was on his good side and got answers. Larry Lasser was initially head of research at Putnam, and since he was now head of all the Putnam funds, he was also put in charge of the Eberstadt funds. This was not what Bob Porter liked and Larry's lack of tact in dealing with the Chemical Fund board, a group of elderly people who were totally convinced of their own importance, started the relationship on the wrong foot from day one. It never got better and eventually the friction between Lasser and the EFM people would lead to the destruction of EAM and EFM.

In the late seventies we heard about a startling development in Holland. It must have been in the fall of 1976 when I returned one evening from the city to find Netty and Adriaan in a state of great excitement in our kitchen. They had just had a phone call from Tilly, who told them that she had left her husband Frans and was in love with our friend Menny Fruitema. They had known each other for many years and they lived near each other in Wassenaar, but we always had thought that Menny and his wife Ella, who were very old friends of ours had a good marriage. We had stayed with them at their house and very much liked their children. They had visited with us on trips they took to the U.S. and we had never discovered any discord. We sensed that Til's marriage was not the best, mainly because Frans became over the years a dull homebody who offered little excitement to Til, who always was a more outgoing and adventurous sort. In the coming months we were visited at Christmas time by Menny, who wanted to take some distance from the home front and think about his situation. He had little chance to do so because there were daily long telephone calls from Wassenaar from both sides. We told Menny that we had great trouble with this situation and would prefer things to stay as they were with Ella. This did not improve our relationship with Tilly, but we felt we could not immediately embrace Menny as our brother-in-law. We knew him very well; I had lived with him in the same house in Leiden and we saw him and Ella often when we were living in Heemstede. We enjoyed Menny as a very funny and entertaining guy who would present a big change for Til. Frans also came to stay with us as he had done every year when he came to New York City with the Dutch delegation for the general assembly of the United Nations. He gave us his side, and we felt very much in the middle of a difficult predicament. On December 23, 1977, Tilly and Menny were married and we gradually got used to the new situation. We had many fun visits with them over the years and enjoyed a cruise in the Windward Islands with them and our family. For Tilly it was a big change, and as she told Netty there was never a dull moment in her new life.

24 : End of The Business Road

T
he decade of the eighties brought dramatic, mostly difficult, changes in my professional life, many positive changes in the life of my family and important changes in our country's economy and national politics. I think it will be best to devote this chapter solely to my experiences with EAM and my hugely diminished business career in the few years following EAM's demise. To separate this part of the story of my life from the history of my family may simplify the storyline and make a clearer distinction between what happened with us as a family and what happened in my business – two very different things.

In the early eighties EAM was a flourishing business and its future was bright. We had more than two billion dollars under management and were quickly moving up to three. The portfolios we managed were mostly the invested reserves of dozens of pension funds of many major U.S. corporations. We now had a research department that worked for the funds and for us and the research director reported to me. We had a research agreement with the Eberstadt brokerage firm that supplied us on a daily basis with their research and investment ideas. For that we paid them a fee in cash, rather than doing business with them, which was a better and more arms-length arrangement. I had hired Leo Clemente as a Modern Portfolio Theory (MPT) expert or quant, as these experts were called. MPT had become a whole new culture that sprang from the academic world and became a factor of overwhelming importance in investment research and portfolio management. Mathematicians began to study the behavior of the market. Their ability to do so was vastly enhanced by the rapidly increasing data processing capabilities of a new tool – the computer.

One basic premise was that all markets acted rationally and that securities were rationally priced. The market was "efficient"–a word that was frequently used. You could calculate the standard deviation of a stock and thus by combining stocks with different standard deviations, compose a portfolio that reached the "efficient frontier" or a maximum safe return with limited volatility. In 1990 three mathematicians,

721

Markowitz, Miller and Sharpe, received the Nobel Prize for economics for their work in this area. The "Random Walk" theory suggested that a stock's past performance gave no useful indication of its future performance. In other words, stock prices performed a random walk through time. One of the ideas that grew out of this theory was that any portfolio, no matter how randomly selected, would perform as well as a carefully structured portfolio of well-researched stocks. You could hang a page of the stock exchange price list, as was then still published daily by the Wall Street Journal, on the wall and throw darts at it. The performance of a portfolio composed of stocks found by the darts would, over time, equal the S&P 500 stock average because the market was rational and would always find a price level for all stocks that was in line with the broader market averages and above all would represent their true value.

For us this was, of course, a troublesome proposition since we had built our business on the premise that we could build a portfolio for our clients based on carefully selected stocks followed by our research analysts that would deliver better than average results with average or less than average risk. Leo went to work to find out what the risk exposure of our portfolios was as measured by Beta, or volatility and Alpha, or risk. We wanted to make sure that all our portfolios would be similar in style and risk exposure and wanted to have a set of data at our disposal that could not be questioned in case our clients asked for them. We had to reckon with the growing number of consultants who began to make serious inroads with our clients. The consultants had discovered the fertile area of pension fund management and the tendency of corporate boards and pension committees to unburden themselves from troublesome decision making by hiring a self- appointed expert who would then tell them which manager(s) to hire and how to measure their performance. The consultants would tear our portfolios apart to find out if we adhered to the investment style we had described in our promotional material. Naturally they embraced MPT with relish because it would enhance their value for their new found clients and diminish the value of our work. And they could justify their fees if they would recommend changes in the stable of managers used by a pension fund.

Now, more than twenty- five years later, it is interesting to note that serious doubts have arisen about the validity of the mathematical theories that governed our business for so long. The crash of 2008 has brought market participants to the conclusion that the market is not rational and that stocks are not or not always priced efficiently.

Earlier, in 1998, the crash of Long Term Capital Management, a Greenwich, Connecticut–based hedge fund raised a huge red flag when it collapsed and caused a $4.6 billion loss. The Federal Reserve had to come to its rescue to prevent this debacle from spreading throughout world markets. For a while LTCM was flying high. It was founded by John Merriwether, an arrogant former partner and head of trading at Salomon Brothers. He recruited two Nobel Prize winners, Myron Scholes and Robert Merton and put them on his board. The fund used absolute-return trading strategies to engage in arbitrage in the bond market, putting massive amounts of borrowed money to work whenever they discovered a discrepancy (a divergence) between U.S. and foreign short- and long-term bonds that were supposed to trade in fixed relationships between each other. They bet that the divergence would turn into a convergence and believed this was a sure thing. When the Russian ruble collapsed, these relationships were suddenly not an absolutely certainty anymore and LTCM capsized. Merrill Lynch wrote in its annual report that "mathematical risk models provide a greater sense of security than warranted." With about $ 2.3 billion in capital LTCM had bet more that a trillion. The markets proved to be irrational and much pain could have been avoided if the people who played the market would have understood that. Unfortunately, we would have to go through many years of excessive trading in which great profits were accumulated out of thin air before we came back to earth in the mortgage credit crisis of 2008. It is not even certain that we have come back down to where we should be since most big banks still have large trading departments that deal in derivatives and other instruments that have no basis in real life and no economic purpose beyond acting as poker chips.

Another, perhaps much more dangerous element, are the firms nobody heard of who operate under the radar and use powerful computers to trade millions of shares in a fraction of a second whenever a small discrepancy is spotted. Cynics say that people like LTCM and other traders know very well what they are doing – they have a good chance at becoming fabulously rich, and since they are "too big to fail." the government (i.e. the taxpayers) will bail them out when things go wrong, only at the cost of some serious public embarrassment for them.

The consultants wanted to interview us continuously and much time was spent by me and my colleagues in satisfying their demands. We knew they were looking for holes in our armor so they could run over to our clients and tell them they had caught us in a misstatement or some other deviation from the rules they had set. A particularly difficult firm to work with was the Frank Russell organization in Tacoma, Washington. I spent time in their office and had lunch with George Russell, who had built a small brokerage firm run by his father into a major pension fund consulting firm. George is a very smart man and a very good and convincing talker. He is now retired from the firm that he built into a very large global investment advisor and investment consultant. Russell even developed now widely used stock market averages known as the Russell Averages and has spread its wings into the emerging market area. We sensed that our struggles with this firm and others stemmed from their inability to position themselves firmly between us and our clients. Over the years, long before the consultants came on the scene we had built generally excellent relationships with our clients. Staying in close contact and socializing with clients in a modest way was something we could not neglect, particularly in difficult markets. As long as clients understood what you were doing and why, and were convinced you always had their best interest in mind, you were likely to keep the account. The consultants sensed this and were jealous of that. In 1984 George Russell would play a small Machiavellian role in the demise of our firm.

Over time we met with some very prominent business people who would attend the meetings we had with their pension fund committees. I always made sure that we explained the often difficult market environment we worked in as best as we could and did not gild the lily, admitted our mistakes if there were any and stuck to the investment approach we used.

Record keeping is an important cornerstone of good portfolio management. You need to know what you own, what its cost is and when you bought it. We could not keep track of our portfolios without using a computer. In the beginning we "outsourced" our monthly appraisals and made changes by hand as we went along through a month. Now we decided to do it in-house. I asked Richard Johnston to take charge of that project, and he succeeded admirably after an intense struggle. Personal computers were just beginning to be used and were not powerful enough to handle all our accounts. So we hired a consultant who worked with portfolio management software he had cobbled together from a package designed for the management of options at a brokerage firm. Software designed specifically for portfolio management did not yet exist. It was far from ideal, but the best we could find. It is inconceivable in today's market that less than thirty years ago things were still so primitive. We benefited from a new trend that brought smaller computers (then called minicomputers) on the market that could be used free-standing in an office and did not need special rooms with all the wiring and cooling the older mainframes required. We bought a Wang computer, designed by a firm that does not exist anymore. The job of keeping our records straight was a major effort that was led by Joan Giannotti who was now our chief administrator and who oversaw a team of four or five young women who all had started out as secretaries and after displaying an aptitude for record keeping and administrative work, were promoted to work for Joan.

When Leo Clemente had completed our MPT system, he hired a young Chinese woman who could do the work for him so he could concentrate on his other skill – analysis of foreign stocks. The world had come full circle from the days when I was trying to get the portfolio people at Brown Brothers interested in foreign investments to the new popularity of foreign investments particularly in emerging markets and in Japan and Europe. Japan had been booming for several decades and its stock market did not seem to have a ceiling. I felt we needed to enter the foreign stock arena, albeit very gingerly. We organized a limited partnership with several foreign advisors to give the effort more substance. I also invited Adrian Cassidy, my friend from Pacific Telephone, now retired, to join the board of this small company. We put in some seed money and started to market it. There appeared to be quite an encouraging level of interest in it among our clients.

To replace Adams, I hired Michael DelPriore who was marketing the portfolio management services of the Bank of New York. Michael was a good choice and proved to be an excellent marketing and P/R man. We decided to hold a client conference somewhere in a nice resort area. The idea was not entirely original, but I think the way in which we worked it out was. We invited our clients to come with their spouses or significant others to a three-day conference where we would pay for their food and lodging and would organize seminars and speakers. We would have several well-organized meetings in the mornings and play golf or provide other entertainment in the afternoon. The spouses were also being entertained. At night we had a nice dinner with a good speaker. Some of the speakers received a honorarium, but others came for free. One of the people we had to pay for was Martin Feldstein, a Harvard professor who later became an important player in the George W. Bush administration. He was an excellent choice. Ed Keeley had the great idea to invite Ross Perot, who at that time ran EDS, a company he had founded and in which we had made a large investment. He flew over in his own plane and wowed the audience. Ross would later on run for president. He lost and by splitting the Republican ticket, pulled George H. W. Bush with him into defeat, allowing Bill Clinton to become president with only 41% of the popular vote.

We structured our seminars and meetings in such a way that our clients would participate in some of them. This gave them an opportunity to share their opinions with their opposite numbers at other companies. Michael took charge of the logistics of these meetings. They were a great success and I believe they created considerable good will. Our real clients were mostly larger corporations, of course, but the pension administrators were the people we dealt with and they were the ones we invited. These people often had a position that was part of the treasurer's department, but a bit on an often neglected side-track and they responded very well to our invitation to be an honored guest. Our first conference was at Seabrook Island near Charleston South Carolina, the second one was at the Breakers Hotel in Palm Beach and the third was at Hilton Head.

At some point around 1979, I was invited to join the boards of the Chemical Fund and the Surveyor Fund. For me this was more a burden than an honor. But it gave me an opportunity to get to know the septuagenarians who populated these boards. They had been treated with great deference by Bob Porter and had gradually become overly impressed with their own importance. The Marsh & McLennan people did not play well to this group and did not handle Bob Porter and his boards very well. When we merged with MMC, the boards had been introduced to the two or three top MMC people and had been addressed by Jack Regan, the CEO. He was an insurance marketing man who had a very good way with people, but as we discovered later, was not a great manager. Together with several other newcomers from Eberstadt and a number of Putnam people I had been invited to attend a day-long seminar in which people representing the major segments of the business explained their operations to the others. It was interesting but not very impressive and I came away with the thought that many of the insurance brokers were good at schmoozing but not very cerebral. The organization was very horizontal with many sectors doing their own thing without much synergy with the others. The leadership was concentrated in a small group, and that made it easy for me.

I had no trouble getting along with Ian Smith and Tom Waylett, both very intelligent men and exceptions to the Marsh rule, but the fund people had to work through Putnam and had difficulties with Larry Lasser who was not used to kowtowing to our fund directors as much as Porter and Dievler did. Larry knew on which side his bread was buttered and spent a great deal of time with Ian Smith. I believe his efforts to get close to Ian and Ian's tendency to deal with people on a very down-to-earth, somewhat casual but still precise way, made Larry think he could do whatever he thought was right. That did not sit well with Porter, who wanted to be treated with deference and as an equal by MMC's top management and not have to struggle to get Ian's ear. In the long run these frictions began to fester with Porter, and he began to work on his board to make another drastic change, i.e. forcing MMC to sell the management contract of Chemical Fund to another firm. After he succeeded in this not very difficult task he turned around and told Ian, "I am no longer in control of my board." Porter got several lead directors on his side, particularly Prof. Roger

Murray. I think Porter thought the threat of losing Chemical Fund would be seen as a major setback by the Marsh people. Unfortunately for him, and as it later appeared also for me, this was not the case. We were no more than a small sideshow for them.

Marsh had had a problem in early 1984 when an internal audit discovered that a woman who ran their company's own short-term cash investments had been cooking the books. She was arrested for fraud. She had lined her pockets and created fictitious returns on the company's short-term bond portfolio that were so good that people like Tom Waylett would ask me frequently why one had to bother with a stock portfolio while this wonder woman achieved much more stable and better results. This affair was all over the press and gave MMC a black eye. The MMC stock had suffered as investors wondered who was in charge and what kind of internal controls the company had. This situation had made Jack Regan gun-shy, and when the Chemical Fund people began to make noises about wanting to cancel the contract, he was inclined to let it go and not fight and risk another uproar in the press. In a special Chemical Fund board meeting I heard that Alliance Capital, a large money management organization, was a likely buyer. I went uptown to see Ian Smith and expressed my deep concern for the future of EAM. Ian assured me that he would not oppose the sale of EFM but wanted to keep EAM. This was a reassuring statement for me and I called my people together to make sure they would stay put and not jump ship. I had, of course, kept my portfolio managers, who were my friends, informed of all the intrigue and back-room dealing that went on for several weeks. As it turned out I did not know everything. Chemical Fund board members had huddled without me and made a deal. I was present when they met with the Alliance people, who assured them they could handle the intricacies of mutual fund administration, which are not easy as the fund business is highly regulated. Alliance had no mutual funds to offer and had correctly decided there was a great and growing demand among smaller investors for fund investment opportunities. I felt calm and reassured as I sat through these meetings until the very last day when a phone call was made to Jack Regan to announce the decision to switch the management contract to Alliance. Regan reacted irritated and abrupt, which was not strange after all the shenanigans he had been forced to go through with what for him was a very small part of the company. He made it clear that he did not want to have anything to do anymore with Eberstadt people and agreed to sell EFM and EAM to Alliance for $10 million. When I heard this, it was as if a trapdoor had opened under my chair. I felt completely betrayed and did not know what to say beyond telling the Chemical Fund board that in my opinion they had made a big mistake and that they had just ruined my career and what was more important, my business. I told them Alliance would not get many of the accounts that were on our books because I knew that most pension funds would refuse to go along with the sale of our business. Alliance was wrong in thinking they could just step into our shoes.

As it turned out, that was exactly what happened. The vast majority of our accounts balked at going along with the change. Only one or two accounts agreed. I left the meeting without waiting for it to end and went back to my office. I had an awful sinking feeling in the pit of my stomach and called Ian Smith to ask what had happened. He told me he had had a terrible argument with Regan and at one point threatened to resign, but Regan had insisted on the course he had chosen and Ian caved in and did not resign. It was a dark November evening and when I called my people together I told them what had happened and realized that at that same moment I had lost control over my staff. It was "sauf qui peut." Nobody felt they would have a career with Alliance and people immediately started to make phone calls to look for other options.

That evening I went over to the hotel of the World Trade Center where Egbert ten Cate, a Dutchman, had invited me to meet him and Mr. Schimmelpenninck, my old boss whom I had not seen in twenty-five years or longer. Ten Cate had been pestering me all day with phone calls saying they were in New York City for only a very brief time and wanted to meet me to see if they could do business with me. He had bought the name of Jonas en Kruseman after the firm had been sold to another larger private bank and wanted to use Mr. Schimmelpenninck's reputation and prestige to build a new business. I told him I was glad to meet them but could do nothing for them since the rug had been pulled out from under me that very same day. Schimmelpenninck had aged considerably and had trouble adjusting to the time change, but we had a nice talk. I told them that I could not invite them over to our house because Netty was in Holland, and I was not a good housekeeper. They said they had no time for that anyway. It was almost spooky to meet the man who had started me on my investment career thirty-four years earlier on the very day it all ended.

When I came home in Riverside that evening, I had dinner with George and Adriaan. They were both working in the city and had taken the trouble to come out and keep me company on this for me very difficult day, a gesture I appreciated immensely. I told them I did not want to do any cooking at home because I did not know how to. Now, many years later, I still have not mastered the art. So we went to a Japanese restaurant in Greenwich. I was still in a daze and picked something from the menu without knowing what it was. The waitress put a small alcohol burner on the table with a pot on top and told me, "you cook." After that dinner I went home and for the first and only time in my life, I had a completely sleepless night. The next day I went up to the Alliance office in midtown New York to have breakfast with David Williams, the CEO of Alliance, and Jon Fossel, his marketing man. The idea was to discuss the transfer of our business and accounts. I told them there was a chance we could keep most of our accounts if they left my business intact. They did not react to this proposal, and it was clear to me that they had other plans. Back in my office I began calling our clients to tell them what had happened. When asked what they should do, I told them I could not vouch for the kind of management they would get from Alliance. Alliance was a perfectly fine firm but I did not work for them and could not tell my clients what style of investment they had. I went uptown and visited with the head of the AT&T pension fund and brought him the same message. He and I had become quite friendly, and in early spring that year Netty and I had played golf with him at Hilton Head. He commented that he had never before had anybody call on him to ask him to please be fired. It was amazing to see how quickly our business unraveled. All my portfolio managers were calling their clients and within days it was all over. Tom Waylett came to visit our office, which he had never done before. He came to pick up the valuable Hudson River prints John Hill had bought some time ago. It was obviously more important for the Marsh McLennan people to salvage these prints than to rescue EAM. I received a call from George Russell, the consultant in Tacoma, who asked me, "how does it feel to be out of business?" A very thoughtful gesture that made me wonder how he had heard the news so soon. My suspicion has always been that he had "consulted" with Prof. Murray about the feasibility of folding our accounts into Alliance.

My business was gone, and I had lost all control over the people who worked for me. I called several meetings with all our employees to brief them on the developing situation and reviewed our future as a business with the portfolio managers. My top people and I had a major problem in that we all had signed a non-compete agreement with Marsh & McLennan, which was still valid. We did not think we could go out and start a business of our own as a continuation of EAM because we could not approach our old clients. We might have succeeded with that but somebody would have come up with the non-compete contract and hauled us into court. Following the lead of Porter and Dievler, several fund people had immediately switched their allegiance to Alliance, and they would not have hesitated to bring it up.

In the following days, people began to drift away. Ed Keeley briefly joined Alliance and managed as far as I know the one or two accounts that came over. Bill

Miller found a home with John Hartwell, a small, well-respected mutual fund and asset management firm. Richard Johnston started out to build a new firm of his own and managed to salvage one or two EAM accounts that declared they wanted to join him out of their own free will. He opened up shop with Bill Huff, who had found a sponsor for a bond firm he started. Several analysts moved over to Alliance and others found better spots elsewhere. I was most concerned with the account administrators and secretaries for whom having a job was an immediate necessity. Luckily, almost all of them found new employment, and I would meet them again in my subsequent wanderings around Wall Street.

The destruction of EAM was for me a very bitter and life-changing experience. It was in a way a pyrrhic victory for Alliance because they got almost nothing in return for what they paid for my firm. It was crystal clear to me that my days as president of a well-respected, large money management firm were over and that a comeback was almost impossible. In hindsight, the timing of the destruction of EAM was also very unfortunate. The Wall Street Journal reported that EFM an EAM had been sold "because of poor performance." This was obviously the explanation given by Alliance. Our performance had not been good for most of 1984, but it was not worse than most of our competitors. We were put out of business in late 1984, and in 1985 a bull market began that would, with one serious very short hiccup in 1987, last for more than fifteen years, bringing great new wealth to investors and especially to those who were handling their money. Individual retirement accounts, or IRAs and later so-called 401Ks became popular bringing many new investors to the market place and money flooded into mutual funds as most investors preferred to leave the management of their retirement portfolio to others. Alliance saw this coming and shifted the emphasis of its business from the management of individual portfolios to mutual funds. The two EFM funds provided them with an important first step in that direction, but the funds would soon disappear in a list of dozens of new ones Alliance would launch over the years. It was clearly an example of very poor timing for Porter, Dievler and their septuagenarians to sell their funds just when they stood at the cusp of what would have been a very profitable growth period for them. John Hill did not go along and kept control of his Energy Fund and moved it over to Putnam, which rewarded him with a seat on the Putnam board of trustees, a very lucrative directorship.

For several years Larry Lasser was the chief executive at Putnam, reaping millions of dollars in income and the Marsh & McLennan annual report would list Larry as the highest-paid executive of the company. Putnam in its heyday provided 14% of

Marsh's total revenue and 23% of its operating income. This all came to an untimely end in 2003 when a Putnam employee informed the SEC of illegal practices that benefited a small circle of preferred clients at Putnam. These people were given the opportunity to buy shares in Putnam funds invested in foreign stocks after the close. This was illegal, as all mutual fund transactions must be concluded before the funds are priced at the close of business on the New York Stock Exchange. By buying these funds invested in foreign markets after the close, on days when they knew New York had closed higher, these people were almost guaranteed a profit since foreign markets almost always followed New York and would open higher the next day, thus giving these new stockholders an immediate profit. They would cash in the next day by selling their holdings, repeating the procedure many times. Several Boston union bosses benefited from this scam and in return brought union pension fund moneys to Putnam. The informer needed police protection when it all came out because union thugs threatened to harm him. There had also been illegal self-dealing by some executives. Larry Lasser resigned. He received a retirement benefit of $15 million and the papers stated he had made more than $5 million in salary and $100 million in bonuses over the five years preceding his retirement. I do not think that he knew about the irregularities but he had obviously done a poor job in controlling his business. Still he benefited hugely from his tenure as Putnam's CEO. John Hill survived this situation and became chairman of the Putnam Fund board vowing to clean up the mess. He is still chairman. Marsh & McLennan sold Putnam Investments in 2006.

After a few days of confusion I retreated to Riverside and was suddenly cast into the role of a retiree, sitting at home with the newspaper, waiting for the mailman to arrive. In February, after a subdued Christmas at home, we went with our entire family to Dorset, Vermont, and stayed at the Dorset Inn for a few days to celebrate my sixtieth birthday. I was very keenly aware that this birthday was in itself a great hurdle for me to start anything new. I would be considered too old for most firms to offer me a new job. Marsh & McLennan offered outplacement consulting to me and my top staff and the others were given some group counseling. Most everybody landed on his or her feet fairly quickly except for me. It would take me some time before I landed a job. This was a difficult situation for me because my income stream, which had been substantial, stopped abruptly, but tuition bills and healthcare insurance charges continued. I also discovered a clearly unfair aspect of the U.S. capital gains tax. In the previous years I had received substantial Marsh & McLennan stock options. Since I was no longer employed by them these had to be exercised promptly. To finance this I had to sell other MMC stock at a big profit and pay capital gains tax over that. So in a year in which my income declined drastically, my tax bill went up!

My friend Doug Campbell, who had his own investment management firm in midtown Manhattan, offered me office space. This was an extremely generous and welcome gesture. It gave me a place in town to go to and the facilities of phones and secretaries, etc., to use whenever needed. I kept going to every investment conference or presentation I could attend and on one such occasion I was listening to a presentation over lunch by Mr. Luns, the former minister of foreign affairs of the Netherlands and former secretary general of NATO. Luns was an amusing speaker who pulled no punches and had an amazingly right-wing point of view for a Dutchman in government service. I happened to sit next to John van Eck, a man I knew vaguely who was of pure Dutch ancestry but had spent all his life in the U.S. and had built up a very successful mutual fund called International Investors. This fund was known as a gold fund. Its portfolio consisted of foreign stocks, but was almost 90% focused on investments in gold mining and metals trading stocks, many of them South African. In the days of rampant inflation this fund became very popular and had seen tremendous growth. John invited me over to see him at his office and after a nice conversation offered me a job as president of a subsidiary he wanted to establish which would diversify his business more and seek to attract pension fund money. Leo Clemente had already landed a job at van Eck's and gave me the impression that I could really achieve something there. So in the spring of 1984 I started at van Eck. The office was on 42nd street, across from Grand Central Station, a great luxury for me after decades of commuting downtown by subway. John was a perfect gentleman, son of a famous Dutch executive, Baron Pantaleon van Eck who was CEO of the U.S. Shell Oil Company. John married late in life. His wife was a charming German lady who gave him two sons, attractive young men who have since then taken over the firm and built it into a successful investment business. Unfortunately, one of them died young. But I would soon discover that the old saying, "you cannot teach an old dog new tricks," also applied to John. He ran his office in a casual, unstructured way, but since he was the sole owner he was in control. Following a jump in the gold price in the days of high inflation, he had handled a huge influx of investors money poorly and had encountered serious problems with the SEC. He had hired a very good administrator, but his office procedures still needed tightening up. John rented a whole new floor in the building for us, and I settled in there with Leo and Bill Jones, another EAM refugee. John's sales staff had been begging for another fund that could serve as an alternative investment for gold bugs who had become disenchanted with the decline in gold prices that had followed the run up. We got that fund going, but I could not organize a disciplined investment approach that everybody adhered to. There were a few people in the office who had been around for a long time and were unwilling to fit into the more structured investment organization I was proposing. The new fund was supposed to be an alternative, non-gold fund, but John immediately put some gold stocks in it, thereby destroying the purpose of the exercise. I had the feeling that John and I were not speaking the same language and that he had agreed to a good overall strategy but was not really interested in implementing it. I felt that life was too short and when I heard from Leo that he was leaving to join Lilia Clemente, his wife, in a new venture, I decided to join them. Lilia had run a very successful internationally invested fund at Paine Webber and wanted to start a firm of her own. As it turned out, I fell from the frying pan into the fire.

Lilia Clemente is the complete opposite of her husband Leo. As calm and reserved, well organized and introverted as Leo is, his wife Lilia is noisy, energetic, extroverted and chaotic. Both had been born and raised in the Philippines and had come to the U.S. to get graduate degrees in economics in Chicago. Lilia has a great sense of humor and is a talented self-promoter. A search for her name in "Google" will give a taste of this talent. For several years she had worked at the Ford Foundation as research director. She joined Payne Webber to provide them with global investment expertise. At Payne Webber she managed the Atlas fund and had achieved very good results in the early eighties when foreign markets were booming and you could hardly go wrong investing abroad, especially in Asia. Lilia had established strong connections with various investment people and firms abroad and wanted to build on these relationships to start her own firm, Clemente Capital. I have often wondered why she was so eager to leave Payne Webber and have sometimes thought she might have felt threatened there by the firm's internal controls that would try to get a better grip on her undisciplined disorganized investment style and enforce stricter compliance with regulatory rules.

What was very important for her firm's future viability was that she had a "sugar daddy" (not in the improper sense of the word) in her connection with John Amos of Columbus, Georgia, the founder of AFLAC, the American Family Life Assurance Company. The company is now the largest provider of supplementary life and health insurance in the U.S. and Japan. John started AFLAC in 1955 with his two brothers. While working with the military in Japan, John perceived a need for health insurance, particularly cancer insurance. He found that many Japanese suffer from stomach and intestinal cancer, which seems to be a genetic and diet-related problem. Somehow John managed to get permission from the Japanese authorities to start selling cancer insurance in Japan. This was a highly unusual achievement in a country that kept itself hermetically closed to outside business interests for many years. They probably thought this company was of little consequence and could be tolerated. John organized a strong sales force that employed not only men, as was then and is still traditional in Japan, but also women. He recruited housewives who would go around their neighborhood and visit with friends to sell insurance. It became an extraordinarily successful business that soon outgrew the U.S. stateside effort. John met Lilia and they struck it off and established a business relationship. John invested in a limited partnership Lilia had set up as a first effort to independently manage global money, and AFLAC became an investor in Clemente Capital, providing us with the funds we needed to get the firm off the ground.

We had to register as investment advisers, find office space and hire people. Particularly the hiring proved to be a difficult issue. Lilia hired people she knew from Philippine connections and promised jobs to others without following through. She made arrangements with people to work for us part-time or half-time, without checking with me, and promised full-time jobs to others without checking if we could pay for them. I was president, but often felt I was running hard to catch up with all the moves. Several times we ran out of money and had to ask AFLAC for more, and when we had our first Christmas party, Lilia organized a luncheon in a much-too-expensive restaurant for which I had to pay with my personal credit card because we had insufficient funds in our checking account to pay with a company check. I managed to find several people who had solid administrative, accounting and mutual fund experience and gave them jobs at Clemente, but over all we had way too many employees. It was difficult to establish even a semblance of a disciplined investment approach, something we could present to larger institutional investors. Had we been able to establish a well-articulated investment policy and a clear global strategy, backed up with whatever meager results we could show, we would probably have succeeded quite well because there was great demand for global investment expertise in the market in those days, and Lilia had excellent contacts all over the world.

As we lurched from one crisis to the next, we did manage to launch a closed-end fund, the Clemente Global Growth Fund, which was listed on the New York Stock Exchange and had a decent board of directors, including my old friend Adolf Sirtema van Grovestins who would fly over twice a year to attend meetings and contributed significantly to our investment knowledge. Lilia got the Ford Foundation's former president, Tom Lennagh, to join the board and I recruited Adrian Cassidy, formerly of Pacific Telephone. We also asked Sam Nakagama, formerly research director at Kidder Peabody, to join as well as Bob Oxnam, the former president of the Asia Society, so we had a respectable group there. Bob was fluent in Mandarin and a true China expert. The introduction of the fund went reasonably well although we had trouble selling it to the public since it was known that most closed-end funds sold at a discount to net asset value immediately after the offering. This also irritated the Japanese investors Lilia had solicited, often with promises that were not realistically achievable. We soon became a target for people who tried to raid closed-end funds, break them open (i.e. convert them into an open-end funds) and cash in on the difference between its market value and asset value. We got into a court fight with the son of T. Boone Pickens, a Texas investor and oil tycoon. The son did not have the firing power his father had and we won in court, but the handwriting was on the wall. Clemente Capital struggled on for several years, but was chronically short on cash because Lilia kept spending more than the firm took in.

In 1988 I made a trip to Japan, Hong Kong, Manila, Singapore and Djakarta, trying to find out what all the connections Lilia claimed to have in these places amounted to and what if anything we could do to improve our business. Netty went along (at my expense) and we had a grand trip. We visited Janet in Kyoto and afterwards took the bullet train to Tokyo where I had a few business meetings and quickly learned that doing business with the Japanese meant you had to do it their way. For instance, if you entered a conference room, you as the visitor could not sit just anywhere, but only as far away from the door as possible to indicate you were not in a hurry to leave. Nothing could be done until you sat in the proper chair. Still fighting a monumental case of jet lag, I sat through meetings in stuffy offices with market analysts who were telling me exactly what their market was going to do for the rest of the year. They were totally convinced that the unprecedented rise in stock prices they had witnessed for years would go on forever. The collapse of Japanese stocks that would come about 15 years later must have been a nasty surprise for them. The only place where I felt we could find some real business connections was Hong Kong, a sophisticated market with many mostly British professionals. I had a good introduction with one of the most powerful Chinese investment groups, but soon discovered they were not interested in doing anything with us, and instead of telling me that up front, they let me come back several times for visits that were almost insulting because whenever I arrived, the person I was supposed to meet was either busy or did not show up, and whatever research in local investment opportunities I could do amounted to nothing.

Jakarta was our last stop. It was odd for me to be back there after forty years of independence. Traces of the Dutch colonial days were visible everywhere for people like us who knew what to look for. But the city now had skyscrapers, and a huge mosque had been built on the beautiful square that used to be a large expanse of grass and trees at the center of the city with the governor general's palace and several Dutch churches and other structures surrounding it. Our hotel was also on the square, and we heard the call to prayer loud and clear, amplified with loudspeakers. In one of the offices I visited, a charming young girl stepped forward and said in Dutch, "Dag Meneer" (Good Day Sir). So they had me pegged. A friendly man who was connected to one of Lilia's sisters, who was herself a successful business person, guided us around town and we visited the Old Dutch fort where it all began. You could climb undisturbed into the tower and get on the roof after removing some old boards. We also hired a driver to bring us up into the mountains to Bogor, on the way to Bandung, where we visited the old very famous botanical garden that was started by the Dutch. The gardens had been kept up somewhat haphazardly. Inside the garden was the palace where the Dutch governor general would stay to enjoy the cool mountain air during the hot season. Nearby were the old graves of former Dutch officials and their wives. On the way up we had stopped for lunch at a small restaurant which had a nice view over the mountains. On the menu we saw "poffertjes," a very Dutch traditional dish. Times change, but many things still linger on.

After my return I made a last effort to get Lilia and Leo to listen to reason and accept my ideas for the survival of the firm, which included the firing of several people Lilia had hired who were not contributing to our investment work and drastic economies on her spending on perks, travel and many other things. This effort did not succeed. Lilia became very agitated and started talking in Tagalog to Leo, who looked helpless. Soon after this I decided to leave. After my departure little changed, Lilia moved the firm to more glamorous and much more expensive offices in the then-new Carnegie Tower and a few years later the firm went broke and closed its doors. Before that happened, I spent some years on the board of the closed-end fund with Adolf. Ultimately the fund was taken over by a group who were seeking a listed company for their own fund and I resigned from the board with some relief.

It was now around 1989 and I still wanted to do something in the investment business. I started a firm of my own which I called "Pilot Rock Investments" after the street where we lived. I soon discovered how hard it is to get something off the ground without any clients. I started a so-called "S" corporation and registered as an investment advisor. Before I could do any serious solicitation work, I found myself working hard for the tax man and the regulators, particularly the Connecticut State ones. Bureaucrats want all businesses to fill in their forms and answer their question-naires and pay upfront registration fees, etc. Nobody wonders how the time and money spent on these inquiries is produced. After a while I linked up with the Lake brothers. Ron and Rick (Frederick) Lake were known to me through the Clemente firm. They had started a business of their own and needed office space and a regis-tered advisor. I was registered and had a small office cubicle in Old Greenwich, and they had accounts that afforded them a start. We hit it off well and I spent some time with them helping them build up their business. They started out with several significant clients, a big difference with my own fledgling efforts. Of all the business I solicited through presentations before groups of friends at the yacht club and other venues, only a meager two or three came on the books, and after about a year or two I decided to call it quits and become a full-time retiree. I was sixty four years old. Time to accept the inevitable.

25 : *Retirement*

The fallacy about retirement is thinking that you are able to relax, travel the world, play golf, sail your boat and do whatever else you like. Travel we did and we took up golf, but relaxing was not a possibility for me, partly because I like to be busy and also because in America many organizations expect you as a retired man to join, to volunteer and spend time working for them and you feel a moral obligation to do that. Soon you find your calendar filling up with dates where you have to be available for a social event, a meeting or some task you have offered to perform. To find time for travel and other recreational activities becomes more and more difficult. In Europe, at least in the Netherlands, people are more accustomed to having all social needs taken care of by government institutions and are much more inclined to lean back and let things take their natural course. Not so in the land of Uncle Sam.

I had been a member of the Riverside Yacht Club since 1964 but had been too busy to be really active in club affairs and be more than a weekend sailor and participant in many social events. We always went on a summer cruise, and when the annual cruise was introduced by the club, we went on that event too and we occasionally took part in races for cruising boats. As we had more spare time, over the years, the club became a very important part of our life and an organization we truly love. It started sometime before my retirement. My good friend Bob Barnum, commodore in 1982 and 1983, roped me in to chair his budget committee. He taught me an important lesson, which was that dealing with volunteer organizations is very different from working in a business environment. You sit on boards with people who are selected for reasons that often do not relate to their ability to manage a business and who are sometimes not used to sit on boards. They waste time with unnecessary or unwanted speeches and many are in love with the sound of their own voice.

After working several evenings to put the budget together with my committee, I had to present it to the board of governors, who then would question many of our numbers and assumptions. It was in my view, particularly odd, that the treasurer and/or other board members, who would have to work with the budget throughout the year were not involved in its design but felt free to criticize it in the board meeting. In my second year I proposed that the committee be eliminated and replaced by a group of governors and committee chairs working under the chairmanship of the treasurer. And so it has been for ever after. Later I became a governor myself and the next year treasurer of the club, first under Commodore Bob Curtis and later under Mike Smith. Bob was a gregarious "townie," as they call people who are born, bred and work in Greenwich as opposed to the commuters and the fly-by-night operators of investment firms that moved into town for tax reasons. Bob knew everybody and was a very good sailor. He found Don Marsden willing to become assistant treasurer with me. Don and I and our wives became good friends. It is customary for the assistant treasurer to follow the treasurer after his two-year term was up. However, Don decided to move to Branford to be closer to his beloved Yale so I served another two-year term under Michael Smith, a very capable man. Mike worked as a sales executive for a major paper company and traveled all over the world.

My stint as the club's money man for Bob Curtis started with an immediate crisis. The office of the club was staffed by two ladies, both named Lorraine. Lorraine West handled membership administration and Lorraine Remnitz was the bookkeeper. Both had been loyal employees for many years and knew all the ins and outs of the club's affairs and all the administrative peculiarities. Nobody else did. Unfortunately Lorraine Remnitz died of a heart attack a few weeks after I stepped into my job, and we were faced with a huge problem. We had to keep the administration going without knowing the first thing about it. Don had a brilliant idea. He told me that the young barkeeper in the Yard Arm Bar, a native of the Philippines, had earned an accounting degree in his homeland. So we asked Mel (Melando) Agudo if he would be interested in trying out for club accountant. Obviously he was. In 1988 personal computers were beginning to become more widely used, and Mel owned one and had worked with it at home. I decided to ask Mel to start from scratch and switch everything over from what amounted to a quill-pen system to the digital age. He did that successfully and soon we were the first private club in Greenwich to have an electronic bookkeeping system. Mel became very successful in his job and was made comptroller after a year or so. We made many improvements in the club's systems that are still in place, saved money by taking the payroll administration in house and improved controls by installing a computerized time clock system. We also changed the chit system the club used to have with members signing off on unintelligible punch cards for their meals and drinks. The wait staff now punched in orders to the kitchen and members were asked to sign a copy of a small printout that listed everything they had ordered. This eliminated the time wasted in arguments with members who claimed they were charged for things they had not ordered. Most important, Mel produced many management reports that for the first time gave us a clear and timely insight in the club's business. Mel stayed with the club for many years until he returned to the Philippines, where he now runs a hotel he owns.

A highpoint for us was the club's centennial celebration in 1988. There were many parties culminating in a ball in costumes of the immediate post–Civil War period. The club was organized on May 25, 1888, by its first commodore, George I Tyson, and ten friends, many of whom had served in the same unit in the Civil War – the 3rd Brigade of the 1st Division of the V Corps – and elected to use its pennant for our burgee. The origins of the club and its burgee were known, but I pride myself on having made at least a small contribution to keep its history going by writing about it. After Mike Smith's tenure as commodore ended he was succeeded by Jim Vaughn. I was succeeded by Jim Farrell as treasurer and had still one year left of my obligation to serve as a governor. At RYC we had for years enjoyed a newsletter called "The Burgee," which was started by Chape Lawson a former vice commodore who is a gifted writer. Chape built the Burgee into a very readable monthly document full of interesting articles and quirky comments he wrote with a very special feel for words and for humorous situations. I always enjoyed reading Chape's writings, but others like my old friend Frank Capers harrumphed that they needed a dictionary to read what was going on in the club. When after many years Chape decided to retire as editor

THIS IS OUR IDEA OF HOW PEOPLE LOOKED IN 1888.

I RECEIVE THE TRENARY TROPHY FROM OUR GOOD
FRIEND COMMODORE GERALD ISAACSON.

of the Burgee, two young women took over. They had good computer skills and knew how to write a newsletter, but the Chape flavor was lost. When these two ladies decided they could not do it any longer, Jim Vaughn was in a bind and announced in a board meeting that he would have to discontinue the Burgee if nobody stepped up to the plate to write it. Since I then had the time and thought I could make it work, I volunteered. But I had only a few days to learn how to write in the Burgee format (two columns on a page) and how to use the, then for me, very new Microsoft "Word" software to do it. My first attempt was less than perfect, but gradually I learned, and for eight years I wrote the Burgee almost every month. This became a labor of love for me that gave me great pleasure although it was sometimes hard work to meet a deadline and type the five or six pages of text. It was a document that was produced on light blue paper, with text only, no pictures. Chape had chosen the blue color but that just happened to be the one and only color Xerox copy machines would not accept for pictures or copying and that made duplicating it difficult. Of course digital photography did not yet exist. Towards the end of my eight year tenure as editor, I decided it was time to update the Burgee and make it look better. So we started to print on glossy white paper with a different and nice masthead and more and more pictures. Now the Burgee is a very different periodical with a modern look, lots of pictures and, perhaps unfortunately, less text. It looks great and serves as a very useful medium to bind the membership together. It was the stories about events and mishaps in the club or other things nautical that had given me the most pleasure to write and they are now mostly gone.

In 1996, after I retired from the Burgee and after a decent interval the club honored me by awarding the Commodore Trenary Trophy to me, to my great surprise and joy. This trophy is the highest honor the club can give a member. As is customary, I received a "keeper" model of the trophy. It gave me special satisfaction to receive this particular model because it was built by

our good friend David Osler. For several years he had been making models for the trophy, which is awarded annually at the club's spring commissioning. Mine was the last one he could make as he was gradually overcome by the horrible affliction of PLS (Primary Lateral Sclerosis), which has kept him immobilized in bed, unable to speak or move his limbs for what is now more than thirteen years.

Netty and I visit him weekly and never fail to marvel at his ability to cope with his problems and still enjoy life despite the very limited scope it has for him.

Adriaan was still in Brussels when the decade of the eighties started. He did not really hate it there, but he was, as far as we could see, not very happy either. The job was basically to assist with the start up of a local office of Continental Insurance. It brought no progress or excitement and his boss was a narrow minded Belgian who was deathly afraid of competition and throttled Adriaan's progress. The climate of Belgium's capital, notoriously gloomy and cloudy also did not help. But he did meet some nice Americans who became lifelong friends. As good Europeans, the Belgians and Dutch are not very open to strangers and kept their doors closed. Adriaan frequently visited his relatives and grandparents in Wassenaar, which was very much appreciated by them and gave him an opportunity to get to know his cousins better. I suspect that he did not mind being transferred in 1980 to Panama City, a sunnier and more interesting place. To illustrate Ade's travels over the years it may be of interest to follow a small Dutch Biedermeyer cabinet that Netty had in her room when she was a young girl. When we lived in Heemstede, we used it as a sideboard in our dining room and subsequently moved it to Riverside. We gave it to Adriaan and he took it to New York City and on to Brussels. It now went back across the pond for a third time, to Panama. In future years it would travel back to Greenwich, from there to New York City, thence to California and now it is with Ade in his house in Harrisburg, North Carolina. Luckily most of these moves were paid for by the companies Adrian worked for. Otherwise it and many other possessions may have ended up in some second hand furniture store.

In 1980 Rich graduated from Brunswick School and was accepted at Trinity College in Hartford, a good school he would enjoy very much. It was at Trinity that he developed his lifelong love for the theater and for performing in plays.

The moralistic and hapless President Carter built another obstacle on his road to reelection by boycotting the Moscow Olympics. The Russians had invaded Afghanistan and the boycott was in protest of that. It was a move that was not appreciated by the American public. We would, of course, hear much more about that strange country, Afghanistan, in the years to come. In March of 1981 Ronald Reagan, our new president, was shot by a deranged young man. Luckily he survived. When this happened, Netty and I were enjoying a brief vacation on Captiva Island in Florida with Janet and Rich. We were in the middle of a round of golf when an announcement came over the loudspeaker system that the president had been shot. We had visions of the drama surrounding the death of Kennedy and the national trauma it caused. This time there was a better outcome. Reagan was soon seen waving from his hospital room and was reported to have said to his doctors, "I hope you are all Republicans."

In the spring of 1981 George graduated from the Columbia School of Architecture in an enormous and impressive ceremony in which degrees were presented to hundreds of Columbia College students as well as people from various graduate schools. While taking pot shots at leaders is more common in the U.S. where almost anybody can buy a gun and exercise his right to bear arms, it is not an exclusively American phenomenon. On the day of George's graduation we were all abuzz about an assassination attempt on the pope in Rome. This also did fortunately not succeed, but it did serious harm to the pontiff. George started life in New York City in the manner customary for young people in Gotham. On a Sunday afternoon and with the help of his brothers, he moved quickly and surreptitiously into a rent controlled apartment of a friend who had moved to California. Once George was inside the little hovel, the rules state that the landlord could not raise the rent or evict him. His brothers came back shaking their heads and saying they would never want to live in a place like that.

Adriaan quit his job at Continental Insurance because life in Panama, while pleasantly old colonial in style, offered no prospects whatsoever for advancement. He lived in a very nice apartment there, had a company car and the services of an office factotum, a man called Napoleon, who would pick him up from the airport when he returned from the U.S. no matter how late at night. His boss was a retired army officer who was a prime example of the people who had for decades enjoyed cushy jobs in the Canal Zone, doing little beyond socializing in their club and on the golf course. Adriaan had found a job with the treasurer's office at Anaconda Ericsson in Greenwich, so he could return home and enjoy life here with his old friends. The

Swedish Ericsson Telephone Company, in a classic reaction by a mature company to market trends that were already passé, had bought the telephone wire business of Anaconda Copper Co., thus becoming a major factor in the U.S. hard wire telephone business, just when the new era of wireless communications and optical fiber was appearing over the horizon.

Meanwhile Janet had moved through the Greenwich Academy with good academic results and a great deal of sports activity. She had been class president for several years and when asked by me why she wanted to be in such a leadership position, she responded, "because I want to be in charge." We thought she was clearly destined to be in an executive position in her future career. It did not turn out that way, but what is better, a good life or decades of stress, office politics and personal pressures? She ended her Academy years by being vice president of the school. When graduation day came in 1982, Netty and I had volunteered to be chaperones of the graduation ball, which took place in the Manursing Beach Club. When we arrived at the black-tie event, the ball was ready to start and huge stacks of speakers were ready to blast out ear-splitting "music" as was and is still customarily required for the amusement of younger people. It was in the middle of the week and my prospects were for a night of maybe two or three hours of sleep before I had to catch the train to New York City again. To my great relief the speakers blew out the entire electric system of the club after about two hours and appeared irreparable. Thus ended this festive ritual in a big disappointment for Janet and her friends, but not for us.

Janet had been accepted at Union College in Schenectady, New York. A good school with many engineers and President Chester Arthur among its alumni. We had never heard of this president, but a statue on campus attested to his historical significance. Arthur was vice president under Garfield and when the latter was assassinated he moved up. He sported a big, handlebar moustache and had a background as a party hack, but when he became president, he changed his stripes and served as a remarkably incorruptible leader who cleaned up the civil service, much to the chagrin of his former buddies.

Janet settled down quickly at Union and in no time found a group of women friends, started to play field hockey, joined a sorority and moved into the party scene. These efforts to quickly establish a hectic social life resulted in a letter with an "Academic Warning" which arrived at our doorstep and according to Janet prompted me to make a phone call in which I told her that if she did not shape up right away she could go to a secretarial school and get a job. This did the trick, and since then we never had anything to worry about in her academic performance. Janet related this story to me when I was in my eighties. I had completely forgotten it.

At Trinity Rich joined the DKE fraternity, known for its hard-partying frat boys and started to live in their house off campus. I don't think he was the hard-partying kind, but he did find many friends there. We visited him there once, saw his room and wondered why anybody would want to live in such a horrible dilapidated place. Rich seemed to like it and began to be active in theatre arts. He had done some very good acting in Brunswick and now could expand on his work there. In his final college years he had roles in five plays. Richard graduated in the year George and Maggie decided to separate and pursue their careers on their own.

We also witnessed the beginning of the disintegration of the Soviet Union. President Leonid Brezhnev died, and as is customary in Russia, was carried in an open casket to his grave by a group of doddering elderly Soviet leaders. He was succeeded by Andropov, also an ancient man who died two years later, and his successor Chernenko, no spring chicken either , lasted less than a year after him. Seeing one procession after another of grim old men in fur hats stumbling along with the coffin of a comrade gave the impression that the regime was on its last legs and it was. The younger and much livelier Gorbachov, who came along in 1984, would leave a much more vigorous impression. He reformed the regime drastically with a movement called "glasnost" that provided more transparency and openness. This would ultimately lead to the implosion of the Soviet Union and the end of the cold war as we had known it for forty years. The death of Brezhnev was the first event in a long series of disparate happenings that would bring this major change about. The eighties will forever be remembered as the decade in which the cold war ended.

A strange discovery in London, which seemed in a way related to the cold war, touched me because I had known the man at the center of the tale and at the end of the rope. On a winter night the Italian banker Roberto Calvi was found dead, hanging off the Black Friars Bridge near the City of London with a noose around his neck. When I was at Brown Brothers Harriman, I had visited him twice. He was atypical for an Italiann – very calm and quiet and unable to speak English. I would speak with him with the help of a translator or using German from time to time. It appeared that he had commanded a large unit of the Italian army on the eastern front near Stalingrad. When it became clear that all was lost there, he managed to load his unit on a train and trundle back to Italy. At least that was the story I heard. His men and many Italians revered him for this. He became a banker at the Banco Ambrosiano, an important private bank with very strong ties with the Vatican. We did not do much

746

business together, but he was as helpful to me as he could. In 1981 an inquiry by the Italian Ministry of Finance revealed that the bank was hiding more than a billion dollars in losses, and there were funds missing that had been secretly moved outside the country in violation of the then-prevailing foreign exchange rules. Calvi himself was accused of moving several millions to his own account outside the country. During the investigation he was told to stay in the country, but he escaped under a false name with a false passport. Two days later he was found hanging in London. The British authorities decided it was a suicide, but the Italians who have a much more lively imagination in situations like this, discovered that he could not possibly have hanged himself because of the way in which the scaffolding, of which he was found hanging, was constructed. For years Italian magistrates followed up and in 2002 they tried to convict a group of Mafiosi of murdering Calvi. From statements made by some of the Mafiosi, it became clear that Calvi was indeed murdered, but there was insufficient evidence to convict anybody. Several books were written about the case and a movie was made that was suppressed by the Vatican. In the years since his death, Calvi was often called God's banker and other names tying him to the Vatican, which suffered a significant loss in the bank's collapse. After the cold war ended, it was revealed that the Banco Ambrosiano had been used by the Vatican to transfer money to the Polish anticommunist movement. John Paul II, the pope we had at that time was Polish and cared about the struggles of his compatriots to free themselves. It was also revealed that Calvi was a member of a secretive Freemasons organization that wielded significant influence in Italy. This seems odd given the Catholic Church's centuries-old opposition to the Freemasons. Calvi's death remains a mystery wrapped in all kinds of enigma's and suspicions about Mafia involvement, the Catholic Church's ways of acting below the radar, and the Freemasons doing the same.

Iran invaded Iraq in 1983, starting a bloody war that lasted several years and was mostly ignored by the West. But it opened a cycle of turmoil and war in the Middle East that is continuing to plague us. The U.S. embassy in Beirut was attacked by a suicide bomber, then a new phenomenon. There were seventeen deaths. The U.S. invaded the small island nation of Grenada. We visited that island in our first Caribbean cruise on the Island Belle and loved it. In the interim a strongly left-leaning authoritarian government had taken over and was smothering all hope we would see a democratic government there. The presence of a number of American youth in a medical school, who had to be protected from communist aggression, gave the Reagan administration enough cause to send in the airborne troops to eliminate the government and replace it with a more democratic one, friendly to us.

Richard went to Austria, benefiting from an opportunity to spend a semester abroad. He enjoyed Vienna and stayed with a nice landlady who told him she was impressed with my ability to speak German when we called him and she answered the phone. We omitted telling her that I learned to speak German during the occupation in Holland where Austrians ruled the roost. Rich would occasionally send us humorous postcards signed "your Sohn." It was not clear to us what he learned from the Austrians, but it was a mind stretching experience for him.

Rich graduated from Trinity in 1984 with a major in history and found a job with Video Productions in West Hartford, a small struggling outfit. A year later he would find a job with ESPN, then a beginning cable network focused on sports. Rich became a mailroom employee and occasionally worked as a driver of the company limo. In subsequent years he would move up into real TV work, first as a video tape librarian and then as a studio technician. ESPN was located in Bristol, Connecticut, a town it obviously chose for its reservoir of cheap labor, not its bucolic charm.

The market started a seven-months decline of 15% in early 1984. This poor investment environment would not help the situation surrounding the destruction of my business later that year. But family life went on. To our horror George casually resigned from a job with a good architect's firm to travel to China and teach architecture to Chinese students during the summer. George explained to his hand wringing parents that in the architectural profession it is quite normal to make frequent employment changes, and firms will hire people when they have a new big project, only to let many of the new hires go when the project is done. Janet used her semester abroad by making use of the "Semester at Sea" project which involved a voyage around the world in a ship specifically equipped for that purpose. She went to Korea, China, Hong Kong, Sri Lanka, Egypt and Greece and ended up back in Florida around Christmas time. She had a fantastic experience that may have planted the seed for her future global roaming. Unfortunately the trip ended on a sour note. Janet and two other girls had met a trio of Greek boys who invited them over to their apartment and when they got back outside, the car with their cameras was missing and the Greeks were gone.

In early 1985 Netty and I began to get seriously worried about my parent's ability to live alone in their house. We had stepped up the frequency of our visits and started calling regularly to find out what was going on. I had to take Pa's car away from him. It had been left unused in the garage so long that it did not move anyway. We learned from our friend Kitty Witteveen that there was a group of ladies in Wassenaar who would come and visit with elderly people to keep them company and make sure they were coping all right. We started with that group and found a few very nice ladies who would come for a small fee. It was difficult to explain to Ma what these people were and to make sure she would not start treating them as servants. This arrangement did not last long. On another visit I found Pa and Ma had slipped into a disheveled state. They were in need of haircuts and had lost a lot of weight because they were eating poorly. The house was not clean despite the weekly visits of a cleaning lady who was prevented by Ma from using suitable cleaning implements.

I decided to make arrangements for live-in help. The group I found was connected to the visiting team. It was a solid organization run by a very nice lady in The Hague. The helpers had to be paid in cash "under the table." The Dutch tax people seemed to know about this but tolerated it because there was a severe shortage of beds in government run homes for the elderly. There is very little in the Netherlands that escapes the eagle eyes and long arm of the tax people. I found my good friend Eelco Apol willing to handle the household expenses and pay the ladies. All was set, the first lady arrived to introduce herself, and she told me she would come in about five days and stay for a week. Then she would rotate weekly with two other women. I went home happy to have resolved a difficult situation. But after a few days I got a phone call telling me that my parents would not let the helper into the house. My mother, who was always very suspicious of strangers and got more difficult in that respect as she got older, did not want a stranger in her house and kitchen. Pa went along with her opposition to avoid problems. I had no choice but to fly back again. It was the Fourth of July weekend and I could go back and forth in three days. Once there I raised hell and told them how much of a problem they were creating for me and themselves. It was very tough to treat my parents that way, but it was necessary. Once the lady was inside and started cooking a nice meal, all problems were over and for the next twelve years a group of good people would take excellent care of my parents.

When George and Maggie had finalized their divorce, George decided to buy a condo on 13th Street. We thought it would be best if I was the buyer because I could use the tax deduction the mortgage would yield while George having not much income had no use for a gimmick like that. So we had to meet with the board of this strange building where we had a serious conversation with the lady who was president. She received us in her messy little apartment with her bicycle leaning against the kitchen table. She was an artist of some sort like many other residents in that building. Dressed in my Wall Street uniform, blue suit and tie, black shoes and armed with my attaché case, I had to prove that I had enough income to pay the maintenance fee of the apartment. George thought it a very good buy because he was on the top floor and had roof rights so he thought he could eventually expand his one bedroom abode into the roof above him. In the meantime, the roof had been freshly tarred and in the summer heat the tar would melt and drip through the planks of George's ceiling onto the ratty carpeting below. The seller was a lady with considerable financial problems, and at the closing I was squeezed into a little room with a large group of people. There were tough-looking IRS guys, various lawyers, people from Bloomingdale's and other places where she owed money. I was asked to write a series of checks for all these people and a small one with the residue for the owner. A few years later I was called in by the New York State tax people who suspected I was using my Connecticut address as a foil to escape their taxes and was really living on 13th Street. I sent them a letter with pictures of the entrance door of 13th Street with the garbage bags piled up on the sidewalk and a homeless man snoozing in front, together with one of our house in Riverside with the rose garden in bloom. After George moved out, I was stuck with this prime property. Later Janet would live there for a while, and after that I found a renter, a Ms. Berkowitz who had constant complaints, did not pay her rent and disappeared without leaving a forwarding address. I was ecstatic when the apartment was finally sold to another architect, who also had plans to renovate and use the roof rights. I hope he did.

My decision in 1986 to leave Van Eck and join the Clemente's was a bad one. Clemente is now bankrupt and Van Eck is a large, prosperous investment organization run by one of John's sons. In the previous year Ferdinand Marcos, the authoritarian president of the Philippines, had been pushed out by a popular uprising. What sealed his fate was the murder of Benigno Aquino, a popular politician who had lived in exile in the US and had returned to the Philippines to take charge after Marcos. Upon his arrival at the Manila airport, Aquino was murdered on the tarmac. His widow Corazon Aquino became president and enjoyed immense popularity in the country as well as abroad. The Philippines seemed to have entered a period of democracy and economic growth that inspired many people all over the world. Lilia Clemente's father, who was a lawyer, had been associated with Aquino and was chosen to join a commission to rewrite the constitution of the Philippines, which had been altered beyond recognition by Marcos. Marcos enjoyed a mild form of protection from the Reagan administration and was allowed to stay on the Hawaiian Islands. He had run a kleptocracy and the excesses of his household, and especially of his wife Imelda, became world famous. She was said to have a collection of a thousand pairs of shoes. The Marcos owned a large townhouse in New York City that had been taken over by the Aquino people. Netty and I visited the empty house one evening with Lilia and Leo, let in by a buddy of theirs who had a key. We marveled at its kitschy interior and extravagant display of wealth. We took a small elevator up to the top floor to see a disco room Imelda had built there. The elevator got stuck for a while, and we realized we were alone in the building and nobody would find us for quite a while if we could not get out. Luckily the elevator went up after we pushed a few buttons.

Janet graduated from Union College that year with a double major, economics and art history. Soon after graduation she left for Japan to try to live there for a while, teaching English. We had considerable misgivings about this plan but realized we now had an adult daughter who chose her own path through life. She arrived in Tokyo and found the hotel rates there way above her budget so she moved into some sort of youth hostel and from there to Osaka, where she managed to get a work permit and found a job teaching English. Two remarkable achievements for a non-Japanese-speaking young woman in a country that is far from hospitable to foreign workers seeking employment, but where people yearn to speak English and flock to language schools. These language schools were interested in hiring native English speakers. She felt it helped she was a blond, a much sought after attribute in a country where everybody has black hair. Also she was smart enough to dress for business for her interview and not casually, as she noted some of her contemporaries did. Janet went to work in Osaka but commuted to Kyoto where she lived. Kyoto is a beautiful, unspoiled traditional Japanese city that was not bombed during the war because, as the story goes, President Roosevelt had visited there and ordered the air force to spare it.

At home, Adriaan left Ericsson and started a firm of his own marketing specialized software for the preparation of tax returns by tax consultants. He called his firm Abacus. He worked hard to get it off the ground but after struggling for a year had to give it up. The entire world of electronic data processing was in a tremendous flux in those years and many entrepreneurs managed to carve out very profitable niches, but many others discovered that their niche was not unique enough or were bypassed by new technology. The latter happened to Adriaan.

1987 Saw the first serious signs of extreme market volatility, a phenomenon that has stayed with us since then and that has gotten more worrisome as the years went by. The Dow Jones climbed for the first time above 2,000 and in April reached 2,400. It briefly rose to 2,700 in August, only to start a 41% decline from there. It surged back to 2,568 in September and on October 19, a day we would later call Black Monday, it dropped 508 points or 22.6% in one day, the biggest one day decline in history. At Clemente Capital, we did not know what had hit us. A visitor to our office was so distraught and disoriented that he crashed into a glass door, hurting his face badly.

In the winter of 1988 when Netty and I made a swing through the Far East we visited Janet in Japan and found her happily ensconced in a very small rather primitive house in Kyoto which she shared with two or three other Gaijin (strangers). We toured with her around the city, which seemed to consist of thousands of temples with a few houses interspersed among them.

Shortly after our return from our trip through Asia, on March 10, 1988, Pa died at age ninety-five. He had been in hospital with a broken hip, the usual problem with elderly people who fall while going to the bathroom at night. He was transported back home, where he had nursing help around the clock. Adriaan and I came over right away after Eelco Apol called us with the sad news. We were there when the funeral director came to fetch Pa to carry him out of the house he had lived in for almost forty years and where he had spent many good years in retirement. We had a very large turnout at Pa's funeral, many more people than we expected. Netty came with George and Richard. Janet was too far away. The two Bas's were there from Friesland and there were many good friends of ours who had taken the trouble to honor my father. Oc and Minny van Crugten came from the south, a long trip. Little did we know that this would be the last time we saw Minny, who died of cancer some years later. She was a dear friend. Since there were few of Pa's contemporaries left, I chose to include a brief review of his life and

career in my eulogy. Tineke also spoke and thanked Pa for what he had done for her when she had great difficulties with her divorce. Pa was cremated and we asked the crematorium to save his ashes until Ma would follow, which would take almost ten years. Ma seemed strangely detached during the ceremony. She would spend her remaining years in the same mental state with few cares in the world.

A happier event was the marriage of George and Diane Elisabeth Alexander on June 17, 1989 in our rose garden.. George had hired Diane in 1985. At that time he and two friends, Harry Kendall and Steve Byrns, all classmates of the Columbia Graduate School of Architecture, had started a firm of their own, called it BKS Architects, and rented space in New York City from a landlord who specialized in renting office space to independent architects. He provided desks, copy machines for drawings (cad cam – computer aided design/computer aided manufacturing – did not yet exist). So when Diane came looking for a job and entered a large room filled with architects, she thought she was interviewing with a large firm. When George and she got serious, he had to ask her to leave because of what he perceived as a conflict of interest. So at the wedding there was a contingent of people from George's then somewhat larger firm and people from the firm where Diane worked. It was a very happy affair that went off extremely well thanks to the work Netty and Diane had done. We met Diane's family and have remained friends with them ever since. The marriage ceremony took place in our rose garden and we had a big tent in our front yard for the party. There were many people from Holland and many good American friends present. Several people spoke, but brother-in- law Menny was successfully prevented from speaking.

The decade ended on a very hopeful note for our family, George and Diane were married, Adriaan had joined Merrill Lynch where he started his successful career in insurance risk management for financial institutions, Richard would soon leave ESPN to go to Boston, Janet had returned from her adventures in Asia and worked for Nippon Steel in New York and Netty and I started to enjoy my retirement with some serious traveling.

The world had seen a minirevolution in China with the student uprising in Tiananmen Square in Beijing. This was harshly and bloodily suppressed by the Chinese army. I believe the student rebellion signaled that the Chinese economic wonder has serious underlying flaws, which may in the long term bring more upheavals and serious problems for the Peoples Republic of China. In Eastern Germany there erupted a sudden change as the isolation of the Iron Curtain countries began to unravel following big upheavals in the Soviet Union that would result in its demise. People from East Germany started driving their smoky little Trabant cars to Hungary and abandoning them at the Hungarian–Austrian border that had suddenly been opened by the Hungarians. Within a short time, the Berlin Wall came down and all East Block communist governments collapsed. The West and mainly the U.S. had simply bankrupted the Soviets by outspending them on defense. The house of cards fell down and millions of people were suddenly free. An event of enormous importance in the history of our world.

26 : Looking Back, Before The Finish Line

Now in my late eighties it is easier to think about the past twenty years than to peer into the future because it is pretty obvious that the future cannot bring much good. So let me start with a brief synopsis of the happenings in our family. We have had the joy of welcoming two grandchildren in this world. Diane presented us on April 8, 1991, with a grandson George Alexander and on January 6, 1994, with a granddaughter Eloise Jeannette. These two are now young people who are our pride and joy. What else is there to live for than one's children and grandchildren? George and Diane moved from the 13th Street hovel to a nice loft apartment George designed on Lafayette Street. As their family grew, they somewhat reluctantly moved to the suburbs. They found a nice old house in Mamaroneck where they have lived for many years as true suburbanites. George designed an addition to this house that doubled its size. Diane made its garden into

OUR PRIDE AND JOY FOR MORE THAN THIRTY YEARS WAS OUR ROSE GARDEN.

a wonderful peaceful retreat, and she and George gradually upgraded the interior. George's firm prospered and grew. He designed a large number of buildings, mostly in New York City. His work includes a synagogue, two libraries and a luxury condominium building for which he received national recognition from the AIA (the American Institute of Architects.)

Alexander and Eloise went to the public schools in Mamaroneck. In the fourth or fifth grade, Alexander stepped into the principal's office and said, "I think we should organize a science fair." The principal agreed and they are now still having science fairs in that school. At an early age Eloise developed a talent for theatre and musicals. She went through grade school appearing in leading roles in several musicals. Some of the tunes are still in my head. In high school she continued doing plays and musicals with singing and dancing performances. We attended all her performances and continue to do so. She will probably continue to be on stage in college, but her main interest now is photography. Making interesting photographs with digital cameras is now a completely different discipline from the print photography I grew up with. There is virtually no limit to the number of pictures you can take in contrast to the old days when you had to be careful not to run out of film, and developing film and making prints could be expensive. Now pictures, if saved on a computer, are free, and Eloise fires away at her subjects, taking as many shots as she likes while weeding out the results afterwards, with often surprisingly impressive results. I am still locked into the old film mindset that allows at most two or three shots of the same subject.

In his final year at the Mamaroneck High School, Alexander earned a National Merit Scholarship that was, of course, a great honor, but it also means that he is a very smart student, apparently not only in the eyes of his grandparents. The honoree never mentioned this achievement to them. His father had to do that. In addition it is a nice financial assist towards the inevitable burden of tuition payments for him. He applied for early admission to Macalester College in St. Paul, Minnesota, and was admitted without a hitch. He never suffered the agony of having to apply to many schools and waiting several months before receiving the results.

The severe economic downturn we experienced in 2008, which took many years to play out, stemmed from an incredible nationwide real-estate bubble, and that also unavoidably affected BKSK (Byrns, Kendall, Schieferdecker and Kravis), George's architectural firm. While he and his partners employed more than thirty architects in its peak year, they had to slim down to a shortened workweek with about eighteen for several years before being able to start growing back to more than thirty again in late 2011. Since then his office has had almost more work than they can handle and he had more than forty architects at work in early 2012.

In September 2011 Alexander went to Norway for a semester abroad. He seems to have developed a strong affection for the Scandinavian countries despite their often horrible climate and the somber dark winters. At the end of his time in Oslo, he traveled to Sweden, Denmark, Finland and the Baltic States and returned home via Iceland, a country that was slowly recovering from a financial calamity caused by a real estate investment frenzy that bankrupted its entire banking system in 2008. The Icelanders had all gone from fishing to banking and were now returning to fishing again. Alexander seems to have understood what happened there and I hope his visit to this peculiar little country and learning about its strange nationwide dalliance with international banking, will eventually spark an interest in economics and bring him around to taking some courses in the dismal science. I have been pleading with him to do that for years.

Adriaan left Merrill Lynch in 1990 when he was recruited by the Wells Fargo bank in San Francisco. He initially settled in a cookie-cutter house in a development full of exactly similar houses in Richmond, across the bay from the city. After a few years he bought a much nicer house in the Oakland Hills, above Berkeley. This very attractive house had a spectacular view of San Francisco and the Bay Bridge. As he prospered, Adriaan began to develop a hobby he is still pursuing; the accumulation of large, old, mainly American automobiles, such as Cadillacs and Lincoln Continentals of the size and type Germans call *Amerikanische Straszen Kreuzer*. Netty and I became aware of this – for our frugal Dutch minds – incredibly wasteful pursuit when we received a Christmas card from Adriaan showing him in a bright red Santa costume, waving at us from the driver's seat of a huge bright red Cadillac convertible with tailfins. That was his way of announcing his new hobby to his family. This car was eventually traded for another one and many more would follow over the years. The parade of outsize vehicles included several Rolls Royces, a stretch limousine, and a huge bus-sized RV (Recreational Vehicle) and has at this writing not abated. It is his hobby and he enjoys it. Enough said.

The Wells Fargo bank was and is a very well-managed bank that grew its business partly through acquisitions, and Adriaan became adept at absorbing the insurance risk management departments of the banks that were taken over. This led to a Wall Street Journal front page article that was published on October 9, 1996, under the title "Darwin's Delight: Seven Office Mates at a dying bank ask: 'who will survive?' " It deals with the heart-wrenching emotional ups and downs people go through when their business is taken over in a bitter buyout and new management steps in. Christopher Addieg, a chain-smoking, nervous man in his fifties who runs the Corporate Insurance Department at First Interstate Bancorp lives in fear of a decision to be made by Adriaan, his opposite number at Wells Fargo. His ulcers are barking. The article's writer pours on the dramatic scenes in the lives of several employees and especially Mr. Addieg. He describes how he and his wife worry about the future and how he fears he may end up in the plumbing supplies department at Home Depot. He writes – "The following morning, Adriaan Schieferdecker, head of Wells Fargo's insurance operation, visits Los Angeles as he has done a handful of times since the merger announcement. The office is atwitter as the 6 foot, 6 inch executive lopes down the hallway, enters Janet White's office and closes the door." He then describes how Adriaan goes about telling people what the future may bring for them and what their options are. Adriaan offers Janet a job in San Francisco, which she declines, and hints at a short-term consulting job at Wells for Addieg. Then follows another long recitation of Addieg's family troubles, his physical problems and finally of a trip to San Francisco to meet with Adriaan to go over a number of issues. He spends the prior evening in a bar and the next morning he is finally in Adriaan's office." Mr. Schieferdecker closes the door and walks around to his desk. He takes a deep breath and begins to speak. 'Chris,' Mr. Schieferdecker says, 'we want to keep you on.' " The article then moves slowly to its surprise denouement. "On August 5, Mr. Addieg's first day of work in San Francisco, he learns that Mr. Schieferdecker is leaving Wells Fargo to direct corporate insurance at BankAmerica Corp. Three weeks later Mr. Addieg is named to fill Adriaan's position." I guess the writer of this article was really hoping to be able to pull at the heartstrings of his readers with a story of a little guy crushed by a merger of big corporations. It did not work out that way this time.

Adriaan became quite successful at BofA, and in 1999 when it merged with Nations Bank in Charlotte North Carolina, he moved reluctantly to this southern outpost where work would become the dominating factor in his life. He bought a sizeable house on the shore of Lake Norman, a large artificial lake that offered boating opportunities. But he discovered that temperatures in summer were beyond what is pleasant on a boat. So he moved away from the water to another house in Harrisburg where he is closer to his office, has more land and where he built a nice swimming pool in his backyard. Always the showman, Adriaan bought a life-size fiberglass replica of the famous Greek headless statue of the winged Nike of Samothrace of which the original resides in the Louvre. It sits at the head of his pool.

The man who delivered it to his house said: "I bet you were mighty angry when you found out they broke the head off." Nations Bank was the gobbelor and BofA was the gobbelee, but the new entity kept the name Bank of America. Adriaan is now one of the very few old Bank of America people who survived the merger. He has had many opportunities to make use of his knowledge of corporate takeovers as the bank became more and more aggressive in its desire to grow to be the biggest financial institution in the country. The bank bought Merrill Lynch when that company was in deep trouble and the government encouraged them to step in. Later they over-reached and acquired the disastrous mortgage company Countrywide, which almost brought the bank down in the financial crisis of 2008. The events following the crisis seriously affected the bank and made Adriaan's daily life much more stressful. He is now making plans for his eventual retirement.

Richard decided to leave ESPN in 1990 and took a job with the Christian Science Monitor in Boston. He liked living in Beantown and the job offered considerably more perspective than ESPN. Unfortunately the Monitor is now a mere shadow of its old self. What was once one of the best newspapers in the country is now published daily on line and only weekly in print. The paper decided, as it turned out much too late, to move into television. It had already a presence in radio. Rich had an interesting opportunity there to help build up a 24-hour news and information TV operation from scratch. Unfortunately it did not work out that way. The operation was closed down in 1992 after suffering significant losses. Richard started free-lancing and met Julie Anathan, a young nurse who became his live-in girl friend and later his bride. In 1993 they moved to Arlington and a year later to Somerville. On June 3, 1995, they were married on Nantucket where Julie's father, Jim Anathan, had a house. This was a wonderful event which was attended by many good friends of ours and Tilly and Menny as major and very visible representatives of our family. Til and Menny were living at that time in Curaçao, where they had moved to avoid the high Dutch taxes. The island of Curaçao is a former Dutch colony and for many years its economy was totally dependent on one large refinery Shell had built there to process Venezuelan oil. When the refinery was closed, the island had to find other sources of income. One of the ideas was to act as a tax haven for offshore corporations and another plan was to attract Dutch pensioners who were interested in becoming permanent residents and offer them very favorable tax treatment. On April 4, 1994, Menny's seventieth birthday was celebrated with a huge party that lasted several days and was attended by about thirty good friends from Holland plus Menny and Til's children and Netty and me. This was a memorable party with tours of the island, lunches, dinners, boat trips and a barbeque on the beach at sundown. All this was well planned and offered many opportunities for Menny to show his skills as a good host and entertainer.

On Nantucket we gave a party for all attendees on the evening before the wedding in the small Life Saving Museum outside the town. We also hosted a rehearsal dinner in a local restaurant where the Schieferdecker family embarrassed Richard with a singing presentation of some incidents in his life that he would rather forget. The wedding was in a local church and the official party was in the golf club. Rich and Julie moved to California where Rich attended San Francisco State University's Multimedia Studies Program. At first they stayed with Adriaan, but after a while they found their own abode in an incredibly small house they rented in nearby Oakland. Julie worked as a nurse at Alta Bates medical center in Berkeley. Rich graduated from SFSU in 1997, and moved back to Boston in the following year. This surprised us, but as Rich later explained, he really did not like life in California and longed to be back East. But before this happened, Netty and I made several nice visits to California, staying with Adriaan and enjoying the company of our California contingent. One year Janet came over from Holland and joined us all for Christmas. This was an eyeopener for her and may well have planted the seeds for her later decision to move to California. The climate is certainly better there than in Holland in December.

After their return to the Boston area Rich and Julie bought a house in Cohasset that they fixed up with great taste and much effort. Richard got a job with an outfit called BaliHai Entertainment where he became operations manager. This company developed interactive learning programs for children. Unfortunately not enough children liked the product and the company had to fold its tents. Rich then joined MedSAFE, a company that specialized in providing doctors, dentists, hospitals and many other institutions in the medical and related fields with guidance in navigating through the myriad rules federal, state and local authorities have developed to promote safe and responsible procedures. The company had grown rapidly by providing its services mainly through communication by representatives and hard copy documents. It now wanted to go digital. Richard became their communications and graphics designer. Unfortunately MedSAFE had stacked its board with Harvard Business School graduates who urged management to seek more rapid growth and finance it with large bank loans. As a result of this risky strategy, the company went belly up in 2002, burdened by excessive interest costs. Richard had now accumulated a track record of joining three enterprises that all went out of business. As a consequence of this he may have learned more about the business world than if he had stayed put with one firm. But it did not make his life much easier. He decided to start working on his own and is now working successfully as an independent provider of internet services for a retailer of high-end outdoor furniture and other luxury goods in Cambridge.

One day Netty and I received an upsetting call from Richard who told us that he and Julie were going to separate. Apparently Julie had decided that she could not continue married life with a member of the other sex. This was, of course, a shocker for us. We were quite fond of Julie although we always had some trouble getting really close to her because she had always kept a high wall around her personality. We understood that it must have been a terrible struggle for her to come to this point in her life and we respected that. On the other hand, we knew that Rich had suffered a gut-wrenching blow that left deep wounds. He loved Julie very much and we knew that he was deeply hurt. Some of his siblings were angry at Julie and felt she should never have married Rich. We did not share that opinion. We realized that she was a person with deepseated problems and mixed-up emotions and that there were many facets to the relationship that we could not and would not fathom. We just had to leave the situation for what it was and try to help repair the damage for Rich. It was immediately obvious to us that attempting to reconcile Julie and Richard was impossible so we tried as much as we could to help our son overcome this very difficult moment in his life. The nice house in Cohasset was sold and the divorce became legally effective in 2005.

Rich bought a condo in a refurbished, charming, old school house in Somerville, right on the border of Cambridge. He and Julie remained good friends and saw each other from time to time. We kept hoping Richard would cut his ties with Julie and find somebody else to share his life with and were delighted when Richard met Toyoko Kawabata in 2009 and after a short courtship, married her in 2011. This was a second marriage for both and there was much less pomp and ceremony. But it was a wonderfully warm affair in what used to be the mansion of the commandant of an old arsenal near Boston. There were quite a few relatives present and several old friends. We also had occasion to meet some of the friends Rich and Toyoko had made in the Boston area. Right after the ceremony, the pair flew to Japan to meet with Toyoko's mother, brother and two aunts. They brought Toyoko's bridal dress and Rich's groom's suit for a low key reenactment of the Boston event. Toyoko's father had unfortunately died several years ago in a traffic accident and her mother suffers from severe diabetes and lives in a nursing home. The two aunts are her mother's sisters. Toyoko and Rich now live happily in Rich's apartment in Somerville. Toyoko fits wonderfully well into our family and we enjoy her sense of humor and active participation in our family's activities. She came to this country to study music at a college in Boston. She played the trumpet, apparently very well because she played in several professional jazz ensembles. Unfortunately "she blew her lip out," as musicians call the problem that arises when a trumpeter damages his or her lips. This problem is a career ending event so Toyoko had to find something else to do. She now works as a tour guide for Japanese travelers who are visiting the Boston area. Every year a stream of mostly older Japanese arrives in the U.S. and is toured around by Toyoko's company in Boston before or after visiting New York City and Washington, D.C.

Janet became our most adventurous and most well-traveled family member. She ended her stay in Japan with a trip around South East Asia, including Hong Kong, Nepal – where she trekked into the foothills of Mount Everest – Burma (then still an almost inaccessible dictatorship) and Thailand. After returning to Japan she went to Hokkaido, the northern most island of Japan, where she spent a month with a farming family. Back in New York City in 1988 she found a job with Nippon Steel as a financial analyst. Two years later she decided, correctly, that to succeed in business she should get an MBA. She applied to several business schools and was accepted at Wharton and the London Business School. She chose the latter because it had more of an international flavor. So in 1990 she moved to London and stayed at first in Hempstead with our dear friends Edith and John Boynton before starting at the school. Janet earned her M.B.A. in 1992 and was recruited by the large multinational Dutch Philips company. She started work as an internal consultant there in their plant in Best. A year later she became a marketing manager and was sent to Singapore where Philips was trying to establish its South–East Asian foothold for its medical systems division. Life in Singapore was pleasant, but the job turned out to be a problem. She worked for an Englishman who seemed to be one of those people who impresses his bosses with skillful presentations, building an aura of sophistication and worldly savoir faire, but who operates in a totally disorganized manner without achieving any tangible results. She asked for and got a transfer back to the Netherlands where she worked as a business manager for the Ultrasound division again in Best. During that period Janet visited her grandparents in Wassenaar every month, which was for us a wonderful way of staying connected with the increasingly more difficult situation there.

Janet quit Philips in 1997, an unheard of event for the company where nobody ever was fired and nobody ever quit. It seems her career was not progressing the way she wanted, and the Dutch climate did not help either. She moved to California and found a job with the E-Myth Academy, a career building and consulting firm, as sales manager. A year later she was laid off, an unexpected rude shock for her. She regrouped by attending a "What Color is Your Parachute" workshop and started her own practice in career counseling and acquired new skills in studying Neuro–Linguistic Programming (NLP) a mainly California- based school of thought that helps people to be more effective in their careers by improving their ability to think clearly and express themselves better. She bought a nice condominium in Sausalito where we visited several times and got acquainted with her two dogs.

In 2004 Janet completed all the course work and student teaching to earn teaching credentials in the state of California, sold her condominium and moved to Vallejo, a depressing little town on the opposite side of the bay from Sausalito. She rented a house there to be closer to the school where she started working. Vallejo has since then been in the news as one of the first communities that declared bankruptcy. Its expenses for pensions and other entitlements for its police and firemen rose to 80% of the town's budget and became unmanageable. Janet chose to start working with severely emotionally disturbed children and taught 5th grade in the Sunrise Elementary School, Mt Diablo Unified School District. Her adventures there could fill another book. Suffice it to say that she had taken on a very difficult task under an ineffective principal for very little pay. It became such an emotional burden for her that she decided to return to working for herself as an NLP practitioner. She bought a nice house in the Oakland Hills, surprisingly close to the house where Adriaan had lived before he went to North Carolina. Janet got caught in the housing crash of 2008–2010 and had to give her house up. She returned to Marin County where she now lives.

The year 1997 was a grim one for us. We went three times to Holland for three funerals. First my mother died in January. Then we had the sad and painful end of Tilly in July and in October we said good bye to Mammie. Pul had a lot of work in settling Mammie's not uncomplicated estate. He did a good job. Over the years we have tremendously enjoyed our friendship and frequent visits with Pul and Monique (Moon) van Basten Batenburg, the wonderful woman with whom Pul shared the last thirty years of his life. Pul's marriage to Eveline van Laer was not a good one. We think that Eveline's behavior was the sole reason for their problems. They had two children, Eelco and Fleur, to whom Pul was devoted, and it was hurtful for him that he could not spend more time with them since Eveline and Dicky van Sinnighe Damsté, her second husband, were living in the Far East where he worked for Shell and from where they sent the children to Swiss boarding schools. The academic results they achieved as a result of this multicultural upbringing were less than stellar, and they seem happier now that they live in Holland. Eelco married Lieke Romme in a joyful, but somewhat chaotic wedding. They now have two children, Kiki (a girl) and Tymen (a boy). Fleur has two children from a relationship with Joost Bellaert, an older man that was (we think) terminated a few years later. They are a boy named Willem and a girl named Emma.

When they were still married, we did not see much of Eveline and Pul. They revolved in their own little society world in Wassenaar and Eveline was not very interested in building a relationship with us or with Tilly and Frans, who were at that time living nearby. After their divorce, Pul became a different man. He was much opener and warmer and often came over to stay and sail with us. It got even better after he and Moon started to live together in Oosterbeek with Moon's two daughters Tet (Juliette) and Men (Germaine). These two young women became great favorites of ours. Unfortunately Moon is unable to fly long distances so she only managed to visit us once. After Pul's retirement they started spending a good part of the year in France. They first owned a house in a compound where many other Dutch people lived and where familiarity started breeding contempt. Then they found a really beautiful house in Opio where Netty and I stayed several times. In 2009 we went over to visit them because Pul had been diagnosed with cancer, and although he was on the mend, we wanted to see him. We saw him once more in Holland where they had a nice flat in The Hague, a place where we often enjoyed their hospitality on trips to Holland. Things got worse in the summer of 2010. Pul and Moon were back in Opio where he was treated for his cancer which had flared up and metastasized. We went there during the last two weeks of his life and had a very good visit. Since we all knew that the end was near, we went to Holland to await it. After Pul's death on July 1, 2010, Netty realized that she was now the only survivor of a family of six. We are still frequently in touch with Moon and see her when we go to Holland.

☙

Then there is travel to look back to. It is not only a pleasure to go on a trip, there are also the good memories that are created and stay with you in the years afterwards. When it became clear to us that it would be best for me to really retire, Netty and I decided that we should use our new found free time to do some serious traveling beyond the many visits we made to our ailing parents in Wassenaar. We took a trip to the Near East organized by the Metropolitan Museum of Art. It was a great success. We first went to Egypt where we boarded a small very comfortable ship, saw Luxor and Abu Simbel and then sailed to Jordan by way of the Sinai Peninsula. Petra in Jordan was a place we would dearly love to see again. It is unforgettable.

We then went on a long-distance trip to New Zealand and Australia. A travel agent helped us find families in both countries where we could spend a night to get a flavor of the people there. We really enjoyed staying in Sydney with Jacky (formerly Bryan) and Raymond Tobias. Up farther north near Brisbane we visited with Wim and Ineke Opstelten, the couple that had become friends of mine in Indonesia.

Several years later the Opsteltens came from Australia to the U.S. West Coast to join us on a trip to Alaska. We cruised on a small ship from Juneau around the Inland Passage area and then came back to Seattle for a drive into the Canadian Rockies and a return to San Francisco by way of Yellowstone Park.

Other trips on ships brought us to the Galapagos Islands where we saw the stunning animal life and passed through the Panama Canal. We went to Berlin and from there by riverboat to Prague and Budapest.

Our friends Kitty and Willem Witteveen came to visit and we organized a car trip with them from Houston along the Gulf Coast to Washington, D.C. where they stayed with friends before returning to our house.

Kitty and Willem also made a memorable trip with us through Tuscany and Umbria. They picked us up in their car at Pul's and Moon's house in Opio. We drove with them into Italy in pursuit of works by Piero della Francesca, visiting all the museums and churches where we could find paintings and frescoes done by this famous early Renaissance artist. Willem had carefully planned our itinerary and it was wonderful to have a fixed goal when visiting a museum. We had read up on this remarkable artist who was one of the first to use true perspective in his work.

The festivities surrounding the bicentennial of the Lewis and Clark expedition generated intense interest all over the country. We visited Janet and drove up to Portland, Oregon, to join a small ship that traveled on the Columbia River all the way up almost to the Idaho border and back with many detailed explanations on several historical sites. After we came back in Portland we rented another car and drove on along the coast to visit Lucas and Agna de Clercq in the Seattle area.

We reacquainted ourselves with our Dutch roots on a summer cruise down the Dutch waterways in a barge we chartered together with our friends Ruurd and Elaine Leegstra and Romano and Pat Vanderbes. For Ruurd it was a visit to the country he left as a small child, but where his parents lived and were raised. For Romano and Netty and me it was the place where we grew up. We boarded the "Broedertrouw" in Haarlem and chugged down the Spaarne, passed the windmill where Eelco and I had capsized, to the Kager Plassen where I had often sailed and on to Leiden. There we visited the places where I had lived as a student. Passing Voorburg we saw the building where the Montessori school used to be and ended up in Delft. On we went to Rotterdam and from there with a wide swing along the big rivers, first east on the Rhine, then north on the IJssel to Friesland where we got stuck in a storm that prevented the skipper from completing the circle that would have brought us to Amsterdam. We saw Holland at its best because we visited small towns where nobody ever goes and stayed away from the crowds that are now part of life everywhere in the Netherlands, a seriously overcrowded country. It was a lovely cruise despite the antics of the strange woman who was cooking for us and flatly refused to serve anything to us other than exactly what she had planned.

A large group of mostly Riverside Yacht Club friends went on several major trips under the very competent leadership of Beth Geismar, daughter of our friends Dick and Pat Geismar. We joined them on a trip to South Africa, where we started in Cape Town. We had gone to Cape Town a week before the tour started, to visit Jan de Clercq and his lady friend Veronica Foulkes. Veronica is, as she calls herself in the – to our ears – charming South African Dutch language, a *"boere meissie"*, (a farm girl). Not exactly. She is a very sophisticated lady who runs a stud farm where she breeds race horses. She also owned a nice apartment in Cape Town where we stayed. Jan and Veronica took us all over the place and also offered a group of friends who had arrived in town ahead of our tour a memorable day in the country by driving all of us around in two small Volkswagen buses. When the tour started, we went to Ngala wildlife preserve, near Kruger Park, where we saw an abundance of wildlife, took a two day train ride in a luxury train out of Pretoria and flew over to the Chobe Park in Botswana where we saw more wildlife, to end up with a visit to Victoria Falls. A fantastic trip that whetted our appetite for Africa and wildlife safaris. I came home with good pictures of the "big five," elephants, rhinos, lions, a leopard and hippos, rounded out by giraffes, monkeys, wildebeest and many birds. Fabulous!

With the same group we went to Russia, first St. Petersburg, then on the Volga by riverboat to Moscow. Another memorable trip in a country that was long seen as our archenemy and now seemed just like us in many aspects of daily life. The scenery was different of course, the museums incredible and the majesty of places like the Hermitage and the Kremlin overwhelming. A somewhat less dramatic but also interesting trip with the RYC group took us to Morocco and Spain.

But before Morocco we made another major excursion with the Leegstras and Elaine's sister, Susan Ricci, to China. We followed the circuit everyone seems to make in either direction. Starting in Shanghai, we went to the Yangtze River, near the new big Great Gorges Dam. There we boarded a river boat, which took us to Chongquing. From there we flew to Xian, to the site where the terracotta soldiers were found. An unforgettable sight, with thousands of soldiers and their horses sculpted in great detail. Every soldier's face is different from all others. We ended up in Beijing from where we visited the Great Wall and saw the Forbidden City and Tienanmen Square festooned with a large picture of Chairman Mao.

With Rob and Liesbeth Laane we made a very special cruise on the Norwegian Hurtigruten Line (the post boat) which runs from Bergen northward, stopping at many small towns and villages en route. We ended up at the North Cape and flew back to Denmark for a few days in Copenhagen.

To warm up in winter time we made several sailing expeditions to the Caribbean, mostly sailing with friends and mostly on trips meticulously organized by our friend Fred Waldron. Fred would rent a catamaran and invite three couples to join him and Debbie Gesner. We went to Antigua, Nevis, Puerto Rico, Guadeloupe and St Martin. All smooth sailing and no serious mishaps.

In 1990 we started an every-five-year tradition of taking our entire family on a trip. When I turned sixty-five and Netty sixty we chartered a sailboat that could carry us all plus Til and Menny on a cruise from St. Lucia to Petit Saint Vincent and back. The longest stretch of open water we had to cross came on the first day. It was the passage between St. Lucia and St. Vincent. Unfortunately we encountered a gray and very windy day for the initiation of Tilly and Menny to offshore sailing. While we were busy trimming the sails and enjoying the ride, bouncing around on not insignificant waves, Adriaan looked over at Tilly and Menny, who were sitting side by side in the cockpit, pale-faced and holding hands. He said, "Dad, Tilly and Menny are scared sh…less." This became a historic pronouncement in our family. Soon much of the pressure was relieved when we passed close by a small sloop with a tiny outboard and three islanders in it who waved enthusiastically at us. For the rest it was a memorable cruise. Rich made a nice video of it.

Five years later we had a bigger family because Alexander and Eloise had arrived. We rented two small houses in a vacation colony in Noorwijkerhout in Holland. We saw quite a bit of the country and made timely visits to both great-grandmothers who would die in 1997.

Again five years later, we rented a nice large house on St. John were we could enjoy the island and its beaches. Diane's parents also joined us there. Lois and Dick Patch had rented a house nearby and often joined us on island excursions. It was on this vacation that I earned my scuba diving certification and made several dives with Janet who had learned this sport in the Far East.

On the next trip, in 2000, we all went to Belize. We stayed in a simple hotel there that was located on the ocean and offered swimming, scuba diving and inland expeditions into the jungle and trips to Mayan ruins.

When I turned eighty in 2005, we splurged on a trip to the Big Island in Hawaii. Adriaan had bought a nice piece of land there near Hilo and was thinking of eventually building a house there for his retirement. After testing out the idea for several years, he abandoned this plan and sold his land for a very good price. We again rented a house there and explored the interesting island from top to bottom. What made the trip for me was a moment on top of Mauna Kea volcano, where we were watching the sunset, and Alexander dropped down on the ground and laying on his back looked at the sky and said, "this is so cool!" The old folks stayed home, but the young ones went on an evening hike across the lava fields to see the Kilauea Volcano in action. We saw it all from the air a few days later when we chartered a small plane that flew us over the entire island and also showed us nearby Maui Island. The whole trip was an unforgettable outing for us.

In 2010 the big recession had hit and we were worried about what the future would hold in store for us retirees without a pension, who were dependent on an investment portfolio. So we arranged a much simpler family retreat. We rented a house in Booth Bay Harbor, Maine. The house was a big old family place that had great appeal for us and worked well for our entire family. Now that our finances have recovered somewhat, we may stage another, probably final, big splurge, but that is still in the planning stage.

Netty and I have always been very fond of making long-distance car trips through the US. Our ramblings have brought us to many out-of-the-way places, often surprisingly interesting. So when Lucas and Agna de Clercq called us to ask if we were interested in a sailing cruise in the San Juan Archipelago in September 2008, we eagerly accepted and told them we would drive up to their house on Whidbey Island, northwest of Seattle. It took a while to get there. We stopped in Chicago, where I had often been on business, but never as a tourist. We visited with Diane's parents in Minneapolis and saw Macalester College where Alexander wanted to go. In North Dakota we saw Little Round Top, the scene of Custer's last stand. As we

AFTER 50 YEARS, L TO R OCTAVE, EELCO, NETTY, ME, LUCIA, FRITS.

were driving along, the economy and our markets began to deteriorate seriously and the first rumblings of what would become the Great Recession became apparent. It was sobering for me as a former Wall Streeter to notice that the news we could pick up on the TV in motels often ignored the stock market, and when we stopped for lunch somewhere in, say Montana, nobody seemed to care or even know about it. During the entire trip it was impossible to pick up any stock exchange reports on our car radio. Lucas had chartered a roomy cruising sloop in Anacortes, and we spent a week on the waters there, marveling at the enormous size of this cruising area and its innumerable number of nice anchorages and hospitable islands, mostly in Canada. Once back on a dock in the U.S., my cell phone worked again and I could call Adriaan to ask him what was happening in the markets. He told me the Dow Jones was down 500 points that day. It was a surreal experience to stand there and look at the lovely harbor we were in and realize the world was changing, perhaps permanently. We drove to Janet by way of Oregon and Crater Lake National Park, and from San Francisco to LA, where we saw the Getty Museum that was built in recent years by what was once one of my favorite clients. There we saw paintings by Frans Hals of Lucas **After 50 years, L to R Octave, Eelco, Netty, me, Lucia, Frits.** and Feina de Clercq, ancestors of our friends. The Rijks Museum in Amsterdam had sent these paintings to the Getty for restoration. Realizing it was futile trying to build a really meaningful collection by purchases in the now, very elevated world art market, the Getty has focused over the years on creating a world class art restoration establishment. We told the friendly reception lady at the museum that we had just been on a cruise with Lucas de Clercq, which baffled her a little. From LA we went due east and ended up with Adriaan. It may sound odd, but we would love to do a similar trip again, anytime.

ↇ

A major milestone in our life was reached on June 30, 2001, when we celebrated our fiftieth wedding anniversary. It so happened that this day fell on a Saturday so we could organize the festivities around a weekend and have a big party on the exact date on which we were married. We invited a large number of people and were humbled to learn that almost all the members of our generation who had attended our wedding in the Netherlands were coming. Eelco Apol came as well as Frits Greup with his wife Dini. Pul was there and also two of Netty's first cousins, Hans and Alexander van Someren Gréve. From my side of the family, we had Jetty and Kees Kraaijeveld. My old friend Octave van Crugten came with his second wife Henriette, and Lucia LeFèvre, Netty's cousin and bridesmaid, also arrived with her husband Billy Zeverijn. We started out on Friday with an evening at our house for those who came from far away. We had set a party tent behind our house for the dinner and Erik Boot, younger brother of my friend Ab, presented a slide show there, mainly showing pictures of his family with a surprising number of shots that included me. On Saturday evening we had our big party at the yacht club with about 120 people in attendance. It was a blistering hot day, but I think most of our guests had a better time than I because I was constantly busy and moving around a lot. We had a raw bar on the lawn and dinner inside with an old-fashioned dance band who played music we older people recognized as music and could handle on the floor. Rich videotaped the whole affair and George spoke as oldest offspring. He did it well, mixing humor and emotion that brought several of our lady friends to tears. Other speakers were Lucas de Clercq and Pul and me, of course, thanking everybody for coming and Netty for giving me fifty wonderful years.

On Sunday we had a brunch at our house, after which everyone marched down to the Harbor Point dock where the Brandaris with Adriaan and me on board arrived, ready for a baptism ceremony to be executed by Eloise. This ceremony did not quite succeed because Eloise was overcome with shyness, but the bottle eventually broke and we steamed away with a large number of guests aboard.

It is sad and painful to reflect on the fact that all the members of our bridal party, Octave, Eelco, Frits, Lucia and Pul are now no longer with us.

We recently celebrated our sixtieth anniversary with our family in Maine. Our offspring presented us with a very good and intimate dinner in an Inn in Camden. No more big parties in these more uncertain times.

We also have a major change in our lifestyle to look back upon. As we began to face the inevitable march of time we realized we should not make the same mistake my parents made and stay too long in our house and then find out that it was too late to move elsewhere. We loved our house, the neighbors, and the location of the neighborhood and had the services of many helpful souls at our disposal, some of whom had worked for us for almost forty years, but we realized more and more that in the coming years living in our house would become a real burden. Although we had regular visits from our gardener, our tree man, our pool man, our sprinkler people and many other tradesmen, the garden still required our constant attention in summer. Also, scheduling and checking up on all the helpers was a full-time job, and we wanted to be free of the maintenance chores a house inevitably requires. In the gardening department, our rose garden with some two hundred bushes gave us a lot of work. It was a beautiful formal garden, a throwback to the estate that had once occupied what was now Harbor Point, and we tremendously enjoyed working in it, but it was hard work and we realized we could not keep doing that forever. So we decided to start thinking about either an apartment or a place like Edge Hill, the continuing-care facility that was in the planning stages nearby on the Stamford border.

Our good friends, Marjo and Dries Woudhuysen, had faced the same dilemma several years earlier and had ended up buying an apartment in Indian Harbor House on Steamboat Road in Greenwich. We often visited there and liked the place. After Dries's unexpectedly early death, we all realized it had been a good and timely move for them. On one of our visits to Marjo she mentioned that an apartment of the same size as hers was for sale and invited us to take a peek. It was a ruin. The owner had started a halfhearted renovation, but had neglected to ask the building's board for permission and had also not taken the trouble to obtain a building permit from the town. He was told to cease and desist and decided to sell. Since interior walls had been torn down, wires hung from open ceilings and parquet flooring was buckled up after some major leaks, the place looked awful and we could get it for a reasonable price. We realized we could do our own renovation and asked George to take a look. By then George and his partners had built their firm into a significant presence in the New York City architectural world and it was a question whether he would be willing to take on a small job like ours. Luckily he accepted us as clients. George took a look and said he could do something nice with this place. We bought it and started the painful process of dealing with a contractor. George had a great deal of experience working with apartments in the city and our local contractor pretended he also had worked with apartment construction, but he soon proved to be less qualified than we thought. After much delay he delivered a very good product, but it was a struggle and George had to rap his knuckles many times. It was my impression that our local contractors are used to what is called "stick building," that is erecting houses mostly made of wood where differences of a few inches in height or width can be easily overcome. In our apartment where we had much built-in cabinetry designed by George that came from elsewhere and where everything had to fit together with less than an eighth of an inch to spare, the contactors were sorely tested.

It took a while to sell our house in Riverside, and we had to endure the unpleasantness of a buyer reneging on a firm and accepted bid, just in time for not losing his deposit. The ultimate buyers were a nice young couple who planned to "scrape" the house as that, now very common practice, is called. However, the new owner works in the financial markets and his outlook for future gains seems to be less rosy, so the house is still standing, much to our delight. The move from a house to an apartment with less than half the square footage was traumatic and complex. We had to get rid of many possessions and found that some items, such as beds, are not easily disposed of. In the event, the apartment was not ready when we had to vacate our house, and we had to spend several weeks as guests of friends who rescued us. We are now already more than six years in our apartment and do not regret having made the move if only because we now realize it would have been physically very difficult for us to go through such an ordeal at this time.

❧

This story would be incomplete without a look back at the world of finance in which I found a good and interesting career and at the extraordinary challenges it presently faces. On my bookshelves are a number of good books that deal with both the good old days that preceded the crisis years and the tumultuous times we have recently lived through. The titles of these books tell the story of the way our markets have evolved over the centuries and the heart stopping events we have survived in the past decades. There is the classic Extraordinary Popular Delusions and the Madness of Crowds, which dates back to 1841 and describes the tendency of people to follow a trend like lemmings and by doing so, create a bubble which is bound to burst. We saw this happen in the collapse of the U.S. real estate boom and meltdown of the mortgage market in 2008. The Reminiscences of a Stock Operator was first published in 1923 and seemed to predict what would happen in 1929. Nobody understood that there was a speculative bubble that caused the great depression. Then there are the more humorous books written in the good days of the sixties and seventies, such as the Money Game and the Tao Jones Averages, Parkinson's Law and the Peter Principle. Don't we all wish those days would never have gone away? The use of more irreverent titles began with Den of Thieves, a description of the insider trading scandal of Ivan Boesky and the bond market manipulations of Michael Milken that brought down the firm of Drexel Burnham Lambert. We also read Predators Ball and Barbarians at the Gate in those days. A beginning of more serious rumblings in the market place is reported in Liars Poker a book that shines a sharp light on the problems in Salomon Brothers and the trading mentality of its principals. This book reflects the change in culture in the Street when more and more money was being made by trading while old, sounder business traditions went by the wayside as well-established banking and stock market regulations were eased. Two companies that were in the past good clients of EAM, Houston Natural Gas and Northern Natural Gas merged to fend off increasingly aggressive corporate raiders, the folks that were driving up stock prices and often disrupted good businesses. The merger produced a company that later became known as Enron and under new, morally corrupt management reached a market value of $63 Billion in 2001 and became the biggest corporate bankruptcy in history. A book entitled The Smartest Guys in the Room describes this disaster. The stock market boomed under the new and less restrictive regulations, but towards the end of the first decade of the new century a tsunami of bad news resulting from bad congressional action, bad corporate decisions and bad actions by trusted institutions and fraudulent behavior by many market participants began to roll over us. The demise of Bear Stearns, the firm that went belly-up in early 2008, is described in House of Cards. (The title is a play on the habit of the CEO of Bear to participate in high-level bridge tournaments while his firm was collapsing.) Need I say more about the way the world began to look at what was once a respectable business in which I spent a lifetime? But there was more. The Myth of the Rational Market told readres, after the fact of course, about the demise of the Modern Portfolio Theory, the idea that markets behaved rationally, an investment philosophy that governed investment thinking for about two decades and spawned several Noble Prize winners. And then there is the Trillion Dollar Meltdown. This book describes the collapse of Lehman Brothers which triggered the biggest bear market and massive worldwide economic collapse. In more recent years we breathlessly read titles like Reckless Endangerment, a harrowing analysis of the way in which the mortgage bond market debacle triggered the great meltdown of the housing market.

I think it all began for equity investors with "Mayday," May 1, 1975, when fixed commissions on the New York Stock Exchange were abolished and replaced with negotiated commissions. The idea was obviously a good one; it was to break the market cartel that had benefited for decades from a noncompetitive fixed price system. There was much handwringing about this at the Eberstadt firm, and several research oriented firms similar to ours closed their doors after a while, unable to find new sources of revenue for the research reports they produced. Eberstadt survived very well, but its way of doing business had to change drastically. Its trading room became a place where actual traders had to make deals with numerous market makers rather than just phoning in orders to the floor of the exchange. As commission rates went down, we had to insist on much bigger orders to get paid for the research we offered. The market also spawned trading houses that worked large volumes of big trades for very small commissions and institutional investors had to establish their own trading rooms to ensure they would get the best price at the best commission level. For a time it looked as if the little guy who was supposed to be the main beneficiary of lower commissions would be left by the wayside because nobody was interested in him anymore. But that changed with the emergence of firms like Charles Schwab that built a huge business out of serving small investors at cut-rate prices. Ultimately the market moved to "Net" trades, where the compensation of the intermediary was included in the price. The trading floor of the NYSE became less and less important, as most of the volume circumvented the Big Board and moved to the "off board market." Computers replaced clerks who posted prices by hand and wrote trade slips for each transaction. Still later prices were also set by electronic means. The NYSE has not remained in limbo. It moved to a merger with a group of European stock markets and formed Euronext, a company that eventually may be publicly owned. The price of a seat on the exchange which had fallen from $510,000 in 1969 to $35,000 after Mayday, is now well over $2,000,000. Still it remains a question why the NYSE will be able to continue to exist in its present form while the over-the-counter market has grown to be enormously more important under the NASDAQ banner.

The culture of the brokerage and investment banking firms changed over the years. What was always a very proper business, run by people with a "white shoe" background who had the interest of their clients in mind and who adhered strictly to the ethics of the business, was now much more influenced by traders who have by nature a short-term horizon and are more at home in the rough and tumble of day-to-day market making. The partnerships of big firms are now dominated by traders and the all-encompassing derivatives business in which esoteric securities are traded and only understood by the insider crowd has hurt the ethical standards of many firms. As the business became more and more competitive and profit margins became thinner, the emphasis shifted to trading for the firm's own account with the interest of clients moving to the background.

Deregulation of the banking system began seriously during the Clinton administration when politicians from both parties pressed for the abolishment of the Glass Steagall Act, which regulated the banking business. Historically, banks were supposed to gather deposits and make loans. When money-market funds and other cash gathering instruments such as short term, so-called Euro Bonds, became popular, the banks saw their deposits melt away and demanded to be allowed to operate in that sphere, too. They moved into the mutual fund and the investment banking business and much more important, started trading and playing the market for their own accounts. These were all areas from which they had been expressly excluded by Glass Steagall. The Bush Jr. administration, supported by a Democratic majority in Congress, moved aggressively forward on the deregulation front and encouraged bank mergers so that U.S. banks could compete better with large foreign banks. The real estate bubble was fed by the explosion of cheap mortgages for everyone and burst in 2008 when we learned that mortgage banks and commercial banks had gone way too far in selling mortgages to people who could not afford them. Masses of unsophisticated buyers had been induced to over-extend themselves under the assumption that the value of their houses would continue to go up, thus allowing them to come out clean.

When the economy and the housing market weakened seriously, the bubble burst and an avalanche of defaults and foreclosures was triggered. The real calamity was in the way in which the mortgage bankers had financed themselves by bundling mortgages into marketable securities, so called "securitization." and selling these sub-par loans to investors as triple A bonds. The rating agencies abdicated their responsibilities by granting hugely over-optimistic ratings to these pieces of paper called Collateralized Debt Obligations or CDOs. Investors who wanted to protect themselves against default of their CDOs, bought Credit Default Swaps. These securities were issued by insurance companies who promised to pay the holder in full if the CDO issuer defaulted. Then traders stepped in and started buying default swaps without actually owning the underlying securities, gambling on the defaults that many people now saw coming. This induced insurance companies like AIG to over-extend themselves by issuing too many default swaps. A major role in this worldwide debacle (American CDOs were sold all over the world) was played by Fannymae (FNMA) and Freddymac (FNMAC). These two formerly government guaranteed companies got into serious trouble during the crisis and were returned to government ownership, at huge expense to the taxpayer. Fanny and Freddy were the largest buyers of mortgages and had also grossly over-extended themselves. Politicians were leaning on them to be more lenient in buying up questionable mortgages under the slogan, "everybody has the right to own his own house," and discrimination in denying mortgages to poorer people was illegal. They still had the aura of government protection and enjoyed all kinds of privileges such as the right to have only small reserves against the loans they made. Whenever Congress tried to dig into their books, they resisted and were helped by politicians they supported with generous campaign donations. When the roof caved in and this true house of cards collapsed, Fanny, Freddy and AIG had to be propped up with large government loans. The stock market crashed and a huge financial debacle swept over most of the western world. Beyond the Lehman collapse and over-extended mortgage banks in the U.S. we had whole countries go broke on their own peculiar financial shenanigans. Iceland, Ireland, Portugal, Greece, Spain and Italy are all in serious financial trouble. All over the world countries except China are now facing a mountain of debt, and the politicians do not seem to want to do anything about it. The U.S. debt, federal, state and municipal together, represent an enormous burden that will take decades to pay off, restructure or reorganize.

It is interesting to reflect on the fact that this historically unprecedented situation would never have occurred if we had not found the Chinese ready and willing to finance our borrowings. China wanted to become a manufacturing giant and needed a market for its goods. It succeeded miraculously well in reaching its goal, but it now has weakened the U.S. Treasury to such an extent that it is questionable whether it will be able to continue flooding us with its products. Our politicians will have to grasp the nettle and come to understand that the days in which being a politician means getting government money for one's constituents, or in other words, the days of giving, have come to an end; we now must have the days of taking away. The stock market on which Netty and I depend for our daily living expenses has recovered miraculously and at this writing seems not to be in danger of collapsing again. But we will have to get accustomed to living in a country where the government has to borrow 40 cents for every dollar it spends and where the future looks to be fraught with risk. Not a pleasant feeling for people our age. The world has changed since the Great Recession started and we are in uncharted waters. We worry not only about our own future, but more so about the financial future of our children and grandchildren.

A much more pleasant part of our life to look back on is our fifty years of being on the water in the twelve boats I have owned and loved. I do not think Netty took to the water as well as I did, but she became a good sailor and a particularly good navigator, and she tolerated my passion for yachting for more than fifty years. It is a good and well-established tradition among my yachting friends to regale ourselves with tales of fogbound voyages, storm and rain and disasters with rigging or engine failures, of rocks hit, of docks crashed into and of unexpected swimming excursions. For this memoir I want to leave mishaps behind and concentrate on the innumerable times we have experienced great pleasure from being on the water. Because the pleasures yachting brings are a very good reason for so many people (mostly men) to be enraptured with being on the water for most of their lives.

There was the time on the Kaag Lake (Kager Plassen), during the war, when we had one of the, for Holland, rare brilliantly sunny days with a nice breeze. I had invited a bunch of friends for a sail in the "Skua" and we had a grand old time. We barreled all over the lake. The boat behaved well and the breeze was just strong enough to make her move nicely. As we shoved the boat into the reeds and the mud on shore (as is done in a country where there are no rocks), we saw two German soldiers who had rented a sailboat and came much too close to our liking, and we yelled at them like you do in a boat and they yelled back, and tacked away. Obviously they knew how to sail, but how would we know that? They were in uniform, complete with hobnailed boots. Good for the varnish job on that boat. We went for a swim and had lunch and sailed back to our marina. All went so well that day that I still enjoy thinking about what a good day we had, and particularly about having fun irritating those krauts.

In America, in our 15 ft. Mercury, the Half Moon, we did not go far off shore, but we had some very good summer days on the water with our two little boys. Rich and Janet had not presented themselves yet. I took movies of the boys diving over board with their life preservers on. These outings were the beginning of our effort to teach our children about boats and sailing. I pride myself on having given all our children a good indoctrination to sailing. They all enjoy the sport and made it part of their own lives. George and I regularly raced the Half Moon in the Greenwich Cove Racing Association with little success. But there was the one glorious day when we anchored near the Indian Harbor Yacht Club mooring field and were having lunch when the IHYC launch came by and asked if we needed a tender. We said, "No, thank you," and proudly pointed to the little Dutch flag in our rigging which was red white and blue in horizontal stripes and not vertically as the French and the "T" for "tender" flag. "This is the Dutch flag, from Holland" we said, surprised that not everybody knew that.

The Eclipse was a 22-ft., mini cruising boat which slept our entire family of four with considerable contortionistic effort. It was a Pearson Electra. With the larger 28 ft. Triton, also built by Pearson, it was one of the first larger fiberglass boats on the market. We thought the Triton was an enormous boat and looked at it with envy. The Tritons became an immensely popular class; the Electras were not so successful. However, the builder took the Electra hull and removed the much-too-narrow cabin to create the Ensign, a nice day sailer with a big cockpit that became a large and very popular racing class. With the Eclipse I took Adriaan with three friends for an over-night in Lloyd Harbor, all the way across the Sound, a real big cruise for us then. We cooked our own meal and went to bed for a cool night, wrapped up in the spinnaker because I had forgotten to bring blankets.

The 30-ft. Volante, a prewar wooden boat of the Malabar Jr. class, was our first real cruising boat. She served us well for several summers despite the problems we had at the outset. Once on a beautiful summer day, Netty and I went out alone and when we were half-way over to Eaton's neck, the wind died as it is apt to do in the Sound in summer. We drifted around a bit and then decided to go skinny dipping. We had a lovely swim and after climbing back on board, dried ourselves off in the sun. The engine must have worked well that day, because I have no memory of frustrating delays on the way home. Just a nice summer afternoon on the water.

We had the Postiljon built new for us in the winter of 1968. This 30-ft ketch was a true sea boat, not very fast but very stable and reliable with a good diesel engine. One of them circumnavigated the globe. In the years we owned her, we made several great cruises. We really liked this boat. She was fun to sail, behaved well in heavy weather, and since she was a ketch we could always take the mainsail down and proceed with jib and jigger, much to Netty's relief. I could single-hand her in that configuration and did so several times for a Saturday afternoon sail. We took the Postiljon to Nova Scotia and on the way back from Maine we sailed for a couple of hours with the boat perfectly balanced sailing on a broad reach at a good clip with nobody touching the helm. Somewhere I have a movie of that. On that same cruise we had the good luck of getting a stiff breeze out of the north east as we were homebound, steering towards the Cape Cod Canal. We had the spinnaker up all day and we made very good time. You do not forget days like that. When Janet and Rich came along, we made shorter cruises but still managed to get to the Cape Cod area with them. Unfortunately I do not have a photographic memory, but I do remember a nice evening at anchor in Hadley Harbor with the kids playing in the inflatable dinghy.

After we sold the Postiljon I owned two smaller day sailers both named Janet S. I liked this name, but it bothered Janet because she would have to ask the launch man

THE GOOD LIFE. RACING STRIDER IN THE NYYC CRUISE IN MAINE.

to bring her to a boat that had her name. So after the last Janet S was sold I switched to the name Gazelle, after the speedy animal of course but also because it was the brand name of a well-known Dutch bicycle manufacturer, makers of my first real bike. The first Gazelle was a Tartan Ten, a pure racing boat we never cruised. George was by then starting as an architect in the city and liked coming out with friends to race. He tried very hard but had little success. His friend Bob Lane would step off the boat and pronounce every time "dead last again." I have a good picture of the first Gazelle under sail with me and Janet. That day we went out for a last sail before she left for Union College as a freshman to begin a new chapter in her life. I knew by then from our experience with our boys that this was the day that Janet's school days and parent dependent life were over. A nostalgic moment, but I remember that outing also as a nice brisk sail. Trying to get a better shot at cruising and still be able to go racing I traded the Tartan for a J 30, a very nice boat of a popular racing/cruising class we also named Gazelle. The racing results were not much better, but the cruising was. The Riverside Yacht Club had started to organize the yearly long distance cruises and we have participated in almost all of them since then. The boat was new when we went on the cruise with Thijs de Clercq as crew Electronic navigation aids were then just beginning to appear, and I had Loran on this boat that would pinpoint your position by obtaining a continuing radio fix from two or more land-based beacons. Unfortunately I was very busy in those days and had not had the time to focus on learning how to operate this new gadget. We ended up in a thick fog and dropped anchor close to the breakwater of the haven of refuge called Duck Island. In the fog we heard voices and knew we were surrounded by friends. The next morning we found ourselves snugly anchored in the Sound, outside the breakwater. No harm done, it was calm and the cruise was great fun. The last sailboat we owned was a boat we really loved. Strider was a J34C, the cruising version of a fast racing hull. We cruised this boat extensively and found it very comfortable and good to spend a week or so in. We had a large number of glorious sails in her. Once Netty and I were at the Shelter Island Yacht Club in the fork of Long Island. We decided to go home and try to reach Port Jefferson, a favorite stop for going east or west, about four to five hours sailing from home. We left early to make the tide change in the Race and had a very strong breeze of about 20 knots. After we came through the Race and entered the Long Island Sound, we were on a close reach with a reef in our main. We had the current with us and were making more than six knots over the ground in fairly calm seas with grey clouds and occasional rain. As we barreled along we reached Port Jeff around three in the afternoon. The boat was moving so well and we were having so much fun that we decided to keep going, and that evening we were home in our own beds. Very proud of our achievement. We had never been able to traverse the entire Long Island Sound in a sailboat in one day and in the following years were never able to repeat that feat.

Once the annual cruise of our club visited New York Harbor and parts of the New Jersey shore near Rumson. This was a truly original departure from the usual "always go East" routine. We sailed most of this cruise with our friends Hal and Mary Jane Frost. They had to leave earlier, so the last day when we had to race home from Manhasset I was short on crew and borrowed two young boys, Hal Park's grandson and his friend. Hal owned a slow Bounty Yawl and the boys were delighted to sail in a fast boat. After the start, the whole fleet took the Long Island shore side of the Sound, traditionally the side that has the best breeze. I had a hunch the other side would be better so we stayed on the north side. We caught a good breeze, had the tide with us and saw the entire fleet flounder along the other side. We finished first with a wide margin. This was the one and only time in my life that I would get a first. The boys were ecstatic and had to wait hours before their grandfather Hal arrived. I won a glass bowl with the words FIRST on it that I kept on a shelf in my den. Years later, when we started our kitchen renovation, the contractors started to bang away at our walls and the glass bowl slowly wiggled to the edge of the shelf. Netty rushed into the den, just in time to see it crash down into a thousand pieces. Now I cannot prove anymore that I did have a first.

George and Diane often took Strider out for a cruise. They liked to go in early September, just after the summer rush when everybody else was back at work. When Alexander was born, they were somewhat limited in their cruising aspirations, but as soon as the little boy was a sturdy baby, he went along. Strider had a quarter berth, almost fit for two, sticking half way below the cockpit. They made a pen out of that for Alexander and he was happy as a clam being in there and participating in the cruise. I do not recall how I ended up sailing with George and Diane, without Alexander, from somewhere in Buzzards Bay to Riverside. But we decided to do this nonstop with George and me alternating while Diane would help out and take care of our care and feeding. I was on watch in the early part of the night with George and Diane asleep. We were in the Block Island Sound, it was very still so I must have been using the engine, and there was no other vessel in sight. The Volvo engine we had was reasonably quiet and pushed the boat along at about five knots. I sat there in the very quiet night under a brilliantly lit, starry sky and somehow I thought about my parents. My mother had died recently and my father ten years ago. Suddenly

I felt connected to them as if they were nearby. I enjoyed that sensation and let it linger until it faded. I have never in my life experienced such an almost surrealistic experience; there was nothing dramatic or spooky about it, just a pleasant encounter with the spirits of people I had been very close to.

As the burden of the years began to creep in upon us, it became clear that we would not be able to handle a sailboat much longer. Strider was a very convenient boat with lazy jacks to catch the mainsail as it came down and a roller furling jib that made the job of furling sails easy, but still there were the winches to crank when tacking and the anchoring and dock lines to handle in relatively confined spaces. In short, we decided to switch to a power boat. Strider went to George and Diane, who used her for several years until they found that they really liked to sail in Maine and that they did not have the time to bring a boat up there and home afterwards.

My idea of a power boat was to get a boat with water jet propulsion, which was a new thing. It made cruising in Maine very easy because the boat had no props and no rudder so she would be able to speed right over all the lobster pots. After considerable research, I found the Legacy Company that made jet boats. They advertised that their high-quality power boats could be equipped with either jet or propeller propulsion. We took a test ride with one of their 31-foot jet boats, and ordered a 41-foot one from them. We called her Brandaris after a famous Dutch lighthouse that dates back to 1594 and is still in operation. What we did not know was that ours was the first jet boat of that size they had built. It was a very luxurious boat compared to what we were used to in a sailboat. It had two engines, a generator, AC and all kinds of good new electronics. It had two cabins and two heads, a microwave in the galley and all sorts of other conveniences. I guess we were carried away by the general mood of optimism, of rising stock markets and of general prosperity. We were dreaming of using this boat to go down to Florida, to keep it there in a marina and spend time on it in winter. It was all a beautiful dream. We had three incidents where our engines froze up and we had to limp back to a harbor for repairs. It appeared that the shafts that drove the big jet pumps were poorly aligned and would overheat and freeze, thus stopping the engines.

We had the big party for our fiftieth wedding anniversary and that summer we went on a cruise up the Hudson River to Troy with Agna and Lucas de Clercq. Everything went as planned and we had a great trip. I have a picture of Netty standing on the bow in a New Jersey marina with the World Trade Center in the background. About seven weeks later, the two towers would come down in the worst terrorist attack the U.S. ever suffered. In the fall, just before September 11, we decided to start our first cruise to Florida. Ruurd Leegstra went with me on the first leg, which was going to get us to Annapolis. After leaving New York harbor, on our way to Atlantic City a third freeze-up occurred, this time, in mid-ocean. We brought the boat into Barnegat Bay, and I called the builder saying we were leaving the boat in a yard there and were going home. It was now his problem to do something about it. I told the builder to sell it. That took a while, but was eventually done. A costly experiment and so much for wintering in Florida.

After a decent interval, I stepped up to the plate again and decided to get a really simple, very seaworthy powerboat. A Maine lobster boat was the answer. Thus another Strider was born, a 31-foot boat, a Duffy that slept two and could carry a big crowd in its very roomy cockpit for a day trip. She was built by the Atlantic Boat Company in Brooklin, Maine a wonderful, very Down East operation. She had one single, very strong, diesel engine, cruised at 17 knots and carried us all over the Sound and beyond. This was a boat I really loved to own and take around. We had her for four years and then Netty decided that she did not have sea legs anymore since she had a knee replacement, which made her feel less secure when standing on a moving platform. We brought Strider to Maine and asked the builder to find a buyer. I took that trip to Maine with Richard. We left from New Bedford, where we had left her after a fun RYC cruise. Rich and I left under fairly rough conditions under gloomy skies. The trip from the Cape Cod Canal to Gloucester was memorable. The seas were big, the wind was blowing, but our lobster boat carried us without any hesitation or trouble. The next day we reached the Portland, Maine, area and after that we were in Booth Bay. We used Strider in the Booth Bay Harbor area when we rented a house there. She was sold the next spring, but I stipulated we wanted to use her for another few weeks when we had rented another house, this time in Rockport. It was there that we met the new buyer and said good-bye to a lovely boat and to our years in yachting. The buyer had a Dutch name and said he would christen her "Dutch." That pleased us.

ᑢᓚ

As I now approach the finish line of my story and of my life, I realize that the word "I" appears most frequently while the name of my cherished wife Netty only shows up occasionally. I have struggled with this and wanted at first to make this memoir the story of our life, not just my life, but that was impossible for the simple reason that even while we have now spent more than sixty years together, we are still two separate individuals who each have their own thoughts and reactions to events. I understood I could never even attempt to reflect Netty's perspective on our life's ups and downs. You never know the inner thoughts of another human being, no matter how close you are and how effortless your relationship develops over the years. I grew up in a very straight-laced family with a mother who was quite dominant and a father who was more distant. My father only could show his great attachment to me and later to my family and particularly Netty, by his actions, not his words. It took him a long time to get to the point where he could show true affection to us and our children. When I was a boy, my mother was always highly critical of my lack of motivation for school work and gave me many tongue lashings for that, but she never encouraged me to do better.

When I lived in America and became quite successful in the investment business, they seemed to view my progress as normal and to be expected and did not seem to wonder where all my investment knowledge came from. I guess they thought, "he has finally applied himself to his career and learned his lessons." I do not blame my parents for that. They were, like me, products of the environment and the age in which they lived. Until I met Netty, I had no clue of what a female was all about. I did not understand the way in which women thought, what motivated them most and what they liked and what they did not care about. Netty taught me all that. It took years, and I can only be grateful for the patience she had with me as a young husband and father.

Netty came from a larger family. She had one sister and two younger brothers. Her mother was also a more dominant factor in her life, but her father was different from mine, softer, more involved with his children and incredibly loving. Her father was less of an "achiever" than mine and certainly less inclined to an active lifestyle. I guess Mammie saw her role as the one who had to be the more assertive one since her husband was such a gentle soul. So Netty's perspective on the world of the male was different from what she found when she married me. It began right away with the strenuous hikes I organized during our honeymoon in Austria, which were far from gentle walks and segued into many adventures such as sailing in boats with failing engines, a screaming skipper and lots of cold water cascading into the cockpit. She took it all in stride and continued to try to appeal gently to my common sense, which suggested waiting a day until the wind might calm down a bit.

Our decision to move to America was a joint one, but my interest and my career were the deciding factors. It all has worked out very well, but it cannot have been easy for her, at first being left in a small house she hated with two little boys and the job of getting a family household going in, for our Dutch body temperature settings, a very hot summer. We have always disliked the terms "homemaker" or "stay at home Mom" and found they were needlessly condescending. Modern society almost requires women to have a job on top of running a household, and we have seen some admirable examples among our friends of women who were doing just that. But we also have seen how marital stress and child development problems emanated from Mom having a stressful job and Dad being unable to fill the gaps in the upbringing of the children. So we have always felt that being the organizer of a household with, in our case, four children and a commuting husband who left around 6:15 a.m. to return only after seven p.m. with frequent business trips in between, was a full-time job. The result is a cohesive well balanced family. And that is almost completely due to all the work Netty has done in the sixty years that we have been together. With her common sense, love for her family and me and good leadership skills, she has managed to make me a better husband and father. May the Lord grant us more good years together.

###

Together in Maine in the summer of 2010

TOGETHER IN MAINE IN 2010.
SITTING, NETTY WITH TIGGER OUR FAVORITE GRAND DOG AND ME. STANDING L TO R. ELOISE, TOYOKO, RICHARD, ADRIAAN, JANET, GEORGE, DIANE, ALEXANDER.

About the Author

In this memoir George Peter Schieferdecker (who has always used Peter as his first name), describes the high and low points of his life. Born and educated in The Netherlands Peter lived through the German occupation of his country during World War II. After the war he served in the Dutch army in Indonesia. Back home he married Jeannette (Netty) van Kleffens and started a career in finance in Amsterdam. Better opportunities brought him and his family to the United States in 1958. He spent the rest of his career in Wall Street and ended up running an institutional portfolio management company responsible for close to three billion dollars in assets. Since their arrival in America Netty and Peter have lived in Greenwich CT where they raised three sons and a daughter and are now the proud grandparents of Alexander and Eloise.

Acknowledgements

I must first of all thank Netty, my wife, for putting up with me for more than sixty years and if that was not enough, still have the energy to read my manuscript with great care. She caught many factual errors and corrected a multitude of misspellings. Without the enormously useful professional help of Cinny Coulson I could never have completed this memoir. As soon as I mentioned its existence to her she volunteered to edit it for me. I owe a great debt of gratitude to her. I thank George Shaddock who came to my assistance in the final stages when he made his intimate knowledge of the publishing business available to me. He encouraged me to take the plunge into a world that was completely unknown to me. He gave me a strong arm to lean on and always patiently answered a multitude of questions. These three have been of immeasurable help to me.

34746351R00448

Made in the USA
Lexington, KY
17 August 2014